ART DECO COMPLETE

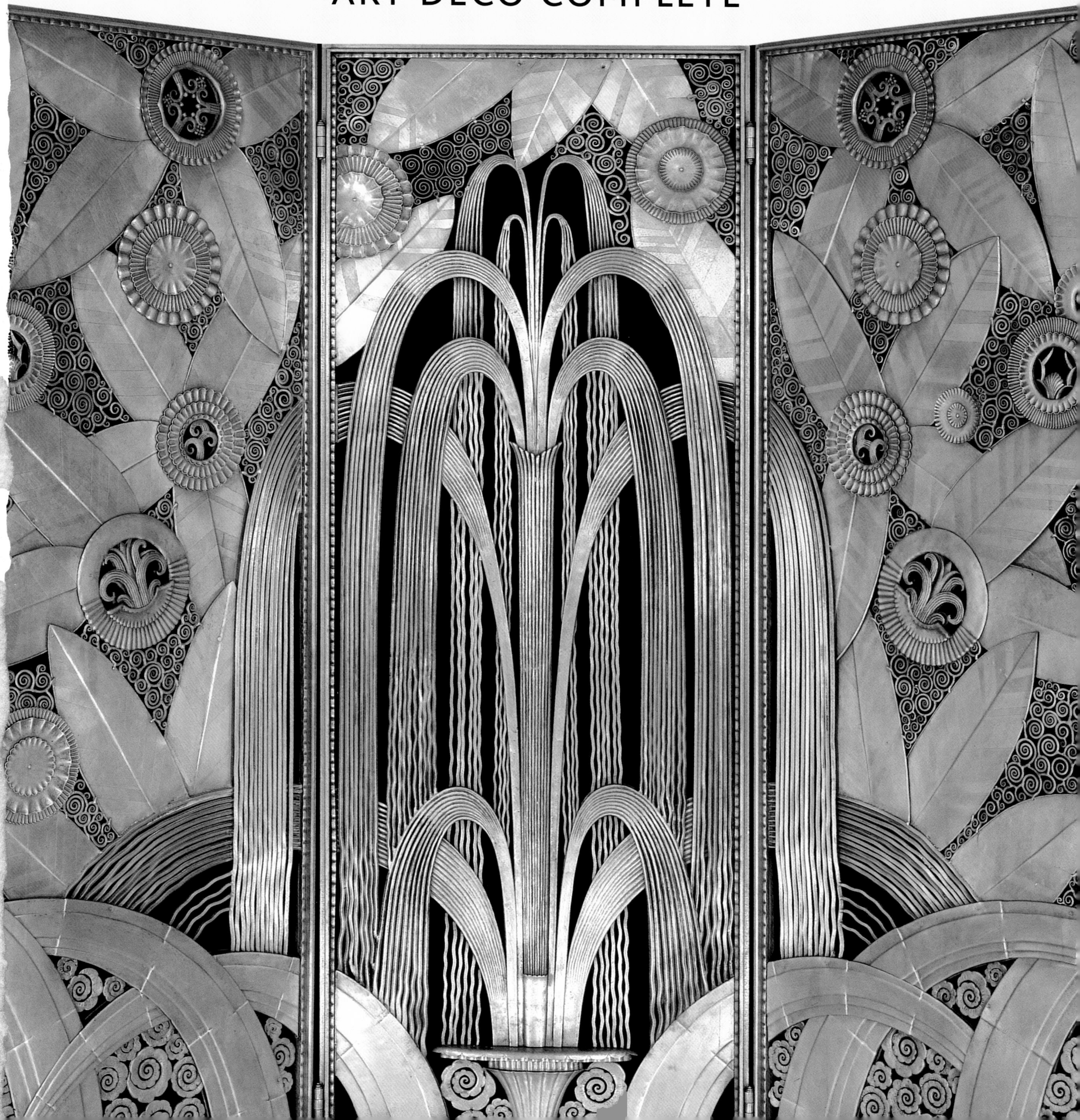

TO STANLEY BARON, LONGTIME FRIEND AND MENTOR

ART DECO

COMPLETE

THE DEFINITIVE GUIDE TO THE DECORATIVE ARTS
OF THE 1920S AND 1930S

ALASTAIR DUNCAN

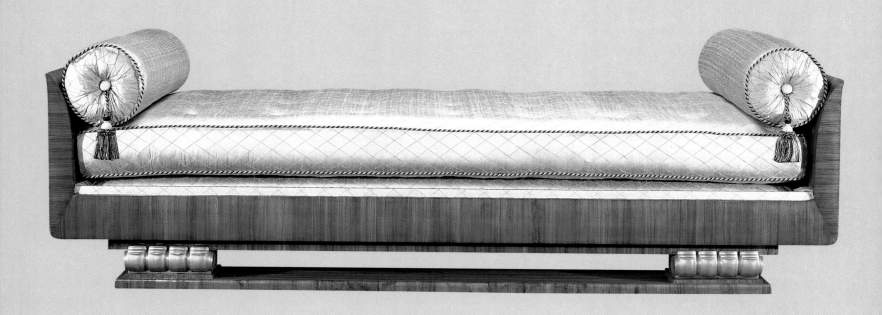

ABRAMS, NEW YORK

page 1

EDGAR BRANDT

L'Oasis screen, wrought iron with
gilt-copper detailing, included in
Brandt's stand at the 1925 Exposition
Internationale, Paris.

page 2

**SIMONET FRÈRES
(ALBERT AND CHARLES)**

(*right*) Chandelier in silvered-bronze
and glass prisms, *c.* 1925.

EDGAR BRANDT

(*left*) Serpent vase, patinated copper
with silver inlay, 1913.

page 3

JACQUES-ÉMILE RUHLMANN

'Bloch' day-bed, *bois de violette*
with gilt-bronze mounts, *c.* 1926.

DAUM FRÈRES

(*below*) Selection of glassware, *c.* 1925.

Cataloging-in-Publication Data has been applied for and may be obtained from
the Library of Congress. ISBN: 978-0-8109-8046-4.

Copyright © 2009 Thames & Hudson Ltd, London

First published in the United Kingdom in 2009 by Thames & Hudson Ltd, London

Published in the United States of America in 2009 by Abrams, an imprint
of ABRAMS. All rights reserved. No portion of this book may be reproduced, stored
in a retrieval system, or transmitted in any form or by any means, mechanical,
electronic, photocopying, recording, or otherwise, without written permission from
the publisher.

Printed and bound in China

10 9 8 7 6 5 4 3

Abrams books are available at special discounts when purchased in quantity
for premiums and promotions as well as fundraising or educational use.
Special editions can also be created to specification. For details, contact
specialsales@abramsbooks.com or the address below.

ABRAMS
THE ART OF BOOKS SINCE 1949
115 West 18th Street
New York, NY 10011
www.abramsbooks.com

CONTENTS

INTRODUCTION

In the history of the applied arts in modern times, Art Deco is a special chapter, one that has been characterized by multiple theories about its origins, its significance and its influence. Because of many seemingly contradictory factors, an exact definition of the style and its scope has proved elusive.

At the time when it made its first appearance before a large general public in 1925 at the Paris Exposition Internationale des Arts Décoratifs et Industriels Modernes, it was described by many critics as a movement radically opposed to Art Nouveau, which had held sway since the 1890s. This is a view no longer supported because in some ways, taking into account its use of ornamentation, exotic materials, bright colours and unfailingly high-grade workmanship, Art Deco might almost be described as an offshoot of Art Nouveau, which had run its course soon after the end of the First World War. But in fact it is a style that defies the easy confinement of its flowering to the period between, say, 1920 and the outbreak of the Second World War, as used to be widely claimed. A fair number of works that are now included among the finest examples of Art Deco, by JACQUES-ÉMILE RUHLMANN, Paul *Iribe, and

Paul *Follot, for example, were produced either before the outbreak of war in 1914 or indeed during the war. Nor did Art Deco run into a dead end in the early 1930s in the face of the Great Depression, as the construction of various buildings, at least in the USA, proves.

The present view is that we cannot define Art Deco as a single homogeneous style, but rather as one that encompassed a great variety of influences from Eastern and Western art, from ancient Egypt to the imagined future, and from the geometric to the non-symmetrical. This diverse Art Deco style has, moreover, been expressed not only in the applied arts, but also in sculpture, architecture, photography, fashion and industrial design.

In this book, the term 'Art Deco' is used broadly to describe the decorative style exhibited in the Paris Salons between the two world wars. The Salons – spread over the calendar year, as they still are today – provided artists across the entire spectrum of the fine and applied arts with the vehicle by which to bring their most recent creations to the attention of the critics and the general public, as well as those government and museum officials who were authorized to acquire works of art for

their respective institutions. Long before the turn of the century, the Salon had established itself as a much-revered annual event, one sanctioned by the state and carefully governed by committees and juries to ensure that traditional academic standards were met and maintained from year to year. Continuity was considered a prerequisite and radical designs were routinely rejected, which meant that change, when it came, was gradual.

Art Deco in the Paris Salons was an exciting concoction of luxury, leisure, exoticism and conviviality. It suited the mood of the post-war period when people enjoyed a sense of liberation and were avidly in search of the adventurous, the daring and the new. Another – albeit more austere and functional – design movement that is often included within the definition of Art Deco, as it is here, has acquired the term 'Modernism' to distinguish it from the 'high-style' Parisian variety. The Modernists' creed was rooted in a more intellectual view of society: that the future of humankind lay not in handcrafted works for the elite minority, but in the evolution of the machine, and therefore in mass production.

Among the many strands that went into the advent of Art Deco were the avant-garde painting movements that characterized the progressive early 20th century in its opposition to the academic realism of the recent past: Fauvism, Russian Constructivism, Cubism, De Stijl and Italian Futurism. Another impetus was derived from the Ballets Russes of the impresario Diaghilev, with its use of brilliant colours and unfamiliar designs that exhilarated *le tout* Paris when it arrived there in 1909.

The Art Deco artists found an important source of inspiration in the findings published after Howard Carter's discovery of Tutankhamun's tomb in November 1922. Motifs such as ziggurats, the lotus, winged discs, obelisks, scarab beetles and vultures, not only of Egyptian origin but Mesopotamian as well, were eagerly adapted. A similar mix of pre-Columbian ornamentation, including Mayan and Aztec temple bas reliefs, was borrowed from South American sites. But it was West Africa that had the greatest impact of exoticism on Art Deco designers, who made full use of ethnographic forms and patterns found on the artifacts imported into Europe in the late 19th and early 20th centuries from such colonial territories as Gabon, Dahomey, the Ivory Coast, Ghana and the Congo.

It is obvious that there are important contradictions within the Art Deco lexicon: on the one hand, special items meticulously produced from rare and luxurious materials, intended for an elite, cosmopolitan and wealthy clientele, and on the other, mass-produced wares in new low-cost materials, such as synthetic plastics and chromed metal, aimed at the broader popular market – works that have no surface decoration but whose forms are themselves decorative, such as those streamlined automobiles and kitchenware that were so popular in the 1930s. By the same token, the area now called South Beach in Miami has become a magnet for people eager to gape at Art Deco architecture simply because of the brilliant colours (such as orange and purple) used to paint the flat façades and walls, whereas the Chrysler Building in New York City ranks as an example of the same style because of its profuse ornamentation.

The result of all this is a highly complex visual language, one that has generated debate on whether there can be a catch-all phrase to characterize Art Deco; whether, in the final analysis, any single term can be used to define such a wide array of influences and practices. Nevertheless, to most observers the Art Deco label remains the most,

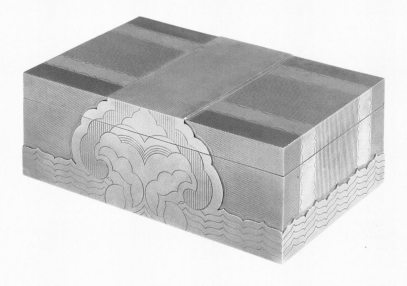

if not the only, appropriate title to apply to the decorative arts of the inter-war years. Three decades after the style's resurgence through publications, exhibitions and auctions, 'Art Deco' retains a strong resonance for a large lay public. On this issue, it is worth noting that the genie long ago escaped from the bottle, and it no longer makes sense to deny the use of the term to works that have been identified as such in countless periodicals, books and exhibitions. According to this viewpoint the diversity of the style can be considered a positive quality rather than an indication of its ideological incoherence, and therefore it presents an intriguing challenge.

The label 'Art Deco' itself is lifted from the title of the 1925 *Exposition Internationale des Arts Décoratifs, a monumental global exhibition dedicated to the decorative arts. This event had been planned ten years earlier but had to be postponed because of the First World War. When the road was finally cleared for its launching, it was on a wave of post-war French nationalism, and unsurprisingly it was perceived as a platform on which to promote French design and to reassert France's claim to be the arbiter of international style and taste. Although Germany and the United States did not participate (for different reasons), most of the European nations did and the exposition was a great success.

The city of Paris itself was a major attraction. The main pavilions were located in the heart of the city over seventy-two acres. Most of them were dominated by French exhibitors, who were given prime locations in the Esplanade des Invalides. Here the most important Parisian department stores held court, each vying to appear more opulent than the next. The Grand Palais and the Petit Palais – iconic architectural symbols of the last major Paris exhibition, in 1900 – served as backdrops for lavish design installations, while visitors to the fair entered through twelve unique entranceways, each designed by a different artist or firm. The Eiffel Tower was temporarily converted into an advertisement for the automobile firm Citroën, its logo sparkling in lights over the city below.

The 'high style' or *art de luxe* of the Parisian drawing room reached its apex during the Exposition, as craftsmen and dealers displayed their works of art in sumptuous settings intended to appeal to a rich

vein of pleasure and diversion. For the first time in a major international exhibition, decorative and applied arts were emphasized above all else, and the consumption of goods was implicitly linked to a consumer's ability to express individuality.

A new development in the 1920s was that the leading Paris department stores, which had traditionally done no more than market the output of various furniture manufacturers, began to set up their own art studios with their own designers, thus offering the potential customer a greater choice of objects and at the same time increasing their profits. Some of the most prominent designers, such as Paul Follot, René *Prou, MAURICE DUFRÈNE and Robert *Block, were hired to manage these studios under names like *Pomone, *Primavera and *La Maîtrise, and thus to promote their own work.

The rise of leisure travel in the 1920s and 1930s provided the era's artist-designers with new challenges and opportunities to create entire environments for an audience eager for adventure in the most deluxe and up-to-date surroundings. The ocean liners constructed during this period embodied the opulent quintessence of the Art Deco style. No ship better demonstrated the emphasis on luxurious interiors than

the French liner *Normandie*. Launched in October 1932, exactly three years after the Wall Street crash, as the largest ship in the world, it featured in its interiors the work of numerous French designers. JEAN DUNAND, René *Lalique, Jacques-Émile Ruhlmann, SÜE ET MARE and Raymond *Subes all participated, and CASSANDRE (Adolphe Mouron) devised a remarkable poster advertising the new vessel. Travel posters, which often relied upon decorative motifs in order to create works of bold sophistication, served as graphic tools to glamourize travel to exotic and romantic destinations. Train travel became another alluring modern mode of transportation, and the streamline aesthetic that turned into a hallmark development of American Art Deco could be seen in designs for train cars and stations as well. The *Pioneer Zephyr*, built in Chicago in 1934, featured a highly polished corrugated stainless steel exterior to emphasize the train's speed and power, while providing passengers with an interior composed of clean lines and a luxurious sleekness.

As it proliferated to Europe's colonial outposts, including India, Australia, New Zealand, Ethiopia and South Africa, the Art Deco style took on national or regional inflections, often after a five- or ten-year delay. Its central themes and motifs were often assimilated to those of the indigenous culture, or supplemented by them. In many faraway places, Art Deco was seen first as a symbol of Modernism through

the medium of Hollywood films. Information disseminated in recent years by the network of Art Deco societies that has sprung up globally since the 1960s reveals how the vast international appeal of the Art Deco style had spread by the early 1940s, much of it transforming the style's stereotypical French grammar of ornament into assortments with local currency.

Just as the Art Deco style had supplanted Art Nouveau in France, it in turn began to give way to Modernism in the late 1920s, a development that had been sown at the very moment of its triumph at the 1925 Exposition Internationale in Paris. The main thrust of Art Deco ideology was that function must dictate form, and this was a precept followed by most of the schools of design that evolved in later years. But the extreme views that certain early Art Deco designers promoted about decoration and craftsmanship met with a less favourable reception.

No more than a year after the intense global excitement that surrounded the 1925 Exposition Internationale, a group of designers who became known as Modernists, including ROBERT MALLET-STEVENS, *Le Corbusier, Francis *Jourdain, PIERRE CHAREAU and René *Herbst, raised their banner in support of what they saw as the future of their *métier* in the new machine age and the potential benefits to be derived from mass production. They represented a faction that decried the creation of exquisite and expensive objects solely for the enjoyment of the elite upper class. They sought to redefine the role of the artisan working with hand tools, as they had since time immemorial, to produce unique works of luxury, and to promote instead a decorative style more appropriate to the needs and the nature of the period.

In the late 1920s, this movement was able to increase its influence, although a number of artist-designers, while agreeing with its basic principles, were not prepared to accept unequivocally its rigid functionalism. In 1928, Paul Follot, a veteran and much-respected designer, expressed a popular sentiment:

> We know that 'necessary' alone is not sufficient for man and that the superfluous is indispensable for him . . . or otherwise let us also suppress music, flowers, perfumes . . . and the smiles of ladies!

MARCEL COARD
(*below*) Settee, palisander with ivory inlay
and caned basket-weave borders.

In effect, this was the prevailing opinion at the time. Even though it was possible, as the more extreme Modernists seemed to imply, that ornamentation might be eliminated entirely from the design vocabulary, it would be exceedingly difficult to persuade their usual customers to accept such an abrupt revision of their tastes. What emerged was a compromise: machine-made items came to replace the handcrafted objects of the past, but an element of decoration was retained, even though, ironically, it often had to be finished by hand.

Functionalism had a longer history outside France, for it had dominated decorative arts ideology in some European countries since the turn of the century. In 1907 Hermann Muthesius, among others in Munich, had formed the Deutscher Werkbund, devoted to extending the concepts of geometry that formed the basis of the earlier Vienna Secessionist and Glasgow movements. In contrast to both the French Art Nouveau repertoire of flowers, insects and willowy maidens and Germany's own similar Jugendstil, the Werkbund sought to establish a link between traditional craftsmanship and mechanization. This involved the formulation of standards of mass-production applicable to the newly emerging machine culture and allowing qualified designers to be infiltrated into industry. As these steps were implemented, the status of ornamentation became a matter of secondary concern. The establishment in 1919 of the Bauhaus in Weimar was a more advanced stage in the Werkbund's ideals, and it was the Bauhaus strain of Modernism that exerted a major influence on the decorative arts in the USA in the late 1920s.

The Bauhaus also played a part in the changes that began to take place in the decorative arts after the end of the war in the Scandinavian and other European countries. Ornamentation was largely restricted to design in France; it was even viewed as a Gallic eccentricity in some of the art periodicals of the period. Only in the USA did the French variety of 'high-style' decoration find a degree of support, as American architects used it in their design of important skyscrapers and, in particular, movie houses. The interior decoration of Radio City Music Hall in New York of 1932, for instance, is probably the prime example of the French style of Art Deco on American soil.

JOHAN VON STEIN
(*below*) *Rotterdam Lloyd*, lithographic
poster, 1931.

**HAROLD VAN DOREN
AND JOHN GORDON RIDEOUT**
(*right*) 'Air King' radio in red Plaskon,
for the Air-King Products Co., early 1930s.

In conclusion, it must be re-emphasized that the issue of Art Deco's broad reach – the overlap between it and Modernism and other contemporary design styles – has not yet been altogether resolved, and probably never will be, as there remains a lack of consensus among the experts on what term, or terms, best encompass it. How is one to formalize the variety and/or unity of such a complex phenomenon, a style that serves to describe both luxury goods and utilitarian items? Yet even if Art Deco's devotees can agree to disagree on its stylistic boundaries, they will not disagree that much of it has a refreshing 'snap' and compelling nostalgic charm. In its approach to this issue, this book opted to include pieces of borderline Art Deco design, leaving to the reader the choice of whether to accept them as such.

NOTE TO THE READER

Each of the main media (or group of media) used during the Art Deco period has a chapter in Part 1 ('Media and Masters'), beginning with an overview of the materials, styles and designers associated with that medium, followed by biographies of the most prominent designers or companies in the field. Entries for other influential designers, companies and organizations appear in Part 2 ('A–Z of Designers, Artists and Manufacturers'). Biographies are ordered letter-by-letter, ignoring spaces, hyphens and accents. Individuals are listed under their surnames; company and organizational names that begin with a forename appear under the forename (for example, Oscar Heyman & Bros is under 'O').

Cross-references are included to assist the reader in locating individual biographies. A cross-reference to a biography in Part 1 is indicated by small capitals (for example, 'PIERRE CHAREAU'), while one to a biography in Part 2 is indicated by an asterisk (for example, 'Chana *Orloff'). Words in bold or bold italic (for example, '**chaser**' and '*galuchat*') are terms that appear in the glossary.

PART 1

MEDIA AND MASTERS

FURNITURE AND INTERIOR DECORATION

That Art Deco furniture was quintessentially French, and specifically Parisian, is a fact that becomes evident as models from the period are analysed. Almost nothing of comparable design or quality was produced in the 1920s outside France. In America, designers were inspired more by German and Austrian Modernist prototypes than by the 'high-style' examples issuing out of the Paris Salons.

The roots of Art Deco furniture are to be sought in the French *ancien régime* and the work of late 18th-century cabinet-makers such as Riesener, Roentgen and Weisweiler, a comparison actively encouraged by JACQUES-ÉMILE RUHLMANN and Jules *Leleu, among others. After the exuberant Art Nouveau era, in which furniture designers were considered to have strayed far from the proven path of traditional French taste, there seemed to be a need for a return to purity of form and refinement. Designs were simplified, and carved detailing scaled back. Harmony was now considered to lie in the graceful proportions of a chair leg or the understated ivory banding along its apron. The harsh doctrine espoused by the Austrian architect Adolf Loos at the start of the 20th century — that ornament equalled crime — had been prescient: decoration, however, was not altogether abandoned after the excesses of the *fin de siècle*. It remained an integral part of Art Deco furniture. Beauty in the home, it was argued, was essential to man's psychological well-being.

In examining their productions during the inter-war years, Art Deco furniture designers can be divided into three different strains: traditionalists, individualists and Modernists. The traditionalists looked back in their designs to the French cabinet-making heritage of the 18th and early 19th centuries. Jacques-Émile Ruhlmann was the most celebrated and influential designer among them. Although many of his most renowned works were designed before 1920, his furniture is today considered the epitome of the Art Deco style and its finest expression, as much for its unimpeachable forms as for its judicious interplay of lavish materials.

Ebony, with its jet black surface, buffed repeatedly to draw out its innate colour, was the furniture-maker's favourite wood, which led by the 1920s to its scarcity within the industry. Cabinet-makers had to make

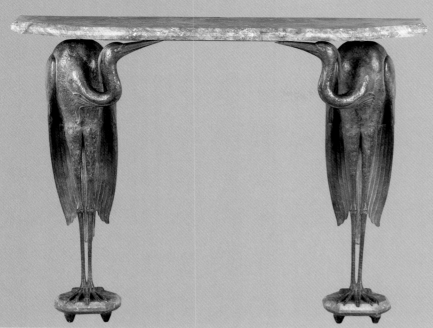

do either with ebony veneers or with substitute woods. For Ruhlmann, and others, the most popular substitute was Macassar ebony, from the island of Celebes in Indonesia. Other important tropical veneers were Brazilian jacaranda (*palissandre de Rio*), which often alternated with a range of indigenous veneers: amaranth, amboyna, mahogany, violetwood and maple. To provide further variety, these could be applied in juxtaposition with a contrasting burl wood, such as maple or ash. Three exotic species — palmwood, calamander and zebrawood — had to be used sparingly if their highly distinctive grains were not to visually overpower the viewer.

The Art Deco furniture designer drew readily also on other materials to broaden his decorative repertoire, thereby adding extra touches of opulence: in particular, lacquer, **galuchat** (shagreen), ivory and wrought iron. Of these, lacquer largely survived the 1920s, after which it was replicated increasingly by industrial synthetic varnishes. *Galuchat* is the skin of a small spotted dogfish; it could be left in its unbleached state, varnished or tinted to accentuate its granular surface pattern. Snakeskin and animal hides, such as ponyskin, were used in a similar manner. Ivory, absent from furniture design in 1900, was revived to give grace and refinement to drawer pulls, **sabots**, key escutcheons and the slender chute that outlined the curve on a cabriolet leg. Wrought iron also underwent a resurgence, its unyielding mass becoming as malleable as putty when serving as furniture, light fixtures and architectural elements.

The partnership of SÜE ET MARE was formalized in 1919 in the Compagnie des Arts Français. Their furniture was inspired by the past, and they considered the style of Louis-Philippe to be the most recent legitimate one. As Mare explained in 1920:

> It responded to needs which we still have. Its forms are so rational that the motor-car designer of today who draws the interior of a car uses them unconsciously. We are not reviving it; we are not deliberately continuing it, but we find it while seeking out simple solutions, and through it we bind ourselves to the whole of our magnificent past. We are not creating a merely fashionable art.

SERGE CHERMAYEFF

(*opposite*) Cabinet, lacquered wood and silver leaf, *c.* 1930.

DOMINIQUE

(*right*) Salon furniture for Mme L., in Indian palisander and *galuchat*, *c.* 1928.

Süe et Mare's armchairs, with their tufted and tapestried Aubusson upholstery, were lush and inviting. Other models could be Baroque or even Rococo.

An even more convinced traditionalist, Leleu pursued a decorative style hallmarked by a devotion to impeccable cabinetry, harmony and the finest materials available, such as walnut, Macassar ebony, amboyna and palisander. Marquetry decoration, never overbearing, was in ivory, *galuchat* or horn. Lacquer was introduced in the late 1920s, as were brass and mother-of-pearl inlays. These were followed by smoked glass panels and metal mounts in the 1930s. The last were, however, restricted, as Leleu believed that, unlike wood, they did not improve with age.

Paul *Follot, who had been employed as a designer in Julius Meier-Graefe's short-lived gallery La Maison Moderne in the early 1900s, made the transition from the Art Nouveau aesthetic with great facility. His furnishings shown at the 1912 and 1913 Salons incorporated a stylized basket of fruit and summer blooms motif today considered an Art Deco icon. In 1923 he was appointed director of the design studio, *Pomone, and in 1928 joined Serge *Chermayeff at Waring & Gillow in Paris. As an **ensemblier** during these years, he designed a wide range of furnishings in a Neoclassical and aristocratic style. The rich effect of his designs derived in part from brightly coloured and tufted damask or velour upholstery on gilt-wood frames.

MAURICE DUFRÈNE, the artistic director of *La Maîtrise, the design studio of the large Paris department store Les Galeries Lafayette, played a prominent role in providing machine-made editions of furniture at inexpensive prices, believing that this need in no way diminished aesthetic standards. At the 1925 Exposition Internationale des Arts Décoratifs et Industriels Modernes, examples of his work were on view literally everywhere.

Likewise a traditionalist, but one who developed a most distinctly personal style, was ARMAND-ALBERT RATEAU, whose works are today among the most prized by Art Deco collectors. Drawing especially on the Orient and antiquity, Rateau created a menagerie that included birds,

insects and animals interspersed with acanthus and marigolds. Early oak furnishings gave way to bronzeware enhanced with a **verde antico** patina. Despite being excluded from the 1925 Exposition Internationale by virtue of the fact that he was not a member of any of the Paris Salons, Rateau nevertheless devised a way in which his creations were on view in some of the entrants' displays, a strategy that served him well, as examples of his works were chosen for the travelling exhibition that toured eight American museums the following year. He is today known most for the interiors he created for Jeanne *Lanvin's apartment in the rue Barbet-de-Jouy in Paris, and his residences for the American couple, George and Florence Blumenthal, and the Duchess of Alba.

The decorating firm of *Dominique – a partnership formed between André Domin and Marcel Genevrière in 1922 – produced an extensive range of fabrics, furnishings, carpets and metalware. In addition to the annual Salons, the firm participated in the 1925 Exposition Internationale and, from the next year, at the annual exhibitions of 'Les Cinq'. Its furniture designs, in a selection of traditional woods accented largely with ivory banding, were invariably refined and logical. The 1930s witnessed a dramatic shift to synthetic fabrics, including artificial silk and Rodhia canvas.

Similar in style to Dominique was the decorating firm of *DIM, established in 1919 under the direction of René *Joubert, Georges *Mouveau and (later) Philippe *Petit. The firm's traditional approach was often influenced by the Louis XVI and Restoration periods. Its editions, mainly for prestigious clients, were small, and its use of warm woods, such as palisander, walnut and Macassar ebony, imparted the desired feeling of luxury. Decoration was provided most successfully by the incorporation of large panels of burled veneers, such as fernwood, which had a most pronounced grain. Marquetry, always understated, was confined to ivory or coralwood crossbanding or trim.

Initially the furniture of Léon-Albert *Jallot, one of the older generation of 1920s decorators, involved formal 18th-century shapes with heavily carved floral decoration. But from 1919 he abandoned this style,

DOMINIQUE
(*below*) Chest of drawers in rosewood
with ivory inlay, mid-1920s.

PIERRE-ÉMILE LEGRAIN
(*left*) Curule stool in black lacquered wood
and *galuchat*, exhibited at the 1923 Salon
of the Société des Artistes Décorateurs, Paris.

ERIC BAGGE
(*opposite*) Dining-room ensemble in
bois de placage with ivory inlay, exhibited
at the 1925 Exposition Internationale, Paris.
Marketed by Saddier et ses Fils.

relying instead on decorative burled veneers for contrast. Marquetry,
in ivory or mother-of-pearl, enhanced the wood's rich grain. In 1921 Jallot
was joined by his son Maurice. Together they displayed at the Salons
for many years, both singly and in partnership, and also at the 1925
Exposition Internationale. Until the mid-1920s their furniture was
produced in wood, sometimes enhanced with *galuchat* or **coquille d'œuf**.
From 1926, however, they faced the problem common to all **ébénistes**:
whether to adjust to, or to fight, the revolutionary introduction of glass
and metal into their *métier*. They chose the former policy, introducing
a distinctive range of furniture using stainless steel. Lacquered doors,
psyches (cheval mirrors) and screens were perennial favourites, with
motifs ranging from monkeys and angular fish to pure geometry.

André *Groult's reputation as an Art Deco exponent is based
mainly on the woman's bedroom he exhibited at the 1925 Exposition
Internationale. Its veneered chest of drawers with ivory banding became
one of the talking points of the Exposition. The remaining furniture,
in a mixture of *galuchat*, ebony and velour upholstery, exuded femininity
and sumptuousness.

Although Paul *Poiret is best known as a couturier, he was
also a successful interior designer. In April 1911 he founded the École
MARTINE, for girls from the working-class suburbs of Paris. The girls were
encouraged to study nature and sketch flowers. Poiret used their ideas
in a wide range of textiles (carpets, wallpapers and upholstery fabrics),
which evoked the Louis-Philippe style in their vivid palette and patterns,
the latter rendered with a refreshing naïveté. An extensive variety of
furnishings, such as tables, pianos and vitrines, was added in the 1920s.
For the 1925 Exposition Internationale, Poiret moored three barges in
front of the Quai de la Seine, and these served as his pavilion.

In 1925 the traditionalist JEAN-MICHEL FRANK chose the field of
interior design as his profession. He was independently wealthy and well
established in Paris's fashionable inner circle, and his association with
Adolphe *Chanaux and other gifted artist–craftsmen, including Alberto
and Diego Giacometti, Salvador Dalí and Christian Bérard, brought him

instant celebrity and many eminent clients. It is Frank's veneers that distinguish his work, as did his conception of interior decoration being architectural. He was interested in the finely tuned relationship between the length of a sofa and that of a mantelpiece, which in turn related to the dimensions of the windows and the height of the ceiling. He also believed that a space looked better if it contained very little furniture. A story survives of Jean Cocteau's comment on leaving Frank's sparsely furnished apartment on the rue de Verneuil: 'A nice young man. Very nice, in fact. Pity the burglars got everything.'

Outside France, 'high-style' Art Deco was only infrequently adopted in furniture. In Germany, Bruno Paul applied the French fashion for contrasting veneers in custom-made pieces from 1914, but with little exuberance. In England, Sir Ambrose *Heal, Sir Edward Maufe and Betty *Joel incorporated similarly conservative interpretations into their Modernist designs, as did the Russian émigré Serge Ivan *Chermayeff. In the United States, Art Deco was rejected by the public as too flamboyant for traditional tastes. In New York, only the Company of Mastercraftsmen produced a series of marquetry and ivory-inlaid pieces that drew a direct influence from Paris, particularly the works of Dufrène and the large department stores. Also in Manhattan, Joseph *Urban created some theatrical chair models which he displayed at the opening of the Wiener Werkstätte showrooms in 1922. These were inspired more by the Vienna Secession than by Paris, however, in their choice of colour and inlays. In Chicago, Abel Faidy designed a similarly ornate suite of lounge furniture for the Charles and Ruth Singleton residence, in 1927. Others whose designs for wooden furniture in the 1920s sometimes reveal a restrained Parisian influence were Eugene *Schoen, Hermann Rosse, Ilonka *Karasz, Jules *Bouy, Herbert Lippmann, Ely Jacques Kahn, Robert Locher and Winold Reiss.

The category of individualists is reserved for those furniture designers whose brilliant and unique concepts put each into a class of his or her own. For example, Irish-born EILEEN GRAY entered London's Slade School of Fine Art in 1898, in her free time learning the art of Oriental lacquer. In 1902 she headed to Paris, where she installed herself five years later in a flat at 21 rue Bonaparte. This she retained for the rest of her life. Lacquer was her primary interest, and she sought out the Japanese master Sougawara to perfect her rudimentary training. Lacquer continued to dominate her work until around 1925, when she introduced chromed tubular steel and aluminium increasingly into her furniture. An articulated chaise-longue in steel, leather and sycamore preceded a similar model by *Le Corbusier, and her tubular chairs those of Ludwig *Mies van der Rohe and Marcel *Breuer. As Gray recalled in a 1973 interview with Éveline Schlumberger in Connaissance des Arts, 'My idea was to make things for our time; something which was possible but which no one was doing. We lived in an incredibly outdated environment.'

Another lacquer exponent was JEAN DUNAND (see under Silver, Metal, Lacquer and Enamel), whose lengthy career spanned three distinct phases: sculpture, metalware and lacquerwork. He turned to lacquerwork in 1909, realizing that its lustrous gloss and lively colours would go well with his metalware. By 1913, panels were painted with overlapping triangles and chevrons; in the early 1920s such ornamentation was expanded to meet the demand of a broadening clientele. Every decorative style was now embraced on the panels – realistic, stylized and abstract figures and landscapes, as well as fantastic animals by Jean *Lambert-Rucki. Jean *Goulden, François-Louis *Schmied and Paul *Jouve supplied further designs. The application of panels of coquille d'œuf (crushed eggshells) to many surfaces added greatly to the appeal and novelty of Dunand's work.

The cartoons of the graphic artist PIERRE-ÉMILE LEGRAIN (see under Paintings, Graphics, Posters and Bookbinding) came to the attention of Paul *Iribe, who invited him to collaborate on various projects, including the commission in 1912 to redecorate Jacques *Doucet's apartment in Neuilly. This, in turn, launched Legrain's career as a bookbinder, during which time he designed also a range of unique pieces of furniture that he exhibited at the 1923 Salon of the *Société des Artistes Décorateurs and, the following year, in an interior designed by PIERRE CHAREAU entitled 'La Réception et l'Intimité d'un Appartement Moderne'. Inspired especially

by African tribal art and Cubism, Legrain's furniture blended primitivism with powerful angular and stepped forms, a novel mix rendered in unexpected combinations of materials.

Marcel *Coard's furniture was also strongly influenced by tribal art, in his case Oceanic as well as African, and he generally used oak (often coarsely hewn), Macassar ebony and palisander. What particularly marked out these pieces as being by Coard was his selection of veneers and encrusted materials. *Cabochons* of lapis and amethyst served as further decorative accents. Coard's ornamentation was always subordinate to form: the contours of his furniture remained unbroken.

Finally, among the individualists there was EUGÈNE PRINTZ. Originally, he was a producer of 'style' pieces but switched to contemporary furniture at the time of the 1925 Exposition Internationale. He made his début as a Modernist with a bedroom in rosewood at the 1926 Salon of the Société des Artistes Décorateurs. His considerable creativity and his innovations produced a highly distinctive, crisp style dominated by arches and perpendiculars with constrasting dark woods and bright metal mounts.

The final group of Art Deco furniture designers in the inter-war years was the Modernists. In applying their interpretation of the ascendancy of the machine to their creations, they were rejecting the restrictions inherent in the Neoclassical discipline. Metal was their material of choice, whether used in combination with wood or not. In France the most notable of these artists were Louis *Sognot, Robert *Block, Pierre Petit, René *Prou, Michel *Dufet and PAUL DUPRÉ-LAFON. Then, in the late 1920s they were joined by a number of progressive architects who had begun to engage in furniture design, among them: René *Herbst, ROBERT MALLET-STEVENS, Jean *Burkhalter, Pierre Chareau, André Lurçat, Le Corbusier, CHARLOTTE PERRIAND and Jean-Charles *Moreux.

French Modernist furniture consisted primarily of chromed tubular components designed for inexpensive mass-production. Except for those of Chareau, many of the designs produced in the modern idiom are so similar that attribution is impossible without documentation.

Chareau made his début at the 1919 *Salon d'Automne and was renowned for his logical solutions to furniture design, creating a series of basic parts that with slight changes could be adapted to numerous models. Most pieces were made of a mixture of wood and wrought iron, whose raw lines were relished, not concealed, and the iron supports were treated with a light patina. Chareau's most important works came towards 1930: in 1927, a golf club at Beauvallon, and in 1929 the Grand Hôtel in Tours.

Beyond France, Modernism soon became the prevailing philosophy. Amédée Ozenfant and Le Corbusier's manifesto, *Après le cubisme* (1918), had broad appeal for progressive furniture designers in its advocacy of a universal style stripped of ornament. The architect-designers associated with the Bauhaus were Marcel *Breuer, Mart *Stam and Ludwig *Mies van der Rohe, who developed a range of cantilevered tubular metal seat furniture that is today considered a classic of 20th-century design. In Scandinavia, designers such as Bruno *Mathsson and Alvar Aalto preferred to incorporate Breuer's functionalism in mass-production with traditional materials, such as wood.

In the United States, the Bauhaus-inspired European strain of machine-made, mass-production metal furniture found acceptance in the late 1920s, in preference to the earlier 'high-style' Art Deco of Paris.

In metal furniture, DONALD DESKEY emerged as America's leading designer, combining the luxury of French Modernism with the technology of the Bauhaus. For his interiors for Radio City Music Hall in 1932, he set convention aside in a display of ostentation intended to buoy a Depression-racked nation seeking refuge in movies and live entertainment. The German *émigré* Karl Emanuel Martin (Kem) *Weber was virtually the only decorative arts designer to embrace the Modernist creed on the West Coast. His style was extremely eye-catching, as in the suite of green-painted bedroom furniture enhanced with Hollywood-style metal decorative accents that he designed for the John W. Bissinger residence in San Francisco.

**LÉON-ALBERT AND
MAURICE-RAYMOND JALLOT**

(*opposite*) Pair of armchairs for a reception
hall, palisander with leather upholstery, 1920s.

HENRI AGUESSE

(*right*) Lady's desk in red lacquer and *coquille
d'œuf* with metal mounts, exhibited at the
desk competition at the Union Centrale des
Arts Décoratifs, Paris, 1927.

PAUL-THÉODORE FRANKL is known primarily for his skyscraper
furniture inspired by the setbacks on the tall buildings which soared
above his mid-town Manhattan gallery. His choice of finishes on some
of his furniture – red and black lacquer, gold- and silver-plated metal,
and gold and silver leaf – evoked that employed by the Secession
movement in his native city, Vienna.

By the mid-1930s, it was evident that metal had won the battle
with wood for the domestic American market. Among those who used
it imaginatively were Gilbert *Rohde, Wolfgang and Pola *Hoffmann,
Warren *McArthur, Jr, Walter Dorwin *Teague and the lighting specialist
Walter *von Nessen. Walter *Kantack, a New York metalware manufacturer,
also produced inspired pieces of tubular metal furniture, as did the
architect William Lescaze, of Howe & Lescaze.

ROSE ADLER

(*left*) Table in black lacquered wood, *galuchat*
and tinted glass, *c.* 1930.

GASTON SUISSE

(*above*) Pair of side tables in black lacquered
wood and *coquille d'œuf*, *c.* 1921.

PIERRE CHAREAU

DONALD DESKEY

MAURICE DUFRÈNE

PAUL DUPRÉ-LAFON

JEAN-MICHEL FRANK

PAUL-THÉODORE FRANKL

EILEEN GRAY

ROBERT MALLET-STEVENS

MARTINE (PAUL POIRET)

CHARLOTTE PERRIAND

EUGÈNE PRINTZ

ARMAND-ALBERT RATEAU

JACQUES-ÉMILE RUHLMANN

SÜE ET MARE

(*below*) Fashionable 1920s Art Deco furniture finishes: (from left to right) eggshell (*coquille d'œuf*); ivory; shagreen (*galuchat*).

PIERRE CHAREAU (1883–1950)

Born in Le Havre into a family of ship owners, Chareau completed his architectural studies before joining a Paris-based English firm, which he left in 1914 to enlist. In 1919 he made his début at the Salon d'Automne, where he displayed a bedroom and office for Dr Jean Dalsace, for whom he undertook his most celebrated architectural commission, the 'Maison de Verre', ten years later.

He established himself in the 1920s, from his studio–showroom at 54 rue Nollet, participating in the annual Salons, 'Les Cinq' and, as co-founder, the *Union des Artistes Modernes (UAM) exhibitions. Chareau received both private and public commissions, including interiors for Mme Thérèse Bonney, ROBERT MALLET-STEVENS, Edmond Fleg, Mme Reifenberg and Mme Kapferer. Among his most important works were a golf club at Beauvallon on the Riviera, in 1927; the Grand Hôtel in Tours, in 1929; and, two years later, the 'Maison de Verre', at 31 rue Saint-Guillaume in Paris. The last, which he designed in collaboration with the Dutch architect Bernard Bijvoet, was of revolutionary design, with walls made of glass bricks and an interior with sliding partitions.

Chareau participated in the 1925 *Exposition Internationale as both an architect and a decorator. On the Esplanade des Invalides he designed the furniture manufacturers' gallery, in which he retained a stand to display a range of wrought-iron plant racks. His office–library in the Ambassade Française pavilion received wide attention for its palmwood panelling and

desk, the latter a double construction that incorporated extra filing space. Collaborators were listed as Louis Dalbet (wrought iron), Jean Lurçat (carpets), Jacques Lipchitz (sculpture), Hélène Lantier (textiles) and PIERRE-ÉMILE LEGRAIN (furniture garniture and book-covers). Elsewhere at the Exposition he designed a dining room in Gabonese *bilinga* (orangewood) for a colonial habitation. From 1932 to 1938, he continued his research, concentrating on the development of mobile room partitions and screens. In 1937 for Djemel Anik, a dancer and friend, he designed a small country house, which included a new system of heating ducts. In the same year he participated in the UAM pavilion at the 1937 Exposition des Arts et Techniques. When the Second World War broke out, Chareau moved to London, settling finally in New York, where in 1945 he received an important commission from the young American painter Robert Motherwell to build a house and studio in East Hampton from two large Quonset huts, which stood as a triumph of architectural expediency until it was razed in 1985. Chareau remained in New York after the war and died there in 1950.

Logical architectural solutions to furniture design were Chareau's forte. Models consisted of basic components that with slight modification could be adapted to multiple needs.

(*below*) Desk with curved bookshelf and mobile circular top, mahogany with wrought-iron mounts, late 1920s.

Linen cupboards, bars, filing cabinets, hearth fenders and desks incorporated the same fundamental structure, and additional elements extended their usage. No attempt was made to mask an item's functionalism: the contours of the wood and metal were left brazenly undisguised.

Most of his pieces were made in a combination of wood and iron. The woods were warm and highly buffed to offset the coldness and austerity of the metal – palisander, amourette, walnut, sycamore and violetwood. The iron supports were cast in broad sheets, treated with a light patina, and bolted together. Chair upholstery was in velour, pigskin or, rarely, sable fur. Cushions were credited to Chareau's English wife, Dollie, who administered his business.

Chareau is perhaps best known for the light fixtures he designed for the Grand Hôtel in Tours – their shades being constructed of overlapping slices of alabaster placed at angles to each other. The design was repeated in table, floor and hanging models. Many of his interiors were shown in contemporary reviews such as *Les Arts de la Maison*, *Intérieurs Français* and *Intérieurs VI*.

(*opposite above*) Desk and chair with roll-top storage unit, Cuban mahogany with wrought-iron mounts; and (rear) linen chest in sycamore with wrought-iron mounts, c. 1927.

(*opposite below*) Table–desk, comprising modular units MB771, MB773 and MB774, Cuban mahogany.

(*above*) Ensemble including a wrought-iron plant stand, three armchairs, a metal centre table with swivel top, and a bookcase in Cuban mahogany and wrought iron, late 1920s.

(*right*) Bedroom exhibited at Lord & Taylor, New York, 1928; the furnishings in palisander with wrought-iron mounts; sculpture by Jacques Lipchitz and carpet by Jean Burkhalter.

(*opposite*) Selection of furniture, including a stool and nesting table in Cuban mahogany, and 'La Religieuse' floor lamp, model SN31 in metal and alabaster, introduced in 1923 and exhibited at the 1925 Exposition Internationale, Paris.

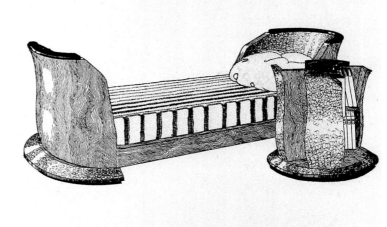

(*middle left*) Armchair with adjustable back, model MF220; Macassar ebony with leather upholstery, c. 1922.

(*middle right*) Sketch of a daybed and bookcase; palisander and amourette, exhibited at the 1923 Salon d'Automne.

(*right*) Desk, model MB233; Macassar ebony, for the living room of a private commission, c. 1920.

DONALD DESKEY (1894–1989)

Deskey was one of the giants of the industrial design movement in the USA. Born in Blue Earth, Minnesota, his formal education included a degree in architecture from the University of California at Berkeley and painting instruction at the Art Students League in New York City and the Art Institute of Chicago. Two trips to France helped to narrow his focus to interior design. He was enrolled at the Académie de la Grande Chaumière in Paris in 1921–22, returning three years later to visit the 1925 *Exposition Internationale, an event that triggered his decision to establish himself in New York. This was as a propitious choice. In 1926 a selection of his painted screens was commissioned by PAUL-THÉODORE FRANKL to serve as partitions in Frankl's interiors; another was commissioned for a window display at Saks Fifth Avenue.

In 1927 Deskey formed an association with Phillip Vollmer, a local businessman. The pair opened a studio, Deskey–Vollmer, Inc., at 114 East 32nd Street in New York City, which remained in operation until the early 1930s; its emphasis was on the design and manufacture of modern tables and lamps. Commissions were received from wealthy private clients such as Adam Gimbel, president of Saks Fifth Avenue; Mrs Edward Titus (better known by her professional name, Helena Rubenstein); Abby Aldrich Rockefeller, for whom Deskey designed

a modern print gallery and boudoir; and John D. Rockefeller, Jr., for whom Deskey produced a picture gallery, ceramics room and print room. In the early 1930s, as the Depression began, Deskey switched his attention to large manufacturers such as the Ypsilanti Reed Furniture Co. and the Widdicomb Furniture Co., for which he designed a wide range of furniture, textiles and rugs for mass-production. The Donald Deskey archives at the Cooper-Hewitt Museum indicate that more than four hundred of his furniture designs went into production from 1930 to 1934.

Deskey's 'Man's (Smoking) Room' at the 1928 exhibition of the American Designers' Gallery, a short-lived organization of which he was a founder-member, drew enthusiastic praise from contemporary critics for its utilization of new materials such as vitrolite, cork and aluminium. Other materials incorporated by Deskey into his interiors showed his continuing fascination with new product design, including Bakelite, Formica, Fabrikoid, parchment, chromium-plated brass, spun and brushed aluminium and transite (an asbestos-factory waste material that he applied to movable partitions). This search for novelty became a hallmark of his career as an industrial designer, in which he focused also on materials for packaging, prefabricated housing and modular homes. His choice, in 1931, of aluminium foil wallpapers for the men's smoking lounge on the second mezzanine in Radio City Music Hall showed his continuing preoccupation with modern materials for modern interiors, to the point that his selection of a material frequently determined its function in the general market for years to come.

In 1932 Deskey completed his best-known commission, that of the interiors of Radio City Music Hall in Rockefeller Center. Following a competition sponsored by Todd & Brown to select an interior designer for the project, Deskey convinced the project manager, Samuel L. Rothafel (known better by his nickname 'Roxy'), of the advantages of the modern style over that of the exuberant Portuguese Rococo style, the preferred decorative vernacular for motion-picture palaces at the time. The project included thirty lobby areas, smoking rooms, retiring rooms, foyers and lounges. To complete it,

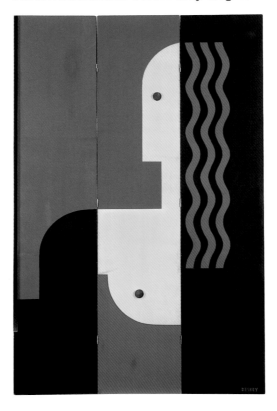

Lysistrata screen, lacquered wood and chromed metal, designed for the dining room of the Gilbert Seldes apartment, New York, c. 1930.

Deskey gathered together some of the foremost artists of the day – painters, sculptors, muralists and craftsmen – who together under his direction created a work of monumental national importance – one that propelled America into Modernism's vanguard. Above the theatre, Deskey crowned the complex with an ultramodern gem of his own creation: Roxy's apartment. The light fixtures – table, floor and wall models – in the apartment's living room and dining room played a dominant role in creating a simple, yet opulent, ambience. In brushed aluminium and black Bakelite, they provided sharp, yet gracious colour accents against the rooms' soaring panelled cherrywood walls, gold ceilings and chestnut carpets.

Although largely forgotten through the years by the art community, Deskey was re-discovered in the 1980s at his retirement home in Vero Beach, Florida. Initially he was reticent to acknowledge his pioneering role in the nascent field of industrial design in the 1930s, so he downplayed his achievements. However, he accepted the label 'Modernist' as a synonym for what he described more accurately as 'Functionalist', even though he rejected out-of-hand the phrase 'Art Deco', a pejorative term that to him described the ornamental excesses of 1920s Paris.

Living room, with cherrywood panelling and furnishings in lacquered and veneered wood, Bakelite, and brushed aluminium, in the apartment designed for S. L. ('Roxy') Rothafel above Radio City Music Hall, c. 1931.

(*right*) Lounge furniture, including an armchair in aluminium manufactured by the Ypsilanti Reed Furniture Co., *c.* 1931.

(*opposite*) 'Man's (Smoking) Room' with cork walls, the furniture in steel, pigskin, aluminium and glass, manufactured by S. Karpen Bros.; exhibited at the American Designers' Gallery exhibit, New York, 1928.

(*left*) Three-panel screen, oil paint and metal leaf on canvas manufactured by Deskey–Vollmer, Inc.; commissioned by Mr and Mrs Glendon Allvine for their home in Long Beach, Long Island, *c.* 1929.

(*above*) Prototype table clock, chromium-plated metal and opaline glass, manufactured by Warren Telechron Co., Ashland, Massachusetts, *c.* 1930.

(*above*) Apartment for Mr and Mrs Adam
Gimbel, New York, *c.* 1929.

(*right*) Adjustable bridge and coffee table,
aluminium with Bakelite top; manufactured
by Deskey–Vollmer, Inc., *c.* 1930.

(*opposite*) Bench and floor lamp in aluminium,
Radio City Music Hall, New York, *c.* 1933.

MAURICE DUFRÈNE (1876–1955)

Dufrène was born in Paris to a father in the wholesale commodities business. In 1887 he left his philosophy courses at the École Communale and switched to the École Nationale Supérieure des Arts Décoratifs. After this he joined a modern print house, where he was introduced to Julius Meier-Graefe, who offered him employment in 1899 in the studio of his Maison Moderne. There he joined the ranks of such august designers as Henry van de Velde, Victor Horta, Charles Plumet and Tony Selmersheim. Dufrène surged to the forefront of the modern design movement, in 1904 becoming a founding member of the *Société des Artistes Décorateurs, through which he exhibited for thirty years. Nobody made the stylistic transition between the Art Nouveau and Art Deco periods more gracefully or with greater versatility. Dufrène taught composition at the *École Boulle from 1912 to 1922, and in 1919 he returned to the Salons as an independent decorator. In 1921 he was appointed artistic director of *La Maîtrise, which opened the following year and which was to produce large editions of furniture at inexpensive prices.

His designs were shown extensively at the 1925 *Exposition Internationale; in addition to the La Maîtrise pavilion, his works could be viewed in a small salon in the Ambassade Française pavilion, in a stand for the furrier Jungmann et Cie, and in an entire row of shops on the Pont Alexandre III. The following year, Dufrène published an album of plates of the interiors shown at the Société des Artistes Décorateurs, and, in 1937, a similar album on the interiors at the Exposition des Arts et Techniques. In the 1930s his earlier predilection for woods yielded gradually to metal and glass. He died in Nogent-sur-Marne.

Pair of *bergères gondoles*, upholstered mahogany; exhibited at the 1913 Salon d'Automne, Paris.

(*far right*) Side chair, Macassar ebony and mahogany inlaid with mother-of-pearl and ivory, *c.* 1920.

(*right*) Table, palisander inlaid with mother-of-pearl and fruitwood, *c.* 1921.

Cabinet, mahogany inlaid with mother-of-pearl, *c.* 1920.

(*opposite*) Interior of La Maîtrise pavilion at the 1925 Exposition Internationale, Paris.

(*left*) Armchair in bentwood, marketed by La Maîtrise, 1920s.

(*above*) Smoker's table, illustrated in *Petits Meubles Modernes*, Paris, 1929.

(*right*) *Semanier*, burled elm and calamander, exhibited by Les Galeries Lafayette in La Maîtrise pavilion at the 1925 Exposition Internationale, Paris.

PAUL DUPRÉ-LAFON (1900–1971)

Born in Marseilles, to Edmond Dupré and Valentine, *née* Lafon, Dupré-Lafon studied at the city's École des Beaux-Arts. In 1923, on receiving a diploma in interior decoration and architecture, he moved to Paris. He completed his first furniture designs in 1925, the year that he met his future wife, Odette Hirtzmann, daughter of a colonel in the infantry. In 1928 – the year of their marriage – he installed himself on the rue Lauriston. From the late 1920s until 1932, Dupré-Lafon formed a collaboration with Hermès, which he retained for his leather accessories and upholstery.

In 1929 he completed his first *chef d'œuvre*: a private residence on the rue Rembrandt, which was reviewed by Bernard Champigneulle in the April 1935 issue of *Mobilier et Décoration*. From 1932 to 1937, he undertook numerous commissions for a wealthy private clientele, including the bankers Dreyfus and Rothschild. Dupré-Lafon designed complete interiors, including the walls, for private homes and villas, many pieces of which were *pièces uniques*. His furniture, always comfortable, made up for its absence of ornament by its emphatically modern forms and richness of materials: warm woods, parchment, leather, lacquer, copper, steel, stone, glass and *métal noirci*.

Dupré-Lafon's second major commission came in 1938: a private residence on the avenue Foch, Paris. Except when he was mobilized between 1940 and 1945, Dupré-Lafon continued in business until 1971. Throughout his career, he avoided the annual Salons and the 1925 and 1937 Expositions, thereby reducing his public exposure to a minimum. His characteristic style was clean, functional and anonymous, and invariably with a certain *puissance*, stylistically similar on occasion to works by Jean Royère, *Saddier et ses Fils, Maurice Champion and Jean *Pascaud. Dupré-Lafon died in Boulogne-Billancourt.

Dupré-Lafon's personal office desk, chair and wastepaper basket; lacquered pearwood, red leather with gilt-metal mounts, 1928. The desk lamp by Poul Henningsen.

(*right*) Period photograph of a Dupré-Lafon interior, showing a variant of the desk shown below.

(*below*) Fall-front desk, parchment with leather and gilt-metal mounts, probably late 1930s.

(*right*) Desk, oak, parchment and leather with steel and gilt-metal mounts, late 1930s.

(*left*) End table in mahogany, metal and red leather, 1940s.

(*above*) Table, gold-leaf on wood with iron and steel feet, probably late 1930s.

(*right*) Smoker's table, rosewood with chromed-metal mounts, *c.* 1940.

(*above*) Desk and chair, spruce with leather upholstery and lacquered bronze mounts, late 1930s/early 1940s.

JEAN-MICHEL FRANK (1895–1941)

Born in Paris, Frank was the third son of Léon Frank, a German Jew who had settled in the French capital to establish a stock brokerage in partnership with a Mr Wolfsohn. Frank grew up on the avenue Kléber, and attended the Lycée Janson de Sailly from 1904. The outbreak of the First World War brought the emigrant family into conflict with its German relatives. Frank's brothers fought on both sides of the war and were killed within a week of each other. His father then committed suicide and his mother was admitted into an insane asylum, where she died in 1919. His cousin Anne Frank, the author of *The Diary of Anne Frank*, died in a Nazi concentration camp.

In 1920 Frank found himself alone, supported by a substantial inheritance from his mother.

He appears to have spent the next five years eradicating the past, travelling extensively and establishing himself in Paris's fashionable inner circle, a milieu that would serve him well in his decorating business. In 1927 he commissioned Adolphe *Chanaux to decorate his apartment at 7 rue de Verneuil. The partnership survived until the Second World War – the furniture being produced at Chanaux's workshops in the Ruche section of the rue Montauban. Beyond this liaison, Frank drew on other well-established collaborators to enhance his reputation. Included in a stellar group were the brothers Alberto (1901–1966) and Diego Giacometti (1902–1985), whom from 1934 he commissioned to provide a wide range of furnishings, including light fixtures, vases, andirons and chimneys, in plaster and

Salon, including a selection of furnishings in straw marquetry, vellum and shagreen; for Templeton Crocker's residence in San Francisco, *c.* 1928.

bronze – the latter material being cast by Alexis Rudier; Christian Bérard did the carpet designs; Paul Rodocanachi, the furniture; Émilio Terry, both furniture and interior designs; Ernest *Boiceau, both carpets and objects; Salvador Dalí, both furniture and screens; and even Pablo Picasso produced screens and fabrics. These artists put the stamp of fashion on Frank's work.

What did Frank himself design? The answer lies somewhere in the middle ground: he concerned himself primarily with an object's form and historical influences, leaving its exact design and execution to others. His style evolved from his respect for French traditionalism; the resulting furniture had stiff functional proportions, its decoration being limited to flat surface areas. Like other Modernists – Georges *Djo-Bourgeois, André Lurçat and Maurice Barret – Frank reduced furniture to its simplest expression, but, unlike them, he remained faithful to the principles of refinement and luxury, believing people needed an environment of warmth and elegance for their psychological well-being. He maintained that there exists a finely tuned architectural relationship between the scale and the dimensions of a piece of furniture. In short, less furniture was more.

An early valued commission was the apartment for Elsa Schiaparelli on the rue Barbet de Jouy; Frank later designed her shop in the Place Vendôme and her townhouse on the rue de Berri. Other clients included Vicomte Charles de Noailles. By 1930, he was known widely within the Paris plutocracy as an arbiter of taste in interior design, his client list providing a 'who's who' of high society. Frank's veneers distinguished his works from those of his contemporaries. These were rendered in earth tones and were lavish in appearance, and included straw marquetry, vellum, parchment, snake- and sharkskin, suede, cane and gypsum, which Frank applied to walls, furniture, doors and chimney surrounds. Lamp bases, if not in bronze or plaster by the Giacometti brothers, were in curved strips of ivory or were hewn from rock crystal, quartz or alabaster. Curtains and fabrics were by Broenne or Mme Cronen-Fels, lace by Selloes and leather by Hermès.

In early 1939, when faced with the German invasion of Paris, Frank left for South America. He settled in Buenos Aires, where he found patronage and friendship in Mme Eugenia Errazuriz and other local clients. His Paris workshops and gallery were closed while he awaited the outcome of the war. The fall of Paris, followed by the Nazi requisition of part of his inventory on the rue Montauban, dashed his hopes of returning. He was encouraged by a lectureship offer from the New York School of Fine and Applied Art and sponsorship by Mrs Archibald Manning Brown, and so moved to the USA. In March 1941, in one of the deep bouts of depression that had punctuated his life, Frank jumped from a New York building to his death.

(*below, left and right*) Hinged nest of tables, wood overlaid with straw marquetry, *c.* 1930.

(*left*) End table, wood overlaid with straw marquetry, *c.* 1930.

(*below*) Armchair veneered in *galuchat*.

(*right and below*) Cabinet, wood overlaid with
shagreen, manufactured by Adolphe Chanaux,
late 1920s.

(*top*) Armchair and side table, wood overlaid
with shagreen, c. 1927.

(*above*) 'Pineapple' table, sanded and limed
oak, c. 1938–40.

(below) Grand piano, wood and shagreen,
probably late 1930s.

(left) Stool, carved oak, c. 1930.

PAUL-THÉODORE FRANKL
(1886–1958)

Born in Vienna, Frankl studied architecture at the Vienna Technische Hochschule for one year before transferring to the engineering faculty at the University of Berlin. Military service interrupted his studies, for which he received a diploma in architectural engineering in 1911. A brief apprenticeship and stint in Copenhagen followed before Frankl set off for the USA in 1914. His first commission served as a propitious start to a career in the design field: a beauty parlour in the Modernist idiom for a Mrs Edward Titus, later known professionally as Helena Rubenstein.

Frankl established his firm, Frankl Galleries, at 4 East 48th Street in Manhattan, listing himself as an architect in the 1916–17 New York business directory. His initial offering included a mix of his own furniture designs and imported fabrics and wallpapers, much of which until the mid-1920s was in a quiet contemporary style. Only with the introduction of his line of skyscraper furniture in 1926–27 did Frankl draw the attention of the international press. The dramatic stepped contours and verticality of his skyscraper bookcases and desks mirrored those of the cathedrals of commerce rising in every American metropolis. Not only were they symbolic of the boundless potential of the new architecture – structures that would scrape the sky – but they were also considered by the critics a forceful and novel expression

of late 1920s taste – one that effectively addressed the shortage of urban living spaces. As he himself explained:

> In my own creations for the modern American home, I have kept within the architectural spirit of our time. The straight line is the most important feature. They call my chests of drawers, my dressing tables, my bookcases, 'skyscraper' – to which I blushingly bow. Why not skyscraper furniture? After all, space is as much a premium within the home as it is outside of it. Why have a bookcase take up half your floor in squat, rigid formality when your bookcase can rise toward the ceiling in vertical, pyramidic beauty with an inviting informality that should go with the books people actually read.

Frankl quickly assumed the role in America of Modernism's most ardent crusader and spokesman, publishing five works that attested to his commitment across a broad front of the decorative arts. In one of these, *New Dimensions* (1928), he extolled the skyscraper as 'a

Dressing table bench in lacquered wood, c. 1927.

distinctive and noble creation . . . a monument of towering engineering and business enterprise', a philosophy that he abruptly retracted in 1932 as the harsh effects of the Depression took root. Now it was 'but a passing fad. The tallest of them, the Empire State, is but the tombstone on the grave of the era that built it . . . Skyscrapers are monuments to the greedy.'

Much of Frankl's 1920s furniture was manufactured in a mix of colourful lacquered wood offset with shiny metal panels and mirrored glass. In the early 1930s, however, he turned his attention to metal furnishings. His tubular chromed chairs and consoles from this period, while meeting the strict standards of functionalism that he espoused, lacked the charm and individuality of the earlier wood pieces.

(*above left*) Cabinet in lacquered wood, aluminium and brass, with Bakelite top, *c.* 1930.

(*above right*) Man's cabinet and wall mirror, red and black lacquered wood with gold and silver plated discs and silver-leaf trim, *c.* 1930.

(*right*) Pair of 'Skyscraper' bookcases,
California redwood with nickel-plated trim,
late 1920s.

(*left*) 'Skyscraper' bookcase in painted wood,
late 1920s.

(*below left*) Pair of 'Skyscraper' chests of drawers in wood with ebonized trim and green lacquered interiors, *c.* 1930.

(*below right*) 'Puzzle' desk and chair in red lacquered wood with silver-leaf drawers and silvered-metal handles, *c.* 1927.

(*bottom*) 'Skyscraper' bookcase in ebonized wood with red lacquered trim, *c.* 1926–27.

EILEEN GRAY (1878–1976)

Gray, a young Irish woman who had adopted the French capital as her home in 1907, made her début at the Salon of the *Société des Artistes Décorateurs in 1913 with a display of lacquered household wares. This intensely shy but determined loner-by-choice worked outside the mainstream of the loosely-knit Paris community artists, designers and craftsmen, shunning its cliques, schools and movements. Gray was therefore, in 1913, something of an enigma in her male-dominated milieu: a gifted non-conformist with a gritty work ethic, one whose novel skills quickly drew the attention of the renowned couturier and art collector Jacques *Doucet, whose patronage established her earliest career – as an artist–designer in lacquer. While embracing the medium's labour-intensive traditional Oriental techniques, Gray produced until the early 1920s a selection of furnishings decorated with a highly personal mix of mythological themes and contrasting abstract imagery. Many of these, including freestanding geometric screens, wall panels and a 'Sirène' chair, show a high degree of luxury and theatricality, qualities then in vogue among the wealthy arbiters of taste who served as her client base.

By 1920 Gray was ready to forgo her decorative pre-war style in favour of a more formal and functional brand of Modernism, one forged by a sense of economy. What gradually diminished was the marriage of figurative and symbolist imagery and the highly individualistic essays in abstraction that had characterized her earlier creations. Whereas the sumptuous tactile surface of the lacquer remained, it now served as a sensuous counterpoint to the crisp angularity of her new designs. The opportunity to give full play to her evolving Modernist ambitions was afforded by the commission from Mme Mathieu-Lévy, a high-society milliner, to refurbish her apartment on the swanky rue de Lota in Paris. Gray responded to the challenge of creating an entire environment by blending bizarre opulence and pared-down sleekness, a combination that effected a systematic yet curious harmony, as it did again in the interior she presented at the 1923 Salon entitled 'A Room–Boudoir for Monte Carlo'. Introduced into the Mathieu-Lévy interior was one of Gray's most ingenious concepts, a lacquered wood screen comprising a grid of articulated blocks that could serve either as wall panelling or as a room divider. With its blocks closed, the screen was employed to encase the interior's walls; with them open, it provided a subtle interplay of solids and voids. The model was reproduced in various colours, and was offered by Gray through her Jean Désert gallery at 217 rue du Faubourg Saint-Honoré, Paris, until its closure in 1930. The screen is now considered a seminal 20th-century design in its ability to serve equally as furniture, architecture and sculpture.

By 1925 Gray was well into the third phase of her career, in which architectural concepts figured increasingly in her pursuit of radical solutions for modern living. Wood was an immediate casualty, abandoned to technology's newest industrial materials. Chromium-plated tubular steel, perforated sheet-metal, cork and cellulose were pressed into service as Gray applied a triple formula – that of the economy of space, material and cost – to her designs for furniture, many of which remained prototypes to be put into standardized production later. Drawing readily on the cutting-edge designs and advice of the era's hierarchy of progressive architects – notably, *Le Corbusier, Walter *Gropius, Marcel *Breuer, members of De Stijl and, around 1930, the *Union des Artistes Modernes (UAM) – Gray created a repertory of unadorned and self-consciously modern furnishings, including tilt-top tables, cantilevered stowaway storage units, retractable walls and room partitions, plus a host of appliances and other gadgets that extended, folded, pivoted or were otherwise adjustable to maximize their space-saving potential. Many models were created specifically for the interiors of the two

(*opposite*) Screen in black lacquered wood, the model introduced, *c.* 1925; breakfast table, model E-1027, with adjustable top in tubular chromed metal, for the guest room in the residence of the Governor of Roquebrune, *c.* 1926–29; and a carpet, 1920s.

(*below*) 'Transat' chair, model E-1027, included in Gray's house in Roquebrune, France, *c.* 1925–30.

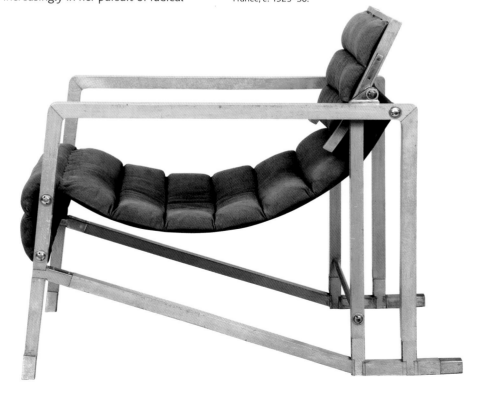

villas she designed and built for herself in southern France: the first, entitled 'E-1027', in Roquebrune between 1927 and 1929; and the second, called 'Tempe à Pailla', in 1934 at Castellar, 4 kilometres from Menton. Both served her as laboratories of Minimalist design, and remain timeless in their utter modernity.

The 1972 auction of the Doucet collection in Paris, four years before her death at age 98, brought the name of Eileen Gray to the eager attention of a discerning new generation of collectors of 20th-century design, including Yves Saint Laurent and Andy Warhol. Appreciation of the designer's astonishing skills — from the exquisite lacquered confections of her early career to the rigorously intellectualized works that followed — has continued to expand following recent biographies and the arrival of newly discovered works by her on the market. In a 2005 Paris auction, six unrecorded examples of her 'Sirène' armchair, commissioned originally by one of Gray's associates, realized more than one million euros *each* in spirited bidding — proof of the designer's unchallenged standing in the pantheon of 20th-century designers.

(*below*) 'Serpent' chair for Mme Mathieu-Lévy, *c*.1933.

(*bottom*) Interior for Mme Mathieu-Lévy's apartment on the rue de Lota, Paris, including the 'Serpent' and 'Bibendum' chair models, 1933.

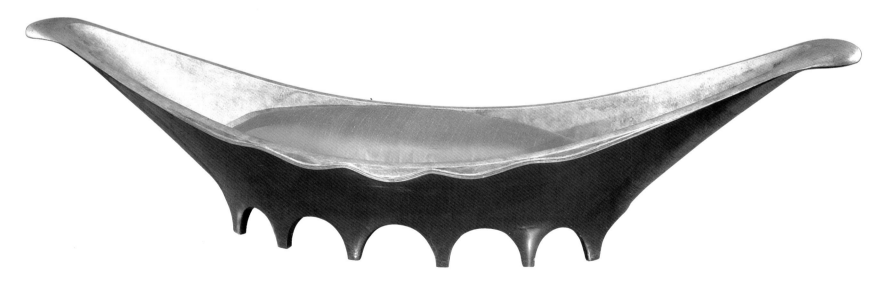

(*top and above*) *Pirogue* (canoe) sofa,
lacquered wood and silver leaf, designed
c. 1919–20, included in the salon in Mme
Mathieu-Lévy's apartment, 1933.

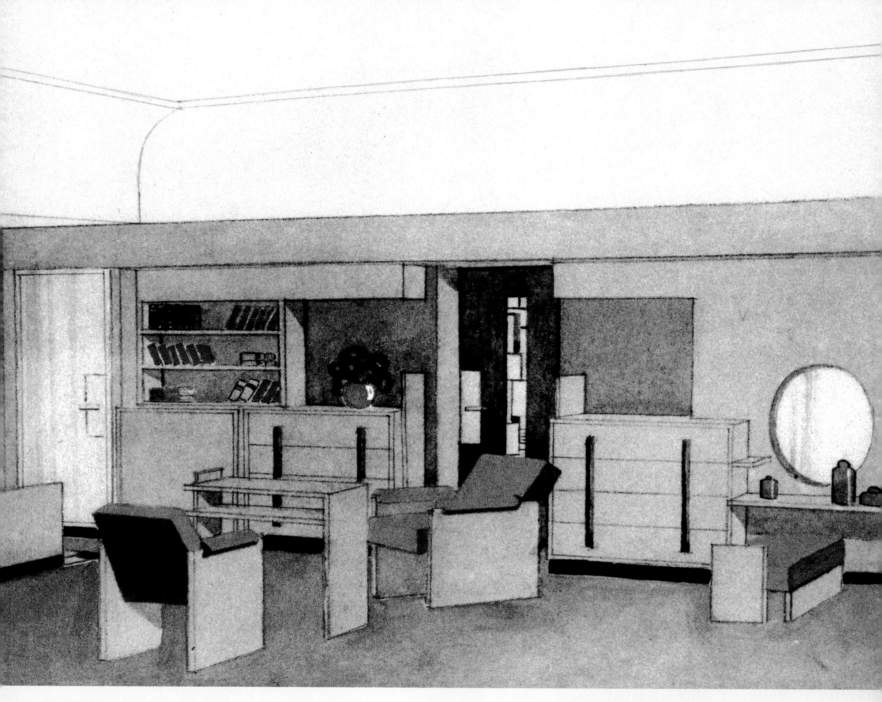

(*above*) Rendering of the furniture for a room
with two beds, illustrated in *Répertoire du
Goût Moderne IV*, Paris.

(*right*) Low table in walnut, chromed metal
and etched glass, late 1920s.

ROBERT MALLET-STEVENS
(1886–1945)

Born in Paris, Mallet-Stevens took the surnames of his father, Maurice Mallet, a painting appraiser, and of his maternal grandfather, Arthur Stevens, a Belgian. His childhood in Maisons-Laffitte was followed in 1905 by enrolment at the École Spéciale d'Architecture, to which he returned in 1924 as a professor. Mallet-Stevens graduated in 1910, and spent the remainder of the pre-war years engaged in architectural and interior design projects, limiting himself to such blueprints as 'Une Cité Moderne', which he showed at the 1912 *Salon d'Automne, and a thesis published in the Belgian magazine *Le Home*. An early and enduring influence was Josef Hoffmann who, in 1905, had designed the famous palace for Mallet-Steven's uncle, Adolphe Stoclet, in Brussels.

After the war, Mallet-Stevens established himself by designing a wide range of private residences, theatres, cinemas, shops, offices and public gardens, the most renowned of which were a villa for the Vicomte de Noailles in Hyères (1923–25), six villas on a street in Auteuil which bears his name (1926–27) and a casino at Saint-Jean-de-Luz (1928).

At the 1925 *Exposition Internationale, Mallet-Stevens was a resounding success, participating in five different projects, including a studio for the Société des Auteurs de Film, a winter garden for which the Martel brothers constructed Cubist trees in reinforced concrete, and a hall in the Ambassade Française pavilion. In 1930 Mallet-Stevens was appointed president of the newly formed *Union des Artistes Modernes. He participated in the 1935 Exposition de Bruxelles and the 1937 Exposition des Arts et Techniques. With the advent of the Second World War, he virtually ceased work, and moved with his family to south-west France, where he died of a protracted illness.

Among the most notable of Mallet-Stevens's furniture designs were garden chairs in green-painted tubular steel and canvas, and a series of office furniture. He used a mix of woods and metal, the latter sometimes executed by Labormetal. Not all of the furniture that bore his name was designed by Mallet-Stevens, however; contributors included Georges *Djo-Bourgeois, PIERRE CHAREAU, René *Prou, *Dominique, Blanche-J. *Klotz and members of the Bauhaus. For fabrics, Raoul *Dufy provided designs; for carpets, EILEEN GRAY and *DIM.

Mallet-Stevens placed great significance on the role that illumination should play in his interiors, preferring either natural light from stained-glass windows by Louis *Barillet or artificial illumination, often on the advice of the lighting engineer André Salomon, commissioned from JEAN PERZEL (*see under* Lighting), *Genet et Michon or Jacques *Le Chevallier.

(*below*) Dressing table in sycamore and polished metal, *c.* 1932.

(*top*) Low table in tinted oak, *c.* 1927.

(*above*) Director's desk in teak; designed for La Société Paris-France, 1929.

(*above*) Desk with inset leather writing surface and recessed nickel-plated metal pen trays, for Mallet-Stevens's residence in Auteuil, *c.* 1928; the chair in lacquered tubular steel manufactured by Labormetal, *c.* 1929; the desk lamp by Jacques Le Chevallier; the floor lamp by Damon, late 1920s; the lacquered screen by Jean Dunand.

MARTINE (PAUL POIRET)

Paul *Poiret's boundless creativity as a couturier spilled over into the field of the decorative arts. In April 1911, following visits to the Wiener Werkstätte and the Palais Stoclet, Poiret founded the École Martine in Paris. Named after one of his daughters, the school took in its first class twelve-year-old girls recruited from the Parisian working class. Poiret's individualism is reflected in the school's charter: students were assigned rooms in his own house, where he personally instructed them in the study of nature. There was no formal tuition, and no teaching staff. The girls were encouraged to visit the Jardin des Plantes and to make sorties into the countryside, sketchbooks in hand. Progress was measured in competitions set and judged by Poiret himself, the best designs of

Dining room for a hunting lodge, in peroba and polished sycamore, exhibited at the 1923 Salon d'Automne, Paris.

which were converted into fabrics printed on cylinder presses by Paul Dumas or into carpets manufactured by Fenaille. The results were spectacular, capturing the spontaneity and freshness of nature. Daisies, poppies, cornflowers and baskets of begonias soon blossomed in kaleidoscopic profusion on carpets, wallpapers and upholstery fabrics. The flower became the pretext for conveying colour, and the students' untutored imaginations and *naïveté* the means of revealing it in unprecedented combinations.

Raoul *Dufy shared Poiret's enthusiasm for the scheme and participated in many of its design projects. The two worked together for many years – initially in a teacher–protégé relationship and then as partners, renting a studio on the avenue de Clichy to print their fabric designs, where the chemist Zifferlin developed colours, lithographic inks and aniline dyes.

Poiret participated at the Salons for many years, both independently and from 1912 in association with the École Martine, which was given the corporate name La Maison Martine, when items went into production. The initial focus was on carpets; the 1920s brought an extensive range of other furnishings: pianos, lampshades, cushions, vitrines and lacquered and marquetry tables. Poiret's furniture was largely Cubist in style, the wood painted in single vibrant colours without further decoration. Seat furniture was piled high with sumptuous tasselled cushions and bolsters. The school's furniture designers included Mario Simon, Léo Fontan and, of course, Poiret himself.

For the 1925 *Exposition Internationale, Poiret devised a masterly means to capture the limelight: three barges, entitled *Amour* (Love), *Délices* (Delights) and *Orgues* (Pipe Organ), anchored in front of the Quai de la Seine. Fitted with plush interiors designed in collaboration with Dufy, La Maison Rosine and La Maison Martine, the vessels drew wide acclaim, providing a fitting capstone to the couturier's career. Painted furniture, characteristically exotic in style, was set off against plush carpets decorated with vibrant flower sprays on warm green and orange-red grounds.

Poiret and the École Martine continued to exhibit at the Salons, in 1927 presenting a deluxe cabin Chantilly for the ocean liner *Île-de-France*. The following year, the school displayed a dining room designed by Yves Chudeau. Because it was disciplined and unspectacular, it lacked the spontaneity and flamboyance of earlier works.

(*right*) Pair of commodes in wood veneered
in shagreen, 1920s.

(*above*) Commode in silvered wood with
incised decoration by Léo Fontan, 1923.

CHARLOTTE PERRIAND
(1903–1999)

Born in Paris, Perriand attended the École de l'Union Centrale des Arts Décoratifs. Her début as a decorator appears to have taken place at the 1926 Salon of the *Société des Artistes Décorateurs, where she displayed a living-room corner with furniture in amboyna and palisander, and a carpet by Marianne Clouzot. The functional and modern ensemble is unremarkable except that it resembles certain models by EUGÈNE PRINTZ at the time. Her decision the following year to join *Le Corbusier and Charles-Édouard *Jeanneret catapulted her to world attention. In the furniture for her attic bar – 'Un Bar sous le Toit' – at the 1927 *Salon d'Automne, the previous year's veneered woods were abruptly replaced by sheets of chromed steel, aluminium and slabs of glass. Clearly, readings of Le

Corbusier's *Vers une architecture* and *L'art décoratif d'aujourd'hui* of 1923 and 1925, respectively, had made her a fervent disciple. Perriand's furniture was now stripped to its essentials, purged of all unnecessary decoration.

She remained with Le Corbusier and Jeanneret until the end of the 1930s. As the three exhibited, in most part, as collaborators, it is difficult to credit their designs individually. Perriand, who until her recent death was an adviser to the Italian furniture manufacturer Cassina, had always stressed the collaborative effort. Contemporary magazines, however, contradicted this modest recollection in crediting the introduction of certain models, especially the 'Grand Confort' armchair, directly to her. A founding member of *Union des Artistes Modernes in 1930, she was still listed as a member in 1955. Certain interiors and individual pieces were credited to her in the society's literature: for example, a 'Habitation d'aujourd'hui' at the 1936 Salon des Arts Ménagers. A modern house, illustrated in *Répertoire du Goût Moderne*, incorporated a favourite Perriand theme: facilities for both work and recreation. Functional kitchens, office space and bathrooms were juxtaposed with an exercise room, bar and solarium. A spartan phonograph and typewriter in surviving photographs remind the reader of the prevailing architectural idiom.

At the outbreak of the Second World War, Perriand accepted an invitation from the Japanese minister of commerce and industry to exhibit in Tokyo and Osaka. She remained in self-exile until 1946, and then returned to France to work both with Le Corbusier and independently. She continued to experiment with metal furnishings, her designs manufactured in Jean Prouvé's studios.

Swivel chair in chromed tubular steel and leather, 1928, marketed by Thonet and exhibited at the 1929 Salon d'Automne.

(*below*) Buffet, mahogany veneered
with *bois de violette*, chromed metal and
sandblasted *dalle de verre* panels, *c*. 1927.

(*right*) Side detail of buffet below.

(*opposite*) Card table, mirrored glass and chromed metal, 1926.

(*left*) Salon in burl amboyna and palisander; fabrics by Marianne Clouzot, 1926.

(*above*) Ensemble by Le Corbusier, Jeanneret and Perriand. Illustrated in Francis Jourdain's *Interieurs*, pl. 17.

(*left*) Lady's desk, polished palmwood
for the Château de Grosbois of the Princesse
de la Tour d'Auvergne, *c.* 1928.

(*below*) Table in palmwood veneered with
Gabonese ebony, on oxidized metal feet,
c. 1930.

(*opposite*) Small salon, Brazilian rosewood
and palmwood, for the Château de Grosbois
residence of the Princesse de la Tour
d'Auvergne, *c.* 1928.

EUGÈNE PRINTZ (1889–1948)

Paris-born Printz was the son of a cabinet-maker in the Faubourg Saint-Antoine, whose firm reproduced a range of *ancien régime* styles, especially Louis XV and XVI. Printz later opened his own atelier at 12 rue Saint-Bernard, where he continued to manufacture 'style' pieces, mostly for interior decorators. He even drew on the 18th-century tradition of providing maquettes – his in cardboard – for the client's approval. Printz's decision to switch to contemporary furniture appears to have come at the time of the 1925 *Exposition Internationale, in which he participated only minimally, sharing the credit with Pelletier and James for the furniture in PIERRE CHAREAU's office–library in the Ambassade Française pavilion.

He made his début as a Modernist at the 1926 *Société des Artistes Décorateurs with a bedroom in rosewood. His reputation grew rapidly; by 1930, his highly personal style attracted praise from the critics, after which he showed his work in most of the era's major expositions, including the 1935 Exposition de Bruxelles and the 1937 Exposition des Arts et Techniques. After the Second World War, Printz joined Jules *Leleu, Léon-Albert and Maurice-Raymond *Jallot, *Dominique and René *Prou in the group Décor de France.

Printz's style shows great energy and innovation; a charming interplay of arches and perpendiculars predominate, the crispness of the design accentuated by the contrast between dark woods and bright metal mounts. Many of his pieces were illustrated in such magazines as *Sièges Contemporains* and *Petits Meubles du Jour*. Two aspects of his work bear mention: his modular tables, with three-, five- or six-hinged elements, which could be positioned in a straight line or compressed to form a bookcase, and his system of folding doors (*portes-accordéon*) on large cupboards.

From his showroom at 81 rue de Miromesnil in the fashionable 8th *arrondissement*, Printz sought out an elite clientele. Included were the Princesse de la Tour d'Auvergne, Princesse de Wagram, Vicomte de Richemont and Baron Rudolphe d'Erlanger. State commissions included the Musée Permanent des Colonies in Vincennes, the Cité Universitaire in Paris and interiors for the Société Générale. Other distinguished customers were Marshal Lyautey, Jeanne *Lanvin and the actor Louis Jouvet, for whose productions *Jean de la Lune* and *Domino* he designed sets. Preferred woods were *palmier*, Gabonese ebony, kekwood, sycamore and violetwood; mounts were in copper, steel, bronze and wrought iron, and their surfaces were oxidized, silvered, patinated, lacquered or incised.

JEAN DUNAND (*see under* Silver, Metal, Lacquer and Enamel) was a frequent collaborator, providing lacquered and chased decorative panels for Printz's cabinet doors. A catalogue published by the firm in 1934 showed a wide selection of interiors and furniture. Customers were invited to choose their favourite woods. Editions ranged from five for the most elaborate pieces, to thirty for smaller items. A distinctive feature of the interiors was their use of a circular ceiling cupola to provide indirect lighting. The same catalogue offered items by Henri Cros, Dunand, Jean *Mayodon, André *Metthey and François *Pompon.

(*above*) Smoker's table in palmwood, 1930.

(*right*) *Secrétaire à abattant*, Brazilian rosewood with lacquered and incised metal panels by Jean Dunand, *c.* 1935.

(*right*) Living room, including an armchair in black lacquered wood, designed for Marshall Lyautey's reception hall in the Musée des Colonies, Paris; exhibited at the 1933 Salon of the Société des Artistes Décorateurs.

(*below*) Table in walnut with hinged sections, 1928.

(*right*) Armchair in palisander with copper feet, upholstered in satin, c. 1930.

(*left*) Writing table in palmwood veneered
in Gabonese ebony, on oxidized metal feet.

(*above*) Bookcase in palmwood and
sycamore on copper feet; the doors in copper
with inlaid silvered decoration, c. 1927–28.

(*right*) Magazine holder in wood and metal, late 1920s.

(*far right*) Chair in black walnut, *c.* 1929.

(*above*) Bedroom in palmwood, exhibited at the 1926 Salon of the Société des Artistes Décorateurs, Paris.

ARMAND-ALBERT RATEAU
(1882–1938)

Rateau was born in Paris, where between 1894 and 1898 he studied sculpture at the *École Boulle. In 1905 he was appointed director of the design studios of La Maison Alavoine et Cie, for which he supervised decorating commissions for clients such as *Tiffany & Co. in the Place de l'Opéra, and the Hôtel Pereire on the rue de Faubourg Saint-Honoré. Among the firm's residential commissions were two in the USA, for W. K. Vanderbilt and George and Florence Blumenthal. Rateau was mobilized in 1914, and served for the duration of the war, after which he resigned from La Maison Alavoine and established his own decorating company on the boulevard Berthier in Paris's 17th *arrondissement*. The meteoric success he achieved in the next years suggests that he had formulated the plans for his future meticulously and well in advance of his departure from Alavoine, perhaps through many empty hours of trench warfare along the nation's borders.

The years from 1919 to 1922 witnessed many of Rateau's most inspired creations, which he designed for a select group of elite clients. The first of these were the Blumenthals; a fortuitous reunion on board the ocean liner *La Savoie* on a trans-Atlantic crossing, in November 1919, forged a business relationship that led first to the commission to furnish the patio area of the indoor swimming-pool in their Manhattan townhouse, and later to further decorating commissions for their homes in Auteuil, in the Paris suburbs, and one near Grasse in the Alpes-Maritimes section of south-eastern France –

the Château de Malbosc. The Blumenthals were in every way representative of the clients to whom Rateau gravitated throughout his career: they were immeasurably wealthy, successful and socially prominent. (George Blumenthal was a senior partner of Lazard Frères in New York, and later dedicated himself increasingly to philanthropic causes in France, for which he was appointed a grand officer of the Légion d'Honneur by the French government in 1934.)

A second major client was immediately forthcoming – Jeanne *Lanvin, who was in 1920 nearing the pinnacle of her fame as a couturier. Celebrated before the war for her matching mother-and-daughter garments and waisted *robes de style*, Lanvin embarked in the new decade on some fresh ventures, including the refurbishment of the bedroom, boudoir and bathroom in her *hôtel particulier* on the rue Barbet-de-Jouy on the Left Bank, and the formation of two new companies, Lanvin-Décoration and Lanvin-Sport. For all of these, Rateau was chosen to design interiors, which he implemented through a large and comprehensive furniture-making workshop called the Ateliers Neuilly–Levallois at 23 rue Gide in Levallois on the outskirts of Paris, which he purchased two years later. It employed about one hundred artist–craftsmen divided among seven or so workshops, including those for cabinetry, metalworking, stucco and plaster, marble and alabaster, fabrics and weaving, wood panelling and carving, and gilding, lacquering and decorative painting.

During the hectic early 1920s Rateau accepted other decorating commissions in Paris, including ones for the Hôtel de Crillon in the Place de la Concorde and the interior of an apartment for the Comtesse de Beaurepaire on the boulevard Saint-Germain. In these Rateau effectively placed his interiors alongside some that were purely traditional in style. This ability to blend his distinctly Neoclassical, yet modern, designs with existing ensembles within a home was the successful basis for much of Rateau's work, and a measure of his brilliance. The bathroom that he designed c. 1925–26 for the Duchess of Alba's residence in Madrid – the Liria Palace – showed further this ability to mix the new with the old: his interior included a sumptuous mix of Siennese marble, bronze

(*above*) Jeanne Lanvin's bedroom in her residence on the rue Barbet-de-Jouy, Paris, disinstalled c. 1965, and reassembled in the Musée des Arts Décoratifs, Paris.

(*opposite below*) Coffee table, model 1209, bronze and marble, c. 1920–22.

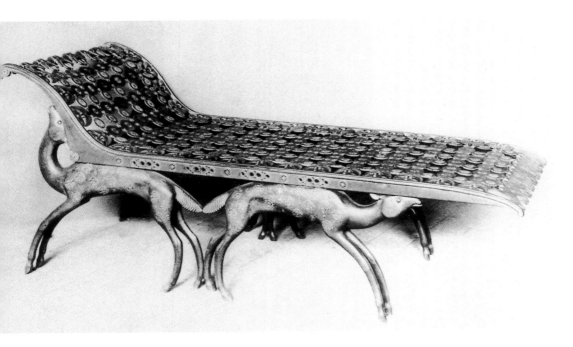

(*left*) Chaise-longue in bronze, model 1385, designed for the terrace of Jeanne Lanvin's boudoir and displayed in the stand of La Maison Callot Soeurs at the 1925 Exposition Internationale, Paris.

(*below*) *Torchère* in bronze, for Jeanne Lanvin's residence on the rue Barbet-de-Jouy, Paris, 1920–22.

(*above*) Ensemble displayed at the Metropolitan Museum of Art, New York, in 1926, including a six-panel wood screen in engraved gold lacquer entitled 'Coursing in the Forest'; seat furniture designed by Paul Plumet and upholstered in tapestry by Braquenié et Cie; a low table, a pair of bronze floor lamps, and a small leopard-skin rug.

furniture and appurtenances, and lacquered panels that in its evocation of past styles blended perfectly into the palace's existing décor.

The 1925 *Exposition Internationale presented Rateau with both a challenge and a dilemma. Clearly too important an event to miss, his entry was complicated by the fact that he was not a member of any of the societies who exhibited at the annual Salons, and was therefore ineligible to participate in the joint displays presented by their members at the Exposition, especially that of the *Société des Artistes Décorateurs, who showed their works in a giant pavilion named L'Ambassade Française. Rateau's solution was shrewd: he lent examples of his furniture to exhibitors grouped in the Grand Palais under the heading of 'La Couture et La Joaillerie', for use in their displays. These included, among an impressive showcase of modern French fashion, Jeanne Lanvin (for her stand 'Jenny'), the Callot sisters, Madeleine Vionnet, Paul *Poiret and Elsa Schiaparelli. Also on view at the Exposition for two weeks at the Arnold Seligman gallery in the Place Vendôme was the bathroom he had designed for the Duchess of Alba, a masterstroke that provided valuable coverage in both fashion magazines and decorative arts revues.

In attempting to define Rateau's style one might more easily determine what it was not. It was not, first, quite like anything produced by any of his contemporaries in France, or anywhere else for that matter. None of the period's standard grammar of decorative ornament is evident, such as the sharply angular or elongated geometric stylizations that adorned most of the items displayed at the annual Salons, now broadly defined as Art Deco. Yet Rateau's favourite motifs have a distinct, even if not typical, 1920s look. These include a delightful range of flora and plants, such as marguerites, acanthus and palm trees, rendered in the designer's highly personalized style. The same distinction applies to his zoological creations; his butterflies, gazelles, pheasants and greyhounds, all of which, while evoking the distant past, convey an indisputable modernity under his hand. A great deal of humour, charm and whimsy are also readily discernible in these creatures – elements lacking in most of the decorative designs of the period.

(*above*) Wash stand, bronze and marble, c. 1925.

If not therefore a typical Art Deco designer, as the term is today loosely defined, how then might Rateau be categorized? He should not, like JACQUES-ÉMILE RUHLMANN and Jules *Leleu, be described as a traditional Modernist, as the term is now taken to identify those 1920s designers who drew their inspiration primarily from the cabinet-making legacy of the French 18th-century **ébénistes** who served the Bourbon court. Rateau's style in most part found its inspiration in far earlier antecedents, those of the Hellenistic, Greco-Roman, Etruscan and Roman ages. The answer is something of a paradox: he was a Neoclassical Modernist. Bronze, Rateau's signature material, was used extensively in antiquity as its strength permitted an extreme lightness of design — the same lightness and grace that are discernible in Rateau's bronze furnishings. Like those of antiquity, Rateau's bronze furniture avoids the appearance of innate mass and unwieldiness in its slender proportions and elegant forms. To embellish his creations, Rateau resorted to the similar array of lavish materials employed by other noted designers at the time: ivory

(*above*) Ensemble displayed at the Metropolitan Museum of Art, New York, 1926, including an example of the bronze 'fish' chair designed for the Blumenthals' swimming pool in their New York residence, *c.* 1920; a pair of bronze floor lamps with alabaster shades, a bronze dressing table with mirror, and a bronze *guéridon*.

(*left*) Dressing table in bronze with marble top.

for light switches; carved alabaster and rock crystal for lamp shades; and black marble for table tops. His upholstery fabrics, mostly in silk, were 18th-century in inspiration, with formalized floral or linear patterns offered in a sedate palette.

Rateau remained extremely busy in the late 1920s and early 1930s, his client list retaining a sprinkling of titled aristocrats, many from outside France, such as the Baron and Baroness de Klitzing at La Tour-de-Peilz on Lake Geneva. Although the economic momentum and optimism of the previous decade slowed dramatically in Europe throughout the 1930s, reducing Rateau's work schedule along with those of all designer–decorators, a steady stream of clients continued to seek him out, some as far away as Rio de Janiero and Buenos Aires. His premature death in February 1948 was observed with respect and sadness by those who had observed at first hand his polite demeanour and creativity.

(*above*) Pair of lacquered wood and bronze doors designed for Rateau's residence on the Quai de Conti, Paris, *c.* 1930.

(*left*) Armchair in ebonized wood.

(*below*) Chaise-longue, model 1193a, in gilt-ash with silk upholstery (originally ocelot), designed for the Duchess of Alba's bathroom in her Madrid residence, the Liria Palace, *c.* 1925.

JACQUES-ÉMILE RUHLMANN
(1879–1933)

Had France of the 1920s been a monarchy, Ruhlmann would have held the position of *ébéniste du roi*. No work as fine as his had been seen for 125 years. Drawing inspiration directly from the 18th century, he was a strict traditionalist, keeping his forms elegant, refined and, above all, simple. Although many of his most celebrated works were created before 1920, his furniture is today considered the epitome of the Art Deco style, and its finest expression. He was born in Paris to François and Valentine Ruhlmann, originally from Alsace. In 1900, after completing his studies and three years of military service, Ruhlmann joined his father's painting, wallpaper and mirror business at 6 rue du Marché Saint-Honoré. His early responsibilities were primarily to oversee the firm's timber inventory and to coordinate its business negotiations, but by 1903 he was interested enough in furniture design to pay visits to various cabinetry shops in the area, such as Gevens, Stauffacher and Laberthe. In 1907 he married Marguerite Seabrook and his father died.

Ruhlmann made his début at the 1910 *Salon d'Automne with a selection of wallpaper designs, and in 1911 he exhibited a similar display at the *Société des Artistes Décorateurs. In 1912 he moved the family business to larger quarters bordering on two streets, the address being given as both 19 rue Maleville and 27 rue de Lisbonne. Continuing the firm's previous stock-in-trade – paintings, mirrors and light fixtures – Ruhlmann set aside special facilities for his deepening interest in furniture design, of which he showed

his first models at the 1913 Salon d'Automne. It was an inauspicious moment, certainly, with war less than a year away.

The First World War provided Ruhlmann with the opportunity both to refine his designs and to obtain a significant head start on those of his contemporaries who saw active service. He was intensely productive during this period and designed such masterpieces as the 1916 corner cabinet (*encoignure*) in ebony, its door veneered with a large basket of stylized blooms. Produced in both three- and four-legged versions, the model stands today at the acme of Art Deco taste. In 1919 he went into partnership with Pierre Laurent, a friend and paintings specialist, and they formed Les Établissements Ruhlmann et Laurent. Laurent was placed in charge of the rue Maleville decorating works, which included silks, carpets, textiles and lighting, while Ruhlmann retained the rue de Lisbonne space as a furniture showroom. In the same year they purchased an industrial building at 14 rue d'Ouessant in the 15th *arrondissement*

and installed a cabinetry workshop on the third floor. Over the next nine years the firm expanded slowly, recruiting artisans with the assistance of André *Fréchet, director of the *École Boulle, and Fenot, a noted *ébéniste*. Eventually the entire building was taken over for workshops, storerooms and offices. A new and more modern workshop employed thirteen artisans and two machinists, headed by a Monsieur Avon. Monsieur Schlesser was placed in charge of veneers, among other things.

By 1920 Ruhlmann's reputation was established. From 1913 to 1924 – more than half his entire career as a furniture designer – Ruhlmann's designs were executed by a range

(*opposite*) Office displayed at the Exposition Coloniale, Paris, 1931; including *vases réflecteurs* by Raymond Subes.

(*below*) 'Bloch' model daybed, *bois de violette* with gilt-bronze mounts, *c.* 1926.

(*bottom*) 'Cabanel Basse-Boule' coffee table, Macassar ebony inlaid with ivory and amaranth, the model introduced *c.* 1918–19.

(below) 'Coffret d'or', Macassar ebony applied with gold leaf and inlaid with ivory, the door's central panel sculpted by Albert Binquet, c. 1928.

of *ébénistes* in the Faubourg Saint-Antoine, including Haentges Frères and Fenot. Only the rarest and most exquisite materials were used in his furniture. Rich veneers, such as palisander, amboyna, amaranth, Macassar ebony and Cuban mahogany, were inlaid with ivory, tortoiseshell or horn. Dressing tables were embellished with leather, **galuchat** or parchment panelling; silk tassels on drawer pulls added a further touch of elegance. On rare occasions, pieces were sent to JEAN DUNAND's workshops to be lacquered, and in the late 1920s and early 1930s pieces were sometimes sprayed with a protective coating of cellulose in the rue d'Ouessant workshops.

The 1925 *Exposition Internationale catapulted Ruhlmann to the forefront of the

modern French decorative arts movement. The nation heaped accolades on the man who demonstrated to the world France's superiority in its most prized tradition – furniture. After nine years in the furniture-making business, he was pronounced an overnight success, but in those years he had been known only to a privileged minority, a situation that radically changed with his Hôtel du Collectioneur at the Exposition, as many thousands of visitors flocked through its monumental doors to gaze in awe at the majestic interior described in its catalogue, with more than a little understatement, as 'a residence for a rich collector'. The building was designed by Ruhlmann's close friend, Pierre Patout, its success derived in part from the talents of the celebrated group of artists who assisted in the project: Émile-Antoine Bourdelle, François *Pompon, Robert *Bonfils, JEAN DUPAS, Gustave-Louis *Jaulmes, Maurice-Raymond *Jallot, Francis *Jourdain, Henri *Rapin, JEAN PUIFORCAT, EDGAR BRANDT, ÉMILE DECOEUR, Jean *Mayodon, Jean Dunand, Claudius *Linossier, FRANÇOIS-ÉMILE DECORCHEMONT and PIERRE-ÉMILE LEGRAIN, to list only the better-known. The firm's own principal designers were credited in the introduction to Jean Badovici's 1924 *Harmonies intérieurs de Ruhlmann*; included were Stephan, Huet, Bougenot, Picaud, Lardin, Lautelin and Denise Holt.

(right, above) Side table, palisander inlaid with ivory, the model introduced 1915–20.

(right, below) Silver cabinet, Macassar ebony inlaid with ivory, c. 1919.

It is perhaps necessary to stress that Ruhlmann had no formal training in cabinet-making and that his technical knowledge was never more than superficial. He made drawings in ink, often on a scale of 2/100th, which provided front, elevation and profile views of pieces. These were passed to a draughtsman to be rescaled at 1/10th, and from there into the cabinet-maker's blueprint. Numerous examples of Ruhlmann's preliminary sketches were reproduced in Léon Moussinac's 1924 *Croquis de Ruhlmann*, in which fifty-four plates bear witness to his ingenuity.

Apart from the 1925 Exposition Internationale and the two annual Salons, Ruhlmann exhibited in Milan, Madrid, New York, Athens and Barcelona, as well as in the 1931 Exposition Coloniale. In 1934, a year after his death, a retrospective was staged at the Pavillon de Marsan in Paris. The accompanying catalogue provided a long list of prestigious clients, including the Élysée Palace, David Weill, Jacqueline Francell, the *Île-de-France*, Monsieur Mollinie, the Paris Chamber of Commerce and the Maharajah of Indore.

In view of the fact that his reputation rested largely on his use of sumptuous veneers, Ruhlmann reacted with remarkable equanimity to the post-1925 advent of metal into the furniture field. Yet metal mounts appeared on his furniture from the mid-1920s; he justified his adoption of metal as a way of countering the problems inherent in the modern centrally heated home, particularly the damage caused to wood veneers by dry heat. His desk in 1932 for the Maharajah of Indore provides a fine example of the successful incorporation of metal, its princely proportions embracing chromed-metal accessories such as a telephone, swivel lamp and wastepaper basket. This and his other furniture were beyond the means of all but the most prosperous; he justified his exclusiveness repeatedly by arguments such as that quoted in the catalogue for the 1928 Lord & Taylor Exposition of Modern French Decorative Arts, held in in New York:

> The movement to develop a contemporary style in interior decoration will only come fully into its own when people of moderate incomes become interested, but owing to the fact that costly experiments must first

be made in furniture *de luxe*, before this renaissance in decoration can be effected, it is necessary that this art be developed under the patronage of the wealthy, just as the art of the older epochs was developed under the patronage of the courts.

Ruhlmann therefore left to others the challenge of producing well-designed but inexpensive furniture for the middle classes. He died at the relatively young age of fifty-four, at which point the firm was dissolved. Laurent retained the painting side of the business and Ruhlmann's nephew, Alfred *Porteneuve, established his own decorating firm in which he created works in the Ruhlmann tradition.

(*below*) Ensemble including a cabinet and chair from the Grand Salon of Ruhlmann's Hôtel du Collectionneur at the 1925 Exposition Internationale, Paris.

(*bottom*) Ambassador's desk in palisander, shagreen, ivory and silvered bronze; manufactured by Adolphe Chanaux and displayed in the office–library in the Ambassade Française pavilion at the 1925 Exposition Internationale, Paris.

(opposite) Loggia with furniture in palisander for Jacqueline Francell, exhibited at the 1930 Salon of the Société des Artistes Décorateurs, Paris.

(below left) Console table, Macassar ebony inlaid with ebony and ivory, c. 1921.

(below right) Tall case clock, 1922.

(bottom) 'Tardieu' desk, black lacquered wood with silvered-bronze mounts and wastepaper basket, exhibited at the 1929 Salon of the Société des Artistes Décorateurs, Paris, in a study–bedroom for a Crown Prince, the Viceroy of India; later purchased by André Tardieu, then the French Prime Minister, hence its name.

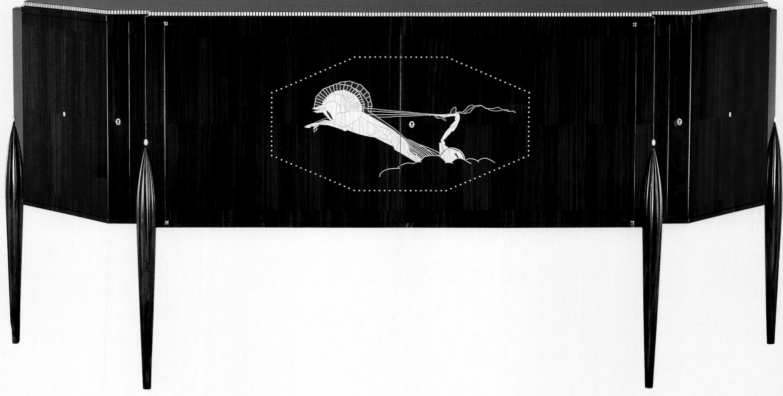

(*top*) Dressing table, amboyna and gilt
and silvered bronze, 1920s.

(*above*) *Meuble au Char*, Macassar ebony
inlaid with ivory, the model exhibited at
the 1919 Salon d'Automne, Paris.

(*below left*) Jewelry cabinet, burl amboyna
inlaid with ivory, *c.* 1913.

(*below right*) *Fuseau* fall-front desk, amaranth
and shagreen inlaid with ivory, *c.* 1926.

(*below*) Cabinet, burl amboyna inlaid with ivory and with silvered-bronze feet, similar to the model commissioned by the Élysée Palace, Paris, 1920.

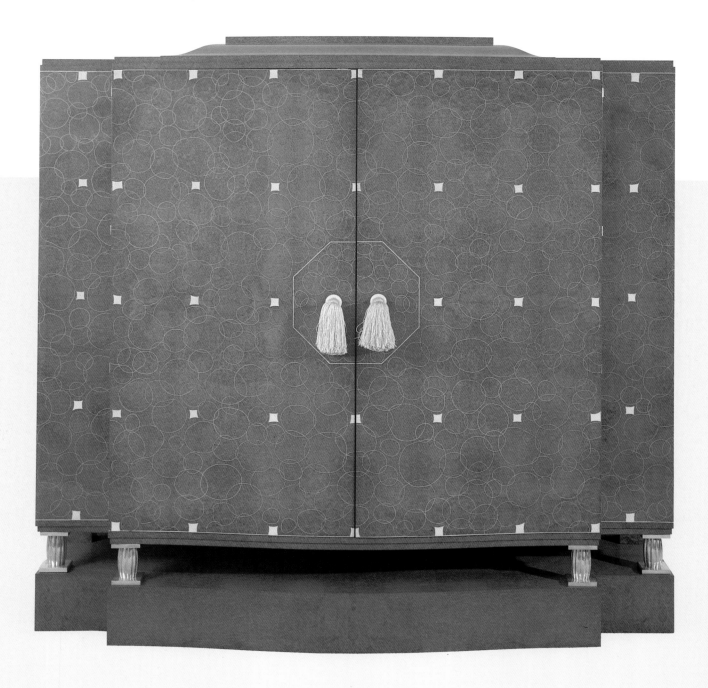

(*top*) Salon with furniture in Macassar ebony and amboyna, for the architect Molinié, 1920s.

(*above*) Chaise-longue in Macassar ebony with silvered-bronze feet, the model exhibited in Ruhlmann's Hôtel du Collectionneur at the 1925 Exposition Internationale, Paris, and again at the 1928 Salon of the Société des Artistes Décorateurs, Paris.

SÜE ET MARE

Louis Süe (1876–1968) first collaborated with André Mare (1887–1932) immediately before the First World War, though their relationship was not formalized until after the war. Süe was born in Bordeaux. His father, Eugène Süe, was a doctor who persuaded him to pursue a medical career at the city's polytechnic. But the son's passion was for the arts, and he left in 1895 for Paris, where he discovered Impressionism, then all the rage. He enrolled at the École des Beaux-Arts, and received his diploma in 1901. Further studies in architecture completed his education. Now ready to put his diverse talents to the test, Süe exhibited paintings at the Salon des Indépendants and the *Salon d'Automne, and designed houses in the rue Cassini (1905) in collaboration with Paul Huillard. In 1910 Süe formed an association with Paul *Poiret, decorating the latter's houseboat *Nomade* and his residence on the avenue d'Antin. In 1912, after Poiret had established La Maison MARTINE, Süe formed his own decorating firm, L'Atelier Français, on the rue de Courcelles. He served on the Eastern Front during the First World War, and on his return formed with André Mare the

Belle France decorating firm at 22 avenue Friedland, a prelude to their Compagnie des Arts Français at 116 rue du Faubourg Saint-Honoré. Numerous commissions followed, both architectural and decorative, including that of the cenotaph in the Arc de Triomphe.

André Mare was born in Argentan. Studies in painting at the Académie Julian were followed in 1903–04 by participation at the Salon d'Automne and the Salon des Indépendants. By 1910, Mare had begun to place an increasing emphasis in his Salon exhibits on the decorative arts, including bookbindings, furniture and complete ensembles. From 1911 to 1913 he collaborated with an imposing list of artists: Raymond Duchamp-Villon, Marie *Laurencin and Jacques Villon, among others. He exhibited his controversial 'Maison Cubiste' in 1912. With the outbreak of war, Mare volunteered, and his wife Charlotte executed his furniture, carpet and fabric designs until the armistice. His relationship with Süe was formalized in 1919, when the Compagnie des Arts Français was established, which the partners promoted as 'évolution dans la tradition'.

With different talents and temperaments, Süe et Mare forged a highly successful business venture, described by Jean Badovici in his introduction to *Intérieurs de Süe et Mare* (1924) as an 'admirable association of two dissimilar

(*above*) Commode in Macassar ebony inlaid with mother-of-pearl and silver, commissioned by the actress Jane Renouardt, c. 1926–27.

(*right*) Desk chair, Macassar ebony inlaid with mother-of-pearl and silver, commissioned by Jane Renouardt, c. 1926–27.

minds which combined the best of their qualities to put them in the service of Beauty'. One key to their success lay in their team of collaborators, which included Gustave-Louis *Jaulmes, Paul *Vera, Charles Dufresne, Drésa, Pierre Poisson, MAURICE MARINOT, Richard *Desvallières, Charles *Martin and Bernard Boutet de Monvel, each free either to create individual works or to participate in group projects.

Süe et Mare produced a great variety of furnishings and objects: clocks, ceramics, lamps, fabrics, wallpapers, carpets and silverware. Important clients included the director of the Théâtre Danou, the duke of Medina Coeli, the countess of Goyeneche, Charles Stern, Marcel Kapferer and Jacques *Doucet. Their furniture was traditionally inspired, with traces of Louis XIV, Louis XV, Restoration and Louis-Philippe evident, especially the last, of which in a 1920 interview with Léon Deshairs, published in *Art et Décoration*, Süe et Mare declared:

> The Louis-Philippe style, for a long time
> favoured in the provinces, is the most
> recent to date of French styles. It is rather
> clumsy, but earnest, logical, welcoming...

(*top*) 'Delompré' revolving pedestal table, carved ebony, c. 1926.

(*above*) Console in wrought iron with marble top, commissioned by Louis Blériot, mid-1920s.

We are not reviving it; we are not deliberately continuing it, but we find it while seeking out simple solutions, and through it we bind ourselves to the whole of our magnificent past.

The partners developed their theories further in a 1921 manifesto, *Architectures*. From the 1830–48 era they adopted the qualities of comfort that the period's cabinet-makers had built into their austere furniture. Süe et Mare's armchairs were lush and inviting, and their tufted colourful velour upholstery offered comfort and luxury while evoking the past. Other models were Baroque, even theatrical. Their imposing desk in Gabonese ebony – exhibited at the 1925 *Exposition Internationale

and later purchased by the Museum of Modern Art, New York – incorporated **ormolu** feet cast as elongated fronds, an updated version of Rococo cabinetry.

The firm's exhibit at the 1925 Exposition Internationale, 'Le Musée d'Art Contemporain', had eclipsed all of their earlier work and received great acclaim. Comprising a rotunda and gallery, it was decorated by a wide team of collaborators. Colour and sumptuousness abounded – the furniture was in carved giltwood and upholstered in Aubusson tapestry. Elsewhere, Süe et Mare furniture was part of a number of other exhibitions, including the Ambassade Française pavilion, the Parfums d'Orsay boutique, the Salle des Fêtes and the Pleyel and *Christofle–Baccarat stands.

(*above left*) Chest of drawers, rosewood and Macassar ebony with gilt-metal mounts, c. 1925.

(*above right*) Linen chest (*chiffonnier*), palisander and burled wood with marble top, exhibited in the Grand Salon of the firm's 'Un Musée d'Art Contemporain' pavilion at the 1925 Exposition Internationale, Paris. The vase by Edgar Brandt.

The partnership lasted until 1928, when Jacques *Adnet assumed the firm's directorship. Mare returned to painting, while Süe continued independently as an architect and *ensemblier* until the Second World War. During the 1930s, his commissions included shops, stage-sets, offices and private houses. He settled in Istanbul during the war, where he lectured at the Academy of Fine Arts. He later returned to France and retired to the Gascony region, near Bordeaux.

(*above left*) Desk, model No. 712, in mahogany, designed for a M. Moreau, 1923. The clock in gilt-bronze designed for Süe et Mare by Paul Vera and modelled by Pierre Poisson, *c.* 1921.

(*above right*) Storage cabinet in mahogany with burled wood veneer, early 1920s.

(left) Ensemble including a cheval mirror in Macassar ebony with gilded frame and an armchair in Macassar ebony, shown in La Compagnie des Arts Français' display at the Exposition of Modern French Decorative Arts at Lord & Taylor, New York, 1928.

(right) Lady's desk in Macassar ebony inlaid with mother-of-pearl and silver, part of an ensemble for the actress Jane Renouardt, c. 1926–27.

(*right*) 'Joussein' dressing table (open),
Macassar ebony inlaid with ivory, and chair,
early 1920s.

(*below*) 'Mongolfier' side chair in palisander,
early 1920s.

(*right*) 'Joussein' dressing table (closed).

(left) Secrétaire à abattant, Macassar ebony inlaid with ivory, c. 1920.

(below) Three-piece suite of salon seat furniture, gilt-wood with tapestry designed by Édouard Benedictus and manufactured by Beauvais, c. 1925.

(*right*) Table in Macassar ebony, early 1920s. The sculpted bronze heads by Scarpa.

(*below*) Settee in gilt-wood upholstered in Aubusson tapestry, representing the story of Paul and Virginia from a design by Charles Dufresne, the model included in the Grand Salon of the firm's 'Un Musée d'Art Contemporain' pavillion at the 1925 Exposition Internationale, Paris.

SCULPTURE

European sculpture from the inter-war years can be divided roughly into two categories: commercial, large-edition statuary, commissioned from sculptors as decorative works for the domestic market by *éditeurs d'art* and foundries such as *Etling et Cie, *Le Verrier, *Arthur Goldscheider and *Les Neveux de J. Lehmann; and works created by avant-garde artist–sculptors, often as *pièces uniques* or in small editions, which fall into that indefinable grey area between the 'fine' and 'applied' arts.

Commercial sculpture mainly comprised a seemingly inexhaustible number of works in bronze or mixed-media materials that served to beautify a mantelpiece or boudoir; as such, they fulfilled much the same function that figurines in porcelain, **biscuit de Sèvres** or terracotta had performed in the elegant salons of 18th-century high society. Now, however, models were invariably produced in different sizes, and often in a variety of materials and finishes, to accommodate the tastes and pocketbooks of an expanded bourgeoisie. Since these were marketed as objects of desire, they were sold by jewellers and department stores rather than by art galleries. Despite their blatant appeal, such works were often exquisitely crafted, and many today have enormous period charm, capturing the spirit of the Art Deco era more poignantly than other, more serious, works. Their subject matter derived from popular culture, often the current idols of its theatre, sports and fashion worlds, so these works provide the collector with a faithful depiction of early 20th-century society. Included were the chorus lines at the Moulin Rouge and the more *risqué* cabarets in Montmartre. Exotic figures and dancers associated with countries such as Egypt, Mexico and Russia also served as inspiration, reflecting the Parisian interest at the time in the Orient, Léon *Bakst's costumes, Paul *Poiret's dress designs and the dance crazes of the new Jazz Age.

Thanks to the invention by Achille Collas in the mid-1800s of the pantograph, a machine that was capable of scaling down or enlarging three-dimensional sculptures while keeping their original proportions, editions were offered in two or more sizes, thereby widening their market appeal. Among these, the category described today as bronze-and-ivory,

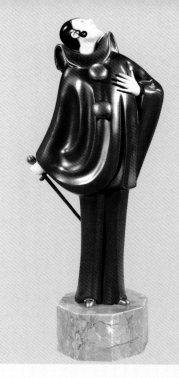

CLAIRE JEANNE ROBERTE COLINET
(*below*) *Ankara Dancer*, patinated bronze and carved and tinted ivory, on marble base, in an edition by the LNJL foundry, Paris, 1920s.

ROLAND PARIS
(*right*) *Pierrot*, cold-painted bronze and carved ivory, on onyx base, 1920s.

or **chryselephantine** (the word derives from the Greek *chrysos*, which means gold, and *elephantinos*, which means ivory, and describes the overlay of gold and ivory employed in classical Hellenistic statuary) represents the pinnacle of the genre. To promote the use of ivory, the Belgian government in the late 1800s initially offered this material from its African colony, the Congo, free to artists. To this end, exhibitions of works in ivory were staged in Antwerp and Brussels (1894) and in the colonial section of the 1897 Exposition Universelle, held in the Brussels suburb of Tervuren. By 1900 the word chryselephantine was extended to encompass any material combining ivory with another substance, such as bronze, wood, rock crystal or lapis lazuli.

In the 1920s and 1930s chryselephantine sculpture in Paris was dominated by DEMETRE CHIPARUS, a Romanian *émigré* who had followed his countryman Constantin Brancusi to the French capital. Impeccably crafted, in **chased** and polychromed bronze accented with minutely carved ivory faces, his figurines were inspired by the worlds of fashion and the theatre. Similarly inspired were his competitors, of which there were many, including Pierre *Le Faguays, Maurice *Guiraud-Rivière, Marcel *Bouraine, Alexandre *Kelety, Claire Jeanne Roberte *Colinet and Raoul-Eugène *Lamourdedieu, all of whose choice of subjects was similar to Chiparus's, but whose postures were often rendered in a more fluid or angular Art Deco style. Additional finishes could be introduced to provide variety, such as naturalistically shaded detailing applied in **cold-painted** enamels to the ivory, as well as **damascening**. With this ancient technique, which originated in the Syrian capital, a precious metal was inlaid into another metal (usually bronze), to provide it with a decorative pattern, such as a floral border on the hem of a gown.

In Berlin a similar school of bronze and ivory sculptors grew up around JOHANN-PHILIPP (FERDINAND) PREISS and his firm, Preiss–Kassler, formed in 1907. Preiss personally designed most of the models produced by his firm, which closed during the First World War. It re-opened in 1919, at which time its style began to shift away from the classical toward the depiction of contemporary children, acrobats, dancers and athletes,

for which it is best known in an Art Deco context. These statuettes and groups, like their French counterparts, often depicted current theatrical and sporting personalities; for example, the aviatrix Amy Johnson, who served as the model for Preiss's 'Airwoman'. These figurines were representative of active and emancipated women, and they bore no resemblance to the then-current model for womankind projected by Nazi propaganda – that of the submissive Teutonic wife and adoring mother. Among the artists who provided models for Preiss–Kassler were Paul Philippe, Otto *Poertzel, R. W. Lange, Hans Kassler and the avant-garde artist Rudolf Belling. The styling of their work was in such harmony with the firm's existing mode that they are often virtually indistinguishable.

Austria – specifically Vienna – developed its own style of chryselephantine works and small decorative bronzes that combined the more theatrical poses of the French works and the softer surface treatment and scale of German sculptures. Viennese artists, such as Josef *Lorenzl, Gerdago (Gerda Iro) and Gustav *Schmidtcassel, provided typical examples. Bruno *Zach, the best-known Austrian chryselephantine sculptor of the inter-war years, worked in an openly erotic style, though the overt sensuality of his burlesque girls and dancers from the *demi-monde* was softened by the tongue-in-cheek humour and sophistication of his stylization. His cigarette-smoking women in leather suits are given a girlish air by the addition of enormous bows in their hair. Others, wearing teddies and garters and carrying whips, are wittily unthreatening. The works of Zach, and others, were cast by the *Friedrich Goldscheider manufactory, whose firm also produced polychromed cast plaster and ceramic versions of the bronze and ivory dancers that it marketed, thereby broadening the selection it presented to its clientele. Unidentified today by sculptor or foundry, as the individual pieces were invariably unmarked, was a 1920s Austrian edition in **spelter** of stylish young women whose mechanized skirts would ratchet up when activated by a switch, to titillate the viewer.

Beyond those whose biographies appear in this chapter, there remained in the inter-war years a host of large-edition sculptors who embraced at some time, and with varying intensity, the Art Deco grammar of decorative ornament in the execution of their commercial work. Although many of these sculptors received recognition in their lifetimes, no ready historical information on them is available. They are known only by their signed works that appear intermittently in the marketplace. Included in this category of commercial sculptors are Paul Philippe, Édouard Drouot, Fayral (Pierre Le Faguays), A. Godard, Giorgio Gori, Raymonde Guerbe, Pierre Laurel, Roland Paris, Georges Omerth, Lucille Sevin and Sibylle May.

The second category of European sculpture from the inter-war years was in the avant-garde style. In France in the 1910s, sculptors found themselves in a middle ground between the 'fine' and 'applied' arts. To compound this identification problem, modern art at the time was unpopular, sustained not by the state – traditionally the medium's principal patron – but only by a handful of progressively minded connoisseurs. For this reason, avant-garde sculptors were invariably too impoverished to have their works cast in bronze. Works were made in materials such as plaster, terracotta, wood or stone, and were often unique, limiting the recognition and income that bronze editions would have generated.

By the First World War, Modernist sculpture had broken with Victorian romanticism and naturalism. In their place was a spirited mix of three-dimensional abstract styles drawn from the parent movement in painting, in which angular, faceted and simplified planes predominated. In Paris, many Modernist sculptors exhibited at Léonce Rosenberg's Galerie de l'Effort Moderne, for some time the prime venue for non-academic, that is, anti-establishment works. Today, the works of these sculptors continue to defy easy categorization. Some pieces, for example, by Alexander Archipenko, Constantin Brancusi, Amedeo Modigliani and Henri Laurens, are allied to the period's vanguard painting movements. The works of others, such as GUSTAVE MIKLOS, Josef *Csáky and Jean (Louis) *Chauvin, are seen generally as 'decorative', aligned stylistically more with the furnishings displayed at the annual Salons of the period. But the distinction is often arbitrary.

FAYRAL (PIERRE LE FAGUAYS)
Séduction, patinated metal, issued in an edition
by Max Le Verrier, 1920s.

Many avant-garde sculptors expressed themselves through the simplification of mass and detailing in a manner that showed the influence of Cubism and Constructivism. Included in this category is Miklos, whose portrait busts of tribal women and birds are especially forceful; both dignity and sensuality are conveyed by their attenuated, rounded features. Preferred materials were diorite, bronze, wood and copper, to which, like Csáky and Léon *Indenbaum, Miklos often applied a brilliant polished sheen.

Csáky set off from Budapest for Paris in 1908, walking most of the way. A pioneer of three-dimensional Cubism, his first avant-garde works appeared in 1911 (all but three of these were later destroyed). Volunteering for action in 1914, he returned to sculpture in 1919 with compositions of cones, cylinders, discs and spheres reminiscent of the work of Fernand Léger. These early essays were followed by works of rectilinear form, in which the subject was modelled out of a single block. Due to the prohibitive costs of bronze casting, these works were usually rendered in plaster or papier mâché. Csáky varied his Modernist style repeatedly in the 1920s, creating perpendicular portrait busts in which certain features were sliced off. Details, where not truncated, were broken down into angular planes. On some pieces, raised and lowered arms provided a fine contrapposto balance. Towards 1930 the sculptor turned to a more figural form of expression, moving away from the rectilinear to more fluid full-bodied compositions.

Moving from Poland to Paris around 1911, Jean *Lambert-Rucki took an atelier with Miklos in the rue de la Grande-Chaumière. Because at times he was close to poverty, he created his sculptural works in a cheap, sometimes curious variety of materials, including wood, polychromed terracotta, stucco and segments of mosaic glass. As in his paintings and decorative panels for JEAN DUNAND (*see under* Silver, Metal, Lacquer and Enamel), Lambert-Rucki's sculpture showed a highly distinctive style in which subjects – often top-hatted theatre-goers and their escorts in Paris's Montparnasse and Montmartre bohemian quarters – were portrayed in silhouette. Other preferred themes, including liturgical instruments, African masks and Modernist animals convey an air of fantasy and lively humour.

The style of JAN and JOËL MARTEL was similar to that of Csáky; bold Cubist images predominate, often rendered in reinforced concrete, reconstituted stone, cement, ceramics or hewn from slabs of granite. Trained in monumental sculpture, the Martel twins created several important works for the 1925 *Exposition Internationale, including a set of concrete trees for a garden designed by ROBERT MALLET-STEVENS (*see under* Furniture and Interior Decoration), which was much acclaimed by the critics, and some bas reliefs for the Porte de la Concorde.

Others who created works in the Art Deco idiom included Ossip *Zadkine (another Cubist-inspired sculptor) and Chana *Orloff, who produced a range of abstract figural and animal sculpture showing an increasing machine influence from 1925. Another Eastern European resident in Paris, Béla *Vörös, is known primarily for his bronze and granite groups of pigeons and musicians rendered in a bold and lightly abstract manner. His simplified forms show a slight Cubist influence in their distortion of the human body. Traces of African tribal art and primitivism are also evident. Part of the *œuvre* of Jean (Louis) Chauvin likewise qualifies as Art Deco. Although most of his subjects were reduced to a pure form of abstraction, similar to the work of Jean Arp and Constantin Brancusi in their simplification, some examples showed understated angular definition.

Following a long line of distinguished predecessors, such as Antoine-Louis Barye, Pierre-Jean Mené and Emmanuel Frémiet, Art Deco *animalier* sculptors adopted the changes introduced into the medium in the early 1910s by Rembrandt Bugatti and Paul *Jouve. Bugatti and Jouve preferred to portray animals impressionistically, achieving their effects in part by kneading or scraping the clay and leaving finger marks in it. Fur and feathers were suggested rather than realistically reproduced. In the 1920s *animaliers* developed this concept by reducing explicit detailing even further: images were given a bas-relief appearance in an attempt to streamline and stylize shapes and surfaces. Features were only hinted at in the overall shape of the animal.

GERDAGO
(*group below*) Exotic dancers, cold-painted bronze and carved ivory on onyx bases, 1920s.

GERDAGO
(*bottom*) Exotic dancer, cold-painted bronze and carved ivory, 1920s.

PAUL MANSHIP
(*opposite*) Group of birds, gilt-bronze on lapis lazuli bases. From left: a crowned crane, concave-casqued hornbill, black-necked stork, Goliath heron, flamingo and pelican, all 1932.

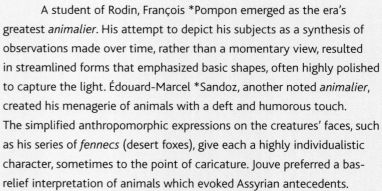

A student of Rodin, François *Pompon emerged as the era's greatest *animalier*. His attempt to depict his subjects as a synthesis of observations made over time, rather than a momentary view, resulted in streamlined forms that emphasized basic shapes, often highly polished to capture the light. Édouard-Marcel *Sandoz, another noted *animalier*, created his menagerie of animals with a deft and humorous touch. The simplified anthropomorphic expressions on the creatures' faces, such as his series of *fennecs* (desert foxes), give each a highly individualistic character, sometimes to the point of caricature. Jouve preferred a bas-relief interpretation of animals which evoked Assyrian antecedents.

In the United States, resistance to an Art Deco sculptural style gave way only slowly, in large part due to the enduring popularity of the Beaux-Arts traditions of the late 19th century, exemplified by the work of Augustus Saint-Gaudens and Frederick William MacMonnies. Another reason was that the Art Deco style was only one of several interrelated avant-garde movements, spearheaded by immigrant sculptors, which occurred simultaneously in the fine arts in America between 1910 and 1930. Waves of talented sculptors arrived in those years, all hoping that 20th-century avant-garde art would be afforded the same degree of tolerance in their adopted homeland that it had been given in Europe. Among those from France were Gaston *Lachaise and Robert *Laurent; from Russia, William Zorach, BORIS LOVET-LORSKI and Alexander Archipenko; from Poland, Elie Nadelman; from Germany, Wilhelm Hunt *Diederich and seventeen-year-old CARL PAUL JENNEWEIN; from Sweden, Carl *Milles; and from Yugoslavia, Ivan Mestrovic. At the same time, the cream of America's young sculptors were crossing the Atlantic in the opposite direction to complete their training in Europe.

America's rejection of Modernism was deep-rooted. Her public was conservative, as was her academic community. Neither was prepared for the avant-garde movement in painting, let alone in sculpture. The National Sculpture Society, founded in response to the public's enthusiasm for the monumental outdoor statuary at the 1893 World's Columbian Exposition in Chicago, continued to represent the most

conservative faction of American sculpture. Local sculptors who were tempted to explore the Modernist expression were often deterred by the fact that the society controlled the allocation of important public commissions, scholarships, prizes and appointments. The human figure, drawn from classical art, remained the medium's primary means of expression. Sculpture virtually missed the impact of the famed 1913 Armory Show, which was so decisive for contemporary American painting. That form could exist independently of content, and could express purely aesthetic or personal ideals without regard to representation, was a belief that progressed far more swiftly on canvas than in bronze or stone. Traditional American sculpture was simply not ready for the abstract Modernist art that confronted it from 1910: Cubism, Constructivism, Futurism and later the machine aesthetic and French Art Deco.

Garden sculpture provided an important middle ground between the Modernist and the customer, because abstraction of the animal form was more palatable to most than distortion of the human figure. Growing demand for such sculpture helped to develop a cohesive group of artists, many of them women, whose style increasingly resisted traditional academic strictures. Emphasis was still placed on form, but it was now more spontaneous and lightly humorous, in many instances incorporating imagery employed by avant-garde artists in Europe. They used repeated patterns, streamlined form and mythological subjects interpreted in a contemporary, and sometimes Art Deco, style. Harriet Whitney Frishmuth, Edith Barretto Parsons, Janet Scudder, Edward McCarten, Eugenie Frederica Shonnard and John Clements Gregory were among those who became known for this type of transitional sculpture.

In the 1920s three factors came together to facilitate the introduction of a distinct 20th-century style of American sculpture: the arrival of avant-garde artists from Europe; the return of the most recent wave of young American sculptors trained in Europe, who were keen to provide their own (often watered-down and cautious) interpretations of vanguard European art; and the development of a new form of architecture – the setback skyscraper.

It is impossible to overemphasize the effect on Modernist American sculpture of the work of immigrant avant-garde sculptors. Only two of these – Lovet-Lorski and Diederich – worked consistently in the Art Deco idiom, but all in their different ways influenced and inspired younger artists. Elie Nadelman, in particular, whose monumental talent dominated the medium in the USA from the moment he arrived after the First World War, produced work of an unclassifiably individual avant-garde style, and this encouraged a host of young sculptors to shorten or forgo their traditional training.

Like Nadelman, other immigrant sculptors, such as Lachaise and Laurent, produced the occasional masterpiece in the 1920s style, among a larger body of more abstract works. The human form and realism – the traditional means of sculptural expression – were embraced by these artists only to varying degrees. Their vision was of the new industrial age, and they looked for more contemporary symbols with which to express it, often turning for inspiration to the early works of artists such as Pablo Picasso and Georges Braque.

Immigrant Modernist sculptors brought with them to the USA a firm belief in the technique of direct carving, as opposed to bronze casting, as the main means of sculptural expression. Both Europe and America had always favoured bronze over other materials, so the preference for carving was partly a reaction against academic tradition which, in the 1920s, still limited the direct carver's success to a small audience, often courted through one-man exhibitions. Laurent, William and Marguerite Zorach, José de Creeft, Heinz Warneke, John Flanagan and Chaim Gross, among others, promoted the use of primary materials such as stone, wood and alabaster in which the artist was involved in the entire creative process.

Second only to the far-reaching influence on American Modernist sculpture of the immigrant sculptors came that of young American artists themselves. By tradition they completed their training in Europe, usually in Rome or Paris. The education offered at both these centres was acceptable, despite the fact that their approaches were fundamentally

PAUL PHILIPPE
Turkish Girl, cold-painted bronze and carved
ivory, 1920s.

different. By the 1920s, Rome's emphasis on antiquity was increasingly seen as outmoded, whereas Paris offered a vibrant academic tradition spanning everything from the École des Beaux-Arts to the annual Salons. Most importantly, the French system had developed a built-in tolerance for radical thought and expression.

Of the young American sculptors returning from Europe, Paul *Manship was the best prepared as he had spent six years in Italy studying the iconography and techniques of archaic and Greco-Roman sculpture and developing a highly personal interpretation of antiquity – one seen by academicians as fresh and at the same time a proper continuation of the American tradition. By 1925 he was pre-eminent within the sculpture establishment, having by then achieved the highpoint of a supremely expressive individual style, which in retrospect was exemplary Art Deco.

The coming of the skyscraper gave avant-garde sculptors a new vehicle for their art. Architects rejected fussy Beaux-Arts decoration, demanding fresh images and forms to accent their soaring new structures. Sculpture's interrelationship with architecture was analysed, its function and relevance were discussed. Understatement was seen to be the key: sculpture's role was to soften the harsh transitions between a building's separate, often stepped, parts. Several sculptors responded imaginatively to this task, most notably René *Chambellan and Lee Lawrie, both of whom displayed a dynamic blend of Modernism in works for the façade of Rockefeller Center.

No American sculptor is identified today more with the skyscraper than John *Storrs, who moved freely between figurative and abstract art, drawing both on classical iconography and on a blend of themes from 20th-century abstract art: Cubism, French Modernism and the machine aesthetic. In the 1920s he created a series of highly distinctive architectural pieces inspired by skyscrapers, including 'Forms in Space No. 1' and 'Study in Forms', in which he explored the simplification of form into planes and volumes.

PAUL PHILIPPE
Fan Dancer and *Tambourine Player*,
cold-painted bronze and carved ivory, 1920s.

DEMETRE CHIPARUS

CARL PAUL JENNEWEIN

BORIS LOVET-LORSKI

JAN AND JOËL MARTEL

GUSTAV MIKLOS

JOHANN-PHILIPP PREISS

DEMETRE CHIPARUS (1889–1947)

Chiparus was born in Dorohoi, in north-east Romania near the Ukrainian border, into an upper-class family. In 1909 he left his native country forever when he travelled to Florence, where he studied sculpture, drawing and painting with the sculptor Raffaello Romanelli. In 1912 he went on to Paris, where he enrolled in the École des Beaux-Arts and studied part time in the atelier of the academic sculptor Antonin Mercié. (Somewhere around this time he changed his first name from 'Dimitri' to the Gallic 'Demetre'.)

He made his début at the 1914 Salon of the *Société des Artistes Français, and, following the First World War, set up his first studio at 24 rue Barrault in Paris's 13th *arrondissement*. He participated at the 1923 and 1928 Salons.

Early works included groups of small figures, such as neighbourhood children at play and other conventional subject matter. Soon, however, these yielded to larger and more sophisticated models of exotic dancers, period personalities and poised, fashionably dressed Parisian women.

Chiparus is known primarily for his many figures and groups in bronze and ivory, which he modelled in plasteline, to which he then sold the reproduction rights to *éditeurs de bronzes d'art* and foundries such as *Les Neveux de J. Lehmann and *Etling et Cie, which at the time possessed their own ivory-carving workshops. The bronze components on these works were highlighted with various enamels in the process known as **cold-painting**. Gold-

Karmorna, patinated, parcel-gilt and silvered bronze on an onyx base, 1920s.

and silver-plating provided artistic diversity. These works sold in fashionable resort centres such as Cannes and Deauville and, in London, through Phillips & MacConnall. In addition to bronze and bronze-and-ivory, a relatively small number of Chiparus models were offered in terracotta, porcelain, **spelter** and marble.

Many Chiparus compositions show a strong Orientalist influence in their costumes, jewelry, headgear and poses, as in his depictions of *Civa* (Shiva, the Indian creator god), *Dancer of Kapurthala*, *Bayadère*, *Cleopatra* and *Semiramis* (the mythical Assyrian queen). Performers in the music halls and cabarets of Montmartre, such as the Dolly Sisters (Hungarian twins who performed at the Théâtre de la Souris and the Folies Bergère),

Isadora Duncan, and Vaslav Nijinsky and Ida Rubinstein in their dance routines in Diaghilev's Ballets Russes provided further inspiration for Chiparus's models. Chiparus also drew on illustrations in period fashion magazines. Among his better-known subjects were pierrots, clowns, harlequins and children. His portrayals in bronze and ivory of the 1920s/1930s Paris music-halls included *Almeria*, *Yambo*, *Kora* and *The Girls*, the last a line of five chorus-line dancers considered by many to be his most inspired creation.

In 1928 at the height of his career, Chiparus moved his atelier to the new home he had acquired in Neuilly-sur-Seine. Faced with rising financial concerns from the mid-1930s, he was forced some years later to sell

the house and move back to the Trocadero quarter in central Paris. With the onset of the Second World War in 1939 matters deteriorated further as business came to a virtual halt. In 1947 he died of a stroke.

Leotard Dancer, cold-painted bronze and carved ivory on an onyx base, 1920s.

The Girls, cold-painted and carved ivory
group of chorus-line dancers, on an onyx
base, 1920s.

(*below*) *Semiramis*, patinated and cold-painted bronze and carved ivory on a marble base, 1920s.

(*right*) *Civa*, patinated and cold-painted bronze and carved ivory on an internally lit onyx base, 1920s.

(below) *Testris*, cold-painted and carved ivory figure on a marble base, 1920s.

(right) *Yambo*, gilt-bronze and carved ivory figure on a marble base, 1920s.

(*below*) *Tango*, cold-painted and carved ivory pair of dancers on a marble base, 1920s.

(*right*) *Book Lady*, cold-painted and carved ivory figure, on a marble base, 1920s.

CARL PAUL JENNEWEIN
(1890–1978)

Although Jennewein's career spans most of the 20th century, it was his earlier work that had a strong Art Deco quality. Born in Stuttgart, he moved in 1907 to the USA, where he studied at the Art Students League in New York from 1908 to 1911, before returning to Europe and the Middle East for two years. While in New York he was apprenticed to Buhler & Lauter, a firm of architectural sculptors and modellers retained by McKim, Mead & White. He remained with the firm from 1907 to 1909, during which time he executed the Pompeiian decorations commissioned for the home of John D. Rockefeller, Jr., at his residence at Fifth Avenue and 55th Street. This was followed by a series of murals for the dome of the Church of the Holy Spirit in Kingston, New York, plus commissions for the Dudley Memorial Gateway,

Harvard University and four murals for the lobby of the Woolworth Building.

In 1916 he received the Prix de Rome, and returned to Europe for four years of advanced study. A highly important commission was forthcoming on his return to the USA: that of the pediment of the west wing of the Philadelphia Museum of Art, which he executed in the Hellenistic style in polychromed terracotta. On a return trip to Rome to formulate his design for the pediment, he created an enduring Art Deco classic, 'The Greek Dance', which was cast in bronze in an edition of twenty-five, with a smaller number in silver. Other freestanding works at the time showed his affinity to the prevailing Modernist style. In the 1920s and 30s he worked on several federal office buildings then under construction in Washington, DC. Notable among these was his sculptural ornamentation for the Department of Justice Building on Pennsylvania Avenue, for which he designed four allegorical marble statues depicting the four elements, in addition to various reliefs, pediments and decorative elements. At the time he was retained also by McKim, Mead & White to create statuary for the Arlington Memorial Bridge.

In the 1930s, he created several powerful Modernist works, many in New York, including the entrance to the British Empire Building in Rockefeller Center (1933), a charming Modernist frieze for the entrance to the apartment building at 19 East 72nd Street (1937) and four stone pylons representing the four elements for the 1939 New York World's Fair. A review of Jennewein's work reveals a dichotomy: small works were rendered in the Modernist style and architectural ones in a traditional style – the latter necessary to procure public commissions.

(*left*) *The Greek Dance*, gilt-bronze on a marble base, *c.* 1926.

(*opposite*) Four sculptures, including *Philomela* by John Gregory, cast in bronze by the Roman Bronze Works (*above left*), 1922; Gregory's figure of a nymph, cast in bronze by the Roman Bronze Works (*above right*), 1922; *Lyric Muse* by Paul Manship (*below left*); and Jennewein's bronze group *Mimi and the Squirrel* (*below right*), *c.* 1925.

(*above left*) *Cupid and Crane*, bronze group;
the model introduced in 1924 as a
companion piece to *Cupid and Gazelle*.

(*above right*) *Cupid and Gazelle*, bronze group,
c. 1918–19.

(*right*) *Water*, plaster study for one of the 'Four Elements' figures on the Department of Justice building, Washington, DC, 1932–34.

(*above*) Eagle relief for a federal office building, New York, 1935.

BORIS LOVET-LORSKI (1894–1973)

Born in Lithuania, Lovet-Lorski studied at the Imperial Academy of Art in St Petersburg, where he worked briefly as an architect before emigrating to Paris and then again, in 1920, to the USA, where he became a naturalized citizen in 1925. Settling in New York, he worked out of a studio at 131 East 69th Street and exhibited his works in at least three of the city's art galleries: Wildenstein & Co., Reinhardt and the Grand Central Art Galleries. He also participated at the *Salon d'Automne in Paris, where he sculpted his entries in space shared in a local artist's atelier. He used an exhaustive range of materials, including bronze and other metals, plaster, linden wood, Egyptian granite, Carrara marble, slate, Mexican onyx and jade. Lovet-Lorski drew on a heady mix of Modernist, Oriental, tribal, archaic (Greek and Cretan) and Teutonic influences in the creation of works that fall into two main categories: portrait sculpture and the female figure, most of which were directly carved in preference to being modelled and cast. The majority of his works, rendered with the geometric precision of a Cubist, are dynamic. No other sculptor in America caught the prevailing French Art Deco mood as effectively or as forcefully.

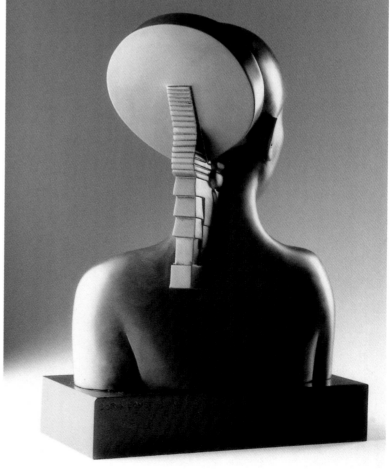

(*above*) *Polynesian Lady*, black Belgian marble, 1920s.

(*right*) *Polynesian Lady* (rear view).

(*opposite*) Bust of a young girl, white marble, c. 1927.

(*top*) Bust in black Belgian marble, 1920s.

(*above*) *Rhythm*, group in black Belgian marble, late 1920s.

(*above left*) Three-quarter length nude, black
Belgian marble, 1920s.

(*above right*) Plaster model for a fountain, 1929.

JAN AND JOËL MARTEL
(both 1896–1966)

These identical twin brothers were born in Nantes (Vendée), where they were raised, before moving to Paris in 1911. There they enrolled first at the Lycée Carnot and then at the École Nationale Supérieure des Arts Décoratifs in 1912. During the First World War, Jan was mobilized and sent to the front in Verdun, while Joël was exempted due to ill-health. On returning to their home town at the end of the hostilities, they received numerous commissions to commemorate the war dead in Eure-et-Loir and Vendée. Settling in Paris in 1919, they participated in the first Salon des Jeunes. Their work soon came to embody the spirit of the French Art Deco style, in terms of its novel use and ready interchange of materials, sophistication and neatness of design, and constant implementation of fresh ideas. Exhibiting at the Salon des Indépendants from 1921, the Martel twins employed Cubist concepts to achieve volumetric solutions. At the 1925 *Exposition Internationale, their grouping of concrete trees, *arbres schématiques*, for the garden designed by ROBERT MALLET-STEVENS brought critical acclaim, as did the selection

of terracotta and porcelain figures that they designed for the pavilion of the Manufacture Nationale de *Sèvres, for which they continued to provide designs until 1938. They were founding members of the *Union des Artistes Modernes (UAM) in 1930, and participated also in the 1931 Exposition Coloniale and 1937 Exposition des Arts et Techniques. Their last work was a bust of their friend *Le Corbusier, modelled shortly after his death. The brothers died in Paris in the same year, one from an accident, the other following a long illness: Jan in March and Joël in September 1966.

(*opposite*) *Joueur de polo*, artist's proof in bronze case by the Susse Frères foundry, 1930.

(*below*) Lion, sheet metal, late 1920s.

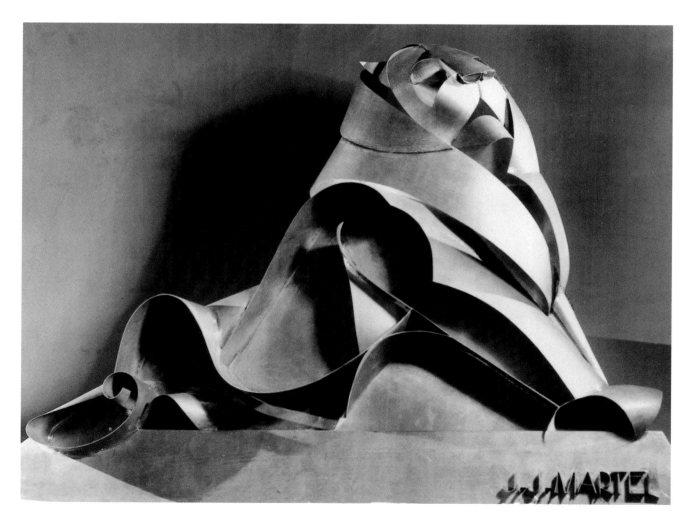

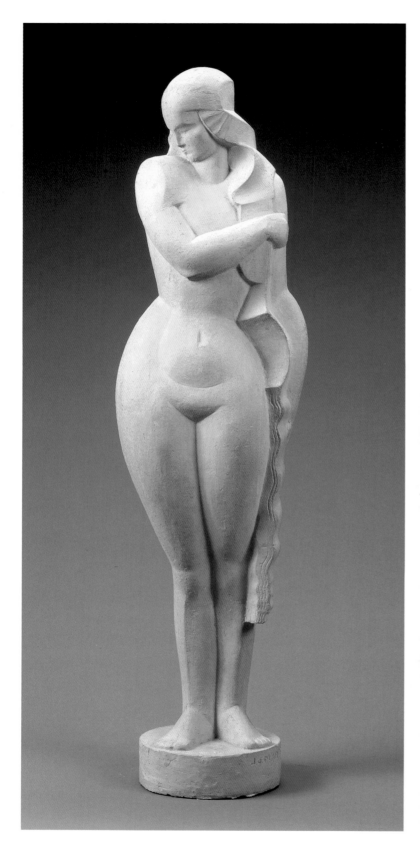

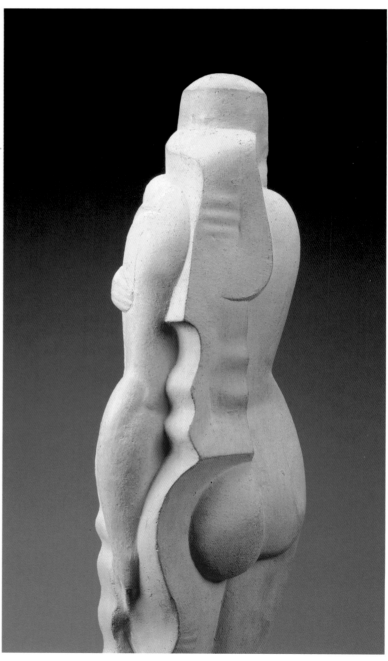

(*above and right*) *Nu de femme*, artist's proof
in beige Lakarme (a synthetic material similar
to Bakelite), displayed at the Union des Artistes
Modernes inaugural exhibition, Paris, 1931.

(*below, left and right*) *Joueuse de luth*, executed in terracotta by La Manufacture Nationale de Sèvres, 1935, from the model created in 1932 for the monument to Claude Debussy, erected in the Bois de Boulogne, Paris.

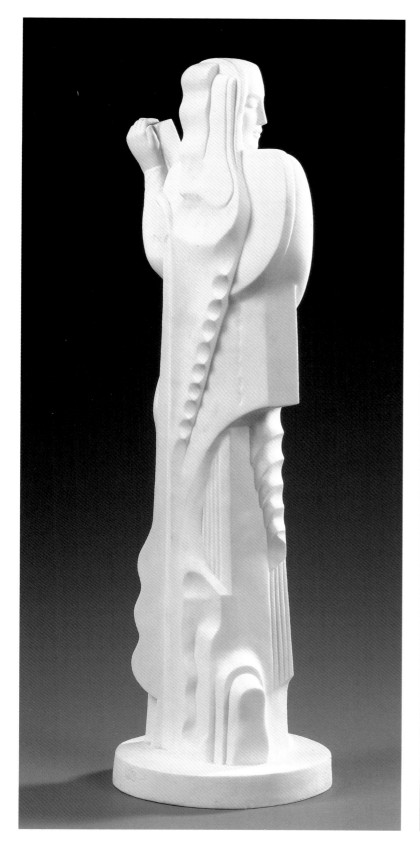

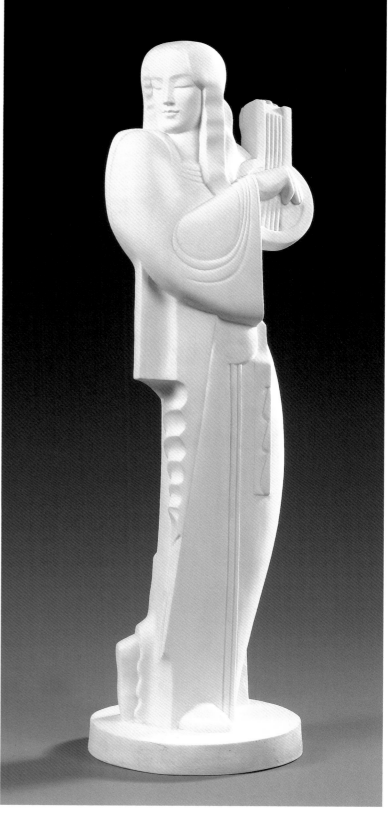

GUSTAV MIKLOS (1888–1967)

Born into a lower-income family in Budapest, where he studied painting under László Kimnach at the School of Art and Design, Miklos arrived in Paris in 1909. He was reunited there with his countryman Josef *Csáky, and attended classes on architecture taught by Henri Le Fauconnier at the Académie de la Palette. From 1910 he exhibited at the *Salon d'Automne, where he was drawn to the Cubist works shown by fellow participants, and in 1913 and 1914 showed at the Salon des Indépendants. In 1914 Miklos enlisted in the Bataillon de Volontaires Étrangers, and served in Salonika and Macedonia, where he became fascinated by Byzantine art, including its mosaics and enamelled liturgical objects. These he interpreted from around 1922 in a Cubist manner. He acquired French citizenship in 1923, around which time he made the acquaintance of Jacques *Doucet, who commissioned him to design various items for his apartment in Neuilly. These included carpets, stained-glass windows and some sculpted accessories, such as drawer handles for PIERRE-ÉMILE LEGRAIN's furniture.

After the First World War, Miklos had returned to his atelier on the rue Saint-Jacques and had begun to work in *champlevé* enamels

(1920), then bas reliefs in *repoussé* metal (1922), until finally he abandoned painting altogether in search of new means of artistic expression. His work incorporated a variety of media including copper, stone and plaster, in which he combined early Christian influences with the Cubist aesthetic. He exhibited sculpture for the first time at the 1923 Salon d'Automne, including non-figurative works in polychromed wood. At the 1925 *Exposition Internationale, he displayed works in numerous disciplines, including jewelry and book illustrations. Three years later, his one-man show at the Galerie de la Renaissance on the rue Royale, Paris, was received with great acclaim by the critics; it included thirty pieces of sculpture in diorite, bronze, silver and wood. A participant in the *Union des Artistes Modernes (UAM)'s inaugural exhibition in 1930, Miklos exhibited with the group until the Second World War, when, in 1940, he left Paris permanently to live in the countryside. He settled in Oyonnax, near the Swiss border, where he taught as an auxiliary professor at the École Nationale Professionnelle des Matières Plastiques. He remained there until 1952.

(*opposite*) *Divinité Solaire*, polished gilt-bronze, cast by the *cire perdue* process by the Valsuani foundry in 1971 from the original modelled in gilt-plaster in 1928.

(*below*) Pair of enamelled gilt-bronze andirons on an oak and metal cabinet designed by Pierre-Émile Legrain for Jacques Doucet, 1924.

(left) *Jeune fille*, transparent black-patinated bronze with black-painted detailing, cast by the *cire perdue* process by the Valsuani foundry, 1927.

(above) *Tête de reine*, unique piece, black-patinated bronze on a marble plinth, exhibited at the Union des Artistes Modernes inaugural exhibition, Paris, 1930.

(opposite) *Tête de femme*, black-patinated bronze with gilded detailing, 1932.

JOHANN-PHILIPP PREISS
(1882–1943)

Preiss was born in Erbach, a town in the Odenwald about 16 kilometres from Frankfurt and known traditionally for its ivory-carving trade. The second of six children, whose mother came from a family of ivory carvers, Preiss attended the gymnasium in nearby Michelstadt. After his parents died within months of each other when he was fifteen years old, he was placed in the care of a maternal uncle, a journeyman ivory carver, under whom he began his apprenticeship in 1898. On completion of his training in Easter 1901, Preiss attended the Königliche Akademie der Künste in Berlin, where he studied under the ivory carver Michael Kern. After working briefly in Milan, he joined the firm of Karl Haebler in Baden-Baden in 1905, where he remained until 1907. While there, he met Arthur Kassler, with whom he went into business. Naming the partnership Preiss–Kassler (PK), they set up their workshop in 1907 at Lenbacherstrasse 1 in the Friedrichshain section of Berlin. Early production concentrated on academic subjects such as children, religious themes and jewelry, all carved entirely in ivory. Preiss placed himself in charge of design; Kassler that of finances. By 1910 there were two ivory carvers on the staff; by the outbreak of the First World War in 1914 this number had risen to six. Preiss designed most of the firm's models himself, and his very personal style became almost a national one. His figures were small in scale and exquisitely finished and detailed, some appearing on clocks, inkstands and dishes, or serving as bases that supported lampshades.

The partners survived the war and in 1919 re-opened the business at a new address, Oranienstrasse 126. When bronze and ivory in combination became fashionable in the realm of domestic household statuary at that time, the firm commissioned the Gladenbeck foundry in Berlin to cast the bronze components in its pieces. Initially, the subject matter for these was inspired by Hellenistic sculpture – for example, Aphrodite and Phryne – but, buoyed by the emerging prosperity and optimism of the 1920s, the firm began to look to the real-life women of the day to serve as its models. National outlets included retailers such as the Wertheim department store in Berlin and the Leipzig trade fair; as part of its expanding foreign trade, Waring & Gillow and the Phillips & MacConnall gallery sold its wares in London.

Popular Preiss figures included idealized young women in gymnastic poses, with titles such as 'Meditation', 'Spring Awakening', 'Beach Ball' and 'Lighter than Air', the last inspired by the English dancer Ada May. Serving as models also were real-life celebrities, including tennis sensation Suzanne Lenglen, the Olympian ice-skater Sonja Henie, who was well known to the German public, and Brigitte Helm, who starred in the film *Metropolis*. The rise of the Nazis in the 1930s impacted negatively on the firm's business, as Preiss was not a party sympathizer. On his death in 1943, Preiss–Kassler was liquidated, and in 1945 the workshop was bombed.

(*right*) *The Swirling Dress*, cold-painted bronze and carved ivory, on a marble base, 1920s.

(*opposite*) *Flame Leaper*, model 1152, cold-painted bronze, carved ivory and resin, on a marble base, 1920s.

(*right*) *Spring Awakening*, cold-painted bronze
and carved ivory, 1920s.

(*left*) *Sun Worshipper*, cold-painted bronze
and carved ivory, 1920s.

(*opposite*) Group of bronze and ivory figurines,
including (top, left to right) *Mandolin Player*
by Preiss, *Miro* by Demetre Chiparus and
Jockey Girl by Bruno Zach; (bottom row)
Woman Rower by Preiss, *The Riding Crop*
by Zach and *Columbine and Harlequin* by
Otto Poertzel, all mid-1920s.

PAINTINGS, GRAPHICS, POSTERS AND BOOKBINDING

The paintings of the inter-war years are difficult, if not impossible, to define in an Art Deco context. Most artists of the period employed a range of avant-garde techniques to solve traditional problems of design and composition. Almost every Modernist artist, for example, employed Cubist-inspired forms of abstraction and the bright colours of the Fauves. Artists whose work falls beyond the scope of this book, such as Fernand Léger, Henri Matisse, Maurice de Vlaminck and Kees van Dongen, at times incorporated Art Deco motifs in their works on canvas and paper.

These factors blur the boundaries between painters who qualify as Art Deco artists and those who do not. There are, however, two main criteria by which individual painters can be judged to fall within the Art Deco movement. First, most Art Deco artists were not in the vanguard of the painting world; that is to say, they were not themselves innovative but rather drew on themes introduced by other Modernist artists in the early years of the century. Second, their works on paper were decorative, designed to fit into and complement the fashionable ensembles of the period. They were created to conform to the style of the furnishings of the room in which they would hang. In this, Cubism, in some bastardized form or other, became the *lingua franca* of the era's decorative artists.

JEAN DUPAS is in this way typical of the true Art Deco artist. Many of his canvases were displayed at the decorative arts Salons rather than those for paintings alone. They were, in the final analysis, decorative rather than artistic compositions. (The same interpretation can be applied to the book illustrations and posters of the period, many of which contained images found on contemporary ceramics, glassware and sculpture.)

To most devotees, the pinnacle of the Art Deco style in painting is represented by TAMARA DE LEMPICKA, who studied in Paris with Maurice Denis, a disciple of Cézanne and an ex-founder-member of the Nabi group, and with André Lhote, a proponent of Cubism. She developed a highly personal, sometimes icy and enigmatic style in which contrasting angular images and bright colours predominated. The Cubist influence is obvious, as is her use of chiaroscuro to enhance the dramatic impact.

JEAN-GABRIEL DOMERGUE
(*left*) *Elegante au Diamant*, oil on canvas, 1928.

GUSTAVE MIKLOS
(*below*) *Tête Cubiste*, gouache and ink on silver paper, 1922, exhibited at the Léonce Rosenberg Galerie de L'Effort Moderne, Paris, 1923.

In painting as in sculpture, some artists in the 1920s adopted a Modernist style in their portrayal of animals. The premier *animalier* painters were Paul *Jouve, Jacques *Nam and André Margat. Unlike their 19th-century predecessors Eugène Delacroix and Théodore Géricault and, towards 1900, Alfred Barye and Rosa Bonheur, who depicted animals in their natural habitat, the 1920s artists chose to treat their subjects in isolation, often silhouetted against a white ground. Felines — leopards and panthers, in particular — snakes and elephants were popular, all painted in abrupt and faceted brushstrokes to reveal their innate power and rhythm.

In the world of graphics, book and fashion magazine illustrators of the First World War years anticipated the Art Deco style that evolved in Paris after the war. Inspired primarily by the 1909 arrival in Paris of Diaghilev's Ballets Russes and by the vivid stage and costume designs of Léon *Bakst and Natalia Goncharova, French commercial artists introduced the same orgy of colours and *mélange* of Russian, Persian and Oriental influences into their designs for book illustrations, fashion plates and theatre sets. Couturiers such as Paul *Poiret provided further opportunities by commissioning artists to illustrate promotional materials for their latest fashions. By the outbreak of the First World War, Bakst-inspired **pochoirs** and aquatints dominated the pages of Paris's foremost fashion magazines, *La Gazette du Bon Ton*, *L'Illustration* and *La Vie Parisienne*, which drew on the talents of a myriad of commercial artists, including Georges *Barbier, Eduardo Garcia *Benito, Robert *Bonfils, Umberto *Brunelleschi, Charles *Martin, André-Édouard *Marty, Bernard Boutet de Monvel and Pierre Brissaud. These artists mixed 18th-century pierrots, columbines, powdered wigs and crinolines with depictions of demoiselles clad in the latest *haute* creations. From the early 1920s, the lightly sensual maiden of these early post-war years was abruptly transformed into a chic *garçonne*, coquettish, wilful, sporty and usually brandishing a cigarette as a symbol of her new-found emancipation.

Elsewhere in Europe, the French Art Deco graphic style received only a sporadic and mixed reception. In Germany, the fashion magazine *Die Dame* followed the lead of its French counterparts in generating 'high-styled' advertisements and illustrations, including work by the German-born illustrator Baron Hans Henning von Voigt, who used the pseudonym Alastair and produced haunting images inspired by Edgar Allan Poe.

In the second half of the 1920s, the French Art Deco graphic style reached the USA, where it quickly evolved into a Modernist idiom in which the machine's influence was increasingly felt. Fashion magazines, such as *Vogue* and *Vanity Fair* (both owned by Condé Nast), *Harper's Bazaar* and *Woman's Home Companion*, included French stylization in their advertisements. Editors commissioned European illustrators, including ERTÉ, Georges *Lepape and Eduardo Garcia Benito, to contribute cover designs. Other periodicals, such as *The New Yorker*, and later *Fortune*, tended to use a more geometric and industrial style, especially for their covers – a style that noted designers such as Joseph *Binder and Vladimir *Bobritsky (both European *émigrés*) and the native-born William Welsh, John Held, Jr. and George Bolin also embraced in the 1920s. Rockwell Kent pursued a light Art Deco graphic style in his woodcuts for book illustrations. John Vassos, the country's premier Modernist designer, gave his designs a powerful linearism.

The 1920s poster artist drew on the rich and enduring turn-of-the-century tradition of Henri de Toulouse-Lautrec, Théophile-Alexandre Steinlen, Jules Chéret and Alphonse Mucha. Works ranged from the transitional 'high-style' interpretations of Leonetto *Cappiello prior to the First World War to the rigorous, geometric compositions of CASSANDRE a decade later. Most designers favoured as their point of departure the soft-edged, whimsical stylizations of Cappiello, whose work spanned the years 1900 to 1925. Jean *Carlu, Charles *Loupot, Charles *Gesmar and PAUL COLIN, in Paris, for example, embraced a light and engaging graphic style that traced a clear progression from their *fin-de-siècle* forebearers.

Beyond the French capital, poster artists adopted the Art Deco style in varying degrees. In Belgium, the Swiss-born Leo *Marfurt and

René Magritte, who worked as a magazine and advertising illustrator before he turned to Surrealism, created some vibrant Art Deco poster images in the mid-1920s, as did two other Low Country artists, Willem Frederik Ten Broek and Kees van der Laan. In Switzerland, Otto *Baumberger, Herbert *Matter and Otto Morach designed for the swank men's clothing store PZK, as did Ludwig *Hohlwein, Germany's most prolific and popular poster artist, whose preference was for virile, notably Aryan, male images.

In the 1920s, commercial art became a bona fide profession which, in turn, gave birth to the graphic artist. In 1900, posters had been created largely to announce theatrical events: music hall, burlesque and cabaret. After the First World War, their use was extended to promote travel, sports meetings and art exhibitions, such as the annual Paris Salons at the Musée Galliera and the Grand Palais. In Germany and Italy, the poster also became a significant tool for Fascist propaganda.

New and improved manufacturing techniques created a surplus of consumer goods in the 1920s, as supply exceeded demand. Dynamic design therefore became an essential tool by which to persuade customers to buy a particular product. The poster, which reached the general French public in its ubiquitous *colonnes d'affiche* (kiosks), became a major advertising medium, directly competing with radio. Powerful symbols and advertising techniques were sought. Poster design was simplified, its images reduced to the essentials of product and brand name. Sharply linear compositions, floating on flat areas of background colour, quickly drew the eye. Other gimmicks helped to gain attention, such as aerial or diagonal perspectives. New sans-serif type faces streamlined the message.

The Art Deco poster artist took inspiration from many of the movements in avant-garde painting of the early years of the century. Cubism and Futurism, in particular, provided powerful new advertising tools. Cubism added fragmentation, abstraction and overlapping images and colour. Futurism contributed the new century's preoccupation with speed and power, translated brilliantly by poster artists into potent images of the era's giant new ocean liners and express locomotives. From the De Stijl and Constructivist movements came pure line, form and colour. By borrowing and mixing some of the concepts of these rather esoteric, intellectual movements, the poster artist helped not only to bring them to general notice but also to make them more comprehensible to the public at large.

Brilliant interpretations of the Art Deco poster were produced outside the main European countries, but with less frequency. Marcello Dudovich and Marcello *Nizzoli, in Italy; Maciej Nowicki and Stanislawa Sandecka, in Poland; and Alexander *Alexeieff, Austin Cooper, John Stewart Anderson and Greiwirth, in Britain, all on occasion captured the buoyant inter-war mood of Paris with verve and imagination in their own countries.

Bookbinding too was a scene of considerable interest at this time. Not since the hand-illuminated manuscripts of the Middle Ages had book design drawn such creativity as in the 1920s. Suddenly convention was swept aside as first PIERRE-ÉMILE LEGRAIN and then a host of other French binders transformed the age-old craft into a vehicle for Modernist design. Most observers were unaware, in fact, that binding had ever attained a high degree of artisanship. The world of book collecting and connoisseurship was a confidential one in which an exclusive group of bibliophiles commissioned works from binders in relative secrecy. By tradition, books in France prior to the First World War were published with flimsy paper covers (as they still largely are). To preserve a favourite volume, the serious collector had to retain a binder to provide a more durable cover. Invariably in leather, this was lightly adorned with a gilt-tooled floral or arabesque design. The binding's primary function was to protect the text; it was not, in itself, considered as a means of artistic expression.

Credit goes to Legrain for revolutionizing the art. Without prior experience, and largely self-taught, he introduced a vigorous blend of Modernist motifs and materials into his designs, to the delight of his

EMMERICH WENINGER
(below) Greta Garbo, Der bunte Schleier ('The Painted Veil'), lithographic poster, 1934.

ALDO SEVERI
(right) Untitled, oil on canvas, 1920s.

first client, the couturier Jacques *Doucet, who commissioned him to provide bindings for his collection of works by contemporary authors. Legrain's ignorance of traditional techniques worked in his favour, allowing him to make free use of his creativity and to introduce into the medium materials used at the time only in the field of avant-garde cabinet-making.

Bookbinding became, in effect, an extension of the Art Deco *ébéniste*'s craft, as exotic skins and veneers were interchanged in the search for modernity. Hides such as snakeskin, *galuchat* and vellum were added to the basic material, Moroccan leather. Other decorative accents were provided in innumerable ways. The binding could be inlaid with a mosaic of coloured leather sections, or with gold, silver or platinum fillets, or decorative plaques could be applied in sculpted or veneered wood, lacquered gold or silver, enamelled porcelain, or bas-relief bronze or ivory. The encrustation of mother-of-pearl, cork, tortoise-shell or semi-precious **cabochons** provided further aesthetic possibilities. Unique, or in a limited edition, works came with a matching sleeve (*chemise*) and slipcase (*étui*).

Some binders even donated the hand tools used on each binding to the patron as an effective selling ploy, and when, as frequently occurred, a binder was commissioned by more than one client to bind the same book, each was provided with his own unique design. In short, the craft was totally revitalized. It was not uncommon for a client to wait two years for a completed commission, particularly after the First World War, when it became the accepted thing for a cover's design to encompass all three of its elements: the front, back and spine. Previously, attention had been paid primarily to the front and, less importantly, the spine.

Beyond Legrain, Paris was home to a multitude of premier binders working in the Modernist idiom. Foremost among these was another Doucet protégée, ROSE ADLER, as well as Georges *Cretté, René *Kieffer, PAUL BONET, FRANÇOIS-LOUIS SCHMIED, Lucien and Henri *Creuzevault, Georges *Canapé and Robert Bonfils. Less known are the works of

Paul Gruel, André Bruel, Geneviève de Léotard, Charles Lanoë, Jeanne Langrand, Yseux, Louise Germain and Germaine Schroeder, whose creations in many instances matched those of their more celebrated colleagues. Enrolment at Paris's École Estienne, a technical school devoted entirely to the art and craft of the book – printing, type cutting, binding and typography – swelled in the excitement generated by the craft's revival. Exhibitions, such as the 1925 L'Art du Livre Français, provided further prestige and exposure.

Many binders collaborated on commissions with artist–designers, even, on occasion, with other binders. Schmied, in particular, was so versatile that he participated on commissions as binder, artist or artisan. JEAN DUNAND (*see under* Silver, Metal, Lacquer and Enamel) was likewise active, creating lacquered and **coquille d'œuf** plaques, as was the *animalier* artist Jouve, who contributed designs for ivory and bronze panels.

For the most part, the inter-war binder drew on the same repertoire of Modernist motifs employed in other disciplines. Combinations of lines, dots, overlapping circles and centripetal or radiating bands were used to create symmetrical or asymmetrical compositions. Raised panels, achieved by the use of thick boards, introduced a sculptural element, and vortex and spiral patterns provided a three-dimensional perspective. Toward 1930, the influence of the machine and new technology became increasingly felt, particularly by Bonet, who emerged after Legrain's death in 1929 as the medium's most brilliant exponent. His sculptural and all-metal bindings of 1931–32 were followed shortly by an even more revolutionary technique: Surrealist photographic images transposed on to leather covers.

Beyond France, bookbinding remained conservative. Very few examples in the Art Deco style were produced in other countries, although in the USA John Vassos designed a few starkly modern bindings in which bright enamels replaced the coloured leather mosaics used in France.

ROSE ADLER

PAUL BONET

CASSANDRE
(ADOLPHE MOURON)

PAUL COLIN

JEAN DUPAS

ERTÉ (ROMAIN DE TIRTOFF)

PIERRE-ÉMILE LEGRAIN

TAMARA (DE) LEMPICKA

FRANÇOIS-LOUIS SCHMIED

HENDRIKUS T. WIJDEVELD
Architecture/Frank Lloyd Wright, lithograph
poster, 1931.

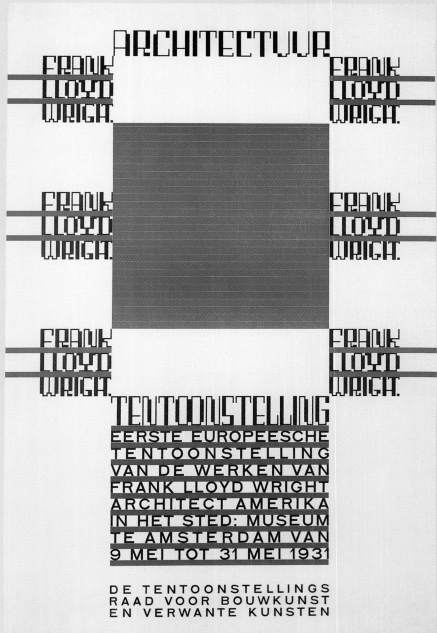

ROSE ADLER (1890–1959)

Paris-born Adler entered the Villa Malesherbes division of the city's École de l'Union Centrale des Arts Décoratifs in 1917, where she studied under Andrée Langrand. She remained at the school until 1925, from 1923 taking extracurricular instruction in binding and gilding from Henri Noulhac at his atelier.

Throughout her career, Adler created a wide range of decorative objects, including jewelry, small toiletry items, clothes and furniture, but today she is almost exclusively known for her bindings. A rare ebony table, commissioned by Jacques *Doucet in the 1920s for his studio in Neuilly and now in the collection of the Virginia Museum of Fine Arts, Richmond, Virginia, shows the same inspired mix of exotic and precious materials – sharkskin, metal and enamel – that she created in her bindings.

A selection of Adler's earliest bindings were included in an exhibition of work from students at the École Nationale Supérieure des Arts Décoratifs at the 1923 Salon of the *Société des Artistes Décorateurs. These impressed Doucet,

who purchased three examples, thereby beginning an association that was to continue until his death six years later. Adler's bindings for Doucet, in many ways similar to those employed at the time by PIERRE-ÉMILE LEGRAIN, consisted largely of non-figurative, geometric compositions executed in brilliant inlays of colour embellished with incrustations of mother-of-pearl, metal strips, hard stones, and animal or snake skins. Like Legrain, Adler made full use of the letters in the book's title by combining them in complex overlapping configurations. Often the sizes, colours and typefaces of each letter were different. She believed that the cover's design should always serve the text, and that a binding should be judged by how successfully it persuaded the reader to open the book.

After Doucet's death in 1929, Adler concentrated on other major commissions, both for private book collectors and for libraries and institutions such as the Bibliothèque Nationale, the Bibliothèque Littéraire Jacques Doucet, the Victoria & Albert Museum and the New York

Les Amis nouveaux (Paul Morand), leather with gold-tooling and pierced duralumin panels, 1927.

Public Library. At that time, her style underwent a distinct change. The arresting colours and imagery of the earlier designs were replaced by a more refined and simplified range of covers executed in combinations of leather, often without incrustations of other materials. She had by now identified herself fully with the avant-garde movement in architecture, painting and the decorative arts headed by Pierre Robert, PIERRE CHAREAU, ROBERT MALLET-STEVENS, Étienne *Cournault, JEAN PUIFORCAT and others, an evolution that can be clearly traced in her binding designs.

Adler showed her work at salons and exhibitions throughout her career. She exhibited independently at the Salon of the Société des Artistes Décorateurs from 1924 to 1929, when

(left) *Tableau de la boxe* (Tristan Bernard), inlays of leather with gold-tooling, 1922.

(middle) *Eupalinos l'âme et la danse* (Paul Valéry), inlays of calf and crocodile, with gilt-tooling, 1923.

(opposite) *Chéri* (Colette), inlays of leather with gold-tooling, 1925.

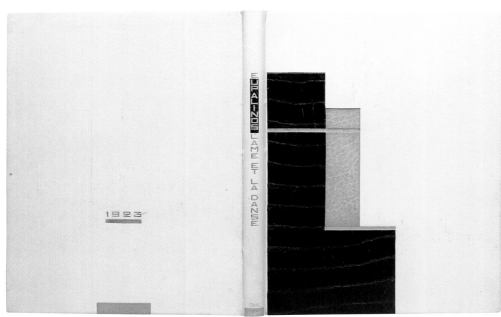

she transferred to the newly formed *Union des Artistes Modernes (UAM). She also participated in the 1925 *Exposition Internationale, the 1931 Exposition Internationale du Livre, the 1937 Exposition des Arts et Techniques and the 1939 Golden Gate Exposition in San Francisco.

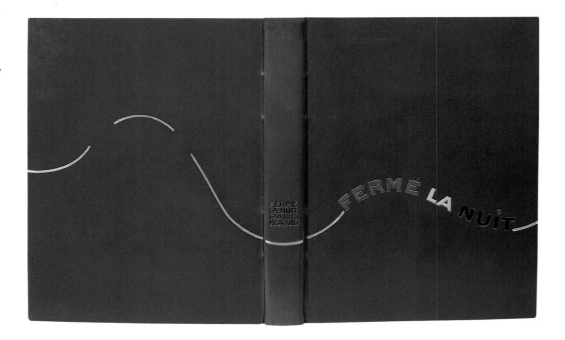

(right) *Fermé la nuit* (Paul Morand), inlays of calf with gold- and silver-tooling, 1920s.

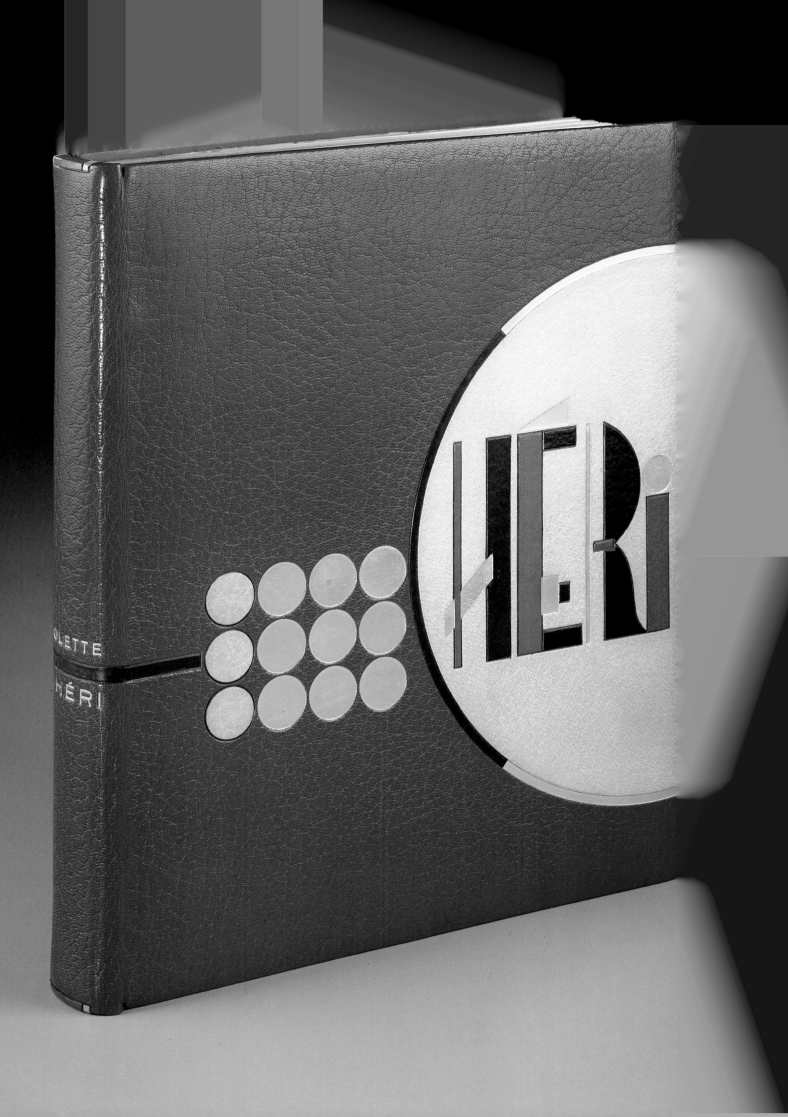

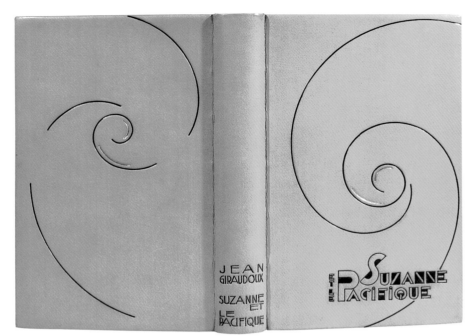

(*left*) *Suzanne et le Pacifique*
(Jean Giraudoux), inlays of calf with
gold- and silver-tooling, 1930.

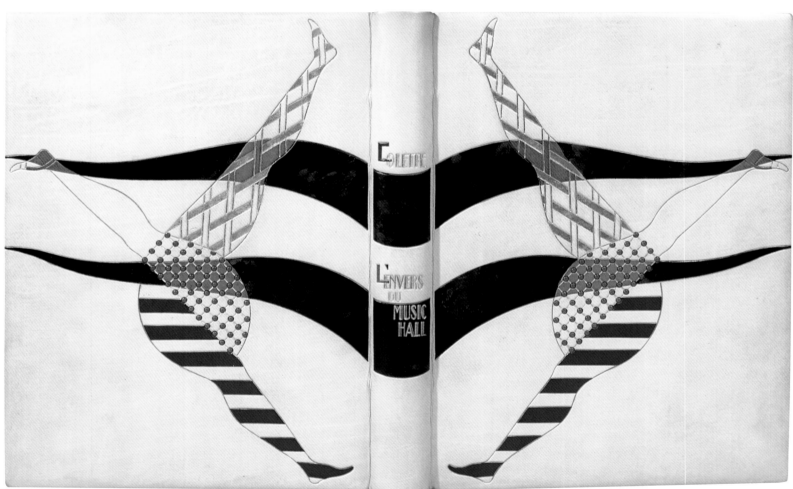

(*above*) *L'Envers du music-hall* (Colette),
inlays of leather and calf with gold-
and silver-tooling, 1929.

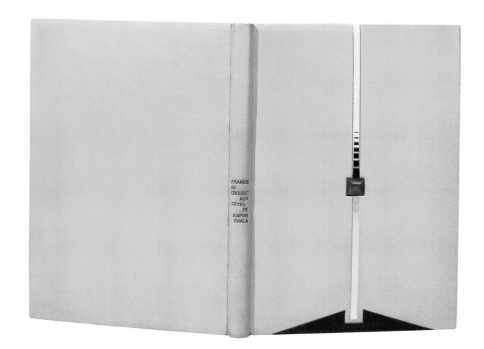

(*right*) *Aux Fêtes de Kapurthala*
(Francis de Croisset), inlays of leather
with gold-tooling and an inlaid emerald
cabochon, 1930.

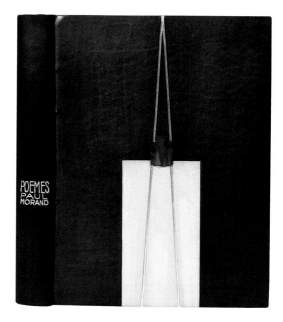

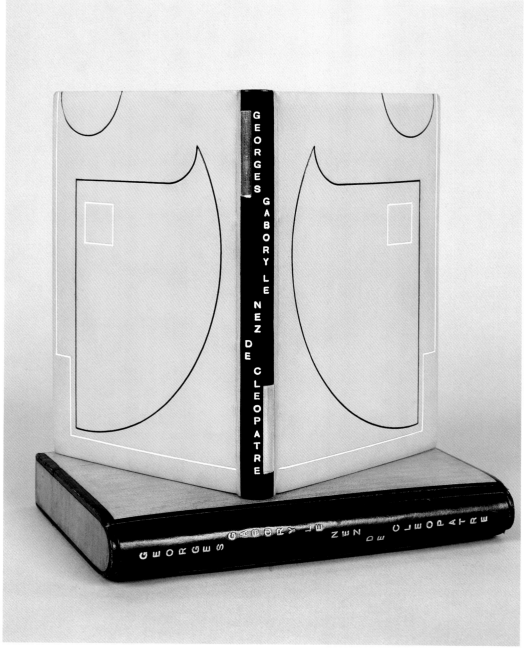

(*above*) *Poémes* (Paul Morand), inlays
of calf with palladium and an inlaid sapphire
cabochon, 1920s.

(*right*) *Le Nez de Cléopâtre*
(Georges Gabory), inlays of leather with
gold- and silver-tooling, 1922.

PAUL BONET (1889–1971)

Born in Paris to Belgian parents from Namur, Bonet attended the École Communale de la rue des Blancs-Manteaux from 1895 to 1903, before taking up an apprenticeship in an electrical shop from 1904 to 1906. At this time he discovered that his real interest lay in painting and, on the advice of Jean-Paul Laurens, he asked his father if he could enrol at the Académie Julian, a request that was denied. Three years later, still determined to pursue a career in the arts, he became a modeller of wooden fashion mannequins, employment that was interrupted by military service from 1910 to 1912. In 1914, his father died and Bonet volunteered for action. Wounded near the Belgian border, he was sent to hospital in Montpellier and then demobilized. He returned to Paris to take up his old job.

Bonet first turned to bookbinding in 1920, when an acquaintance invited him to design simple covers for his modest collection. Bonet proposed half-bindings in *galuchat*, which were executed by a local binder. Bookbinding remained a hobby for him until 1924, when the decorator Mathieu Gallerey persuaded him to exhibit his works. He was presented to Henri Clouzot, the conservator at the Musée Galliera, who was preparing the L'Art du Livre Français exhibition for the following year. Clouzot agreed to display a few of Bonet's designs, which Gallerey arranged to have executed by students at the École Estienne. At the end of 1925, when further examples of his designs were accepted by the jury of the *Salon d'Automne, Bonet decided to take up

Nuits de Paris (Francis Carco), inlays of leather with gold-tooling (bound by Maurice Trinckvel, gilded by Jules-Henri Fache), 1927.

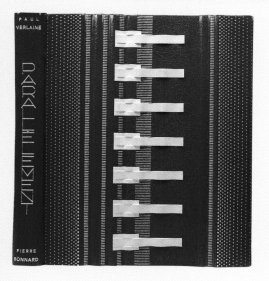

the craft professionally. The following year he made his début at the Salon of the *Société des Artistes Décorateurs. The public responded initially with indifference, but between 1927 and 1929 one collector in particular, R. Marty, supported him. In 1930, a business reversal caused by the Depression forced Marty to sell his entire collection. The auction, conducted by Auguste Blaizot at the Hôtel Drouot, included fifty-two Bonet bindings. The bibliophile world awoke to the sudden realization of his genius.

At the 1928 Salon, Bonet had gained the confidence of a second client, Carlos R. Scherrer, a businessman from Buenos Aires who spent part of each year in his Paris office. An avid collector of bindings, rather than books *per se*, Scherrer quickly emerged as Bonet's principal customer and patron, commissioning most of his major works in the 1930s. By 1931, Bonet was firmly established, exhibiting at Raoul Simonson's invitation in Brussels. He also bound manuscripts and Surrealist works for the Belgian collector René Gaffe. In the same year, he designed his first truly major bindings, which were bound by Ferdinand Giraldon with gold fillet work by André Jeanne.

Throughout his career Bonet readily acknowledged his debt to PIERRE LEGRAIN — evident in his 1920s linear designs. From 1930, however, his introduction of daring novel effects quickly established him as a master in his own right. His preoccupation with the letters in

(*top*) Complete 14-volume set of works by Georges Courteline, inlays of leather with gold-tooling, 1928.

(*above*) *Le Serpent* (Paul Valéry), inlays of leather with gold-tooling (bound by Maurice Trinckvel, gilded by Marcel Bailly), 1927.

(*left*) *Parallèlement* (Paul Valéry), leather with gold-tooling, platinum and ivory (bound by Ferdinand Giraldon, gilded by André Jeanne, the ivory carved by Raby), 1933.

the book's title as the principal elements of its design, for example, was one of his major contributions to the field. He designed more than forty different covers for Apollinaire's *Calligrammes* alone, each a dynamic variation on a common theme. His Surrealist bindings also conveyed on photographic film the disturbing images engendered by the writings of André Breton and Paul Éluard. Equally ingenious was his creation of the irradiant design, which provided a three-dimensional optical illusion in the use of undulating lines radiating from a common centre. His sculpted bindings for Picasso's illustrated editions of Buffon's *Natural History* and Balzac's *Le Chef-d'œuvre inconnu* were strikingly original.

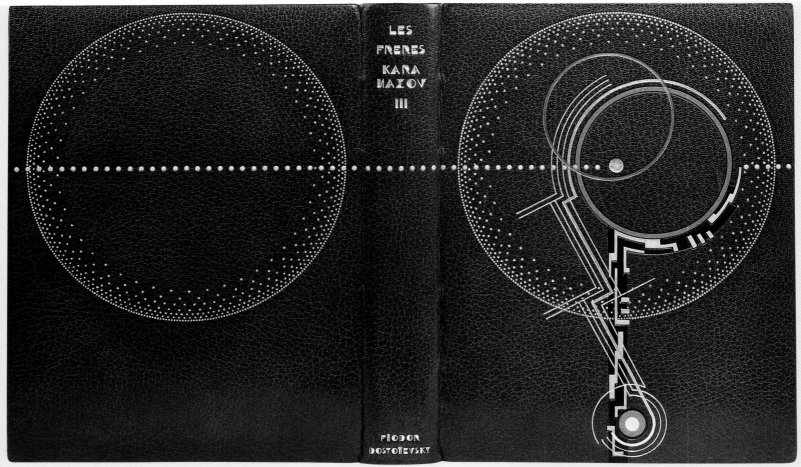

Collaborating with ***orfèvriers*** and jewellers (Egouville, Pierre Boit and GUSTAVE MIKLOS), Bonet introduced nickel, steel, gold platinum and **duralumin** into his covers. His leather was handled by various binders, including René Desmules, Clovis Lagadec, Henri Lapersonne, Maurice Trinckvel and Charles Vermuyse; and his gilding by Roger Arnoult, Roger Cochet, Charles Collet, Raymond Mondange and Guy Raphael.

(*top*) *La Petite ville* (Yan Bernard Dyl), inlays of leather (bound by Maurice Trinckvel), 1927.

(*above*) *Les Frères Karamazov* (Fyodor Dostoevsky), one of three volumes with inlays of leather, gold-tooling and palladium, 1929.

(*left*) Calligrammes (Guillaume Apollinaire), inlays of leather and enamelled duralumin, 1932.

(*below left*) Calligrammes (Guillaume Apollinaire) inlays of leather, 1943.

As was the case with many other binders, Bonet's commissions fell off in the 1930s, the economic recession of 1934–35 forcing him to resort in his free time to his old profession of modelling mannequins. However, the 1937 Exposition des Arts et Techniques witnessed renewed interest in and support for bookbinding, as fresh clients were drawn to the medium. Bonet's exhibit charmed and astonished visitors with its new techniques and audacious designs.

During the Second World War, he continued to execute commissions, adding designs for commercial *cartonnage* bindings to those for his private clients. In 1943, as a measure of Bonet's pre-eminence within the field, the publisher Georges Blaizot published a monograph on him that coincided with an exhibition of his

bindings at the Galerie Renou et Colle. After the war, Bonet's fame increased further with his introduction of a new series of *Calligrammes* covers and, in 1949, his famous lion's head configurations. The following year he was appointed a *chevalier* of the French Légion d'Honneur.

(*left*) Calligrammes (Guillaume Apollinaire), inlays of leather, palladium and blind-tooling, 1930.

(*above*) Journal d'un fou (Nikolai Gogol), inlays of leather with gold-tooling, 1932.

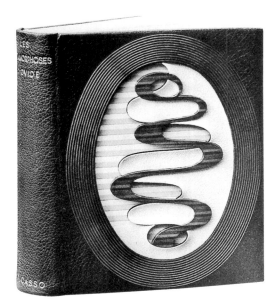

(left) Les Métamorphoses (Ovid), inlays of leather with sculpted detailing and gold-tooling, 1937.

(opposite, above left) La Treille Muscate (Colette), inlays of leather with gold-tooling, 1942.

(opposite, above right) Le Chef-d'oeuvre inconnu (Honoré de Balzac), inlays of leather with sculpted detailing and gold-tooling (bound by Ferdinand Giraldon, gilded by André Jeanne), 1944.

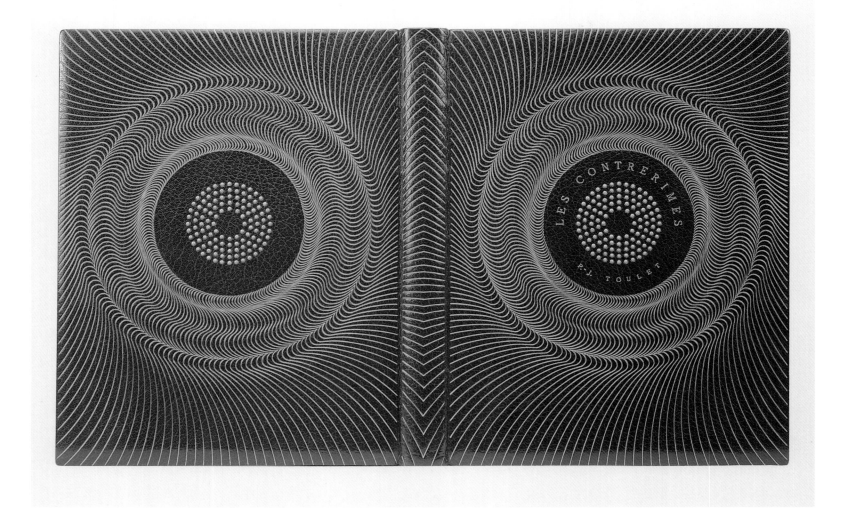

(above) Les Contrerimes (P. J. Toulet), leather, gold-tooling and palladium (bound by René Desmules, gilded by André Jeanne), 1939.

(opposite below) Tartarin de Tarascon (Alphonse Daudet), pierced leather with gold- and blind-tooling, 1942.

CASSANDRE
(ADOLPHE MOURON) (1901–1968)

Generally acknowledged as the finest posterist of the 20th century, Adolphe Mouron – who adopted the professional name of Cassandre – was born in Kharkov, Ukraine, the son of a Bordeaux wine merchant whose business was in Russia. He moved in 1915 to Paris, where he studied at the Académie Julian in preparation for a career in painting, with architecture as a second choice. However, early on he realized that he was drawn rather to the applied arts and, in particular, poster design.

By the early 1920s Cassandre was an accomplished painter, posterist, theatre designer and typographer. He designed his first poster, for Au Bûcheron (1923–24), after which he worked until 1928 for the Hachard printing office. At the 1925 *Exposition Internationale,

L'Intransigeant, lithographic poster, 1925.

he was awarded a *grand prix* for poster design. Applying the Cubist and Symbolist principles he had absorbed in his studies, together with his architectural training and the Art Deco stylizations just then coming into fashion, Cassandre developed a variety of typographic, photographic and other visual effects that virtually defined the 1926–35 decade in poster design. Crisply defined lines and angles, intriguing perspectives and conspicuously legible lettering produced images of startling impact

and aesthetic appeal that channelled the viewer's eyes and mind to the essence of the message. Of his medium, Cassandre wrote:

> The poster requires total self-effacement. The artist cannot *express* himself in the poster – and even if he were able to, he would have no right to do so. Painting is a *goal* in itself. The poster is only a means, a means of communication between the seller and the public – somewhat like a telegraph. The poster artist is like a telegrapher: he does not *draft* messages, he *despatches* them. No one asks him what he thinks; all he is asked to do is to communicate clearly, powerfully and precisely.

Numerous posters bear testimony to the accuracy, power and clarity of his poster designs, including *Chemin de Fer du Nord*, *L'Oiseau Bleu*, *Lys Chantilly*, *United States Lines*, *L'Atlantique*, *Côte d'Azur*, *Wagon-Bar*, *Nord Express*, *Étoile du Nord*, *Normandie*, *Paris*, *Triplex*, *Bonal* and *Dubonnet*.

In 1930, with Charles *Loupot and his friend Maurice Moyrand, Cassandre founded the Alliance Graphique, which functioned simply as a design studio. Moyrand administered it and arranged for its printing operations, which were done almost entirely by the firm of L. Danel in Lille. The Alliance Graphique was disbanded in 1934 after Moyrand's death in a car accident, after which Cassandre concentrated on new type faces and other typographical work. Following a 1936 one-man show at the Museum of Modern Art in New York, he remained in the USA, where from 1937 to 1939 he designed covers for *Harper's Bazaar*. Following this, he returned to France where he almost completely abandoned posters for advertising, theatre design and painting. He committed suicide in 1968.

(*right*) *L'Atlantique*, lithographic poster, 1931.

(*right below*) *LMS Best Way*, lithographic poster, 1928.

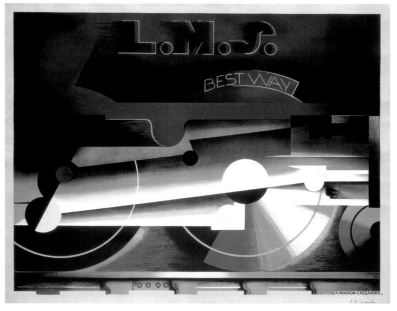

(*above*) *Wagon-Bar*, lithographic poster, 1932.

(top) *Dubonnet, à l'eau*, 1934.   (above) *Dubonnet, hiver vin tonique*, 1936.   (opposite) *Triplex*, lithographic poster, 1931.

LE VERRE

TRIPLEX

S'ÉTOILE MAIS N'ÉCLATE PAS

PAUL COLIN (1892–1985)

Born in Nancy, Colin moved to Paris in 1913, where he developed into a fine painter, posterist and designer of costumes and stage sets. After the war, Colin began his career as the decorator of a young and struggling music hall – the Théâtre des Champs-Élysées. By 1925, his clear and succinct designs, appreciated by performers and promoters alike, established show business advertising as his speciality. His poster for *La Revue Nègre*, which introduced Paris to Josephine Baker, signalled the start of his long association with the American dancer and other black American entertainers, including jazz musicians.

Colin created more than 1,400 posters, and designed costumes and stage sets for the Paris Opéra and Comédie Française, as he immersed himself in these and other theatres and music halls. He exhibited at the *Salon d'Automne, the 1925 *Exposition Internationale and the 1931 Exposition Coloniale. In 1926 he opened the École Paul Colin, a school for the graphic arts, where he taught for nearly forty years. Notable in his vast portfolio of work was *Le Tumulte noir*, published in an edition of 500 (1929), in which he personally hand-coloured the illustrations in the **pochoir** process. In addition to his theatrical posters, Colin created ones for charities, the Liberation of Paris in 1945, commercial products, the travel industry and various government agencies. With CASSANDRE and Jean *Carlu, his designs dominated the 1930s French poster scene.

Leroy Opticien, lithographic poster, 1938.

(*opposite*) Four sketches from *Le Tumulte noir* portfolio, 1929.

ANDRÉ RENAUD

"SUCCÈS" 7, Imp.ⁱᵉ Marie-Blanche. Paris. H. CHACHOIN Imp 1929

PAUL
COLIN

(*opposite*) *La Revue Nègre*, lithographic
poster, 1925.

(*above*) *André Renaud*, lithographic poster, 1929.

Les Perruches, oil on canvas, exhibited in
the Grand Salon of Ruhlmann's Hôtel du
Collectionneur at the 1925 Exposition
Internationale, Paris.

JEAN DUPAS (1882–1964)

Bordeaux-born Dupas studied at the city's École des Beaux-Arts, later transferring to the École des Beaux-Arts in Paris. Listed at the Salons from 1909, he was awarded the Prix de Rome the following year for his *Éros vainqueur de Dieu Pan*. In Rome Dupas studied at the French Academy under Carolus Duran and Paul-Albert Besnard. His distinctive Art Deco graphic style, in stark defiance of his training and the spirit of the jury's award, evolved during his sabbatical in Italy. The early 1920s witnessed two important works, *Jugement de Paris* and *Les Antilopes*.

Besides a huge volume of works on canvas and paper, Dupas designed posters, book illustrations, brochures and catalogue covers, and decorated porcelain wares for the Manufacture Nationale de *Sèvres. For the

His distinctive elongated style, termed at the time *en tuyau de poêle*, brought occasional censure from the critics, which Dupas addressed in a 1928 article in *Creative Art*:

> I do not aim at a systematic deformation . . . but one must realize that a painted decoration is part of an architectural scheme, and hence it demands scale and strong vertical lines . . . Here, in the art of the South, the figures are tall, slim and distinguished. For me elongation is not even a stylization, but rather a means of expression.

Explaining his style further, Dupas wrote: 'Why are there so many voluminous robes in my pictures? Not because I have a special predilection for them, but merely because they are useful to me.' His other compositional devices included tall fanciful hats and birds in flight.

Dupas's preferred subject matter was fashionable young women in idealized and extravagant settings, with elaborately coiffed hair and bouffant dresses, capturing the glitter and sophistication of the 1920s. Many of these are mixed-media compositions, combining watercolours, gouache, pastel, ink and chalk. Dupas was elevated to the Académie des Beaux-Arts in 1941, and the following year was appointed a professor at the École des Beaux-Arts, where he taught painting until 1952.

Palais de la Nouveauté, lithographic poster, 1925.

grand salon of the ocean liner *Normandie*, he designed a large mural depicting the history of navigation executed in *verre églomisé* by the glassmaker Charles Champigneulle.

Dupas is today best known for his oil painting *Les Perruches*, which hung over the mantel in RUHLMANN's Hôtel du Collectionneur at the 1925 *Exposition Internationale; at that Exposition he also displayed *Les Vins de France* in the Bordeaux pavilion. Other commissions included murals for the Salle des Fêtes de la Bourse du Travail in Bordeaux, the Église du Saint-Esprit in Paris and the Salon de l'Argenterie at the Royal Palace in Bucharest.

ROUSSEAU FRÈRES. IMP. BORDEAUX.

BAL DES ÉTUDIANTS
ALHAMBRA - 8 JANVIER 1927

Association Générale des Étudiants reconnue d'utilité publique. (Décret du 14 Décembre 1924)

(*top left*) *Untitled*, ink and watercolour on brown paper, for Saks Fifth Avenue, New York, 1929.

(*above*) *Bal des étudiants Alhambra*, lithographic poster, 1927.

(*top right*) *Untitled*, ink and watercolour on brown paper, 1932.

(*right*) *Untitled*, ink and gouache on paper, 1928.

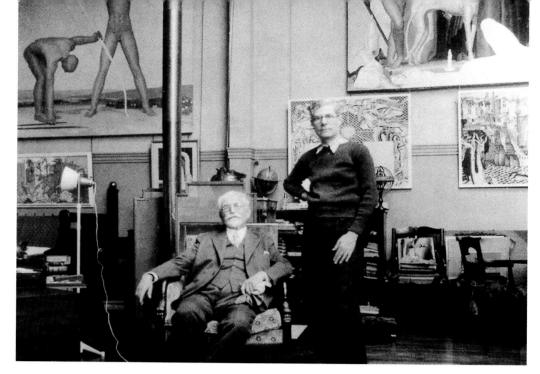

(*right*) Dupas in his atelier with Alphonse
Mucha, probably 1920s.

(*right*) *Untitled*, pencil and crayon on paper,
probably a study for *Les Perruches*
(see p. 156), *c.* 1925.

ERTÉ (ROMAIN DE TIRTOFF)
(1892–1990)

Born in St Petersburg, Russia, the son of an admiral, Romain de Tirtoff studied painting in his native city in 1906 with the portraitist Ilya Repin. In 1912, he moved to Paris, where he furthered his studies at the Académie Julian under Jean-Paul Laurens. The following year he worked briefly for the dressmaker Caroline, and submitted fashion sketches to Paul *Poiret, who hired him to create costumes for his first theatrical production, *Le Minaret*. At this time, he also contributed fashion sketches to *La Gazette du Bon Ton* and adopted as his signature the pseudonym Erté, derived from the French pronunciation of the capital letters R and T in his name.

In 1914, now a resident of Monte Carlo, Erté provided covers, fashion pictures and illustrated columns for *Harper's Bazaar*, for which his first cover appeared in the January 1915 issue. He also produced similar material for the fashion shop of Henri Bendel and the B. Altman & Co. department store, both in New York. In 1916, he signed an exclusive ten-year contract with *Harper's Bazaar*, which was owned by William Randolph Hearst. He also created the costumes for the revue *Les Merveilles de l'Orient*, starring Maurice Chevalier and Mistinguett, at the Théâtre Fémina, Paris, in 1917. In 1925, Erté moved to Hollywood, where he designed film sets and costumes for Metro–Goldwyn–Mayer and Cecil B. DeMille. This was followed in 1926 by a second ten-year contract with *Harper's Bazaar*. From 1929 to 1930, he produced fabrics and dresses for the Amalgamated Silk Corporation in New York.

Throughout his career – from the mid-1910s to 1966 – Erté continued to design costumes and sets for diverse stage productions in London, Milan, Blackpool, Berlin, Naples and New York. In 1968, shortly after the Art Deco collector revival began, he was rediscovered by SevenArts Ltd, a division of the Grosvenor Gallery in London, for which a new series of lithographs and statuettes served to re-establish his celebrity. In 1990, he died of kidney failure in Paris following a trip to Mauritius.

(*above*) Cover design for *Harper's Bazaar*, 1929 Christmas issue, gouache and pencil on paper.

(*opposite*) *Bain du Soleil*, cover design for *Harper's Bazaar*, gouache on paper, June 1930 issue.

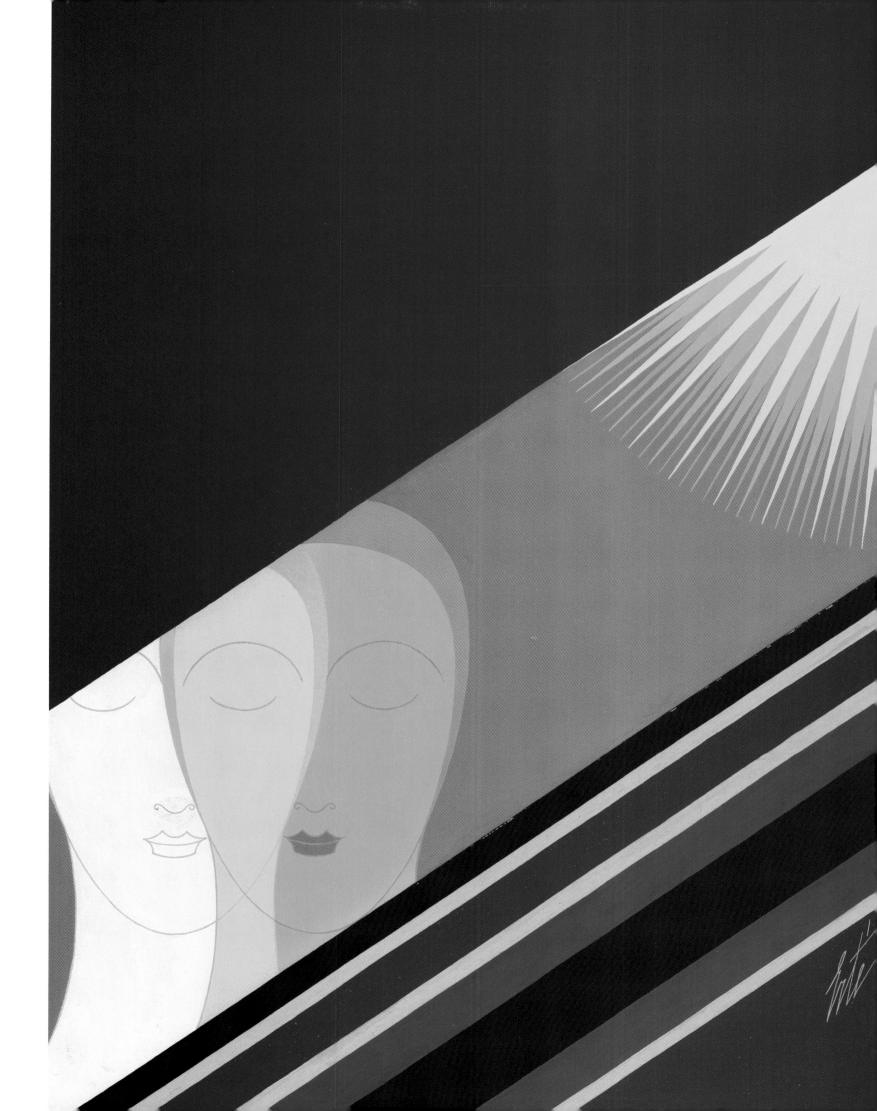

(*right*) *L'Arc en ciel*, cover design for *Harper's Bazaar*, gouache on paper, April 1930 issue.

(*above*) *Alcazar de Paris*, lithographic poster, 1920s.

(*right*) *Vénus moderne*, gouache on paper, c. 1928.

(*below*) *The Twin Sisters Curtain*, gouache
on paper, later version of the design
introduced in 1926.

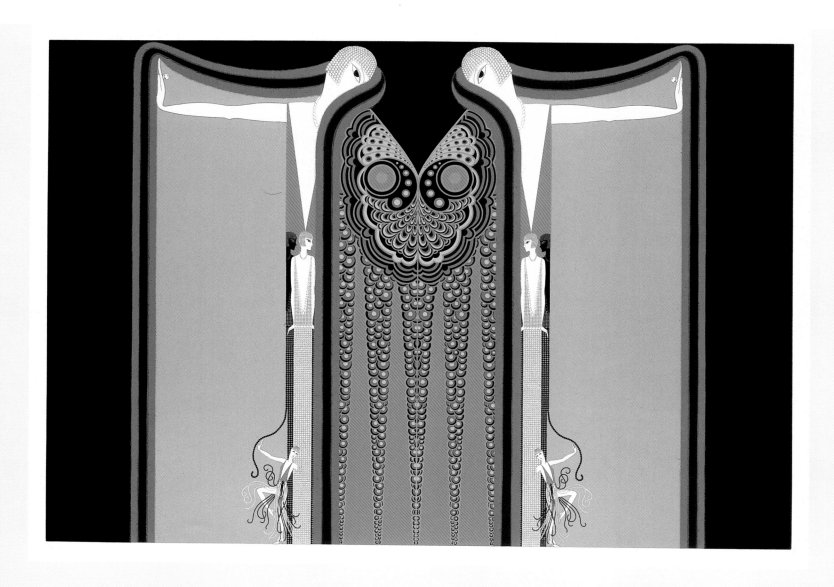

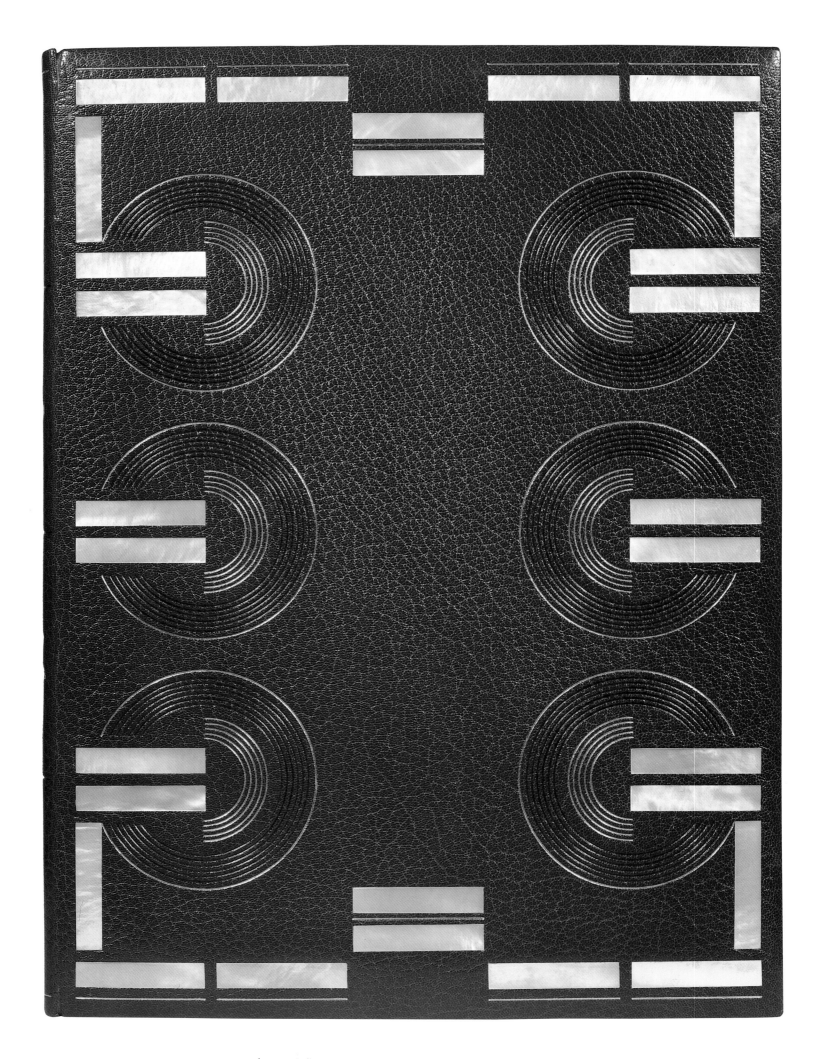

PIERRE-ÉMILE LEGRAIN
(1888–1929)

Legrain was born in Levallois-Perret on the outskirts of Paris, the son of a prosperous distillery owner and a Belgian mother who entered him in the Collège Sainte-Croix in Neuilly. He began at an early age to suffer from the chronic health problems that recurred throughout his life and led to his premature death in 1929. Poor health may have contributed to his decision at twelve years of age to leave school and pursue his studies independently. In 1904, determined to become an artist, he entered the École Germain-Pilon in Paris to study painting, sculpture and theatre decoration.

In the next four years Legrain underwent considerable hardship, caused by the failure of the family business and his father's subsequent death. However, his fortunes improved in 1908, when he was invited by Paul *Iribe to submit cartoons for the latter's satirical revues, Le Témoin, L'Assiette au Beurre, Le Mot and La Baionnette. Impressed by the young man's creative skills, Iribe invited him to collaborate on various projects, including dress designs for Jeanne Paquin, jewelry for Robert Linzeler and Modernist furnishings and interior settings for Iribe's progressive clientele. The last included the commission in 1912 to decorate Jacques *Doucet's apartment at 46 avenue du Bois, Paris, in the modern style. Because of the impending war and various differences of opinion with the couturier Paul *Poiret, for whom he designed fashions, Iribe in 1914 decided to leave for New York.

When the First World War began, Legrain volunteered for action but was declared medically unfit and assigned to the home guard in the Paris suburbs. Toward the end of 1916, after demobilization, he found himself in the capital unemployed and without prospects or money. Remembering Doucet from the Iribe commission, he sought out the couturier to ask for work. His timing was propitious, as Doucet had decided to bind his recently formed collection of works by contemporary writers in appropriate Modernist covers, and he offered Legrain 300 francs per month to begin the project. Totally ignorant of the craft, but in desperate financial need, Legrain agreed. A makeshift studio was set up in his patron's dining room, where Legrain began to design Modernist covers for works

by Suarès, Gide, Jammes, Claudel and Doucet's other favourite authors.

In 1919, now married and living at 9 rue du Val-de-Grâce, Legrain began to accept commissions from other collectors. His liaison with Doucet had been hugely successful, but both had strong temperaments and opinions on the suitability of certain designs, which had strained the relationship. At this time, also, Doucet developed a passion for Surrealism and began to pursue this new interest, thus easing

(opposite) L'Art d'aimer (Ovid), leather, gold- and blind-tooling, and inlaid mother-of-pearl, executed by Jacques-Antoine Legrain, 1935.

(below) Sketch for the cover of Daphné et Chloé (Longus), watercolour and ink on paper with pencil notations, 1920s.

the way for Legrain to seek other patrons. Perhaps to facilitate the transition, Doucet exhibited twenty of his Legrain bindings at the 1919 Salon of the *Société des Artistes Français. The response was unparalleled in the history of the medium. Collectors turned with renewed enthusiasm to the modern style, and Legrain gained many new clients, including Baron Robert de Rothschild, Louis Barthou, Hubert de Montbrison, Baron R. Gourgaud, Georges and Auguste Blaizot, and the Americans Florence Blumenthal and Daniel Sickles. Until 1923, Legrain's maquettes were bound by René *Kieffer, after which they were distributed among Georges Canapé, George Huser, Salvador David, Georges Levitsky, Henri Noulhac, Germaine Schroeder and Stroobants.

In 1923, Legrain established his own workshop within the premises of the decorators Briant et Robert at 7 rue d'Argenteuil, from where he moved in 1925, first to a basement on the avenue Percier, and then to 304 rue Saint-Jacques. During this period he gradually built up his own team of binders and gilders, including André Jeanne, Charles Collet, Desmoules, Aufschneider, Dress, Vincent and Lordereau. In the late 1920s, hoping to extend himself into the entire field of book production as commissions continued to grow, he planned a final move to the Villa Brune, where he could house printing presses and a bindery. On 17 July 1929, the day of the scheduled move, Legrain suffered a fatal heart attack.

In a meteoric career covering scarcely a dozen years and roughly 1,300 designs for book covers, Legrain had single-handedly revolutionized the age-old craft. His influence was as great on his generation of binders as had been that of Henri Marius-Michel (1846–1925) on the preceding one.

To the majority of today's Art Deco collectors, however, Legrain is far better known as a furniture designer. His commissions in this idiom included Doucet's new studio in Neuilly, as well as work for friends of his mentor, including Jeanne Tachard, a noted milliner, for whom he furnished two apartments at 41 rue Émile Ménier. So well did his African-inspired furniture complement her tribal art collection that she retained him to decorate her villa and grounds at La Celle-Saint-Cloud. Another

(below) Daphné (Alfred de Vigny), inlays of leather with gold-tooling, 1924.

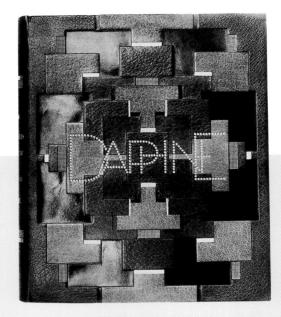

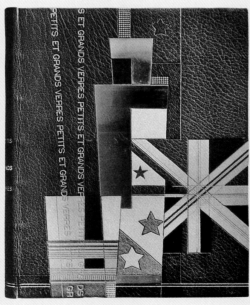

(above) Petits et grands verres (Toye et Adair), inlays of leather, gold-tooling and palladium.

client was Pierre Meyer, for whose house on the avenue Montaigne Legrain designed the celebrated glass and copper Pleyel player piano shown at the 1929 exhibition of Les Cinq at the Galerie de la Renaissance. Other noted commissions were from Maurice Martin du Gard (a suite of rooms); the Vicomte de Noailles (a bedroom); the 'Princesse G. de G.' (houses on the rue Villejust, Paris, and at La Celle-Saint-Cloud); Mme Louis Boulanger; and Suzanne Talbot. Small commercial orders filled the gaps: leather camera cases for Eastman Kodak, cigarette boxes for Lucky Strike and Camel, and a desk set for the Élysée Palace.

The inspiration for Legrain's furniture was drawn primarily from two sources: African tribal prototypes (including Ashanti and Dahomey throne chairs, neck-rests and chieftains' stools) and Cubism – the latter which he translated into three-dimensional angular and stepped forms that, owing to their generous scale, had a pronounced masculine look.

Legrain's furniture, like his bindings, incorporated lavish materials and contrasting colours. Palmwood, with its coarse, open grain was particularly suited to his African-inspired pieces, while highly buffed palisander and ebony brought opulence to his Cubist designs. Whenever possible, he exploited the tactile qualities of his materials. Metal and glass were juxtaposed with *galuchat* or animal hides on chairs and consoles. Colour was added by expanses of lacquer or small detailing in enamel or mother-of-pearl. In his interiors, the walls complemented the furniture – their surfaces panelled in cork, parchment, corrugated card or oilcloth.

Legrain showed examples of his furniture alongside his bindings in the 1920s at the annual Salons, at the 1925 *Exposition Internationale, at the exhibitions of Les Cinq from 1926 and at the inaugural *Union des Artistes Modernes (UAM) exhibition in 1930.

(opposite, above) La Soirée avec M. Teste (Paul Valéry), snakeskin with inlays of leather and gold-tooling, 1922.

(opposite, below) Poèmes à l'eau-forte (Louis Legrand), inlays of leather with gold- and blind-tooling, undated.

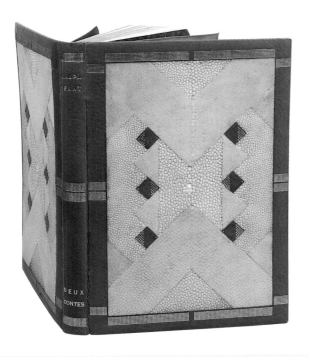

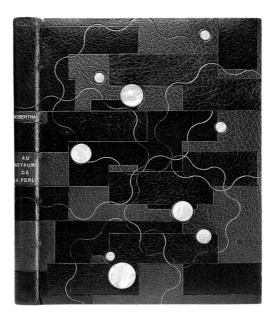

(*far left*) *Deux contes* (Guy de Maupassant),
leather and sharkskin with gold-tooling,
undated.

(*left*) *Au Royaume de la perle*
(Léonard Rosenthal), inlays of leather,
gold- and blind-tooling and inset mother-
of-pearl cabochons.

(*above*) *Théâtre complet* (François de Curel),
six-volume set, inlays of leather and
palladium (bound by René Kieffer), 1919.

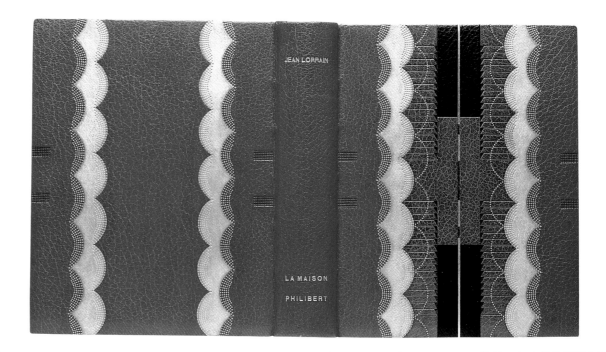

(*right*) *La Maison Philibert* (Jean Lorrain), inlays of leather with gold- and blind-tooling, 1925.

(*left*) *Trois Filles de leur mère* (Pierre Louÿs), inlays of leather and gold-tooling, 1926.

(*above*) *Daphné* (Alfred de Vigny), inlays of leather, gold- and blind-tooling and palladium, 1926.

TAMARA (DE) LEMPICKA
(1898–1980)

Warsaw-born Tamara Gorska was one of three children of Malvina, *née* Decler, and her husband Boris Gorski. She married Thadeus Lempitzski (Tadeusz Lempicki), a Russian, in St Petersburg in 1916, just before the February Revolution that propelled the Bolsheviks to power.

After her husband was seized and imprisoned, Lempicka left Russia via the Finland Station. Reunited, the couple moved in 1918 to Paris, where their daughter, Kizette, was born. Following her decision to become a painter, Lempicka enrolled at the Académie de la Grande Chaumière. She moved shortly to Montparnasse, where she frequented the cafés used by the city's artistic *demi-monde* to rendezvous, making the acquaintance, among others, of Maurice Denis and, later, André Lothe, both influencing her evolving style. She cultivated friends and within months executed some dozen portraits. In the search for a gallery owner who would represent her, she was successful with Colette Weill, who exhibited and sold her first paintings. These she signed 'Tamara de Lempitzki' or, employing the Polish feminine ending, 'de Lempitzka'. She then set out to paint the portraits of Europe's moneyed bourgeoisie, nobility and aristocracy, including the Comte de Furstenberg-Hendringen, the Duchesse de la Salle, the Marquis Sommi Picenardi and Gabriele d'Annunzio, the celebrated Italian novelist, poet and playwright with whom, like several other of her subjects, she had a romantic dalliance.

In the mid-1920s, with her canvases on view at the *Salon d'Automne, Salon des Tuileries and the Salon des Femmes Peintres, members of the artistic community were taking note. By 1927, at the height of her powers, Lempicka portrayed the leading lights of *Les Années Folles* with a cold and impersonal painterly technique that came to exemplify the Art Deco style. Following her self-portrait, *Tamara in the Green Bugatti* (1925), she completed a series of powerful portraits in which her subjects were seen against a backdrop of skyscrapers, including *Andromeda* (c. 1929), *Mrs Alan Bott* (1930), *Mme Boucard* (1931), *Adam and Eve* (1932) and *Suzy Solidor* (1933), who had become a friend and lover. In this, and other works, there exists a hint of homoeroticism, one that no doubt mirrored Lempicka's own bisexual nature.

Lempicka's highly distinctive and compelling style can be seen in roughly one hundred portraits executed from 1925 to 1939. Inspired by the concepts of Cubism, which she humanized, her male subjects reveal their cold detachment and impenetrable personalities. Her female portraits, conversely, project an overt decadence, smouldering sexuality and, in older subjects, a lingering desirability.

In 1929, after her marriage had dissolved, Lempicka undertook several portrait commissions in New York. Back in Paris from 1931 to 1939, where the Depression had begun to take hold and a sombre mood now prevailed, she continued to paint the rich and famous. Included among her subjects were the Queen of Greece and King Alfonso of Spain. She also toned down her neo-Cubism a bit. Lempicka continued to exhibit at the city's galleries, including the Galerie Zak, Galerie Colette Weill and the Galerie du Cygne. In 1933, she married Baron Raoul Kuffner, and in 1939 left with him for the USA, where she stayed in Hollywood the next year and then returned to New York. After Baron Kuffner's death in 1962, she settled in Houston to be near her daughter, Kizette. In 1978, Lempicka moved to Cuernavaca, Mexico, where she died two years later. Her paintings during her twilight years lacked the dynamism of the inter-war era; in their place, she produced an unremarkable series of floral still-life compositions.

Modele Assise, oil on canvas, late 1920s.

(opposite) Printemps, oil on canvas, c. 1928.

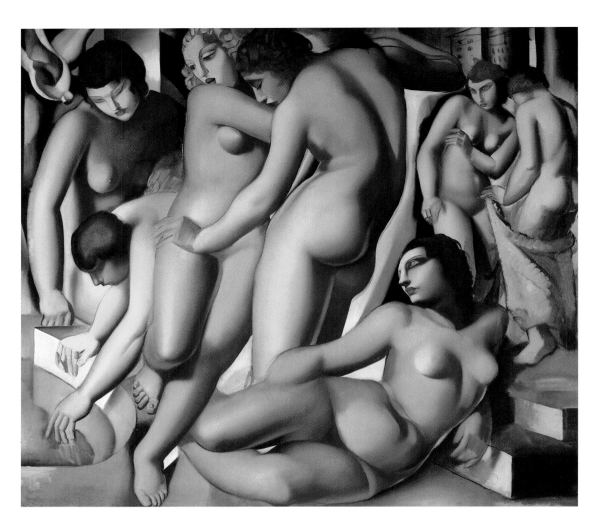

(left) Women Bathers, oil on canvas, 1929.

(below) Portrait of the Marquis d'Afflito,
oil on canvas, 1925.

Irene and her Sister, oil on canvas, 1925.

FRANÇOIS-LOUIS SCHMIED
(1873–1941)

(opposite) *Le Cantique des cantiques*, leather with lacquered and *coquille d'oeuf* metal panel executed by Jean Dunand (bound by Georges Cretté), 1925.

Schmied was born in Geneva, Switzerland, to an ex-colonel in the French Algerian army and his Vaudoise wife. He studied at the city's École des Arts Industriels as an apprentice wood engraver under Alfred Martin, and spent his spare time researching illuminated manuscripts and incunabula at the Geneva municipal library. In 1895, after five years of tuition, he moved to Paris, where he earned a living by cutting wood blocks for the commercial house of Georges Aubert. Joined three years later by his friend JEAN DUNAND (*see under* Silver, Metal, Lacquer and Enamel), Schmied continued his career as an engraver, and at the same time developed his skills as a painter and illustrator. From 1904 he exhibited wood engravings at the *Société Nationale des Beaux-Arts. In 1911 one of the exclusive books clubs – the Société du Livre Contemporain – commissioned him to engrave and print Paul *Jouve's watercolour illustrations for Rudyard Kipling's *The Jungle Book*. The project, interrupted by the First World War, was completed in 1919.

During the war Schmied enlisted in the French Foreign Legion and was wounded in the trenches at Capy on the Somme, losing his right eye. Having been demobilized, he returned to Paris to resume his career and to complete *The Jungle Book*, which was received with great acclaim by bibliophiles for its precise colour reproductions of Jouve's sketches. To achieve such precision, Schmied established his own printing plant, purchasing a Stanhope platen

hand-press. Sometimes twenty to twenty-five colours were used in a single illustration, each requiring a separate image engraved on a wood block. A single page from some books, such as *Le Paradis musulman*, which employed forty colours, took almost a month to print.

After the war, Schmied applied himself increasingly to the total production of deluxe editions – to their illustrations, typography, typesetting, page design and printing. He did not, however, bind all of his books; some were published in unbound sheets encased in a slipcover in the normal manner of French illustrated books, allowing the purchaser to select his own preferred binder. By 1925, his atelier at 12 rue Friant in Paris had become too small to house his expanding operation, and he moved

into larger premises at 74 bis rue Halle. His eldest son, Theo, himself an accomplished engraver, supervised the firm's four or five wood engravers. In addition to the Stanhope hand-press, there were four Italian Nebiolo printing presses.

The 1920s witnessed Schmied's most sumptuous works, often issued in editions of between twenty-five and one hundred for members of France's elite book clubs. The earlier works, in particular, were exuberant in their use of vibrant colours and fantastic imagery, revealing the artist's fascination with North Africa and Orientalism. Some illustrations were hand-coloured in Dunand's atelier; others were coloured by *pochoir* by Jean Saude. Further artists, such as Jean *Goulden, Georges *Barbier, Jouve, Sureda and Bergue, were commissioned

Peau-brune (François-Louis Schmied), inlays of leather with gold-tooling and palladium, 1931.

to provide illustrations for books that Schmied did not himself illustrate. During this period, he participated in several exhibitions, in particular the annual shows staged at the Galerie Georges Petit by himself, Dunand, Goulden and Jouve. As a member of the Société Nationale des Beaux-Arts and the *Société des Artistes Français, Schmied also displayed his works in their annual Salons. In 1927, he held a one-man exhibition of paintings and bindings at the Arnold Seligman gallery. Schmied's clients included Henri Vever, Barthou, Miguet, Chouanard and – a favourite author of his – Dr Joseph-Charles Mardrus.

The collapse of the world economy following the 1929 Wall Street crash had dire repercussions for Schmied, as the demand for expensive books diminished sharply. In addition, examples of his earlier works began now to appear on the secondhand market. To protect their value (and, thereby, his reputation), Schmied attempted to repurchase as many of these as he could, which contributed to his impending bankruptcy. By 1935, the workshop on the rue Halle was closed; in April of the same year an auction of his book inventory was held at the Hôtel Drouot, Paris. Schmied decided to exile himself, settling in Tahanaout, an outpost in the Moroccan desert south of Marrakesh. The bookbinder Lucie Weill was among the last to visit him there, although he returned to Paris in the late 1930s on several occasions to oversee the execution of outstanding book commissions, including *Faust* and *Le Tapis de Prière*.

(*below*) *La Création* (Dr Joseph-Charles Mardrus), in collaboration with Gonin et Cie, 2 vols, inlays of leather, gold- and blind-tooling, and a lacquered panel, 1928.

(above) *Le Livre de la vérité de parole*
(Dr Joseph-Charles Mardus), inlays of leather
with gold- and blind-tooling, 1929.

GLASS

In the years between the two world wars, the distinction made between glass as an artistic medium and as a utility household item became more pronounced. Once the concept of Modernism emerged in the late 1920s, glass was increasingly used in both furniture design and architecture; in fact, it became a fundamental component of the new design aesthetic. In rejecting traditional materials and modes of decoration, alternative media were introduced or explored to meet the functionalist aims of the day. As a result, French designers in the Art Deco era produced a tremendous variety of forms and decoration in glass, and they did this under the leadership of MAURICE MARINOT and RENÉ LALIQUE, who jointly succeeded Émile Gallé as the nation's leading *maître verriers*.

The work of Marinot is now considered to have been the major inspirational design source for decorative glass after the First World War. Trained as a painter, he acquired the skills of his adopted profession quickly and was soon executing his own designs. He worked with virtually no interruptions during the war, experimenting with translucent enamels as an alternative to opaque varieties of glass. This led to a transitional period in which he continued to employ enamelled ornamentation on the outside surface of the glass while experimenting with ways to apply it internally. By 1923, Marinot had rejected all types of extraneous decoration, including the use of enamels, in order to explore both hot and cold glass-making techniques. This allowed him to work with the vitreous glass mass itself. The objects of his mature years were extremely sculptural, while retaining the brute force of his early Fauve paintings.

Of Marinot's many followers, Henri *Navarre created furnace-worked glass with heavy walls and internal decoration in the form of swirls and whirls of colour, internal granulations and *intercalaire* textures. These effects were achieved by the use of powdered metal oxides patterned on the **marver** on to which a *paraison* of viscous clear glass was then rolled. The application of a second layer sealed the decoration. Navarre's palette was more sombre than Marinot's, and his surfaces were more heavily adorned with applications pressed on to, or wrapped around, the body.

Like Navarre, André *Thuret began to experiment in glass in the 1920s after working as a glass technician. His work incorporated the same thick walls employed by Marinot in clear glass enhanced with internal air bubbles. His style, however, was more adventurous in its range of shapes and colours; the semi-molten mass was either pinched into contorted or undulating shapes or was rolled on to metallic oxides on the marver to produce multicoloured whorls and patterns. Another Marinot disciple – Georges *Dumoulin – made a series of waisted vessels with internal colour and bubble effects in which trailing, serpentine spirals were applied around the perimeter of the glass. Jean Sala, the son and protégé of Dominique Sala, also applied a bubbled *intercalaire* form of decoration to his 'Maflin' series.

Aristide *Colotte joined the Cristallerie de Nancy in the mid-1920s as a modeller. His early designs included moulded radiator mascots and statuettes, but experimentation soon led to enamelled and painted glassware enhanced with etched detailing. By 1928, his style had become distinctly unconventional, more suited to wood or metal in its choice of sculpted forms and techniques. Favourite themes included animals and birds, and a considerable body of religious subjects, to which Colotte often applied powerful geometric motifs such as bolts of lightning or spiralling bands engraved deeply into the freeform mass of crystal.

Lalique began his career as a graphic artist and then became a jeweller. His discovery of glass occurred in the course of his search for new and less expensive materials for his jewelry. He experimented with vitreous enamels and glass cast by the **cire perdue** (lost wax) method, and it was in the latter technique that he produced his first all-glass object – a tear-shaped vial with stopper – between 1893 and 1897. In 1906, Lalique designed glass *flacons* for the parfumier François Coty, which he had executed by the Legras glassworks; within two years he had taken over a glassworks in Combs-la-Ville and, at the end of the First World War, another in Wingen-sur-Moder.

Lalique's success prompted a similar line of glassware from other designers, including the *éditeur d'art* *Etling et Cie, in opalescent glass

with a bluish tint. Like Etling, the firm of Holophane in Les Andelys produced a range of opaline glass *bibelots* and tablewares under the name of Verlys. Lighting specialists such as the firms of Sabino, SIMONET FRÈRES (*see under* Lighting) and *Genet et Michon generated similar lines of Lalique-inspired glasswares, as did Pierre *d'Avesn, who had worked for Lalique between 1916 and 1926 before establishing himself at the Cristalleries de Saint-Rémy. Another imitator was André *Hunebelle, who designed moulded vases *à la Lalique*, often in a luminescent opaline glass.

A different direction in art glass was pursued in the inter-war years by DAUM FRÈRES in Nancy. The firm re-opened in 1919, after the First World War, and grew in prestige as the region's other glasshouses closed or faltered. It produced an industrial line of thick-walled, large vases in transparent and opaque coloured glass, some of which were deeply etched with bold geometric motifs and on occasion blown into a bronze or wrought-iron armature. After 1930, the walls on Daum's glass became thinner and the etching shallower. Daum Frères also produced cameo vases and lamps in crystal or single colours, etched with stylized designs of animals, repeating floral patterns, sunbursts or swirls, invariably against a roughly etched background.

Charles and Ernest *Schneider established their glassworks in 1913 at Épinay-sur-Seine, where they created large, colourful vases and lamps decorated with internal bubbles and mottled or marbled colour effects. Some pieces were adorned with boldly coloured glass trailings fashioned into stylized flora; others with engraved geometric whorls. Some combined techniques to mimic realistic scenes from nature, such as painted goldfish on a translucent bubbled ground simulating an aquarium. Opaque black and orange glassware was also sold under the trade names Charder and Le Verre Français or, without a signature, with an embedded *millefiori* cane.

Marcel *Goupy followed the enamelling style of Marinot's early work, designing a range of vessels in colourless or transparent coloured glass on which the decoration was rendered in bright enamels painted on both the outside and inside surfaces. His decorative motifs ranged from stylized birds, flowers and animals to landscapes, mythological figures and female nudes, in a style resembling that of SÜE ET MARE (*see under* Furniture and Interior Decoration). Less known, but often equally 'high-style', were the enamelled commercial glasswares of Delvaux and André *Delatte.

Auguste *Heiligenstein became proficient in enamelling under Goupy, for whom he worked for four years. His elaborately detailed and brilliantly coloured vessels reflected the 1920s revival of Neoclassical themes in the Art Deco idiom. Draped women among flowers became a favourite theme, often rendered in a combination of enamelled, engraved and etched techniques. Jean *Luce, too, used enamelled stylized floral designs to embellish his early glassware, but shortly afterwards rejected enamelling in favour of abstract patterns engraved or sandblasted in contrasting matt and polished finishes. Some models incorporated mirrored or gilded surfaces engraved or sandblasted with symmetrical, eye-catching geometric patterns.

Another style of Art Deco glass design was **pâte-de-verre**. Although its revival in France was initiated at the end of the 19th century, it did not peak until the 1920s and 1930s. *Pâte-de-verre* is made of finely crushed pieces of glass ground into a powder mixed with a fluxing catalyst that facilitates melting. Colouring is achieved by using tinted glass or by adding metallic oxides after the ground glass has been melted into a paste. In paste form, *pâte-de-verre* is as malleable as clay, and is modelled by being packed into a mould, where it is fused by firing. It can likewise be moulded in several layers or refined by carving after it has annealed.

FRANÇOIS-ÉMILE DECORCHEMONT brought the greatest recognition to *pâte-de-verre*. A ceramist by training, he was inspired in 1902 to experiment with the material on seeing the **pâte-d'émail** (enamelled paste) works of the turn-of-the-century pioneer Albert-Louis Dammouse. Around 1909, Decorchemont began to work in the *cire perdue* method of casting, producing thin-walled vessels with decorative details cut into their surfaces. A year later he was using **pâte-de-cristal**, having rejected

DELVAUX
Vase in clear glass with enamelled decoration, 1920s.

the thin walls and ethereal decoration of his earlier models. By 1920, his style had become increasingly bold, progressing to the stylized asps and grotesque masks of the early to mid-1920s and, finally, to the highly geometric images and jewel-like palette of his mature years.

JOSEPH-GABRIEL ARGY-ROUSSEAU employed several dozen artisans to execute his designs. He manufactured a wide range of decorative objects in a colourful and opaque *pâte-de-verre* of a very light weight and high clarity. The waning public interest in the technique from 1929 led to the dissolution of his firm, La Société Anonyme des Pâtes de Verre d'Argy Rousseau, in the early 1930s. Almeric *Walter, a former ceramist, likewise embraced *pâte-de-verre* as his preferred medium. He joined Daum Frères in the early 1900s, where he produced sculpted household items and jewelry pendants in collaboration with Henri *Bergé and the firm's other modellers.

Glass produced in the rest of Europe was derivative of the styles and techniques developed in France in the 1910s, with one exception. In Scandinavia, and specifically at *Orrefors in Sweden, glass designers brought a novelty and energy to the medium. During the First World War, the Svenska Slojdforeningen (Swedish Society of Industrial Design), inspired by the ideas of the German socialist critic and theorist Hermann Muthesius, launched a campaign to introduce high standards of design into mass-production through the union of art and industry. Orrefors was the first to capitalize on the new movement, hiring Simon *Gate and Edvard *Hald to design a fresh line of art glass both in its newly developed **Graal** technique and in engraved crystal. In the 1930s, the firm's glassware became heavier and more massive following the move to functionalism introduced at the 1930 Nordiska Kompaniet (NK) exhibition in Stockholm; engraved detailing was pared back as economic austerity began to impact on consumer spending.

In Belgium, the Val Saint-Lambert glassworks, near Liège, reopened after the First World War. In the early 1920s, it introduced a series of vases decorated by Léon Ledru and engraved by Joseph Simon with 'high-style' motifs. Entitled 'Arts Décoratifs de Paris', each crystal body was overlaid in transparent coloured layers cut with repeating geometric patterns. Other noted Val Saint-Lambert designers included Modeste Denoël, Charles Graffart, Félix Matagne, René Delvenne and Lucien Petignot.

In Central Europe — Austria and Czechoslovakia, specifically — glass remained tradition-bound in the inter-war years, despite occasional forays into Modernist design by the Wiener Kunstgewerbeschule, J. & J. Lobmeyr, Moser and the technical schools of Steinschönau, Bor-Haida and Zwiesel, in Bavaria. In particular at Bor-Haida (now Novy Bor), 60 kilometres north of Prague, a vigorous Parisian 'high-style' range of geometric motifs, including black and burgundy sunbursts and lightning bolts, was applied to cocktail and lemonade services comprising decanters with matching liqueur glasses or tumblers. Invariably unsigned, and often misidentified today in the marketplace as Baccarat, these are believed to have been designed by Karel Palda and Alexander Pfohl. Beyond these, restraint remained the catchword in commercial glass production in the region.

In Britain, efforts at a contemporary idiom were lacklustre except for the work of Keith *Murray, a New Zealand architect who turned his hand to glass design in the 1930s for Stevens & Williams in Brierley Hill, Staffordshire.

In the USA, the glass industry suffered a decline after the Art Nouveau flourishes of Louis Comfort Tiffany, but two companies did produce some successful designs based on the Art Deco style in France: the Steuben and Libbey glass companies.

At Steuben, Frederick *Carder's work of the 1920s and early 1930s was based on the Parisian vernacular of Art Deco ornament. Made of acid-cut translucent glass, his expensive limited editions of art glass included images and patterns derived from the 1925 Exposition Internationale des Arts Décoratifs et Industriels Modernes. In 1933, Carder was replaced by a new principal designer, the sculptor Sidney *Waugh. The coloured glass line that Carder had developed was eliminated, and only items in colourless crystal were made.

STEUBEN GLASS CO.
(below) Bowl in cased black and alabaster glass, 1920.

HALD FOR ORREFORS
(right) Orrefors, 'Ball-Playing Girls', model No.176, engraved bowl with underplate, designed by Edvard Hald, 1920.

UNIDENTIFIED MANUFACTURER
(opposite above) Decanters in black enamelled glass by unidentified manufacturer, Czechoslovakia, 1920s.

SCHNEIDER
(opposite below) Vases in cameo glass produced under the firm's tradename 'Le Verre Français', 1920s.

The Libbey Glass Co. was in the vanguard of 1930s American commercial glass design. Around 1933 it introduced a novelty cocktail glass, 'Syncopation', with an angular stem inspired by Cubism. The firm's 'Embassy' pattern, designed by Walter Dorwin *Teague and Edwin W. Fuerst in the late 1930s, was similarly Modernist, with slender fluted columnar stems that took their imagery from Manhattan's skyscrapers.

In France, Modernist tendencies were heralded by L'Esprit Nouveau, a group of progressive designers and architects led by Amédée Ozenfant and *Le Corbusier, whose radical pavilion at the 1925 Exposition Internationale generated confusion and censure. One of the period's most extensive architectural applications of glass was that of the Maison de Verre, designed by PIERRE CHAREAU (see under Furniture and Interior Decoration) as both a clinic and private residence. Wired glass was introduced for internal partitioning, and slim square glass Nevada bricks were used in the elevations to separate the interior spaces and to diffuse the daylight. Following the formation of the *Union des Artistes Modernes (UAM) in 1930, glass was widely incorporated by members into their interiors. Notable was the bent chromed-metal and glass furniture of ROBERT MALLET-STEVENS (see under Furniture and Interior Decoration) and the luxurious glass bed and other furniture created by Louis *Sognot and Charlotte Alix for the palace of the Maharajah of Indore.

In Britain, glass was also used extensively in Modernist architecture. This was exemplified by its gradual incorporation of glass into progressive architecture: for example, in Erich Mendelsohn and Serge *Chermayeff's De La Warr Pavilion at Bexhill-on-Sea (1935–36); Wells *Coates's Embassy Court flats in Brighton (1935); and Ellis & Clarke's Daily Express Building in London (1929–32). British designers also used glass in interiors, primarily in hotels and other public areas: for example, Oliver Bernard's back-lit glass panelling for the entrance to the Strand Palace Hotel (1929–30); Oliver Milne's use of mirrored-glass panelling in the remodelled Claridge's Hotel (1930); and Basil Ionides's all-glass Savoy Theatre foyer, which included spectacular illuminated glass columns executed by James Powell's Whitefriars Glassworks.

The influence of the Bauhaus was strongly felt in the USA due primarily to the fact that many prominent German, or German-trained, designers and architects emigrated to America in the inter-war years, including Ludwig *Mies van der Rohe, Walter *Gropius, Marcel *Breuer, Josef Albers and László Moholy-Nagy. Under their influence, glass became a symbol of modernity. Mirrored and glass cocktail cabinets, frosted glass panelling and glass-panelled chairs became fashionable Modernist artefacts. Among native-born designers, DONALD DESKEY (see under Furniture and Interior Decoration) employed glass in a variety of ways: in architecture as glass bricks to provide indirect lighting; and in furniture as glass tops and shelves to achieve transparency. Similarly, Gilbert *Rohde and Karl Emanuel Martin (Kem) *Weber used glass in their furniture designs. An end-table by Weber, for example, utilized circular panels of glass separated horizontally by vertical silvered supports to create multiple transparent spaces that were compared to the Constructivist works of Naum Gabo and Antoine Pevsner.

JOSEPH-GABRIEL ARGY-ROUSSEAU

DAUM FRÈRES

FRANÇOIS-ÉMILE DECORCHEMONT

RENÉ LALIQUE

MAURICE MARINOT

JOSEPH-GABRIEL ARGY-ROUSSEAU (1885–1953)

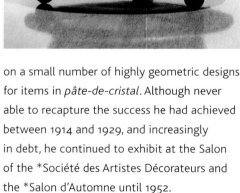

Born in Meslay-le-Vidame (Eure-et-Loir), Rousseau studied at the École Nationale de Céramique in Sèvres from 1902. Fellow students included Jean Cros (the son of the *pâte-de-verre* artist Henri Cros) and Nicolas Platon-Argyriades (later a painter and artist in ceramics and glass). On graduating in 1906, Rousseau took over the direction of a small ceramics research laboratory and soon thereafter opened his own small workshop. Following his marriage to Platon-Argyriades's sister, Marianne, in 1913, Rousseau adopted the first four letters of her surname, thereby naming himself Argy-Rousseau.

He made his début at the 1914 Salon of the *Société des Artistes Français with a display of *pâte-de-verre*, and later that year, following the outbreak of the First World War, he enlisted as a national defence engineer. In 1919, Argy-Rousseau began to produce a range of scent bottles in clear glass with enamelled decoration. Two years later he formed a limited company in partnership with Gustave Moser-Millot, the owner of a gallery at 30 boulevard des Italiens, Paris, and a glassworks at Karlovy Vary in Bohemia. Entitled La Société Anonyme des Pâtes de Verre d'Argy-Rousseau, the firm's workshops were initially at 52 avenue des Ternes, and from 1923 at 9 rue du Simplon. In addition to the production of a great variety of household accoutrements in *pâte-de-verre* – table lamps, chandeliers, night lights, bonbonnières, bowls, vases and ashtrays – as well as jewelry, the studio worked to develop *pâte-de-cristal*, a more translucent material. Argy-Rousseau

executed his models in wax, then handed them over to his assistants for mass-production. Among others, the sculptor Marcel *Bouraine was commissioned to provide models for figurines for execution in *pâte-de-cristal*. Stylistically, Argy-Rousseau's designs ranged from Neoclassical (masks, Greek dancers) to Art Nouveau (flora, insects, reptiles) and Modernist (overlapping geometric patterns). In addition to the Moser-Millot gallery, outlets in the French capital included the galleries Goupil et Cie, Briche, Manoury and the Salon des Arts Ménagers.

Argy-Rousseau was unable to survive the economic crisis of 1929; his studio dissolved on 31 December 1931, from which time he continued to work in his own small workshop at 10 rue Cail. In later years he concentrated

on a small number of highly geometric designs for items in *pâte-de-cristal*. Although never able to recapture the success he had achieved between 1914 and 1929, and increasingly in debt, he continued to exhibit at the Salon of the *Société des Artistes Décorateurs and the *Salon d'Automne until 1952.

(*above left*) Table lamp, model No. 29-09, in *pâte-de-verre* decorated *d'angles aigus*, with wrought-iron mounts 1920s.

(*above*) Night light (*bibelot lumineux*) in *pâte-de-verre* with wrought-iron mount, 1920s.

(*opposite*) *Danseuse*, statuette in *pâte-de-cristal* with bronze mount, designed by Marcel Bouraine, 1920s.

(*opposite*) 'Libations', vase in *pâte-de-verre*, c. 1924.

(*above*) Selection of *pâte-de-verre* pendants on silk cords, 1920s.

DAUM FRÈRES

Jean Daum (1825–1885) was born in Bischwiller (Bas-Rhin). He was a solicitor who included among his clients several glassworks in Meisenthal and Saint-Louis. With the outbreak of the Franco-Prussian War in 1870, his family became refugees, moving in with one of his wife's uncles at Sarralbe (Moselle). After the war, Jean chose to stay in France, moving to Dombasle and then Nancy in 1876. Following a series of unsuccessful business ventures, he acquired the glasshouse Verrerie Sainte-Catherine, which had opened in 1875 to manufacture watch glasses, plate glass and tableware, with unsecured financing that he had provided. In 1878, when the owners were unable to repay him, Jean took possession of the glassworks, plus its contents, leasehold and the option to purchase the freehold. Lacking in technical expertise when he took over the operation, which he renamed Verrerie de Nancy, Jean engaged the former manager of the Sars-Poteries works to run the technical side while he attended to its administration.

Towards the end of 1879 his eldest son, Auguste (1853–1909), came to his rescue. Born in Bitche, Auguste studied there and then in Metz and Nancy before moving to Paris, where he enrolled in the law faculty at the University of Paris. On graduating, he returned to Nancy to become a solicitor's clerk, but his father's problems at the glassworks persuaded him to forgo his chosen career and to join him. Quickly familiarizing himself with the glassworks' operations, Auguste reduced its overhead costs while expanding the market for its products.

Jean Daum's second son, Antonin (1864–1931), who had studied in Lunéville and Nancy and then at the prestigious École de l'Union Centrale des Arts Décoratifs, joined the firm in 1887, taking responsibility for its production. Following the 1889 Exposition Universelle in Paris, where its exhibit was favourably reviewed by the critics, the firm participated again in the 1893 World's Columbian Exposition in Chicago, the 1895 Libre Esthètique exhibition in Brussels and the 1900 Exposition Internationale in Paris. No doubt at first under the giant shadow of Émile Gallé's *cristallerie*, the early art glass of Daum Frères was predictably parallel, but inferior, to that of its celebrated neighbour. Gradually, however, a more sophisticated and individual repertoire

of shapes and finishing techniques emerged, the latter including *martelage* (a hammered finishing effect), *jaspé* (mottled glass), *intercalaire* and *marqueterie*. The firm also developed its own palette. Less vivid than that of Gallé, its emphasis was usually on autumnal hues, such as ochres, oranges, sepias and burgundies. At the time, also, a *pâte-de-verre* workshop was set up under Henri *Bergé and Almeric *Walter.

In 1909, the year of Auguste's death, his son Paul (1888–1944) joined Daum Frères, which until then had embraced Art Nouveau's

(below) Vase in moulded glass with etched decoration, 1920s.

anthology of flora as its preferred means of ornamentation. On Paul's arrival, however, the firm turned to simpler forms – a decision dictated in part by changing consumer taste. Designs became less fussy, with monochromatic hues replacing the blended naturalistic palette of the *fin de siècle*.

The works were closed at the outbreak of the First World War in 1914, and when they re-opened in 1919, the designs became even simpler, often in thick-walled opaque coloured glass with gold or silver inclusions. Further ornamentation was provided by trapped air bubbles or abstract intaglio-carved patterns, the vessels sometimes housed in reticulated metal mounts provided by Louis *Majorelle, EDGAR BRANDT (*see under* Silver, Metal, Lacquer and Enamel) or André *Groult. Thick-walled transparent coloured glass with deeply cut patterns, usually geometric in concept, became popular, their surfaces often polished and acid-etched. Executed under Paul Daum's supervision, a selection of these were included in the Daum Frères exhibit at the 1925 Exposition Internationale to wide acclaim. In the same year, Antonin's son, Michel, joined the firm as a chemist and engineer. He, in turn, introduced colourless crystal and a sculptural quality into the firm's repertoire.

(*above*) Selection of moulded and etched glassware, 1920s.

(*left*) Vase in moulded and etched glass, 1920s.

During the German occupation of France in the Second World War, the plant was forced to close. Paul Daum was deported to a concentration camp, where he died. Daum Frères re-opened in 1946 with Auguste's youngest son, Henri, in charge of administration. Now only crystal was produced; glass *per se* was discontinued. In 1962, the limited company founded in 1925 was converted into a public one named the Cristallerie Daum, with Michel Daum as its president. The family administers the firm to this day.

(*opposite*) Selection of moulded and etched glass vases, 1920s.

(*below*) Selection of moulded glassware with etched decoration, 1920s.

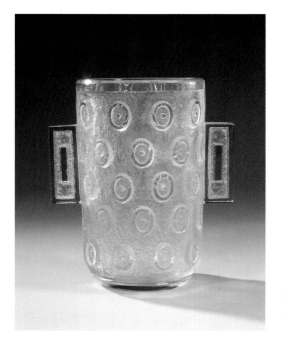

(*far left*) Moulded and etched glass vase, 1920s.

(*left*) Moulded and etched glass vase with wrought-iron mount, 1920s.

FRANÇOIS-ÉMILE DECORCHEMONT (1880–1971)

Born into a family of Normandy artists in Conches-en-Ouche (Eure), Decorchemont studied at the École Nationale Supérieure des Arts Décoratifs, Paris, between 1896 and 1900, while painting and learning the pottery craft in a small ceramics workshop set up in his parents' home. Between 1900 and 1903, he created a number of stoneware vases in a muted Art Nouveau style and began to experiment with *pâte-de-verre*, drawing inspiration from the work of Albert-Louis Dammouse. His first experimental pieces were in a fine opaque glass paste known as *pâte-d'émail*. He made his début at the 1903 Salon of the *Société des Artistes Français, and within four years succeeded in creating a true *pâte-de-verre* paste, employing powdered glass purchased from the Cristalleries de Saint-Denis. By 1910, he had also perfected a genuine *pâte-de-cristal*. Decorchemont closed his kilns in 1914, returning in 1919 to produce similar pre-First World War wares for a few years. His 1920s wares, some of which he offered through the Maison *Geo. Rouard, showed considerable simplification in their increasingly geometric forms and newly developed finishes.

Decorchemont was eventually able to make his own glass, to which he added metallic oxides to achieve different colour effects. Around 1920, he developed a formula for a hard translucent substance composed of crystal, in which he combined metallic oxides with silica, examples of which were displayed at the 1925 Exposition Internationale. From 1933 until the outbreak of the Second World War, he was increasingly preoccupied with the manufacture of *pâte-de-verre* stained-glass windows; from 1935 to 1938, he worked almost exclusively on windows commissioned by the church of Sainte-Odile in Paris. The Second World War again interrupted his work. Despite being sixty-five years old at the end of the hostilities, Decorchemont continued to work productively for another quarter century, both in glass and *grès* (earthenware).

(*opposite*) 'Scarabée' vase in *pâte-de-verre*, c. 1915–20.

(*below*) 'Rhinoceros' and 'Locust Beetle' vases in *pâte-de-verre*, c. 1915–20.

(*right*) Bowl in *pâte-de-verre*, 1920s.

(*below*) Vase with chameleon handles in *pâte-de-verre*, the model introduced in 1922, this example 1924.

RENÉ LALIQUE (1860–1945)

Lalique was born at Ay (Marne) and left the Lycée Turgot (near Vincennes) at sixteen years of age, having shown a great aptitude for draughtsmanship. In 1876, he apprenticed himself to Louis Aucoq, a leading Paris gold- and silversmith. During his apprenticeship he attended courses at the city's École Nationale Supérieure des Arts Décoratifs, two years later travelling to England, where he completed his training in a two-year stay at Sydenham College. Lalique returned to Paris in 1880, working first for the jeweller Auguste Petit and then in association with an old family friend, Varenne. During this time he supplied jewellers such as CARTIER (see under Jewelry), *Boucheron, Destape and Aucoq with models, while studying sculpture with Justin Lequien. In 1885, he joined Destape as its manager, a year later taking over the business. Now his own master, Lalique soon abandoned the traditional canons of the medium, the start of a journey to the pinnacle of the bijouterie profession during the Art Nouveau epoch. At the 1900 Exposition Universelle, his name became world-famous.

The medium of glass soon drew Lalique's attention, however, and he began to experiment with it in his workshop in the rue Thérèse, where he incorporated clear and coloured glass into his jewelry. In 1902, he rented a small workshop at Clairefontaine, near Rambouillet, which he equipped and staffed with four glassmakers. Using the **cire perdue** process, he modelled figures and vessels in glass. From that moment, he moved increasingly into the realm of glass as he abandoned that of jewelry.

Around 1905, Lalique incorporated engraved glass into his designs for mirrors, textiles, paper knives and other small items, and in 1907 was commissioned to design labels for an edition of perfume bottles for the parfumeur François Coty. He also designed the bottles themselves, which were executed by the *Legras et Cie glassworks. The following year Lalique rented the Verrerie de Combs-la-Ville, a glassworks at Combs (Seine-et-Marne), which he subsequently purchased. More perfume bottles followed – for Coty, Forvil, Worth, Orsay and Roger et Gallet. The Armistice in 1918 led to the return to France of Alsace and part of Lorraine, where Lalique purchased his second glassworks, a large factory at Wingen-sur-Moder (Bas-Rhin), close to the German border. At fifty-eight years of age, Lalique was about to embark on a second career.

Lalique showed his glassware in his own pavilion at the 1925 Exposition Internationale, which served as a triumphal event for him – as had that in 1900. He also designed and manufactured a glass table, stemware and candlesticks for the *Sèvres pavilion, and the monumental illuminated fountain in front of the Cour des Métiers pavilion. In 1927, he provided moulded glass light fixtures for the first-class dining room designed by Pierre Patout on the ocean liner Île-de-France, while continuing to exhibit at the *Salon d'Automne and that of the *Société des Artistes Décorateurs. In the 1920s, his series of thirty-plus car mascots was introduced, and in the 1930s he executed some monumental commissions, including the glass chapel displayed at the 1931 Salon d'Automne. Lalique also designed entire sections of wall panels and light fixtures for the Normandie in 1935. In 1937, the glassworks at Combs-la-Ville closed, and during the Second World War the Wingen-sur-Moder factory was taken over by the invading German forces. Lalique died shortly after the Liberation.

(opposite) Selection of moulded glassware. Top, from left: 'Lézards et Bleuets', 'Milan' and 'Perruches'; Centre: 'Serpent', 'Monnaie du Pape' and 'Languedoc'; Bottom: 'Courges', 'Albert' and 'Soucis'.

(below) Selection of car mascots. From left: 'Longchamps' (introduced 1929), 'Cinq Chevaux' (1925), 'Tête d'Aigle' (1928), 'Tête de Paon' (1928) and 'Comète' (1925).

(*left*) 'Oxford', four-branch candelabrum in moulded glass, introduced 1928.

Lalique's vessels, which incorporated exceptionally high relief and finely detailed decoration, were made in three ways: by blowing glass into moulds by mouth; mechanically by an *aspiré-soufflé* (or *pressé-soufflé*) process; or by casting with a stamping press. The base material used was demi-cristal – glass with a 50 per cent lead content that was left clear or was coloured with metallic oxides, sulphides and chlorides to produce an array of exquisite, jewel-like colours ranging from emerald green to ruby red. Opalescent effects were obtained by sandwiching a layer of opaque white glass between two layers of coloured glass. Other forms of decoration were achieved: by painting or staining with enamels; by frosting with acids; by 'antiquing'

(*above*) 'Ceylan' vase in moulded opaline glass, introduced 1924.

(*right*) 'Palestre' moulded vase, introduced 1928.

or simulating the effects of ageing; by exposing the glass to metallic oxide fumes under a muffle; or by polishing with rouge or high-speed buffers.

In addition to glass jewelry, illuminated wall panels, statuettes, fountains and *luminaires*, Lalique's output included an exhaustive selection of household accoutrements, including vases, trays, compotes, clock cases, decanters, light fixtures and *bibelots lumineaux*. Designs were pictorial, covering the gamut of art-historical themes from antiquity to the present day. Lalique's grammar of decorative ornament was equally varied: abstract geometric patterns, naturalistic or stylized animals, flowers, human and mythical subjects, and towards the end of his life, increasingly religious in nature.

(*above*) 'L'Oiseau de feu', in moulded and tinted glass on an illuminated metal base, introduced 1922.

(*left*) 'Le Jour et la nuit', clock in clear and frosted glass on a silvered-metal illuminated base, introduced 1926.

(far left) 'Gros Scarabées', moulded glass vase.

(left) 'Salmonidés', moulded glass vase.

(above) 'Archers', moulded glass vase.

(right) Panel in moulded and etched glass for the John Wanamaker Men's Store, Broad Street and Penn Square, Philadelphia, 1932.

Elevator door in moulded glass and nickel
silver, for the lobby of the Oviatt Building,
Los Angeles, 1928.

MAURICE MARINOT (1882–1960)

Born in Troyes, Marinot moved in 1901 to Paris, where he trained as an artist and exhibited, while studying with the group later known as 'Les Fauves'. Failing to graduate, he persuaded his parents nevertheless to send him to the city's École des Beaux-Arts, where he studied under Fernand Cormon, a painter. In 1905, he returned to Troyes, never again to leave. He displayed paintings at the *Salon d'Automne between 1910 and 1913, exhibiting also in these years at the Salon des Tuileries. A visit in 1911 to the small Viard glassworks at Bar-sur-Seine managed by his friends, the brothers Eugène and Gabriel Viard, prompted an immediate career change; he displayed a selection of his first creations in glass at that year's Salon des Indépendants.

Marinot presented his first major selection of glassware at the 1913 Salon d'Automne, some of which was shown within a liqueur table in André Mare's exhibit (*see* SÜE ET MARE). Adrien Hébrard, the well-known founder, became his sole agent, displaying his works in his gallery on the rue Royale. Among his first clients were the Musée du Luxembourg, Baron Robert de Rothschild and Mme Louis Barthou. These early wares comprised clear glass decorated in coloured enamels with stylized flowers, swags and birds.

Mobilized during the First World War, Marinot returned in 1919 to his bench at the Viard works. There he continued to employ enamels until 1923, even though he realized that the conventional application of opaque paints to the glass surface masked its innate beauty,

thereby rendering the technique counter-productive. His search was for the means by which to decorate the glass mass itself, thereby eliminating all extraneous ornamentation. By 1922, the problem was largely resolved: the shapes and internal decoration on his glassware determined its appeal.

In the 1920s and 1930s, Marinot's work divided itself roughly into four categories. First were the vessels he designed immediately after his rejection of enamelling. These are characterized by heavy, thick walls that incorporate deeply etched or internal decoration, the latter consisting of air bubbles, smoky tints, streaks of muted colour or a 'sandwich' effect in which a layer of speckled or spiralling colour was inserted between the inner and outer layers of clear glass.

The second category comprised etched pieces that were very deeply acid-cut with powerful, almost savage, abstract geometric motifs in which the acid-treated textured areas contrast with the polished and smoothed raised areas to maximize the refractive effects of the light. The third category included glassware worked at the furnace, in which heavy applications of molten glass emphasized form. Marinot modelled some of these into formalized masks. The fourth category comprised his bottles and

(*opposite*) Bottle with stopper, model No. 1411, cased glass with internal aeration, *c*. 1927.

(*below*) Bottle with stopper, model No. 1997, etched glass, 1931.

flacons, either shaped on the wheel or sculpted into chunky free-form shapes at the kiln, which incorporated the artist's characteristic spherical or hemispherical stoppers and internal decoration.

Marinot's exhibit at the 1925 Exposition Internationale, where he displayed *hors concours* in Hébrard's stand and in SÜE ET MARE's (*see under* Furniture and Interior Decoration) pavilion, received wide acclaim. In the same year he staged his first exhibition in New York.

In 1937, the Viard factory closed down and Marinot never again worked in glass, in part due to failing health caused by working for so many years in proximity to the furnaces. A final show of his works was staged by Hébrard at the 1937 Exposition des Arts et Techniques. In 1944, Troyes was liberated by the Allies.

In the preceding bombing, however, Marinot's atelier was blown up, destroying some 2,500 paintings and much of his glass. Only the pieces that had been stored at the home of his sister, Hélène, were saved. Throughout these years, Marinot continued to paint and to exhibit his canvases at galleries such as the Galerie Charpentier, in 1948.

(*below*) Selection of stoppered bottles in cased glass with aerated and/or textured interior decoration, 1920s.

(*left*) Vase in clear glass with enamelled decoration, 1913.

(*below left*) Vase in clear glass with enamelled decoration, 1914.

(*below*) Flacon, clear glass with applied and enamelled decoration, *c.* 1913–14.

CERAMICS

In an examination of the ceramics of the Art Deco period, it is tempting to limit the discussion to the 'high style', which dominated the annual Salons and the 1925 *Exposition Internationale des Arts Décoratifs et Industriels Modernes. However, this important element of the decade's decoration – characterized by the mannered female form accompanied by attenuated silhouettes of animals against a background of conventionalized flowers, volutes or geometric motifs – represented only one facet of the wealth of artistic talent found in the Modernist ceramics of the inter-war period. A clearer picture of the full range of Art Deco ceramics emerges if related wares of the 1919–39 period are divided into three more or less distinct categories. First, and most important, are the creations of the artist–potters, direct heirs to the reform movements of the late 19th and early 20th centuries. Second are the wares of the more traditional manufactories, some of which had been in continuous production since the introduction of porcelain into Europe in the 18th century. And third was the birth of industrial ceramics – wares designed expressly for mass-production, the offspring of a marriage between art and industry unknown in the 1800s.

The inter-war artist-potters attempted to counter the poor artistic and technical standards within the ceramic industry in the late-Victorian era, which had been created by the emergence of a large and prosperous bourgeoisie whose purchasing power fuelled the manufacture of vast numbers of inexpensive, badly made wares. Artistic reformers, such as John Ruskin and William Morris, assigned a higher moral and artistic significance to handmade pieces, elevating the craftsman to the status of artist and thereby ennobling his creations. 'Art Pottery' became a distinguished art form by which the craftsman was seen as virtuous, while the machine and its products were castigated as the roots of a social evil. Equally important at the time was Europe's gradual awareness of Orientalism. The beginnings of this cross-fertilization with the Far East were apparent in the Japanesque wares introduced to the English consumer market in the 1880s by factories such as the Worcester Royal Porcelain Co., and in the early 20th century's fascination with Oriental

GERHARD SCHLIEPSTEIN
Prince and Princess, group in glazed hard-paste
porcelain, for Rosenthal Porzellan, 1925–26.

glazing techniques in the works of Ernst Seger in Berlin, Auguste Delaherche and Ernest Chaplet in Paris, and Adelaide Robineau and the *Rookwood Pottery in the USA.

After the First World War the potter was effectively involved in all phases of production – design, modelling and glazing – in a manner often hard to distinguish from that of his immediate forebears in the Arts and Crafts Movement. At no point were higher levels of technical virtuosity achieved than in the French ceramics of the years preceding and following 1920. The mastery of the glaze became paramount, but this preoccupation with technical perfection came at the expense of artistic innovation, and it was left to the British and to Viennese-inspired Americans to breathe new life into this aspect of the medium in the period preceding the Second World War.

The work of the French potter André *Metthey provided an important link between the reformers and the early modern period. Although the great body of his work was executed prior to the First World War, his wares incorporated many of the motifs that became the standard vernacular for Art Deco artisans. Working initially in stoneware and then in **faïence**, Metthey invited prominent artists of the School of Paris to decorate his wares. More significant from a technical standpoint was the work of ÉMILE DECOEUR, whose stoneware and porcelains were noted for a pronounced unity of form and decoration. Preoccupied at first with exquisite *flambé* glazes with incised decoration carved into rich layers of coloured **slip**, his style evolved gradually in the 1920s towards monochromatic glazes which by their brilliance effectively precluded the need for any further ornamentation.

Émile *Lenoble's work was strongly reminiscent of Korean and Sung wares. Mixing kaolin to produce stoneware of exceptional lightness, he created geometric and conventionalized floral motifs suitable for simple forms. Such decoration, incised into the vessel or its slip, was often used in conjunction with a refined celadon glaze.

The work of Georges *Serré was profoundly influenced by a sojourn in the Orient, where he taught and developed a fascination with Khmer

JACQUES-ÉMILE RUHLMANN
Vase in soft-paste porcelain on a gilt-bronze
foot for La Manufacture Nationale de Sèvres,
painted by Maurice Herbillon, *c.* 1930.

and Chinese art. He produced massive vessels incised with simple geometric motifs and glazed to resemble cut stone. Jean *Besnard was inspired by native traditions for his distinctive glazes, some of which he developed to resemble the delicacy of lace. Other models incorporated moulded or incised animals and birds in a more robust technique applied with a thick glaze. Séraphin *Soudbinine, a Russian *émigré* and protégé of Rodin, worked in porcelain and stoneware, producing vessels that were predictably three-dimensional. In Boulogne-sur-Seine, Edmond Lachenal began to work with *flambé* glazes in the early years of the century, gradually developing a technique in which the glaze was manipulated to mimic the geometric precision of **cloisonné** enamel. His choice of colours included a brilliant turquoise blue often imposed on a crackled ivory or beige ground. Henri *Simmen, one of his students, used incised symmetrical decoration to enhance his glazes.

Jean *Mayodon's faïence wares were noted for their painted figural technique and crackled glazes, many designed for him in 'high-style' Art Deco by Marianne Clouzot. Tiles were a Mayodon speciality, including the commission for many areas of the ocean liner *Normandie*. The simple bulbous forms by RENÉ BUTHAUD invited a similar type of figural decoration. Buthaud worked in Bordeaux, and his Modernist imagery has often been linked to the painterly style of JEAN DUPAS (*see under* Paintings, Graphics, Posters and Bookbinding), a friend and neighbour, who depicted a similar range of languorous maidens in lightly titillating poses on his canvases. Stylistic qualities notwithstanding, Buthaud's technical capabilities were evident in the thick **craquelure** and **peau de serpent** glazes he mastered in the early 1930s. Also outside the French capital, Félix Massoul, at Maisons-Alfort, worked with a bright palette of metallic glazes, often in collaboration with his wife, Madeleine.

In Belgium, native-born Georges Guérin (1896–1954) worked for the Société des Grès de Bouffioulx in Châtelet, where he employed running glazes in a vibrant blue and brown palette, some with metal overlays that he applied to individually modelled, hand-thrown vessels.

He participated at the 1925 Exposition Internationale and 1937 Exposition des Arts et Techniques, Paris.

The Wiener Werkstätte provided a forum for artisans in a variety of different fields. Founded in 1903, its early style was severe and uncompromising, but, perhaps in reaction to the deprivations of the First World War, a spontaneous style evolved in its ceramic workshops. Throughout the 1920s, Susi *Singer, Gudrun *Baudisch-Wittke and Valerie (Vally) *Wieselthier, among others, worked in a highly idiosyncratic style characterized by coarse modelling and bright discordant drip-glaze effects. At the 1925 Exposition Internationale, these artists were joined by Michael *Powolny and Josef Hoffmann, who displayed their modern ceramics through the Wiener Keramik workshops.

In the USA, the impact of the Austrian school was felt through the teachings of Julius Mihalik, who emigrated to Cleveland. A number of his students found employment at the Cowan Pottery Studio in Rocky River, west of the city. These included VIKTOR SCHRECKENGOST, Waylande de Santis *Gregory and Thelma Frazier. Schreckengost's exposure to Viennese ceramics was direct: he studied under Powolny at the Wiener Keramik in 1929. Schreckengost — a part-time saxophonist — is best known for his series of 'Jazz' punch bowls, executed at the Cowan Pottery. He had a profound influence on 1930s American ceramics: his entries at both the Cleveland May shows and the Ceramic National exhibitions drew repeated praise and awards. His designs, inspired always by his studies in Vienna, were often strong and colourful, and always witty.

Trained as a painter, Carl *Walters did not turn to ceramics until 1919. His clever animal figures, produced in editions, relied on strong modelling techniques and glazes derived from sources as diverse as American folk art and Egyptian faïence. William Hunt *Diederich, better known for his elegant metalwork, also executed pottery. Characteristic were animal forms in silhouette, reminiscent both in style and technique of the transparent washes found in early Mediterranean earthenware. The painter Henry Varnum *Poor turned to pottery in part from economic necessity. Inspired by primitive ceramics, he at first produced simple

MAURICE GENSOLI

(below) Sirènes et Tritons, vase in soft-paste porcelain for La Manufacture Nationale de Sèvres, painted by André Plantard, c. 1933.

CHARLES CATTEAU

(right) Selection of glazed earthenware vases for Boch Frères, c. 1925.

tableware items but gradually shifted towards more profitable architectural commissions. For the latter, his style remained basically unchanged, relying on the decorative value of the slip and **sgraffito** decoration.

The inter-war years in America witnessed the growth and maturity of the Cranbrook Academy of Art, founded in 1932 in Bloomfield Hills, Michigan. The academy is well known as a catalyst for the post-Second World War studio movement. Remarkable, in a ceramics context, were a cool and elegant dinner service by Eliel *Saarinen, for Lenox, and the serene and austere creations of Majlis (Maija) *Grotell, which in their tactile quality and careful glaze manipulation showed her mastery of Oriental kiln techniques.

The state manufactories of France and Germany – the second category of related inter-war wares – experienced general artistic stagnation in the 1920s and 1930s. Throughout the 19th century such firms had become bastions of conservatism, creating expensive ornaments for the well-off, rather than trying to promote a Modernist audience. It was left in part to the Scandinavians, whose boundaries between art and craft were less rigid, to integrate the aesthetics of the potter's wheel with the grammar of Modernist ornament.

Other European potteries, with widely varying capabilities, turned their attention to the possibilities of the modern style. These ranged from the French-inspired interpretations of Belgian firms to the divided efforts of the British, who produced both modern wares and period reproductions, and to various other Continental and American firms whose products revealed a thinly veiled attempt to capitalize on the 1925 style. Ironically, it was the last-mentioned which served most to popularize Art Deco and, by vulgarizing it, to precipitate its decline.

The inter-war years are generally conceded to have been artistically dry for the Manufacture Nationale de *Sèvres, despite its continuing efforts towards modernization. Under the direction of Georges Lechevallier-Chevignard from 1920, the factory participated in the 1925 Exposition Internationale, with items commissioned from independent artist–designers and architects whose principal expertise lay outside the

SUË ET MARE
(*below*) Covered tureen in glazed earthenware
for Primavera, manufactured by the faïencerie
Marcel Meran de Montereau, early 1920s.

field of ceramics. Rather more successful, in a Modernist context, was the stylish tableware produced by Theodore *Haviland et Cie, of Limoges. By commissioning works from outside artist–designers, such as Suzanne Lalique and Jean Dufy, there was an obvious attempt to adapt a contemporary decorative vocabulary to traditional forms. Marcel *Goupy, known more for his glass designs, created dining services in porcelain and glass. Jean *Luce, another artist whose creations in glass overshadowed his achievements in ceramics, designed tableware for Haviland in a light Modernist style. A delightful selection of small *animalier* porcelain wares, in biscuit or glazed, by Édouard-Marcel *Sandoz, was also issued by the firm.

In the 1920s, the large Paris department stores generated an extensive range of household ceramics designed by their own studios. At *Pomone, Charlotte *Chauchet-Guilleré, Madeleine Sougez, Marcel Renard and Claude Lévy created lightly decorated tablewares and accessories in faïence to complement their furnishings. At *La Maîtrise (Les Galeries Lafayette), MAURICE DUFRÈNE (*see under* Furniture and Interior Decoration), Jean and Jacques *Adnet, Paul Bonifas and Mlle Maisonne offered a similar line of table-top wares executed for the store by Fau et Guillard and *Boch Frères Keramis. At the firm of *Faïenceries de Longwy, a vivid palette outlined in black in a style derived from North African tiles was successfully integrated in the 1920s with images such as leaping gazelles and formalized flora.

The potteries of Robert *Lallemant, dating from the 1920s and early 1930s, reflected the vogue in France at the time for angular forms. The large number of his wares fashioned as lamp bases attests to his purely decorative intent. A similar series of crisply angular forms and bird figures was designed at the time in white-glazed *grès* by Jean and Jacques Adnet. The Paris retailer *Robj sold figural decanters and other ceramic *bibelots* created by a variety of designers. Vaguely Cubist and often quite charming, these were intended to be collected in series.

With the closure of the famous Vienna Manufactory in the 19th century, only the Augarten firm and *Friedrich Goldscheider remained to play a significant role in Austria's production of modern-style porcelain

HALL CHINA CO.
(*below and opposite*) Teapots in earthenware
with red Chinese glaze, from left: 'Airflow'
(1940), 'Football' (1938), 'Doughnut' (1938),
'Rhythm' (1939) and 'Automobile' (1938).

wares. Augarten produced a limited selection of decorative wares designed by Josef Hoffmann and Ena Rottenberg. In the 1920s, Goldscheider's range of ballerinas and pierrettes, some from models by Josef *Lorenzl, achieved a certain gaiety and popularity. At the 1925 Exposition Internationale, the firm's Paris branch, *Arthur Goldscheider, displayed a more stimulating range of ceramic dinner wares, statuettes and lamp bases designed for it by Eric *Bagge, Édouard *Cazaux and Sybille May.

In Belgium, the modern style was vigorously adopted by the firm of *Boch Frères Keramis, in La Louvière. Charles *Catteau, the firm's principal Modernist designer, worked in a brilliant turquoise blue glaze on crackled ivory grounds reminiscent of Edmond Lachenal's earlier palette.

At the Società Ceramica *Richard-Ginori factory in Doccia, Italy, the architect Giovanni (Gio) *Ponti introduced wares with highly mannered Modernist decoration into the firm's classical repertoire from 1923. In Turin, Eugenio Colmo turned to ceramics as a hobby and decorated white porcelain blanks with a forceful range of Art Deco images in vibrant colours.

In Germany, only the Berlin manufactory espoused an interest in 20th-century design. The nation's oldest and most esteemed porcelain factory, the Staatliche Porzellan-Manufaktur Meissen, chose largely to sit out the Modernist movement.

England, too, chose largely to eschew progressive design in preference for her rich legacy of traditional styles. Yet those artists who took the trouble to transpose the modern decorative idiom into industrial wares did so to considerable acclaim. Notable among these were Eric *Slater, at Shelley Potteries, and Susie *Cooper, who produced her own simply decorated services. In 1931, Cooper accepted an offer from Wood & Sons' Crown Works to execute shapes of her own design. She produced dozens of tableware designs decorated – in deference to the British consumer's innate conservatism – with subdued abstract or geometric jazz-style patterns in muted tones. At the other end of the spectrum, CLARICE CLIFF's 'Bizarre' tableware, produced by the Newport

Pottery from 1928, has come to symbolize the decorative exuberances and excesses of the Art Deco style in its use of colour, geometry and eccentric shapes. Clever marketing schemes and moderate prices helped to popularize her wares. But her later employment of artists such as Vanessa Bell and Duncan Grant, who were already engaged in pottery decoration, and others such as Sir Frank Brangwyn, Graham Sutherland and Laura Knight was less successful. Critics likened the idea to 'eating off pictures', and the project was quickly abandoned. At Josiah Wedgwood & Sons, the ceramic designer Daisy Makeig-Jones (1881–1945) introduced a great variety of 'Fairyland Lustre' patterns on bone china between 1915 and 1920; these received critical acclaim. Although often included today at auction within the Art Deco category, in fact they qualify more as Victorian-type fantasy wares with folklore influences.

In Sweden, Wilhelm *Kage was artistic director at the Gustavsberg porcelain works. His 'Argenta' stoneware included 'high-style' Art Deco chased silver images applied to green-glazed grounds that resembled *verde antico* bronze. In Norway, the geometry of Nora Gulbrandsen's designs for the Porselaensfabrik in Porsgrunn clearly reflected the modern aesthetic.

In the USA, the foremost potteries of the Midwest were too conservative to embrace the new idiom. Whereas the Rookwood Pottery encouraged individual decorators to familiarize themselves with Paris's newest fashions through contemporary art reviews, its continuing financial vicissitudes from the mid-1920s prevented it from full commitment to anything new and risky. The same reticence applied to the *Fulper, Newcomb, Van Briggle and Grueby potteries – all in various stages of decline since their celebrated 1900 years. Only *Roseville had the temerity to produce a spirited line of new designs, entitled 'Futura', inspired by the terraced contours of Manhattan's skyscrapers.

Perhaps most significant to the development of a 20th-century aesthetic was the birth in the inter-war years of industrial ceramics and the professional industrial designer. That the profession is seen today as the inter-relationship between art and industry is the result

of attempts in numerous fields – not the least of which is ceramic design – to prove that good design could be both economical and functional. The true industrial ceramics of the 1930s, non-derivative in form and generally devoid of decoration, lost none of their character through mass-production. Throughout the decade, there occurred a gradual acceptance of functional forms coupled with modern industrial techniques. The machine, seen decades earlier as the antithesis of good design, became the vehicle that facilitated the mass-production of well-designed works. The turning point in this development can be traced to the establishment of the Bauhaus in Weimar in 1919. Although no body of ceramic works evolved at the Bauhaus to rival, say, the metalware designs being created there by Marianne *Brandt or Ludwig *Mies van der Rohe, the school's ceramics are noteworthy for their wholehearted rejection of tradition and the marriage of art and craft, as stated in Walter *Gropius' original manifesto.

The only German manufactory to show a significant interest in functionalism was the Staatliche Porzellan Manufaktur in Berlin. Its most direct link to industrial design was in the employment of ex-Bauhaus pupil Marguerite Friedländer-Wildenhain, who designed the simple, classic shapes of the 'Halle' service of 1930, in which plain banding was the only form of decoration. Trude Petri's 'Urbino' service of 1930 was more remarkable. In production for some thirty years, it was among the first to rely on neither colour nor ornament for commercial success. Also in the functionalist mode was Dr Hermann Gretsch's 'Arzberg 1382', for the Arzberg porcelain works. Devoid of ornamentation, showing soft, rounded silhouettes, the service was first shown at the 1930 Deutscher Werkbund exhibition, where it won a gold medal, signifying a growing interest in unornamented form, without neglecting porcelain as a costly and formal material.

Eva Stricker-Zeisel is one of the most noted 20th-century industrial designers. Although her mature work generally belonged to the post-Second World War period, her designs for the Schramberger Majolikafabrik in the 1920s incorporated several geometric motifs

associated with Modernism. Throughout the 1930s, a somewhat softening geometry was reflected in her work in Berlin for Christian Carstens Kommerz, in the Soviet Union for Lomonosov Porcelain and Dulevo Ceramics, and in the USA for the Bay Ridge Specialty Co. and Riverside China.

In Britain, Keith *Murray's designs from 1933 for Wedgwood were truly avant-garde. He designed large numbers of non-derivative shapes in which ornament consisted exclusively of turned or fluted motifs. A selection of matt glazes provided textural interest.

It was left primarily to the Americans to explore the phenomenal sales potential of mass-production. The most accomplished, and one of the bestselling, tableware services was Frederick *Rhead's 'Fiesta', designed for the Homer Laughlin Co.. Introduced in 1936, the simple geometric shapes of 'Fiesta' were offered in five bright colours. In production for more than thirty years, the line was an overwhelming success, helping to precipitate a revolution in industrial design. Russel *Wright's ideas also had a profound effect on the public perception of 'good design'. His American modern dinner service was conceived in 1937, introduced by Steubenville Pottery in 1939 and marketed by Baymor until around 1959. In its biomorphic forms and subdued colours it presaged the work of post-Second World War organic designers.

WIENER WERKSTÄTTE
(*opposite*) Selection of table wares in glazed
terracotta, decorated by Hilda Jesser, 1920s.

RENÉ BUTHAUD

CLARICE CLIFF

ÉMILE DECOEUR

VIKTOR SCHRECKENGOST

RENÉ BUTHAUD (1886–1986)

Born in Saintes (Charente-Maritime), Buthaud studied engraving and painting at the École des Beaux-Arts in Bordeaux and then, from 1903, at the École des Beaux-Arts in Paris under Gabriel Ferrier. He was later awarded both the Prix Chenavard and the Prix Roux. After the First World War, Buthaud returned to Bordeaux, determined to concentrate on clay as his primary medium. After exhibiting at the 1920 Salon of the *Société des Artistes Décorateurs, in Paris, he was invited to direct the *Primavera ceramic workshop at Sainte-Radegonde in Touraine, where he experimented with glazing techniques. He developed simple stoneware forms thrown for him by local potters, to which he applied crackled glazes. These he displayed at the Paris Salons and the 1925 *Exposition Internationale.

In 1926, Buthaud was back in Bordeaux, where he opened his own atelier, and in 1931 he was appointed a professor of art at the École des Beaux-Arts in Bordeaux. He exhibited through *Geo. Rouard in Paris from 1928 until he ended his career in 1965. In the 1930s he created a line of commercial wares which he considered of secondary quality; these he signed *J. DORIS* to distinguish them from the works that he showed at the Geo. Rouard gallery.

Buthaud's preferred subject matter was idealized young woman, either mythological or fashionable and current, whom he rendered in a distinctive Art Deco painterly style. Other favoured motifs were athletes, floral garlands and kinetic geometric compositions. Influenced by African tribal art, he developed a lustred and crackled **peau de serpent** glaze around the time of the 1931 Exposition Coloniale in Paris. He showed his versatility in a lengthy career through the creation of numerous **verre églomisé** murals and panels and other graphic works, including posters in support of the Bordeaux wine industry.

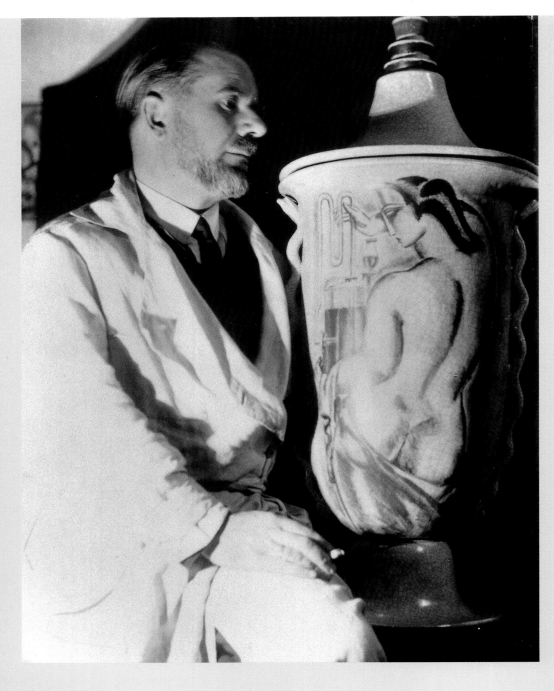

Buthaud at work in his atelier, 1920s.

(*right*) Vase in glazed earthenware exhibited at the Exposition Coloniale, Paris, 1931.

(*below left*) Vase in glazed earthenware, *c*. 1930.

(*below right*) Covered urn in glazed earthenware *c*. 1930.

Cliff was born in Tunstall, Staffordshire, the fourth of seven children of an iron moulder. She attended the High Street Elementary School and Summerbank School in her native town. Her first job, in 1912, was a three-year apprenticeship as an enameller at the firm of Lingard Webster & Co., based at the Swan Pottery in Tunstall. This she left in 1915 to join Hollingshead & Kirkham at the Unicorn Pottery, where she developed a talent for ceramics while in the lithography department. During these years, her parents sponsored her attendance at evening classes at the Tunstall School of Art and the Burslem School of Art.

With the advent of the First World War, Cliff left Hollingshead & Kirkham for Burslem-based A. J. Wilkinson Ltd, which traded as Royal Staffordshire. There she worked initially in freehand decoration. Around 1920, Cliff's painterly skills were recognized by the decorating shop manager, who also improved her modelling skills, which played a major role in her later success. Cliff exhibited at the 1924 British Empire Exhibition. After 1925, she was given her own studio in which to experiment, at the Newport Pottery – a small pottery purchased by Wilkinson in 1920, away from the main production area.

In 1927, Cliff attended the Royal College of Art, London, where she enrolled in modelling, figure composition and life drawing classes. After a quick trip to Paris, she determined to produce colourful Modernist designs, and experimented in secret over the ensuing months.

Vases decorated with various 'Bizarre' patterns, glazed earthenware, 1920s.

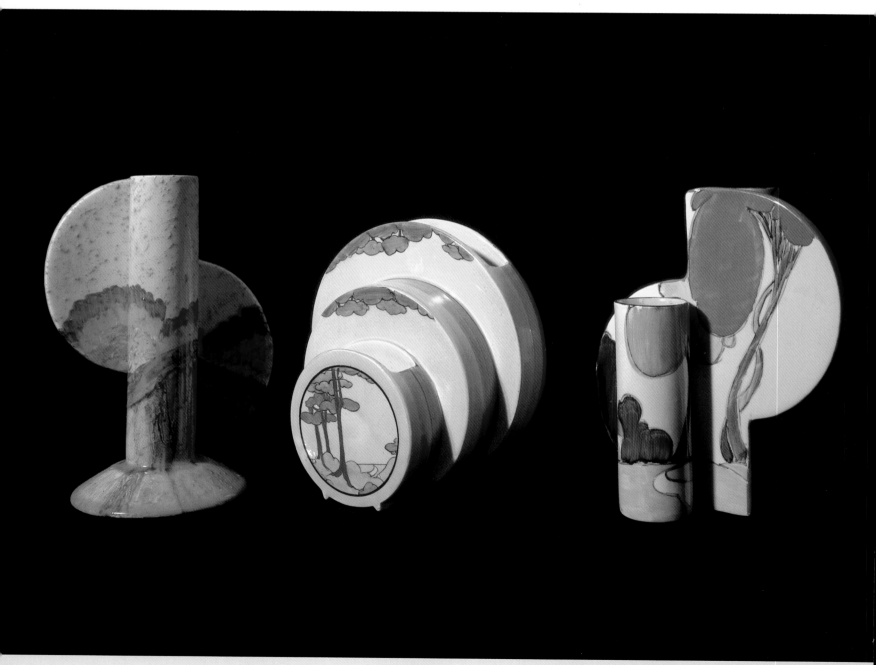

The first of her hand-painted geometric patterns, entitled 'Bizarre', was shown to the public in August that year and quickly established her name within the industry. Despite initial criticisms that it was vulgar and too advanced for the market, it sold briskly and remained in production until 1939.

Further patterns, which proved equally popular for their eye-catching stylizations and lightheartedness, were soon forthcoming, including 'Crocus', 'Diamond', 'Mondrian' and 'Castellated Circle'. Some of these were produced on streamlined old Wilkinson forms. They were followed by newly modelled ones, including 'Cone', 'Stamford' and 'Eton'. Soon a wide range of new designs and shapes was in production, offered to the nation's households through such upmarket department stores as Harrods, Liberty, Waring & Gillow and Selfridges. In 1930, her most productive year, Cliff was appointed artistic director at both A. J. Wilkinson and the Newport Pottery. She experimented constantly; new patterns included 'May Avenue', 'Orange Roof Cottage' and 'Windbells'. In the mid-1930s, however, sales began to fall off and some patterns were phased out.

After the Second World War, Cliff attempted to revive A. J. Wilkinson's sales, especially in the USA. One of her first new designs was 'Bristol', in 1948. As consumer tastes had changed since the war, her designs were therefore more conservative, their earlier frivolity and vibrant palette absent. Included among her new models, in response to customer demand, was a cup on a larger plate for eating while watching television. In 1964, following her husband's death three years earlier, she sold A. J. Wilkinson and the Newport Pottery to W. R. Midwinter Ltd. In 1999, the centenary of her birth, a major exhibition was staged at the Wedgwood Visitors' Centre accompanied by a new publication on her life and work. To today's collector, Cliff's works epitomize the Art Deco movement in British ceramics.

Tea service in the 'Coral Firs' version of the 'Bizarre' pattern, glazed earthenware, 1920s.

Selection of glazed earthenware, including
a Viking ship in a 'Bizarre' pattern and
four cut-outs of musicians and dancing
couples; all designed for A. J. Wilkinson Ltd,
Newport Pottery, 1920s.

'Killarney' in a 'Bizarre' pattern, including
a bowl, sugar sifter and shaker, honey pot
and mustard pot.

ÉMILE DECOEUR (1876–1953)

Decoeur was apprenticed in 1890 to Edmond Lachenal (1855–1930) at his Châtillon-sous-Bagneux studio. In 1901 he abruptly rejected the prevailing Art Nouveau idiom in favour of austere forms inspired by classic Oriental prototypes. After a brief association with Fernand Rumèbe, Decoeur opened his own studio in 1907 at Fontenay-les-Roses, where he worked exclusively in stoneware and then also in porcelain. He produced the purest Chinese-inspired pottery of his generation – his work being characterized by thin clotted glazes rendered in sublime blue, pearl grey, celadon and ivory tones.

In the inter-war years, Decoeur was judged to be one of France's most accomplished potters, with a preference for Chinese-style vessels with simple symmetrical shapes decorated with painted, *champlevé* or incised underglaze patterns such as spirals, whorls and formalized flower sprays. From 1939 to 1948, he was associated with the *Sèvres manufactory, principally as a consultant and model designer, after which he retired to his atelier at Fontenay-les-Roses, where he continued his research on how to combine enamels, glazes and **engobes**.

Vases decorated with plant motifs, c. 1903, showing the degree to which Decoeur embraced the organic Art Nouveau style in his early career and the severe transition to his post-war style.

(*below*) Vases in glazed stoneware, *c.* 1930.

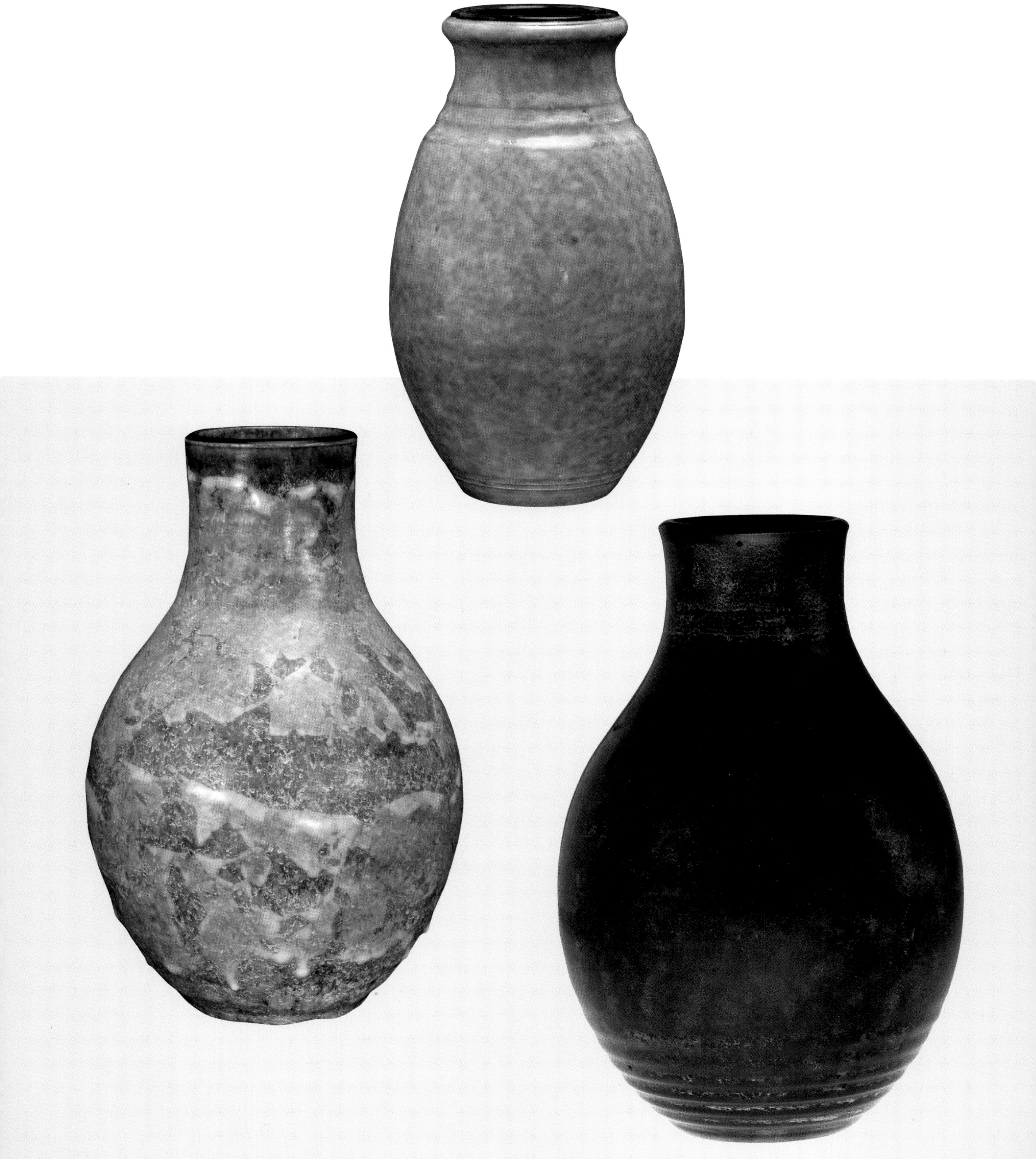

Vase in glazed stoneware, c. 1930.

(*left*) Vase in glazed stoneware, *c.* 1930.

(*right*) Vase in glazed stoneware, *c.* 1930.

VIKTOR SCHRECKENGOST
(1906–2008)

Raised in a family of potters in Sebring, Ohio, Schreckengost worked in a local pottery before enrolling in 1924 to study cartoon-making at the Cleveland School of Art. Changing his focus to ceramics, he studied under Paul Travis, Walter Sinz and a visiting teacher, the Austrian designer Julius Mihalik. Schreckengost's appreciation of the Viennese school, and of the travelling International Ceramic Exhibition which opened at the Cleveland Museum of Art in 1929, persuaded him to undertake postgraduate work at the Kunstgewerbeschule in Vienna. There his instructor was Michael *Powolny, who taught him how to model directly in clay. Returning to Cleveland in 1930, Schreckengost taught at the School of Art and also worked with the small group of artist-designers retained by the

when he had heard Cab Calloway at the Cotton Club in Manhattan. Glowing street lamps, champagne and cocktail glasses, neon signs in Times Square, skyscrapers, musical instruments and notes are arranged in a continuing narrative around the bowl. Using Schreckengost's template, Cowan put the bowl into production, employing a **sgraffito** technique in which artisans scratched its designs into the **engobe**. In its final stage, an Egyptian blue glaze was added to provide a nocturnal glow. About fifty examples of the 'Jazz' bowl were produced, each today considered an icon of American Art Deco design. Humour, evident in the bowl, and satire are present in much of Schreckengost's work – his means to undercut the traditional earnestness of the medium.

*Cowan Pottery Studio in their last-ditch stand against bankruptcy. When Cowan closed in 1931, Schreckengost designed items for large-scale manufacturers of ceramic tableware, such as the American Limoges Ceramics Co., for which he created the first modern mass-production dinnerware, 'Americana'.

In 1930, Schreckengost was commissioned by Eleanor Roosevelt to design a bowl in celebration of her husband's re-election in New York's gubernatorial election. Delighted with the piece, entitled 'Jazz Bowl', she ordered a second example, which Schreckengost again decorated with images recalling a night

By the mid-1930s, Schreckengost had turned his attention to industrial design. With the engineer Ray Spiller, he designed the first cab-over-engine truck for Cleveland's White Motor Co. Later in the decade, he designed a Mercury bicycle for Murray-Ohio, which in 1949 became the world's largest manufacturer of children's toys. In the 1940s, he produced designs for children's pedal cars and toys. In the Second World War, Schreckengost was recruited by the US Navy to develop a system for radar recognition. Although he retired from industrial design in 1972, he continued to teach at the Cleveland School (now Institute) of Art and to paint and model in clay.

(*above left, centre and right*) Summer, *Fall* and *Winter*, modelled in red clay with green engobe and slip clay, three of four figures in the 'Four Seasons' series, 1938.

(*opposite*) Water, modelled in red clay with green engobe and slip clay, one of four figures in the 'Four Elements' series, 1939.

(*right*) 'Jazz' punch bowl, glazed porcelain with sgraffito decoration, manufactured by Cowan Pottery, commissioned by Eleanor Roosevelt, 1931.

(*opposite*) *Jeddu*, bust in painted plaster, 1931.

(*above*) 'The Hunt', punch bowl and plates, underglaze decoration on white porcelain, manufactured by Cowan Pottery, 1931.

LIGHTING

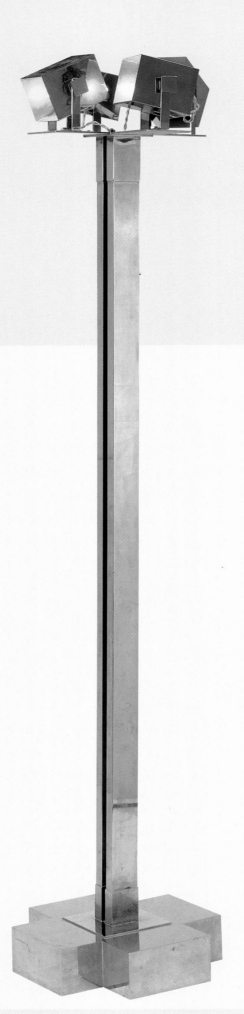

DESNY
(*right*) *Torchère*, nickel-plated metal, *c.* 1930.

PIERRE CHAREAU
(*far right*) 'La Religieuse' floor lamp, model No.
SN31, painted metal and sliced alabaster,
designed for the Hôtel Tours, 1923.

(*right*) Table lamp, chromed metal and frosted
glass, late 1920s.

The distinction between lighting in the Art Nouveau and Art Deco periods
could hardly have been more pronounced. The first fashion to disappear
after the First World War was the *fin de siècle*'s blended naturalistic
palette: the azure blues, moss greens, magentas and lavenders; these were
replaced by achromatism, in designs that relied on factors other than
colour for their effect. By etching, enamelling or sandblasting the surface
of the glass, the designer could orchestrate the light; by pressing or
engraving it he could achieve sculptural effects; and, by combining such
processes, he could obtain any number of optical nuances. In place of
the spectrum there was milkiness and limpidity.

Between the wars, the mounts on lamps likewise changed:
a range of metals – initially wrought iron, then increasingly nickel- and
chromium-plated alloys, steel and aluminium – replaced the turn-of-the-
century champion material, patinated bronze, because with their bright
sheen they represented far more effectively the aspirations of the new
machine age. At the same time there was considerable discussion about
the role of illumination in the modern interior, much of which focused
on the merits of indirect as against direct lighting and of function as
against ornamentation. Professional groups, such as the Société pour
le Perfectionnement de l'Éclairage, were established to gather and
disseminate information for the homeowner on recent developments.
By 1925 there were fifteen magazines worldwide that concentrated on
the science of photometry. Of these, *Lux*, published from 1928, provided
its French readership with information on the photometric values of
light, including foot-candles, lumens, lux and intensity. Angles of reflection
were measured, as were the coefficients of the transmission of light.
This preoccupation with interior illumination created, in turn, a new
vocation – that of the lighting engineer.

From 1920, lamp designers had ample opportunity to display their
creations: a Grand Concours de la Lumière was hosted in Paris in 1924
by the Union Syndicale de l'Électricité; the 1925 *Exposition Internationale
des Arts Décoratifs et Industriels Modernes provided another excellent
showcase. In the 1930s, five Salons de la Lumière were staged in Paris:

in 1933, 1934, 1935, 1937 (as part of the Exposition des Arts et Techniques)
and 1939. As well as these, the annual Salons provided a forum in which
most decorative artists and designers participated.

JEAN PERZEL was lighting's foremost Modernist exponent in the
inter-war years. Exclusively a designer and manufacturer of light fixtures,
he aimed to use light so that it appeared evenly on different surfaces
and at its maximum luminosity. To achieve this he developed special glass
for the insides of his lampshades. In later years, he used lightly tinted
enamels to match the colour schemes in certain interiors.

Also in Paris, *Damon placed a similar importance on the correct
type of glass for lighting purposes. Claiming that frosted glass was not
perfectly translucent – the points of light formed by the bulbs being
clearly visible through the glass – the firm created a special variety,
verre émaillé diffusant, which it housed in metal armatures. Damon also
commissioned designs from Boris *Lacroix, Gorinthe and Daniel Stephan,
among others. A similar line of fixtures was produced at the time by
the brothers Eugène and G. L. Capon.

EDGAR BRANDT (*see under* Silver, Metal, Lacquer and Enamel)
worked with several glassmakers, but was best served by DAUM FRÈRES
(*see under* Glass). From the mid-1920s, the firm produced a range of
heavy glass shades, often acid-etched with stylized floral or geometric
motifs, and these were well suited to the assertiveness of Brandt's
ironwork. The period's other ***ferronniers*** followed suit. Paul *Kiss,
*Nics Frères, Adelbert-Georges *Szabo, Édouard and Marcel *Schenck
and Raymond *Subes all produced fixtures comprising glass and iron.

EDGAR BRANDT AND DAUM FRÈRES

(*opposite, above left*) Chandelier, wrought iron and moulded and etched glass, 1920s.

DAUM FRÈRES

(*opposite, below left*) Table lamp, moulded and etched glass with wrought-iron mount, 1920s.

EILEEN GRAY

(*opposite, right*) Floor lamp in lacquered wood and parchment, designed for a bedroom–boudoir in a house in Monte Carlo, 1922. Illustrated in *Intérieurs français*, Jean Badovici, 1925, pl. 18.

UNIDENTIFIED AMERICAN DESIGNER

(*right*) Desk lamp, chromed metal and copper, mid–late 1920s.

Daum Frères created some wonderful lamps of its own. Glass shades, shaped like mushrooms, coolie hats or elongated phallic forms, rested on matching spherical or cylindrical glass bases. Models in frosted white and amber glass, often etched with forceful linear patterns, were especially popular. Of equal importance to the glass fixtures by Daum were those by RENÉ LALIQUE (*see under* Glass), in which flowers and fruit predominated. Lalique also produced an enchanting series of *luminaires* in moulded clear glass – panels and sculptural pieces with lighting housed inside their bronze bases – decorated with peacocks, jousting knights and swallows in flight.

Albert Simonet, of the firm SIMONET FRÈRES, one of the oldest bronze houses in the French capital, was among the first to realize that electricity required an entirely new lighting aesthetic, not simply one that revamped gas and candle models. By the mid-1920s, the firm had replaced its editions of bronze fixtures with a selection of contemporary glass ones that drew acclaim and awards at the 1925 Exposition Internationale. The sculptor Henri *Dieupart designed many of the firm's pressed-glass shades.

The Maison DESNY (*see under* Silver, Metal, Lacquer and Enamel) designed a host of ultramodern light fixtures that in their stark perpendicularity echoed International Style architecture. These were in chromed metal alone or in chromed metal housing slats of green-tinted glass. The firm's designs for general interior illumination were aimed specifically at eliminating centralized points of light; wall brackets, chandeliers and floor lamps incorporated inverted reflector bowls that concealed the naked bulbs and projected the light upwards. Where localized light was required – either for reading purposes or to illuminate a prized object or painting – the firm offered a range of genre spotlights. Desny also designed a series of illuminated *bibelots* in clear glass and/or metal, which had no other function than to brighten a dark corner. Limited in number, the lamp models created by Jacques *Le Chevallier matched those of Desny in their brazen *machinisme*.

ALBERT CHEURET designed a wide range of 'high-style' Art Deco lamps in which overlapping slices of alabaster were secured by bronze mounts cast as birds, flowers or plants. His distinctive style blended influences from nature and antiquity in a sumptuous and exotic manner.

In the USA, the new philosophy on domestic illumination, when it finally arrived in the late 1920s, was pursued with at least as much zeal as in Europe. First, however, it had to wait for the public to change its attitude towards Modernism in the entire field of interior decoration. This did not occur until 1926, when an exhibition of items from the 1925 Exposition Internationale travelled to eight American cities. Lamp fixtures began to show a Modernist influence only after the nation's department stores joined the drive towards a contemporary style, in so doing relinquishing their traditional reliance on European leadership in all decorative matters. Those who at some point designed light fixtures in the Modernist idiom included DONALD DESKEY (*see under* Furniture and Interior Decoration), Ilonka *Karasz, Walter *von Nessen, Eugene *Schoen, Wolfgang and Pola *Hoffmann, Walter *Kantack, Kurt Versen, Gilbert *Rohde and Robert Locher.

Von Nessen was the USA's premier Modernist lamp designer, and he was especially successful in the retail trade in the early 1930s, when most businesses were retrenching. His lamps, in particular, were greeted enthusiastically because of their novelty, both in form and in choice of brilliant metallic finishes. Functional and artistic, their bold linear contours matched the most avant-garde of von Nessen's European

Deskey showed his versatility in several lamp designs which rivalled those of von Nessen in ingenuity. Some of his lamp bases, especially, were astonishingly abstract. One was composed of a spiralling shaft of chromium-plated brass which led the eye to the light source above. Another, in brushed aluminium, consisted of a series of square horizontal ribs echoing the box-like structures of International Style architecture. A further example, with a serrated front inset with rectangles of frosted glass panels, appears to have been directly inspired by the work of Perzel.

Kantack, another leading lighting exponent, complemented his output of Modernist fixtures from 1928 to 1932 with monthly issues of his firm's magazine, *The Kaleidoscope*, in which he set out his tenets for contemporary domestic illumination. His lamps matched his concepts: they were crisply angular, bright and functional.

In the forefront of Modernist American lighting design, Kurt Versen created various table and floor models with polished chromed mounts. His lampshades used a mix of opalescent glass, Bakelite, cellophane, Lumerith and, his favourite material, toyo paper. Versen's best-known models incorporated hinged shades that flipped upwards to provide either direct or indirect illumination.

Among the other metal craftsmen and small studios to turn their hands to contemporary lamp design were John Salterini and the Lancha Studios in New York City, both of whom produced wrought-iron fixtures with frosted glass shades in a manner distinctly similar to that of Paris metalworkers such as Gilbert *Poillerat, Nics Frères, and Adelbert-Georges Szabo. Paul Lobel, another metalworker, was also drawn to the medium, though his designs in copper and wrought iron showed greater innovation in the sculptural bases than in the lamps *per se*.

counterparts. Angular shades in frosted glass or parchment were mounted in chromium-plated metal, brass or brushed aluminium. To soften this machine-age aestheticism, decorative accents were added in Formica, Bakelite and rubber discs. Both direct and indirect lighting requirements were accommodated by shades that could tilt, rotate or turn fully upwards. A particularly functional concept came to fruition in von Nessen's 'Lighthouse' lamp model, which was made of two sections that could be lit together or independently.

JACQUES-ÉMILE RUHLMANN
Table lamp in silvered bronze and beaded glass, the model included in the dining room in the Hôtel du Collectionneur at the 1925 Exposition Internationale, Paris.

ALBERT CHEURET

JEAN PERZEL

SIMONET FRÈRES

ALBERT CHEURET (*fl.* 1907–28)

Nothing is known of Cheuret's upbringing beyond his being trained in sculpture by Jacques Perrin and Georges Lemaître. He participated regularly at the Salons of the *Société des Artistes Français from 1907, at some point establishing his atelier at 11 avenue Franco-Russe, in Paris. At the 1924 Salon he showed a pair of 'Pearl' sconces, a 'Pebbles' floor lamp and a 'Bird of Paradise' chandelier. These, as in many of his fixtures, were composed of bronze mounts that housed sharply angled and overlapping slices of alabaster. At the 1925 *Exposition Internationale, he occupied stand 33 on the Pont Alexandre III, listing himself as a *statuaire–décorateur*. Included in his display was a range of bronzeware, of animal and bird figures, furniture, clocks and a wide variety of light fixtures – ten examples of which were illustrated the following year in an issue of Le Luminaire et les Moyens d' Éclairage Nouveaux dedicated to lamps shown at the Exposition.

Cheuret's designs have an unmistakable freshness and charm. Beyond light fixtures, he produced console tables, radiator covers, pedestals, *guéridons*, mirrors and mantel clocks. One of the last-mentioned was strikingly designed as the head of a Pharaonic dignitary with flaring coiffure – no doubt in celebration of Howard Carter's 1922 discovery of the Tutankhamun tomb – and is now firmly established as an Art Deco icon. Other decorative themes were herons, aloes and cacti.

(*above*) 'Paons' chandelier, patinated bronze and alabaster, *c.* 1925.

(*below*) 'Aloès' chandelier, patinated bronze and alabaster, *c.* 1925.

(*right*) 'Cigognes' chandelier, patinated bronze and alabaster, *c.* 1925.

(*above left*) *Torchère*, silvered bronze and alabaster, the model exhibited at the 1925 Exposition Internationale, Paris.

(*right*) *Torchère*, patinated bronze and alabaster, *c.* 1925.

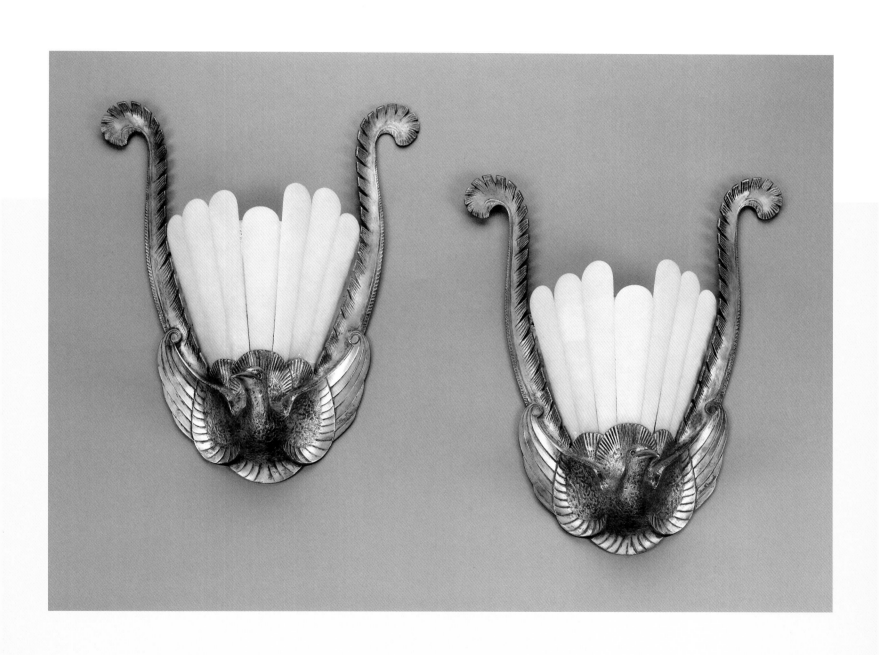

Pair of wall sconces, gilt-bronze and alabaster,
c. 1925.

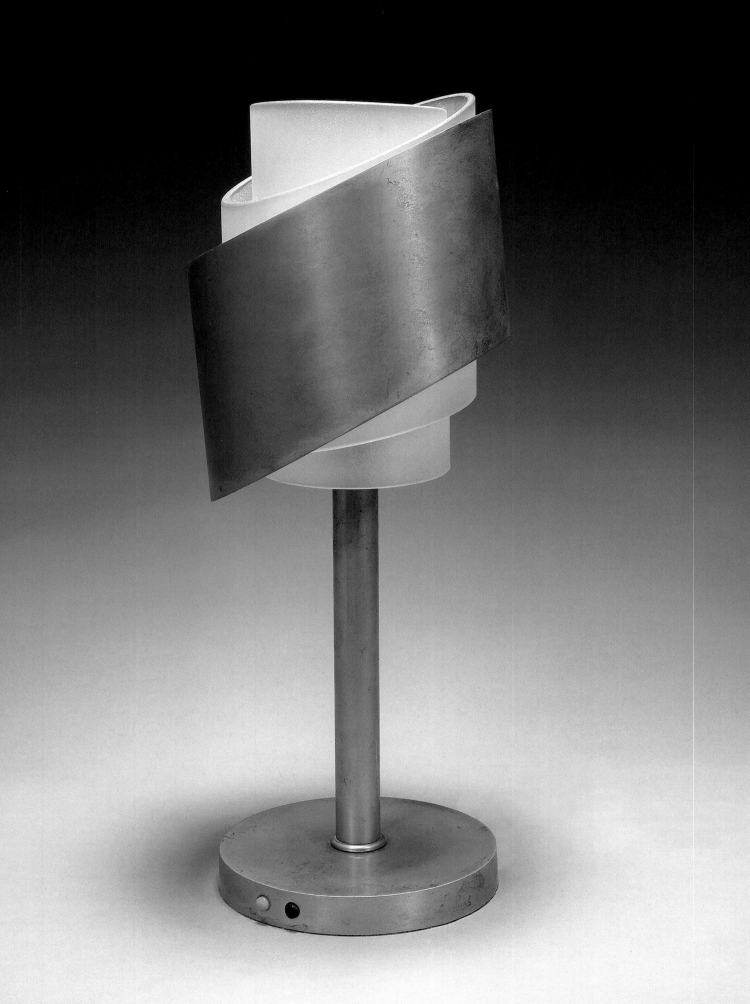

JEAN PERZEL (1892–1986)

Perzel was born in the Bavarian town of Bruck, and his family moved to Paris when he was ten. Volunteering in 1914, he served for the entire war, afterwards returning to Paris to take up what had been his father's and his grandfather's profession – glassmaking. It was then, as Perzel recounted in a 1928 *Lux* article, that he first realized the potential of light fixtures since they were no longer simply transformed oil-lamps or candlesticks. Drawing inspiration from his own profession – that of stained-glass windows – he conceived his first lamps in the manner of old unpainted Romanesque church windows. Perzel described the idea as follows:

> It would be pretentious to say that I would like to treat electricity in the way that the old stained-glass artists treated the sun, but that is what I tried to do. I wanted to mask entirely the luminous source in using its rays; from which came my research into the relative opacity of nacreous and frosted glass.

Perzel's influence in domestic lighting burgeoned from this seminal stage. Exclusively a designer and manufacturer of light fixtures, he had a two-fold philosophy: first, to ensure that the light playing on uneven surfaces did so equally, and, second, to achieve maximum utilization of the light source's rays. To ensure that the light was transmitted uniformly, Perzel developed a specially frosted (that is, sandblasted) glass for the inner surface; a coating of enamel was then applied to this, for decorative effect. By this means not only was the light equally filtered but also his preferred standards of opacity and milkiness were met. In later years, lightly tinted enamels, such as beige and pink, were applied as required. Another form of glass,

(*opposite*) Desk lamp, nickel-plated metal and frosted glass, *c.* 1928.

(*above left*) Table lamp, silvered metal and glass, *c.* 1928.

(*right*) Table lamp, chromed metal and opalescent glass, *c.* 1930.

though seldom used, was a more translucent prismatic variety. Perzel's mounts, always judiciously designed for their secondary and supportive role, were in metal, sometimes nickelled or lacquered.

Perzel concentrated his production on large editions of a limited number of designs. Lacking the range of light fixtures, for example, of *Genet et Michon or *Sabino, his output consisted mainly of table lamps, chandeliers, wall brackets and ceiling lights, though he occasionally produced ceiling *dalles*, columns and illuminated tables. Based on pure geometry, his shades were often polygonal, both in their overall shape and in the units of which they were composed. Others were conical, spherical, cylindrical or rectangular, always with a sober

elegance and often of an astonishing modernity. Commissioned to provide lighting for the ensembles of other decorators – for example, Léon-Albert and Maurice-Raymond *Jallot, Lucien *Rollin, *Tétard Frères and the architect Michel Roux-Spitz – Perzel also enjoyed an elite international clientele, including Henry Ford in Detroit, the Savoy Hotel in London and the King of Siam in Bangkok. He participated in the *Salon d'Automne from 1924 to 1939, the *Société des Artistes Décorateurs from 1926 to 1939, the 1925 *Exposition Internationale and the 1930s Salons de la Lumière.

(*left*) Selection of lamps and an illuminated table, *c*. 1925.

(*below*) *Torchère*, metal and glass, *c.* 1930.

(*right*) Ceiling fixture, frosted glass panels with chromed-metal mount, late 1920s.

(*above*) Illuminated table, nickel-plated metal and sandblasted glass, 1931.

Championed by *Mobilier et Décoration* in numerous articles between 1924 and 1931, the firm Simonet Frères was pre-eminent in the lighting field in the inter-war years. Its success was built around the partnership of Albert Simonet (*fl.* early 1920s–1935) and Henri *Dieupart (*fl.* early 1920s–1935). Charles Simonet (d. 1929) appears to have been either on the management side of the firm or a sleeping partner; no mention is made of him artistically.

A bronze worker by profession, Albert Simonet's first lighting designs incorporated very little glass, but, following his association with the sculptor and glassmaker Dieupart, the predominance of the bronze mounts was steadily replaced by that of glass. This evolution was to result, by 1933, in the almost total eclipse of metal; it was used only as an armature to house the magical pressed glass. Expounding on the most recent photometric results obtained from French laboratories, Simonet claimed that the shapes of his lamps were determined by 'coefficients of utilization' – that is, the dimensions, end-use and coloration of the rooms for which the fixtures were to be designed. These could be mathematically, psychologically and scientifically computed. For his part, Dieupart executed Simonet's designs in moulded glass, the uniformity of which was obtained by passing a current of compressed air through the glass as soon as it had been poured into the mould. Renouncing bright colours, Dieupart left most of his glass untinted. His raised motifs were

introduced not only for decorative purposes but also for their light-refractive powers. Motifs were almost entirely floral – convolvulus, thistle, bracken, honesty, hydrangea, hortensia, aloe, lily of the valley and marguerite – but in the 1930s they became more geometric – lozenges, rhomboids and squares.

Exhibitions in which Simonet Frères participated included: the first Exposition d'Art Moderne at the Pavillon de Marsan and the great lighting competition staged by the Union Syndicale de l'Électricité, both in 1924; the 1925 *Exposition Internationale, in which the firm had a stand in the Grand Palais; the fifth Exposition de la Décoration Contemporaine Française (1931); and the second Salon de la

Lumière in 1934. The firm's range of light fixtures was extensive: a large number of chandeliers, ceiling lights and wall brackets, often *en série*, were produced, in addition to illuminated friezes, cornices, ramps and *bouts de table*. In collaboration with the ceramist G. Henry, the firm manufactured a bronze pedestal table with a translucent porcelain top.

(*above*) Period illustration of the chandelier and matching pair of sconces, designed for the living room of a wealthy home, awarded first prize at the Grand Concours de la Lumière in Paris, 1924.

(*above*) Slighly different model of the
chandelier illustrated on p. 242, in silvered
bronze and glass prisms, c. 1925.

(*opposite*) Chandelier in silvered bronze and
moulded satin glass, *c.* 1925.

(*above*) *Monnaie du pape* chandelier, silvered
bronze and moulded and stained glass, *c.* 1925.

TEXTILES

About 1925 the role of textiles within an ensemble was reconsidered: should they be designed independently of the furnishings that they would complement, or should they act merely as a decorative accent and, by definition, play a secondary role in the colour and design of the ensemble? In general, textile design had taken second place to other disciplines in the decorative arts. However, as the inter-war period progressed, wallpapers and, later, fabrics and rugs gained in importance, since they were often the only note of pure decoration in increasingly austere and utilitarian interiors.

A caveat is in order here: the fragility of both fabrics and carpets means that few examples have survived from the 1920s and 1930s, and those that do exist have often suffered a degree of discoloration. This fact can often mislead today's observer as to the decorating scheme and the artist's use of colour. Although the study of *pochoirs* or colour reproductions from the period can help to clarify the designer's original intention, these are sometimes as faded as the fabrics themselves. What becomes clear in an analysis of the printed fabrics and rugs of the Art Deco period, however, is that different disciplines shared common qualities of colour, texture and pattern.

Tastes in colour changed more rapidly in the field of textile design than in any other medium. In the 1920s, vivid, sometimes discordant shades of lavender (Lanvin blue), orange-red (tango) and hot pink were juxtaposed with lime greens and chrome yellows to generate a psychedelic palette rivalling that of the 1960s. Such colours dominated Parisian textile design at the time and were partly due to a post-war impulse to celebrate, but even more to do with the overwhelming influence of Sergei Diaghilev's Ballets Russes and its brightly coloured, exotic costume and scenery designs by Alexandre Benois and Léon *Bakst. These had an immeasurable impact and helped bring about an aesthetic of 'colour for colour's sake'. In the late 1920s, the pendulum began to swing the other way. A new conservatism emerged, which encouraged more neutral schemes in interior design. The Depression ushered in the muted, albeit luxurious and costly

interiors of decorators such as JEAN-MICHEL FRANK (*see under* Furniture and Interior Decoration) in Paris and Syrie Maugham in London. Colour accents were restrained. Most popular were tones of charcoal, bottle green and a shade of dusty brown referred to on the Continent as ***tête de nègre***. The exuberance of the 1920s Jazz Age yielded to the disquiet of the 1930s.

As colours became less vibrant, texture grew more important. Indeed, the most significant contribution of the late 1920s and 1930s to textile design may have been the growing belief that the material itself was of primary importance. The Modernists therefore virtually abandoned printed or other 'applied' decoration — now seen as a cheap substitute for hand-woven fabrics — and concentrated instead on the innate qualities of the fibre. Good weaving alone was expected to draw out the beauty of the fibre through its texture. This attitude was fuelled in part by the philosophy of the Bauhaus weaving workshop, the full effects of which were felt after the First World War in the mass-production of rather non-descript woven fabrics.

Interest in the early 1930s was focused on varied weaves, the use of unusual materials such as raffia and jute, the qualities of hand-knotted, fringed area rugs and the sculptured carpets such as those designed by Marion *Dorn. At the same time, synthetic fibres such as rayon and acetate were developed, and these could be woven into a wide variety of textiles which simulated the textures of traditional linen weaves, silk and wool. In emphasizing the decorative qualities of extremely coarse or 'natural' textiles, Modernism reversed the trend of the industry. The strident pastiches of the early 1920s yielded to an era of almost apologetic hues and non-representational patterns. In Germany, pale striated geometric fabrics became popular, as did wallpapers with minute monochromatic detailing.

In the 1920s textile patterns showed the influence of the new exoticism, and they included motifs from the Near East, Africa, the Orient, folk art, Cubism and Fauvism. The emphasis on flat graphic decoration was felt most strongly in Continental Europe and in the USA.

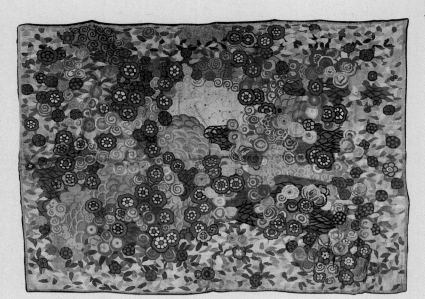

ÉDOUARD BENEDICTUS
Wool carpet manufactured in Aubusson, 1920s.

JULES LELEU
(*opposite*) Suite of salon furniture upholstered in Aubusson tapestry, c. 1930.

In the world of inter-war woven fabrics and printed papers, Paris's most celebrated couturier and ***ensemblier*** – Paul *Poiret – was one of the seminal figures in the promotion of the exotic and colourful Art Deco style. The most successful sketches from the students in his École MARTINE (*see under* Furniture and Interior Decoration) were translated into fabrics by Paul Dumas and into carpets by the firm of Fenaille. These were then sold at Maison Martine. Essentially colourful and frivolous, the Martine style evoked the exoticism of the Ballets Russes, ancient Persia, the South Sea Islands and, to a limited extent, the more decorative elements of the Vienna Secession.

Raoul *Dufy, another of Poiret's early designers, created fabric designs that drew on the narrative and pictorial 18th-century style in which figures were portrayed in various outdoor pursuits within arabesques or floral borders. Patterns included 'La Danse', 'Le Pêcheur' and 'Le Moissoneur'. Dufy's other designs show the facility with which he interpreted decorative fruit and floral trelliswork of the kind associated with Indian calicoes and, somewhat later, subdued geometrics.

Sonia *Delaunay rivalled Dufy as a textile designer, producing a range of radically Modernist and colourful fabric and rug patterns, in addition to stage and costume designs.

Many French artist–decorators designed wall-coverings, drapery and upholstery materials in printed silks, cotton and linen – damasks, brocades, brocatelles and lampas – to complement their interiors. The catalogues of the annual Salons in the inter-war years list textiles by designer–decorators such as André *Groult, Francis *Jourdain, JACQUES-ÉMILE RUHLMANN (*see under* Furniture and Interior Decoration), René *Gabriel, René *Herbst, SÜE ET MARE (*see under* Furniture and Interior Decoration), Pierre-Paul *Montagnac, Fernand *Nathan, Maurice-Raymond *Jallot, Jacques *Adnet, Tony Selmersheim, Paul *Follot and MAURICE DUFRÈNE (*see under* Furniture and Interior Decoration).

Patterns were divided broadly into two categories: floral and geometric – the latter often comprising overlapping blocks of colour or abstract linear motifs, at times combined with animal or anecdotal motifs. In addition, the Paris department stores' own studios provided a matching range of light Modernist designs to supplement their furnishings. Among these were *Pomone (Follot, Germaine Labaye, Marcel Bovis and Mme René Schils); *La Maîtrise (Dufrène, Léon Marcoussis, Daragnes, Crozet and Mme Lassudrie); *Primavera (Sigismond Olesiewicz, Mme Madeleine Lougez and Paul Dumas); and *Studium-Louvre (Jean *Burkhalter and Étienne *Kohlmann).

The French were considered masters of the art of tapestry. By tradition, tapestry screens had been used to define interior space and to lend warmth to interiors. However, the 18th- and 19th-century concept of the tapestry as a woven reproduction of a painting stifled artistic initiative until the emergence of Jean Lurçat, who in the 1930s designed hangings in his signature Surrealist style for tapestry manufacturers in Aubusson and seat furniture upholsterers in Beauvais. Lurçat conceived his panels as abstract compositions which accentuated the interplay of colours. He also advocated the use of relatively coarse fibres, which reduced production costs and lent themselves to dramatic, tactile compositions. Tapestries and rugs executed under the artistic direction of Marie Cuttoli at Aubusson were also popular, representing a continuation of the tradition of the *trompe-l'œil* reproduction of paintings by modern artists such as Pablo Picasso, Georges Braque, Henri Matisse, Fernand Léger and Georges Rouault, whom Cuttoli commissioned to submit cartoons.

In the 1920s seat furniture and screens upholstered in tapestry were widely produced by interior decorating firms and department stores. Süe et Mare, in particular, offered furniture upholstered in tapestry designed in both neoclassical and Modernist styles by Paul *Vera, Gustave-Louis *Jaulmes, Marianne Clouzot, Marguerite Dubuisson and Maurice Taquoy. At La Maîtrise, Dufrène retained Jean *Beaumont to design colourful tapestried chair upholstery and screens, which were executed by the nation's traditional tapestry and carpet manufacturers – the Manufacture Nationale de la Tapisserie de Beauvais, the Manufacture Nationale des Gobelins, various Aubusson manufacturers, Braquenié et Cie and *Mybor – all of which retained their own design staff.

The *Normandie provided a spectacular commission for French **tapissiers** to upholster all of the seat furniture in the ocean liner's grand salon. Against a backdrop of theatrical splendour, including Dupas's silvered and gilt **verre églomisé** murals and Beaumont's 20-foot lengths of curtain decorated with cerise wisteria, were hundreds of abundantly stuffed chairs and canapés upholstered in tapestry (designed by Émile Gaudissart (1872–1957) and executed in Aubusson), depicting flora from various French colonies. The lavish ivory and olive tones on vivid orange-red and grey grounds, set against the silver and gold leaf of the murals, produced an image of grandeur unrivalled in the 'floating palaces' of any other nation.

In Britain there was growing interest in the 1920s in modern textiles and printed papers. Some noteworthy examples of this were the geometrically patterned fabrics produced by William Foxton Ltd of London and the designs of Charles Rennie Mackintosh, Minnie McLeish, F. Gregory Brown and Claud Lovat Fraser, dating from the years following the end of the First World War. Examples of Foxton's fabrics were exhibited at the 1925 *Exposition Internationale des Arts Décoratifs et Industriels Modernes, but it was not until the early 1930s that British textile firms warmed to designs in the modern idiom. One of these was the textile workshop founded by the painter, designer and decorator Allan Walton, in 1925, and bearing his name. Walton commissioned designs by Vanessa Bell and Duncan Grant, Frank Dobson, Cedric Morris, H. J. Bull and Margaret Simeon. Another British textile firm was Edinburgh Weavers, under the direction of Alastair Morton. This included the Constructivist fabric jointly designed by Barbara Hepworth and Ben Nicolson in 1937 among its repertoire of designs.

Bell and Grant's styles of painting translated well into their printed fabrics for Walton, although stylistically they fall outside the context of a study on Art Deco. Their Omega workshops, which had been devoted to the promotion of household furnishings painted with post-Impressionist designs, had closed in 1919. However, the duo continued their efforts in a style that came to depend less on post-Impressionism

and more on purely decorative appeal. From 1913 until the outbreak of the Second World War, they introduced more than a dozen designs which exuded the 'cosy' character of English, 19th-century printed fabrics and at the same time echoed the vogue for fanciful prints current in France in the 1930s. In the 1920s, Bell and Grant also designed needlepoint canvases which were successfully worked by Ethel Grant (Duncan's mother) and the painter Mary Hogarth. These were shown in the 1925 Independent Gallery exhibition, Modern Needlework, and again in 1932 at the Victoria & Albert Museum.

The team of Phyllis Barron and Dorothy Larcher, whose workshop was located first in Hampstead and then in Gloucestershire, was responsible for the revival of interest in printed textiles. Their patterns ranged from Larcher's naturalistic interpretation of flowers traditionally associated with English chintzes to Barron's simple but bold geometrics. Discharge printing, in which acid was used to bleach a pattern on dyed grounds in the manner of Indian calicoes, was one of their specialities. They were joined in 1925 by Enid Marx, who two years later established her own workshop. In 1937 Marx gained wide acclaim for her upholstery designs for the London Passenger Transport Board and for her work for the Unity Design Scheme during the Second World War.

Marion Dorn was best known for her Modernist sculptured carpets, but she also created textile designs. These were influenced by her association with the graphic artist Edward *McKnight Kauffer. Her relatively simple and inexpensive designs of the late 1930s included 'Aircraft', which was used in the interiors of the first-class lounge on the ocean liner Orcades.

No account of British textile development in the 1930s would be complete without mention of Ethel Mairet. Her Gospels weaving studios in rural Ditchling, Sussex, were part of a larger community founded by the typographer Eric Gill. Mairet had a strong belief in the importance of the artisan, and her early weaves reflect her initial distrust of industrial procedures. But encounters with other designers, in particular GUNTA STÖLZL of the Bauhaus, later convinced her that her idiosyncratic weaves

would lose none of their character in the process of mass-production. The fabrics of the post-war era, beginning with the simple weaves of the Utility Design Panel, owed much to Mairet's dedication to weaving as both art and craft.

In Austria, the success of the textile division of the *Wiener Werkstätte, set up as a separate workshop around 1910, led to the establishment of an independent retail outlet in 1917. Textiles and carpets were originally designed as part of an overall scheme for specific interiors only. This was in line with the workshop's overriding principle of *Gesamtkunstwerk* (the concept of the interior as a total environment), but financial considerations eventually made broad commercial production necessary.

Whereas early textiles and carpets designed by Josef Hoffmann and Koloman Moser were rigidly geometric and almost invariably monochromatic or black and white, the Wiener Werkstätte textiles of the late 1910s and 1920s grew increasingly colourful, employing whimsical decorative motifs characteristic of the workshop's designs in other media. In the USA, the Werkstätte of America Inc. retailed decorative textiles, including table linens, at their New York branch and through Marshall Field's department store in Chicago. Their imaginative lacework and embroideries combined traditional techniques with a brilliant use of colour. Popular motifs included the fanciful floral prints of Mathilde Flogl, Camilla Burke and Franz von Zülow, and the African-inspired geometry of Maria *Likarz-Strauss, in addition to the eccentric 'Spitzbarok' patterns of Dagobert *Peche.

Wallpapers were also produced for the Wiener Werkstätte by Salubra-Werke and Flammersheim & Steinmann. Peche created a large selection of wallpaper designs in 1919, and again in 1922 – one of which was selected for the catalogue cover to the Austrian design section of the 1925 Exposition Internationale. Peche's colleague Likarz-Strauss created a portfolio of wallpaper designs in 1925, while examples of Flogl's work were included in the workshop's collection in 1929. During this period the Wiener Werkstätte's imaginative wallpaper patterns were enormously popular. Literally thousands were produced by Peche, Hoffmann, Flogl, von Zülow, Ludwig Heinrich Jungnickel, Arnold Nechansky and the Rix sisters Kitty and Felice. Hoffmann's designs from the mid-1920s simplified the eye-catching herringbone and dash patterns of his pre-war style.

In the light of the October Revolution, Soviet designers took a fresh look at textile decoration and attempted to develop an entirely new aesthetic vernacular. Motifs symbolic of the Revolution – often of considerable charm despite such titles as 'Electrification', 'Industry' and 'Waste Utilization' – were used by designers such as Varvara Stefanova. She developed her artistic philosophy in her work with Alexander Rodchenko while designing simple geometrically patterned fabrics for the first state textile factory in Moscow with Liubov Popova. Her later wallpaper designs were distinctly Constructivist.

In Germany, textiles were rescued from oblivion by the legacy of the Bauhaus. Weavers such as Stölzl and Anni *Albers, whose careers flourished post-Second World War, helped to implement change in the field of textile design and production. In fact, much of the post-war textile industry owed its success to the Bauhaus aim of developing 'prototypes for industry'. The focus was on materials – the decorative effect of each fibre judged both by its colour and texture and by its ability to convey tactility. Material was given preference over all other factors as the key to successful industrial production.

Stölzl single-handedly directed the Bauhaus weaving workshop from 1926 to 1931, and it was through her talent and guidance that the mass-production of Bauhaus designs became a reality. The workshop's early designs demonstrated an affinity for the colour theories of one of its instructors, Paul Klee, whose teachings helped to free the Bauhaus artists from their lingering pre-war notions concerning the application of conventional pattern and ornament. Outside the Bauhaus, Modernist printed and hand-woven fabrics were produced at the Kunstgewerbeschule, the industrial art school at Halle and the Deutscher Werkbund. Notable individual designers were Bruno Paul, Fritz A. Brehaus and Richard Lesker.

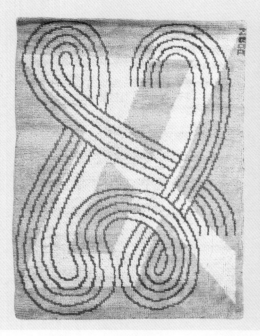
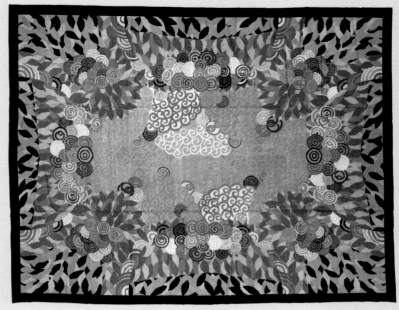

Modernist Belgian fabric designers appear to have been inspired mostly by their German neighbours in their choice of a muted palette. Jaap Gidding and Paul Haesaerts, at the Studio de Saedeleer, produced linens and tapestries decorated with Peruvian Indian and tribal African motifs on geometric grounds. At the Vanderborght Frères mill, Sylvie Féron created dynamic geometric patterns composed of overlapping triangles, zigzags and squares. For the 1925 Exposition Internationale, Darcy designed roller-printed wallpaper and geometric and fanciful floral patterns on a pallid ground for the Société des Usines Peters-Lacroix.

Although the acid colours of early French Art Deco fabrics were initially perceived as too bold for the conservative American public, the inclusion of French textiles in exhibitions at the Metropolitan Museum of Art, New York, in 1926, and the nation's department stores from 1928, led to the gradual understanding that Modernism was more than a passing fancy. Larger retailers began to offer a modest selection from Aubusson manufacturers, Cornille Frères, Bianchini–Férier and others.

At the time there were only a handful of specialist textile designers of note in the USA: Ruth *Reeves, Henriette Reiss, Zoltan Hecht and Louise (Loja) *Saarinen. Small firms that added Modernist lines to their traditional repertoire included Nancy McClelland and M. H. Birge & Sons Co.

Three exhibitions were staged in New York in the late 1920s and early 1930s to promote the Modernist movement – those of the American Designers' Gallery, Contempora and the American Union of Decorative Artists and Craftsmen (AUDAC). At these, carpets were exhibited by Hermann Rosse, Wolfgang and Pola *Hoffmann, Eugene *Schoen, Joseph *Urban, Henry Varnum *Poor and DONALD DESKEY (see under Furniture and Interior Decoration), as part of their own interiors or those of others. Of the fabrics shown, most were executed by small rural weaving communities, such as the New England Guild, the Connecticut Handicraft Industry and the Contemporary American Artists Handhooked Rugs Guild.

The Hungarian emigrant sisters Mariska and Ilonka *Karasz applied the exuberance of the new palette to traditional folk art motifs. The influence of Fauvism is apparent in the colours and patterns of their needlework. The work was executed by Mariska to designs by Ilonka. Another folk-inspired American artist was Lydia Bush-Brown, who revived the batik technique in a blend of stylized Middle Eastern and modern motifs. In tapestry wall hangings, Marguerite Zorach and Lorentz Kleiser emerged as the nation's pioneer Modernist designers.

The work of Ruth Reeves reflected the continuing search in America for a native vernacular appropriate to modern decoration. Reeves's association with Fernand Léger in the 1920s in Paris left the firm stamp of Cubism on both her woven and her printed designs. In 1930 the Fifth Avenue furniture dealers W. & J. Sloane exhibited twenty-nine of her designs – a sign of the confidence American firms were beginning to show in the economic viability of the new style. 'Figures with Still Life', 'Manhattan' and 'Electric' displayed Reeves's interest in the vigorous interrelationships of geometric forms. Among her most successful works was the repeating abstract design in her carpets in Radio City Music Hall. Reeves translated her designs into roughly a dozen types of fabric, including chintz, monk's cloth, voile, velvet and muslin.

Deskey – America's premier Modernist designer of the period – created textiles that exhibit his fascination with asymmetrical geometric forms. The photographer Edward Steichen produced a unique range of silks for the Stehli Silk Corp., in which everyday objects lit from various angles were reproduced photographically in black and white to create powerful machine-age images.

By 1930, the modern textile movement had hit its stride in the USA, its tenet being simplicity of form and colour. No finer example of this simplicity was provided than 'Triptych', a printed linen fabric in three complementary hues of yellow, by Jules *Bouy.

In the 1920s, rugs had provided a decorative accent to the lavish interiors of the Paris ensembliers – Dufrène, Follot, Süe et Mare, Ruhlmann, Jules *Leleu, Gabriel, Nathan and Jourdain – while Groult, among others, designed carpets to complement their decorative schemes. Towards the end of the decade, rugs often provided the only element of warmth and ambience in the austere, metal-dominated interiors

UNIDENTIFIED ARTIST
Silk shawl, 1920s.

presented by PIERRE CHAREAU (*see under* Furniture and Interior Decoration), Georges *Djo-Bourgeois and René *Herbst at the initial exhibitions of the *Union des Artistes Modernes (UAM), in the early 1930s.

Modernist rugs and carpets, like Modernist fabrics, displayed a selection of floral, abstract and non-figurative patterns. Designs were executed by: Aubusson (Édouard *Benedictus, Paul Vera, Henri *Rapin, Paul Deltombe and Louis Valtat); Mybor (Louis Marcoussis, Josef *Csáky, Léger and Lurçat); La Maîtrise (Dufrène, Jacques and Jean Adnet, Suzanne *Guiguichon, Marcelle Maisonnier, Raoul Harang, Jean Bonnet and Jacques Klein); La Maison Martine (Raoul Dufy); Pomone (Follot); *DIM (Drésa, Boberman and Follot); Primavera (Olesiewicz and Colette Gueden); Süe et Mare (Paul Vera and André Mare); and Chareau (Lurçat and Burkhalter). Other designers of merit appear to have worked independently: Marcel Coupé, Mlle Max Vibert, Maurice *Matet, Mme S. Mazoyer and Mme Henri Favier.

French painters occasionally applied their talents to carpets – mixing abstract and Cubist styles. Noteworthy were the artists commissioned by Cuttoli (for her Maison Mybor) and the painter Marie *Laurencin, who translated her gay floral compositions into carpet designs for Groult. The finest-quality carpets were *au point noué* (hand knotted). As synthetic fibres made their entry into the medium, experimental pieces in cellulose and vegetable fibres were shown at the Paris Salons, as were new washable linen materials.

The most successful rug and carpet designs in Paris were those of IVAN DA SILVA BRUHNS. Drawn to Berber and Moroccan textiles shown in the French capital during and immediately after the First World War, da Silva Bruhns also borrowed American Indian motifs for his early works. From the mid-1920s, however, his style evolved into a powerful Cubist-inspired geometry. His palette included beige, rust, ochre and grey tones. Cubism also played a role in the Modernist designs of Hélène *Henry, who was retained by Jourdain and the architects ROBERT MALLET-STEVENS (*see under* Furniture and Interior Decoration) and Chareau.

EILEEN GRAY (*see under* Furniture and Interior Decoration) used carpets to relieve the severity of her late 1920s interiors. Her crisp, angular designs were displayed at the annual Salons, and through her gallery, Jean Désert. Similar in design to those of Gray were the carpets introduced by MAISON DESNY (*see under* Silver, Metal, Lacquer and Enamel) to complement its metal furnishings.

In Britain, rugs and carpets were retailed by a number of decorating firms in the subdued and comfortable Modernism of the late 1930s. The geometrically designed rugs of graphics designer Edward *McKnight Kauffer were used in interiors created by David Pleydell-Bouverie and Raymond McGrath. Betty *Joel, who initially used rugs designed by da Silva Bruhns, later made her own models. These, woven in China, were an extension of her understated furniture. The painter Francis Bacon designed carpets to complement his own interior schemes.

The expatriate American Marion Dorn earned the nickname 'architect of floors'. Beginning in the early 1920s with designs for batik fabrics, her first collaborative efforts were with McKnight Kauffer and were executed by the Chelsea weaver Jean Orage. In 1929, their designs for the Royal Wilton Carpet Factory in Wiltshire were exhibited at the Arthur Tooth gallery. In 1934 Dorn established her own firm, Marion Dorn Ltd, specializing in handmade and custom-designed rugs. Her skilful integration of different piles added textural interest to McKnight Kauffer's brilliant geometric patterns.

In Germany, some geometric patterned rugs were made by the Bauhaus's Stölzl and Albers, while other rugs in the Modernist idiom were created by Edith Eberhart (in a style reminiscent of Stölzl's), Marie Hannich (who designed rugs with powerful images of boats, cars and buildings in a rigid geometric manner), and Brehard Hesse and Hedwig Beckemann (who also worked in a geometric style).

In the USA, three specialized exhibitions helped to stimulate modern carpet design: shows at the Art Center, New York (1928), the Newark Museum (1930) and the Metropolitan Museum of Art, New York (1931). Here, avant-garde European textile designers were seen by the

LOUIS MARCOUSSIS

(*left*) Wool carpet for the entrance foyer in Jacques Doucet's residence in Neuilly, *c.* 1926.

PAUL IRIBE

(*below*) Wall fabric design in block-printed silk, for André Groult, 1912.

American public for the first time. The quiet symmetry of the German designers (Bruno Paul, Ernst Böhm and Wilhelm Poetter) contrasted with the more spontaneous and colourful works of McKnight Kauffer and Dorn, the sophisticated and exotic geometrics of da Silva Bruhns and the naïve florals of Maison Martine.

The Cranbrook Academy of Art in Bloomfield Hills, Michigan, played an important role in the dissemination of Scandinavian ideals to a generation of American weavers whose work came to prominence after the Second World War. Saarinen's weaving studio was established in October 1928, to complete special commissions, and in 1929 a weaving department was founded. This was staffed by Scandinavian expatriates to execute commissions by architects and designers such as Frank Lloyd Wright. Saarinen's style, and indeed Cranbrook's weaving style in general, was marked by a restrained palette and an absence of either sharp geometry or purely representational motifs. When American mills such as Stephen Sanford & Sons and the Bigelow–Hartford Carpet Co. finally became convinced that the modern idiom was more than a fad, they commissioned designers to work in a mode largely derivative of the European Modernists. There was also a market in the USA for rugs woven in China with subdued Art Deco patterns.

IVAN DA SILVA BRUHNS

GUNTA STÖLZL (STADLER-STÖLZL)

GEORGES DJO-BOURGEOIS
Wool carpet, handwoven with cotton warp,
c. 1930.

IVAN DA SILVA BRUHNS
(1881–1980)

Born in Paris of Brazilian parents, da Silva Bruhns was working as an artist–decorator when he was drawn in 1920 to carpet design by a commission from Louis *Majorelle. His early designs were conventional; garlanded fruit and flora, in a variation of the 17th-century Savonnerie style adopted by Jules *Coudyser (with whom da Silva Bruhns formed an early partnership), Édouard *Benedictus and MAURICE DUFRÈNE.

Da Silva Bruhns revolutionized both carpet manufacture and design. After dissecting an Oriental rug, he developed his own variation of the *au point noué* stitch. This was described by Marcel Weber in a 1924 article on the artist in *Art et Décoration*:

> Each of the spots of colour is made
> by tying a slip knot around the strands
> of the warp thread. After weaving, the
> juxtaposed knots are covered by rings
> which are then cut with scissors.
> This reveals the strands that will form
> the pile of the carpet.

Da Silva Bruhns taught his technique to an artisan, whom he installed in a village in the Aisne département to set up a studio of local weavers. In 1925, he founded a workshop entitled La Manufacture de Savigny, in the Paris suburb of Savigny-sur-Orge (Essonne), for which he opened a showroom in the city. He concerned himself mainly with two aspects of production: the colour selection of the wool; and the preliminary watercolour maquette – the latter traced in microscopic detail on to squared paper. It was the first time that 20th-century design had been applied to carpets: geometric patterns composed of overlapping rectangles, lozenges and chevrons on earth-toned grounds, and Cubist elements. His palette was sober: indigos, browns, pinks, greys and apricot, which met precisely the carpet's function within an ensemble that the *Mobilier et Décoration* critic described in 1928 as:

> . . . providing the harmony which
> is struck between the colours of the
> furniture and the tapestries – its
> fundamental bass note whose rich and
> warm resonance helps create a sum of
> varied and carefully wrought sensations
> like an orchestral chord.

No further measure of the esteem in which da Silva Bruhns was held by his colleagues at the Salons is needed than a list of those who incorporated his carpets into their exhibits: Jules *Leleu, Pierre-Paul *Montagnac, Paul *Follot, JACQUES-ÉMILE RUHLMANN, Bouchet, Eric *Bagge, *Fréchet, EUGÈNE PRINTZ and René *Prou, to name only the most important. Other commissions came for the nation's ocean liners – the *Île-de-France*, *Atlantique* and *Normandie* – plus French embassies and the United Nations agency in Geneva. Da Silva Bruhns also exhibited on his own until the late 1930s. Two addresses were given for him in the inter-war years: 3 avenue du Château, Neuilly; and 9 rue de l'Odéon, Paris.

Wool carpet woven by La Manufacture de Savigny, c. 1927.

(*right*) Wool carpet, *c.* 1930.

(*below*) Wool carpet, 1920s.

(*right*) Wool carpet, 1920s.

Wool carpet made by
La Manufacture de Savigny, 1920s.

(*below left*) Wool rug, *c.* 1930.

(*below right*) Wool carpet, 1920s.

(*bottom left*) Wool carpet made by La Manufacture de Savigny, probably late 1920s.

(*bottom right*) Wool rug made by La Manufacture de Savigny, 1920s.

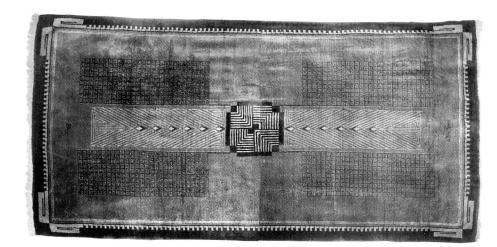

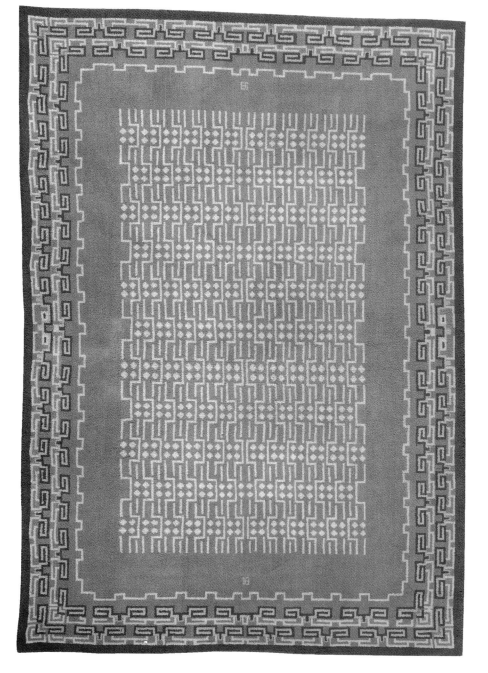

GUNTA STÖLZL (STADLER-STÖLZL) (1897–1983)

Adelgunde 'Gunta' Stölzl was born in Munich and attended decorative painting, ceramics and art history classes at the city's Kunstgewerbeschule from 1913 to 1916. During the First World War she served as a Red Cross nurse, resuming her studies in Munich on the cessation of hostilities. In 1919 Stölzl was interviewed by Walter *Gropius, who hired her to run the women's weaving workshop at the Bauhaus, a position she assumed the following year. Two years later, after attending dyeing courses at Krefeld, she established dyeing facilities at the Bauhaus and passed the school's journeyman examination as a weaver.

In 1925, following the Bauhaus's move to Dessau, Stölzl was elected a craft master in a process by which the students chose their instructors. She was again promoted, in 1927 – this time to *Jungmeister* (young master). Transforming her workshop into a profitable venture (the only one to become so at the school), Stölzl created her own weavings while continuing to teach. Of note during this period was her '5 Chore' ('5 Harnesses') wall hanging using the Jacquard technique. Contemporary accounts of her skills were unanimous: she was the quintessential weaver – her technical command of her craft unsurpassed and her colour sense unerring. Many of her compositions comprised a chequerboard matrix, by which she introduced the subtle interplay of graduating tonalities that characterized her finest works.

Stölzl's career began to unravel following her marriage in 1929 to a Palestinian Jewish architect, Arieh Sharon, to whom she bore a daughter that year. In 1931, she was forced to resign from the Bauhaus along with two colleagues – Gertrude Preiswerk and Heinrich-Otto Hurlimann – after a letter, written by a Nazi Party member whose daughter she had been obliged to dismiss from her weaving class, was sent to the mayor of Dessau complaining about her supposedly scandalous private life. Suddenly unemployed, Stölzl joined her two colleagues in the formation of a small weaving shop, called S-P-H Stoffe, across the Swiss border near Zürich. There she continued to create works for a variety of clients while participating in exhibitions, such as that of the Werkbund in Stuttgart, where in 1932 she showed coverings, curtains and upholstery.

Following the dissolution of S-P-H Stoffe in 1933 and her divorce three years later, Stölzl joined the Association of Swiss Women Painters, Sculptors and Craftswomen, through which she displayed her weavings. In 1942 she married Willy Stadler. She remained active until 1969.

(*opposite*) Wall hanging in cotton, wool and linen fibres, 1922–23.

(*below*) Wall hanging in linen, wool and rayon fibres, 1923–25.

'5 Chore', jacquard wall hanging in cotton,
wool, rayon and silk fibres, manufactured
at the Bauhaus (Dessau), 1928.

(*below*) 'Black-White' wall hanging in linen and rayon fibres, 1923–24.

(*right*) Wall hanging in linen, wool and rayon fibres, 1923.

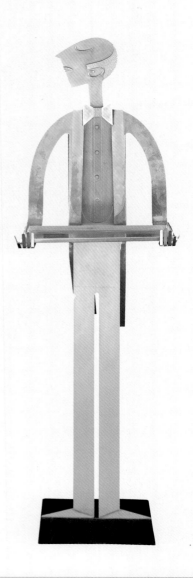

SILVER, METAL, LACQUER AND ENAMEL

Silverware designers had to be more cautious than their counterparts in other disciplines because they had a more conservative clientele. The Modernist philosophy of eliminating surface decoration could not be applied at will. What emerged was a transitional 'Modern Class' style, a marriage between new and old – one that was dignified, understated, rational and safe rather than bold.

By virtue of its colour, silver is a 'dry' material. To give it life without the use of surface ornament, the 1920s Modernist silversmith had to rely on an interplay of light, shadow and reflection created by contrasting planes and curves. Another way to enrich its monotone colour was by incorporating semi-precious stones, rare woods, ivory and glass. Towards the 1930s, **vermeil** or gold panels were applied to the surfaces as an additional means of embellishment. When used with restraint, so as not to overwhelm the balance and purity of the design, these materials added warmth, sumptuousness and textural contrast.

JEAN PUIFORCAT emerged as the doyen of the Art Deco silversmiths. From a very early stage, he concentrated on trying to unify design and function. Superfluous ornamentation was pared away in the pursuit of a purely functional form of design. This, he found, could be achieved largely by using fundamental geometric shapes. Combining elegance and simplicity, he generated a formidable range of silver tea services, flatware and hollowware, table-top objects and liturgical pieces. Included were streamlined cruet dishes, *chocolatiers*, chalices and sword guards adorned with lapis lazuli, ivory, ebony and crystal. The term Cubist was sometimes loosely applied to his style, but he preferred to call it 'mathematical'.

A latecomer to the field of silver, Jean Tétard abandoned simple geometric shapes for a combination of more complex flattened forms made of identical sections joined by flat conforming bars. Although these designs required a high degree of technical skill, they allowed him great freedom of expression. His only concessions to ornament were beautiful sculpted handles in rare woods that seemed to grow out of the silver. Tétard's development of serpentine surfaces, in which concave and convex planes were alternated to create the impression of spiralling

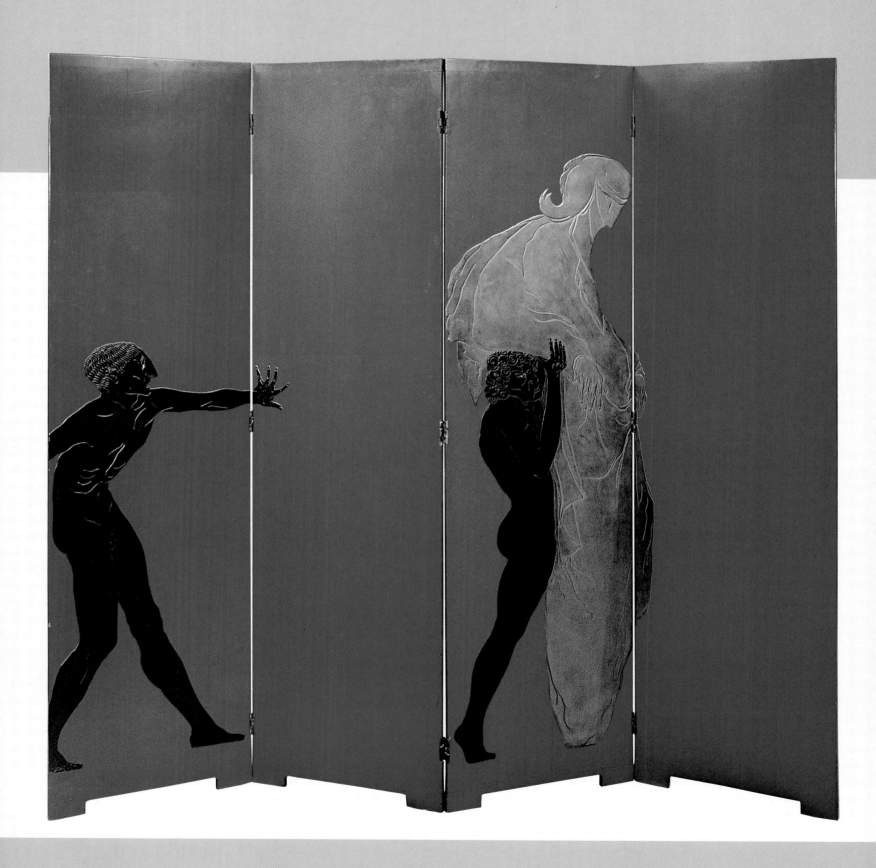

EILEEN GRAY
'Le Destin', four-panel wood screen in red
lacquer with bronze and silver applications,
the reverse with an abstract geometric design,
commissioned by Jacques Doucet, 1914, and
exhibited at the Exposition de Paris, 1929.

movement, was particularly dramatic. Biographical information remains scant for many individual silversmiths and companies active in the inter-war years in the French capital, including Fouquet–Lapar, *Lapparra, *Ravinet–d'Enfert and *Boin–Taburet, all of which exhibited Modernist works at the Salons.

Silverplate, produced by *galvanoplastie* (electroplating), was virtually indistinguishable from real silver. It was developed in the 1840s by Charles Christofle, whose firm of *Christofle purchased all existing French patents and the originating one from Elkington & Co. in England. In 1855, Pauline de Metternich, wife of the Viennese ambassador to the French court, dined with Napoleon III. When she complimented him on the silver, he replied, 'Dear Ambassadrice, it is a luxury that everyone can now afford. I have on my table not one piece of sterling silver. It is all by Christofle.' Branches in London, Vienna and Philadelphia carried the firm's name to foreign markets.

Several individual jewellers and jewelry companies were drawn to silver as a means of extending their talents. Jean *Després created silver and pewter bowls, bonbonnières, tureens and flatware that were starkly simple and almost brutal in their Modernism, with heavily hammered surfaces and boldly hewn bolts and rivets. Gérard *Sandoz also produced a limited number of distinctive objects of forceful design, to which lizardskin, *galuchat*, enamels and ivory added refinement. Among the large companies, CARTIER (*see under* Jewelry), *Van Cleef & Arpels, *Boucheron, Mellerio and *Chaumet followed suit with a stunning array of objects that overstepped the traditional boundaries between jewelry and silver. Elaborate Art Deco objects of *virtu* were created in which elements made of semi-precious stones were mixed with silver and gold. Cartier's famous 'mystery clocks' provided perhaps the most extreme example of this marriage of the two disciplines.

The design of clocks in general underwent a stylistic revolution once they were electrified. Now they were small enough to sit comfortably on tables with other objects and to hang on inaccessible parts of walls, because they would not require winding. Most Art Deco designers abandoned the circular clock face in favour of strong vertical and horizontal ones. Some modified, or even abolished, the traditional hands, replacing them with balls on moving plates or stationary points on a rotating dial of numbers. Great attention was also paid to the design of the numbers themselves. Roman and Arabic numerals became outmoded and were replaced by combinations of vertical or horizontal rectangles, circles and arcs.

In Belgium, Germany and Denmark there were isolated exponents of the Art Deco style in silver. In Brussels, Marcel Wolfers, son of the famous Art Nouveau jeweller and silversmith Philippe Wolfers of *Wolfers Frères, designed a range of angular and bulbous tea services and flatware in the Modernist idiom. In Germany, some of the period's most profoundly important and exciting designs in silver and metal were produced by the staff and students at the Bauhaus. In Copenhagen, Georg Jensen emerged as a major figure in 20th-century silver, despite the fact that he was not a great innovator. His major accomplishment lay in turning handcrafted modern silver into a successful commercial enterprise by producing it at a cost that made it available to the new bourgeoisie. In 1904, he founded the silversmithy *Jensen, where he was joined by the painter Johan *Rohde. The firm introduced the ideals of William Morris to 20th-century Scandinavian art, and Harald *Nielsen, who joined the firm in 1909, brought with him a functional style derived from the Bauhaus. Sigvard *Bernadotte, son of the king of Sweden, was Jensen's most influential designer in the 1930s, producing hard-edged pieces characterized by incised parallel lines.

Silver design in the USA was less receptive than other areas of the decorative arts to European, especially French, Modernist influences. To Americans, silver was still something passed down from generation to generation; it implied a certain snobbish entitlement. *Tiffany & Co., the largest and most prestigious manufacturer of fine silver in the country, executed very few pieces in the contemporary idiom. Even these did not make an appearance until the mid-1930s, after Louis Comfort Tiffany, the firm's artistic director and a fierce antagonist of Modernism,

GEORG JENSEN
Tea pot and creamer in silver with ebony
handles, designed by Johan Rohde, 1919.

had died. Gorham, another important silver manufacturer, was likewise reluctant to abandon traditional styles. Edward Mayo was appointed head of the firm in 1923, and he tried to bring new inspiration by hiring the Danish silversmith Erik *Magnussen, who worked for Gorham from 1925 until 1929. Magnussen produced designs that took their inspiration from innumerable sources: Jensen's lingering Art Nouveau style, Constructivism, Cubism and the skyscraper, the last of which inspired his 1927 tea service, 'The Lights and Shadows of Manhattan'. The industrial designer Norman *Bel Geddes also created a 'Skyscraper' cocktail service and a 'Manhattan' serving tray, but these were done in a linear style that was almost Scandinavian in its restraint.

The *International Silver Co. in Connecticut retained outside designers such as Gilbert *Rohde and Eliel *Saarinen to create silver, silverplate and pewter hollowware and flatware that reflected new trends in the decorative arts. One of the most noteworthy silversmiths working independently in the USA in the inter-war years was the German-born Peter *Müller-Munk. His designs were modern without being extreme, reflecting a European sophistication that attracted many private clients. But with the Wall Street crash of 1929 the silver market declined precipitously, opening the way for a variety of imitation metals, such as silverplate, chrome and nickel.

The most successful manufacturer of mass-produced chrome and nickel accessories was the *Chase Brass & Copper Co. of Waterbury, Connecticut. It hired prominent designers such as Walter *von Nessen, Albert *Reimann, Gilbert Rohde, Russel *Wright and Rockwell Kent, to create a line of Modernist-inspired cocktail and smoking accessories for the mass market. The Apollo Studios, a division of Bernard Rice's Sons, based in New York City, likewise entered the Modernist market with its 'Shadowart' series of hollowware, designed for it by Louis M. Rice in 1928. Mention should also be made of Reed & Barton, in Taunton, Massachusetts, and the Wallace & Sons Manufacturing Co., in Wallingford, Connecticut, both of which introduced similar series of contemporary hollowware in the late 1920s.

Among the other metals, wrought iron enjoyed a golden age in France during the inter-war years. The spare, clean lines of the new style in architecture lent themselves particularly well to decorative ironwork. Wrought iron was used on the exteriors of buildings for grilles, window guards and doors, and in the interiors for balustrades, railings, fireplace furniture and a wide range of furnishings, including light fixtures, console tables and screens. Elevator cages became the focal decorative point in lobbies, their ornamentation carefully matched to nearby railings and entrance doors. Only in their attempt to design traditional pieces of furniture, such as tables and room dividers, did Modernist wrought-iron artists sometimes apply too heavy a hand and produce a piece that over-powered other furnishings in an ensemble. Because of the metal's innate heaviness, it was often at its best when used as an accent piece.

In wrought iron, the Art Deco style divided itself chronologically into two broad categories. The first, following the lead of the *fin-de-siècle* designers, drew its inspiration from nature: birds, flowers, greyhounds, gazelles, clouds, fountains and sunbursts were translated into a style in which elongation and exaggeration of form predominated. The second category was a more architectural style which emerged after 1925 and in which the sleek lines of machinery, aeroplanes and steamships were increasingly evoked.

The period's pre-eminent ironworker was EDGAR BRANDT, who created grilles and fixtures for numerous private homes and hotels, as well as for notable public commissions and ocean liners. Between commissions, Brandt exhibited non-architectural metalware, such as radiator covers, lamps and consoles, at the annual Salons. For the 1925 *Exposition Internationale he made not only the Porte d'Honneur but also on his own stand his celebrated 'L'Oasis' five-panel screen in wrought iron highlighted with brass accents. The screen displayed the facility with which Brandt interchanged materials such as wrought iron and bronze, in the 1920s, and also gilt-copper; later, he included steel, aluminium and the alloy 'Studal'.

Mantel clocks in gilt and silvered bronze,
c. 1925.

Raymond *Subes was second only to Brandt in the scope and quality of his work. As artistic director of the leading architectural construction company Borderel et Robert, he was responsible for commissions for hotels, exhibition halls, churches, monuments and cemeteries in the 1920s. It was in the eye-catching lines of a hotel's stairway balustrade or on anonymous building façades that Subes's considerable skills were fully utilized. His choice of materials matched Brandt's: a basic preference for wrought iron, at times exchanged for patinated copper, bronze and, in the 1930s, aluminium and oxidized or lacquered steel. Subes also exhibited furnishings at the annual Salons.

Jules and Michel Nics were Hungarian-born brothers who worked in Paris under the name of *Nics Frères, producing a complete range of domestic decorative ironwork characterized by a highly conspicuous *martelé* (hammered) decorative finish and a rather excessive and *passé* use of naturalistic motifs. They rejected die-stamping and file work, and affirmed themselves instead as masters of the hammer, and thereby, of the craft's pre-industrial past.

The metalworker Richard *Desvallières produced some extraordinary pieces in the 1920s in a transitional style that carefully balanced the massive presence of Art Deco design and the sinuous lines of the *fin de siècle*. Paul *Kiss collaborated with Brandt early in his career, and his work displays a similarly lyrical quality, though it differs in character. Other serious and dedicated wrought-iron workers of the time included the father-and-son team of Édouard and Marcel *Schenck, Adelbert-Georges *Szabo, Louis *Gigou, Charles Piguet, Michel Zadounaisky, Louis Katona, Fred Perret, Gilbert *Poillerat, Édouard Delion, Robert Merceris and Paul Laffillee.

Byzantine art was a continuing influence on Claudius *Linossier, whose shimmering metallic surfaces evoked the mosaics of Hagia Sophia in Istanbul and of St Mark's basilica in Venice. He also studied alloys, and his understanding of these enabled him to achieve the various tonalities of silver that gave his pieces their understated richness. But the outstanding element of Linossier's work was his use of metal encrustation. He refused to use acids, as they did not produce permanent colours. Instead, he concentrated on the flame, causing the inlays to expand and merge slightly into one another, creating soft tones of faded rose, silvery white, grey, pinks, yellows, mauve and a jet black. The finished piece revealed the natural qualities of the metals, and also bore the subtle traces of the hand that had formed it.

Maurice *Daurat preferred to work in pewter, a soft metal, ductile and extremely supple, which in his hands achieved the status of a new-found material. He exploited its almost flesh-like surface, sombre shadows and the irregular reflections of light from random hammer marks. All of these imparted to the finished piece a warmth more appealing to him than the cold gleam of silver. His designs became increasingly pared down, emerging finally as studies in form and simplicity. Daurat's only concession to ornament could be a band of round beads at the base, or a scrolled handle. He intended his pieces to be admired rather than used, and indeed their weight often rendered them impractical.

Almost every Paris decorating firm worked with *Fontaine et Cie, which had created attractive hardware for more than one hundred years. It was the only company willing to take the financial risks involved in making well-designed hardware in editions large enough to permit reasonable prices. One of the reasons for its success was that it commissioned designs from prominent sculptors and decorators, such as SÜE ET MARE (*see under* Furniture and Interior Decoration), who designed mirror frames, fire screens, clocks and a full line of decorative hardware for Fontaine in their characteristically full-bodied stylizations of natural forms, and *trompe-l'œil* depictions of pleated fabric executed in gilded, silvered or bronzed copper. More Modernist than the work of Süe et Mare was the work of the furniture designer René *Prou, whose style included geometric motifs worked in various finished metals that gave their surfaces an interesting play of light. Other notable artist–designers retained by Fontaine included Émile-Antoine Bourdelle, Aristide Maillol, Joseph-Antoine *Bernard, Paul *Jouve and Pierre Poisson.

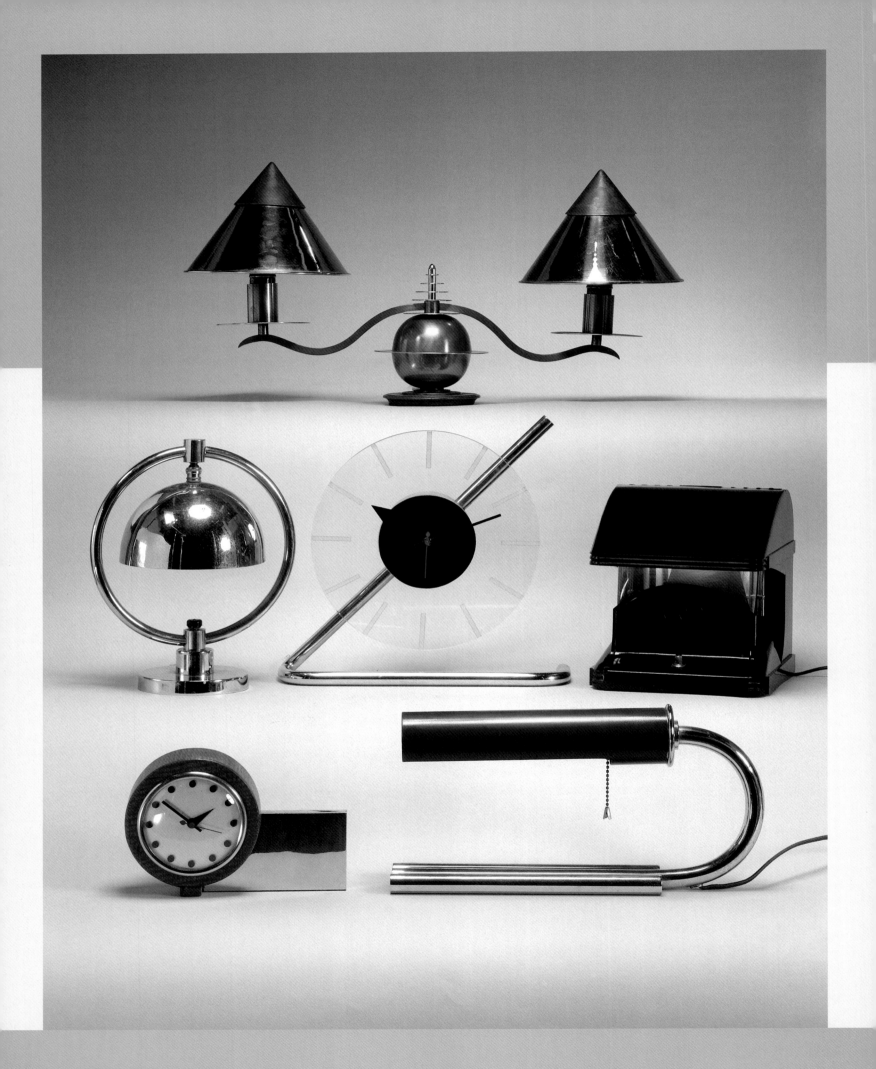

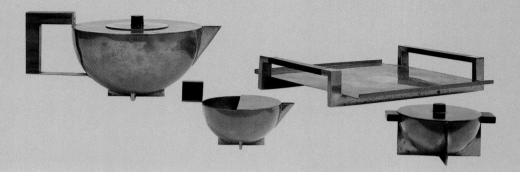

At first the USA lagged behind France in its adoption of metalwork for interiors. By the late 1920s, however, after the influence of the 1925 Exposition Internationale and the opening of Brandt's New York office, Ferrobrandt, metalwork had become immensely popular. A number of American designers and craftsmen produced a great variety of both interior and exterior ironwork.

Oscar *Bach was perhaps the only ironworker in the USA endowed with the technical prowess of the great French *ferronniers*. Born in Germany, he emigrated to New York in 1914. He was proficient in many styles of metalwork and metals, and in the interchange of copper, aluminium, bronze and chromed-nickel silver to provide colour and textural contrasts. Bach worked on many of Manhattan's most outstanding buildings, including the Chrysler and Empire State Buildings and Radio City Music Hall.

William Hunt *Diederich, a Hungarian *émigré*, was a successful designer in several areas but was especially attracted to metalwork. His simple, two-dimensional cut-out images of figures and animals seem snipped out of the iron. Jules *Bouy came from France to the USA as the manager of Ferrobrandt. He was no doubt strongly influenced by Brandt's work, but brought a more forceful interpretation of machine-age angular design to a wide variety of domestic metalware and wooden furniture for a moneyed clientele in and around New York City.

Meanwhile, in France, the huge interest in Japanese art, spawned in the late 19th century, contributed greatly to the resurgence of interest in lacquer. JEAN DUNAND, who developed into the most important artist to work in the medium, was tutored by a famous Japanese lacquer artisan Sougawara, which effectively changed his career from that of metalworker. Dunand was able to develop shades of yellow, green and coral lacquer that had always eluded Japanese artisans, and to produce top-quality lacquer at a relatively low cost. To achieve the so far elusive colour of white, he developed the intensely laborious art of *coquille d'œuf*, in which particles of crushed eggshell were inlaid into the uppermost layers of the lacquer.

Dunand applied lacquer to his metalwork vases in arresting geometric patterns that provided a series of vibrant new Art Deco images. He later extended its use into screens and panels, collaborating also with furniture designers such as JACQUES-ÉMILE RUHLMANN (*see under* Furniture and Interior Decoration), Jacques *Leleu and EUGÈNE PRINTZ (*see under* Furniture and Interior Decoration) on panels and doors for their cabinetry.

One of Dunand's associates, Jean *Goulden, became an outstanding master of the art of *champlevé* enamelling. His highly sophisticated objects are simple in shape, with powerful Cubist volumes and flat planes painted with sharply contrasting enamels in abstract or representational designs. His preferred metals were gilt-copper, gilt-bronze, silvered-bronze and sterling silver.

Beyond the French capital, enamelling emerged in the 1920s as a significant art form in Limoges, known exclusively until then for its manufacture of porcelain. Camille *Fauré was the town's pre-eminent enamel exponent in his creation of dynamic overlapping geometric patterns applied mostly to vessels and plates. Also in the Limousin region, Jules Sarlandie and his son Robert as well as the husband-and-wife team of Alexandre and Henriette Marty applied a largely floral decorative vernacular to their enamelwares.

LOUIS KATONA
Fire-screen in wrought iron with parcel-gilt
detailing, c. 1925.

EDGAR BRANDT

MAISON DESNY

JEAN DUNAND

JEAN PUIFORCAT

LOUIS KATONA
Fire-screen in wrought iron with parcel-gilt
detailing, c. 1925.

EDGAR BRANDT (1880–1960)

Born in Paris, the son of a director of a mechanical engineering firm, Brandt was educated at the École Nationale Professionelle de Vierzon. On graduating, he established his own studio, laying the foundation of his subsequent emergence as the outstanding ironsmith of the inter-war years. At the turn of the century, while still in the shadow of the celebrated *ferronnier* Émile Robert – to whom credit for the 19th-century revival in metalware is due – Brandt began to exhibit through the annual Salons. He adopted the prevailing Art Nouveau style, designing wrought-iron and bronze furnishings and architectural elements with floral motifs into the mid-1920s, at which point he introduced into his repertoire the sharply angular motifs which had heralded

EDGAR BRANDT

Entrance door in wrought iron with gilt-bronze application, for Cheney Bros., 181 Madison Avenue at 34th Street, New York, c. 1925.

the new decade. Favourite early themes were the pine cone, eucalyptus, gingko, rose and serpent, the last-mentioned reproduced in a series of 'La Tentation' lamps. The 1930s brought stark Modernism – overlapping scrollwork and diagonal sunbeams.

Private commissions came quickly for Brandt – a large number being from architects who retained him to create grilles and fixtures for private houses and hotels. A notable public commission was a First World War monument, *La Tranchée des Baïonettes*, near Verdun, in 1921. Brandt maintained a fruitful collaboration with its architect, Henri Favier, for many years. Others with whom he worked were André Ventre and Richard Bouwens van der Boijen. Further prestigious commissions were afforded by ocean liners, in particular, the *Paris, Île-de-France and *Normandie.

Between commissions, Brandt exhibited regularly in the 1920s at the Salons of the *Société des Artistes Décorateurs and the *Salon d'Automne, showing a seemingly limitless range of non-architectural metalware such as grilles, lamps, radiator covers and consoles. The 1925 *Exposition Internationale provided him with numerous opportunities to display his work, beginning with the event's imposing point of entry, the Porte d'Honneur, designed by Favier and Ventre. Brandt's own stand on the Esplanade des Invalides offered a broad range of wares, while other works were dotted throughout the Exposition: grilles in the Hôtel du Collectioneur pavilion; gates in the Pavillon National Monégasque; the shop of the magazine *L'Illustration*; the Pavillon de la Renaissance; and light fixtures in the *Sèvres exhibit. The following year Brandt participated in the Exhibition of Modern Decorative Arts at the Metropolitan Museum of Art, New York, returning to the city for the 1927 Macy's Art-in-Trade Exposition and the 1928 Lord & Taylor Exposition of French Decorative Arts.

A 1926 firm's catalogue listed two Paris addresses: 101 boulevard Murat (workshop) and 27 boulevard Malesherbes (showroom). Two overseas showrooms were also listed: 3 George Street, Hanover Square, London, and Ferrobrandt, at 247 Park Avenue, New York. The catalogue illustrated a considerable variety of items, including Brandt's celebrated 'Oasis'

screen and 'L'Âge d'Or' doorway, the latter being a virtuoso work in pierced wrought iron adorned at its centre with gilt-bronze Classical figures.

The apparent ease with which Brandt transformed a bar of pig iron into the most ephemeral flower spray belied the material's innate lack of malleability, yet he succeeded in taming it, making it at once robust and plastic, bold and frivolous. His dexterity is amply shown in the facility with which he interchanged materials; most frequently, in the 1920s, wrought iron and bronze, with more ambitious works enhanced with gilt-copper motifs that provided a light accent of richness. Later came steel, aluminium and, around 1934, the alloy 'Studal'. Occasional collaborators included the sculptors Max Blondat and Badory, and the metalworkers Pierre Lardin and Gilbert *Poillerat. Ancillary materials were ordered from the period's foremost manufacturers: glassware from DAUM FRÈRES; porcelain from the Sèvres manufactory; and crystal from Pantin. Marble and alabaster, for lampshades and the tops of consoles, were shipped from Italy.

(*above*) View of Brandt's stand on the Esplanade des Invalides at the 1925 Exposition Internationale, Paris.

(*right*) *Potiche* in silvered bronze, the model included in Brandt's stand at the 1925 Exposition Internationale, Paris (*above*).

(*right*) Fire-screen in wrought iron, 1920s.

(*below*) 'L'Oasis' five-panel screen, in collaboration with Henri Favier, wrought iron with gilt-metal applications, exhibited at the 1925 Exposition Internationale, Paris (*see opposite page, top*).

Ensemble displayed at the Exhibition of
Modern Decorative Arts at the Metropolitan
Museum of Art, New York, 1926, including
a pair of Oriental floor lamps in wrought
iron and alabaster, a *Noblesse* console
table in wrought iron and marble; and a
'Transition' wall mirror. The sculpture is
by Émile-Antoine Bourdelle.

(*opposite above*) Console in wrought iron
with marble top, mid-1920s.

(*opposite below*) Console in wrought iron
with marble top, late 1920s.

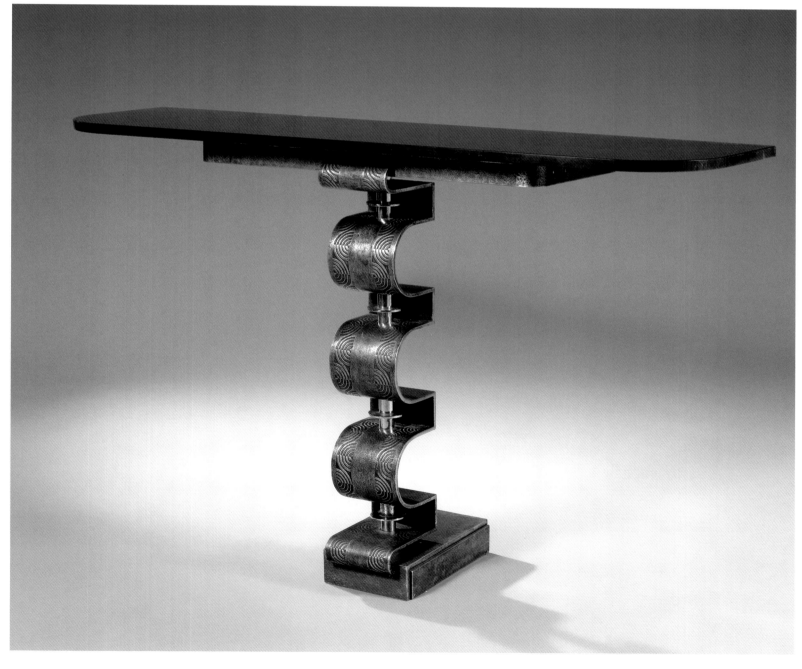

(*left*) Charger with serpent handles in wrought iron, 1920s.

(*below left*) *Cobra dressé* pedestal in gilt-bronze, wrought iron and marble, *c.* 1926.

(*below right*) *Torchère* in wrought iron and alabaster, *c.* 1925.

(*opposite*) Serpent vase in hammered wrought iron, *c.* 1922.

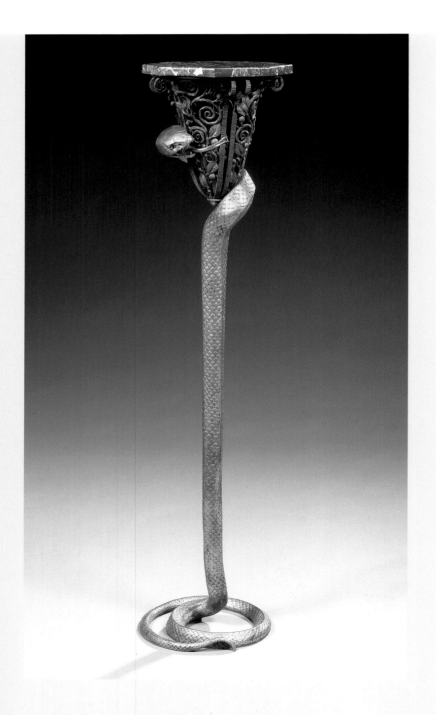

The confusion surrounding the history of Maison Desny has persisted longer than that relating to any other individual designer or design firm of the inter-war years, and it continues to haunt today's researchers. Only *Lux* – a monthly journal published in Paris between 1929 and 1937, in which developments in the field of domestic and commercial illumination were chronicled – contained articles and quotes credited directly to 'Desny'. Information on the firm, therefore, remains vague, but it appears that it was established by two designers, Desnet and René Nauny, from the contraction of whose names 'Desny' was derived. The two were friends who earned pocket money as quick-sketch artists for the circus. They formed a business partnership under the financial auspices of one

firm's business, in which it made furniture including aluminium mobile bars, floor lamps, abstract rugs and murals. However, Maison Desny is far better known for its editions of small-scale functional objects, such as covered boxes, *coupes*, cocktail sets and centrepieces, designed as extensions of the ultramodern interiors in which they were to be housed.

By 1931, the firm could boast a select clientele which included Georges-Henri Rivière, Pierre David-Weill, Mlle Thurnauer and the Belgian royal family. On occasions, it collaborated on interior design commissions with ROBERT MALLET-STEVENS and JEAN-MICHEL FRANK (*see under* Furniture and Interior Decoration), Georges *Djo-Bourgeois, André Masson and Alberto and Diego Giacometti.

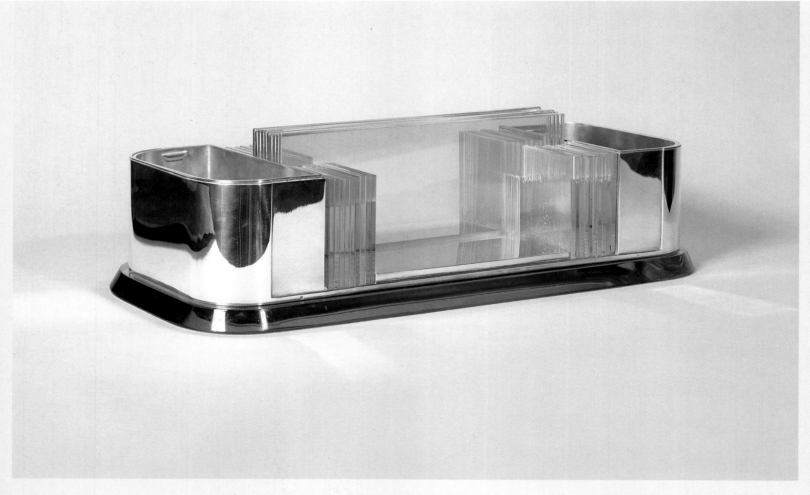

Letter rack with flanking *jardinières* in silver-plated metal and tinted glass, c. 1930.

M. Tricot in 1927, establishing themselves at 122 avenue des Champs-Élysées in Paris.

Shortly after its creation, the firm was commissioned to design an office for a Paris businessman. Begun in 1928, the project included a range of metal and wood furnishings. This and other interiors have survived in period illustrations to document this aspect of the

Desny's works represented progressive Machine Age industrial design at its most powerful. In this, the crisp symmetrical interplay of perpendicular shapes and contrasting planes carefully balanced against the item's intended function provides a ready form of identification. The firm excelled, especially, in its design for light fixtures. Editions of table and floor models, chandeliers and wall brackets, the latter sometimes with anglepoise arms, contained reflecting bowls that localized the light. Charming but less functional were the *bibelots lumineux* – some models with tiers of lime green glass panels, which served no other purpose than self-illumination.

Maison Desny remained in business until the mid- to late-1930s. The successful collaboration of its two gifted designers ended with the death of Desnet in 1933. Some time later, in association with Jean Painlevé, son of the French minister of war, Nauny founded the first sea aquarium in France, in Ploumanach. It remains unclear for how long he chose to design without the collaboration of his late colleague.

Four-piece tea service with conforming tray in silver-plated metal and wood, *c.* 1930.

Coupe in chromed metal with rosewood handles (*left*), and *coupe* in chromed metal with vermeil interior (*right*), late 1920s.

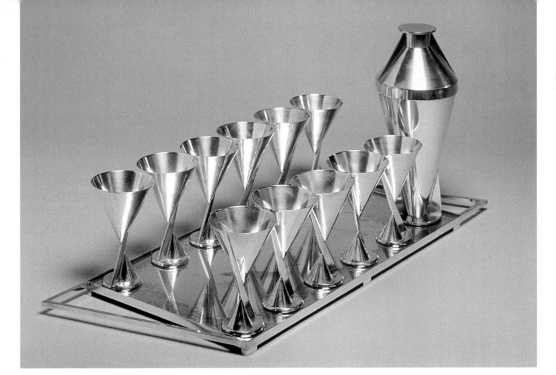

Cocktail service comprising a shaker, twelve goblets and tray, silver-plated metal and mirrored glass, 1929–30.

Cocktail cabinet in veneered sycamore with chromed-metal mounts, c. 1930.

Desk container in nickel-plated metal,
designed by Robert Mallet-Stevens, c. 1928.

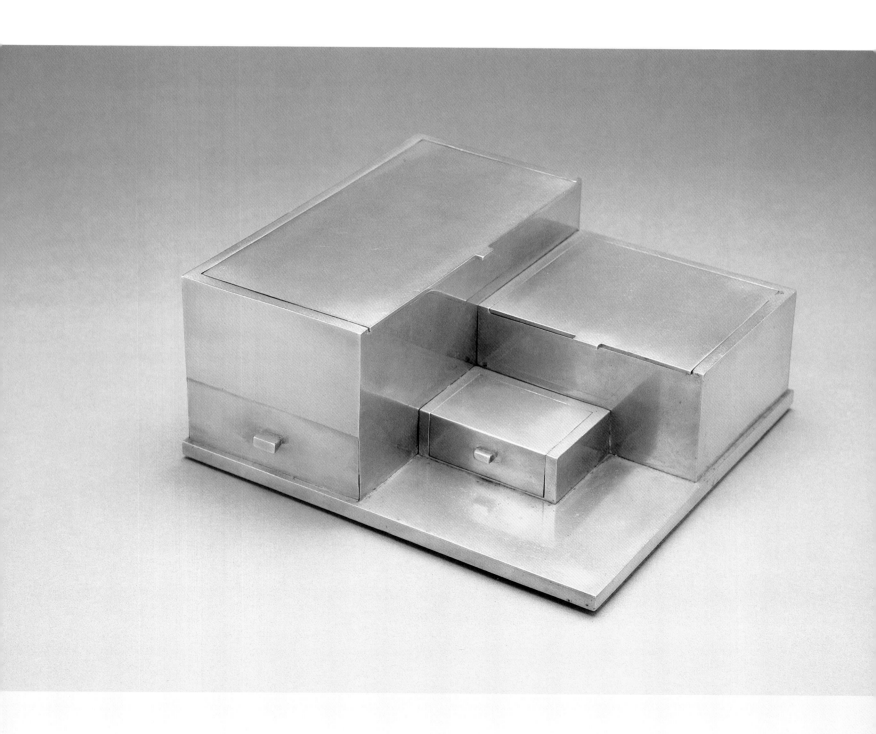

JEAN DUNAND (1877–1942)

Dunand was born in Lancy, Switzerland, to French parents; his father was a gold smelter in the clock-making business. Enrolment at the École des Arts Industriels in Geneva was followed in 1897 by a scholarship for advanced study in Paris. On his arrival there, Dunand was reunited with some old Swiss friends, Boutet de Monvel and Carl Albert Angst. The latter introduced him to his employer, the noted sculptor Jean Dampt, who took him on as an apprentice. Until 1902, Dunand studied sculpture and mastered its materials: bronze, plaster, stone and ivory. His career then spanned half a century and can be divided into three relatively distinct phases: sculpture, metalware and lacquerwork.

He appears to have established himself in a small studio near the Porte d'Orléans in 1903, and made his début at the Salon of the *Société Nationale des Beaux-Arts in the same year. Two years later Dunand showed a selection of Art Nouveau metal vases with designs in *repoussé* copper, followed by vases, book covers, jewelry and even fabric designs in various engraved and encrusted metals.

The transition to lacquer came in 1909 when Dunand first saw the lacquered creations of Paris-based Japanese artisans. He was immediately drawn to the medium, recognizing its lavish gloss and vibrant palette as the ideal embellishment for his metalware. An exchange followed – Dunand trading his hammering technique for the secret formulae of lacquer application. In 1912 he became associated with the Japanese master Sougawara, who had worked with EILEEN GRAY since 1907. Dunand applied his lacquer in the Oriental manner, an onerous procedure involving over twenty coats of lacquer, sanded between applications. He used this lacquering process on his furniture and metalware, either polished to a high sheen or treated with a rough chipped surface finish known as *laque arrachée*. On the outbreak of the First World War, Dunand enlisted as a Red Cross volunteer. After the armistice, he moved to larger quarters at 70 rue Hallé, where he could have metal, cabinetry and lacquer workshops.

The invention of *coquille d'œuf* as a decorative motif has been credited to Dunand. This technique was developed as a dramatic

(*below*) Dunand in his atelier working on *La Chasse*, a panel for the ocean liner *Normandie*, c. 1935.

(*right*) *La Conquête du cheval* panel in gold lacquer, a smaller copy of the one in *La Chasse*, a series of murals for the smoking room on the ocean liner *Normandie*, c. 1935.

substitute for the colour white, which could not be obtained through the vegetable dyes used to create lacquer. The eggshell's impact was most pronounced on a contrasting red or black lacquered ground.

He drew on the talents of associates to decorate some of his work, including Jean *Lambert-Rucki, Jean *Goulden, FRANÇOIS-LOUIS SCHMIED (see under Paintings, Graphics, Posters and Bookbinding) and Paul *Jouve. Infrequent collaborators were Ernest Bieler, Henri de Waroquier, Georges Dorignac and Serge Rovinski. Many of his works were shown at the Salons in ensembles presented by other exhibitors; for example, Michel Roux-Spitz, Léon Boucher, Théodore Lambert and ROBERT MALLET-STEVENS. He also provided lacquered finishes for other cabinet-makers – most importantly JACQUES-ÉMILE RUHLMANN and EUGÈNE PRINTZ (see under Furniture and Interior Decoration).

Dunand grasped every opportunity to show his works throughout the 1920s and early 1930s, not only at the Salons but also at the Galerie Georges Petit, the Galerie Jean Charpentier, the Maison *Geo. Rouard and the Salon des Tuileries. At the 1925 *Exposition Internationale, he designed the smoking room in the Ambassade Française in collaboration with Charles Hairon and Léon-Albert *Jallot. For the Hôtel du Collectioneur, Dunand provided lacquered panels and *dinanderie*. In 1928 he participated in the Lord & Taylor Exposition of Modern French Decorative Arts in New York, returning in 1929 for a two-man show with Jean Pellenc at the Rosenbach Gallery. Major clients included the milliner Mme Agnès, for whom he designed a complete interior, jewelry and scarves. Other benefactors included Jeanne *Lanvin, Madeleine Vionnet and Ambassador Philippe Berthelot. Further commissions were afforded by the ocean liners Île-de-France, *Atlantique and *Normandie.

Dunand's evolution from small metalware objects to large lacquered-wood furnishings can be traced in his changing choice of decoration. By 1913, the earlier *repoussé* flora on his copper vases had yielded to painted overlapping triangles and chevrons, and, by 1921, to a mix of African and Oriental figures, abstractions, realistic landscapes, stylized flowers, exotic fish and birds, and Lambert-Rucki's menagerie of fantastic animals.

In 1925, Dunand was joined by his elder son, Bernard. The outbreak of the Second World War brought family tragedy. Bernard was mobilized and captured. The second son was killed in action. As raw materials became increasingly scarce, Dunand was forced to close his workshops shortly before his death in 1942.

(*left*) Mural wood panel in *laque arrachée*, 1930s.

(*above*) *Figures and Deer by a Fountain*, mural panel in lacquered wood inlaid with *coquille d'œuf, c.* 1924.

Occasional table in lacquered wood
inlaid with *coquille d'œuf*, designed by
Jean Goulden, 1923.

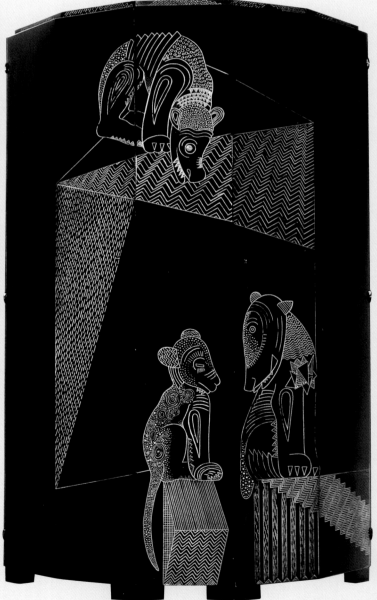

(*above*) *Kingfishers* , Four-panel wood screen
in silvered *laque arracheé*, exhibited at the
Galerie Georges Petit, Paris, 1928.

(*right*) Cabinet in black lacquered wood with
decoration by Jean Lambert-Rucki, included
in Dunand's smoking room in the Ambassa
de Française pavilion at the 1925 Exposition
Internationale, Paris.

Commode in lacquered wood with ivory trim and *sabots*, c. 1935.

Bed in lacquered wood inlaid with mother-of-pearl, designed for Mme Bertholet, 1930.

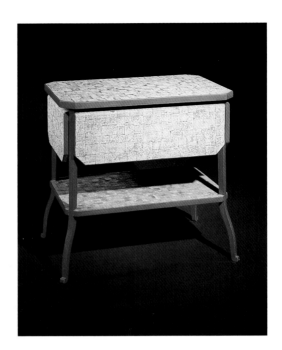

(*top left*) Drop-leaf table in red lacquered wood inlaid with *coquille d'œuf*, 1923.

(*top right*) Table, lacquered wood inlaid with *coquille d'œuf*, c. 1925.

(*above*) Table by Jacques-Émile Ruhlmann with ivory *chutes* and *sabots*, the lacquered and inlaid *coquille d'œuf* top by Dunand, 1920s.

(*right*) Side table in lacquered wood,
the top inlaid with *coquille d'œuf*, 1920s.

Mobile folding cocktail bar in lacquered
metal, *coquille d'œuf* and chromed metal,
designed for Lawrence Rigby, 1928.

(*below left*) Lacquered and patinated metal vases, one with *dinanderie* decoration, 1920s.

(*below right*) Lacquered metalware inlaid with *coquille d'œuf*, 1920s.

(*bottom*) Selection of lacquered metalware inlaid with *coquille d'œuf*, 1920s.

(*below left*) Three vases in patinated metal with *dinanderie* decoration, on tripod mounts, *c.* 1914–15.

(*below right*) Winged vase in patinated and lacquered copper, 1931.

(*right*) Vase in lacquered metal inlaid with *coquille d'œuf*, *c.* 1926.

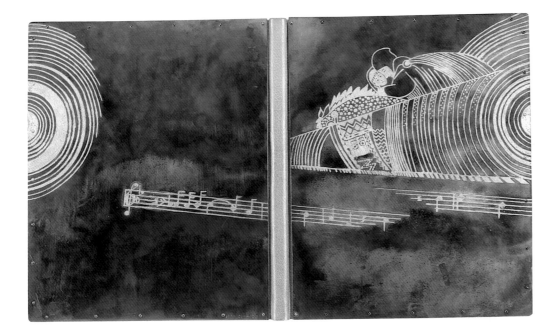

(left) Binding for *Le Roi des aulnes* (Johann Wolfgang von Goethe), leather with etched and lacquered metal panels, 1920s.

(below) Lacquered metal panel inlaid with mother-of-pearl, designed by Jean Lambert-Rucki for *Paradis terrestres* (Colette), bound by Georges Cretté, *c.* 1932.

(left) Lacquered metal doublures for *Le Livre de la vérite de parole* (Dr Joseph-Charles Mardrus), bound by François-Louis Schmied, 1929.

(top) Doublure in polychromed mother-of-pearl
for *Peau-brune* (François-Louis Schmied),
bound by Georges Cretté, 1931.

(above) *Woman Bathing*, panel in lacquer
and gold-leaf with incised detailing, illustrated
in *L'Art Vivant*, December 1930 issue.

JEAN PUIFORCAT (1897–1945)

Tea service, silver and cut-crystal, the model introduced in 1925.

The heir to a family silversmithing business that originated in 1820, Puiforcat established himself as the unrivalled *orfèvre* of the 20th century in an abridged and itinerant career disrupted in part by two world wars. He was mobilized at the start of the First World War, and returned to his native Paris after the hostilities had ended. There he joined his father, Louis-Victor, at the workshops in the Marais district of the French capital. Puiforcat also studied at the atelier of a local sculptor, Louis Lejeune. Self-taught as a silversmith, Puiforcat searched for a contemporary aesthetic from which superfluous forms and ornamentation would be purged, especially the aberrant ones associated with the then *démodé* Art Nouveau movement. Only in the reduction of its design to its basic

function could an object realize its inherent beauty. This search for rational forms and purity of line and proportion was conceptually similar to that pursued at the time by the Bauhaus.

Puiforcat made his debut at the 1921 Salon of the *Société des Artistes Décorateurs. His evolving style was distinguished by the sharp contours and richly buffed surfaces on his silverware. Forms and proportions were based on mathematical formulae in which the straight line predominated. The industry's state-of-the-art mass-production techniques were eschewed: all surfaces were subjected to the time-honoured cycle of manual planishing and hammering. Luxurious materials, such as Brazilian rosewood, crystal, lapis lazuli, ivory, jade and rock crystal, were added selectively as handles and mounts.

These, along with *vermeil* (gilding), served
as colour accents that played off the smooth
surfaces of the silver.

Towards 1925, Puiforcat moved his family
away from the mainstream to Saint-Jean-de-Luz
on the Côte Basque. At the 1925 *Exposition
Internationale, he served as a member of both
the admissions and awards juries. In addition,
his works were displayed in several pavilions,
including that of JACQUES-ÉMILE RUHLMANN
(*see under* Furniture and Interior Decoration)
and one shared with the ceramic retailer
*Geo. Rouard. By now an acclaimed Modernist,
Puiforcat associated with the group of kindred
spirits who came together in France in the late
1920s to challenge the status quo at the annual
Salons. Among this group were *Le Corbusier,

(*top*) Tea set with tray, silver and rosewood, 1937.

(*above*) Tea service with samovar and tray,
silver and Brazilian rosewood, 1928.

(right) Clock in nickel-plated metal and white marble, designed for the clockmaker/jeweller Hour–Lavigne, 1932.

(opposite) Clock in nickel-plated metal, grey marble and tinted green glass, designed for the clockmaker Hour–Lavigne, 1927.

the furniture and interior designers CHARLOTTE PERRIAND, René *Herbst, PIERRE CHAREAU and ROBERT MALLET-STEVENS and the bookbinder PIERRE-ÉMILE LEGRAIN.

During this period, Puiforcat displayed his works in three annual Salons – those of the Société des Artistes Décorateurs, the *Société des Artistes Français and the *Salon d'Automne – plus international exhibitions and private art galleries. There he exhibited alongside other metalworkers, including *Tétard Frères, and jewellers, RAYMOND TEMPLIER, Gérard *Sandoz, JEAN FOUQUET, Jean Serrières, Robert Linzeler and the Maisons *Cardeilhac and *Lapparra. In 1928 Puiforcat resigned from the Société des Artistes Décorateurs to become a founder member of the breakaway group, *Union des Artistes Modernes (UAM), which staged its first exhibition in 1930.

About 1931, Puiforcat substituted the curve for the straight line in his designs; the set square and the ruler yielded to the compass. Now it was the circle, sphere, cone and cylinder, and segments thereof, which served as his preferred decorative vernacular. As he explained, 'I continue to think that the circle, which explains the entire world, is the ideal figure. And the curve, which approaches it, is nobler than the straight line.' His mastery of the curved line manifested itself in his triumphal display at the 1937 Exposition des Arts et Techniques in Paris, which included a selection of liturgical wares. For these, within a category of metalware stylistically unchanged throughout history,

Puiforcat managed to provide a contemporary design idiom without offending the entrenched conservatism of church ministry.

Increasingly obsessed in the late 1930s with the spectre of the impending hostilities, Puiforcat left his daughters in a Swiss boarding school, sold the house in the Basque country, and, after various delays, moved first to Spain, then Cuba and, in 1940, to Mexico, where he was joined by his wife and children the following year. Settling finally in Mexico City, he had his designs for silver flatware, table-top items and jewelry manufactured locally; they were sold mainly on the American market through upmarket retailers such as Saks Fifth Avenue and the John Rubel Fifth Avenue jewelry salon. Following the armistice in 1945, Puiforcat returned to Paris, arriving on 24 October. He died the following day after a party in his honour. His father outlived him by ten years.

(below) Clock in nickel-plated metal and grey marble, designed for the clockmaker and jeweller Hour–Lavigne, c. 1930.

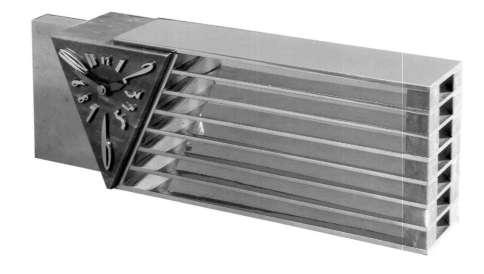

JEWELRY

The Art Deco style in jewelry traced its origins to the turn of the 20th century, when the Art Nouveau movement liberated the medium from its Victorian straitjacket. By 1900, the diamond's long reign was brought to an end by *bijoutiers* such as RENÉ LALIQUE (*see under* Glass), GEORGES FOUQUET and Henri Vever, who introduced semi-precious and even valueless materials into their Belle Époque jewelry designs. The traditional French jewelry houses – known collectively as 'La Haute Joaillerie' and clustered along Paris's rue de la Paix, Place Vendôme and rue Royale – awoke to the realization that horn, tortoise shell, ivory, enamel and mother-of-pearl had laid siege to their stock-in-trade of diamonds, rubies, emeralds and sapphires. And although the Art Nouveau style, including its jewelry, was too ornamental and flamboyant to sustain the public's interest for long (by 1905, its more extreme manifestations were on rapid retreat at the annual Salons), the world of fashion continued to embrace its use of the semi-precious gemstone.

By the 1920s, the previous hierarchy of stones had to a large extent been overthrown: jewellers no longer selected stones for their carat weight alone; now it was their colours or decorative values that took precedence and they experimented with these qualities as a painter does with his palette. Stones that had been unfashionable or neglected were rediscovered; for example, the topaz, aquamarine, amethyst, rock crystal, turquoise and tourmaline. From the Far East came enamel, lacquer, mother-of-pearl, coral, onyx and Chinese jade. Thrown into the mix, also, was the fact that conventional jewellers were not the only ones now to apply themselves to the medium: artist–designers such as JEAN DUNAND (*see under* Silver, Metal, Lacquer and Enamel), GUSTAV MIKLOS (*see under* Sculpture), JEAN PUIFORCAT (*see under* Silver, Metal, Lacquer and Enamel), Jean *Goulden and Jean *Lambert-Rucki brought their multifaceted talents to bear in the creation of a broad range of Modernist jewelry.

The great influence on Art Deco jewelry was Paris fashion prior to the First World War, so much so that a study of contemporary fashion is a prerequisite to an understanding of why certain types of jewelry evolved in the inter-war years. More than any other couturier, Paul

*Poiret transformed dress design, freeing the female figure from the constricting bustles, crinolines and whalebone corsets of the Victorian era. 'It is unthinkable', he wrote, 'for the breasts to be sealed up in solitary confinement in a fortress-like castle like the corset, as if to punish them.' His revolutionary designs, rejecting all superfluous ornamentation, transformed the female silhouette. Suddenly, dresses were long, tubular and relatively unadorned. In 1917, a line of low-waisted models replaced Poiret's slim, high-waisted dresses. Hemlines fluctuated for the first five years of the 1920s, ranging from the ankle to the calf. Then, in 1925, skirt lengths shot up to just below the knee – the length now generally associated with the era – and dropped to mid-calf in 1929. The silhouette became longer and flatter, suppressing all curves. This long, lean look adopted variously by the era's other noted couturiers – Madeleine Vionnet, Jeanne *Lanvin, Jean-Charles Worth, the Callot sisters, Gabrielle (Coco) *Chanel and Jacques Heim – necessitated a similarly simple, minimal line of jewelry.

Not only hemlines fluctuated. The neckline and the back of the dress also moved up and down, the latter plunging almost obscenely low. To accentuate the vertical line of the tubular dress, jewelry designers introduced long, dangling necklaces. *Sautoirs* of pearls and strings of beads were worn down the back, over one shoulder or wrapped around an arm. Necklaces, with suspended pendants and tassels, hung as far as the stomach or, on occasion, even to the knees. In the 'Roaring Twenties', a long necklace and short tunic dress were *de rigueur* for modern dances, such as the tango, Charleston and foxtrot.

The First World War introduced women into the workforce. Certain types of work, such as assembly-line production in armaments factories, expedited women's liberation from constrictive clothing, giving them a freedom that they would not surrender after the war. There was also a need to conserve heavy fabrics for the troops, which hastened women's acceptance of a softer, slimmer silhouette. The introduction of light materials such as rayon and muslin had an impact on the design of jewelry. New, lighter designs, often mounted in platinum, replaced heavy jewelry, which lightweight fabrics could not support.

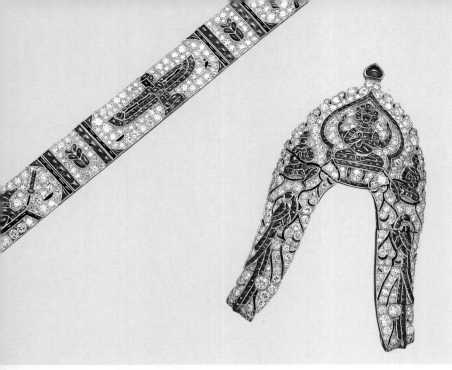

VAN CLEEF & ARPELS
Bracelet and shoulder clip, rubies, emeralds, sapphires, onyx and diamonds mounted in platinum, 1924.

To match the sleek new look, hairstyles were shortened, ushering in the boyish *garçonne* look. These changes in hair fashions also directly influenced jewelry design. Closely coiffed hair, for example, exposed the ears and neck, allowing the introduction of pendant earrings, which by 1929 had grown so long that they touched the shoulder. The cloche hat, which made its entry in the winter of 1923, was another symbol of the Art Deco period; it completely covered the head from the eyebrows to the nape of the neck, and was secured with a brooch buckle or hat dart. Because long hair or hair pinned back in a bun or chignon distorted its shape, women cut their hair into the new bobs and shingles. This, in turn, eliminated the need for the large combs, hair pins and formal tiaras and diadems of the Belle Époque era. When venturing forth without her cloche, the fashionable new woman enhanced her mannishly cropped hair with clips of stones, worn flat against the head or with a bandeau. For evening wear, the bandeau, adorned now with an aigrette, was worn on the hairline or set back on the crown of the head, like a halo.

The typical dress of the period was sleeveless, allowing the jewelry designer free rein to decorate the wrist and upper arm. Several types of bracelets evolved. Most popular were flat, flexible, narrow bands, decorated with compact, stylized designs of flowers, geometric patterns or exotic motifs, worn four or five at a time. Towards the end of the 1920s, these bands became wider. Large square links of coral, rock crystal, onyx and *pavé* diamonds were accentuated with emeralds, rubies, sapphires and other cabochon gems. Bangles or slave bracelets were worn on the upper arm or just below the elbow. Like the wrist bracelets, several of these were worn at a time. A variation for evening wear consisted of loose strands of pearls held together by a large pearl-studded medallion from which additional strings of pearls were suspended. This, too, was worn above the elbow.

The sleeveless dress and the craze for sports which evolved in the 1920s helped popularize the watch bracelet. Jean *Patou introduced the *garçonne* look into high fashion when he outfitted the tennis star Suzanne Lenglen, who came to typify the snappy new look. By day, the wristwatch was plain, with a leather or ribbon strap. The evening variety resembled a richly jewelled bracelet set with pearls and diamonds, mounted in enamelled or bicoloured gold. An example from the period by *Tiffany & Co. was set with diamonds and onyx mounted in platinum. The pendant and chatelaine watch, suspended from a ribbon or silk cord, became popular between 1925 and 1930. An example by *Van Cleef & Arpels shows the Eastern influence, with its jade, lacquer and Oriental motifs. A version for evening wear, suspended from a *sautoir* chain, was studded with pearls, diamonds and coloured gems, its case embellished with diamonds.

The new couture also did away with muffs and gloves, leaving fingers and wrists free to display a dazzling new array of matching ring and bracelet models, the latter often being articulated or worn in multicoloured sets, like bangles. Rings tended to be massive, signet-style designs, composed of a single central stone bordered by a band of small *pavé* diamonds, cabochons or semi-precious stones. The popularity of the fan for evening wear provided an additional opportunity to show off the latest in ring fashions. A large ring by Suzanne *Belperron, in carved chalcedony set with a single Oriental pearl, captured the new mood precisely. Other designers offered widely different solutions; Jean *Després, for example, combined crystal, gold and silver in abstract geometric patterns influenced by Cubism and African masks. The most versatile jewelry accessory of the inter-war era was the brooch, used not only as a corsage ornament but also to adorn belts, hats and shoulders. Almost every jeweller offered brooches designed on the theme of the stylized floral bouquet or basket of fruit, and the cascading fountain.

Another inspiration for the Art Deco jewelry designer was provided by the riot of colours which burst on to the Parisian scene before the First World War. Léon *Bakst's stage sets and costumes for the Ballets Russes, which opened in the French capital in 1909, were a kaleidoscope of oranges, bright blues and greens, which eclipsed the diaphanous, rather evanescent *fin-de-siècle* palette. The world of fashion was also seduced by the Ballets Russes' emphasis on Persian and Oriental motifs. In avant-

LACLOCHE FRÈRES
(*below*) Vanity case, enamelled gold, frosted crystal, coral, rose diamonds and lapis lazuli, 1920s.

CHARLTON & CO.
(*right*) Compact in enamelled gold and pearls, 1923; earrings by Black, Starr & Frost, diamond and coral mounted in platinum, 1926.

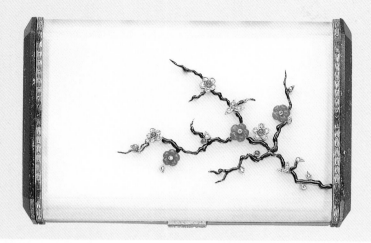

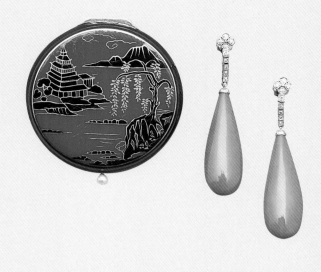

garde painting, the Fauves, who had first exhibited as a group at the 1905 *Salon d'Automne, similarly promoted the use of vibrant colours. The period's preoccupation with brightness manifested itself in jewelry design in the search for a matching palette in stones, many of which were exotic: for example, coral, jade, amber and onyx.

Art Deco jewelry motifs in the 1920s drew primarily on the vanguard painting movements in the first decade of the 20th century for a decorative vernacular. The Cubist and Constructivist movements, in particular, in their division of form into flat and overlapping geometric images, provided a major source of inspiration. Superfluous details were eliminated in the pursuit of simplification. In 1909, the Italian poet Filippo Marinetti published the *Futurist Manifesto*, which heralded the machine, urban life and speed as the visual expressions of a new reality. The Dutch painter Piet Mondrian took Cubism a step further, into Neo-Plasticism. Through abstraction, he freed forms from any suggestion of objective reality. As early as 1913, several of these new concepts were evident in jewelry design, particularly in France. In the USA, where Modernism in jewelry design was resisted fiercely for many years, a critic for *The Jewelers' Circular Weekly* asked, in 1913, 'Will the new movement in painting and sculpture – the strange, misunderstood, misinterpreted, and often ridiculed tendency in art – be reflected in the forthcoming jewelry of the Summer and Fall?' and went on to conclude that a 'vital impulse toward something new and simple is apparent on every hand'. This impulse reached its peak at the 1925 *Exposition Internationale des Arts Décoratifs et Industriels Modernes, in which the USA declined to participate due to doubts that it could meet the Modernist mandate established for entry.

In the early and mid-1920s, the principal motifs in Art Deco jewelry design were simple geometric forms – the polygon, circle and oval – which were often juxtaposed or overlapped to create complex linear configurations. Abstract patterns, derived from the architecture of ancient civilizations, such as Babylonian ziggurats and stepped Mayan and Aztec temples, likewise found their way into the contours of jewelry design.

Sir William Flinders Petrie's archaeological excavations in the first decade of the century started an Egyptomania that was accelerated by Howard Carter's hugely publicized discovery of Tutankhamun's tomb in 1922. The clean lines in hieroglyphic calligraphy reiterated the linear concepts that had begun to emerge before the war. Van Cleef & Arpels, among others, introduced stylized Egyptian motifs, such as the god Horus, lotus, ibis, scarab and sphinx, in a series of matching bracelets, shoulder clips and brooches. Stripped of their symbolic significance, these images brought a light femininity and exoticism to jewelry design. For these pieces, diamonds, rubies, emeralds and sapphires were interchanged with neutral stones such as onyx.

Further exotic influences were drawn from France's African colonies. Tribal masks and statuettes were translated into brooches by designers such as Jean Fouquet and RAYMOND TEMPLIER. Josephine Baker's successful *Revue Nègre* helped to popularize this interest, which was promoted further in the jewelry exhibition 'Les Arts Précieux' at the 1931 Exposition Coloniale. Jewellers also turned to Persia for inspiration in their creation of jewelry designed as turbans or as details from carpets and miniatures in a characteristic palette of rose pinks, jonquil yellows, mauves and cherry reds. From the Far East, jewellers and fashion houses borrowed pagodas, dragons, Chinese ideograms and fishermen on junks for their brooch designs.

As noted, Art Deco was principally a French movement. In America, the style was only reluctantly assimilated into jewelry design. Tiffany & Co., the nation's leading jewelry establishment in the 19th century, created some objects in the new style but without the crisp angularity of the Paris houses. Other jewelry firms produced items in the new idiom, but, again, without the panache of their French counterparts: for example, *Black, Starr & Frost and Udall & Ballou in New York; J. E. Caldwell & Co. and Bailey, Banks & Biddle in Philadelphia; and C. D. Peacock and Spaulding–Gorham Inc. in Chicago. Within these limitations, Art Deco jewelry in the USA followed a similar path to that taken in France: lightness and economy in the early part of the decade;

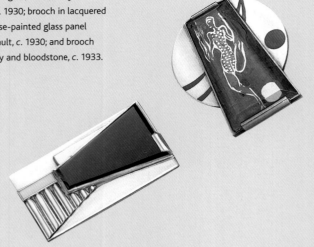

JEAN DESPRÉS
From left: Brooch in gold, silver, ivory
and bloodstone, *c.* 1930; brooch in lacquered
silver with a reverse-painted glass panel
by Étienne Cournault, *c.* 1930; and brooch
in gold, silver, ivory and bloodstone, *c.* 1933.

massiveness worn in quantity towards the end. In 1924, the major Paris houses displayed their most up-to-date creations in the French exhibition at the Grand Central Palace in New York, and though American jewelry design did not derive direct models from this exhibition, it did later become more geometric.

One genuinely new stylistic development can be discerned in American jewelry at the time: the stepped outline made its début on a few pieces, coinciding with the emergence of the skyscraper, which was transforming the skylines of major cities across the country. The image first appeared in jewelry when the Chrysler Building and the Empire State Building were under construction in the early 1930s.

Costume jewelry differs from fine jewelry in that it is made out of base metals or silver, set, for example, with marcasite, paste or imitation stones. In the 1920s, the introduction of synthetic substances brought the price of artificial jewelry within the reach of the general population. Since it was inexpensive, it had the advantage over precious jewelry that it could be discarded when styles changed. Included now with such inexpensive natural materials as amber, mother-of-pearl, tortoise shell and cultured pearls were a host of synthetic products such as galalith, celluloid, plastics, rhodoid, Perspex and Bakelite – the last-mentioned an inflammable synthetic resin named after its inventor, L. H. Baekeland. Considered at first only a substitute for natural materials, Bakelite gradually became appreciated in its own right as a major component in costume jewelry. Its palette included butterscotch, pea green, maroon and orange, either plain or with a marbled finish. Glass and *pâte-de-verre* pendants and brooches by Lalique, JOSEPH-GABRIEL ARGY-ROUSSEAU (*see under* Glass) and Almeric *Walter reinforced the fact that good design could trump a piece of jewelry's intrinsic worth.

The French dress designer Coco Chanel championed the use of costume jewelry from the early 1920s. In the 1930s, a rival of hers – the Italian fashion designer Elsa Schiaparelli – created a great stir in the French capital, where she set up a boutique at 21 Place Vendôme, which sold accessories and jewelry under her own label, including bizarre

spectacle frames and telephone bags. Drawing on the talents of some of the era's foremost designers and artists, such as Christian Bérard, Jean Cocteau, Salvador Dalí, Kees van Dongen, Alberto Giacometti and Man Ray, Schiaparelli's fashion line incorporated lively, imaginative designs and an extravagant palette. Christian Dior followed suit in the 1940s.

Exquisite accessories for the well-dressed woman of the period were produced by Van Cleef & Arpels and CARTIER, among others. Influenced by Chinese, Japanese, Persian and medieval art, these *objets d'art* combined precious stones with a mix of coloured gemstones, enamel and lacquer. The small cigarette cases designed by Gérard *Sandoz, Dunand and Paul-Émile *Brandt introduced a further type of decoration by incorporating crushed **coquille d'œuf** panels. Whatever its intended use, each item was also a miniature work of art.

The *nécessaire* (vanity case) took its form from the Japanese *inro* (a small case that contained compartments for medicines). Although small, it accommodated all essential accoutrements: mirror, compact, lipstick and comb. Mostly rectangular, oblong or oval, and hung from a silk cord, *nécessaires* were often decorated with Persian and Chinese hunting scenes, pagodas, birds of paradise or Egyptian temples in a lavish mix of materials. In 1930, the *nécessaire* was enlarged into the *minaudière* by Alfred Van Cleef, who gave it the name after witnessing his wife *minauder* (simper) into the mirror. The *minaudière* replaced the evening bag, *pochette* and daytime dress bag. Cigarette, lipstick and card cases were decorated with the same mix of materials.

Art Deco handbags were made of luxurious fabrics or exotic skins with gold or platinum frames and clasps. Gemstones embellished with faceted or cabochon rubies, emeralds, sapphires and diamonds studded the frames. Semi-precious stones, carved with Egyptian and Oriental motifs, were used for the clasps. Evening bags by *Lacloche Frères and *Chaumet were embroidered with sequins sewn on to the fabric. *Mauboussin designed elaborate evening bags with diamond and emerald clasps to match brooches and bracelets.

JEAN GOULDEN
(*left*) Box in silver and *champlevé* enamel, 1927.

AUGUSTE BONAZ
(*below*) Necklaces in galalith, *c.* 1923–24.

The Art Deco style was applied also to men's jewelry, but with less flare. Pocket watches were given geometric dials and mounted in platinum set with onyx, diamonds, pearls, emeralds, rubies and topazes. Watch chains consisted of cylindrical links enhanced with polished or faceted stones. Cufflinks incorporated the same general shapes. Jean Fouquet designed a notable pair of cufflinks with enamelled Cubist motifs, while Black, Starr & Frost's selection included onyx cufflinks with diamond borders.

The top jewelry houses included in their repertoire a range of luxury goods comprising the same materials as their pieces of personal adornment: table-top items such as paperweights, pen trays, lighters, match boxes, photograph frames, toiletry receptacles and clocks had precious and semi-precious stones set against a background of enamelled *guilloché* gold, coral and mother-of-pearl. Unsurpassed in the clock category were Cartier's 'mystery clocks' in which the hands appeared to float in space. These were in reality attached to a rock crystal disc with a notched metal rim driven by worm-gears concealed in the base or the frame of the clock case. Cartier apparently made close to one hundred examples of this clock between 1913 and 1930.

As in most disciplines of the decorative arts, the 1925 Exposition Internationale represented the pinnacle of 'high-style' Art Deco in French jewelry. Beyond France, however, the style had few adherents, and the foreign entries did not on the whole reflect the geometric style which had dominated modern taste in Paris since the First World War.

Georges Fouquet of La Maison FOUQUET was elected chairman of the selection committee for the Exposition's *parure* section. Under his leadership, the committee decided that only works of new inspiration and originality would be accepted. Objects had to be submitted anonymously; the names of the designers and firms whose works were chosen were omitted from the showcases. Of the nearly four hundred entries, comprising individual jewellers and companies, only thirty were accepted under the Modernist label mandated for acceptance. The principal exhibitors were Chaumet, Dusausoy, Fouquet, Lacloche Frères,

Linzeler & Marchak, Boivin, Mauboussin, Mellerio, *Ostertag and Van Cleef & Arpels. Frédéric *Boucheron was represented with creations by Lucien Hirtz, Masse and John Rubel, which included two remarkable corsage ornaments characteristic of the Art Deco style. Both were of scalloped lapis lazuli, jade and onyx, combined with matt coral and turquoise within diamond-studded borders in geometric patterns resembling miniature mosaics.

The artist–jewellers Raymond Templier, Paul-Émile Brandt and Gérard Sandoz contributed outstanding examples in new and original materials. Maison Fouquet was represented by the architect Eric *Bagge, the graphic artist CASSANDRE (ADOLPHE MOURON) (see under Paintings, Graphics, Posters and Bookbinding), the painter André *Leveillé, Louis Fertey and Georges Fouquet's son, Jean, who had joined the family firm in 1919. Leveillé and Fertey received grand prix awards, and Cassandre and Jean Fouquet honourable mentions. Leveillé's designs recalled the overlapping images in Picasso and Braque collages, while Cassandre adapted the mandolin, a motif popularized by Picasso, into the design for a brooch.

In 1929, the Exposition des Arts de la Bijouterie, Joaillerie, Orfèvrerie was held at the Musée Galliera in Paris. Only one truly novel piece of jewelry was displayed – a large diamond-studded tie-pin by Van Cleef & Arpels. The diamond now once again reigned supreme, cut in the new baguette style and juxtaposed with contrasting stones. Boucheron introduced a baguette-cut diamond bracelet, edged with sapphires, while Mauboussin incorporated diamonds on to the tassel of a large sapphire collar. The coloured diamond, out of fashion since the late 19th century, also returned to favour. Lacloche Frères displayed a brooch and bracelet set with canary diamonds.

By 1930, the abstract geometric configurations of the 1925 Exposition Internationale had evolved into mechanistic forms based on industrial design and machine parts. The engineering principles inherent in car and aeroplane construction inspired a new decorative vocabulary for jewelry, including crankshafts, cams, gears, cogs and ball bearings.

These forms were often executed in stainless steel or chromed metal, which was appropriate in a chastened economic climate. Being symbolic of the Machine Age, they usurped the medium's conventional materials of gold, silver or platinum. In the vanguard of the new asceticism were Jean Fouquet, Sandoz and Templier, who switched from the *Société des Artistes Décorateurs in the late 1920s to the vanguard *Union des Artistes Modernes (UAM), where they were joined by Jean Després and Brandt.

The Wall Street crash struck a fatal blow to the sales of luxury items. After 1929, multiple-use jewelry (made of two or more components which could be dismantled and used separately) came into vogue. Pendants could double as brooches or be attached to lapels. A double barrette was constructed from two linked parts which could be worn separately. Tiffany & Co. designed a necklace which came apart to form either a pendant and two bracelets, or a pendant and a choker.

As the economic effects of the Depression deepened, firms were hesitant to produce new items which might prove difficult to sell. In 1931, when entries were solicited for the Exposition Coloniale in the Bois de Vincennes outside Paris, only twenty-three firms participated. Although some exhibited jewelry embellished with colonial themes such as African masks, most contributed objects from existing inventory. Throughout the 1930s, major jewelry houses cut back their staff or closed. In 1936, Art Deco's grandest house, the Maison Fouquet, ceased major production. In the USA, Tiffany's remained open, but with a skeleton staff. By the mid-1930s, the industry had begun to rebound, its designs inspired now increasingly by aerodynamics – a public obsession at a time when air and land speed records were repeatedly toppled. The streamlined new jewelry forms included narrowly spaced serpentine bands or rows of fins that alluded to speed.

JEAN DESPRÉS

(*opposite, left*) Necklace in silver and ivory, probably 1920s.

SIMMEN-BLANCHE

(*opposite, right*) Coupe, ivory with rock crystal handles, *c.* 1910.

UNIDENTIFIED ARTIST

(*below*) Necklaces in chromium-plated metal and Bakelite, *c.* 1925.

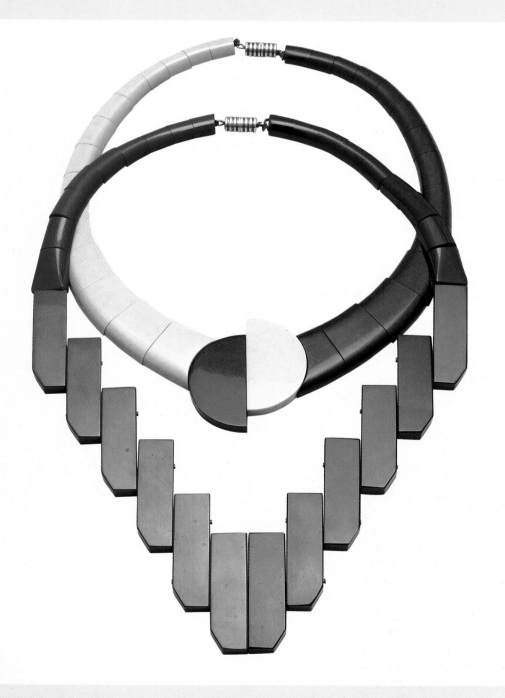

CARTIER

FOUQUET

RAYMOND TEMPLIER

Four successive generations of the Cartier family established the Maison Cartier as a jewelry dynasty. Louis-François Cartier (1819–1904) opened his first jewelry shop at 29 rue Montorgueil, Paris, in 1847, from where he moved in 1853 to 5 rue Neuve-des-Petits-Champs. He became the favourite jeweller of Princesse Mathilde (a cousin of Napoleon III) and Empress Eugénie. In 1859, the Maison Cartier moved to 9 boulevard des Italiens. On the retirement of Louis-François following the Franco-Prussian war, his son Alfred (1841–1925) succeeded him. Alfred, in turn, was followed by his three sons: Louis (1875–1942), who moved the Paris showroom in 1899 to 13 rue de la Paix; Pierre (1878–1965), who established the New York branch in 1909; and Jacques (1884–1942), who administered the London branch (which opened in 1902). In 1945, Jean-Jacques, one of the founder's great-grandsons, was placed in charge of the London operation; three years later Claude (1925–1975), another great-grandson, was appointed president of Cartier in New York.

The years 1900–15 witnessed the triumph of La Maison Cartier, which was patronized by crowned heads of Europe, maharajahs, Oriental potentates and a 'who's-who' of the industrial world's *nouveaux riches*, including American tycoons such as the Vanderbilts, Morgans, Goulds and Astors. In 1910, branches were added in Moscow and the Persian Gulf, and in 1913 the firm introduced the first of its celebrated mystery clocks.

At the beginning of the century, partly through the impact of the Ballets Russes, Maison Cartier began to adapt the 'high-style' ornamentation and palette that came to dominate the Paris Salons in the early 1920s. Louis Cartier, the creative genius within the family, worked closely with the firm's various designers, notably Charles Jacqueau and Jeanne Toussaint, who provided the technical expertise to transform his designs into practical models. These, in turn, were sent to a network of top Paris workshops, such as that of Maurice Couet, a clock technician whose grandfather had worked for Breguet. Louis is credited with many of the firm's innovations in these years, such as the introduction of platinum into *haute joaillerie* and the promotion of such luxury goods as pendulettes, *nécessaires* and powder compacts.

At the 1925 *Exposition Internationale, the firm did not participate with the other jewellers in the Grand Palais, instead opting to exhibit with the fashion houses in the Pavillon de l'Élégance. In a dizzying array of jewelry, including ear clips, bracelets, tassel pendants, necklaces, fibula brooches, jabot pins, chokers and stomachers, there were three pieces that the press corps considered of special merit: a *décolleté* brooch, an emerald-studded shoulder ornament and the 'Berenice' tiara. For these, and for the bejewelled objects of *virtu* on view, Cartier offered a range of ornamentation as varied as the items themselves: Islamic art (stars and geometrical themes derived from carpets), chinoiserie (dragons, chimeras, pagodas and Buddhas); Egyptology (Tutankhamun-inspired temples, hieroglyphics, sphinxes, the god Horus, scarabs, lotuses and sarcophagi); and the prevailing 'high-style' Art Deco (baskets of fruit and flowers in carved gemstones).

Cartier continued to generate spectacular new works throughout the 1930s and to open new branches (Monte Carlo in 1935, and Cannes in 1938). In 1940, during the German occupation of Paris, it moved its operations temporarily to Biarritz.

In 1972 and 1974, Cartier's Paris and London operations were purchased by the same investor group, and in 1976 another group acquired the New York operation. Three years later, the three were merged.

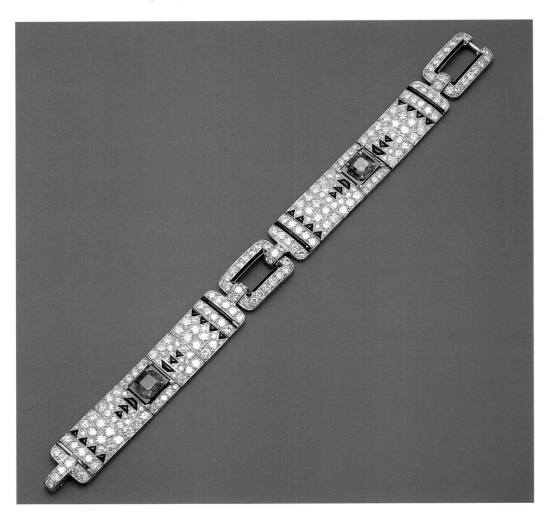

(*opposite*) Bracelet in diamonds and emeralds, *c.* 1925.

(*above*) Brooch in diamonds, rubies, emeralds, sapphires and onyx mounted in platinum, *c.* 1921.

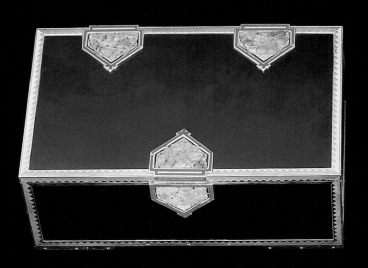
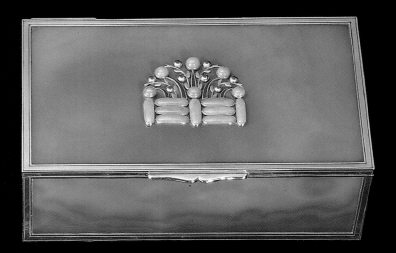

(*opposite*) (*above left*) Casket in onyx, jadeite, diamonds and enamel, *c.* 1930; (*above right*) casket in agate, jadeite, coral and enamel, *c.* 1930; (*below left*) Chinese-style *bonbonnière* in *laque burgauté*, coral and enamel, 1925; (*below right*) Chinese-style *bonbonnière* in *laque burgauté* and lapis lazuli, 1925.

(*right*) Mystery clock in rock crystal, mother-of-pearl, diamonds, coral and enamelled gold, 1926.

(*above*) Cigarette box in gold, silver, enamel, lacquer, coral, onyx and diamonds, 1920s.

(*right*) Sarcophagus-style jewelry casket in coral and lacquer with gold and silver mounts, 1920s/1930s.

FOUQUET

Born in Alençon, Alphonse Fouquet (1828–1911) moved to Paris as a young boy, where he underwent an apprenticeship with a novelty jeweller in the Marais district. Working independently from 1860, often in collaboration with other jewellers, he exhibited at the 1878 Exposition Internationale before opening a showroom in avenue de l'Opéra the following year. In 1891 he was joined by his son, Georges Fouquet (1862–1957), and by his son-in-law, who together helped the Maison Fouquet adjust stylistically to the Art Nouveau impulses initiated by RENÉ LALIQUE (see under Glass) in the mid-1890s. Alphonse retired in 1895, later writing his memoirs, *Histoire de ma vie industrielle*, under the pseudonym Jules Dragon.

Georges was born in Paris. On succeeding his father, he determined in 1899 to consolidate Fouquet's position within the market by retaining the designer Charles Desrosiers (a teacher at a drawing school in Paris and a jewelry designer) and the graphic artist Alphonse Mucha to provide the firm with progressive jewelry designs for its exhibit at the 1900 Exposition Universelle. A year later, Fouquet opened the showroom at 6 rue Royale, designed by Mucha with a street façade in a rampant Art Nouveau style.

In the immediate post-war years, Georges redirected the firm's naturalistic designs towards a more Modernist idiom, emphasizing geometric shapes and a more vibrant palette. He was joined after the First World War by his son, Jean Fouquet (1899–1984), and a team

of designers that included Louis Fertey (the studio's overseer), Desrosiers, Eric *Bagge, CASSANDRE (see under Paintings, Graphics and Bookbinding) and the painter André *Leveillé. These were followed in 1936 by Jean *Lambert-Rucki, who contributed Cubist and tribal art designs.

Fouquet played a leading part in the 1925 *Exposition Internationale and in later exhibitions. After the closure of the firm in 1936, Georges continued to work for his regular clients. The firm's archives and designs were bequeathed to the Musée des Arts Décoratifs, Paris.

Paris-born Jean studied classics and literature before joining his father at the Maison Fouquet in 1919. A gifted Modernist designer, he exploited to the full the emerging taste for abstract compositions in jewelry and *objets d'art*. Making his international debut at the 1925 Exposition Internationale, Jean published *Bijoux et orfèvrerie* in 1928. From 1925, he participated in numerous exhibitions for Fouquet as well as under his own name at the *Salon d'Automne in 1926 and 1928, and at the Salon of the *Société des Artistes Décorateurs in 1928. He became a founding member of the *Union des Artistes Modernes (UAM), with which he exhibited from 1930 to 1932. Between the closure of the Maison Fouquet in 1936 and his semi-retirement in 1961, Jean worked with private clients, for whom he designed jewelry, mostly rings that were of simple and bold square form. His early use of precious stones gave way increasingly to hard stones, including rock crystal, onyx and aquamarines, which he mounted in platinum, silver, and white and yellow gold, accented with black lacquer. Notable were his series of *demi-parures* and *roulement* à *billes* (ball-bearing) bracelets rendered in a uncompromising modern style. Jean finally retired in 1974.

Jean Fouquet

(*left, abo*) Pendant in platinum, diamonds, sapphires and black onyx, 1927.

(*left*) Pendant and chain in polished platinum, cabochon sapphire and diamonds, 1929.

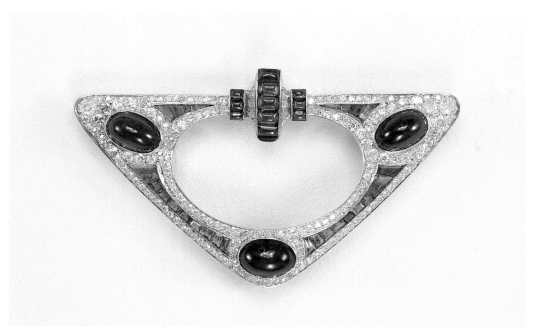

Georges Fouquet

(*top left*) Brooch in diamonds, sapphires, and emeralds mounted in platinum, *c*. 1922–23.

(*top right*) Necklace in rock crystal, onyx, diamonds and seed pearls mounted in platinum, *c*. 1925.

(*above*) Pendant in diamonds, jade and onyx, 1920s.

(*left*) Necklace in rock crystal and diamonds mounted in platinum, *c*. 1925.

Jean Fouquet

(*below*) Bracelet in white gold, diamonds and jade, 1928–29.

(*bottom*) Bracelet and ring in gold and topaz, c. 1937.

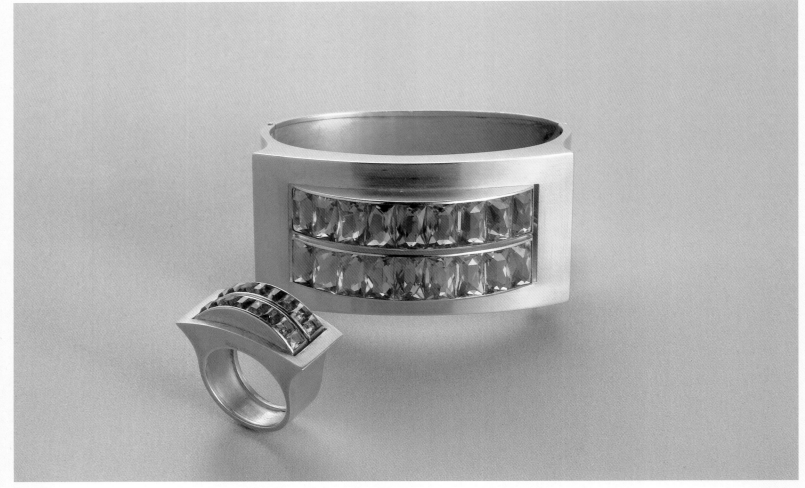

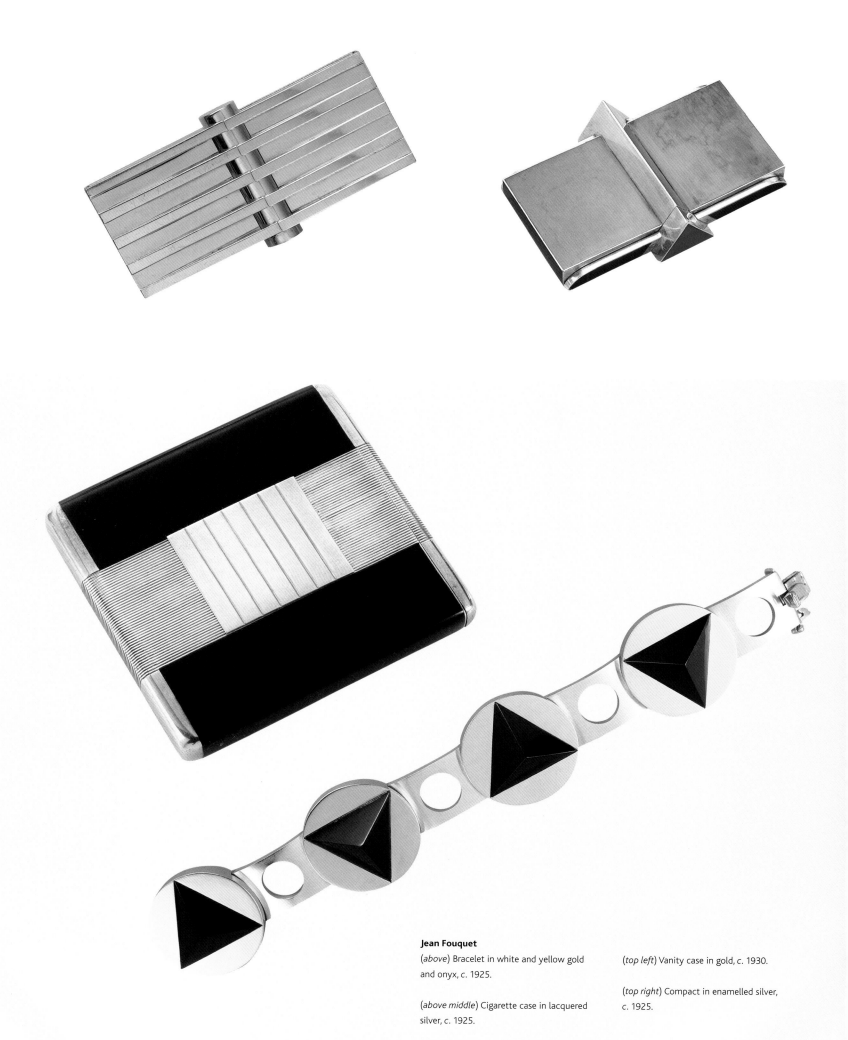

Jean Fouquet

(*above*) Bracelet in white and yellow gold and onyx, *c.* 1925.

(*above middle*) Cigarette case in lacquered silver, *c.* 1925.

(*top left*) Vanity case in gold, *c.* 1930.

(*top right*) Compact in enamelled silver, *c.* 1925.

RAYMOND TEMPLIER (1891–1968)

Born in Paris into a dynasty of ***bijoutiers–joailliers***, this grandson of Charles Templier (who had founded the family jewelry house in 1849) studied at the city's École Nationale Supérieure des Arts Décoratifs from 1909 to 1912, during which time he began to exhibit at the Salons of the *Société des Artistes Décorateurs. Raymond joined his father, Paul, in the business in 1919.

Raymond Templier's designs, based on strict mathematical formulae, were for the most part resolutely geometric. He favoured enamel, lacquer and semi-precious stones, such as peridots, brilliants and aquamarines, mounted in platinum. Within his jewelry repertoire, Templier became known for his diadems and pendant earrings. In 1928, he designed the famous ***parure*** worn by the actress Brigitte Helm in Marcel L'Herbier's film *L'Argent*. A founder member of the *Union des Artistes Modernes (UAM), in 1929 he took over the Maison Templier's administration from his father in 1935.

Also in 1929, Marcel Percheron, likewise a graduate of the École Nationale Supérieure des Arts Décoratifs, joined Templier. For the next thirty or so years they collaborated in the creation of minutely detailed geometric jewelry designs. Templier did not work directly in the firm in the last years of his life, at which point it was administered by Percheron.

(*above*) Cigarette case in lacquered silver inset with *coquille d'œuf*, 1928.

(*top*) Bracelet in enamelled silver, *c*. 1927.

(*above*) Bracelet in silver, *c*. 1930.

(below) Four sketches of rings designed
by Templier, c. 1930.

(below) Brooch in diamonds and enamel
mounted in platinum, c. 1935.

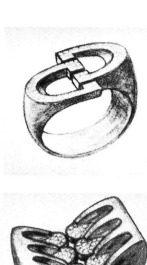

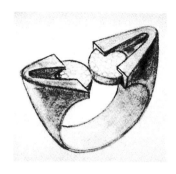

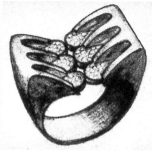

(right) Bracelet with detachable brooch
in diamonds, gold, silver, platinum and onyx,
c. 1925–30.

PART 2

A–Z OF DESIGNERS, ARTISTS AND MANUFACTURERS

Jacques Adnet

(*right*) Nest of tables in oak
veneered with parchment,
c. 1937.

A

Adler, **Rose** (1890–1959). *See under* Paintings, Graphics, Posters and Bookbinding.

Adnet, **Jacques** (1900–1984)

Jacques and his twin brother Jean were born at Châtillon-Coligny, in Burgundy. They spent their adolescence in Auxerre, attending the municipal school of design, in 1916 transferring to the École Nationale Supérieure des Arts Décoratifs in Paris, where they studied architecture under Charles Genuys. After graduation, Jacques worked briefly for Tony Selmersheim, perfecting his cabinetry skills. On being demobilized after the First World War, the twins joined *La Maîtrise, where MAURICE DUFRÈNE became a mentor and close friend. From 1923, the twins worked together on numerous projects, sharing credit at the Salons under a joint name: J.-J. Adnet.

In the 1920s, the Adnets designed a selection of ceramic table-top wares, mainly figurines and animals, in an angular style for La Maîtrise; these were manufactured by the Faïencerie de Montereau in a crackled ivory glaze. At the 1925 *Exposition Internationale, the twins had their own stand on the Esplanade des Invalides as well as exhibiting in the Ambassade Française and La Maîtrise pavilions. Three years later, they parted company: Jacques accepted the directorship of the Compagnie des Arts Français, while Jean remained at La Maîtrise, where he became a sales manager for Les Galeries Lafayette.

Jacques changed the charter of the Compagnie des Arts Français, rejecting its emphasis on the past. As noted by Louis Cheronnet in his monograph *Jacques Adnet*, published in 1948 by *Art et Industrie*:

> His aesthetic preoccupations are different. Born with the century, he feels no nostalgia. His only thought is that this century, whose new beauty is slowly revealing itself in photography and the cinema, a

century of the precision machine and of speed, a century of the aeroplane, electricity and steel, must discover in design meaningful analogies in greater harmony with its means and outward appearance.

By 1928 Jacques's style was distinctly avant-garde, comparable even with the work of contemporaries such as Jean Lurçat, Louis *Sognot and Michel *Dufet. His initial furniture incorporated woods – often exotic species, such as peroba and bubienga – but underwent a sharp transition in 1930 to chromed metal, the shelves and doors embellished as before with a combination of mirror, leather, *galuchat*, parchment and – his favourite medium – smoked glass. Designs became increasingly streamlined; the mounts, never pronounced, were now barely visible. A rigidly functional aesthetic was pursued, with ornamentation pared away wherever possible. A 1930 quote summed up the battle being waged: 'What a lot of work to achieve simplicity.'

Imbued with *Le Corbusier's belief that a house is a *machine à habiter*, Adnet's light fixtures – mainly chandeliers and desk lamps, based on sharp geometric design principles – showed the same philosophy of stark functionalism and novelty that he applied to all aspects of his ensembles, such as his chromed nickel tubular furniture. In one chandelier the metal rods that protrude from a central column to house the tubular frosted bulbs are perpendicular to the column; in another they are triangular; while in a third the rods and tubular bulbs are opposed to one another in zigzag fashion. Almost nowhere is there a concession to ornamentation, the influence of contemporary *machinisme* being ever-present.

In the late 1920s Jacques exhibited several interiors at the Salons that were marketed by *Saddier et ses Fils. Within five years, many decorators had adopted his *machinisme*, claiming it as their own. The 1930s brought a wide range of prestigious commissions, including state ministries, universities and ocean liners.

His collaborators included Édouard *Schenck (nickel and glass), Mme Léone Huet (carpets and fabrics), Louis *Gigou (furniture mounts), Jean *Besnard (ceramics) and J. & L. Bernard (paintings). At the 1937 Exposition des Arts et Techniques, Jacques collaborated with René Coulon on the Saint-Gobain pavilion, which had glass brick walls. He remained at the Compagnie des Arts Français until it closed in 1959, at which point he accepted the directorship of the École Nationale Supérieure des Arts Décoratifs.

Albers, **Anneliese (Anni)** (1899–1994)

Born in Berlin-Charlottenburg, Albers (née Fleischmann) studied weaving at the Kunstgewerbeschule in Hamburg and in her native city before entering the Bauhaus in Weimar in 1922. There she studied under Johannes Itten and Paul Klee and experimented with silk, cotton and linen yarns for weavings, hangings and textiles. Her philosophy was that the raw materials and their components should become the source of beauty without being overpowered by the design. At the Bauhaus she met Josef Albers (1888–1976), a teacher, writer, sculptor, painter and colour theorist, whom she married in 1925, the year the school moved to Dessau.

In 1933 the couple emigrated to the USA, where Josef had accepted a position on the faculty of Black Mountain College near Asheville, North Carolina. There, until 1949, Albers made weavings, developed new textiles and taught. In 1950, the Albers moved to New Haven, Connecticut, where Josef had been appointed chairman of the department of design at Yale University's School of Art.

One of the foremost textile designers of the 20th century, Albers revolutionized the look of the modern household. Central to her philosophy was the series of Art Deco hand-knitted rugs that she designed and executed. Among the books she authored were *On Designing* (1961) and *On Weaving* (1965). She added printmaking to her repertoire in 1963.

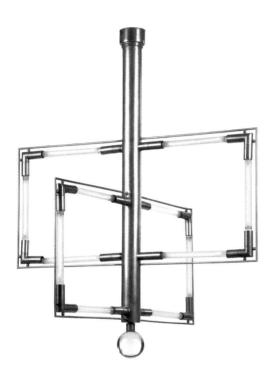

Jacques Adnet

(*top*) Ceiling fixture, nickel-plated copper with frosted glass tubes, for La Compagnie des Arts Français, late 1920s.

(*above*) Chandelier, nickel-plated copper with frosted glass tubes, for La Compagnie des Arts Français, c. 1929.

(*right*) Table lamp, pewter with glass globe, 1929.

Alexandre Alexeieff
The Night Scotsman,
lithographic poster, 1932.

Alexeieff, Alexandre (1901–1982)

Born in Kazan, Russia, Alexeieff spent his early childhood near Istanbul, where his father served as a military attaché. In 1921 he left for France, where he studied illustrative art and animation before working as a commercial artist and poster designer.

In 1930 Alexeieff married Claire Parker (1910–1981), a wealthy American student with whom he formed a life-long partnership directing animated short films and commercials. These employed a pin-screen technique that produced images resembling a mezzotint. A chronicle of his work, entitled *Alexeieff – Itinerary of a Master*, edited by Giannalberto Bendazzi, was published in 2001.

Amphora

In 1892 the firm of Reissner, Stellmacher & Kessel was founded in what is now the town of Trovany in the former Turn–Teplitz region of Bohemia for the commercial manufacture of porcelain and stoneware. Its partners were Hans and Carl Reissner, Edward Stellmacher and Rudolf Kessel. The factory's site was chosen for its proximity to Dresden in eastern Germany, which had a long and distinguished tradition of ceramic manufacturing.

Making its international début at the World's Columbian Exposition of 1893 in Chicago, the firm produced porcelain with *flambé* glazes and elaborately sculpted works in terracotta. Some were decorated by Michael Mortl and Arthur Strasser with gold detailing and inset hard stones. In 1905, when Stellmacher left to set up his own business, the company continued as the Reissner & Kessel Amphora Works until 1910, when Kessel also departed. Renamed the Amphora Werke Reissner, the firm continued through the inter-war years and the Second World War before being nationalized by the Czech government in 1945.

Among Amphora's standard repertory of revivalist designs was a line of household accessories, including figurines, jardinières, vases and toiletry items, designed in the Modernist idiom. In the inter-war years, as previously, the firm's wares were marketed under the trade name Amphora, but were referred to also as 'Teplitz', like those of the many other ceramic manufactories in the Turn–Teplitz region, which included the Imperial Technical School for Ceramics & Associated Applied Arts where many of Amphora's designers and artisans were recruited.

Arbus, André-Léon (1903–1969)

Born into a family of Toulouse cabinet-makers, Arbus attended the city's *lycée* before entering the École Militaire de Saint-Cyr to study law. His free hours were spent in his father's cabinetry workshop at 34 rue de Metz. Ill health forced a switch from the military academy to the École des Beaux-Arts, where Arbus met the sculptor Henri Parayre, who became a friend and mentor. On graduating, Arbus joined his father, whom he succeeded on the latter's retirement. He immediately eliminated the firm's stock-in-trade, 18th-century furniture styles, replacing them with a range of modern designs, labelling himself both a Modernist and a decorator. Arbus never practised cabinetry himself, content to leave the execution of his sketches and maquettes to the firm's journeyman *ébénistes*.

Arbus made his début at the Salons in 1926, and moved to the capital four years later, where he opened his gallery, L'Époque, at 22 rue la Boétie. He participated in the Salon of the *Société des Artistes Décorateurs, the *Salon d'Automne and the Salon des Tuileries, as well as La Galerie des Quatre-Chemins. Collaborators included Paule Marrot (upholstery), Marc Saint-Saëns (a painter and fellow Toulousian), Vadim Androusov (sculpted decoration in wood, gesso and terracotta), Belmondo (bas reliefs), Gilbert *Poillerat (wrought iron) and *Bagues Frères (lighting).

The 1930s generated countless commissions and an unanticipated bonus – the Prix Blumenthal in 1935. Arbus continued to seize every opportunity to exhibit: among the most prestigious venues were the 1935 Exposition de Bruxelles, the 1937 Exposition des Arts et Techniques and the 1939 New York World's Fair. The post-war period brought an even busier schedule – the ministries of Agriculture and Armaments joined the ever-expanding list of clients.

Arbus rejected painting and marquetry as forms of furniture ornamentation, preferring to decorate his furniture with a combination of finely grained veneers, parchment, *galuchat*, lacquer or bleached animal hide. The furniture's frame, often in sycamore with key plates and mounts in metal, generated the intended aura of sumptuousness. His inspiration was classical – in most part Louis XVI and the First and Second Empires. His light, angular forms proved popular but were not distinctive; they are today often difficult to distinguish from those of his co-exhibitors, especially Jean Prouvé, Étienne *Kohlmann and Pierre Petit. Much of Arbus's finest furniture was manufactured in the 1940s and 1950s. He remained in Paris until his death.

Argy-Rousseau, Joseph-Gabriel (1885–1953).

See under Glass.

Arthur Goldscheider

Opened in Paris in 1892, this French branch of the Viennese firm *Friedrich Goldscheider incorporated a showroom at 45 rue de Paradis and a bronze foundry in the city's outskirts. Four years later a further showroom was opened at 28 avenue de l'Opéra, where many of the firm's Austrian products were offered.

When Arthur Goldscheider was placed in charge of the French operation, one of his goals was to cultivate works by French sculptors and foreign sculptors living in France. At the outbreak of the First World War, Arthur severed all connections with the parent firm and became a naturalized Frenchman. After the war, he set up two artistic groups: L'Évolution, which organized exhibitions of its members' designs; and La Stèle, which produced and marketed their works.

Amphora

(*far right*) Glazed earthenware vase, *c.* 1930.

(*right*) Glazed earthenware vase, designed by Max von Jungwirth, 1920s.

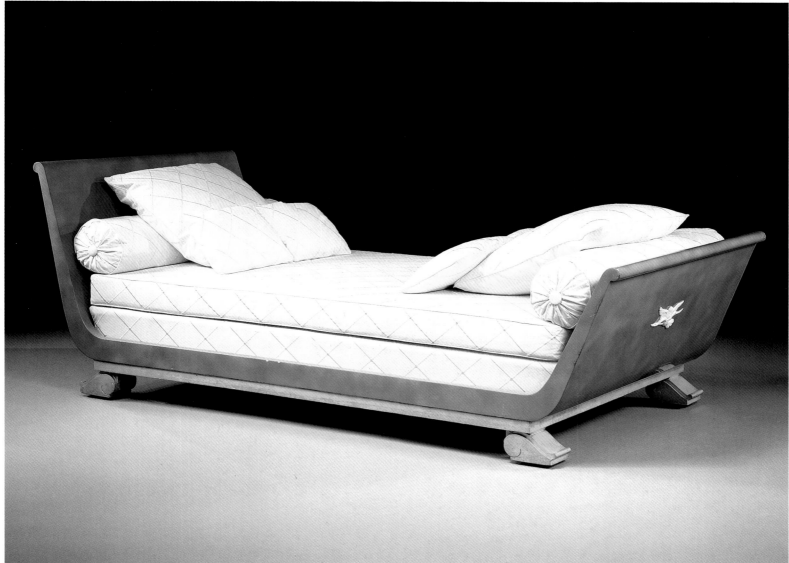

André-Léon Arbus

Lacquered and gilt-wood daybed, with carved ivory dove medallion by Vadim Androusov, c. 1937.

Émile Just Bachelet

(*below left*) *Femme nue voilé*, carved ivory on marble base, 1930s.

(*below right*) *Venus et l'Amour*, carved ivory, 1920s.

(*right*) Condor in glazed terracotta, executed by the Manufacture Nationale de Sevrès, *c.* 1939.

Oscar Bruno Bach

(*right*) Selection of light fixtures, patinated bronze and metal, two with Steuben 'Aurene' glass shades, 1920s.

Félix Aublet
Table lamp in nickel-plated metal, 1930.

For the 1925 *Exposition Internationale, Eric *Bagge was retained to design the Goldscheider pavilion, which included sections for La Stèle to display sculpture, and L'Évolution to show decorative objects in other disciplines. Represented in these displays were works by Pierre *Le Faguays, Sibylle May, Éduoard *Cazaux, DEMETRE CHIPARUS, Claire Jeanne Roberte *Colinet, Marcel Bouraine, JOËL MARTEL, Max Blondat, Alexandre *Kelety, Raoul-Eugène *Lamourdedieu, Pierre-Charles *Lenoir, Fanny Rozet and Carlo Sarrabezolles.

Asplund, Erik Gunnar (1885–1940)

Stockholm-born Asplund is now considered one of the pioneers of modern Scandinavian design. In 1909 he received a diploma in architecture. Rejecting Neoclassicism in the 1920s, he promoted an architecture of steel and glass. Pursuing this philosophy in his furniture designs, Asplund formulated simplified, well-balanced and expressive shapes, such as his 'Senna' chair (1925) in walnut upholstered in leather (manufactured by David Blomberg of Stockholm) and the 'Goteborg 1' and 'Goteborg 2' chair models in 1934 (both produced by Cassina).

As an architect, Asplund designed numerous housing complexes, shops, the Stockholm Municipal Library, the Town Hall and Palace of Justice in Gothenburg, and the crematorium in a cemetery south of Stockholm (1936–40). He also designed the Swedish pavilion at the 1925 *Exposition Internationale and others for the 1930 Stockholm Exhibition.

L'Atlantique. See Normandie.

Aublet, Félix (1903–1978)

The son of the Orientalist painter Albert Aublet, Aublet studied at the École des Beaux-Arts, Paris, and in the atelier of the painter Fernand Cormon. He made his début as a designer in 1928 in Zurich, where he exhibited an adjustable chair in tubular metal. At the 1931 Exposition Coloniale in Paris he showed further furnishings in tubular metal, and in the following year he created a mechanical table in steel and tubular metal for the Parisian apartment of François Pernod.

Aublet is today known almost exclusively for his light fixtures, including a *torchère* with an upturned shade in nickelled metal. His best-known table model was an adjustable shade, mounted on a weighted spherical base held within three talon-like arms that allowed it to swivel or tilt in any direction. It was produced in two sizes and with various finishes: the larger in **vieil argent** coated in Duco – an artificial lacquer impermeable to heat and cold.

B

Bach, Oscar Bruno (1884–1957)

Born in Breslau, Germany, Bach studied at the city's Catholic gymnasium (1890–98) and the Königliche Akademie der Künste in Berlin (1898–1902), during which time he completed a four-year apprenticeship in metallurgy and metallic art. He then joined a Hamburg foundry. At the age of eighteen he completed his first major commission: a Bible binding in wrought metal encrusted with jewels and precious stones ordered by the British government as a gift for Pope Leo XIII's Vatican library. After working in Berlin (1904), where he designed the architectural metalware for the City Hall, and in Venice (1908), Bach participated in the 1911 Turin Exposition, where he won a *grand prix*. The following year he set sail on the SS *Argentina* from Trieste for New York, where he joined his older brother, Max, who had emigrated in 1904.

The two opened a studio at 257 West 17th Street in Manhattan. The reputation of the business grew as orders poured in for residential and commercial ornamental metalware from interior designer firms and architects – the latter including Herman Brookman, Harvie T. Lindberg and Charles B. Delk. By 1922, Bach's studio was located at 257 West 77th Street. The following year it moved to 511 West 42nd Street, and then to 610 Fifth Avenue. A long-running feud during these years involved copyright issues with Bertram A. Seger, who had financed Bach's initial business and later purchased his studios. Eventually it was resolved in court.

Bach's solid grounding in European art enabled him to produce works spanning the range of revivalist styles, from Gothic to American Renaissance to Modernist. Included were entrance grilles, mantels, stairways, light fixtures, radiator grilles, furniture, candlesticks, andirons, bookends, memorial plaques and liturgical objects such as pulpits and lecterns. Interchanging materials and techniques to achieve the contrasting textural and colour effects sought for each piece, Bach worked in enamelled and *repoussé* copper, bronze, aluminium, chromed nickel steel and **duralumin** – a shiny aluminium-copper-manganese alloy introduced into the market in the early 1930s, which he favoured for his later Modernist works.

Among a host of commissions, many today still unidentified, were: decorative metalware for two American Lines ships, the *Washington* and the *Manhattan*; the Bank of New York & Trust Co. at 48 Wall Street (c. 1929); the Chrysler Building (a chromed nickel directory board and show windows, 1931); the Earl Carroll Theater (1931); the Empire State Building (1931); Radio City Music Hall (four exterior plaques designed by Hildreth Meiere, 1932); and Temple Emanu-El (sanctuary lanterns). A 1928 monograph by Matlack Price, *Design & Craftsmanship in Metals: The Creative Art of Oscar B. Bach*, chronicled and paid tribute to his work.

Bachelet, Émile Just (b. 1892)

Little is known of the early life and training of the French sculptor Bachelet, who today is best known for his Art Deco-styled depictions of mythological legends

Léon Bakst

(*above left*) *Caryathis*,
lithographic poster, *c.* 1916.

Georges Barbier

(*above right*) *Clotilde &*
Alexandre Sakharoff,
lithographic poster, 1921.

Louis Barillet (attr.)

(*right*) Skylight in leaded glass,
late 1920s.

Eric Bagge
Dressing table, sycamore with ivory trim, 1920s.

carved out of entire elephant tusks: for example, *Vénus et l'Amour* (c. 1934). Bachelet was a member of the *Société des Artistes Décorateurs, where he exhibited a range of life-size animal carvings, including ducks, guinea pigs, condors and chickens, in stone, ***grès*** (stoneware) and bronze cast by the Valsuani foundry.

Bagge, Eric (1890–1978)
Born in Antony (France), Bagge trained as an architect, presumably in Paris, and then lectured at the École des Arts Appliqués. His participation in the annual Salons began after the First World War, with furniture designed in collaboration with Bernard Huguet. Despite their spartan Louis XVI provincialism, these ensembles and single pieces were reviewed favourably by the critics. Bagge created further furniture in partnership with René *Prou, Jean Fressinet, Peters and Georges Bastard, much of which was manufactured by the firm of G.-E. & J. Dennery and marketed through such retail outlets as *Mercier Frères, *Saddier et ses Fils, Contenot & Lelièvre, Établissements Guinier, *La Maîtrise, André-Léon *Arbus and, in the 1930s, Atelier des Champs-Elysées and Maison P. Blache.

Diversification followed as Bagge presented carpets, wallpapers and fabrics in his Salon exhibits. His carpets were manufactured by Marcel Coupé and retailed by Lucien Bouix; wallpapers and fabrics were made by Robert *Bonfils or Leroy, and marketed through Lucien Bouix. Jacques *Gruber and F. Chigot were commissioned to design stained-glass windows, which became a signature decorative accent in Bagge's interiors.

At the 1925 *Exposition Internationale, Bagge designed a dining room for the exhibit of Saddier et ses Fils, a desk exhibited at the Société de l'Art Appliqué aux Métiers and, in collaboration with René Prou, a boudoir and adjoining bathroom in the Ambassade Française pavilion. At the Exposition he also revealed his training as an architect with the stands he designed for the jeweller Henri Dubret, the publishers L. Rouart

and J. Watelin and the furriers Guélis Frères. Bagge's larger buildings included the pavilion for the sculpture dealer *Arthur Goldscheider and the parfumier Jacquet. A 1929 article in *Mobilier et Décoration* listed Bagge as the newly appointed artistic director of Mercier Frères. The accompanying illustrations showed interiors with clean lines that were sober yet forcefully avant-garde.

Bagues Frères
Based in Paris, Bagues Frères had outlets in Brussels, London and New York. In a 1928 advertisement in *Mobilier et Décoration*, the firm listed its range of products as ancient and modern light fixtures, *objets d'art* and ironwork. Categorization of its light fixtures is as difficult as attempting to evaluate the quality of its work. In addition to the advertised modern and old styles – in particular Louis XIV and Empire – Bagues Frères also produced lights in 'modernly designed Louis XIV girandoles' and a mishmash of revivalist designs that today appear stylistically muddled, if not vulgar.

A favourite material was crystal beads – clear or opalescent, or, as in the chandelier Bagues Frères designed for Jeanne *Lanvin, in topaz and amethyst tones – housed in bronze mounts and shaped as gigantic fruit or petrified jets of water. Other designs were less successful, including one designed as a windmill, and another as a birdcage in glass and gilt-bronze with electric candles positioned around the cage's perimeter. In 1932 the firm's commission for the ocean liner *L'Atlantique* included four large reflecting vases for the lounge. Bagues Frères participated in the 1934 Salon de la Lumière et l'Éclairage in Paris and the 1937 Exposition des Arts et Techniques.

Bakst, Léon (1866–1924)
Born in St Petersburg, Bakst attended the city's Imperial Academy of Fine Arts (1893–96) before moving to Paris, where he studied further with Albert Edelfelt. He returned around 1900 to St Petersburg,

where he joined the Mir Iskustva (World of Art), an avant-garde movement that published an art magazine by that name, with which Sergei Diaghilev was associated. By now an accomplished painter, set designer, textile and costume designer, and illustrator, Bakst returned to Paris with Diaghilev in 1909, where he designed sets and costumes for the Ballets Russes. He held his first London exhibition in 1912.

Barbier, Georges (1882–1932)
Little is known of Barbier's early years or education other than that he was born in Nantes; he emerged, however, as a prolific and versatile artist. Primarily a book illustrator, Barbier also designed textiles, wallpapers, posters, commercial packaging, postcards, and stage and cinema costumes and sets, the last-mentioned including commissions for the Folies Bergère and Casino de Paris. One of his first illustrated albums, *Dances de Nijinsky* (1913), revealed his inspiration in the theatre and, specifically, dances performed by the Ballets Russes.

Barbier also created numerous fashion plates for journals such as *Vogue, Fémina, La Gazette du Bon Ton, Le Journal des Dames et des Modes* and *Comœdia Illustré*. His illustrations were often executed in the ***pochoir*** process or in woodcuts interpreted for him by François-Louis *Schmied. In the late 1920s he worked briefly in Hollywood. He died while at work on a film of Pierre Louÿs's *Aphrodite*.

Barillet, Louis (1880–1948)
A French stained-glass designer and maker, Barillet worked in partnership in the inter-war years with Jacques *Le Chevallier in a studio on the Place Vergennes in Paris. Most of his commissions were generated by architects, especially progressive ones such as ROBERT MALLET-STEVENS, for whom he created stark geometric or Cubist designs in clear and frosted glass. Included in the studio's commissions were a

series of windows portraying the days of the week for the periodical *La Semaine* (1928–29) and abstract ecclesiastical panels for the Capucins de Blois church (1935). In 1930, Barillet became a member of the *Union des Artistes Modernes (UAM), where he exhibited until 1937. Following the Second World War, he was joined by a new partner, Théodore Hanssen.

Baudisch-Wittke, Gudrun (1907–1982)

Born in Pols (Steiermark), Austria, Baudisch studied from 1922 to 1926 at the Österreichische Bundeslehranstalt für das Baufach und Kunstgewerbe in Graz, where she attended the ceramic classes of Hans Adametz. On completion, she was hired as an assistant in the ceramic division of the Wiener Werkstätte. In 1930, she left to open her own design studio in Vienna, where she undertook ceramic commissions until 1936, including a stucco ceiling for the Ataturk Palace in Ankara, Turkey, for the architect Clemens Holzmeister. From 1936 to around 1944 she was active in Berlin, after which she formed her own ceramic workshop, the Keramik Hallstatt, which was administered later by her second husband, Karl Heinz Wittke, whom she married in 1940.

Preoccupied during this period by her work as a stuccoist, Baudisch-Wittke is known in an Art Deco context for the ceramic figurines, busts and masks that she modelled for the Wiener Werkstätte. In their crudeness, imaginative palette and witty portrayal of young women, these were often stylistically indistinguishable from those by Vally *Wieselthier and Susi *Singer.

Baumberger, Otto (1889–1961)

Swiss-born Baumberger was schooled in Munich, Paris and London, before gaining employment in 1914 as a lithographer at the J. E. Wolfensberger printing plant in Zurich. While there he produced nearly all of his hundreds of poster designs, including many travel-related ones. Among his commercial clients were the Seiden–Grieder store, Cinema Speck, Corso restaurants and the Burger–Kehl Co. For Burger–Kehl he designed his classic 1923 poster in which one sees only a PKZ coat and its label – there is no accompanying textual message; the clothier's brand name was so well established that the label said it all.

Baumberger employed a broad range of graphic styles, each tailored to the individual client's needs. Among his commissions were numerous travel posters, to which he applied a sensitive palette and broad strokes to capture the lyrical beauty of the lake or landscape being publicized; for the Künstler Konzerte, he applied a semi-Cubist style in which thumb-snapping, sketchy lines provided the energetic flavour of the music hall; for commercial products, such as Baumann hats, Baumberger's preference was for an almost photographic rendering of the subject. His success lay in his fine grasp of the subject matter; he never allowed his personality to impose itself on how he communicated his client's message.

He produced concert and exhibition posters from 1916 to 1918, and then after the war he became active in stage design; in 1920 he designed sets for theatres in Berlin and Zurich. In the same year, Baumberger took a position as a professor of art in Zurich, which he held until 1959.

Bayer, Herbert (1900–1985)

Born in Haag am Hausruch, Austria, Bayer lacked a formal art education. While apprenticed to the architect–designer George Schmidthammer in Linz, he was exposed to the work of the Vienna Secession and the theories of the early Deutscher Werkbund. Bayer moved to Darmstadt in 1920, where he worked as an architectural draughtsman under Josef Margold at the town's artist colony owned by Grand Duke Ernst Ludwig von Hesse.

Enrolling at the Bauhaus in Weimar in October 1921, Bayer began in Wassily Kandinsky's mural-painting workshop, before branching out into other media, notably typography. At this time, he experimented with contemporary movements, including De Stijl, Constructivism, Dadaism and Surrealism. He spent 1923 travelling, mainly in Italy, before returning to the new Bauhaus facility in Dessau in 1925, where he was appointed the first master of its typography shop. In 1928, he moved to Berlin, where he worked as the art director of the German edition of *Vogue* and at the Dorland Studio, a prominent international advertising agency. His graphic style was always solidly geometric, as in his 1927 poster for Europäisches Kunstgewerbe, in which he combined blocks of colour and the letters in the message's title in eye-catching combinations.

Bayer is credited with the introduction of the Bauhaus techniques of collage, photography and photomontage into the world of commercial art, but by the late 1920s his style was increasingly Surrealist. A close associate of Marcel *Breuer, he visited the USA in 1937 to attend a planning meeting with Walter *Gropius and László Moholy-Nagy, who were organizing an exhibition on the Bauhaus for the Museum of Modern Art in New York. He emigrated to the USA in 1938, where he lived in New York City until 1946, serving as the consultant art director to John Wanamaker and J. Walter Thompson. In 1946, Bayer moved to Aspen, Colorado to become consultant designer for the Container Corp. of America. In 1975 he moved to California, where he died ten years later in Montecito.

Beaumont, Jean (1895–1978)

Not much is known of Beaumont's upbringing beyond that he was born in Elbeuf (Seine-Maritime). Two Paris addresses were listed for him in the 1920s and 1930s – 214 rue du Château des Rentiers and 5 rue Sebastien Mercier – during which time he worked for *La Maîtrise and exhibited at the annual Salons.

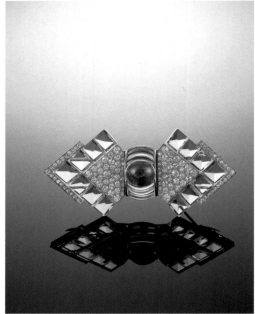

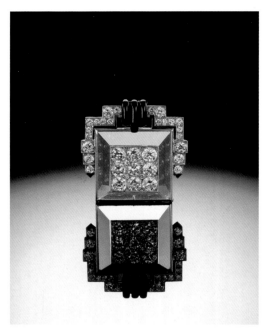

Beaumont worked in numerous media, including porcelain for *Sèvres, enamels, lacquer and posters, but he excelled especially in tapestry, carpet and fabric design, which he rendered in the prevailing Art Deco vernacular. His stylizations captured precisely the period's decorative mood: elongated animals and people among huge flower sprays in a muted palette in which greens, oranges and reds predominated. His tapestry designs were manufactured in part in Aubusson, and the rest were done by the Manufacture de Savigny, the Maison Hamot Frères, Braquenie et Cie and Beaumont's wife. A 1927 article in *Les Échos des Industries d'Art* described a special weaving technique of his by which threads were embroidered on to a reticulated canvas pattern sheet so that the detail stood out in relief. Beaumont's best-known tapestry design, 'Grignon', was commissioned by MAURICE DUFRÈNE for a suite of seat furniture exhibited in the Maîtrise pavilion at the 1925 Exposition Internationale among tapestries and carpets by Édouard *Benedictus, Dufrène, Gabriel *Englinger, Marcel Coupé and Jean and Jacques *Adnet. The cabinet-maker Roumy manufactured the wooden frames for Beaumont's tapestried furniture upholstery. One of Beaumont's major commissions was the large panel *Les Phéniciens introduisent le vin en France* in 1935. At the same time he produced several designs for lacquered panels executed by Louis *Midavaine.

Becquerel, André Vincent (1893–1981)

Born in Saint-André-Farivillers (Oise), Becquerel studied at the École des Beaux-Arts, Paris, under Hector Lemaire and Prosper Lecourtier. Making his début at the Salon of the *Société des Artistes Français in 1914, he was shortly elected a *sociétaire*, and he exhibited a range of small-scale sculptures until 1922. Becquerel specialized in animal figures, especially the big cats, cast either entirely in bronze or in highly styled bronze, and ivory groupings of fashionable Parisiennes. These were manufactured in editions by *Etling et Cie.

Much of Becquerel's work was devoted to models of children among pets or farmyard animals, which, because they were rendered naturalistically, do not fall within the Art Deco genre. Little else of his work appears to have been recorded until 1937, when he was commissioned to create a monumental statue in patinated plaster for the 1937 Exposition des Arts et Techniques, Paris.

Bel Geddes, Norman (1893–1958)

Bel Geddes was born in Adrian, Michigan, and attended the Cleveland School of Art and the Art Institute of Chicago before joining the Chicago advertising agency Barnes–Crosby as a draughtsman. In 1918 he started a successful career in New York as a stage set and window designer before setting up his own industrial design firm in 1927.

Early commissions for domestic products included furniture for Simmons Co. and counter scales for the Toledo Scale Co., both in 1929, and a range of gas stoves for the Standard Gas Equipment Corp. in 1932. His prototype 'House of Tomorrow' (1931), 'Skyscraper' cocktail service and giftware for the Revere Copper & Brass Co. (1937) and his 'Soda King' siphon bottle for the Walter Kidde Sales Co. displayed the ease with which Bel Geddes worked within numerous design fields. His projections of futuristic transportation – streamlined cars, ships and trains, many reproduced in his 1932 book *Horizons* – were widely criticized. *Fortune* magazine described Bel Geddes as a 'bomb thrower', whose designs would cost American industry a billion dollars in retooling. But the public remained entertained and enchanted by his romantic vision, which reached its apex in his Futurama 'Metropolis of Tomorrow' exhibit for the General Motors Highways and Horizons pavilion at the 1939 New York World's Fair.

Bel Geddes did more to popularize the industrial design profession than any of his competitors, despite the fact that almost all of his more outlandish

futuristic renderings remained unrealized. His enthusiasm and panache earned him the title 'The P. T. Barnum of Industrial Design'. His collection of archival materials is housed at the University of Texas, Austin.

Belperron, Suzanne (1900–1983)

Born in the small town of Saint-Claude near Besançon, Belperron became a student at the École des Beaux-Arts in Besançon in 1914. After the First World War, she went to Paris to continue her studies and some time later was hired by Maison Boivin. After the firm's owner, René Boivin, died in 1917, his widow continued the business, assisted by Juliette Moutard and Belperron, who were responsible for its jewelry designs.

In 1933, Belperron joined Bernard Herz at Maison Herz, 59 rue de Châteaudun, Paris. Until then a dealer in precious stones and pearls, the firm turned to jewelry on her arrival and assumed the name Herz–Belperron. Belperron's jewelry designs were realized exclusively by the goldsmiths Groene & Darde, later renamed Darde et Fils. In 1941 Herz was sent by the occupying Nazi forces to a concentration camp, from which he did not return. His son, Jean, became a prisoner of war. In their absence, Belperron administered the firm and when Jean returned he was named an associate. After she closed the firm in 1974, Belperron travelled a great deal and was a familiar presence at cultural and social events in Paris.

Belperron's clients included the Duchess of Windsor, Daisy Fellowes, Mrs Harrison Williams and Hollywood stars of the post-Second World War era. Her favourite gemstone was chalcedony, which she carved into sensual shapes that enhanced its natural luminosity.

Benedictus, Édouard (1878–1930)

Born in Paris to Dutch parents, Benedictus studied painting at the École Nationale Supériere des Arts Décoratifs, Paris, and then at the Technische Hochschule in Darmstadt, before turning his attention

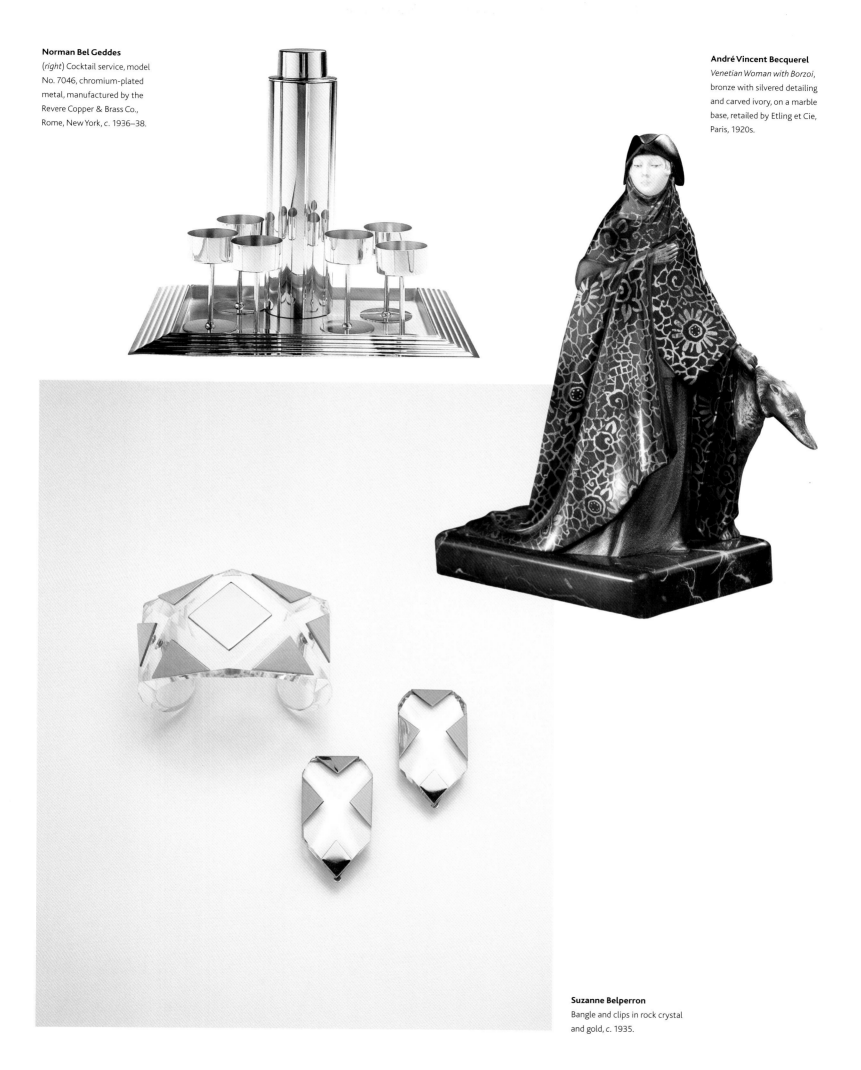

Norman Bel Geddes
(*right*) Cocktail service, model No. 7046, chromium-plated metal, manufactured by the Revere Copper & Brass Co., Rome, New York, *c.* 1936–38.

André Vincent Becquerel
Venetian Woman with Borzoi, bronze with silvered detailing and carved ivory, on a marble base, retailed by Etling et Cie, Paris, 1920s.

Suzanne Belperron
Bangle and clips in rock crystal and gold, *c.* 1935.

Édouard Benedictus
Maquette for a jacquard fabric
pattern, 1920s.

to the decorative arts from 1899. Over the next ten years, he produced a large number of household accessories, especially in inlaid leather. These he displayed at the Salon of the *Société des Artistes Décorateurs in 1902, while providing artwork to Maurice Verneuil, the editor of *Art et Décoration*. In 1910 Benedictus invented Triplex, a type of unbreakable glass.

Following the First World War, Benedictus devoted himself to fabric, wallpaper and carpet design, examples of which he published in three volumes: *Variations* (1923), *Nouvelles Variations* (1926) and *Relais* (1930). These served the textile industry widely in its mass-production of printed fabrics and wallpapers. Inspired initially by plant forms and nature, his patterns became progressively more simple; Benedictus's late 1920s collection was basically geometric.

He participated in the 1925 *Exposition Internationale in the Ambassade Française pavilion, where he displayed textiles and rugs, including 'high-style' compositions depicting colonnades and jets of water, that were manufactured by Brunet & Meunie, Tassinari & Chatel, and the manufactories in Beauvais and Aubusson.

Benito, Edouardo Garcia (1891–1962)
Benito was born in Valladolid, Spain, and studied at the Real Academia Belles Artes de San Fernando in Madrid and at the École des Beaux-Arts, Paris. A painter and graphic artist, his career was launched before the First World War by Paul *Poiret, who retained him to design fabrics, furnishings and decorative objects.

From around 1919 Benito worked in Paris and New York as a book and fashion illustrator for the magazines *La Gazette du Bon Ton*, *L'Homme Élégant* and the furrier Max, among others. From 1921, for about two decades, he designed a large number of covers for *Vogue's* international editions. He exhibited at the Salons of the *Société Nationale des Beaux-Arts until 1934 and

at the Salon des Tuileries in 1923. Benito later became a portrait artist and muralist.

Bergé, Henri (1870–1937)
Born in Diarville (Meurthe-et-Moselle), the son of a lace manufacturer, Bergé studied under Jules-François Larcher at the École Municipale des Beaux-Arts in Nancy. At first freelance, he listed himself as an artist–designer and decorative painter on his business card. From 1895 he participated in the Salon de Nancy exhibitions mounted by the Société Lorraine des Amis des Arts, where he showed landscapes and botanical studies. His address in 1896 was listed as 3 rue Eugène Ferry, Nancy.

In 1905 Bergé signed a limited contract with DAUM FRÈRES, which allowed him to pursue outside work. At its *cristallerie*, he supervised the firm's drawing school for apprentices until the 1930s, and, from around 1906, he designed for Daum a series of table-top items and sculpture, mostly naturalistic in theme, which were executed by Almeric *Walter in **pâte-de-verre**. At the same time, Bergé designed graphic works, such as posters for Maison d'Art Lorraine, and menus, in addition to fabrics, stained-glass windows for an inn and private residence in Maxeville, and ceramics for Mougin Frères in Montreville, near Nancy.

Between 1919 and 1930 Bergé freelanced for Walter, who had become self-employed in 1919, while continuing to work for Daum Frères. Bergé also taught at various schools in Lorraine, including the École Professionelle de l'Est, the Lycée Poincaré and the École Loritz. He participated at the 1925 *Exposition Internationale, where he received a gold medal for the glassware models he designed for Walter.

Bernadotte, Sigvard (1907–2002). *See* Jensen.

Bernard, Joseph-Antoine (1866–1931)
Bernard studied at the École des Beaux-Arts in Lyons and at the one in Paris. Influenced perhaps by his

father, a stonemason, Bernard's preference was for direct carving over modelling. He employed a modified classical style in which excess detailing and ornamentation were eliminated.

He exhibited regularly at the annual Salons, first at that of the *Société des Artistes Français, where he showed an allegorical figure depicting 'Hope Conquered' at his début in 1893, and then at the *Salon d'Automne (1910–27) and the Salon des Tuileries (1923–27). Bernard's frieze *La Danse* for JACQUES-ÉMILE RUHLMANN's Hôtel du Collectionneur pavilion at the 1925 *Exposition Internationale was subsequently purchased by the French state.

Bernhard, Lucian (1883–1972)
Born in Austria, Bernhard studied at the Akademie der Bildenden Künste in Munich. Self-taught as a designer and architect, he worked as a poster artist, typographer, graphic artist and architect, creating furniture, rugs, wallpapers and lighting fixtures, in addition to designing office buildings, factories and houses. He maintained a studio in Berlin.

In poster design, Bernhard is acknowledged as a pioneer in advertising concepts. His first poster appeared around 1903. Between 1910 and 1920, he worked mainly as a designer for the Deutsche Werkstätten Dresden-Hellerau. He was also a member of a group of graphic designers who submitted poster designs on a regular basis to Hollerbaum & Schmidt, a firm known for its progressive advertising posters. In 1920 Bernhard was appointed the first professor for poster art at the Akademie der Künste in Berlin.

Emigrating to the USA in 1923, he settled in New York, where he worked as an interior designer and taught graphic arts at New York University and the Art Students League. With Bruno Paul, Rockwell Kent and Paul *Poiret, Bernhard was a founder of the international design firm Contempora – a group of European Modernist designers working in New York.

Henri Bergé

Desktop accessories in *pâte-de-verre*, modelled for Almeric Walter, 1905–15.

Joseph-Antoine Bernard

Jeune Fille se Coiffant debout, figure in black patinated bronze, cast in 1926 by the *cire perdue* process by Valsuani from the model in marble exhibited at the 1923 Salon des Tuileries, Paris.

Edouardo Garcia Benito

(*above*) *Candee*, lithographic poster, 1929.

Lucian Bernhard

(*right*) *Bosch–Licht*, lithographic poster, 1913.

Jean Besnard
(*opposite, left*) Glazed
stoneware sculpture, c. 1932.

Louis Léon Eugène Billotey
(*opposite, right above*) Study
for *Sacrifice d'Iphigénie*, pencil
and oil on canvas, probably
late 1920s.

Joseph Binder
(*opposite, right centre*) *New
York World's Fair*, lithographic
poster, 1939.

Jean Besnard
(*opposite, right below*) Glazed
stoneware vase, c. 1935.

Émile James Bisttram
*Pearls and Things and Palm
Beach (The Breakers)*,
watercolour on paper, c. 1925.

After Bernhard's departure to New York, his Berlin
studio was managed by Fritz Rosen (1890–1980). The
graphic works, including posters, that were generated
there were signed 'Bernhard Rosen'.

Besnard, Jean (1889–1958)
The son of the painter Paul-Albert Besnard (1849–1934),
Besnard studied folk pottery and produced folk-inspired
faïence with highly idiosyncratic glazes. He is best
known for his granular and printed surface patterns –
the latter often resembling lace or basketry. In the
1920s Besnard participated at the Salons of the
*Société des Artistes Décorateurs, the *Salon
d'Automne and the Salon des Tuileries, showing vessels,
masks and jewelry inspired by primitive African art.

Billotey, Louis Léon Eugène (1883–1940)
Billotey attended the École des Beaux-Arts in Paris
before receiving the Prix de Rome in 1907. During
a three-year sojourn in Italy, he developed a
distinctive Neoclassical figurative style rendered
in a Modernist idiom similar to that of fellow
Prix de Rome recipients JEAN DUPAS, Robert-Eugène
*Pougheon and Jean *Despujols. Although technically
accomplished, Billotey remained unknown to the
public as he bypassed the annual Salons – which were
the conventional means to promote work – except for
brief participation at the *Société des Artistes Français
in 1912–13, 1922 and 1924.

For his subject matter, Billotey selected mainly
mythological themes, such as Adonis, Diana the
Huntress, Venus, Tragedy and, repeatedly, those
of the sacrifice of Iphigénie and the martyrdom
of St Sebastian. He chose to work exclusively on
institutional commissions, among which were the
designs in stained glass for the St Nicolas's Day church
in the village of Villers-Cotterêts. When the Nazis
entered Paris in 1940, Billotey was at work in his Atelier
Raynouard, and he committed suicide.

Binder, Joseph (1898–1972)
Born in Austria, Binder studied at the
Kunstgewerbeschule in Vienna. This graphic artist,
designer, painter and poster artist opened his own
studio in Vienna in 1924, where, until 1929, he designed
posters and packaging for a coffee and tea importer.
The following year saw the first of Binder's many travel
posters: one for the Austrian tourist board, in which
French skiers were invited to try the Austrian Alps.

Between 1933 and 1935, Binder taught design
in New York. During the latter part of his stay
he also undertook freelance and graphic design work.
He created the official poster for the 1939 New York
World's Fair.

Bing & Grøndahl
The Bing & Grøndahl manufactory in Copenhagen was
founded in 1853 by brothers Herman and Jacob Bing
(local businessmen) and Frederick Grøndahl (a modeller
formerly employed at the Royal Copenhagen Porcelain
Manufactory). In 1895, the year Bing & Grøndahl
launched its annual Christmas plate editions ('Jule
Afren'), the firm became a public stock company.
At the time, much of its production was designed in
a predictable, somewhat rehashed, Beaux-Arts style.

A turning point came in 1899 with the 'Heron'
service which, with its curious blend of Japanese
naturalism and Rococo revivalism, created a stir
and helped to usher a modern look into the firm's
repertoire. In the inter-war years, when most of its
designs resembled those of other northern European
potteries, Bing & Grøndahl introduced editions
of high-fired stoneware, some modelled with witty
mythological themes by Jean René Gauguin, son
of the painter.

Although its output of porcelain figurines and
tableware services remained mostly conservative, a
limited series of Art Deco-style wares was created by
Ingeborg Plockross-Irminger, Siegfried and Olga Wagner

and Kai Nielsen. In 1987 the firm, still owned by the
Bing family, merged with Royal Copenhagen.

Bisttram, Émile James (1895–1976)
Hungarian-born Bisttram became one of the American
Southwest's leading painters and teachers in the 1930s
and 1940s. A mixed-media artist, his style evolved
from the classic regionalism of the 1930s that he
employed for various Works Project Administration
(WPA) commissions, to the angular graphic style that
he applied to his Art Deco poster designs, and from
there into abstraction based on dynamic symmetry
theories of the next decade.

Based in Taos, Bisttram was later the founder with
Raymond Johnson of the Transcendental Art Movement,
a New Mexico group that created works exploring
and promoting universal meaning, employing idealistic
forms and colours suggesting sounds.

Bizouard, Valéry (1875–1945). *See* Tétard Frères.

Black, Starr & Frost
Founded as a goldsmithing enterprise in 1810 by
Isaac Marquand on Lower Broadway, New York, the
firm underwent various name changes in the 19th
century as new partnerships evolved. By the 1830s
it was called Ball, Black & Co., which it remained until
it closed in 1876; in the same year, it was purchased
by Robert C. Black, Cortlandt W. Starr and Aaron Frost,
who named it Black, Starr & Frost. In 1912 the firm
moved to 594 Fifth Avenue. In 1929, following the
merger with the Gorham Co., the firm became Black,
Starr & Frost–Gorham.

At the 1939 New York World's Fair, the firm was a
primary exhibitor (with Tiffany & Co.) in the exhibition's
House of Jewels pavilion. It currently maintains
a stock of imported jewelry and precious objects,
in addition to silverware, carriage and bracket clocks,
watches and novelty items.

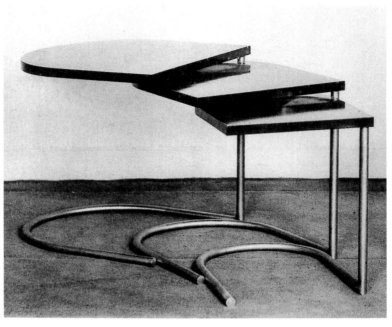

Block, Robert (*fl*. 1925–30s)

Swiss-born Block was the first director of Studio Athelia, which was inaugurated on 15 December 1928 as an adjunct to the department store Trois Quartiers, on the boulevard de la Madeleine, Paris. Its function matched that of *Primavera, *Pomone and *La Maîtrise: to design and mass-produce items for middle- and upper-class income groups. Block's address in 1930 was listed as 60 avenue Malakoff.

His association with Studio Athelia was short-lived; by the mid-1930s various pieces of his furniture exhibited at the Salons were marketed by Gaveau (a lacquered piano), Waring & Gillow (a dining room) and Heal & Son (a desk executed by the Société Industrielle d'Art). Other furniture of Block's, illustrated in *Sièges Contemporaines* and *Petits Meubles du Jour*, shows a strikingly fresh creativity at a time when tubularism had reduced much of what was new to anonymity. Some of the pieces are chic, functional and quite simply a cut above much that was being produced by his competitors. Emphasis was placed on modular designs – *meubles transformables et juxtaposables* – for the city's small apartments.

Bobritsky, Vladimir (Bobri) (1898–1986)

Born into a wealthy banking family in Kharkov in the Ukraine, Bobritsky showed an interest in theatre while at the city's Imperial Art School. He later studied scenic design at the State Dramatic Theatre. He fled Russia in 1917, initially to Turkey, before emigrating to New York in 1921, where he established himself as a fashion illustrator for magazines such as the *New Yorker, Vogue* and *Harper's Bazaar*, working out of a studio on East 50th Street, Manhattan.

Bobritsky was also a painter, book illustrator (especially of children's books), theatre artist (designing costumes and sets) and poster artist. For his posters he employed bold images and colours to draw the viewer's attention. An album of his collected sketches, *Taxco Mexico: 12 Pastels for V. Bobri*, was published in 1949. When among fellow *émigrés*, Bobritsky was an accomplished balalaika and guitar player. He worked until his death in a fire at his home in Rosedale, New York State.

Boch Frères Keramis

In 1841 Victor Boch of the Boch family ceramics works in Luxembourg determined to broaden the firm's market with the establishment of a fine earthenware factory in Belgium. A site was chosen for the Keramis factory at Saint Vaast in the region of La Louvière, 53 kilometres from Brussels and close to natural deposits of pure clay. Boch Frères Keramis opened in 1844. Eugène Boch (1809–1892) and his brother Victor Boch (1817–1920) succeeded each other as head of the works, whose artisans were drawn initially from Luxembourg and then from nearby Belgian pottery works. Production by 1900 was noted for its oyster plates, inspired in part by prototypes from Delft and Italian majolica.

The firm's 1920s earthenware, characterized by its spirited and colourful Art Deco imagery, often in azure blue on an off-white crackled ground, was designed largely by Charles *Catteau and Raymond Chevallier for the design studios of the large Paris department stores, including *La Maîtrise, *Pomone and *Primavera. Boch Frères Keramis participated in both the 1925 *Exposition Internationale and the 1937 Exposition des Arts et Techniques, Paris. It went into liquidation in 1985.

Bofarull, Jacint (b. 1903)

Catalan-born Bofarull studied fine arts before working as an advertising graphic designer. Among the clients for whom he designed posters from the late 1920s were Alfred Dunhill and various sports stores in Barcelona.

A Communist sympathizer, Bofarull designed anti-Fascist propagandist posters, such as *Els Aixafaremi!!!*, during the Spanish civil war of 1936–39. Following Franco's victory, Bofarull fled to France, where he found employment with the daily newspaper *Perpignan Indépendant* until 1950, when he left for Venezuela and Argentina. He later returned to Spain.

Boiceau, Ernest (1881–1950)

Born in Lausanne, Boiceau studied design, painting and architecture at the École des Beaux-Arts in Paris. He worked for several galleries in Paris before the First World War, then opened his own showroom on the avenue de l'Opéra, where he sold furniture upholstery and embroidered fabrics. In 1925 Boiceau moved to a new address on rue Pierre-Charron, where he presented his own creations in a similar range of home furnishings.

From 1926, Boiceau decorated and furnished numerous apartments and *hôtels particuliers* in Switzerland, the USA and France, working in partnership especially with Cécile Sorel in Paris, Louise de Vilmorin at Verrières-le-Buisson and Jérôme and Jean Tharaud in Versailles. In 1928 and 1929, his *pièces uniques* at the *Salon d'Automne were widely acclaimed, and in 1933 he opened a new shop on the avenue Matignon. The Second World War put an end to his business.

Boiceau's furniture shows a predilection for ample and massive forms, some perhaps a little theatrical and some evoking antiquity. He used rare and precious wood veneers mixed with marble, bronze, glass and lacquer. His carpets were woven by *au point dit 'de Cornély'*, a technique invented in 1865, of which Boiceau patented a modified version in 1920.

Boin–Taburet

This conventional *orfèvre-joaillier* business was founded in Paris in 1873 by the silversmith Georges Boin and his father-in-law, Taburet, a manufacturer of decorative objects. La Maison Boin–Taburet concentrated its production in the late 1800s and

Boch Frères Keramis
(*far left*) Vase in glazed earthenware designed by Charles Catteau, 1920s.

(*left*) Vase in glazed earthenware designed by Charles Catteau, 1920s.

Vladimir (Bobri) Bobritsky
(*above*) Magazine cover for *Vanity Fair*, October, 1926.

Jacint Bofarull
(*right*) *Beristain/Dunhill*, lithographic poster, 1932.

Marcel Bouraine
(*right*) *High Priestess*, group in bronze and carved ivory, on marble base, 1920s.

Boin–Taburet
(*below left*) Lamp in silver, onyx, ivory and ebony, 1920s/1930s.

Robert Bonfils
(*below right*) *Salon d'Automne*, lithographic poster, 1928.

salon d'automne

4 novembre 16 décembre
entrée: 5 f
dimanche: 3 f
vernissage: 10 f
éclairé
chauffé
1928 ensembles décoratifs
GRAND PALAIS

Robert Bonfils

early 1900s on deluxe table-top items designed in a mix of revivalist styles, including *tous les Louis* and chinoiserie. A *rocaille* gold centrepiece, awarded a medal at the 1889 Exposition Universelle, was typical of its output.

In the 1920s, as the new Modernist grammar of ornament took root at the Paris Salons, Maison Boin–Taburet introduced into its repertoire a range of contemporary silverware, including tea and coffee services, trays, tureens and candelabra.

Bonet, Paul (1889–1971). *See under* Paintings, Graphics, Posters and Bookbinding.

Bonfils, Robert (1886–1972)

Bonfils entered the École Germain-Pilon in Paris in 1903, three years later continuing his education in the Atelier Cormon division of the École des Beaux-Arts. On graduating he joined the furniture designer Henri Hamm, who introduced him to Paul Gallimard. Gallimard was the co-ordinator of the book section of the annual *Salon d'Automne, at which Bonfils made his début in 1909.

His first book commission, *Clara d'Ellebeuse*, which Bonfils illustrated with *pochoirs*, was shown in 1913. Another important pre-war commission was the tea-room of the large Paris department store Au Printemps, which he decorated with allegorical murals depicting the four seasons. During the First World War he illustrated a three-volume edition of *Les Rencontres de M. de Bréot* with woodcuts. Bonfils later showed his versatility by designing objects in a wide range of materials, including silks for Bianchini–Férier and ceramics for the Manufacture Nationale de *Sèvres. The Musée de la Ville de Paris and the Musée d'Art Moderne today hold selections of his paintings.

In 1919 Bonfils was appointed to succeed Henri de Waroquier as a professor of design at the École Estienne. He taught his students that a binding's design should suggest, rather than provide a precise definition of, a book's contents. He also believed that a book's surface should be flat, without sculptural detailing, encrustations or inlaid metal plaques. His covers were therefore in leather (either plain or with inlays of colour) or vellum, to which he applied – in a simple linear graphic style – enchanting Art Deco imagery of fashionable young women, tribal African masks and musical instruments. In particular, his depictions of women captured the buoyant mood of the 1920s in a poignant and romantic manner. Many of these appeared in *La Gazette du Bon Ton*.

A regular participant in binding exhibitions, Bonfils also took part in the 1925 *Exposition Internationale, for which he was commissioned by the operating committee, Le Commissariat Général, to design one of the event's official posters. This is today his best-known work. Later, Bonfils exhibited at the 1937 Exposition des Arts et Techniques and the 1939 New York World's Fair.

Boucheron

Frédéric Boucheron (1830–1902) opened his first jewelry store in the Palais Royal, Paris, in 1858, and soon acquired fame as a fine technician, creator of beautiful jewelled works and expert in precious stones. In 1893 he was the first jeweller to open a showroom in the Place Vendôme (at no. 26), where he continued to serve society's élite, and where the firm still operates. In the late 19th and early 20th centuries La Maison Boucheron participated in international exhibitions while opening branches worldwide, including one at 180 New Bond Street, London, in 1907, and another in Moscow, which closed on the eve of the Revolution. Frédéric's sons Louis (1874–1959) and Gérard (b. 1910) succeeded him in turn.

Among many highlights in the firm's career, Louis was summoned in 1930 to Teheran by the Shah of Persia to estimate and inventory his jewelry collection, which included the Peacock Throne, a terrestrial globe and orbs. Another wealthy foreign customer in the late 1920s was the Maharajah of Patiala, then ruler of the Punjab, who brought six caskets filled with precious stones of inestimable value to Boucheron in Paris to have them transformed into tiaras, aigrettes, belts, armlets, necklaces *en cascades* and fringes to be worn under the sari.

Maison Boucheron adapted to the Art Deco style with a selection of sumptuous jewelry and accessories in gemstones carved with flowers and fruit within borders of *pavé* diamonds. Lapis lazuli, coral, jade, malachite, onyx and turquoise were interchanged to form a luscious palette. At the 1925 *Exposition Internationale, jewelry by Louis Boucheron was shown alongside pieces by Lucien Hirtz, Masse and Rubel – the firm's other designers.

Bouraine, Marcel (1886-1948)

Born in Pontoise (Seine-et-Oise), Bouraine studied in Paris under Jean-Alexandre-Joseph Falguière. Mobilized in 1914, he was captured in Germany and interned in Switzerland. In 1922 he exhibited at the Salon des Tuileries, and the following year showed also at the Salon of the *Société des Artistes Français and, later, at the *Salon d'Automne. Largely self-taught and one of the most prolific artists of the era, Bouraine's stock-in-trade was domestic statuary: for example, female nudes depicted with or without greyhounds or leaping gazelles. He produced models for Paris's foremost *éditeurs d'art* and founders, including Susse Frères, *Etling et Cie, Max *Le Verrier and *Arthur Goldscheider, often showing in the 1920s with Arthur Goldscheider's La Stèle and L'Évolution groups.

In 1928 Joseph-Gabriel Argy-Rousseau commissioned from Bouraine a number of figurines, mostly female nudes, plus a fountain and illuminated group, which he executed in varicoloured

pâte-de-cristal. At the 1937 Exposition des Arts et Techniques he created a large earthenware statue representing 'Ceramics' for the Sèvres pavilion. Bouraine also modelled a range of mythological female figures, and stylized animals designed as bookends and paperweights – the latter marketed through Alfred Dunhill in New York.

Bourgeois, Édouard-Joseph (1898–1937)

Bourgeois was born in Bezons and studied at the École Spéciale d'Architecture. In 1923 he joined *Studium-Louvre and made his début at their annual Salon. At the 1925 *Exposition Internationale he exhibited two ensembles in the Studium-Louvre pavilion – a smoking room and an office–library.

After 1926 Bourgeois established his own business and developed a group of avant-garde clients. Using modern furniture materials in his designs, he replaced his earlier preference for combinations of wood and glass with tubular metal, aluminium, iron and concrete. His collaborators included Paul-Émile *Brandt and Louis *Tétard.

Bouy, Jules (1872–1937)

Born in France, Bouy established an interior decorating firm in Belgium before moving to New York in 1913. Between 1924 and 1927, he produced furniture for L. Alavoine & Co., a Paris-based firm that provided modern and period-revival furnishings for fashionable Manhattan residences. During these years, he also managed Ferrobrandt, EDGAR BRANDT's New York showroom. By 1928, now established as president and art director of his own firm, Bouy Inc., he received interior design commissions from upmarket New Yorkers such as Lizzie Bliss, Agnes Miles Carpenter and the Dahlstrom family.

In 1931 Bouy designed and manufactured furniture in lacquered and painted wood with steel light fixtures for the summer harp school in Camden, Maine,

run by Carlos Salzedo, a noted harpist and composer. Bouy is best known for his metal lamps and furniture that incorporated skyscraper or other novel machine-age motifs. He participated in Macy's 1927 Art-in-Trade Exposition.

Brandt, Edgar (1880–1960). *See under* Silver, Metal, Lacquer and Enamel.

Brandt, Marianne (1893–1983)

Brandt was born in Chemnitz, Germany, and first studied painting and sculpture at the Weimar Grossherzogliche Hochschule für Bildende Kunst. In 1923 she enrolled at the Bauhaus where the following year she was transferred from the introductory course to the metal workshop at the suggestion of its director László Moholy-Nagy.

Following preliminary studies under Josef Albers and Moholy-Nagy, Brandt became actively involved in production at the Bauhaus workshop. In this capacity she is known primarily for her tea infuser (teapot) of 1924, which, with its push-on lid, non-drip spout and heat-resistant wooden handle and knob finial, was designed for standardized production. Boldly progressive in its simple design and practical construction, the tea infuser is today considered an icon of 20th-century industrial design. Brandt is famous also for her 'Kandem' bedside lamp, which was manufactured by Korting & Matthiesenof Leipzig.

Brandt succeeded Moholy-Nagy at the Bauhaus metal workshop in Dessau between 1928 and 1929. She then left the Bauhaus to work briefly with Walter *Gropius's architectural firm in Berlin on the designs for the Dammerstock housing project. Brandt subsequently joined the Ruppelberg metalware factory in Gotha, Thuringia (1929–32), before withdrawing the following year to Chemnitz, where she returned to painting.

After the Second World War Brandt taught at the Hochschule für Freie und Angewandte Kunst in Dresden and, between 1951 and 1954, in East Berlin at the Institut für Angewandte Kunst.

Brandt, Paul-Émile (b. 1879)

Born in La Chaux-de-Fonds, Switzerland, Brandt moved to Paris, where he studied under Chaplain and Allard. By 1900 he was an established designer and maker of jewelry and *objets d'art*, which he interpreted in a muted Belle Époque style. After the First World War, Brandt adopted the strict geometry and chromatic contrasts of the period's 'high-style' jewelry, utilizing a mix of black enamel, onyx, rock crystal and pearls mounted in white gold or platinum, to achieve the eye-catching compositions that characterized his finer jewelry designs.

Breuer, Marcel (1902–1981)

Breuer was born in Pecs, Hungary, and spent a brief time in Vienna before moving to the Bauhaus in Weimar in 1920, where he studied and eventually lectured. From 1923 he produced stunning innovations in tubular steel furniture, including his famous 'Wassily' chair of 1924 and a modular storage system the next year. From 1925 to 1928 he was employed at the Bauhaus in Dessau as head of its furniture workshop, after which he set up his own architectural practice in Berlin. In the same year he designed the 'Cesa' chair, his own very successful version of the cantilevered chairs pioneered by Mart *Stam and Ludwig *Mies van der Rohe.

Breuer later went to the USA, where he worked as an architect. In 1935 he moved to England, where he founded a partnership with F. R. S. Yorke, and designed furniture for the Isokon Furniture Co. During his stay, he experimented also with moulded and cut-out plywood furniture designs for Heal & Son Ltd. He was in partnership until 1941 with Walter *Gropius,

Jules Bouy

(*right*) Music cabinet in maple, ebonized and green-stained wood with nickel-plated bronze pull handles, *c.* 1925–30.

Marcel Breuer

(*below*) 'Wassily' chair, nickel-plated tubular steel and canvas, manufactured by Standard-Möbel, Lengyel & Co., Berlin, 1927–28.

Marcel Breuer

(*bottom*) Chaise-longue, model No. 313, aluminium and wood, manufactured by Embru-Werke AG., Rüti, Switzerland, *c.* 1935.

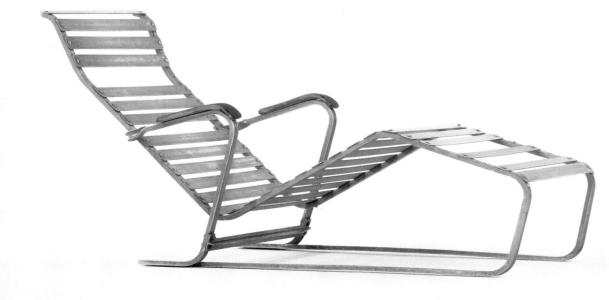

EDMONDE GUY

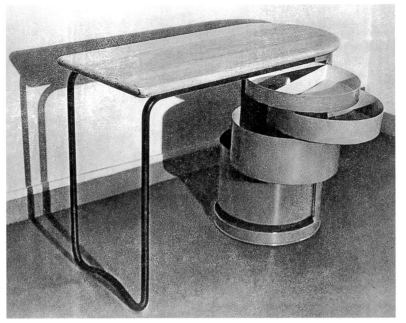

Jean Burkhalter
(*left*) Table in painted tubular steel and polished oak, 1928.

Umberto Brunelleschi
(*far left*) *Edmonde Guy*, lithographic poster, 1928.

whom he joined at Harvard as a professor of architecture in 1937; as teachers the two influenced an entire generation of architects.

Now independent, having moved his office to New York City in 1946, Breuer was commissioned by the Museum of Modern Art, New York, to design a house in its sculpture garden, an event that foreshadowed an increase in commissions. In the 1950s he enlarged his New York office in response to a series of public, institutional and commercial commissions. He retired from active practice in 1976.

Breuer is known now more for his furniture designs than his architecture; his tubular steel chairs, in particular, remain among the most original and iconic designs of the last century.

Broders, Roger (1883–1953)
Born to Danish parents named Brodersen, who were living in the Chamonix–Martigny region on the Swiss–French border, Broders was employed between 1920 and 1930 by PLM Railways, for which he designed numerous travel posters to promote ski resorts such as Saint-Gervais and Gstaad, beaches on the Côte d'Azur and summer boating on Switzerland's lakes. These were rendered in eye-catching 'high-style' compositions, juxtaposing bold colours and brief textual messages with images of chic holidaymakers and stunning vistas.

Brunelleschi, Umberto (1879–1949)
Brunelleschi was born in Montemurlo, near Pistoia in Tuscany, and attended the Accademia di Belle Arti, Florence, in 1899. The following year he moved to Paris, where he found employment as an illustrator and caricaturist with the revues *Le Rire* and *Le Journal des Dames et des Modes*. Between 1906 and 1908, he contributed to *Il Giornalino della Domenica* (the Florentine Sunday newspaper) while exhibiting gouaches for book illustrations regularly at the Paris

Salons and the Venice Biennale, which he participated in until 1942. In 1914 he added set and costume designs to his repertoire, many of the latter for Josephine Baker. His graphic style incorporated delicate detailing, fanciful flourishes and jewel-like colours.

Brunelleschi served for most of the First World War in the Italian army, afterwards returning to Paris as the editor of the upmarket fashion, theatre and lifestyle magazine *La Guirlande*, while contributing to *L'Estampe Moderne*, which showcased the **pochoirs** of many of the period's leading print artists. In the inter-war years Brunelleschi worked also on theatre sets, including those for La Scala and the Folies Bergère.

Buquet, Édouard Wilfrid (*fl.* 1925–35)
No information on Buquet's upbringing and education is apparent in contemporary sources. He is known in an Art Deco context exclusively for his 'Anglepoise' lamps, for which he received a patent in 1927. Equilibrated and fully rotatable, these were produced in a variety of table, wall and floor models incorporated into ensembles by many of the era's progressive architect–decorator–designers, including *Le Corbusier, Louis *Sognot, Marcel *Breuer, Lucien Rollin, *Joubert & Petit, and Marcel *Coard. Handmade in nickel-plated brass and aluminium, the 'Anglepoise' lamp was in the vanguard of 1920s functionalist design, stylistically comparable to the counterbalance models designed by Christian Dell at the Bauhaus.

Burkhalter, Jean (1895–1982)
Born in Auxerre (Yonne), Burkhalter attended the École des Beaux-Arts in Paris, emerging from his studies as a painter, architect and designer. It is as a designer that he is known in an Art Deco context for a diverse range of furniture, household wares, textiles and wallpapers for the **tapissier** Jules *Coudyser, silverware for the Maison Henin, ceramics for *Sèvres and a number of posters. Burkhalter made his début at the

Salon of the *Société des Artistes Décorateurs in 1919, following which he joined *Primavera, where he proved himself a gifted and versatile designer of small household accoutrements, fabrics and endpapers.

At the 1925 *Exposition Internationale, Burkhalter took stand 66 on the Esplanade des Invalides, displaying a range of carpets, posters and fabrics. He also collaborated on the furnishings for a studio and dining room in the Primavera pavilion, and on the Pierre Iman stand on the Pont Alexandre III bridge with his brother-in-law JOËL MARTEL and EDGAR BRANDT. A member of the exhibition's jury, he was awarded a first prize, *hors concours*. Burkhalter turned to furniture design in the late 1920s, producing small items: kitchen tables, ladies' desks, chairs and plant stands. Tables and desks in oak had their supports in chromed or galvanized tubular steel, which twisted and curved back on itself gracefully in its path around the object. Forms were studied, light and functional.

A volume of his textile patterns was published by Alfred Lévy in 1925. Included were **pochoirs** of seventy different carpet and fabric designs in strikingly colourful compositions of abstract plants and animals or co-ordinated blocks of colour.

Burkhalter became a founding member of the *Union des Artistes Modernes (UAM), displaying four tubular tub chairs, marketed by PIERRE CHAREAU, at the group's inaugural exhibition. In later years his range widened to include flower holders and porcelain tableware. Around 1930, he was appointed a professor at the École des Arts Industriels, Grenoble, and, in 1935, director of the École Municipale des Beaux-Arts in Auxerre. He later moved to Limoges, where he taught at the local decorative arts school. Burkhalter was still listed as an active member of UAM in 1955.

Buthaud, René (1886–1986). *See under* Ceramics.

Édouard Wilfrid Buquet
(*above left*) Wall fixture in
nickel-plated metal, with
'Anglepoise' arm, late 1920s.

Roger Broders
(*above right*) *Le Tour du Mt Blanc*,
lithographic poster, 1927.

Jean Burkhalter
(*right*) Armchair with adjustable
back in walnut with ebonized
wood feet, c. 1930.

Georges Canapé
Le Chariot d'Or (Albert Samain),
designed by Robert Bonfils,
inlays of leather, 1920s.

C

Callender, Bessie Stough (1889–1951)

Callender was born near Wichita, Kansas, and studied drawing at New York's Art Students League under George Bridgeman and sculpture at the Cooper Union. In 1926 she moved to Paris, where she worked in the ateliers of Émile-Antoine Bourdelle (1861–1929) and Georges Hilbert (b. 1900), the latter with whom she studied for three years. During her sojourn she spent many hours modelling and sketching animals at the Jardin des Plantes – her style being influenced by the firm, static outlines of Pharaonic Egyptian sculpture.

She participated at the Salon des Indépendants from 1928 to 1931, and showed animalier figures at the *Salon d'Automne. *Etling et Cie manufactured at least one of her sculptures: a semi-nude dancer draped in a sequined cloak, entitled 'Anita', which it offered in both bronze and bronze-and-ivory. In 1930 Callender moved to London, where she stayed for a decade and created works exhibited at the Royal Academy, the Walker Art Gallery in Liverpool and the Bradford Museum.

Canapé, Georges (1864–1940)

In 1865 J. Canapé *père* established his bindery at 18 rue Visconti, Paris, where he specialized in liturgical bindings and half-bindings. In 1880, to expand his business, he purchased the inventory and client list of the last noted Second Empire bindery, Belz–Niédrée. Georges Canapé succeeded his father in 1894, some years later adding a gilding department to provide the firm with full autonomy.

Like his contemporaries – Henri Blanchetière, Émile Carayon, René Chambolle and Affolter – Canapé adopted a restrained version of the Art Nouveau aesthetic around the turn of the century. His compositions comprised floral emblems within formal borders. At the annual Paris Salons, he offered bindings in a new style blended with Classical Revival elements and executed with the technical precision of a long-established bindery.

Canapé was dependent on others to provide the designs for his most important bindings, most notably PIERRE-ÉMILE LEGRAIN, with whom he executed several covers for Jacques *Doucet during the First World War. Doucet's exhibition of Legrain's bindings at the 1919 Salon of the *Société des Artistes Décorateurs included several fine examples by Canapé, including *La Ville* by Paul Claudel and *Portraits* by André Suarès. Noted artists were commissioned to create other cover designs, including Adolphe Giraldon, Georges *Lepape, Georges *Barbier, Jules Chadel, Maurice Denis and Robert *Bonfils. Collectors of Canapé's works, in addition to Doucet, included Henri Vever, L. Comar, William Augustus Spencer and Charles Miguet.

In 1918 Canapé was nominated president of the syndicate of patron–bookbinders. In the 1920s he turned his attention increasingly to the promotion of young binders by helping to modernize the apprenticeship process. In 1927 he took on a gifted young graduate of the École Estienne, A. Corriez, as a partner in his firm. On his death, the firm was divided: the bindery was sold to Esparon, and the gilding department to Henri Mercher.

Cappellin, Giacomo (1887–1968). *See* Venini.

Cappiello, Leonetto (1875–1942)

Born in Livorno, Italy, Cappiello moved to Paris in 1898, where he began his career in the graphic arts as a caricaturist, submitting cartoons of Puccini and Novella to the revue *Le Rire*. This was followed by his celebrated 'Nos Actrices' album for *La Revue Blanche*.

In 1899, Cappiello designed his first poster for the magazine *Frou-Frou*, in which he retained the caricaturist's flair for shock in the employment of flat exaggerated colours and off-beat concepts. The poster proved his true *métier*: he was to create some three thousand over the next four decades. In 1900 he started a business arrangement with the Paris firm Vercasson, which survived until 1916; for it, he produced a new poster design every four days on average! From 1904 Cappiello worked only as a poster artist. Among his posters during the pre-war years were classics such as 'Chocolat Klaus' (1903), 'Cinzano' (1910) and 'Thermogène' (1909). In 1919 he began a new association with the Devambez press.

Cappiello's impact on poster design was entirely novel. He eschewed the meticulous attention to brushstrokes that had been the norm, preferring to employ only a few broad lines and entirely flat and exaggerated colour planes, combined with an irresistibly outlandish image to create a surprising composition that arrested the viewer's attention and etched an indelible image of the product on the mind – the essence of modern advertising. His subjects were always in motion – riding unusual animals, juggling items of an incongruous size or making exuberant gestures. Dynamism was his motto. Today, Cappiello's poster style can be seen as transitional – one that falls halfway between Jules Chéret's Art Nouveau and CASSANDRE's Art Deco.

Cardeilhac

Founded *c.* 1804, the Maison Cardeilhac was initially a manufacturer of cutlery, to which the founder's grandson, Ernest Cardeilhac (1851–1904), added gold- and silversmithing at the turn of the 20th century. (He had apprenticed under Harleux.) The firm's display at the 1900 Exposition Universelle in Paris brought rave reviews, especially for the refined botanical designs of its chief in-house designer, Lucien Bonvallet. In 1927, Ernest's sons, Pierre (1888–1944) and Jacques, assumed the firm's directorship. On Pierre's death, Jacques managed Maison Cardeilhac on his own until 1951, when it merged with *Christofle.

Cardeilhac

Tureens in silvered metal; (*left*)
with jade handles, *c.* 1925,
and (*right*) with ivory handles,
c. 1930.

DEVAMBEZ, 144, Champs-Élysées, PARIS

Leonetto Cappiello

Le Petit Dauphinois,
lithographic poster, 1933.

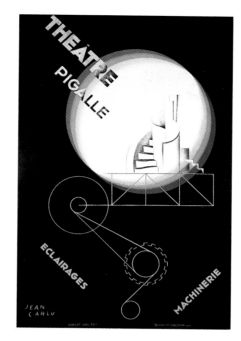

Carder, Frederick (1863–1963)

Born in Brockmoor, Staffordshire, Carder was apprenticed at fourteen in his father's pottery while attending evening classes in chemistry and metallurgy at the Dudley Mechanics Institute. He also studied at the Stourbridge School of Art under John Northwood, who encouraged him to apply for a job at Stevens & Williams at Brierley Hill, Worcestershire, which he joined in 1880 as a glass designer and decorator. When Northwood died in 1902, Carder was passed over as his successor and Northwood's son was appointed as the firm's manager.

Following a tour of German and Austrian glassworks to determine their technical facilities, in 1903 Carder was sent on a further tour of inspection to the USA, where the glass industry, though as troubled as that in the UK, was protected from cheap imports by high tariffs. While in America, Carder visited the town of Corning in New York State, home of both the Corning Glass Co. (a large manufacturer of industrial and table glasswares) and Thomas G. Hawkes & Co. (a small firm, founded in 1880, that produced decorative glassware on blanks that it purchased from the Corning Glass Co.). During his trip, the president of Hawkes persuaded Carder to help him set up a new works, for which they acquired and equipped the local S. W. Payne foundry premises for the production of crystal and coloured glass. The new company was incorporated on 2 March 1903, and named the Steuben Glassworks after the county in which it operated. Carder was placed in charge of the firm's artistic direction.

In 1918, the Steuben Glassworks was sold to the Corning Glass Co., and Carder continued as art director. Until his retirement in 1933, he participated in the creation of numerous varieties of glass in new techniques with varied colours and surface effects, including acid cutback, alabaster, aurene, calcite, intarsia, cluthra, jade, Cintra, Cyprian, Diatreta, Tyrian

and mandarin yellow. From 1932 some of the firm's designs included engraved patterns rendered in a spirited Art Deco style.

Despite the breadth of artistic expression in its glassware, sales at Steuben remained unprofitable in the 1920s, during which time the firm's management and sales divisions were restructured several times. The Great Depression from 1929 further curtailed its market for decorative art glass, and in 1933 Corning Glass Co.'s management, now under Arthur Amory Houghton, Jr., decided to liquidate the Steuben division, thereby eliminating coloured glass from the firm's repertory. Carder finally closed down his workshop in 1959 and died four years later, at the age of one hundred.

Carlu, Jean (1900–1997)

Carlu was born in Bonnières-sur-Seine (Yvelines) and studied architecture at the École des Beaux-Arts in Paris, after which he became a designer, artist and posterist. In 1918 he had his right arm amputated after a tram accident. Following his first poster creation in 1917, Carlu concentrated on the medium after the First World War, while applying his talents to all the graphic arts, including magazine covers for *Vanity Fair*.

The poster that launched his career was 'Mon Savon', in 1925: the triangular shape of a well-tanned brawny bather leads the viewer's attention to the blue soap in his hand, a composition that reveals Cubist influence. 'Pepe Bonafe' and 'Théâtre Pigally' were noteworthy among Carlu's many other posters, in which he adopted a variety of avant-garde techniques, including Cubism, symbolism, abstraction and, in the 1930s, photomontage – the last especially for film posters.

In 1928 Carlu was commissioned to design a poster for La Régie Française des Tabacs (the French tobacco monopoly) and its top cigar brand, named 'Diplomat'. Appropriately, he drew a figure in the image of an

ambassador. For reasons now unknown, the maquette was refused. At about the same time, however, Carlu had been doing some work for a British publisher named Crawford, to whom he showed the rejected maquette. Crawford took it to London, making no changes to the design beyond its name, and sold it to the British firm of Larrañaga, an importer of Havana cigars. The poster was a huge success in England; Carlu designed a subsequent poster for the English cigar firm, making the gentleman appear a little more English. This was not the first time that Carlu had recycled a design in this manner.

From 1932 Carlu became involved in political causes, especially anti-Nazism, and in the late 1930s and 1940s designed related posters in the USA. He also wrote articles and lectured, and designed graphic works for both the 1937 Exposition des Arts et Techniques and the 1939 New York World's Fair. Following 'Stop Hitler Now', his first American defence poster for the Second World War, he produced a number of poster designs for the US Office of War Information. After the war, Carlu remained in New York until 1953 before returning to France to resume his career. He retired in 1974.

Carter, Gertrude Ellen (Truda) (1890–1958)

Born one of seven children to a distinguished entomologist and his wife near Dartford, Kent, Carter (née Sharp) was later affectionately known as Truda. In 1910, she moved to London to enroll on a three-year course at the Royal College of Art. There she met John Adams, a fellow student and gifted potter, whom she married in 1914. During the First World War the couple left for South Africa, returning in 1919 to England, where Adams joined Charles Carter and Harold Stabler in a pottery venture (CSA) launched in 1921 in Poole. Better known as Poole Pottery, the firm experimented initially with red earthenware with a semi-matt glaze, which it introduced the following year.

Influenced by the Art Deco figural stylizations that emerged at the Paris Salons after the First World War, especially those of René *Buthaud, Carter applied a similar decorative vernacular to the ceramics that she displayed in the firm's 1922 début at the British Industries Fair. CSA also participated at the 1925 *Exposition Internationale, where Carter's designs remained imitative of her French counterparts'. She later introduced various forms of abstraction, including Cubism, into her designs.

Divorced from John Adams in 1925, Carter married Cyril Carter in 1929. Over a twenty-year period, she was the creative force behind the patterns that placed Poole Pottery at the forefront of British design. Limited during the Second World War, her production increased again gradually until she retired around 1950.

Cartier. *See under* Jewelry.

Cartier, **Louis**. *See* Cartier.

Cassandre (Adolphe Mouron) (1901–1968).
See under Paintings, Graphics, Posters and Bookbinding.

Catteau, **Charles** (1880–1966)
A ceramic decorator at *Sèvres (1903–1904), Catteau transferred to Nymphenburg (1904–1906), where he specialized in underglaze decoration. He joined *Boch Frères Keramis the following year in La Louvière, Belgium, as design director. Acclaimed for his designs at the 1925 *Exposition Internationale, Catteau served as the technical director of an art institute from 1928 to 1945, before retiring to Nice.

Cazaux, **Édouard** (1889–1974)
Born in Caunelle (Landes), the son of a potter, Cazaux was fourteen when he started to work for a factory in Tarbes that produced architectural and household ceramics. He later found employment in Paris. Military service interrupted his education, but after the First World War Cazaux set up a kiln at La Varenne-Saint-Hilaire, a Paris suburb, where he pursued a career as a potter and sculptor. A monument to the war dead in Biarritz brought early recognition. He became a member of the La Stèle and L'Évolution groups, through which he displayed both his own vases and those he decorated for Sybille May, which were marketed by *Arthur Goldscheider. At the 1925 *Exposition Internationale, he was appointed a member of the jury for ceramics.

In the late 1920s Cazaux met the founder–manager of the Cristalleries de Compiègne, David Guéron, who was in search of a designer for a new line of art glass. Having been hired, Cazaux produced designs until the outbreak of the Second World War for vessels with moulded relief definition in clear, frosted and coloured glass, with polished, sandblasted, tinted or frosted finishes. A member of the *Salon d'Automne from 1923, and the *Société Nationale des Beaux-Arts from 1922, Cazaux was elected a *chevalier* of the French Légion d'Honneur in 1933. In the 1930s he was the foremost designer for *Degué, and in his later years Cazaux produced enamelled pottery, stoneware and sculpture.

Chambellan, **René** (1893–1955)
Chambellan was born in West Hoboken, New Jersey, and studied at New York University from 1912 to 1914, and later at the Académie Julian in Paris. Mobilized in the First World War, he served as a sergeant in the 11th US Army Corps of Engineers. Following the armistice, his vigorous Modernist style, which he rendered in a flat, two-dimensional form for bas-relief works, established him as one of America's foremost architectural sculptors. His work was sought for important public and private commissions, the latter including façades for the American Radiator and Daily News Buildings in Manhattan, both in conjunction with the architect Raymond Hood. Chambellan was also responsible for the Stewart & Co. Building, the Cromwell–Collier Building, the panels in the foyer of the Chanin Building, and the fountain court and ceiling of the RKO Center Theater in Rockefeller Center. In addition to a building's exterior, his designs extended into its lobby to include radiator grilles, postboxes and elevator doors. Much of his work today remains unidentified, because its authorship was concealed under the name of the building's retaining architect.

For the fairgrounds at the 1939 New York World's Fair, Chambellan created the sculpture *The Spirit of the Wheel*, a theme in keeping with the machine-age spirit of the time. His angular style, implemented in a flat, two-dimensional manner for architectural purposes, displayed a more forceful Modernism than that of most of his contemporaries in France.

Chanaux, **Adolphe** (1887–1965)
Throughout his career Chanaux played a brilliant second fiddle to a group of designers who benefited hugely from his creativity, including André *Groult, JACQUES-ÉMILE RUHLMANN and JEAN-MICHEL FRANK. Born in Paris, Chanaux studied painting at the city's École des Beaux-Arts, and after the First World War joined Groult's atelier, where he worked as a cabinet-maker. Chanaux was credited with the execution, if not also the design, of the celebrated anthropomorphic *bombé* chest of drawers included by Groult in his bedroom in the Ambassade Française pavilion at the 1925 *Exposition Internationale.

Chanaux's importance lay in his mastery of the period's most exotic and fashionable materials – *galuchat*, parchment, vellum, ivory, straw marquetry and hand-sewn leather – and the refined manner in which he used them. His history after he left Groult's atelier is uncertain. It is known that he worked for Ruhlmann in the mid-1920s as some of Chanaux's furniture bears both signatures. By 1927, however,

Chanaux had formed an association with the cabinet-maker Pelletier, whom he left after three years to join Frank, whose taste in materials and design matched his own more closely than any of his previous associates. By 1931 they were partners, supervising the workshops on rue Montauban in the Ruche section of Paris. Pieces from this period often bear both branded names.

In 1940, Chanaux left Paris for Arcachon, returning after Frank's death in 1941 to close the Ruche works. In 1943, he was engaged by the *parfumier* Jean-Pierre Guerlain as artistic director until his death.

Chanel, Gabrielle (Coco) (1883–1971)

After their mother died, Gabrielle Chanel (known later universally by her nickname 'Coco') and her sisters were placed in a convent. Chanel began her career in fashion as a seamstress, and later created an unconventional line of women's clothing that was freer, simpler and more comfortable than most in the early part of the century. In 1910 she opened her first fashion boutique, Chanel Mode, in rue Cambon, Paris, and this was so successful that it led shortly to a second outlet opening in Deauville. By 1915 a further one had opened in Biarritz, where Chanel became famous for her simple jersey dresses, which she embellished with costume jewelry. Each season she developed a new accessory line with the assistance of the Gripoix, a husband-and-wife team of jewellers.

In the late 1920s, Chanel introduced a line of jewelry mostly comprising very long ropes of gold chain hung with baroque pearls of all sizes and colours and, on occasion, *pâte-de-verre* crosses. She advocated that these be worn in the day – a distinct departure from the convention of the time. She also designed opera-length strings of imitation stones made of coloured glass which were interspersed with pearls. Around the same time, Étienne de Beaumont, her chief designer, created a selection of *faux* diamond jewelry.

In the early 1930s, to complement her masculine-style clothes and plain sweaters, Chanel introduced military chain trimmings, gilt buttons and a line of heavy Slavic-style gilt chains with huge medallions. As women became more independent, fake jewels gave them confidence in their own taste; no longer did fashion dictate a display of wealth. Following Chanel's success in this field, many of the larger fashion houses followed suit.

After 1932 Chanel was assisted by the Duke of Verdura, a Sicilian nobleman, who initially worked for her as a textile designer and later as a jewelry designer. He created enamelled bracelets adorned with imitation coloured beads and sometimes Maltese crosses assembled in the Gripoix's workshop. Toward the end of the decade, Chanel's 'little black dress' was accessorized with quantities of gilt coins, called 'gypsy necklaces'. After a period of self-exile in Switzerland, Chanel returned to the fashion world in 1954.

Chareau, Pierre (1883–1950). *See under* Furniture and Interior Design.

Chase Brass & Copper

In 1875, Augustus S. Chase (d. 1896) purchased a controlling interest in the USA Button Co. and the following year incorporated it as the Waterbury Manufacturing Co. While continuing to make buttons, Waterbury expanded into the manufacture of industrial brass goods such as lamps and beds, harness ornaments, patented novelties and electrical tubing. On his death, Augustus was succeeded by his son, Henry, under whose management the company grew into one of the nation's biggest consumers of brass, and had its own rolling mill. In 1909 it purchased the Noera Manufacturing Co., a maker of oilers, grease guns and tyre pumps, and the following year changed its name to the Chase Metal Works.

At the end of the First World War, the Chase Metal Works lost its principal customer, the US government,

which had purchased brass and copper for its wartime needs. This forced the firm to launch an aggressive sales campaign to establish a new client base. In so doing, it acquired the U. T. Hungerford Brass & Copper Co. and was itself in turn acquired by the Kennecott Copper Corp. Following a series of further mergers, the firm was renamed the Chase Brass & Copper Co. Inc. in 1936.

By the late 1920s the firm had entered the domestic market, manufacturing low-cost quality housewares such as cigarette boxes, pancake and corn sets, after-dinner coffee services and martini mixers in silvered and chromed metal, brass and Bakelite. Its timing was propitious as chromium provided an affordable alternative to silver in a collapsing economy. For its new product line, Chase Brass & Copper turned to an outside team of designers – including Walter *von Nessen, Albert *Reimann, Lurelle Guild, Charles Arcularius and Rockwell Kent – and an in-house one, Harry Laylon. During the Second World War, these wares were scaled back when the US government again commissioned war materials; at the end of hostilities Chase did not re-enter the consumer market for speciality wares. Today, based in Montpelier, Ohio, it is a leading maker of free-cutting brass rod.

Chauchet-Guilleré, Charlotte (1878–1964)

Born in Charleville (Ardennes), Chauchet-Guilleré (née Chauchet) trained as an artist. She exhibited at the first Salon of the *Société des Artistes Décorateurs, organized in 1904 by René Guilleré, whom she married shortly afterwards. In 1913, her husband, an accomplished art administrator and entrepreneur, established the *Primavera atelier and appointed his wife its artistic director. At Primavera Chauchet-Guilleré supervised a team of designers, including Louis *Sognot. They were as talented as their foremost competitors – *Studium–Louvre, *Pomone and *La Maîtrise – ensuring that they remained in the vanguard of modern taste and materials.

Chaumet

(*opposite*) Compact in diamonds, coral and lacquered gold, c. 1925 (*left*); and chain purse in diamonds and enamelled gold, c. 1925 (*right*).

Christofle

(*right*) Patinated metal vase with *dinanderie* decoration, designed by Luc Lanel, 1920s.

(*Far right*) Group of vases in patinated metal with *dinanderie* decoration, 1920s.

Chauchet-Guilleré exhibited at the Salons under her own name, including a range of bedroom and dining-room ensembles manufactured by Primavera. Salon catalogues list two addresses for her: 13 rue Eugénie-Girard, Vincennes, and 26 rue Norrins. At the *Salon d'Automne from 1922, she also exhibited an ensemble for a ministerial office at the 1923 L'Art Urbain et le Mobilier exhibition.

At the 1925 *Exposition Internationale, she supervised Primavera's exhibit, contributing a bedroom of her own. Elsewhere at the exhibition she took stand No. 68 on the Esplanade des Invalides, where she showed a dining room. Chauchet-Guilleré continued as director of Primavera after her husband died in 1931, and was succeeded in 1939 by Colette Guéden.

Chaumet

The origins of Maison Chaumet can be traced to the jewelry business established in 1780 by Marie-Étienne Nitot (1750–1809), whose most illustrious customer was Napoleon Bonaparte. He appointed Nitot 'Official Jeweller to the Emperor'. In 1815, with the fall of the empire, the founder's son, François-Regnault Nitot, continued the business before choosing the head of his workshop, Jean-Baptiste Fossin, as his successor. Fossin turned it over to his son Jules, who was succeeded in 1862 by Prosper Morel. Morel expanded the firm by opening a branch in London and participating in the era's major exhibitions. Maison Chaumet was launched in 1875 with the marriage of Joseph Chaumet (1852–1928), an expert in gemology, to Morel's daughter Marie; he assumed control ten years later.

During the *fin-de-siècle* period, Maison Chaumet created a stunning array of Art Nouveau jewelry, and in 1907 opened a showroom at 12 Place Vendôme, where it took its place alongside the era's pre-eminent jewelry houses – *Boucheron, *Van Cleef & Arpels and RENÉ LALIQUE. At the 1925 *Exposition Internationale,

it was one of thirty French jewelry establishments selected to exhibit in the *parure* section. On his death, Joseph was succeeded by his son, Marcel (1886–1964). Maison Chaumet is today a member of the LVMH Group owned by Bernard Arnault.

Chauvin, Jean (Louis) (1889–1976)

Born in Rochefort-sur-Mer, Chauvin moved to Paris at eighteen years of age to study at the École Nationale Supérieure des Arts Décoratifs, later studying sculpture under Antonin Mercié at the École des Beaux-Arts. He participated in the *Salon d'Automne and Salon des Indépendants, largely without critical acclaim. His abstract style incorporated fluid, elongated, machine-inspired forms. In later years Chauvin became reclusive, but continued to produce one or two sculptures each year. A retrospective exhibition on his works was staged at the 1962 Venice Biennale.

Chermayeff, Serge Ivan (1900–1996)

A Russian *émigré* educated at Harrow, Chermayeff worked as a journalist before 1924, then became chief designer for the decorating firm of E. Williams Ltd. In 1928, he was appointed director of the Modern Art Studio, which had been established by the London furniture manufacturers Waring & Gillow.

Chermayeff's designs for wood furniture, carpets and household effects, strongly influenced by the 1925 *Exposition Internationale, were often implemented in abstract patterns in black glass, silver cellulose and macassar ebony. From 1931 to 1933, while in private practice as an architect, he designed modern interiors for the BBC, and from 1933 to 1936, in partnership with Erich Mendelsohn, Chermayeff created the De La Warr pavilion at Bexhill-on-Sea. In 1936 he designed unit furniture for Plant Ltd. In 1939, he emigrated to the USA, where he taught design and architecture.

Cheuret, Albert (*fl.* 1907–1928). *See under* Lighting.

Chiparus, Demetre (1889–1947). *See under* Sculpture.

Christofle

Founded in 1830 by Charles Christofle (1805–1863) as a jewelry manufactory, in 1842 the company purchased from the English firm of Elkington & Co. its patent for the *galvanoplastie* (electroplating) process, which enabled it to extend production into the field of silverware. Christofle also introduced into its repertoire from c. 1850 an enchanting selection of *damascened*, enamelled, patinated and *guilloché* techniques to accent the metal. The most celebrated Christofle commission at this time was its centrepiece and dinner service in silverplate for Napoleon III and the Empress Eugénie, which was exhibited at the 1855 Exposition Universelle.

Charles Christofle was succeeded on his death by his nephew Henri Brouilhet, an engineer and art lover (he was one of the founders of the Musée des Arts Décoratifs in Paris). Brouilhet's innovations propelled the firm to the forefront of its market. Most important under Brouilhet's stewardship were the firm's refinements both to the Elkington silverplating process and to the one developed by the Frenchman Herman Jacobi, which had been registered in 1836. It also made advances in the techniques of mechanical damascening and electromagnetic engraving. Brouilhet invented a cost-effective method of manufacturing solid and *ronde-bosse* wares, which enabled the firm to create monumental plated works, including statuary for the façade of the Paris Opéra. At the 1900 Exposition Universelle, the firm presented an improved silver-plating technique, named *Gallia, for a series of its flat- and hollowware.

In the 1920s and 1930s, Christofle suspended some of the Beaux-Arts style items that had been the company's stock-in-trade (and the entire silver industry's), introducing in their place restrained

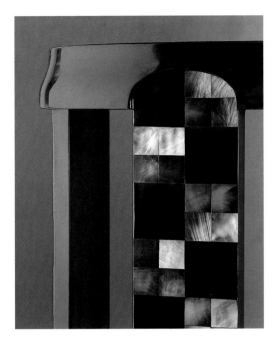

and pared-down Modernist silverware. At the 1925 *Exposition Internationale, the firm shared a pavilion with the Compagnie des Cristalleries de Baccarat. Its address at the time was listed as 56 rue de Bondy, Paris. Included in its display were polychromed bronze and silverplated wares designed by Carl Christian *Fjerdingstad, André *Groult, Jean *Bonnet, Luc Lanel and SÜE ET MARE. Another noted designer commissioned by Christofle in the inter-war years was Gio *Ponti, whose famous candlesticks made of crossed horns were introduced just before the Second World War. Later models were commissioned from Lino Sabattini and Tapio Wirkkala. Now one of the largest worldwide exporters of silverware, Christofle remains under the control of the Brouilhet family.

Clark, Allan (1896–1950)

Born in Missoula, Montana, Clark studied with Albin Polasek at the Art Institute of Chicago, and later with Robert Aiken at the Art Students League in New York. In 1924 he left for Japan to experiment with the technique of polychromed sculpture. After three years of travel and study in the Far East, including trips to Korea, China and later to the Turkestan border with a Fogg Museum archaeological expedition, Clark's sculptures became distinctly exotic, while gracefully marrying Oriental and Modernist influences. His treatment of clothing, in which the garment's folds were simplified into sweeping lines, was particularly successful. A pair of Caucasian figures, 'Forever Young' and 'Forever Painting', issued in editions of fifteen by the Gorham Manufacturing Co., show the same engaging youthfulness and energy.

As most of Clark's works were unique, whether castings or directly carved works commissioned by private clients, the whereabouts of many of them are unrecorded.

Cliff, Clarice (1899–1972). *See under* Ceramics.

Coard, Marcel (1889–1975)

Coard was born in Paris into what he later described as a 'grande bourgeoisie' family. He studied architecture at the École Nationale Supérieure des Beaux-Arts, yet emerged as a decorator, establishing himself in 1914 on the boulevard Haussmann. At the outbreak of the First World War Coard volunteered for action, but was demobilized through illness and spent the remainder of the war in a military hospital passing the time by sketching furniture designs. In 1919, he renewed his career as a decorator.

As fashionable Parisian taste at the time favoured the past, Coard furnished most of his interiors with 18th-century antiques. This expediency explains, in part, his limited furniture production. But an additional reason was that he disliked duplicating his designs, as he explained in an interview in *L'Oeil* prior to his death:

> Such pieces of furniture, exquisitely wrought, were unique, because I have always avoided repeating the pieces I have made. I was never really concerned with large-scale production. These pieces were each made individually with the most beautiful materials I could find.

To maintain such integrity required wealthy clients; for Coard, most importantly, these were Jacques *Doucet in Neuilly and Pierre Cocteau in Touraine. Coard's preferred woods were oak (often primitively cut), macassar ebony and palisander. His selection of veneers and encrusted materials gave his pieces their individualism: parchment, mother-of-pearl, *galuchat*, rock crystal, tinted mirror, marbrite and glass with a silvered ground. Colour accents were added by the use of lapis lazuli and amethyst. Coard's ornamentation, however, was always subordinate to form; the contours of his furniture remained unbroken.

African and Oceanic tribal art and the Orient were ever-present influences on Coard's work. Only PIERRE-ÉMILE LEGRAIN's furniture bore a pronounced

similarity to Coard's, to the point where certain pieces require provenance to determine authorship. Coard was rigidly independent, avoiding both the annual Salons and the small groups, such as Les Cinq, which exhibited intermittently in Paris. Of his contemporaries, only PAUL DUPRÉ-LAFON seemed as intent on privacy. A 1932 monograph in *Art et Décoration* traced some of Coard's important commissions: in addition to his work for Pierre Cocteau, there were private residences near Boulogne and in Paris. The illustrations show, in large part, a restrained Coard – many pieces of conventional, if not nondescript, design serving as a reminder that only in his work for a very narrow avant-garde could Coard's creativity operate unbounded.

The pieces commissioned by Doucet are important today as they show this unbridled Coard. Most of these are now in the Musée des Arts Décoratifs, Paris, or were offered in the 1972 auction of Doucet's collection at the Hôtel Drouot. Two pieces – a table and armchair – were made in collaboration with Josef *Czáky and GUSTAV MIKLOS. Two others – a 'bird cage' table and a *tabouret* – are so similar to contemporary designs by Legrain that the issue of precedence arises. Elsewhere, an armoire in the collection of the Musée des Arts Décoratifs, Paris, is stamped 'Roumy', providing a rare identification of one of Coard's cabinet-makers.

Coates, Wells (1895–1958)

Son of a British missionary in Japan, where he was raised, Coates studied engineering at the University of British Columbia in Vancouver before serving in the First World War as a pilot. After the war he settled in London, where he worked intermittently as a draughtsman and journalist. It was in the latter capacity that he visited the 1925 *Exposition Internationale, where *Le Corbusier's pavilion, L'Esprit Nouveau, influenced him greatly.

Allan Clark

(*opposite, left*) *Study for a Garden Pool*, tinted plaster, 1920s.

Marcel Coard

(*opposite, centre*) Occasional table in lacquered wood applied with mother-of-pearl panels, *c.* 1930.

(*opposite, right*) Detail of the occasional table described above.

Marcel Coard

(*below*) Table in lacquered wood overlaid in *coquille d'œuf*, with chromed metal mounts, *c.* 1930.

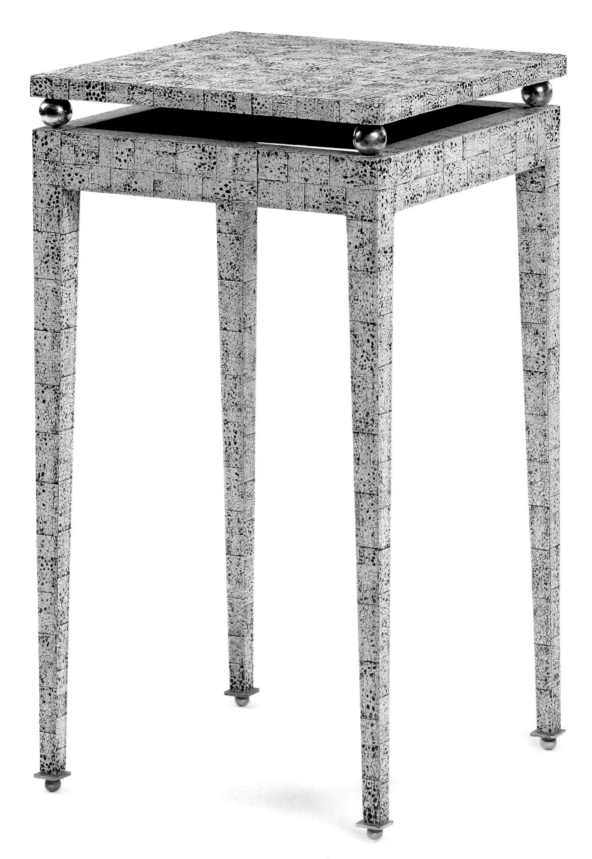

Susie Cooper
(*below*) Charger in glazed
earthenware, 1920s.

Aristide Colotte
(*right*) Vase in moulded, cut
and sandblasted glass, 1920s.

Aristide Colotte
(*opposite, left*) Vases in
moulded, cut and sandblasted
glass, the left one dates to
1928.

Consolidated Lamp & Glass
(*opposite, right*) Selection
of 'Ruba Rombic' tableware,
moulded and cased topaz glass,
late 1920s.

Claire Jeanne Roberte Colinet
(*right*) *Juggler*, gilt-bronze and
ivory, 1920s.

Coates's first major architectural commissions, based on Le Corbusier's concept of a *machine à habiter*, were the Lawn Road flats in Hampstead (1932–1934), built by Isokon, the firm that he had established with Jack Pritchard in 1931 to design and build modular housing and unit furnishings. In 1935 the firm was expanded into the Isokon Furniture Co. to manufacture and distribute additional furniture by other designers. In industrial design Coates's major work was for E. K. Cole, for which he created a series of circular plastic radios (1934–1946), the portable 'Princess' handbag (1947) and plastic electric heaters (1937).

Colin, Paul (1892–1985). *See under* Paintings, Graphics, Posters and Bookbinding.

Colinet, Claire Jeanne Roberte (1880–1950)
Brussels-born Colinet studied in her native city under Jef Lambeaux before moving to Paris, where she exhibited at the Salons of the *Société des Artistes Français from 1913 and later became a naturalized French citizen. She exhibited also at the Salon des Indépendants (1937–40) and became a member of the Union des Femmes Peintres et Sculpteurs. In the 1920s, her residence was listed as 59 rue du Château in Asnières (Seine).

Colinet is best remembered for her works in bronze and ivory, in which she portrayed her models in a far more animated style than that of most of her contemporaries, including DEMETRE CHIPARUS. Her models included an array of female entertainers, such as odalisques, exotic dancers, snake charmers, jugglers and cabaret performers. Notable among her finest works in this genre were the figurines 'Dance of Carthage', 'Theban Dancer' and 'Corinthian Dancer'. Her works were commissioned by at least three Paris manufacturers: *Etling & Cie, *Arthur Goldscheider and *Les Neveux de J. Lehmann (LNJL). Colinet's last recorded Salon entry was in 1945.

Colotte, Aristide (1885–1959)
Born in Baccarat, in Lorraine, Colotte joined the Baccarat glassworks at a very young age and remained there for some years before enlisting in the military. Wounded in action in the First World War, he settled in 1919 in Nancy, where he worked in engraving and **chasing** at the Magasins Réunis. In 1925 he found employment at the Cristallerie de Nancy, for which he designed a number of cast figurines, including automobile mascots. He also etched, painted and enamelled blocks of black glass, before setting up his own atelier at 2 rue Gilbert in Nancy in 1926.

Colotte's speciality was direct cutting, which he did on large heavy blocks of crystal supplied by Baccarat. Carving, grinding and etching techniques, the last-mentioned with hydrofluoric acid, were interchanged as he proceeded. Most of his works were *pièces uniques*, comprising roughly hewn slabs of glass that were deeply carved and etched, then polished, chiselled or filed to create sparkling background effects. By the mid-1930s Colotte's work mainly depicted human and animal figures, often inspired by biblical themes. He first exhibited at the Salon of the *Société des Artistes Décorateurs in 1927. He was awarded the Légion d'Honneur in 1931.

His workshop, which soon employed several workers, extended its production to gold, silver and metal jewelry. At the 1937 Exposition des Arts et Techniques in Paris, Colotte displayed large sculpted works, including a dolphin carved from a 680 kilogram block of crystal. During the Second World War he received a large number of private and public commissions, including the glass sword, 2 metres high, presented by the city of Nancy to Marshal Pétain, who had been appointed President of France with the agreement of the occupying German forces.

In 1944, Colotte was condemned and imprisoned as a Nazi collaborator, and his property was confiscated by the French state. On his release, he moved to Paris and worked as a jeweller. He died penniless.

Consolidated Lamp & Glass
The Consolidated Lamp & Glass Co. of Coraopolis, Pennsylvania, was incorporated in 1893 to manufacture a line of domestic utility glassware, which included *Gone with the Wind* spirit lamps. In 1926, it introduced a line of art glass with relief-moulded designs, entitled 'Martelé', designed by Reuben Haley in a distinctly LALIQUE style.

This was followed two years later by a more successful pattern, 'Ruba Rombic', whose title was described in an advertisement in *Garden and Home Builder* in 1928 as a combination of *rubaic* (meaning epic or poem) and *rombic* (irregular in shape), 'so ultra-smart that it is as modern as tomorrow's newspaper'. Offered in muted monochromatic hues, including smoky grey, lavender, topaz and amber, were pressed tableware, toiletry items, candlesticks, vases and table lamp bases designed in an ultra-modern style that in its interplay of sharp angularities echoed the burgeoning Manhattan skyline.

Affected by the Great Depression from 1929, the plant was closed in 1932, at which time its most popular models were lent to the Phoenix Glass Co. in Monaca, a few kilometres north of Coraopolis, where production was continued. In 1936, when the Consolidated Lamp & Glass Co. re-opened, the moulds were returned. It was closed after a fire in 1963.

Cooper, Susie (1902–1995)
Born into a middle-class family in Milton, just outside Stoke-on-Trent, Staffordshire, Cooper was the youngest of seven children of a justice of the peace. She attended a local school and, from 1918, went to evening classes at the Burslem School of Art, where she was awarded a scholarship to study full time for three years. To further fund her studies, she joined a local pottery, A. E. Gray Ltd, in Stoke, where she was trained as a painter. Some of her designs were included in the firm's display at the 1925 *Exposition Internationale, for which it was awarded a gold medal in lustreware.

Cooper's designs, including the 'Moon and Mountains' pattern (1927), incorporated an enchanting mix of Art Deco and Cubist imagery. Increasingly unhappy with the shapes she had to use as they did not match her designs, Cooper set herself up in 1929 as an independent designer and joined Crown Ducal, a fledgling factory in Tunstall, before moving to Burslem. The success of her tablewares spurred Cooper's search for larger premises, which she found in 1931 at the Crown Works, Burslem, where she worked for the next fifty years.

In the 1930s Cooper introduced a wide range of innovative decorating techniques including crayon and aerographed decoration – the latter often with *sgrafitto* detailing – into her hand-painted earthenwares, which she showed at trade shows such as the British Industries Fair. Among the most popular of her 1930s patterns were 'Dresden Spray', 'Wide Bands', 'Woodpecker', 'Briar Rose' and 'Heliotrope'. New shapes included 'Kestrel' and 'Curlew'. These were practical and functional, easy to clean, poured well and could take all manner of decoration. In the late 1930s, the sale of her wares in the USA was administered through her agent Fondeville & Co., on Fifth Avenue in New York.

During the Second World War, a fire at Cooper's pottery led to its closure. Following the armistice, while it was under reconstruction, she returned to textile design. In the early 1950s, her firm, the Susie Cooper Pottery, purchased Jason China Ltd, based in Longton, but in 1957 this workshop suffered a disastrous blow from a fire in an adjacent building. Cooper nevertheless continued to create ceramics into the 1960s in a subdued and elegant style, some of which were for Wedgwood, who later purchased her firm. A 1987 retrospective exhibition at the Victoria & Albert Museum paid tribute to her career, which, as she continued to work into the 1990s, ultimately spanned seven decades.

Copier, Andries Dirk (1901–1991)

Copier was born in Holland and joined *NV Vereenigde Glasfabriek Leerdam as an apprentice in 1914. There he began to produce glass with new forms and techniques, while studying in Utrecht and Rotterdam between 1917 and 1925. In 1923, he was appointed director of Leerdam's Unica Studio. Awarded a silver medal at the 1925 *Exposition Internationale, he held his first exhibition of Unica wares in Stuttgart in 1927. Under his artistic direction, Leerdam glassware gained considerable recognition in Europe.

Coudyser, Jules (1867–1931)

Lille-born Coudyser was an interior designer who also retailed fabrics, embroideries, lace, wall hangings and carpets through his Paris store L'Art dans les Tapis et les Tissus. At the 1925 *Exposition Internationale, he and Georges Boudart shared a stand, listing themselves as artist–decorators located at 85 rue du Bac. Elsewhere, Coudyser's rugs were included in displays by *Saddier et ses Fils, Ausseur, Eric *Bagge and Georges Champion, among others. In the late 1920s Coudyser was appointed a professor at the Conservatoire des Arts et Métiers, Paris.

Cournault, Étienne (1891–1948)

Born in Malzéville, Cournault studied at the École des Beaux-Arts in Nancy before moving to London in 1920, where he remained for ten years. Although a skilled painter, printer and illustrator, he is recognized more for his work in glass, such as the engraved mirror he created for Jacques *Doucet's Neuilly residence and his enamelled and etched miniature panels for Jean *Després's jewelry. Cournault was a founding member of the *Union des Artistes Modernes (UAM) in 1929.

Cowan, Reginald Guy (1884–1957)

Cowan was born in East Liverpool, Ohio, into a family of potters, from whom he received a practical and

formal training, He established his own pottery studio in 1912 on Nicolson Avenue in Lakewood, near Cleveland, Ohio, after the local gas supply failed in Rocky River, west of Lakewood, where he had lived previously.

At the forefront of the modern movement in ceramic design in America, the Cowan Pottery Studio provided the forum for many of America's most gifted ceramists for ten years (from 1921 until late 1930). In the early 1920s, it began the production of desk-top items – compotes, bookends, figurines and vases – in bright lustred glazes such as cream and marigold, which were distributed through a network of roughly twelve hundred national outlets, including Marshall Field's in Chicago, John Wanamaker's in Philadelphia and Ovington in New York.

In addition to its commercial wares, Cowan's studio produced limited editions of art pottery designed by well-known artists such as Russell B. Aitken, Thelma Frazier, Arthur E. Baggs, Waylande de Santis *Gregory, Paul Bogatay, Margaret Postgate, Edward Winter and VIKTOR SCHRECKENGOST. Following the Wall Street crash in 1929, the quality and volume of the firm's wares began to fall, and it went into receivership in December 1930. Without commercial pressures, artists affiliated with the pottery experimented freely in the interim period before its closure.

Cretté, Georges (1893–1969)

Born in Créteil, Cretté completed his studies at the École Estienne in 1911, and the following year joined Henri Marius-Michel's workshop on rue Pierre-Nicole, Paris, where he quickly emerged as its foremost gilder. His career was interrupted by military service and the advent of the First World War. In 1919 he rejoined Marius-Michel, whose studio had been more or less inoperative due to the master's lingering ill-health.

Henri Creuzevault
Assise (André Pératé), inlays of leather, 1920s.

Josef Csáky
(*opposite, left*) Standing female figure, marble, 1920s.

(*opposite, above right*) Figure of a bird, plaster, c. 1924.

(*opposite, below right*) *Tête de jeune fille*, marble bust included in the Exhibition of Modern French Decorative Arts at Lord & Taylor, New York, February, 1928.

Cretté assumed control and began to direct the flow of new business, an arrangement formalized in 1923 and put into effect in April 1925, a month before Marius-Michel's death. As a mark of esteem for his former employer and mentor, Cretté added to his signature the proud imprimatur, *SUCC. de MARIUS MICHEL*, on many of the bindings that he subsequently created. A member of the *Société des Artistes Décorateurs from 1924 to 1929, his binding masterpieces included *Le Cantique des cantiques* and *Le Livre de la jungle*.

The 1925 *Exposition Internationale introduced Cretté to the public as an independent binder. Adhering initially to the Art Nouveau floral aesthetic, which allowed him to retain Marius-Michel's old clients, he gradually began to promote his own more traditional geometric style, which was built around compositions of gold and blind-tooled fillets. His virtuosity as a gilder drew comparisons with the 19th-century master gilder Trautz, and earned him the soubriquet *maître des filets*. By 1930, Cretté was well established as a modern binder with classical roots – one to whom collectors such as J. André, Baron Gourgaud, Aubert, Barthou and Bussilet brought many of their volumes.

His designs were crisp and in harmony with the texts, composed of repeating symmetrical punched decoration, such as overlapping circles, letters and angled or parallel lines. The incorporation of delicate images, such as ears of corn or arabesques, added enchantment. His mastery of leather brought Cretté various outside commissions, including ones from FRANÇOIS-LOUIS SCHMIED and JEAN DUNAND, whose lacquered panels he bound.

Cretté's style continued to evolve after the Second World War, with the introduction of sharply contrasting inlays of colour on to beige or tan leather grounds. He also pursued the use of recessed or sculpted definition which he had begun in the 1930s.

Creuzevault, Henri (1905–1971)
Born in Paris to an independent binder, Creuzevault served his apprenticeship as a gilder between 1918 and 1920 before joining the family business, which he quickly propelled into the front ranks of the Modernist movement with a broad range of avant-garde designs executed in innovative techniques.

From 1925 Creuzevault's bindings began to incorporate the Art Deco imagery which had became popular at the annual Paris Salons. Henri felt himself to be at one with both the new epoch and the style that dominated it. His youthful and vigorous covers took as their point of departure the revolutionary designs of PIERRE-ÉMILE LEGRAIN. His bindings for *Le Livre de la jungle* and *Les Carnets de voyage en Italie*, executed c. 1926, drew wide praise for their powerful imagery and robust leather covers accentuated with two ribs (in place of the traditional five) which protruded 1 centimetre from the spines. With their accompanying sleeves and slipcases, the books made an imposing and weighty package.

From 1928 Creuzevault was assisted by his younger brother, Louis, who bound his designs. By the mid-1930s, after the workshop had moved to 159 Faubourg Saint-Honoré, Creuzevault incorporated raised or sculptural details in his covers, which were soon described as 'architectural'. The introduction of partial or shaded combinations of colour on the surface of the leather characterized his endless pursuit of novelty. Examples included encrustations of gold and silver, silver and aluminium with blind-tooled fillets, and gold with imitation lacquer.

The death in the early 1930s of his brother Louis had an adverse effect on Creuzevault's work for several years. However, by 1937, when he was awarded both a *grand prix* and a gold medal at the 1937 Exposition des Arts et Techniques, he had established himself as a rival of ROSE ADLER and PAUL BONET in the vanguard of the Modernist movement in French bookbinding –

a position he built on after the Second World War. His covers remained remarkably fresh and experimental, combining abstract and geometric compositions with three-dimensional effects.

In 1946, Creuzevault helped to form the society La Reliure Originale, in whose exhibitions he participated. Ten years later he retired from active bookbinding and turned his attention to an art gallery that he had purchased on the avenue Matignon in Paris. At the time he also created tapestry designs for the Gobelins manufactory.

Csáky, Josef (1888–1971)
Csáky was born in Szeged, near Budapest, and enrolled at the city's Academy of Decorative Arts. Disappointed by its traditional curriculum, he left after eighteen months to pursue an independent career in modelling and direct carving. Initial commissions, including that of a portrait bust for Count Karoly, were followed in 1908 by his departure for Paris. There he made the acquaintance of similar young artists in the Vaugirard quarter; many were associated with the La Ruche group, including Fernand Léger, Alexander Archipenko, Marc Chagall, Chaim Soutine and Henri Laurens. At first Csáky assisted an art dealer while making moulds for sculptors and posing for artists. He participated at the *Salon d'Automne (1911–12), those of the *Société Nationale des Beaux-Arts (1910–11) and the Salon des Indépendants (1913–14, 1920, 1923). He became a naturalized Frenchman in 1914.

One of the first sculptors to adopt the three-dimensional Cubism that painters such as Pablo Picasso and Georges Braque were developing, Csáky applied the same theories of abstraction to his figures. In 1911 he completed his first Cubist portrait bust. By now an ardent publicist for Cubism, he was appointed the secretary of the revue *Montjoie*.

At the outbreak of the First World War, Csáky enlisted in the French army, where he remained until

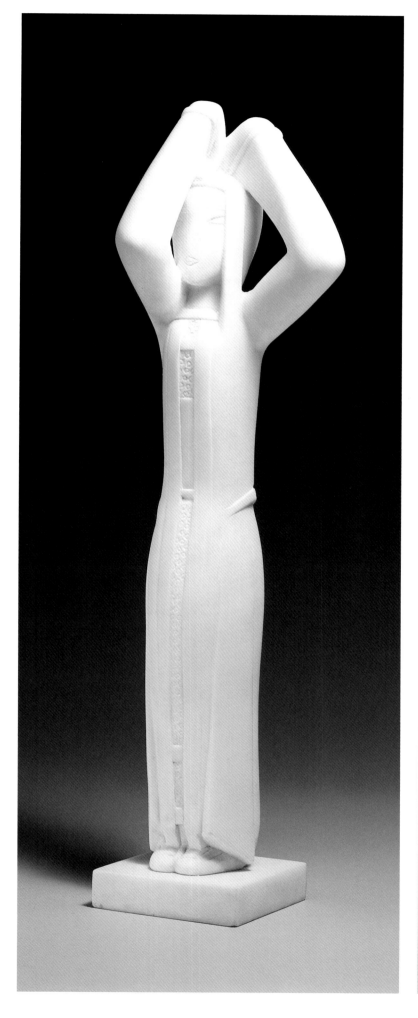

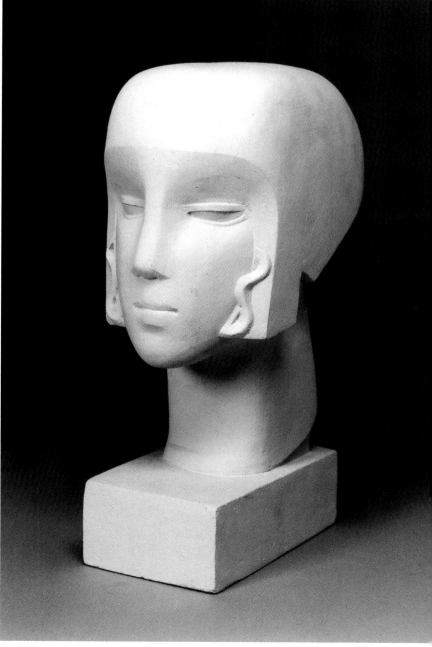

Pierre d'Avesn
(*opposite left*) Vase in moulded glass, 1920s.

Maurice Daurat
(*below*) Coupe in pewter, 1920s.

Damon
(*right*) Table lamp in nickel-plated metal, late 1920s.

D'Argental
(*opposite right*) Vase in etched cameo glass, 1920s.

the armistice. After the war he again focused on the concept of abstraction, in which his compositions were systematically reduced into a series of cones, disks, cylinders or spheres. By 1920 he had begun to model reliefs of geometric patterns, which he highlighted by painting and incising the negative space. Around this time, he signed a contract with Leonce Rosenberg to exhibit at his avant-garde gallery, L'Effort Moderne, at 10 rue de la Baume in Paris.

From 1927 to 1930 Csáky executed several sculptures on the theme of 'the fish' for the house of Pierre Cocteau in the Touraine. In 1927 he also was commissioned by Jacques *Doucet to collaborate with PIERRE-ÉMILE LEGRAIN in furnishing his studio in Neuilly, for which he created sculpture and decorative elements, including a stair balustrade, columns, door handles and carpets. Around 1928, Csáky's style revealed an orientation towards naturalism. Numerous museum and gallery exhibitions followed in the 1930s throughout Europe and in the USA, and his works were acquired by such noted Modernist collectors as Charles de Noailles, Baron Philippe de Rothschild, G. Acheson in New York and Ernest Duveen in London.

A founding member of *Union des Artistes Modernes (UAM) in 1929, Csáky showed with the group until 1932, and also participated at the 1937 Exposition des Arts et Techniques. In 1946, he was appointed a *sociétaire* of the *Salon d'Automne. Despite the importance of his work and his worldwide celebrity, Csáky remained impoverished until his death.

Cuttoli, Marie (1879–1973). *See* Mybor.

D

Damon

Damon was named for its founding lighting engineer, and developed *verre émaillé diffusant*, in which the glass was enamelled on its interior and frosted on its exterior. The resulting hybrid, it was claimed, provided the benefits of both finishes: although transparent, it was of sufficient opacity to conceal the number or position of the bulbs behind it and to provide an even distribution of light. In addition to the founder's own creations, the firm commissioned Jean-Boris *Lacroix, Gorinthe, André Roy, André Basompierre, Georges Martin, Daniel Stephan and Jean Baignères to provide lighting designs for its showroom, located at 4 avenue Pierre 1re de Serbie in Paris's 16th arrondissement, with workshops in Boulogne.

A proponent of functional lighting, Damon marketed a full range of standard fixtures, including illuminated vases, antechamber lanterns and *bouts de table*. The lamps' metal mounts were in gilt or silvered bronze, chrome or nickelled copper.

D'Argental

In 1924, the Cristalleries de Saint-Louis-lès-Bitche, located in the Moselle département, introduced a new line of cameo art glass entitled 'D'Argental'. The name derived from the German village of Münzthal, where the manufacturing glass house had its origins. *Münze* in German means 'coins' and the firm chose the French word, *argent*, meaning 'silver' as the trade name for the new wares.

The majority of D'Argental's designs were in the Art Nouveau genre – vistas of the Vosges mountains and harvesting scenes in two- or three-layered glass – provided by Paul Nicolas, an ex-Gallé employee. However, some examples were made in a stylized Art Deco idiom.

Da Silva Bruhns, Ivan (1881–1980). *See under* Textiles.

Daum, Antonin (1864–1931). *See* Daum Frères.

Daum, Auguste (1853–1908). *See* Daum Frères.

Daum, Jean (1825–1885). *See* Daum Frères.

Daum, Paul (1888–1944). *See* Daum Frères.

Daum Frères. *See under* Glass.

Daurat, Maurice (1880–1969)

Born in Bordeaux, Daurat studied drawing, painting and sculpture at the local art school. Drawn to metalware, he began his career **chasing** jewelry and working in bronze, and at some point established his own studio. Daurat was a participant at the Salons of the *Société des Artistes Français, the *Société des Artistes Décorateurs and the *Salon d'Automne, where he showed objects in gold, silver and pewter, the last becoming his metal of choice. At the 1925 *Exposition Internationale, his works received favourable critical reviews.

Daurat employed traditional ironsmithing techniques in his creation of a wide range of liturgical and domestic wares in pewter, including light fixtures, tea services and jewelry. Eschewing other forms of ornamentation, he applied a mix of robustly hammered and planished finishes to the surfaces of his metals. At the 1937 Exposition des Arts et Techniques in Paris, Daurat served as a member of the International Metalware Jury.

d'Avesn, Pierre (*fl.* 1914–1950s)

D'Avesn was employed by RENÉ LALIQUE prior to the First World War, after which he worked for a number of commercial glassworks, familiarizing himself with the various techniques used in the glass-moulding process. In the mid-1920s he joined DAUM FRÈRES in Nancy. In 1927 Paul Daum established Les Verreries d'Art Lorrain in Croismare (Meurthe-et-Moselle) to mass-produce domestic glassware, placing d'Avesn in charge. The venture comprised Les Verreries d'Art de M. P. d'Avesn and Les Verreries de Belle-Étoile,

Degué
(*below*) Table lamp in etched
cameo glass, 1920s.

Georges de Bardyère
(*left*) Cabinet in oak, *c.* 1928.

Sonia Delaunay
(*below*) Wool carpet, 1920s.

Georges de Bardyère
(*left*) Salon ensemble, late
1920s.

André Delatte
Vase with etched and
enamelled decoration, 1920s.

the latter an existing glassworks which was taken over and expanded. Pieces in clear, frosted, stained or coloured varieties of glass were signed 'P. d'Avesn' or 'Lorrain'. Products included light fixtures housed in metal armatures, and vases, compotes and ashtrays, in moulded glass decorated with stylized Art Deco floral and geometric patterns.

A casualty of the 1929 Wall Street crash and its global economic reverberations, the Croismare works were closed in 1932. D'Avesn went on to work for the Cristallerie-de-Choisi-le-Roi, for which he designed glassware. He was still active in 1951, when models by him were included in the firm's display at the L'Art du Verre exhibition in Paris.

De Bardyère, Georges (d. 1942)

Born in Wassy (Haute-Marne), de Bardyère's date of birth is unrecorded. He participated regularly at the Salons of the *Société des Artistes Décorateurs from 1919 as a decorator–interior designer. Early works were stiff and undistinguished, their understated classic forms lightly decorated with carved bas-relief decoration and ivory veneers. At the 1925 *Exposition Internationale, de Bardyère created more interesting interiors for his stand on the Esplanade des Invalides. He also exhibited at the 1926 *Salon d'Automne, where his furniture was adorned with volutes that drew comparison to the Louis-Philippe themes popularized at the time through the work of SÜE ET MARE.

For his interiors, de Bardyère retained Genet & Michon for his lighting needs, Henri Pinguenet for paintings, JEAN DUNAND for lacquered wares and IVAN DA SILVA BRUHNS for carpets. His choice of woods included burl walnut, palisander, mahogany and amboyna. He displayed at the Salons into the 1930s, with increased emphasis on wallpaper and fabric designs. At the time of his death, his address was listed as 21 rue de Richelieu, Paris, where he had lived for nearly thirty years.

Decoeur, Émile (1876–1953). *See under* Ceramics.

Decorchemont, François-Émile (1880–1971). *See under* Glass.

Degué

La Verrerie d'Art Degué was established in 1926 by David Guéron, the owner of the Cristalleries de Compiègne (a manufacturer of household goods), with the aim of adding art glass to his commercial repertoire.

With its headquarters on the boulevard Malesherbes and a wholesale showroom at 41 rue de Paradis, the firm produced a range of art glass virtually indistinguishable from that of other industrial glass houses in the post-Gallé era, including *D'Argental, André *Delatte, *Muller Frères and *Schneider. The colouration on one of its editions especially resembled the orange-red-yellow palette employed by Schneider, which later sued Degué for breach of copyright. Degué's foremost designer in the 1930s was Édouard *Cazaux. The glassworks closed in 1939 and were later bombed. Guéron himself died during the war.

Delatte, André (*fl.* 1921–30)

Delatte founded a small glassworks at Jarville, on the outskirts of Nancy, in 1921. There he manufactured editions of mould-blown industrial household tablewares decorated with random striations of *intercalaire* (interior colour), and etched cameo wares with floral or landscape scenes so imitative of those manufactured at the time by *Muller Frères and DAUM FRÈRES that the latter initiated breach of copyright suits against him.

Delatte's later editions of Art Deco-style glassware, including enamelled geometric patterns on monochromatic grounds and thick-walled opaque pieces with deeply sandblasted frieze designs, were more innovative. Many of these were signed 'Jarvil', a contraction of the name of the Nancy suburb in which his glassworks was located.

Delaunay, Sonia (1885–1979)

Born in Gradizhsk, Ukraine, Delaunay (née Terk) studied drawing in Karlsruhe before settling in Paris in 1905, where she attended the Académie de la Palette. She married the painter Robert Delaunay (1885–1941) in 1910, and adopted his theories on 'simultaneous contrasts' and his Fauvism to her textile designs, in what became a mutually fruitful collaboration that lasted for many years.

Delaunay's first abstract compositions appeared in 1911, after which she introduced abstraction into her collages, bookbindings, posters, canvases and clothing – the last becoming the rage in the *haut monde* of Paris fashion. She also designed costumes for the Ballets Russes and early films. Her bookbindings, created in collaboration with the era's great Surrealist authors, were judged masterpieces of abstract art.

In 1914 the Delaunays moved to the Iberian peninsula to escape the war. They returned to Paris in 1921, where they socialized with the new literary avant-garde associated with the Dadaists and Surrealists. One of Delaunay's abstract dress designs led to a contract from the Lyons textile firm Bianchini–Férier in 1922. This was followed by her design programme for clothing and accessories, 'La Boutique Simultanée', shown at the 1925 *Exposition Internationale, where she exhibited with the furrier Jacques Heim. (She had opened a Paris boutique with Heim the previous year, at 40 rue Lafitte.)

In a career punctuated by many highs, Delaunay produced her first wool tapestry coats and exhibited her 'fabrics in movement' at the 1924 *Salon d'Automne. In 1929 she designed the furniture for the bachelor apartment in the film *Parce que je t'aime*, joined the *Union des Artistes Modernes (UAM) and published the album *Tapis et tissus*. After 1931 she focused almost exclusively on painting. At the outbreak of the Second World War, the Delaunays left Paris for Auvergnes to escape the Nazis. In 1941, after her

Raphaël Delorme
Baroque Fantasy, oil on
masonite, 1920s.

Jean Després
(*opposite*) Silver necklace,
c. 1925.

husband's death, Delaunay took refuge in Grasse
in south-eastern France. After the war she returned
to Paris, where she worked until her death.

Del Marle, Félix (1889–1952)

Del Marle was born in Pont-sur-Sambre (Nord).
Although a French painter, he was drawn initially to
the Italian Futurist movement, in support of which
he published his 1913 *Manifeste futuriste de
Montmartre*, where he railed against the bohemianism
of his fellow Parisians.

His experiences in the First World War turned
him against the brutality of Futurism, however, forcing
him to search for other styles and philosophies. After
the war, he met several members of the Dutch De Stijl
group, including Piet Mondrian and Theo van Doesburg,
and eventually adopted the forms, if not all the
doctrines, that they espoused. Del Marle promoted
the group's ideas in Lille, and organized and
participated in its exhibitions in 1925 and 1928.

His 1926 living-room suite of furniture for Mme
'B' in Dresden – described by Mondrian as 'the best
application of neo-plasticism' he had seen – included
a wall tapestry, carpet, two chandeliers, sofa and three
chairs. Each piece was composed of rectangles and
squares in black, white and tones of grey, with accents
in the primary colours – red, blue and yellow. From
1946 to 1952, del Marle contributed to the magazine
Art d'Aujourd'hui.

Delorme, Raphaël (1885–1962)

Born in Cauderon, near Bordeaux, Delorme studied
under Gustave Lauriol and Pierre-Gustave Artus
at the city's École des Beaux-Arts before moving
to Paris, where he became a stage designer. Mme
Metalier, a wealthy cousin, offered him the hospitality
of her château at Valesnes in Indre-et-Loire if he
would abandon the stage for easel painting. This he did,
combining in his often fantastical compositions his

love of architectural perspective with statuesque,
somewhat expressionless female models rendered in a
distinctly Neoclassical and theatrical style that showed
his background in set design, on occasion employing
trompe-l'œil and Symbolist effects.

Delorme exhibited at the *Salon d'Automne,
the *Société Nationale des Beaux-Arts and the Salon
des Tuileries, in addition to one-man shows in Tours
and Bordeaux. With practically no commercial success
during his lifetime – he claimed in later years to
have sold only one painting during his entire career,
to the Maharajah of Kapurthala – Delorme was only
'discovered' after his death.

Descomps, Jean-Bernard (1872–1948)

Descomps was born in Agen (Lot-et-Garonne) and
studied at the École des Beaux-Arts in Paris under
Jean-Alexandre-Joseph Falguière, following which he
participated in the Salons of the *Société des Artistes
Décoratifs. In the late 1920s he designed models
for execution in *pâte-de-verre* by Almeric *Walter
(including a plaque of Isadora Duncan) as well
as figurines that were put into ceramic production
by Mougin Frères in Lorraine.

Descomps, Joseph-Emmanuel-Jules (Joe) (1869–1950)

Born in Clermont-Ferrand, Descomps studied under H.
Hiollin before making his début at the Salon of the
*Société des Artistes Français, of which he was elected
a full member in 1893. He designed and executed a
wide range of decorative items in the Art Nouveau
idiom, including jewelry, sculpture and ceramics.

In the 1920s Descomps concentrated on small-
scale sculpture, often Neoclassical figures produced
in bronze and ivory, entirely in ivory or in a low-grade
white metal; these were manufactured by *Etling et
Cie. Many of his pieces, such as *Meditation* and *Scent
of the Rose*, were rendered in a more spirited Modernist

style than the work of his peers. His female nude,
Femme au lotus, welcomed visitors in the vestibule
of the Ambassade Française pavilion at the 1925
*Exposition Internationale.

Deskey, Donald (1894–1989). *See under* Furniture and Interior Design.

Desny. *See under* Silver, Metal, Lacquer and Enamel.

Després, Jean (1889–1980)

Després was born in Souvigny (Allier) to parents who
ran an art and jewelry gallery in Avallon in the Yonne.
He served apprenticeships as a goldsmith initially in
Avallon and then in Paris, where he expanded his
training by working for a jeweller friend of his father's
in rue des Gravilliers. During the First World War,
Després worked as a labourer in a military workshop
that manufactured aeroplane engines. His fascination
with the world of mechanics and industrial design,
with its cold precision and engineered equilibrium,
determined the designs and materials of his post-war
jewelry. As an artist and a theoretician, Després believed
that an object must be inspired by contemporary
aesthetics; in the 1920s and 1930s, this translated into
simple, severe forms without superfluous ornament,
and with no preconceptions regarding materials.

In the 1920s Després participated in most of the
important exhibitions in France as a goldsmith and
jeweller, showing table ornaments, such as cigarette
cases and compotes, in addition to jewelry. His displays
at the 1925 *Exposition Internationale and the 1926
Salon des Indépendants included toiletry items, many
of truncated cylindrical or circular form in hammered
silver. Toward 1930, he created a series of Surrealist
jewelry in collaboration with Étienne *Cournault, who
provided painted and engraved glass panels inserted
into metal mounts. He also participated in the 1936
Artistes de ce Temps exhibition at the Petit Palais.

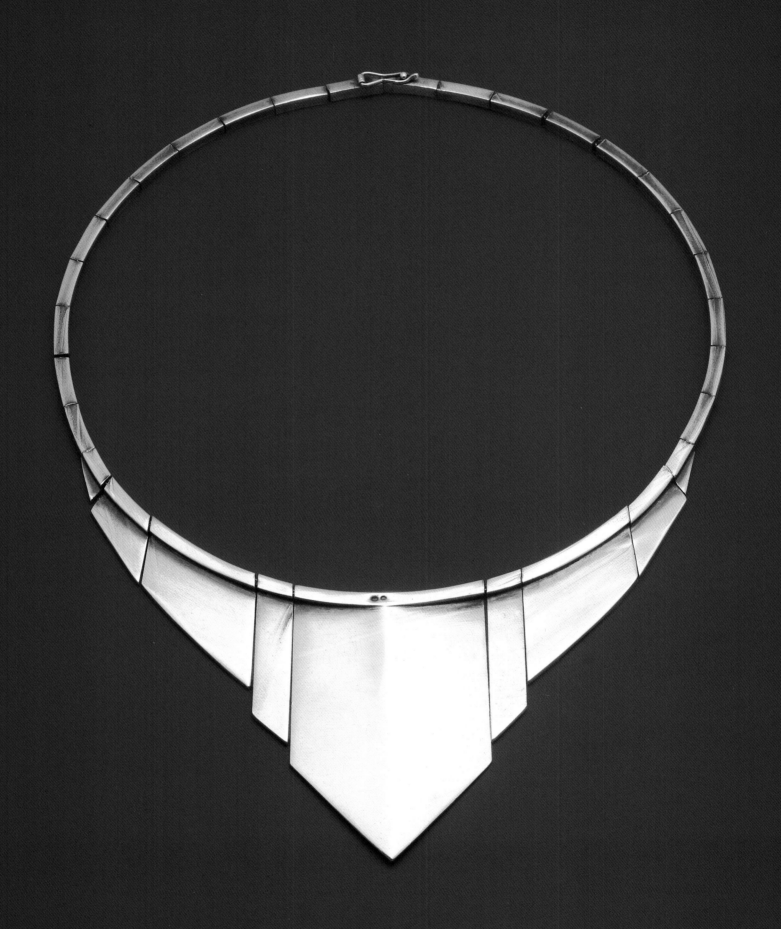

Després managed the gallery Art et la Mode in Paris for many years, as well as his own shop on the avenue des Champs-Elysées and a workshop in Avallon.

Despret, Georges (1862–1952)

Born in Belgium, Despret trained as an engineer and in 1884 inherited a small glassworks in Jeumont (Nord), where in the 1890s he expanded the firm's repertoire with the creation of cameo glassware incorporating trapped air bubbles and abstract surface patterns. In 1899 he began to experiment with the *pâte-de-verre* technique pioneered by Henri Cros.

At the 1900 Exposition Universelle the following year, Despret displayed a selection of bowls in this medium, in which dense opaque-coloured paste produced jewel-like effects. Later models included a series of Tanagra-style figurines, fish and animals in the round, bookends, candlesticks, masks and *bibelots d'art*, designed, *inter alia*, by Jean Goujon, Alexandre Charpentier and Pierre *Le Faguays.

Despret participated in the Salons of the *Société Nationale des Beaux-Arts from 1900 and in some of the exhibitions staged in Europe prior to the First World War. Destroyed during the war, his factory reopened in 1920 with a diminished output. It finally closed around 1937.

Despujols, Jean (1886–1965)

Despujols was born in Salles (Gironde) and studied at Bordeaux's École des Beaux-Arts and later at the institution of the same name in Paris, where he won the Prix de Rome for painting in 1914. In Rome he befriended JEAN DUPAS and Robert-Eugène *Pougheon, both also winners of the Prix de Rome. Together, the three spearheaded the French Neoclassical style of the inter-war years.

As well as exhibiting at the *Société des Artistes Français, the Salon des Indépendants and the Salon des Tuileries, Despujols taught painting at the Fontainebleau American School of Art between 1924 and 1936. He then travelled extensively in the Far East before settling in the USA, where he became a citizen in 1945. Despujols also composed music, wrote poetry and essays on philosophy and metaphysics, and published six illustrated autobiographical volumes.

Desvallières, Richard (1893–1962)

Born in Paris, the son of the painter Georges Desvallières, Desvallières became an ironworker, favouring the *métier*'s traditional techniques over modern ones. Desvallières's items were hand-wrought, which explains his relatively limited output. His grillework was light and charming, often adorned with tasselled curtains or pierced bouquets, stylistically similar to that of Édouard *Schenck, another traditionalist.

Desvallières's address in the 1920s was listed as rue Ernest-Legouvé, Saint-Port (Seine-et-Marne), where he executed a body of work for SÜE ET MARE's Compagnie des Arts Français as well as grilles, fire-screens, sconces and various items of furniture – some quite massive – that he displayed under his own name at the annual *Salon d'Automne. Larger orders included a dining-room table for the architect Jean *Patou in 1924, and a balcony and balustrade in Süe et Mare's pavilion at the 1925 *Exposition Internationale. Ecclesiastical works, such as choir stalls, grilles and reliquaries represented a considerable part of Desvallières's repertoire. In 1933 he executed the interior ironwork for the Église Sainte-Agnès in Maisons-Alfort.

De Tirtoff, Romain (1892–1990). *See* Erté.

Diederich, William (Wilhelm) Hunt (1884–1953)

Diederich was born into a wealthy local family in Szent-Grot, Hungary, and was the maternal grandson of the American painter William Morris Hunt and the grand-nephew of the architect Richard Morris Hunt.

At the age of sixteen he emigrated to the USA, where he lived initially with his mother in Boston while studying at Milton Academy. After a period of travelling back and forth to ranches in Wyoming, New Mexico and Arizona, Diederich entered the Pennsylvania Academy of the Fine Arts in 1906. There he befriended Paul Manship, a fellow student, with whom he spent a summer in Spain. In 1913 his career was advanced by his participation in both the *Salon d'Automne in Paris and the Armory Show in New York. After the latter he staged a one-man show at the city's Kingore Gallery.

Diederich is known mainly for his two-dimensional works in sheet metal, including weathervanes, fire-screens, balconies, railings, boot-scrapers and trivets, executed to his designs by Greenwich Village Blacksmiths. However, he also showed his versatility in a body of sculptural works, fabric designs and ceramics, following a 1923 trip to Morocco during which he acquired examples of native pottery that inspired his ceramic designs.

Diederich's preferred subject matter involved animals, including greyhounds, polo players and jockeys on their steeds, fox hunts, bullfights and ibexes. These he portrayed in a highly idiosyncratic, engaging, and often witty style in which the images were depicted in silhouette. He worked mainly in wrought iron, to which he sometimes added detailing in tin, copper and fly-screening.

Dieupart, Henri (*fl.* EARLY 1920S–35). *See* Simonet Frères.

DIM

The decorating firm of Décoration Intérieure Moderne (DIM) was established in 1919 by René *Joubert (d. 1931) and Georges Mouveau at 19 place de la Madeleine, Paris. Born in Laval (Mayenne), Joubert trained as an architect before moving to the decorative arts. His employment at Maison Jansen, where he

Richard Desvallières
(*opposite*) Console in wrought
iron with marble top, 1920s.

Jean Despujols
(*left, above*) *Le Muguet*,
oil on canvas, c. 1930.

Richard Desvallières
(*left*) Console in patinated
and parcel-gilt wrought iron,
designed for La Compagnie
des Arts Français, 1920s.

William Hunt Diederich
(*top*) Weathervane on stand
in wrought iron, 1920s.

(*above*) *The Jockey*, bronze, 1924.

DIM
Jewelry cabinet in red
lacquered wood inlaid with
coquille d'œuf, c. 1926.

Jean-Gabriel Domergue
(*opposite, above left*) *La
Danseuse de corde*, oil on
canvas, 1931; exhibited at the
Salon of the Société Nationale
des Beaux-Arts, Paris, 1932.

Georges Djo-Bourgeois
(*opposite, above right*)
L'Inhumaine, lithographic
poster, 1924.

was instructed by the Art Nouveau cabinet-maker Léon Benouville, was followed by further experience in furniture-making at Diot & Bouche. Mouveau brought a background in stage design to the partnership, but returned to his chosen *métier* in 1923, when the theatre strike that had led him to seek employment at DIM was resolved.

Joubert ran the firm on his own for a year, with M. Vienot as his technical director. In 1924 he was joined by Philippe Petit (d. 1945), a younger man who had worked briefly at *Primavera after his studies at the École Bernard-Palissy. Joubert was clearly the senior partner, designing most of the furnishings displayed at the Salons under both the firm's name and his own. Petit's role was to create interiors that would soften Joubert's forceful lines by introducing muted colours – green and greys – into their carpets and wallpapers.

Like Paul *Follot and Jules *Leleu, Joubert was a rigid traditionalist, his inspirations often being Louis XVI or Restauration designs. Working for an elite clientele, he kept his editions small – as in the repertoire of phonograph cabinets, mobile cocktail cabinets and plant stands that he introduced in the late 1920s. These were executed in warm woods with veneered ivory or coralwood crossbanding and trim.

The firm took stands Nos. 37 and 39 on the Pont Alexandre III at the 1925 *Exposition Internationale, near the Pleyel stand, which displayed a DIM piano. The firm's dining room in the Ambassade Française pavilion sparked excitement; it was heralded as a *tour de force* of sobriety and harmony. In the mid-1920s DIM moved to 40 rue du Colisée, where it staged its inaugural display on 6 November 1926. Accompanying catalogues show a variety of furnishings, including a wide range of carpets, many Cubist-inspired.

Joubert yielded to the onslaught of metal furniture designs with equanimity. The first glimpses of this shift in his designs came at the 1927 Salons. The next year, a New York cafeteria commission undertaken by DIM

consisted entirely of tubular metal chairs and tables. By 1930 many nickelled metal desks and chairs were evident, as well as radio cabinets and phonographs in lacquered metal and glass. Joubert's death in 1931 led to Petit's resignation from DIM; from then on he and the firm showed separately at the Salons.

Djo-Bourgeois, Georges (1898–1937)

Born in Bezons (Seine-et-Oise), Djo-Bourgeois graduated from the École Speciale d'Architecture in 1922. The following year he joined *Studium–Louvre and made his début at the Salons. For Studium's director Étienne *Kohlmann and consultant designer Maurice *Matet, Djo-Bourgeois filled a gap; now the studio could match the Modernist interiors of Louis *Sognot at *Primavera and, independently, those of Jean Lurçat, CHARLOTTE PERRIAND and ROBERT MALLET-STEVENS. An ardent Modernist, Djo-Bourgeois's philosophy was that in order to furnish a space, one must first un-furnish it. Less was definitely more; in bareness, geometry and equilibrium lay the ingenious solutions to modern living.

At the 1925 *Exposition Internationale, Djo-Bourgeois exhibited two ensembles in the Studium–Louvre pavilion: a smoking room and an office–library. The compact nature of the furnishings drew comment; in particular, the radio–telephone and phonograph built into the sides of a broad divan. His preferred materials included a combination of wood, often lacquered, and glass. Soon the wood in his designs was replaced by tubular metal, aluminium, iron and concrete, while wood panelling was replaced by cork and a plastic composite.

At some point after 1926, Djo-Bourgeois left Studium–Louvre to establish his own business, the address of which was listed by 1929 as 25 rue Vaneau. He cultivated a narrow group of avant-garde clients, including Vicomte de Noailles, the Duke of Harcourt, M. Lahy and M. Lange. Assisted by his wife, Élise,

who designed geometric carpets and cushions that introduced colour into his otherwise spartan interiors, Djo-Bourgeois continued to exhibit at the Salons until his premature death. His last commission was for an interior in a yachtsman's apartment on the Côte d'Azur.

Domergue, Jean-Gabriel (1889–1962)

Domergue studied at the École des Beaux-Arts in Paris under Tony Robert-Fleury, Jules-Joseph Lefebvre, Jacques Adler, Humbert and Flameng before making his début at the Salon of the *Société des Artistes Français in 1906. On winning the Prix de Rome, he attended the French Academy in Rome from 1911 to 1913.

Early landscapes gave way to portraits of celebrities and sleek young socialites, the latter characteristically portrayed with long slender necks and limbs, and sensual lips and posture, as in Domergue's 'Alice Soulie' poster of 1926. In addition to his posters – in the most part for theatres and balls in Europe's capitals – Domergue created fashion plates in which a similar array of stunning women paraded. In 1920, the year he was awarded a gold medal at the Paris Salon, he exhibited at the Royal Academy in London and the Carnegie Institute in Pittsburgh.

Elected to the Académie des Beaux-Arts in 1950, Domergue became a curator at the Musée Jacquemart-André in Paris in 1956. In addition to his work as a poster artist, he created book illustrations and designed costumes for theatre productions and balls in Paris, London, Cannes, Biarritz and especially Monte Carlo, where he resided for many years as a member of the smart set.

Dominique

The Dominique decorating firm was founded in 1922 by André Domin (1883–1962), a self-taught artist born in Caen, and Marcel Genevrière (1885–1967), a trained architect. Located at 104 rue du Faubourg Saint-Honoré, Paris, the firm soon offered a wide range of

Jean-Gabriel Domergue

(*above*) *Cote d'Azur Toute l'Année*, lithographic poster, 1930.

DIM

(*right*) Lady's desk, wood veneered in shagreen and ivory, and with leather writing surface, *c.* 1927.

Dominique
Cabinet, mahogany with sculpted fruitwood door panels, exhibited at the Exposition Coloniale, Paris, 1931.

carpets, fabrics, furniture and wrought-iron wares. Two important commissions were JEAN PUIFORCAT's residence in central Paris and the offices of the Houbigant perfume factory in Neuilly.

A participant in the annual Salons of the *Société des Artistes Décorateurs, Dominique displayed a reception room in the Ambassade Française pavilion at the 1925 *Exposition Internationale, in collaboration with Charles Hairon (furniture carving), Helen Lantier (silk upholstery) and Maison Lunot (an Aubusson tapestry). In the same year the firm was awarded the first prize for its entry in a chair competition organized by the Union Centrale des Arts Décoratifs. In 1926, with PIERRE CHAREAU, PIERRE-ÉMILE LEGRAIN, JEAN PUIFORCAT and RAYMOND TEMPLIER, Dominique exhibited at the Galerie Barbazanges. Known as Les Cinq, the group showed together two years later at the Galerie de la Renaissance (the venue was changed every year; another was the Galerie Georges Bernheim).

For Dominique the 1930s brought a radical shift from conventional furniture materials to synthetic fabrics: Duvetine, artificial silk, Rhodia canvas, and silvered and ultramarine Tricotene. The search now was for the new: crystal handles replaced the existing ones in silver by Puiforcat, *dalles* of glass superseded walnut room-panelling and doors. Modernity was *de rigueur*.

The firm reached maturity in the early 1930s. For the ocean liner *Normandie, c. 1935, it designed the deluxe four-room apartment 'Rouen', in which it incorporated a selection of furniture displayed against parchment walls hung with panels by Daragnes and Le Trividic. Dominique also participated in the 1935 Exposition de Bruxelles and the 1937 Exposition des Arts et Techniques. On Domin's death, the firm was taken over by his son. It closed in 1970.

Dorn, Marion (1899–1964)

Born in San Francisco, Dorn studied graphic arts at Stanford University before moving in 1916 to Paris and in 1923 to London, where she became a freelance designer working with resist-dyed fabrics. Shortly after her arrival she met the American-born graphic designer and poster artist Edward *McKnight Kauffer, whom she lived with and ultimately married in 1950.

Establishing her career as a textile and carpet designer, Dorn staged her first exhibition in 1929. Numerous private and public commissions followed in the 1930s, including textile designs for hotels and the Cunard line (the *Queen Mary* and *Orion*), as her celebrity rose. In 1934 she opened her own showroom in London, Marion Dorn Ltd, through which her carpets were sold. At the time she also supplied designs for woven and printed textiles to leading English manufacturers, including Warners, Old Bleach Linen, Edinburgh Weavers, the Wilton Royal Carpet Co. and Donald Brothers. She is credited with more than one hundred carpets, some of which were woven by Jean Orage in her Chelsea workshop.

Inspired in part by examples shown at the annual Paris Salons, especially by IVAN DA SILVA BRUHNS, Dorn's carpet designs included a repertoire of volutes, spirals, zigzags and other geometric configurations rendered in a muted naturalistic palette. Other compositions incorporated representational images of shells, plants and animals, or Cubist conventions in arresting colours. Such was Dorn's success that she acquired the pseudonym 'Architect of Floors'.

Dorn and McKnight Kauffer returned to America in 1940, where Dorn continued to design fabrics, some produced by Greeff and others by Edwards Fields (1951–62). Dorn died in Tangier in 1964, soon after setting up a studio there.

Doucet, Jacques (1853–1929)

A couturier and art collector, Doucet amassed an impressive collection of 18th-century art and furniture between 1896 and 1910, which he abruptly auctioned two years later. He then turned his attention to contemporary art, furniture and furnishings, including paintings by Paul Cézanne, Vincent van Gogh, Claude Monet, Alfred Sisley, Edgar Degas, Henri Rousseau, Édouard Manet and Pablo Picasso, whose *Les Desmoiselles d'Avignon* he acquired in 1920.

Attending the annual Paris Salons from around 1910, Doucet commissioned furniture, sculpture and bookbindings for his apartment at 46 avenue du Bois (now avenue Foch) from the era's vanguard artist–craftsmen, such as PIERRE-ÉMILE LEGRAIN, EILEEN GRAY, ROSE ADLER, Paul *Iribe, Marcel *Coard, Paul-Louis *Mergier, GUSTAV MIKLOS, Jean-Charles *Moreux, RENÉ LALIQUE, Jean Lurçat, Clément *Rousseau, Étienne *Cournault and Josef *Csáky. Doucet spent the following twelve years adding to his initial purchases.

By 1924 Doucet's new collection – consisting of a mix of modern paintings, Oceanic and African tribal art, and modern furniture – warranted its own space, so he engaged the architect Paul Ruau to design a studio on rue Saint-James in Neuilly, on the outskirts of Paris. The collection, which remained intact after Doucet's death, was auctioned amid wide publicity at the Hôtel Drouot, Paris, in 1972. Works with a Doucet provenance continue to demand among the highest prices in today's Art Deco market – a tribute to his connoisseurship and patronage. A noted bibliophile, his collection of bindings and manuscripts is today housed in the Bibliothèque Littéraire Jacques Doucet, Paris.

Dufet, Michel (1888–1985)

Born in Déville-lès-Rouen, Dufet studied architecture and painting at the École des Beaux-Arts, Paris. In 1913 he established the furniture retailing firm of Meubles Artistiques Modernes (MAM) at 3 avenue de l'Opéra, and the following year he made his début at the Salon of the *Société des Artistes Français. He exhibited again after the war, when he worked in partnership with the painter Louis Bureau, until 1924. Modern furniture reminiscent of JACQUES-ÉMILE RUHLMANN's

Michel Dufet

(*top left*) Commode in
lacquered oak with painted
decoration and marble top,
1920s.

(*left*) Desk and chair in
palmwood and burl ash with
chromed metal feet and
python upholstery, marketed
by Au Bûcheron, *c.* 1930, the
vase by Claudius Linossier.

Marion Dorn

(*top right*) Tufted wool rug,
c. 1930.

(*above*) Tufted wool rug,
manufactured by the Wilton
Royal Carpet Co., 1932.

Michel Dufet
Buffet in walnut with burl
walnut veneers, early 1920s.

was placed in high-ceilinged rooms lined with tall black-and-white-veined marble pilasters topped with carved-fruit capitals. A Louis XVI formality and elegance prevailed.

In 1922, Dufet founded the art magazine *Les Feuilles d'Art*, and in the next year became director of Red Star, a firm of interior decorators based in Rio de Janeiro. At some point between 1922 and 1924, Dufet and Bureau separated – the latter dropping from prominence. Their ensembles had been marketed by P. A. Dumas, to whom Dufet then sold MAM.

A two-year South American sojourn prevented Dufet's participation at the 1925 *Exposition Internationale, but he did exhibit at the 1926 Salon of the *Société des Artistes Décorateurs and in 1927 joined *Le Sylve art studio of the furniture retailer Au Bûcheron, a business dependent on mass-production. He continued to participate in the annual Salons, his displays including prefabricated furniture of varying sizes for use in combination (*meubles juxtaposables*). A significant amount of Cubist influence is readily apparent both in the starkly functional chairs and in their ultramodern settings.

The 1930s brought numerous commissions in addition to Dufet's standard productions for Au Bûcheron. In 1932 he furnished a waiting room for Marshal Lyautey, the commissariat general of the 1931 Exposition Coloniale. Commissions for the ocean liners *Normandie* and *Île-de-France* followed. Synthetic new materials, including **duralumin**, chromed tubular steel, zinc and etched *dalles* of glass paved the way to a new Modernism. At the 1937 Exposition des Arts et Techniques, Dufet collaborated with René *Gabriel on a display in the wallpaper pavilion, following which he was commissioned to design the French pavilion at the 1939 New York World's Fair.

Dufrène, Maurice (1876–1955). *See under* Furniture and Interior Design.

Dufy, Raoul (1877–1953)
Dufy was born in Le Havre and recollected later that he was a reluctant student, initially at the city's École Municipale des Beaux-Arts (1892), and then at the École des Beaux-Arts in Paris (1900). He made his début as a painter at the 1901 Salon of the *Société des Artistes Français, after which he exhibited with the Fauves between 1903 and 1909.

His early painting reflected the group's sensibilities in its expressive use of colour and simplicity of design. At this stage in his career Dufy also illustrated a number of books using woodblocks, etchings and lithographs. For these, as in his woodcut illustrations for Guillaume Apollinaire's *Bestiare* (1908), his graphic style was plain and rustic.

In 1911 Paul *Poiret commissioned Dufy to design fabrics for Maison MARTINE, setting up a studio for him. His designs, intended for translation onto linen, silk, satin, velvet and brocade, were characteristically free-spirited and vibrant. The relationship lasted for ten years, and Dufy was retained again in 1925 to design fourteen large wall hangings for one of the three barges that Poiret used for his display at the 1925 *Exposition Internationale

In 1912 Dufy was hired by Bianchini–Férier – the large textile manufacturer in Lyons – to design dress and upholstery fabrics and printed panels, which he displayed at the annual Salons of the *Société des Artistes Décorateurs from 1921, and later, alongside his paintings, at the *Salon d'Automne and Salon des Indépendants. The agreement with Bianchini–Férier lasted until 1928, after which Dufy designed printed silks for Onondaga of New York from 1930 to 1933.

Known primarily as an artist during a career that spanned a half-century, Dufy showed his versatility frequently: for example, in a series of fabric designs for the fashion revue *La Gazette du Bon Ton*; tapestries for Beauvais; and ceramics for Artigas and *Sèvres. For the 1937 Exposition des Arts et Techniques,

he painted what was then the world's largest picture – 10 metres high by 60 metres wide– on the subject of electricity for the Pavillon de la Lumière.

Dumoulin, Georges (1882–1959)
Born in Vittecreux (Côte d'Or), Dumoulin worked for the jewellers Falize as a young man while studying the arts of goldsmithing and jewelry-making. Specializing in enamelling, he developed his own techniques before joining the Manufacture Nationale de *Sèvres, where he spent eight years as a ceramist, experimenting with chemicals to obtain new glaze effects.

Around 1928, at the age of forty-six, Dumoulin began to experiment with glass, and he exhibited his first pieces at the Palais de Marbre, Paris. Inspired by MAURICE MARINOT's works, he produced a similar range of stoppered bottles with bubbled interior decoration, often using powdered oxides, aventurine and other minerals to achieve a multiplicity of textures, iridescent colours and swirling effects. He also applied external decoration, such as glass trailings. Dumoulin refused to use enamels or to etch or carve his glass, working on each piece only with the glass artisan's conventional tools. He also eschewed the use of moulds; each of his creations was therefore a *pièce unique*.

Dumoulin exhibited at the Salons of the *Société des Artistes Français, receiving an honourable mention in 1913, and at those of the *Salon d'Automne and the *Société des Artistes Décorateurs from 1922. He also staged several one-man shows of his paintings, mostly Breton landscapes. The 1929 Wall Street crash had a significant negative impact on his sales, as consumers reverted to a simpler, less expensive, functionalist style. Dumoulin, however, still showed a few vessels at the 1937 Exposition des Arts et Techniques. A major retrospective of his works was staged in 1944 at the museum of the Conservatoire des Arts et Métiers, Paris.

Raoul Dufy

(*right*) *Ananas*, woven silk damask, probably manufactured by Bianchini–Férier, *c.* 1928.

(*below*) Chair upholstery decorated with scenes on the theme of Orpheus, designed in collaboration with Jean Lurçat and manufactured in Aubusson tapestry by Marie Cuttoli (Mybor), late 1920s.

Hans Rudi Erdt
(*above*) *Problem Cigarettes*,
lithographic poster, 1912.

Gabriel Englinger
(*top*) Boudoir marketed by
the Studio Abran, *c.* 1927–28.

Marc du Plantier
(*right*) Storage cabinet in oak
veneered in shagreen, with macassar
ebony and bronze mounts, *c.* 1937.

Etling et Cie
(*right*) Figurine in moulded
oplaine glass, 1920s.

Dunand, Jean (1877–1942). *See under* Silver, Metal, Lacquer and Enamel.

Dupas, Jean (1882–1964). *See under* Paintings, Graphics, Posters and Bookbinding.

Du Plantier, Marc (1901–1975)
Born in Madagascar, du Plantier studied architecture at the École des Beaux-Arts in Paris and then concentrated on a career in painting and sculpture. He worked as a modeller for Paris couturiers, for whom he created costumes and theatre décor, before switching to furniture design.

Du Plantier's furniture revealed its traditional roots in its Baroque and Consulate forms, to which he added an exotic mix of materials to provide the luxurious elegance that he sought for an elite, often aristocratic clientele: gilded bronze leaf, *galuchat*, parchment and lacquer. In 1940 he decorated several palaces and residences in Spain, followed by further houses and a yacht in France and Algeria. In 1955 he worked for the Elysée Palace. Du Plantier was represented in Paris by the Galerie Yves Gasteau and by the Galerie Neo Senso.

Dupré-Lafon, Paul (1900–1971). *See under* Furniture and Interior Design.

E

École Boulle

Founded in 1886 by the City of Paris in the 12th *arrondissement* as the École Supérieure des Arts Appliqués aux Industries de l'Ameublement, this cumbersome title was later contracted to École Boulle after Louis XIV's celebrated *ébéniste* André-Charles Boulle. André *Fréchet, the school's director from 1919 to 1934, formulated its 1920s charter. Today its function remains fundamentally unchanged: to provide the finest possible instruction for the nation's next generation of cabinet-makers. Students are provided with tuition (a four-year apprenticeship) in three broad categories: furniture, bronze-work and precious metals.

By the early 1920s, École Boulle could boast close to three thousand graduates, many of whom had received recognition far beyond the Faubourg Saint-Antoine, Paris's furniture manufacturing district. In an Art Deco context, its most prominent alumni included Philippe *Genet and Lucien Michon, Raymond *Subes, Louis *Gigou, ARMAND-ALBERT RATEAU, Gabriel *Englinger, and Étienne *Kohlmann, all of whom participated in a student retrospective exhibition at the Musée Galliera in 1923.

In the 1920s, Fréchet initiated frequent competitions among the students and displayed the school's workmanship, whenever appropriate, at the annual Salons, often using his own furniture designs to ensure its entry. The critics were invariably enthusiastic: examples were found to incorporate a blend of harmony, logic and rigorous construction. At the 1925 *Exposition Internationale, the school provided the furnishings for the Salon d'Honneur in the Pavillion de la Ville de Paris. Ten years later it participated also in the 1935 Exposition de Bruxelles, the pieces shown being designed by M. Charlot, Fréchet's successor.

Englinger, Gabriel (1898–1983)

Paris-born Englinger attended the *École Boulle before joining *La Maîtrise in 1922, where he established himself quickly as one of the studio's foremost decorators. He participated in various projects in its pavilion at the 1925 *Exposition Internationale, in collaboration with MAURICE DUFRÈNE and Suzanne *Guiguichon. His carpet, floral wallpapers and upholstered chairs imparted a plush opulence to the pavilion's reception area.

Englinger remained at La Maîtrise for three more years, collaborating on its projects while also exhibiting independently at the Salons. In 1926 he showed a dining room marketed by La Renaissance de Meuble, and a year later at the *Société des Artistes Décorateurs, a bedroom in violetwood and amaranth marketed by La Maîtrise. In 1928 he transferred to the Studio Abran, for which he showed a living room at one of the 1929 Salons. From 1928 Englinger's designs were executed by Veroni and Larcheveque, among others. Some designs appeared stiff; others, such as tubular steel armchairs (1931), were largely indistinguishable from examples by Ludwig *Mies van der Rohe.

Englinger continued to exhibit in the 1930s, joined now by Marguerite Englinger for draperies and embroidered panels. In 1934 he moved to L'Isère, accepting a lectureship in the decorative arts in Grenoble and another in applied design in Voiron. After the Second World War, Englinger returned to the Paris Salons, moving again in 1949 to teach at the École Regionale des Beaux-Arts in Rennes.

Erdt, Hans Rudi (1883–1918)

Born in southern Bavaria, Erdt attended the industrial college in Munich before moving in 1905 to Berlin, where he became a commercial poster artist. His graphic style, like those of Lucian *Bernhard and Ludwig *Hohlwein, is described as *Plakatstil*. Among his more notable posters, whose style anticipated the 1920s Modernism, were those for Automobile Opel (1910), which combined bold unserifed fonts with images reduced to their elemental shapes. During the First World War, Erdt designed propagandist posters for the German government, including 'U-Boote Heraus!' (1917).

Erté (Romain de Tirtoff) (1892–1990). *See under* Paintings, Graphics, Posters and Bookbinding.

Etling et Cie

Founded by Edmond Etling in 1909, the firm of Etling et Cie, located at 29 rue de Paradis, Paris, served in the inter-war years as an important *éditeur d'art* and

Camille Fauré
Selection of enamelled copper
vases, 1920s.

retailer of popular domestic statuettes and *objets d'art* in bronze, glass and ceramic. Under its artistic director Dreyfuss, the firm marketed the works of a gifted stable of contemporary artist–sculptors, including DEMETRE CHIPARUS, Claire Jeanne Roberte *Colinet, Joe *Descomps, Marcel *Bouraine, Maurice *Guiraud-Rivière, Alexandre *Kelety, Pierre *Le Faguays, André *Becquerel and Bessie Stough *Callender. Some of these, including Chiparus, Guiraud-Rivière and Colinet, designed works in all three media.

In addition to its sculptural editions, Etling et Cie commissioned a wide range of decorative household accessories, including figurines, in moulded opalescent glass – many mounted as *luminaires*. Among its designers were Geneviève Granger (b. 1877), Lucile Sévin and her husband Jean-Théodore Delabasse (b. 1902), Geza Hiez and Georges Béal (b. 1884). The firm maintained its own bronze foundry, and also worked with another manufacturer, *Les Neveux de J. Lehmann (LNJL), for its casting needs. Its glassware was produced at the Choisy-le-Roi factory on the outskirts of Paris.

During the Second World War, members of Etling et Cie, including Edmond Etling and his family and Dreyfuss, were deported to Nazi concentration camps, where they died. The firm did not re-open when the hostilities ceased.

L'Exposition Internationale (1925)

The Exposition Internationale des Arts Décoratifs et Industriels Modernes was a long time in the making. Conceived as early as 1907, it was scheduled and rescheduled as the First World War came and went. Planning was begun again in 1919 for 1922, then for 1924, and finally for April to October, 1925.

In a stylistic context, the Exposition came at the moment when the 'pure' or 'high' Art Deco style was approaching its end. The extravagant exhibits staged by individual interior designers and department stores actually brought the curtain down, rather than up, on the movement. Yet few designers felt confident enough to bypass the event, if only because their competitors would not.

The principal designers and manufacturers were spread out along the Pont Alexandre III, the rue des Boutiques, and the Esplanade des Invalides on Paris's Left Bank. The only major exceptions were Paul *Poiret, whose theatrical interiors were housed on three barges moored at the Quai d'Orsay, and *Le Corbusier, whose Esprit Nouveau pavilion was banished to the Right Bank. Represented was the pride of France's modern movement across every artistic discipline.

The major French exhibits were lined up along the Esplanade des Invalides, a park in front of Les Invalides. The exhibition visitor could stroll from one pavilion to another, each with its own expanse of lawn and garden statuary. Pride of place went to the city's department stores – Au Bon Marché, Au Printemps, Les Galeries Lafayette, and Le Louvre – whose art studios designed and furnished their pavilions. Interspersed with these were the private exhibitors, quite unintimidated by their larger neighbors. The critics were unanimous in their choice of JACQUES-ÉMILE RUHLMANN's Hôtel du Collectionneur as the Exposition's most spectacular display. After that, in varying degrees of preference, came SÜE ET MARE's Musée d'Art Contemporaine; the *Société des Artistes Décorateurs' pavilion, L'Ambassade Française, and RENÉ LALIQUE's pavilion.

F

Faïenceries de Longwy

Faïenceries de Longwy was established by the Huart family in 1798 in the provincial town of Longwy (France) near the Belgian border. The company has enjoyed a celebrated history for its ceramics and enamelled wares. The firm's early 1920s production of glazed household *grès*, commissioned in part by *Primavera (the art studio of the large Paris department store Au Printemps), was characterized by a rampant Art Deco grammar of ornament rendered in a vivid palette of coral-red, flamingo-pink, crackled ivory-white and turquoise-blue silhouetted in gold. It drew inspiration from Japanese, Persian and Iznik models. Motifs included formalized flora, the ubiquitous leaping gazelles and birds-of-paradise in lush tropical settings.

One of the firm's designers in the inter-war years, Maurice Paul Chevallier, was credited with the 'Boule Coloniale', a large spherical vessel decorated with highly colourful and condensed compositions rendered in the *cloisonné* technique. Chevallier's brother, Raymond, was a designer with Charles *Catteau at *Boch Frères Keramis, which may explain the stylistic similarity in some of Longwy's wares.

Fauré, Camille (1874–1956)

Born in Périgueux, Fauré served a long apprenticeship locally before moving to Limoges, where he opened a business to produce painted signboards, street signs, cinema billboards and other advertising materials. This led to his experimentation in enamels and the establishment of a studio to create enamelled artworks at 31 rue des Tanneries, which he operated for some fifty years. In later years he was joined by his daughter, Andrée Fauré-Malabre (1904–1985), who continued the studio after his death.

Fauré's pre-war designs were mostly floral, but from the 1920s he introduced bold, abstract, three-dimensional compositions of overlapping circles, arcs and other geometric configurations. Employing the medium's conventional techniques, Fauré mixed powdered glass with chemical pigments, which were then heated into a vitreous paste, applied and fused to a metal base. High-relief definition juxtaposed with carefully blended complementary colours made his

Faïenceries de Longwy

(*right*) Vase in glazed earthenware, for the Primavera atelier of Au Printemps department store, 1920s.

(*below*) Charger in glazed earthenware, for the Pomone atelier of the Au Bon Marché department store, 1920s.

Modernist enamelware production highly distinctive within the decorative arts of 1920s France. Whereas certain artists, such as Pablo Picasso and Georges Braque, translated Cubism into sculptural forms, only Fauré and Jean Goulden applied the concept successfully to domestic enamelwares.

Fix-Masseau, Pierre (1905–1994)

The son of the renowned sculptor Pierre-Félix Fix-Masseau, Fix-Masseau owed much to CASSANDRE, whom he followed closely in his technique of apportioning space with bold linear elements in his poster designs between 1926 and 1928. Fix-Masseau showed a special facility with railway and transportation themes in the posters that he created during the 1930s and the Second World War. Of these, his 'Exactitude' (1932), with its forceful choice of colours and imagery, is considered his finest work.

In 1983 Fix-Masseau was honoured with a retrospective exhibition of a half-century of his work, comprising some 150 posters, at the Bibliothèque Nationale in Paris.

Fjerdingstad, Carl Christian (1891–1968)

Born in Kristiansand, Norway, Fjerdingstad worked as a silversmith in Blaricum in the Netherlands before leaving in 1921 for Paris. There he was employed as a designer by *Christofle, but he also worked as an independent silversmith. Combining French naturalistic ornamentation with the hammered surfaces and rounded forms of contemporary Danish silverware, Fjerdingstad's tableware designs for Christofle in the inter-war years were invariably understated and graceful, such as his 'Cygne' gravy boat and Art Deco-inspired tea service, both introduced in 1933.

Follot, Paul (1877–1941)

Paris-born Follot was the the son of a successful wallpaper manufacturer, Félix Follot. He studied design and sculpture under Eugène Grasset, whom he succeeded in 1904 at the École Nationale Supérieure des Arts Décoratifs in Paris. He spent from 1901 to 1903 at Maison Moderne, working alongside Abel Landry and MAURICE DUFRÈNE. By 1904 Follot had branched out on his own, designing a wide range of household items that allied a Neoclassical discipline to rich decoration; these included clocks, jewelry, furniture, light fixtures and carpets.

Follot's furniture in the pre-war years is classified as 'pure' Art Deco; the Musée des Arts Décoratifs anticipated the importance of his work by purchasing several pieces directly from a 1912 Salon. By the outbreak of the First World War he had installed himself in a home–office built for him by Pierre Selmersheim at 5 rue Schoelcher, Montparnasse.

In 1919 Follot returned to the Salons, showing his furniture, which had been executed by Lucien Rigateau, among others, and was marketed by Coupé. Carpets made by Savonnerie and Cornille Frères added opulence to his ensembles. In 1921 Follot was commissioned to design the first-class dining room on the ocean liner *Paris*. Two years later he was appointed director of the design studio *Pomone, which had been opened by the department store Au Bon Marché. With assistance from colleagues, Follot designed all the rooms in the Pomone pavilion at the 1925 *Exposition Internationale, as well as the antechamber in the Ambassade Française, and he collaborated with René Crevet on the Art et Industrie exhibit.

Follot remained with Pomone until 1928, when he joined Serge Ivan *Chermayeff at the newly established Paris branch of Waring & Gillow, at 130 rue la Boétie. When the firm disbanded its Paris office in 1931, Follot reverted to his role as an independent decorator, continuing to show his ensembles at the Salons. In 1935 he was commissioned to design interiors for the ocean liner *Normandie* and participated in the 1935 Exposition de Bruxelles.

Fontaine et Cie

A manufacturer of locks and related *serrurerie décorative* (household hardware), Fontaine et Cie commissioned prominent decorator–designers in the inter-war years to create a Modernist line of products. These designers included SÜE ET MARE, Paul *Vera, René *Prou, André *Groult, Aristide Maillol, Antoine Bourdelle and Pierre-Paul *Montagnac.

At the 1925 *Exposition Internationale, the firm retained its own pavilion. Its addresses at the time were listed as 81 rue Saint-Honoré and 190 rue de Rivoli, in Paris's upmarket retail quarter. An album of decorative ironwork published by Fontaine in 1930 illustrated more than five thousand accessories – locks, hinges, escutcheons, latches, catches and casement bolts – in a full repertoire of revivalist and contemporary styles.

Fouquet. *See under* Jewelry.

Fouquet, **Alphonse** (1828–1911). *See* Fouquet.

Fouquet, **Georges** (1862–1957). *See* Fouquet.

Fouquet, **Jean** (1899–1984). *See* Fouquet.

Frank, **Jean-Michel** (1895–1941). *See under* Furniture and Interior Design.

Frankl, **Paul-Théodore** (1886–1958). *See under* Furniture and Interior Design.

Fréchet, André (1875–1973)

Born in Chalons-sur-Marne, Fréchet was a professor of art history at the École des Beaux-Arts in Nantes from 1905 to 1911 before moving to Paris to join the faculty at the *École Boulle. In 1919 he assumed the directorship of the school, a position he held until 1934. The following year, aged sixty, he resigned

Pierre Fix-Masseau

(*right*) Exactitude, lithographic poster, 1932.

Paul Follot

(*opposite left*) Grand Salon exhibited at the 1925 Exposition Internationale, Paris, and marketed by the Au Bon Marché department store.

(*opposite right*) Armoire in bird's eye maple and satinwood with fruitwood and mother-of-pearl veneers, exhibited at the 1910 Salon d'Automne.

André Fréchet

(*left*) Dressing table in walnut
with burled walnut veneer,
c. 1924.

André Fréchet

(*right*) Cabinet on stand in
macassar ebony and shagreen
with gilt-bronze mounts,
c. 1935.

Gallia
Tea service in silvered metal
with macassar ebony handles,
1920s.

and accepted a part-time lectureship to teach design
and art history at the Académie Julian.

As a furniture designer, Fréchet is best known
for his association with École Boulle, where he proved
himself to be a most effective administrator and
instructor. He displayed work both in his own name
and in collaboration with the Boulle students,
exhibiting at the Salons from 1919 until the late 1930s.
At the 1922 Salon des Industries d'Art Fréchet
showed an *armoire-psyche* in maple, and his works
were omnipresent at the 1925 *Exposition
Internationale. In addition to participating in École
Boulle's exhibit in the Pavillon de la Ville de Paris,
he displayed four other ensembles marketed either
by the Strasbourg firm of Jacquemin or by
*Studium—Louvre. In the late 1920s, his furniture at
the Salons was marketed through Verot or Jacquemin,
later also through Jeanselme.

In the 1930s Fréchet worked frequently with
Paul Fréchet. Their display at the 1930 Salon of the
*Société des Artistes Décorateurs listed a score of
collaborators. In 1931 his bedroom included a striking
two-tier end-table; this was sold in the celebrated 1975
auction of Karl Lagerfeld's Art Deco collection at
the Hôtel Drouot in Paris. Fréchet was still productive
at the advent of the Second World War.

Friedrich Goldscheider

Friedrich Goldscheider (1845–1897) founded his
namesake firm in 1885 as a manufacturer of porcelain
and majolica wares, and had factories in Pilsen
and Vienna. Later, its range was expanded to include
terracotta and, in 1892, castings in bronze, pewter
and zinc, and works in marble. In the same year,
branches opened in Paris and Florence. In 1894 further
outlets opened in Leipzig and Berlin and, in 1896,
a second showroom in Paris at 28 avenue de l'Opéra.
In 1899 the firm, now based at 7–9 Staudgasse in
Vienna, began to participate in the Paris Salons,

the 1900 Exposition Universelle and other European
exhibitions. At the outbreak of the First World War,
ties between the Viennese head office and the
Paris branches had to be severed – the latter being
renamed *Arthur Goldscheider after the end of the
hostilities. The Viennese operation was administered
by Friedrich's sons Walter and Marcell.

Friedrich Goldscheider exhibited at the 1925
*Exposition Internationale, following which
Marcell set himself up independently in 1928 to
manufacture decorative objects in marble, alabaster
and ceramics created, among others, by the sculptors
Josef *Lorenzl and Stephan Dakon. Following
the Anschluss in 1938, Walter was forced to flee
with his family to England, from where he later
moved to the USA. All branches of the original family
business were closed by 1954.

Fulper

At the family firm of Fulper Pottery Co., in Flemington,
New Jersey, William Hill Fulper began c. 1903
to experiment with decorative glazes and shapes.
By 1909 he had added the 'Vase Kraft' line
of stoneware art pottery to the company's editions
of utilitarian wares.

Like Artus van Briggle and other potters of the
period, Fulper was inspired by Oriental ceramics and
adopted many of their shapes, while setting out to
reinvent their glazes. The Chinese-inspired glazes
were fired in one operation with the green clay body,
which gave Fulper's wares their distinctive look. Later,
a range of other colours and glazes was added to
the company's repertoire – the new glazes were listed
in the firm's catalogues as mirror, *flambé*, lustre, matte,
wisteria and crystal – providing the mass-produced
editions with the seeming individuality of art-pottery
products. These continued to be made throughout the
1920s, but a fire in 1929 destroyed the factory and
the firm was sold in 1930.

G

Gabriel, René (1890–1950)

Born in Maisons-Alfort (Val-de-Marne), Gabriel was
a wallpaper designer by profession but soon branched
out into fabrics and carpets, porcelain decoration, theatre
design and furniture ensembles. He was listed in the
inter-war years at three Paris addresses: one a wallpaper
shop called Sansonnet on rue de Solferino; another at
20 avenue de l'Opéra; and a third at 24 rue Victor Noir,
Neuilly, where he opened his Ateliers d'Art in 1934.

Gabriel exhibited furniture at the *Société des
Artistes Décorateurs from 1919, often showing a
combination of fabrics and wallpapers. His wallpapers
were marketed by Les Papiers Peints de France or
by Nobilis. At the 1925 *Exposition Internationale,
he showed a vestibule for *Primavera and a kitchen
marketed by Les Établissements Harmand. Gabriel also
participated in the Ambassade Française, emphasizing
large editions of furniture for the bourgeoisie, with
multiple interchangeable parts. In 1931 he showed
a *coin de repos* for the ocean liner *Île-de-France* and,
four years later, a suite of Colonial furniture.

It is hard to identify Gabriel's furniture designs
without contemporary photographs to corroborate
authorship, as his furniture was often bland and
anonymous – its impact coming largely from his
colourful wallpapers.

Gallia

Gallia was the trade name registered by *Christofle
for one of its silverplate-making divisions introduced
c. 1900. This subsidiary opened at Saint-Jean-de-Bournay
(Isère) to manufacture inexpensive wares in an improved
pewter alloy made by *galvanoplastie*. Offered in a
wide range of revivalist and contemporary styles was
an inexpensive selection of table-top pieces, including
knife rests, salts, menu holders, egg cups and ice buckets,
some by Édouard-Marcel *Sandoz.

Gate, Simon (1883–1945)

Born into a family of farmers in Västergotland in south-west Sweden, Gate attended the College of Technology in Stockholm from 1902 to 1905 before enrolling at the city's Royal Academy of Art, where he studied painting from 1905 to 1907. Over the next ten years he worked briefly as a portrait painter and illustrator of inexpensive books for the publisher B. Wahlstrom, and then travelled widely before joining *Orrefors in 1916 at the invitation of the firm's director Albert Ahlin. His early years at Orrefors were spent primarily on the development of two techniques: *Graal* and engraving. In 1917 Orrefors hired a second young artist–designer, Edvard *Hald.

In Graal, Gate incorporated compact serpentine designs, scrolled floral patterns and bands of maidens frolicking in pastoral scenes. The technique of enlargement used in this method provided these images with a whimsical and romantic quality through distortion. In engraving, his artistic style was strictly traditional, drawing on classical and Baroque themes: Bacchanalia, cupids, herms and nymphs were painstakingly carved into the surface of the glass in a manner similar to that of early 18th-century Nuremberg, Thuringian and Potsdam glassmakers.

In the 1930s Gate's conservatism began to ease. Uneven, thick-walled vessels in clear glass accented only with bands of colour at the rim or foot show a mild acquiescence to the evolving Modernist aesthetic. However, some of his designs, such as his 1934 'De Frya Elementen' (Four Elements) vase, engraved with a band of nude maidens among thick foliage, incorporate a vigorous Art Deco imagery.

Gaudin, Louis (d. 1936). *See* Zig.

Genet & Michon

Genet & Michon was founded in 1911 by Philippe Genet and Lucien Michon, who described themselves in advertisements as decorator–manufacturers, although they were in fact almost exclusively lighting specialists. Graduates of the *École Boulle in Paris, they made the pressed variety of glass virtually their own, the result of a protracted analysis of the specific needs of the material as an instrument of light. They discovered that thick glass multiplied the reflections of the light – and thus its intensity – more than a thinner variety did, and that this required thickness was most satisfactorily obtained by the technique of pressing the glass. The base compounds of silica, soda and lime were heated to 1,300 degrees Celsius, which transformed the mixture into a vitrifiable paste. This paste was then poured into a steel matrix. Genet & Michon was obviously satisfied with its product, since the composition of the glass (which was kept highly secret) was to remain fundamentally unchanged in the firm's fixtures as late as 1938. The pressed glass was invariably achromatic because the designers reasoned that the introduction of pigmentation would diminish both its brightness and its warmth.

Genet & Michon was credited with two 'firsts'. One was mentioned by Guillaume Janneau in *Le Luminaire et les moyens d'éclairage nouveaux*, his publication on the lighting at the 1925 *Exposition Internationale; he wrote that the firm had been the innovator of the illuminated ramp, designed to border a room at cornice level. The second was recorded in 1926 by Gaston Varenne an art critic for *Art et Décoration*, who maintained that Genet & Michon was one of the 1920s pioneers of the 'suspended illuminated sphere' (the others being RENÉ LALIQUE and JEAN PERZEL).

Over the years, the firm was to engage in virtually every conceivable form of illumination: not only lamps, lustres, wall brackets, tables and epergnes, but also friezes, ceiling *dalles*, door architraves, columns, pilasters, cornices and reflecting vases. These it exhibited at the Salons of the *Société des Artistes Décorateurs (1922–28), the *Salon d'Automne (1922–24) and at a host of other exhibitions: the 1924 Grand Lighting competition; the 1924 Monza exhibition; the 1925 Exposition Internationale; the second and third Salons de la Lumière, in 1934 and 1935; and the Pavillon de la Lumière at the 1937 Exposition des Arts et Techniques. In addition, Genet & Michon was commissioned to provide lighting for the ocean liner *Normandie.

Gennarelli, Amadeo (*fl.* 1913–late 1920s)

Born in Naples, Gennarelli studied there under Lerace before emigrating to France, where he made his début at the 1913 Salon of the *Société des Artistes Français. He generated a large volume of outdoor statuary in marble– including funerary monuments – as well as figurines and groups in bronze and bronze-and-ivory, all executed in a vibrant Art Deco style. Variation was provided by a range of patinated finishes that Gennarelli applied to his works, including *verdigris*, gold and silver.

Geo. Rouard

In 1909 Georges Rouard purchased Jules Mabut's retail shop À la Paix, at 34 avenue de l'Opéra, and changed its name to Maison Geo. Rouard. In 1913 he formed Les Artisans Français Contemporains, a group of contemporary artist–decorators whose works he exhibited. He then hired Marcel *Goupy (whom he had met in 1909) to oversee the production of household accoutrements, mainly in glass and ceramics, in his workshop on rue Vieille du Temple. Designs in porcelain were commissioned from Théodore *Haviland in Limoges.

Regular exhibitions at the shop comprised the works of the period's foremost artist–decorators, including Goupy, Jean *Luce, Auguste *Heiligenstein, MAURICE MARINOT, Henri *Navarre, André *Thuret, Georges *Despret and FRANÇOIS-ÉMILE DECORCHEMONT. Many of these artists also participated in Maison Geo.

Amadeo Gennarelli
(*left*) Nude figure in silvered-bronze on a marble plinth, *c*. 1925.

Simon Gate
(*opposite right*) Vase in engraved and etched glass, for Orrefors, 1934.

Marcel Goupy
(*opposite left*) Enamelled glassware, 1920s.

Jean Goulden
(*below*) Pair of boxes designed by Gustav Miklos, in silvered-metal and *champlevé* enamel, *c*. 1930.

Rouard's display in the pavilion that it shared with JEAN PUIFORCAT and the revue *Art et Décoration* at the 1925 *Exposition Internationale. Goupy remained with the firm until 1954.

Gesmar, Charles (1900–1928)

French-born Gesmar's tragically brief career was inextricably bound to Mistinguett, an aging Parisian music-hall sensation whom he worshipped. At the age of eighteen he was practically adopted by the forty-six-year-old Mistinguett, and until his death he created extravagant costumes, stage sets and programme covers for her and the Casino de Paris and Moulin Rouge. Gesmer's first poster dates from 1916, followed by more than fifty posters that portrayed Mistinguett's uninhibited showmanship and wanton sensuality. He also worked for the Folies Bergère and the Olympia music hall. His zestful and witty style precisely captured the pulse of the Jazz Age's music halls and cabarets.

Gigou, Louis (*fl*. 1920–39)

Known primarily as a locksmith, Gigou exhibited regularly in the 1920s at the Salons of the *Société des Artistes Décorateurs. Drawing both on historical and Modernist styles, he produced a wide range of household fixtures, including door handles, locks, finger plates, escutcheons and a limited selection of light fixtures in **chased** bronze, wrought iron and steel inlaid with copper.

Goulden, Jean (1878–1946)

Born in Charpentry (Meuse) to prosperous Alsatian farmers, Goulden graduated in medicine from the École Alsacienne before moving to Paris in the 1890s to set up his practice. In 1908, following the publication of his thesis on the physiology of a detached heart, he was appointed a hospital consultant in Paris.

Goulden volunteered during the First World War and was assigned to the Macedonian front. After the war, he was invited to stay on by the monks at nearby Mount Athos, a sojourn that exposed him to Byzantine enamelware and, with it, the start of an avocation that would become a second career. On his return to Paris he sought out JEAN DUNAND for instruction in the technique of *champlevé* enamelling. Goulden was quickly accepted into Dunand's circle, whose members included Paul *Jouve, FRANÇOIS-LOUIS SCHMIED and Jean *Lambert-Rucki, and he participated in the group's annual exhibitions at the Galerie Georges Petit at 8 rue de Sèze, Paris, between 1921 and 1932, and thereafter at the Galerie Georges Charpentier. He also exhibited independently at the Salon of the *Société des Artistes Décorateurs in 1929 and 1930, after he had transferred to Rheims to continue his medical career.

Goulden rejuvenated the technique of *champlevé* enamelling, bringing to it a vibrantly coloured and distinctive Cubist style. In addition to a spectacular selection of enamelled silver table-top wares – *coupes*, clocks, cigarette boxes and *coffrets* – he designed enamelled plaques for bindings by Georges *Cretté and Schmied. The identity of the metalworker(s) who executed his designs is apparently unrecorded.

Goupy, Marcel (1886–1954)

Paris-born Goupy studied architecture at the École Nationale Supérieure des Arts Décoratifs, after which he set up a studio at 19 rue Charlot, where he designed decorations for porcelain and pottery. From 1909 he supplied designs for the retailer Maison *Geo. Rouard, which he joined after the First World War as a designer–decorator. While there he displayed his own works alongside those of the firm's stable of artist–craftsmen, including Jean *Luce, Auguste *Heiligenstein, MAURICE MARINOT, Henri *Navarre, André *Thuret, Georges *Despret and FRANÇOIS-ÈMILE DECORCHEMONT.

On Georges Rouard's death in 1929, Goupy became the artistic director of Maison Geo. Rouard and continued to generate patterns for ceramics and glassware until his own death. His pottery designs were executed in Belgium and his porcelain designs by Théodore *Haviland in Limoges.

In addition to a prolific number of glass and ceramic designs, most in an engaging Art Deco style with decorations stencilled or hand-painted onto the vessel, Goupy worked in other disciplines, including silverware. At the 1925 *Exposition Internationale, he displayed his works in several pavilions and was a member of the jury for glassware. He also participated in the Paris Salons from 1926 to 1928 and in the 1929 Contempora exhibition in New York.

Gray, Eileen (1879–1976). *See under* Furniture and Interior Design.

Gregory, Waylande de Santis (1905–1971)

Born in Baxter Springs, Kansas, Gregory studied at the Art Institute in Kansas City and then at the Art Institute of Chicago, before launching his career as a sculptor in bronze under Lorado Taft in Chicago. In 1925–26, he undertook one of his early major commissions in architectural sculpture, designing and executing plaster cast models after Aztec examples for the Hotel President in Kansas City, after which he turned his attention gradually to ceramics.

Gregory worked at the Cowan Pottery Studio in Ohio from 1929 to 1932, before moving to the Cranbrook Academy of Art in Bloomfield Hills, Michigan, where he became an artist-in-residence with his own studio and kiln. In the late 1930s he received two important commissions for the 1939 New York World's Fair: 'The Fountain of the Atoms' and 'American Imports and Exports' – the latter for General Motors. From around 1940 his studio was listed in Bound Brook, New Jersey. In later years he concentrated mostly on *repoussé* metalwork. In an Art Deco context, Gregory is known especially for his 'high-style' figurines in glazed pottery.

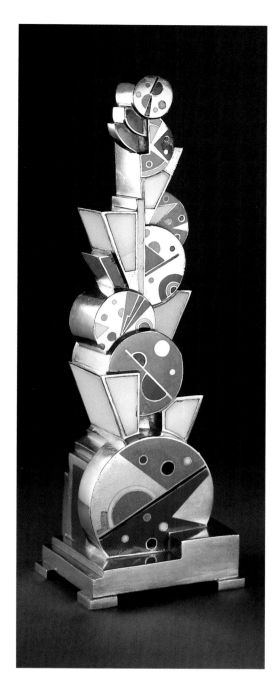

Jean Goulden

(*above*) Table lamp in silvered-bronze, *champlevé* enamel and opalescent glass, late 1920s.

Charles Gesmar

(*opposite*) *Mistinguett*, lithographic poster, 1917.

(*right*) Clock in silvered-bronze, *champlevé* enamel and marble, 1929.

André Groult

(*right*) bedroom ensemble with bed and armchair in veneered shagreen, included in the Ambassade Français pavilion at the 1925 Exposition Internationale, Paris.

André Groult

(*above*) Side chair in wood veneered in shagreen, *c.* 1922.

Waylande de Santis Gregory

(*right*) Three glazed earthenware figures, late 1920s/early 1930s.

Gübelin

(*right*) Clock in chinoiserie style, enamelled silver on onyx base, *c.* 1920.

Gropius, Walter (1883–1969)

Gropius was born in Berlin and studied architecture in Munich and Berlin from 1903 to 1907 before establishing an independent architectural practice in 1910. The Fagus shoe-last factory at Alfeld an der Leine, which he designed in 1910–11 in association with Adolf Meyer, was startlingly progressive in its use of steel and glass in place of conventional load-bearing walls. In 1914 Gropius designed buildings for the Deutscher Werkbund exhibition in Cologne.

After serving in the German infantry during the First World War, he was appointed director of the Kunstgewerbeschule Weimar, which he reorganized into the Bauhaus. In 1928 Gropius resigned from the Bauhaus to set up an office in Berlin. In 1934 he exiled himself to England, where he entered into partnership with E. Maxwell Fry and two years later became the controller of design for the Isokon Furniture Co. In 1937 Gropius moved to the USA, where he taught architecture at Harvard until 1952 and worked with Marcel *Breuer from 1938 to 1941.

Grotell, Majlis (Maija) (1899–1973)

Born in Helsinki, Finland, Grotell studied painting, sculpture and design at the Central School of Industrial Art there before training as a potter for six years with Alfred William Finch. She emigrated to the USA in 1927, where she accepted various positions as a ceramics instructor, including periods at Inwood Pottery (1927–28) and at the Union Settlement (1928–29), both in New York, before furthering her studies under Charles Fergus Binns at the New York State College of Ceramics at Alfred University.

From the early 1930s, Grotell worked as an art instructor at various schools and institutions, including the School of Ceramic Engineers at Rutgers University in New Jersey (1936–38), before accepting the directorship of the ceramics department at the Cranbrook Academy of Art in Michigan (1938–66).

Grotell is known for her brushed-on colour *slips* and glazes, which she applied to clay vessels that she threw on a kick-wheel.

Groult, André (1884–1966)

Groult was born in Paris and made his Salon début *c.* 1910 as a decorator, exhibiting intermittently into the 1930s. His furniture designs, executed by a small group of craftsmen in his atelier at 29–31 rue d'Anjou, Paris, were notable for their sumptuous materials, especially *galuchat* and horn. Notable among his collaborators was the *ébéniste* Adolphe *Chanaux, who for a brief period after the First World War influenced Groult's choice of materials immeasurably. Other artists – including Marie *Laurencin, Charles *Martin, Georges d'Espagnat, Pierre Laprade and Paul *Iribe (before 1914) – were commissioned to provide a range of paintings and murals for Groult's interiors.

Groult's reputation today rests largely on the lady's bedroom he displayed in the Ambassade Française at the 1925 *Exposition Internationale. At once restrained and provocative, it included an eye-catching *bombé* chest of drawers veneered in *galuchat* with ivory banding – its anthropomorphic shape becoming an endless source of conjecture among viewers. Elsewhere in Groult's bedroom, furniture comprising a mix of *galuchat*, ebony and velour upholstery executed by Maison Delaroière et Leclercq imparted elegance and femininity to the ensemble. At the same exhibition Groult also participated in the displays for *Fontaine et Cie, *Christofle–Baccarat, Les Arts du Jardin and the Société de l'Art Appliqué aux Métiers. By the 1930s many of Groult's interiors resembled those of JEAN-MICHEL FRANK – their walls and chairs being veneered in straw paper.

Gruber, Jacques (1870–1936)

Born in Sundhausen (Haut-Rhin), Alsace, Gruber studied first in Nancy and then under Gustave Moreau

at the École National Supérieure des Beaux-Arts in Paris. On his return to Nancy in 1893, he worked initially at DAUM FRÈRES, where he learned the art of glass engraving.

As a founding member of the École de Nancy in 1900, Gruber revealed his versatility in designs for furniture, stained glass, leather, ceramics (for Mougin Frères) and bookbinding (for René Wiener). In 1900 he set up his own studio to manufacture windows and furniture, the latter often inset with maroon cameo glass panels etched with vistas of the nearby Vosges countryside. Gruber closed this studio in 1914.

In 1920 Gruber opened new premises on the Villa d'Alésia in Paris, where he concentrated on secular and religious stained-glass windows rendered in rigorous geometric patterns far removed in spirit from his earlier Art Nouveau style. He exhibited at the 1925 *Exposition Internationale alongside Louis *Barillet and ROBERT MALLET-STEVENS. On his death he was succeeded by his son.

Gübelin

The Gübelin firm began as a watch- and jewelry-making house founded in Lucerne in 1854 by Mauritz Breitschmid, whose daughter married Jakob Gübelin in 1887. Initially the enterprise focused mainly on the production of high-quality timepieces. In 1924 Jakob's son Édouard, in collaboration with the New York jeweller Edmond Frisch, opened a store in Manhattan to develop the firm's American market.

In the following years, additional branches of Gübelin were opened in St Moritz and Zurich as the firm focused its production on *pièces uniques* and limited-edition jewelled watches, including a series of pieces in the Art Deco style offered within a wider range of classical and avant-garde designs. Following the end of the Second World War, Gübelin opened further European outlets.

Guiguichon, Suzanne (1900–1985)

Paris-born Guiguichon joined *La Maîtrise in 1921
and made her début at the *Salon d'Automne the next
year. Much of her work remained anonymous, as her
primary function was to design modern interiors
offered through Les Galeries Lafayette, which may
have inhibited her personal ambitions, perhaps leading
to her decision to become independent in 1929.
Her address in the 1920s and 1930s is listed as 11 rue
Constance. Guiguichon's furnishings were marketed
by various firms, including Compagnie des Arts
Français, La Pepinière and the cabinet-makers Speich
Frères in the Faubourg Saint-Antoine. Collaborators
included Henri Brochard.

At the 1925 *Exposition Internationale, Guiguichon
exhibited two ensembles in the Ambassade Française
and a *coin pour causer* (corner to chat) in an artist's
studio. She participated also in La Maîtrise's pavilion,
sharing credit with Gabriel *Englinger for a living room.
Her furniture designs, executed by Maison Morand et
Angst and Maison Debusscher, were strikingly Art Deco,
yet sober and less feminine than those of other
female designers. Guiguichon continued to exhibit
at the Salons in the 1930s, showing a range of rooms.
She developed a private clientele and worked both
through and outside the Salons until the 1950s.

Guillemard, Marcel (1886–1932)

Born in Paris, Guillemard was a generation older than
most of the young designers and architects in the
vanguard of 1920s style. Early training at the Krieger
cabinetry works in the rue du Faubourg Saint-Antoine,
where he joined Louis *Sognot, imbued him with
a strong sense of the rich heritage of the nation's
furniture – Antoine Krieger being a maker of all 18th-
century styles.

Guillemard later followed Sognot to *Primavera,
where he emerged as a top designer and decorator
from the end of the First World War until his premature
death at the age of forty-six. All his interiors were
marketed through Primavera, which credited him both
independently and in collaboration with Sognot,
Charlotte *Chauchet-Guilleré and Georges *Lévard.
He played an important role in furnishing the
Primavera pavilion at the 1925 *Exposition
Internationale, including a dining room and an office.
Guillemard introduced nickelled tubular furniture into
his repertoire after 1925, showing Sognot's influence
in a series of neat, angular and, above all, functional
interiors at the *Société des Artistes Décorateurs and
the *Salon d'Automne.

Guiraud-Rivière, Maurice (b. 1881)

One of the most versatile sculptural talents of the
inter-war years was that of Guiraud-Rivière, who was
born in Toulouse. Moving to Paris, he studied sculpture
at the École des Beaux-Arts under Antonin Mercié,
working later as a painter, graphic artist and cartoonist
for a number of journals. He made his début at the
Salon of the *Société des Artistes Français in 1907,
and was by the early 1920s an established participant
at the Salons, where he displayed a range of sculpture
in the prevailing Art Deco idiom.

Guiraud-Rivière's models were mostly in **cold-
painted** bronze, the figurines sometimes inset with
carved ivory faces and limbs. One of these, entitled
La Comète, is today considered his *chef d'œuvre*
in its dynamic portrayal of a young woman streaking
across the heavens, her long trailing tresses fashioned
into the comet's tail, her torso resting on a bank
of stylized clouds. This and other works were
commissioned by *Etling et Cie and *Les Neveux de
J. Lehmann (LNJL), for reproduction in bronze. Some
models were also produced in porcelain by *Sèvres or
in ceramics by *Robj, the latter a 1920s merchandiser
of trendy household *bibelots*.

Some of Guiraud-Rivière's subject matter was
drawn from contemporary society, such as the jockey
Max Dearling and unidentified cabaret performers.
Motor-racing drivers, charioteers and steeplechasers
also served as models for his pieces, many rendered
in a distinctly masculine style.

Gustave Keller Frères

Founded in 1851 as a maker of leather dressing cases,
the firm entered the *orfèvrerie* business *c.* 1880,
focusing on silver toiletry articles and hollowware.
A participant in all the major international exhibitions
from 1900, Gustave Keller Frères offered a line of
progressive designs within a broader range of Beaux-
Arts wares. At the 1925 *Exposition Internationale,
its display was listed as 'Keller Fils-Gendre, Successeurs
de Gustave Keller'.

H

Hagenauer

Carl Hagenauer (1871–1928) served his goldsmithing
apprenticeship in the jewelry workshop of Wurbel &
Czokally before establishing his own workshop,
the Werkstätten Hagenauer, in Vienna in 1898.
Initial production, primarily in bronze, included
reproductions of old masters, his own designs and
those of Josef Hoffmann, Otto Prutscher, E. J. Meckel
and others – selections of which he displayed in
the period's international exhibitions.

In 1919 Carl was joined by his son Karl
(1888–1956). Born in Pressburg (Bratislava),
Karl attended the Kunstgewerbeschule in Vienna
and was a highly regarded sculptor in his own right
when he entered the firm, helping to expand
its range of wares and materials. In the inter-war
years Hagenauer's materials included silver, bronze,
copper, ivory, chromed sheet metal and carved wood.
On his father's death in 1928, Karl was joined by
his brother Franz (1906–1986) and his sister Grete
as the firm's directors.

Maurice Guiraud-Rivière

(*top right*) *La Comète*, gilt- and cold-painted bronze, retailed by Etling et Cie, 1920s.

(*above left*) Figure in patinated and parcel-gilt bronze and carved ivory, *c.* 1930.

Hagenauer

(*top left*) Pair of heads in brass, *c.* 1930.

Hagenauer

(*left*) Tennis player, polished bronze, 1930s.

(*above*) Horse and rider wall ornament, patinated brass, 1930s.

Katsu Hamanaka
Writing set in lacquered wood
and silvered-metal, c. 1930.

More so than his father's and brother's work, Franz's designs provided Hagenauer's wares with a distinctive 'high-style' *élan* and lightheartedness. Portrait busts, butlers, mannequins and tribal musicians were fashioned into toiletry items and bar accessories in chromed metal, brass and wood. Their pared-down and elongated forms show the influence of Constantin Brancusi or Amedeo Modigliani and bring a ready chuckle to modern viewers. The firm closed in 1956.

Hald, Edvard (1883–1980)

Born in Stockholm, the son of a Norwegian engineer and businessman who emigrated to Sweden in 1875, Hald studied architecture briefly at a technical college in Dresden before leaving for Paris to pursue a career as a painter. Studies followed in Dresden, Copenhagen (under Johan *Rohde), Stockholm and Paris (in part under Henri Matisse).

Hald made his début as an artist in Stockholm in 1909. In 1917, following a large exhibition of his canvases in Lund, he began to pursue an evolving interest in glass and ceramics. This led, in the same year, to employment at Rörstrand and then *Orrefors.

His style carried the future with him. His simplified Modernist designs were fresh and innovative, in direct opposition to the Neoclassical style favoured by Simon *Gate. Hald concentrated on the drawn line, unlike his Orrefors colleague, whose sculptured approach depended on depth and relief effects. Hald's engraved works, such as 'Ball-Playing Girls' (1919) and 'The Broken Bridge' (1920), show his training as a painter in their flat execution. Some pictures, such as 'The Fireworks Bowl' (1921) and 'Cactus Show' (1927), have a narrative or pictorial content; others are light and humorous.

Hald's history at Orrefors parallels that of the firm itself. For nearly thirty years he had formed a close artistic and personal association with Gate at Orrefors. In 1933, as the Depression began to bite in Sweden, Hald took over the management of the company.

Three years after his retirement in 1944, he was recalled as artistic adviser, and continued to work for the firm until his final retirement in 1978.

Halouze, Édouard (b. 1900)

Nothing is known of Halouze's upbringing and education prior to the end of the First World War, when he emerged as a painter, decorator and illustrator in Paris. There he designed programme covers and advertisements for the city's music halls, and illustrations for *La Gazette du Bon Ton*, *Les Feuilles d'Art* and other fashion revues. With their distinctive Cubist designs, rendered in watercolour, gouache and pencil, his sketches represented the Art Deco style at its most vigorous. In 1941 Halouze published *Costumes of South America*, which included forty hand-coloured *pochoirs* of the continent's tribes in their native costumes.

Hamanaka, Katsu (1895–1982)

Born in Sapporo, Japan, Hamanaka was trained as a lacquer worker, and it is probable that he was lured to Paris in the 1920s by the prospect of ready employment. The revived vogue for lacquer – initiated in part in the pre-war years by EILEEN GRAY, who was trained in the medium by the Japanese lacquer master Sougawara – caused a surge in demand for qualified artisans. JEAN DUNAND and LÉON-ALBERT JALLOT, among others, looked to the Far East for extra technical expertise.

Little is known of Hamanaka's training. He emerged at the Salons in 1929, when he exhibited a range of lacquered tables, screens and boxes. In 1980, frail but elated, he walked into the gallery of a Left Bank Art Deco dealer to announce that he was creator of the lacquered screen on display. The dealer read of his death two years later. A part of Art Deco history had slipped away, almost unnoticed.

It seems from Hamanaka's limited output that he worked alone. His screens incorporate dynamic designs and display considerable technical virtuosity.

Haviland et Cie

In 1839 David Haviland, a young American engaged in the retail china trade in New York, saw an unsigned piece of porcelain that initiated an odyssey to trace its source. The trail led ultimately to Limoges, near the town of Saint-Yriex, where deposits of kaolin – the pure white clay employed in the finest porcelain production – had earlier been discovered. After first importing wares from Limoges into the USA, Haviland then built a factory in the town, from which he exported his wares after 1842. David's son Theodore succeeded him, and from the early 1890s built one of largest and best factories for fine china in the area. Theodore was succeeded in 1936 by his son William D. Haviland, and later by Theodore II – each in turn modernizing the family's factories.

In the inter-war years, the firm of Haviland et Cie retained prominent outside artist–designers to ensure that its wares remained contemporary and competitive. Among these were Édouard-Marcel *Sandoz, Jean Dufy, Solange Patry-Bié and Suzanne Lalique, who was the daughter of René *Lalique and later married Paul Haviland.

Heal, Sir Ambrose (1872–1959)

Heal & Son, Ltd., the London home-furnisher and retailer, began as a feather-dressing business established in 1810 by John Harris Heal. Over the following decades the firm expanded into one of the city's largest suppliers of home furnishings. The son of Ambrose Heal, the firm's owner and a member of the British Bedding and Furniture Manufacturers and Retailers Association, Ambrose Heal, Jr. entered the family business in 1893 and was within three years designing furniture for it. In 1898 he became a partner, in 1907 managing director, and, after his father's death in 1913, chairman. In 1905 the firm was converted into a limited company. A period

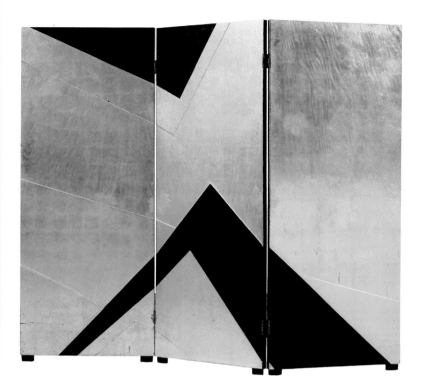

Édouard Halouze
(*left*) Illustration in *pochoir* for a fashion magazine, 1920.

Katsu Hamanaka
(*below*) 3-panel wood screen in gold leaf and black lacquer.

Sir Ambrose Heal
The Horniman Table, walnut on ebonized feet, *c*. 1928.

Poul Henningsen
(*left*) Chandelier in patinated metal and opalescent glass manufactured by Louis Poulsen, *c.* 1930.

(*below left*) Table lamp, model No. PH5/3, in green-enamelled copper and patinated brass, manufactured by Louis Poulsen, *c.* 1927.

Hélène Henry
(*below*) Desk and stool in sycamore commissioned from Pierre Chareau for her Paris apartment, *c.* 1927; the painting by Jean Dunand.

Auguste Heiligenstein
(*opposite left*) Vases in etched and enamelled glassware, *c.* 1925–26.

(*opposite right*) Vase and two flacons in etched and enamelled glass, 1920s.

catalogue showed that the firm focused largely on the Arts and Crafts style, dividing its product line between costly, handmade items and inexpensive machine-made wares aimed at a broader market.

In the 1930s, under the influence of his designers J. F. Johnson, Leonard Thoday, Arthur Greenwood and others, Heal introduced laminated woods and tubular steel into the firm's repertoire of Modernist furniture. In addition to a series of inexpensive furniture by Greenwood and E. W. Shepherd, the firm stocked models by Ludwig *Mies van der Rohe and commissioned new ones from Marcel *Breuer. The company also opened a fabric department. After the Second World War, Heal & Son was the largest exhibitor at the Britain Can Make It exhibition at the Victoria & Albert Museum. In 1984 the company was purchased by Terence Conran.

Heaton, Maurice (1900–1990)

On moving to New York from his native Switzerland at the age of fourteen, Maurice Heaton attended the Ethical Culture School in the city between 1915 and 1919. From 1920 to 1921 he studied engineering at the Stevens Institute of Technology in Hoboken, New Jersey. Heaton was introduced to glass-making through a long apprenticeship under his father, Clement Heaton, a noted English stained-glass artist who had worked in Switzerland before emigrating to the USA.

Working out of his studio in Valley Cottage, New York, Heaton adopted a Modernist style in the late 1920s. He experimented with translucent white enamelled glazes on hand-cut sheets of bubbly glass, which Eugene Schoen and Rena Rosenthal offered through their Manhattan galleries. Heaton also undertook mural commissions, including 'The Flight of Amelia Earhart across the Atlantic' for the RKO Center Theater in Rockefeller Center (the theatre was demolished in the 1950s).

Heiligenstein, Auguste (1891–1976)

Born in La Plaine Saint-Denis on the outskirts of Paris, Auguste Heiligenstein was apprenticed from the age of eleven at the LEGRAS ET CIE glassworks, where he studied various aspects of design and decoration, before pursuing his career at the Prestat and Baccarat works. He worked as a commercial artist after 1910. Mobilized during the First World War, he was awarded the military Légion d'Honneur in 1917.

Following the end of hostilities, Heiligenstein joined Maison *Geo. Rouard, where he executed designs by Marcel *Goupy in enamelled glass. In 1923 he left Geo. Rouard, married the ceramist Odette Chatrousse, pursued a dual career in enamelled glass and ceramics while working out of an atelier at 235 boulevard Raspail, Paris, and made his début at the Salon of the *Société des Artistes Français. He exhibited at Geo. Rouard's gallery until 1926, when he switched to EDGAR BRANDT'S.

From 1926 to 1930 Heiligenstein occupied the post of technical adviser at the Verrerie Ouchon-Neuvesel, the successor to Legras. Now freelance, Heiligenstein executed glass with enamelled decoration by Léon *Bakst for Florence Blumenthal, designed a selection of pieces for the Cristallerie de Pantin from 1931 to 1935 and continued to exhibit at the Salons.

Henningsen, Poul (1894–1967)

Poul Henningsen was born in Ordrup, Denmark, and studied at the Danish College of Technology in Copenhagen between 1911 and 1917. While working as an independent architect in the city from 1920, he designed residences, restaurants and a factory. He also pursued a career as a man of letters, working as a journalist, playwright, poet and editor of the magazine *Kritisk Revy* (The Critical Revue), a forum for left-wing, often polemical, commentaries on current Danish culture.

Henningsen's light fixtures established his international reputation, starting with the 'PH' series, which he showed as prototypes in a Danish lighting competition in 1924 and, in completed versions, at the 1925 *Exposition Internationale in Paris, at which he was awarded a gold medal. The following year he received the lighting contract for the Forum, a large exhibition hall under construction in Copenhagen. The design of the initial 'PH' series, for hanging, wall and table models, was based on his scientific analysis of the shade's function: its size and shape, and the arrangement of its graduating tiers of individual reflectors to ensure the optimum diffusion and distribution of a glare-free light. Manufactured from its inception by Louis Poulsen, initially with white opaline glass shades housed in chromed metal armatures, the 'PH' series was followed by the 'Artichoke' model, designed on the same principles, but with more panels and layers of reflector shades. This and other new models were displayed at the annual Cabinet-Makers' Guild exhibitions in Copenhagen.

Following the outbreak of the Second World War and the decline in sales of his lamps, Henningsen left Nazi-occupied Denmark in 1943 for Stockholm, returning after the armistice. At his death, more than one hundred sketches of his light fixtures were discovered, some of which were put into production by Poulsen.

Henry (Henri), Hélène (1891–1965)

Born in Champagney (Haute-Saône), Henry's upbringing and education are unknown beyond that she was self-taught as a textile designer. In 1918 she opened a workshop in Paris equipped with hand looms to produce modern fabrics, table linen, velvets, brocades and carpets to her own designs. Henry supplied upholstery fabrics to many of the era's pre-eminent furniture designers, including JACQUES-ÉMILE RUHLMANN, PIERRE CHAREAU, MAURICE DUFRÈNE, Francis *Jourdain and ROBERT MALLET-STEVENS, and participated in this capacity in several pavilions at the 1925 *Exposition Internationale, mixing abstract printed patterns with

Ludwig Hohlwein
(*left*) *Café Odeon und Billard Akademie*, lithographic poster, 1908.

Wolfgang Hoffmann
(*below*) Rocking chair in chromed tubular steel and leather, manufactured by the Howell Co., St Charles, Illinois, 1930s.

textured ones. Henry co-founded the *Union des Artistes Modernes (UAM) in 1929. After her death, her workshop was run by her son under the name Tissages Van Melle.

Herbst, René (1891–1982)

The events of René Herbst's early years are sketchy, including details of his education. Born in Paris, he trained as an architect, graduating *c. 1908*, and then gained experience in Paris, London and Frankfurt. From 1919 he applied himself to the challenges of modern living, concentrating on metallic furniture, shop-window displays and interior lighting.

Herbst made his début as a furniture designer at the 1921 *Salon d'Automne, displaying furnishings for a rest area in the Musée de Crillon. He later undertook a wide range of architectural commissions, including cinemas, shop façades, restaurants, offices and aeroplanes. The award of the Blumenthal Prize in 1924 enhanced his reputation, adding credence to his crusade for Modernism. He participated in the 1925 *Exposition Internationale both as member of the jury and as an exhibitor, taking stand 27 on the Pont Alexandre III; he also displayed a mahogany and nickelled metal piano in the Pleyel exhibit, designed stands for Cusenier, Lina Mouton and Les Établissements Siegel et Stockman Réunis. Herbst's address was then listed as 4 rue Chateaubriand, Paris.

From 1926 Herbst began to replace the earlier wood components in his furniture with metal, glass and mirror, and in 1927 he was appointed president of the syndicated chamber of decorative artists, a prelude to his co-founding of the Union des Artistes Modernes (UAM) two years later. At the time, he earned the soubriquet 'Man of Steel'. By 1930 he was competing with Adrienne Gorska, Louis Sognot, Claude Lévy and Émile Guenot for the metal furniture market.

Herbst also placed great emphasis on interior lighting, both direct and indirect, for which he retained André Salomon as his consultant. Notable in this area were his dining-room chandelier at the 1928 Salon d'Automne and, the next year, a curious floor lamp comprising a circular metal disc supported by twin rods. He also pioneered the science of shop-window illumination, including concealed lighting that provided daytime nuances and night-time visibility.

The 1930s brought increased renown. Herbst won the commission to decorate the Maharajah of Indore's palace, and later apartments for the Aga Khan and the prominent art dealer Léonce Rosenberg. He also participated in the 1935 Exposition de Bruxelles. At the outbreak of the Second World War, he volunteered with Jules *Leleu for the French air force and was demobilized the following year. In 1946 Herbst was elected president of the revived UAM.

Hernández, Mateo (1885–1949)

Born in Spain, Hernández began sculpting at the age of twelve, later attending the School of Art and Industry in Béjar, where he worked primarily in stone. His first life-size model, which he carved when seventeen years old, won him a scholarship in Madrid. From there he moved to France in 1913, settling in Meudon where he kept a studio and a private zoo. Although based on real animals, his sculptures, directly carved in stone or wood, are simplified and stylized, as in the life-sized diorite figures of a black panther and peacock that he displayed at the 1925 *Exposition Internationale. Although primarily known as an *animalier*, he also modelled portraits and designed frescoes and lithographs.

Hoffmann, Wolfgang (1900–1969) and Pola (b. 1902)

A son of Josef Hoffmann, Wolfgang studied architecture and the decorative arts in secondary school, followed by studies at a special architectural college and the Vienna Kunstgewerbeschule. On graduating, he worked briefly for local architects, including his father, before emigrating to the USA in December of 1925. A thorough grounding in both architecture and the decorative arts placed Wolfgang at the vanguard of the Modernist movement in America. He opened his studio *c. 1927*, from where he designed a wide range of interiors – wood and metal furnishings, rugs and linens – in collaboration with his Polish-born wife, Pola.

Wolfgang participated in the 1928 and 1929 American Designers' Gallery exhibitions in New York, and also in the 1931 American Union of Decorative Artists and Craftsmen (AUDAC) exhibit at the Brooklyn Museum. At the 1928 Macy's International Exposition of Art in Industry, he and Pola showed a one-room woman's apartment, including a combination desk, dressing table and bookcase unit, as well as a lounge that he had designed for the St. George's Hotel in Brooklyn. Wolfgang's style showed a rigid adherence to functionalism, while Pola contributed the Modernist textile designs for his interiors. The couple also designed modern light fixtures. Their partnership was dissolved in the 1930s when they were divorced. Pola afterwards married the mystery writer Rex Stout.

Hohlwein, Ludwig (1874–1949)

Hohlwein was born in Munich, where he studied architecture at the Fachhochschule. From 1906 he devoted himself primarily to poster design, in which he was self-taught. The first of his menswear designs for the Munich tailor Hermann Scherrer in 1907 launched his career as a poster artist: from that point Hohlwein created more than one thousand examples, many of which became classics. These included designs for PKZ, Wilhelm Mozer, Marco-Polo-Tee, the Munich zoo, Kaffee Hag, Audi automobiles, Panther shoes, Kitty Starling and Riquet tea. Hunting and horse racing were also popular themes. In 1913 a tobacco manufacturer from Hohlwein's home town named a product after him (Hohlwein cigarettes). These commissions were accompanied by numerous advertisements and exhibition, film and propaganda posters, including work in the 1930s for the Nazi party.

A star of German poster art, Hohlwein did not belong to any school or group. Yet he exercised a profound influence on the style that came to be regarded as uniquely German. His starkly composed images with their strong lines and contrasting colour planes were often simplified or compressed into silhouettes and patterns that gave the impression that they were created by woodcuts. The lettering in his typefaces was always in keeping with the theme of the advertisement: for example, bold capitals for the zoo and a delicate, ornate, hand script for Frau Gertrud.

Hunebelle, André (1896–1985)

A leading French designer of moulded glassware in the inter-war years, Hunebelle was clearly influenced stylistically by RENÉ LALIQUE. Born in Meundon (Hauts-de-Seine), he worked out of a studio at 22 rue la Boétie in Paris. Hunebelle's name first appeared c. 1928. He exhibited a range of tablewares with deeply moulded decoration, including symmetrical patterns and stylized leaves, at the Salons of the *Société des Artistes Décorateurs and those of the *Salon d'Automne from 1930. After the Second World War, Hunebelle became a noted film director in France, producing more than twenty films between 1948 and 1978.

I

Icart, Louis (1888–1950)

Born in Toulouse, the son of a banker, Icart attended the city's École Chrétienne des Frères, a Catholic school. Intent on becoming an actor, and without formal art training, he only later realized his true *métier*. On graduating, Icart joined an architectural firm, where he learned basic draughting skills. After military service, he moved to Paris, where in 1907 he found employment at a postcard publishing company.

Within a year, Icart opened his own studio, progressing from postcards to illustrations for such fashion revues as *Le Rire*, *Fantasia* and *La Baïonette*. In 1913 *La Gazette du Bon Ton* staged his first one-man exhibition of etchings, paintings and drawings in Brussels. The following year Icart met Fanny Volmers, a representative for the Paris fashion house Paquin. She was to become his model, inspiration and life companion. During the First World War Icart's work also came to the attention of Maison Valmont, a ladies' hat designer and manufacturer, which retained him to illustrate its catalogues. Mobilized towards the end of the war, Icart served as a pilot in the Tenth Airborne Division, rising to the rank of major.

Icart's subject matter was invariably young women, whom he portrayed in an inexhaustible array of charming, naughty, coy, insouciant, sensuous and romantic poses, sometimes in racing cars or disporting themselves with borzois and poodles in the countryside. Many of these images are now considered to border on kitsch.

At the end of the hostilities, Icart participated in exhibitions at the Paris galleries Wagram and Henaut, which began to export his etchings to the USA, where they became the rage. His first major show in Paris took place in March 1920. Two years later, on a trip to the USA, he met Anton Schutz, the president of the New York Graphic Society, who helped to shape his career in America.

In the 1920s Icart's output was prolific: in addition to hundreds of etchings, he generated drypoints, sketches, drawings, oils, watercolours, lithographs, monotypes, posters, *livres d'artiste* and a considerable volume of erotica. His peak production occurred in the late 1920s and early 1930s. In May 1940, when the Germans invaded France, Icart chronicled the plight of the war's refugees in a harrowing series of oils and monotypes entitled *L'Exode* (The Exodus).

Indenbaum, Léon (1890–1981)

Indenbaum was born in Sievsk, Russia, and studied at the Beaux-Arts School in Odessa from 1909 to 1910. In 1911 he moved to Paris, where he frequented La Ruche, a studio set up originally for Russian *émigrés*, where he worked alongside Marc Chagall, Chaim Soutine, Alexander Archipenko, Amedeo Modigliani and Jacques Lipchitz. In 1912 his display at the Salon des Indépendants caught the attention of Jacques *Doucet, who commissioned from him a bas relief for the dining room in his Neuilly apartment. Executed in marble, this was entitled *Musiciens et Antilopes*. (The piece sold at auction in Paris on 27 October 2004, for 3 million euros.) From 1913 Idenbaum exhibited at the Salon des Tuileries and *Salon d'Automne. His works were sought also by Georges and Marcel Bernard, known for their Impressionist painting collection. From c. 1918 to 1926 he was based in Émile-Antoine Bourdelle's atelier.

Indenbaum used a range of materials, including wood, terracotta and granite. His studies of the human torso were often rendered without heads and limbs, their truncated forms inspired by Hellenistic statuary excavated from archaeological sites.

International Silver Co.

Incorporated in 1898, the International Silver Co. within a year had purchased seventeen small silversmithing works, including the Meriden Britannia Co., the Rogers Manufacturing Co. and the Derby Silver Co. By the early 1900s it had become a large industrial consortium with headquarters in Meriden, Connecticut.

Notwithstanding its size and focus on mass production, the firm provided a surprisingly spirited contribution to the Modernist movement in the late 1920s with a range of hollowware and flatware in sterling, silverplate and pewter through divisions such as the Wilcox Silver Plate Co. and Simpson, Hall, Miller & Co. Popular in the latter's production was Alfred G. Kintz's 'Spirit of Today' silverware series, introduced

(*above*) Set of stem cups with
matching tray, silver and
champlevé enamel, 1930s.

Léon-Albert and Maurice-Raymond Jallot
(*right*) Reception hall in collaboration with Raymond Subes, Charles Despiau, Paul Jouve and Jean Perzel, exhibited at the Salon of the Société des Artistes Décorateurs, 1930.

Paul Iribe
(*left*) *Bergère gondole* in sculpted mahogany, 1914.

Léon-Albert and Maurice-Raymond Jallot
(*above*) Boudoir, late 1920s.

in 1928, which included 'Northern Lights', 'Tropical Sunrise' and 'Ebb Tide', characterized by broad unornamented surfaces within decorative borders, which gave emphasis to contrasts of light and shade.

Key to the International Silver Co.'s success was the mix of outside consultants and in-house designers whom it retained to provide up-to-the-minute models: in addition to Kintz were Eliel *Saarinen, DONALD DESKEY, Paul Lobel, Lurelle Guild, Ernest R. Beck, Edward J. Conroy, Peer Smed, Gilbert *Rohde and Jean G. Theobald. Assisted by Virginia Hamill, an adviser on merchandizing and home furnishings, Theobald contributed designs for three three-piece tea services introduced through the company's Wilcox Silver Plate division in 1928 – a pot, creamer and sugar bowl created as a unified architectural unit housed on a conforming tray – that propelled the International Silver Co. smartly into the medium's avant-garde.

Iribe, Paul (1883–1935)
Iribarnegaray – a name that he understandably contracted to Iribe – was born in Angoulême and trained as a commercial artist. He became famous as a caricaturist for a range of Paris journals, including *L'Assiette au Beurre*, *Le Rire*, *Le Cri de Paris* and *Le Témoin*. His creativity was confined largely to four years, from 1910 to 1914. This meteoric burst of brilliance was followed by relative obscurity.

In the early 1900s Iribe had developed skills as an interior decorator, probably encouraged by Paul *Poiret, for whom he designed a range of jewelry, fabrics, wallpapers and furniture. In 1912 another couturier, Jacques *Doucet, commissioned Iribe to furnish his new apartment in Neuilly, and this established Iribe's reputation as a furniture designer. With his young assistant, PIERRE-ÉMILE LEGRAIN, he designed a range of modern furniture, three pieces of which were donated subsequently to the Musée des Arts Décoratifs, Paris.

Iribe's style provided elegance; whereas a Louis XV flamboyance is evident in the fluid designs of his furniture, its discipline is distinctly of the 1800s. Present also in his designs is a pleasing touch of femininity and comfort. Preferred woods were zebra, with its distinct grain, macassar ebony and mahogany. His favourite motif was the rose, which later became the celebrated 'rose Iribe', a symbol of 'high-style' Art Deco, despite its pre-war conception.

In the winter of 1914, Iribe set sail for the USA for what became a sixteen-year sojourn. He settled in Hollywood, designing giant sets for Cecil B. de Mille. In 1930, aged forty-seven, he returned to France, where he took a studio at 4 avenue Rodin. Until his death, Iribe was engaged intermittently in designing jewelry for Gabrielle (Coco) *Chanel.

J

Jallot, Léon-Albert (1874–1967)
and Maurice-Raymond (1900–1971)
Léon-Albert Jallot was born in Nantes and studied at the École des Beaux-Arts, Paris, which provided him with the basic technical skills of an artist, wood sculptor and engraver. His career began c. 1894, and in 1899 Siegfried Bing appointed him head of the studio that made furnishings for La Maison de l'Art Nouveau on rue de Provence. Léon-Albert therefore participated in the creation of some of the Art Nouveau movement's most prized works, including those designed by the firm's renowned threesome: Georges de Feure, Édouard Colonna and Eugène Gaillard. When Bing's business closed in 1903, Léon-Albert established his own studio at 17 rue Sedaine. His versatility was apparent: carpets, fabrics, lamps and furniture were shown at the Salons of the *Société Nationale des Beaux-Arts.

Léon-Albert emerged in the pre-war years as a master artist–craftsman. His stylistic preference was for traditional furniture: formal, 18th-century shapes decorated with heavily carved floral panels and mouldings. From 1919 he abandoned revivalism, relying for his ornamentation more on burled veneers, especially jacaranda and wild cherry, to provide contrasting compositions. His designs from this period, which were largely transitional, show an easy elegance and *savoir-faire*.

Léon-Albert's son Maurice-Raymond had been born in Paris during the 1900 Exposition Universelle, an auspicious start to a career in the decorative arts. On graduating from the *École Boulle, he joined his father's atelier. At the 1925 *Exposition Internationale, father and son exhibited both singly and in partnership. They contributed furnishings for the Hôtel du Collectionneur, the Ambassade Française, the Société Noël, La Maison de Bretagne and Gouffé-Jeune.

Imbued with the same energetic versatility as his father, Maurice-Raymond displayed a range of ensembles and individual pieces independently at the Salons. His most important commission was for the Hôtel Radio. He designed his furniture in wood – sometimes embellished with *galuchat* or *coquille d'œuf* – in sober and practical shapes. From 1926 Maurice-Raymond faced the challenge common to all *ébénistes*; whether to adjust to, or to fight, the revolutionary introduction of glass and metal into his medium. He chose the former course, introducing a distinctive range of modern furniture into his repertoire: stainless-steel card tables with reversible tops, mirrored cabinets and tea tables. Lacquered doors, psyches and screens became perennial favourites. Long a master of lacquer, he produced screens and decorative panels carved in bas relief with equatorial forest scenes detailed in polychromed lacquers on gold ground.

Maurice-Raymond left his father's studio to gain outside experience before rejoining it in 1930. Léon-Albert retired in the 1940s; Maurice-Raymond continued the family business until nearly 1950.

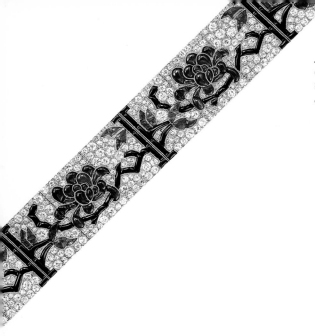

Janesich

(*left*) Chinoiserie-style bracelet in diamonds, sapphires, emeralds and onyx, 1920s.

Alfred Auguste Janniot

(*right*) *Leda and the Swain and the Swan*, charcoal, gouache and gold paint on paper, dated 1926.

(*opposite*) *Diana*, maquette in plaster, 1920s.

Janesich

The watch-making and jewelry house Janesich was founded at the end of the 19th century in Trieste by Leopoldo Janesich, whose grandsons opened a branch in Paris. Before the First World War, the firm's designs were inspired by 19th-century prototypes in which emphasis was placed on a series of diamond- and silver-mounted watches. In the 1920s Janesich introduced a series of Art Deco style accessories that incorporated enamels and semi-precious stones such as jade and lapis lazuli. It closed its doors in 1968.

Janniot, Alfred Auguste (1889–1969)

Born in Paris's Montmartre quarter, Janniot attended the city's École des Beaux-Arts, where he studied under Jean Antoine Injalbert and Antoine Bourdelle. In 1919, following the armistice, Janniot was awarded the Prix de Rome. While in Italy, he developed a Neoclassical style inspired by Greco-Roman mythology and the Bible, to which he applied a distinct Modernist interpretation.

On returning to the French capital, Janniot focused on monumental outdoor statuary, and he received wide acclaim for the group he designed for the entrance to JACQUES-ÉMILE RUHLMANN's Hôtel du Collectionneur at the 1925 *Exposition Internationale. Based on the theme of the Three Graces, the piece was entitled *L'Hommage à Jean Goujon*. Also at the exhibition Janniot created the statuary for the 'Monument aux Morts de Nice' fountain commissioned by the city of Nice, and a polychromed group, *La Vigne*, for the foyer of La Tour de Bordeaux pavilion.

Further prized commissions were forthcoming, including an allegorical *Nymphe de Fontainebleau* group in giltwood for the Grand Salon of the ocean liner *Île-de-France* (1927), and a series of bas reliefs for the Musée des Colonies (1928–31). Janniot's application of an abstract Modernist style to archaic subject matter had matured by 1930 as he undertook a wide range of architectural commissions, including the entrance façade for La Maison Française at Rockefeller Center in Manhattan (1934), a massive fresco in gilded plaster, *Poésie, Beauté et Élégance*, for the ocean liner *Normandie* (1935), façades for the Musée d'Art Moderne and the esplanade of the Palais de Tokyo, both in Paris (1937), and a bronze torso of a woman for the French pavilion at the 1939 New York World's Fair.

In 1945, following the bombing of his Paris atelier during the Second World War, Janniot accepted a professorship at his alma mater – the École des Beaux-Arts. Hailed among academicians, he was linked now with Raymond Delamarre and Carlo Sarrabezolles as worthy successors to the revivalist traditions of Auguste Rodin, Bourdelle and Aristide Maillol.

Jaulmes, Gustave-Louis (1873–1959)

Jaulmes was born in Lausanne and trained as an architect at the École des Beaux-Arts in Paris, before emerging as an artist and decorator of considerable and varied talents, best known for his Art Deco tapestries. Between 1901 and 1905 Jaulmes applied himself increasingly to painting, and later, in collaboration with Messrs Menu et Boigegrain, focused on tapestry. In the interim, he exhibited regularly at the Salons, displaying a wide range of decorative objects, including posters, pottery and book illustrations.

Jaulmes made his tapestry début in 1915, abandoning his rigid painting tutelage for that of the 18th-century traditions of Gobelins, Beauvais and Aubusson. His first works were in **petit point**; multicoloured compositions created by transposing preliminary sketches into brightly tinted wool. The Musée Rodin at the Hôtel Biron commissioned two tapestries during the First World War. Other commissions illustrated in a 1920 article by Léon Deshairs in *Art et Décoration* show allegorical panels depicting Music, Abundance and Floréal.

Furniture commissions included tapestried upholstery for SÜE ET MARE. Jaulmes's designs were classic, inspired by Flemish prototypes from the 1780s: formal garlanded flower sprays and baskets of fruit interlaced with ribbons and draperies, matching the stiff Louis XVI contours of Süe's *canapés à corbeille*. A typical tapestry screen from 1919, depicting two pigeons and fruit on a pink ground, is in the collection of the Musée des Arts Décoratifs, Paris. A number of small-scale furnishings such as chair-backs and screens were woven by Jaulmes's wife, Marie-Georges. He also designed furniture for the decorating firm Damon.

Jaulmes's versatility is seen in his participation at the 1925 *Exposition Internationale. His works were shown in the Hôtel du Collectionneur pavilion, and seven oils depicting 'Les Mois en Fête' were on display in the Salle du Grand Palais, as were murals for the Salle d'Honneur in the *Sèvres pavilion and tapestries for furniture in the Musée d'Art Contemporaine and the Ambassade Française. He also painted murals for the Théâtre du Palais de Chaillot at the 1937 Exposition des Arts et Techniques, the Musée des Arts Décoratifs, Paris, and the proscenium curtain for the Grand Théâtre, Lyons.

Among his commissions were many of monumental size undertaken for the Manufacture Nationale des Gobelins, with which Jaulmes had a longstanding relationship. One project took ten years to complete. His sketches depicting the rivers of France were exhibited at the 1923 Salon of the Société des Artistes Décorateurs, while the completed tapestries were on show at the same Salon in 1933.

His most celebrated work was commissioned by the French state as a gift to the city of Philadelphia, commemorating the USA's assistance of France during the First World War. The panel exemplified the description by Deshairs of Jaulmes's style as 'filling every inch of cloth, leaving no "holes" in the decoration'. The primary intention was not, as it might

at first seem, to cram all possible detail into the composition but rather to use such detail as a means of introducing infinite colour permutations, each an essential component of the whole. Jaulmes remained active until the Second World War.

Jeanneret, Charles-Édouard (1887–1965). *See* Le Corbusier.

Jennewein, Carl Paul (1890–1978). *See under* Sculpture.

Jensen

The celebrated silversmithy that bears his name was founded in 1904 by Georg Arthur Jensen (1866–1935), who was born in Raadvad, Denmark, to a father who was a grinder in a steel knife-blade manufacturing plant. Having started his career in the applied arts as a goldsmith's apprentice between 1880 and 1884, Jensen enrolled in a sculpture course at the Royal Academy of Fine Arts in Copenhagen, after which he worked in ceramics in the workshop of the artist–designer Mogens Ballin, and then in the *Bing & Grøndahl porcelain factory. After the 1900 Exposition Universelle in Paris, in which he displayed pottery with an artist friend, Joachim Petersen, Jensen returned to his initial training in metalware, designing jewelry that in its interlacing organic ornamentation showed a close affinity with the Art Nouveau style then the rage in the French capital. Jensen then set up his own silver workshop in a tiny premesis at 36 Bredgade Street, in a fashionable section of Copenhagen. Shortly after he opened the Jensen silversmithy, the first of his hollowware pieces, a 'Blossom' teapot, made its début – an auspicious start to a career that established Jensen as Denmark's pre-eminent 20th-century silversmith. In 1905 he participated in an exhibition at the Karl Ernst Osthaus Museum in Hagen, among other German venues.

The Jensen silversmithy opened its first foreign outlet in Berlin in 1909, followed by others in Paris (1919), London (1921) and New York (1924) as the demand for its wares expanded worldwide. The collaboration forged in 1907 between Jensen and a fellow Dane, Johan *Rohde (1856–1935), served to broaden the firm's appeal. Unlike Jensen's designs, which evoked a romantic baroque exuberance, those by Rohde were more restrained and sparing in their ornamentation, providing an alternative for those customers drawn to the medium's traditional forms. Rohde was a painter, architect and interior designer and in 1891 he had co-founded the Secessionist group Den Frie Udstilling (the Free Exhibition). It was through this group that he first met Jensen, who in 1897 exhibited sculpture at Den Frie. The two later worked in the Mogens Ballin silversmithy. Rohde's first silver designs, made in 1905, were executed by Jensen, with whom he collaborated again three years later, but it was not until 1917 that he entered into a formal association with Jensen, which lasted until Rohde's death. Rohde is known best for his 'Acorn' cutlery of 1916 and his streamlined pitcher of 1920 (model No. 432), the latter being considered too advanced for its time and not put into production until 1925. During his career, Rohde also designed for other Copenhagen firms.

By the time Jensen retired in 1926, his brother-in-law Harald Nielsen (1892–1977) had already worked for the firm for seventeen years, initially as a **chaser** and later – on Jensen's death in 1935 – as artistic director. His 'Pyramid' flatware, the firm's first Modernist pattern, was introduced in 1926. Nielsen left the Jensen silversmithy after sixty years, in 1969.

Sigvard Bernadotte (1907–2002) joined the Jensen silversmithy in 1930, where he emerged as the firm's foremost Modernist designer during the 1930s; his 'Bernadotte' cutlery pattern was introduced in 1939. He was the second son of Adolf VI, the king of Sweden,

and brother of Ingrid, the queen mother of Denmark. Bernardotte had entered the Royal Swedish Academy of Arts in 1929, and in 1949 he set up a design studio with the Dutch architect Acton Björn.

Joel, Betty (1894–1985)

Joel (*née* Lockhart) was born in Hong Kong, the daughter of an English administrator. Returning to the United Kingdom, and without formal training, she and her husband opened a modest cabinetry shop on Hayling Island, near Portsmouth, shortly after the First World War. There she manufactured a mix of Arts and Crafts and neo-Georgian furniture. By the 1930s, around the time that Joel opened a showroom in Knightsbridge and a cabinetry workshop in Kingston-on-Thames, she had become a disciple of the Modern movement.

Most of Joel's commissions were for a private clientele, including Lord Louis Mountbatten, Coutts Bank, the *Daily Express* and Royal Dutch Shell, but she also designed space-saving and built-in furniture for small inner-city flats. Her designs were progressive: serpentine, stepped and planar forms that mixed light-coloured woods and veneers, steel and glass, at times accented with luxury materials such as ivory for drawer handles. One of her bedroom designs was selected for the 1935 British Art in Industry Exhibition at the Royal Academy of Art, London. Joel was also a designer of carpets and textiles, film and theatre sets, radio cabinets and cast-iron heating stoves. She retired in 1937. Thereafter, her firm continued under her husband's direction.

Joubert, René (d. 1931). *See* DIM.

Jourdain, Francis (1876–1958)

Paris-born Jourdain was the son of Franz Jourdain, an architect. Internships with Paul-Albert Besnard and Eugène Carrière led to Jourdain's first painting

Betty Joel
(*right*) Tufted wool rug woven in China, *c.* 1930.

Jensen
(*opposite left*) Georg Jensen. Silver vase, 1925–32.

(*opposite right*) 3-piece demitasse silver service designed by Jorgen Jensen, *c.* 1933–44.

exhibition in 1897, after which he showed his canvases for several years at the Galerie E. Druet, the Salon des Indépendants and the Salon d'Automne. He also studied painting and gravure with Jacques Villon and sculpture with Joseph Chéret. His exhibit at the inaugural Salon d'Automne in 1903 included several very plain and geometric pieces of furniture, ample testament to his fierce opposition to the prevailing Art Nouveau idiom. Later he would lay claim to being the century's first Modernist, well ahead of the Bauhaus and De Stijl schools.

In 1912 Jourdain opened his Ateliers Modernes, a modest undertaking that employed one artisan. By 1919 matters had improved to the point that he could open a showroom, Chez Francis Jourdain, in rue de Sèze in Esbly (Seine-et-Marne). The furnishings for the showroom were manufactured in a nearby workshop. Jourdain's preferred woods in the early years were walnut, oak, zingana and maple; these were later replaced by steel, aluminium, lacquer and wrought iron.

At the 1925 *Exposition Internationale, Jourdain showed a selection of furniture, light fixtures and carpets in a stand on the Pont Alexandre III. He also decorated a library in the G. Crès et Cie stand, and participated in the Ambassade Française pavilion, for which he designed a physical culture hall and smoking room in collaboration with Georges Bastard, JAN AND JOËL MARTEL, Félix Massoul, Edmond Lachenal and Édouard *Schenck. Jourdain was a co-founder of the *Union des Artistes Modernes (UAM) in 1929. His drawing room at the 1937 Exposition des Arts et Techniques was considered his *chef d'œuvre*; it included modular furniture entitled 'Essai de Désencombrement pour Jeune Travailleuse Intellectuelle ou Manuelle'. One of Jourdain's last commissions was in 1938 – a joint work with PIERRE CHAREAU, Louis *Sognot and Jacques *Adnet. Jourdain retired in 1939 to concentrate on his writing.

Jouve, Paul (1880–1973)

Born in Bourron-Marlotte, near Fontainebleau (Seine-et-Marne), the son of a portrait painter and ceramist, Jouve studied at the École Nationale Supérieure des Arts Décoratifs and the École des Beaux-Arts in Paris, before dedicating his life and career to portraying animals, especially big cats, elephants and birds of prey. In his début at the Salons at the age of sixteen he showed the canvas *Les Lions de Menelick,* and he was only eighteen when he designed a ceramic frieze of animals for the Binet entrance gates at the 1900 Exposition Universelle, Paris. Frequenting the zoos of Paris, Antwerp and Hamburg, Jouve emerged as one of the Art Deco period's foremost *animalier* artist–sculptor– engravers. He participated in the Salons of the *Société des Artistes Français and those of the *Société Nationale des Beaux-Arts.

In 1907, having received a grant from the Société des Peintres Orientalistes, Jouve took up residence in the Villa Abd-el-Tif, a sort of artists' retreat in the French colony of Algeria. Local warfare later precipitated his move to Greece. Following the First World War, in which he was mobilized, Jouve took a trip to the Far East, which included sojourns in Ceylon and Southeast Asia where he sketched the local wildlife.

In addition to canvases, works on paper and sculpture, Jouve worked as a book illustrator, notably for FRANÇOIS-LOUIS SCHMIED's edition of Rudyard Kipling's *The Jungle Book* (1918), in which his drawings were executed in woodcuts, and Schmied's edition of Pierre Loti's *Un Pélerin d'Angkor,* for which he made a preparatory trip to Cambodia to research the illustrations. He also submitted designs to JEAN DUNAND for his screens and panels, and participated in the exhibitions staged in the 1920s at the Galerie Georges Petit in Paris with Dunand, Schmied and Jean *Goulden. Jouve also produced ceramic works.

K

Kage, Wilhelm (1889–1960)

Kage studied painting at the Valand School of Fine Arts in Gothenburg, then with Carl Wilhemsson in Stockholm and Johan Rohde in Copenhagen. Following the recommendation of the Swedish Society of Industrial Design that artists should be integrated into industry to improve the artistic quality of domestic objects and, thereby, to educate consumer taste, Kage left a promising career in poster design to join the Gustavsberg porcelain factory in 1917. He then participated in the firm's display at that year's Homes Exhibition at the Liljevalchs Art Gallery in Stockholm. Kage's designs for Gustavsberg in the 1920s included tableware in earthenware with underglaze decoration, such as the 'Liljebla' service, and unique sculptural works. He was awarded a *grand prix* at the 1925 *Exposition Internationale.

At the 1930 Stockholm Exhibition, Kage introduced his 'Argenta' wares, for which he had shown prototypes in Stockholm in 1926 and in New York the following year. The prototypes had had gold decoration on a blackish green ground, but Kage replaced the gold with silver, which he placed on a range of celadon and bright emerald grounds. 'Argenta' served as an artistic counterpoint to his principal work on utilitarian wares, which were uncompromisingly functional. It was humorous and playful, drawing on an iconography of whimsical Scandinavian folklore themes and up-to-the-minute Art Deco imagery from the Paris Salons. Met by immediate popular acclaim, it remained in Gustavsberg's repertoire for twenty years, selling especially well in the USA.

In the 1930s Kage introduced several other series, including 'Farsta', 'Surrea', 'Praktika' and 'Pyro', all of which sought rational solutions to urban living, such as stackability. In 1949 he was replaced as art director at Gustavsberg by Stig Lindberg, but stayed on in an unofficial capacity until his death.

Paul Jouve

(*opposite left*) *Miroir aure boussois*, glass mural designed for Mme Arlette Dorgere, executed by Gaeton Jeannin, *c*. 1930.

Francis Jourdain

(*opposite right*) Office with furniture in waxed oak, exhibited at the Salon d'Automne, Paris, 1922.

Wilhelm Kage

(*left*) Selection of Argenta tableware in green-glazed stoneware with silver applications, for Gustavsberg. 1920s/30s.

Francis Jourdain

(*above*) Storage cabinet in Brazilian palisander with inlay mounts, 1920s.

Ilonka Karasz
(*left*) Tea service in nickel-plated silver, manufactured by Paye & Baker Manufacturing Co., North Attleboro, Massachusetts, *c.* 1925.

Alexandre Kelety
(*far left*) *Méduse moderne*, bust in patinated and gilt-bronze, 1920s.

(*below*) *Danseuse à la culotte bouffante*, silvered-bronze with damascene detailing, 1920s.

Ilonka Karasz
(*right*) Cover for *Harper's Bazaar*, gouache on paper, 8 January 1927.

René Kieffer
(*far right*) *Contes* (Albert Samain), inlays of leather with gold- and blind-tooling, 1926.

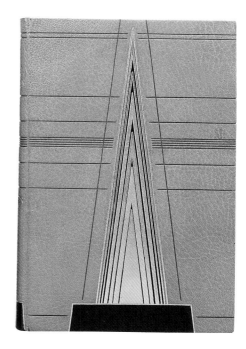

Kantack, Walter W. (1889–1953)

Situated at 238–40 East 40th Street in Manhattan, Kantack & Co. was one of the foremost manufacturers of metalware in the modern idiom in the USA. Its founder, Walter W. Kantack, came to prominence partly through his association with the decorating firm of French & Co., and architectural firms such as Buchman & Kahn and Voorhees, Gmelin & Walker, for whom he provided a wide range of metal furnishings and decorative accessories in sheet and cast aluminium, such as grilles, mirrors and tables. Private commissions included metalware for A. V. Davis's yacht *Elda* and for the Irving Trust Co.'s offices in New York. At the 1929 American Industrial Art exhibition at the Metropolitan Museum of Art, Walter collaborated with the architect Ely Jacques Kahn and the sculptor Edmond R. Amateis on a monumental urn decorated in bas relief with giraffes.

Between 1928 and 1933, Kantack published the quarterly magazine *The Kaleidoscope*, in which his firm's most recent works were reviewed. His light fixtures, crisply angular, bright and functional, were especially noteworthy.

Karasz, Ilonka (1896–1981)

Born in Budapest, Hungary, Karasz attended the Royal School of Arts and Crafts in the city before emigrating in 1913 to the USA. Her sister Mariska (1898–1960) followed the next year. Settling in Greenwich Village in Manhattan, Karasz taught at the Modern Art School on Washington Square South, while selling her hand-dyed and embroidered textiles at a local bookshop-gallery, the Sunwise Turn.

In a prolific and multifaceted career spanning six decades, Karasz designed ceramics (for the Pennsylvania Railroad, manufactured by the Buffalo Pottery Co.), silverware, textiles, wallpapers, furniture (for S. Karpen in Chicago) and graphics. These included illustrations and covers for *Vanity Fair* and the *New Yorker* (186 covers alone for the *New Yorker*

between 1925 and 1973), in a distinctive and engaging style that reflected her self-adopted role as a practitioner and publicist of the Modernist movement. At the 1928 and 1929 exhibitions of the American Designers' Gallery in New York and the American Union of Decorative Artists and Craftsmen (AUDAC) at the Brooklyn Museum in 1931, she showed furnished interiors. Between the 1940s and 1960s she worked almost exclusively as a wallpaper designer, mostly for Katzenbach & Warren.

Karasz's textile designs, executed initially by her sister Mariska, included hand-dyed batiks, needlepoints and embroidered fabrics, many of which incorporated folk motifs. Her mature work was carried by a large number of textile mills and retailers, including Rockledge, Schwarzenbach, Huber & Co., and Ginzkey–Maffersdorf Inc.

Kauffer, Edward McKnight (1890–1954).
See McKnight Kauffer, Edward.

Kelety, Alexandre (d. 1940)

Kelety was born in Budapest and studied under Imre Karoly Simay, the noted Hungarian *animalier* sculptor, before settling after the First World War in Toulouse. He exhibited at the annual Salons of the *Société des Artistes Français and the *Société des Artistes Décorateurs in the inter-war years.

Kelety's designs showed an easy facility with the stylized Art Deco vernacular of decorative ornament then in vogue, with which he enhanced a host of sculptural household accessories, including ashtrays, bookends, perfume burners and table lamps with shades supported by nudes. Much of his output was commissioned by *éditeurs d'art* and foundries, including works in bronze and bronze-and-ivory for *Etling et Cie and *Arthur Goldscheider, in whose stands he participated at the 1925 *Exposition Internationale.

An accomplished mixed-media artist, much of Kelety's *œuvre* has enormous period charm, encapsulating the atmosphere of the Roaring Twenties in its lively depiction of fashion- and theatre-world celebrities. Models were offered by Etling et Cie in more than one material, providing its customers with a broader selection; those in bronze were often accented with **damascened** detailing.

Kieffer, René (1875–1963)

A member of the founding class of the École Estienne in 1889, Kieffer later joined the Chambolle-Duru bindery, where he worked for ten years, specializing in gilding. In 1903 he established his own atelier at 99 boulevard Saint-Germain, later moving to 41 rue Saint-André-des-Arts, and then, in 1910, to 18 rue Séguier, where he remained until his retirement.

Making his début at the 1903 Salon of the *Société des Artistes Français, Kieffer became a disciple of Henri Marius-Michel, moving gradually away from his traditional training toward a more emblematic and modern style. He remained in business during the First World War, emerging afterwards as one of Paris's leading binders. His fine workmanship was now matched by a wide range of progressive designs inspired by PIERRE-ÉMILE LEGRAIN. Between 1917 and 1923 Kieffer executed Legrain's bindings for Jacques *Doucet and gained first-hand knowledge of Legrain's Modernist concepts.

Traditional techniques, such as the use of fillets, blind-tooling and *pointillism*, were mixed with coloured inlays of leather to create eye-catching modern compositions. Kieffer's style continued to evolve in the late 1920s and 1930s, and his earlier mix of figurative and decorative metal panels set into compact linear compositions was phased out. For example, Kieffer's binding for *Les Luxures* by Maurice Rollinat, shown at the 1937 Exposition des Arts et Techniques, incorporated metal discs encrusted with **cabochons** of iridescent

Paul Kiss (Kis)

(*left*) Table lamp in wrought
iron and alabaster, 1920s.

Paul Kiss (Kis)

(*right*) Console in wrought iron
with marble top and lower
shelf, 1920s.

glass. His cover for *Le Roman de Renart*, displayed at
the same exhibition, was inlaid with rows of red glass
beads that simulated rubies.

Collectors of Kieffer's works in the inter-war years
included Dr Henri Voisin, Henri Vever, Jacques Doucet,
and the Comte de Verlet.

Kinsbourg, Renée (*fl.* 1921–31)

Born in Rouen, Kinsbourg moved to Paris, where her
address in the mid-1920s was listed as 85 rue de
Longchamp. A decorator by profession, her interiors
were marketed by Les Arts de France. For the 1925
*Exposition Internationale, Kinsbourg designed a young
woman's bedroom for her stand on the Esplanade des
Invalides; this was in collaboration with A. Berger.
The furniture was executed by the cabinet-makers
Taso & Molino, the wrought-iron fixtures by Leblanc
and the upholstery by Open et Cie.

Kinsbourg's smoking-parlour at the 1926 *Salon
d'Automne featured angular lines that came to
characterize her style. Veneers were sumptuous and
mounts minimal, similar to PIERRE CHAREAU's designs.
In 1926 she also displayed a lady's bedroom in palisander
and lacquer, again retailed by Les Arts de France.

In 1928 Kinsbourg received praise from the critic
Gabriel Henriot of *Mobilier et Décoration* for her
exhibit at the Salon of the *Société des Artistes
Décorateurs. In the same year at the *Salon d'Automne
she exhibited a deluxe cabin for a transatlantic liner.
Practical and compact, the room included storage
units built into its panelling to maximize space. Carpets
were an integral part of her displays, giving warmth
and ambience where the furniture did not. In 1931
carpets that Kinsbourg designed for *Saddier et ses
Fils incorporated a muted palette of greys and beiges.

Kiss (Kis), Paul (1885–1962)

Romanian-born Kiss spent several years in itinerant
jobs in Hungary and Germany before moving to Paris,
where he was granted French citizenship. Collaborating
initially with EDGAR BRANDT, he then opened an
atelier–showroom at 2–4 rue Léon-Belhomme, where
he designed and executed a full range of wrought-iron
furnishings and lighting, including consoles, light
fixtures, radiator covers, gates and a monumental grille
for the palace of the King of Siam.

At the 1925 *Exposition Internationale, Kiss took
stand No. 5 on the Pont Alexandre III, where his display
included a door for the monument to the dead at
Levallois-Perret. He was also commissioned to provide
the entrance door for the Ferand Savary pavilion.
An article in that year's *Mobilier et Décoration* gave
high praise for his work. In 1926, in collaboration
with Paul Feher, Kiss displayed wrought-iron ensembles
at two Salons and participated in an exhibition at
the Musée Galliera charmingly entitled 'Une Petite
Exposition Après la Grande'.

Although Kiss never fully stepped out of Brandt's
shadow, he did produce a substantial amount of high-
quality metalwork which he exhibited through the
*Société des Artistes Décorateurs, the *Société des
Artistes Français and the *Salon d'Automne. His style
was highly distinctive for a material as anonymous
as iron; bands of deeply hammered incisions accented
with black patina were his imprimatur. Kiss's works
were marketed in part by the Société des Toiles de
Rambouillet.

Klint, Kaare (1888–1954)

Born in Fredericksberg, Denmark, Klint enrolled in
painting classes at the local polytechnic in 1903,
after which he studied architecture at the Copenhagen
Technical School under his father, P. V. Jensen Klint.
He also worked as an apprentice to his father and the
Copenhagen architects Kai Nielsen and Carl Petersen,
and in 1914 assisted the latter in designing Neoclassical
furniture for the Fåborg Art Museum. It was during this
project that Klint created one of his most important
designs: a chair in oak with a back-rest in woven cane
inspired by the ancient Greek 'klismos' model. In 1917
he set himself up as an independent furniture designer
and three years later opened his own design office,
undertaking commissions for Fritz Hansen and Rudolph
Rasmussen, among others. In 1924 Klint established
the Furniture Department at the Royal Academy of
Art in Copenhagen, where in 1944 he also became a
professor of architecture. During his design career, he
received many official commissions, including furniture
for the Thorvaldsen Museum from 1922 to 1925.

Unlike many designers of the 1920s, Klint's style
was influenced by English 18th-century prototypes.
His desk chair of 1933 and his X-frame folding chair,
both combining comfort, simplicity and classic design
solutions, are considered among his finest works.

Klotz, Blanche-J. (b. 1885)

Paris-born Klotz was listed in the 1920s at 3 rue de
Miromesnil. A self-taught decorator, her work received
a remarkable amount of coverage for an artist who
mainly participated in the annual Salons of the
*Société des Artists Décorateurs. Her initial designs for
lampshades, cushions and curtains led her to furniture
and, ultimately, to architecture. An office illustrated in
1924 shows the essence of her evolving style: a sharply
angular and functional desk, and chair with square
arms and harmonious beige leather upholstery.

At the 1925 *Exposition Internationale, Klotz
took a stand on the Esplanade des Invalides, where
she showed a hall–studio for a villa in Montagnac.
The furnishings were neat and angular. Klotz placed
emphasis on colour harmony allied to ultramodern
forms. Her interiors were frequently illustrated in
critical reviews, but some designs are now difficult
to distinguish in black-and-white period illustrations
from those by Louis *Sognot and CHARLOTTE PERRIAND.

In 1930 Klotz participated in the inaugural
exposition of the *Union des Artistes Modernes (UAM),

in which she exhibited an office for an executive
in the chemical industry. Her desk at the 1934 Salon
of the Société des Artists Décorateurs was untypical
of her style: its top and frieze in *verre églomisé*
was engraved with zodiac symbols by Pierre and
Jacques Lardin.

Within a year a new direction was evident in the
design of editions of furniture manufactured *en série* by
the cabinet-maker Schmit et Cie on rue de Charonne.
To disguise the concept of a series production, the
client was invited to select the veneer, upholstery
leather and fabrics (by Hélène *Henry) so that no
two pieces were absolutely identical. In addition, most
pieces were bi- or multifunctional. In 1935 Klotz was
commissioned to design cabins for the ocean liner
Normandie. She continued to exhibit at the Salons
into the late 1950s – from the mid-1930s listing herself
by her married name, Mme Klotz-Gilles.

Kohlmann, Étienne (1903–1988)

Born in Paris, Kohlmann came early to his chosen
profession, working as a trainee cabinet-maker at the
Nieuport aviation factory in 1916. A series of career
changes followed in a short period: an apprenticeship
in a technical cabinetry school; a one-year enrolment
at the *École Boulle; and a further twelve months with
an *ébéniste* in the Faubourg Saint-Antoine. All of this
was achieved by the age of twenty, when Kohlmann
joined *Studium-Louvre as a cabinet-maker–decorator.
He was soon appointed its co-director with Maurice
*Matet, a position he held until 1938.

Throughout the 1920s Kohlmann was acclaimed
as much as a cabinet-maker as a decorator. At the 1925
*Exposition Internationale, he contributed a woman's
bedroom with adjoining office to the Grands Magasins
du Louvre pavilion. Many of his interiors were
illustrated in *Meubles du Temps Présent* and *Répertoire
du Goût Moderne*; in sum, he was close to the vanguard
of the Modernist movement.

Kohlmann introduced a line of tubular metal
furniture after 1925. The 1930s brought a chain of
prestigious commissions, several reviewed in a 1934
article in *Art et Décoration* by Paul Laroche, who wrote
that Kohlmann's designs expressed precisely *l'esprit
moderne*. He participated at the 1937 Exposition
des Arts et Techniques and again at the 1939 New York
World's Fair. Kohlmann continued after the Second
World War as an independent designer.

Kosta Glasbruk

Founded in 1742 in the glass-making region of
Småland, Sweden, the word 'Kosta' is a combination of
the first syllables of the family names of its founders –
General Anders Koskull and Georg Bogislaus Stael von
Holstein. Incorporated as a limited company in 1875,
Kosta Glasbruk remains the oldest Swedish glassworks
in production. Among its earliest creations was the
twelve-branch chandelier, dating from *c.* 1760, which
now hangs in a church in Herrakra.

In 1897, Kosta Glasbruk began to produce
editions of cased art glassware adorned *à la Gallé* with
naturalistic themes and a blended palette. The firm
used several noted independent designers, including
Gunnar Gunnarson Wennenberg, Ferdinand Boberg
and Alf Wallander. Following the 1917 Homes Exhibition
in Stockholm organized by the Swedish Society of
Arts and Crafts, Kosta's management recruited well-
known artist–designers, such as Karl Lindberg and
A. E. Boman, to improve the quality of its editions .

In the 1920s a Modernist direction for the firm;s
glass production was charted by a new generation
of designers, including Edvin Ollers, Evald Dahlskog,
Sven Ericson and Elis Bergh. One noted Kosta designer
was Vicke *Lindstrand (1904–1983), formerly of
*Orrefors, who became senior designer in 1950. Today,
Kosta, which includes the sister factories of Boda,
Johansfors and Afors, is best known for its decorative
cut glass and tablewares.

Krass, Christian (1868–1957)

Born in Lyons, Krass studied at the École des Beaux-
Arts in Aubusson before returning to the family's
furniture business in his native city after the
First World War. At some point he served as an
apprentice in one of JACQUES-ÉMILE RUHLMANN's
cabinetry shops, presumably in the 1920s; this is
evident from the unmistakable influence that
Ruhlmann exerted on Krass's furniture designs of
the 1930s. The majority of Krass's models are closely
imitative of those of the *maître ébéniste* – both in
their designs and in their choice of warm woods inlaid
with ivory banding. In 1937 Krass displayed a suite
of furniture commissioned by the Aga Khan at the
Société Lyonnaise des Beaux-Arts.

L

Lachaise, Gaston (1882–1935)

Paris-born Lachaise emigrated to the USA in 1906 after
studying at the city's École des Beaux-Arts. In 1917 he
married his former mistress and model, Isabel Dutaud-
Nagel – the inspiration for the series of oversized
and voluptuous yet geometrically styled portrait busts
that became his trademark. Lachaise also undertook
commissions of animals, notably the figure of a
seal and the 'Dolphin Fountain' which he created for
Gertrude Vanderbilt Whitney in 1924; both of these
revealed the sculptor at his most sensitive and alluring.

Commercial commissions included Lachaise's frieze
for the lobby of the AT&T Building and his bas reliefs
on the RCA Building in Manhattan in 1929, all of
which showed a highly distinctive personal style
as did his large plaster relief for the 1933–34 A Century
of Progress exhibition in Chicago.

Lachaise is today considered one of the major
figures in the development of a Modernist idiom in
American art, although it was only toward the end of
his career that he began to receive critical recognition.

Christian Krass
Cabinet in burled wood
with ivory trim, c. 1930.

Étienne Kohlmann

(below) Desk in palisander and chromed metal with leather writing surface, c. 1930.

Christian Krass

(bottom) Commode in lemonwood with nickel-plated mounts and ivory pulls, 1930s.

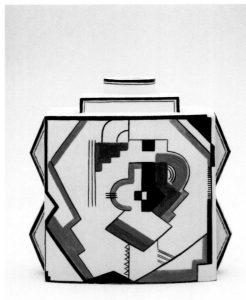

Robert Lallemant
(*far left*) Vase in glazed earthenware, 1920s.

(*left*) Vase in glazed earthenware, *c.* 1925.

Lacloche Frères
(*above*) Lapel watch in diamonds and enamelled silver, *c.* 1926.

Robert Lallemant
(*right*) Vase in glazed earthenware, *c.* 1925.

Lacloche Frères

The jewelry firm Lacloche Frères was founded in Madrid in 1875 by four brothers – Fernand, Jules, Jacques and Leopold – who later opened branches in Saint-Sebastian, Biarritz and Paris (at 15 rue de la Paix). Prominent makers of Art Deco jewelry and *objets d'art*, the firm took over Fabergé's London showroom in 1920 and was chosen by the selection committee in the *parure* section at the 1925 *Exposition Internationale as a participant in the Modernist jewelry section. Included in Lacloche's repertoire of luxury goods were clocks, chatelaines, *étuis*, cigarette cases, powder boxes and pendant watches. The firm's display in the 1929 Exposition des Arts de la Bijouterie, Joaillerie et Orfèvrerie, staged at the Musée Galliera, Paris, drew wide acclaim.

Lacroix, Jean-Boris (1902–1984)

In his diverse career, Lacroix initially worked anonymously in decorating and furniture design, often undertaking complete installations, including the architectural planning of his interiors. He designed wallpapers, worked for a number of fashion houses and designed clothing, accessories and costume jewelry before specializing in lighting.

Lacroix turned his attention to every form of domestic illumination – table lamps, illuminated ceilings and picture frames – which he exhibited from 1927 at the *Salon d'Automne and the Salon of the *Société des Artistes Décorateurs. His designs, executed by *Damon, were either in metal only, with a polished or matt nickel finish, or in Damon's special enamelled diffusing variety of glass. A distinctive feature of Lacroix's fixtures was their multifunctionalism: the same model, for example, could serve as a desk lamp, or, by adjusting its arms, be used to illuminate a sheet of music on a piano, or, with a hooking device attached to its base, be transformed into a wall bracket to spotlight a painting.

In a 1929 article on modern lighting in *Lux*, Lacroix described his line of light fixtures as stop-gap – that is, practical only until the engineers of the future created a source of indirect illumination that would bathe rooms completely in a light that did not emanate from any discernible point. After such a development, light fixtures *per se* would become history.

Lahalle & Lévard

The initial partnership involved Pierre Lahalle (1877–1956) and Maurice Lucet (1877–1941), both of whom were born in Orléans (Loiret) and studied architecture at the École des Beaux-Arts before joining Studio Pascal. In 1903 they branched out on their own, designing buildings and interiors. Their first attempts in furniture design were markedly Art Nouveau – the pieces contoured with sinuous curves and arabesques. Soon, however, relief decoration was replaced by polychrome medallions of fruit and flowers executed in marquetry.

In 1907 Georges Lévard (*fl.* 1903–30), who was born in Bayeux (Calvados) and was a graduate of the École Nationale Supérieure des Arts Décoratifs in Paris, joined Lahalle and Lucet as they expanded their furniture production, in part to meet a growing South American market. Their style at this time was seen as Consulate and Directoire in influence.

In 1919 the trio was still together, exhibiting a range of sober and refined interiors at the Salons, but the partnership dissolved gradually within the next few years. Lahalle was the mainstay during this time, though less fully from 1922, when he was appointed professor of composition at the *École Boulle, occupying the post vacated by MAURICE DUFRÈNE. Lucet departed shortly thereafter, leaving Lahalle and Lévard to operate the business even after Lévard joined *Primavera.

At the 1925 *Exposition Internationale, Lahalle & Lévard had its own stand on the Esplanade des Invalides, displaying a vestibule in collaboration with Ruetsch and Berthelot, Morand, IVAN DA SILVA BRUHNS and Mlle Chaplin. The company also participated with André *Fréchet in *Studium-Louvre, exhibiting a boudoir and reception hall. In the Primavera pavilion, Lévard presented a hallway with furniture by Louis *Sognot and Claude Lévy. Lahalle & Lévard's most celebrated interior was the indoor swimming pool for a villa on the Riviera shown at the 1924 *Salon d'Automne in collaboration with JACQUES-ÉMILE RUHLMANN and Primavera's director, Charlotte *Chauchet-Guilleré. Lahalle & Lévard continued to design interiors into the 1930s, with special emphasis given to coromandel lacquerwork.

Lahalle, Pierre (1877–1956). *See* Lahalle & Lévard.

Lalique, René (1860–1945). *See under* Glass.

Lallemant, Robert (1902–1954)

Born in Dijon, Lallemant studied under Ovide Yencesse at the city's École des Beaux-Arts. From 1921 to 1922 he worked in Edmond Lachenal's atelier before establishing himself in an old workshop at 5 passage d'Orléans in Paris's 13th *arrondissement*.

Lallemant later moved to the Quai d'Auteuil, where, with his wife's assistance, he generated a mix of cream-glazed **faïence** wares, including vases, lamp bases and other table-top accessories. These were ornamented either with lighthearted vignettes depicting popular French singers and peasants clad in 18th-century costumes, or with eye-catching Cubist compositions applied to stepped and angular vessels. Showing a clear affinity for Cubism, Lallemant became a member of the avant-garde movement that came to fruition in the *Union des Artistes Modernes (UAM), exhibiting alongside René *Herbst, *DIM, Georges *Djo-Bourgeois, JAN AND JOËL MARTEL and CHARLOTTE PERRIAND in UAM exhibitions during the 1930s.

Marie Laurencin
Painted decoration on a side chair designed by André Groult and executed by Adolphe Chanaux in ebony and stained tortoise shell, c. 1924.

La Maîtrise (Les Galeries Lafayette)

La Maîtrise was directed by MAURICE DUFRÈNE from its opening in 1922 until 1952. Among its team of artist-designers in the inter-war years were the *Adnet brothers, Édouard *Benedictus, Jean *Beaumont, Édouard *Schenck, Georges Chevalier, Gabriel *Englinger and Suzanne *Guiguichon, as well as manufacturers including the *Faïenceries de Longwy, Maison Coupé, Cornille Frères and *Saddier et ses Fils. La Maîtrise participated in the 1922 *Salon d'Automne and the 1925 *Exposition Internationale, where the firm exhibited through its own pavilion.

Lambert-Rucki, Jean (1888–1967)

Born in Krakow, Poland, Lambert-Rucki was a sculptor and painter who studied under Mehoffer at the city's School of Fine Art before moving to Paris in 1911. Soon a fixture in the city's artistic avant-garde, he became a member of the Section d'Or, a group that included Amedeo Modigliani, Chaim Soutine, Guillaume Apollinaire and Max Jacob. At the outbreak of the First World War, Lambert-Rucki joined the French Foreign Legion and saw action in the Dardanelles. Demobilized in 1918, he exhibited at the Salon des Indépendants from 1920, with the Section d'Or group from 1922 to 1924, at the Léonce Rosenberg gallery in 1924 and at the Salon des Tuileries from 1933.

Greatly influenced by African tribal art and Cubism, Lambert-Rucki used a wide variety of materials in his work, including painted and lacquered plaster, gold and silver leaf, metal and wood. He sometimes covered the wood with gold or silver leaf, or applied mirrored glass or mosaics to it. In the inter-war years, Lambert-Rucki collaborated with JEAN DUNAND on numerous works, providing him with designs for lacquered furniture panels, screens and book covers in an endearing, novel, and often comic or caricature style.

A retrospective exhibition of Lambert-Rucki's work was staged at the Claude Robert gallery in Paris in 1971.

Subjects included clowns, African portrait busts and masks, clerics and biblical characters, and views of Montparnasse that showed top-hatted theatregoers promenading. These were either sculpted in bronze or lacquered wood, or depicted on paper in a montage of overlapping images.

Lamourdedieu, Raoul-Eugène (1877–1953)

Born in Fouguerolles (Lot-et-Garonne), Lamourdedieu exhibited sculpture at the Salons of the *Société Nationale des Beaux-Arts from 1905 to 1914, and then again after the First World War. In the 1920s he participated also at the *Salon d'Automne and that of the *Société des Artistes Décorateurs, and was appointed a professor at the École des Beaux-Arts in Paris.

A member of La Stèle and L'Évolution groups, Lamourdedieu exhibited with them in *Arthur Goldscheider's pavilion at the 1925 *Exposition Internationale, showing a selection of figurines and medals executed in a robust Art Deco style. At the 1937 Exposition des Arts et Techniques, he showed a granite fountain and two massive patinated plaster figures. A retrospective exhibition of his works from 1900 to 1941 was staged at the 1942 Salon of the Société des Artistes Décorateurs.

Lanvin, Jeanne (1867–1946)

Lanvin opened her fashion house on rue du Faubourg Saint-Honoré, Paris, in 1889. Celebrated before the First World War for her matching mother-and-daughter garments and waisted *robes de style*, from the 1920s she embarked on fresh ventures, including the decoration of her *hôtel particulier* at 16 rue Barbet-de-Jouy on the Left Bank, and the formation of two new companies, Lanvin-Décoration and Lanvin-Sport. For all three of these, ARMAND-ALBERT RATEAU was chosen to design interiors. Lanvin's residence, scheduled for demolition in 1965, was saved by Prince Louis de Polignac, who had been married to her daughter

Marguerite and who offered the Rateau interiors to the Musée des Arts Décoratifs in Paris, where they were re-installed.

Lanvin exhibited at the 1925 *Exposition Internationale, the 1931 Exposition Coloniale and the 1937 Exposition des Arts et Techniques, in addition to travelling shows in Prague and Athens in 1927. Her firm's emblem, which depicted Lanvin dressed for a ball with her daughter Marguerite at her feet, was designed by Paul *Iribe.

Lapparra

Henri Lapparra founded his silver-manufacturing business in 1893, listing himself in an early sales brochure as an 'orfèvre-argentier'. Originally a producer solely of high-quality flatware (95 per cent pure silver), Lapparra added a line of hollowware in the 1920s.

Like many traditional silver manufacturers of the era, Lapparra commissioned Paul *Follot and other Modernist designers to provide a selection of progressive models for the company's displays at the annual Paris Salons, the 1925 *Exposition Internationale and the Décor de la Table exhibition at the Musée Galliera in 1930. The firm later merged with C. Souche and is now located at 157 rue du Temple in Paris.

Laurencin, Marie (1883–1956)

Paris-born Laurencin attended the Académie Humbert in that city before starting her painting career. She participated in the Maison Cubiste at the 1912 *Salon d'Automne and exhibited regularly at Léonce Rosenberg's gallery from 1913 to 1940.

Identified for more than twenty years with the avant-garde of the art world, Laurencin included among her friends Guillaume Apollinaire, Pablo Picasso, Georges Braque, Juan Gris, Sonia *Delaunay and Gertrude Stein. In 1914 Laurencin married the German painter Otto von Wätjen. The couple spent the First World War in Madrid, returning in 1920 to Paris, where

Jean Lambert-Rucki
(*left*) *Prosternation*, figural group in mahogany, lacquer, and *coquille d'œuf*, 1925–28.

Raoul Lamourdedieu
(*below*) *Danseuse au voile* in patinated bronze; *cire perdue* casting by Valsuani, 1920s.

Jean Lambert-Rucki
(*bottom left*) *La Visite*, oil on board, 1927.

(*bottom right*) *La Conversation*, oil on board, 1927.

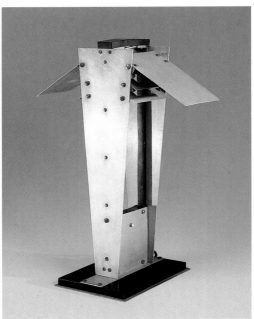

Jacques Le Chevallier

(*far left*) Table lamp in brushed aluminium, late 1920s.

(*left*) Table lamp in aluminium with adjustable hood vents in brushed aluminium and Bakelite, *c.* 1927–30.

Le Corbusier

(*below*) *Fauteuil à dossier basculant*, in collaboration with Pierre Jeanneret and Charlotte Perriand, chrome-plated tubular steel and leather manufactured by Embru Werke AG, Rüti, Switzerland, this model *c.* 1935.

Laurencin achieved great success. In 1924 she designed the sets and costumes for the ballet *Les Biches* by Poulenc, and in 1927 for *À Quoi Rêvent les Jeunes Filles* by Alfred de Musset at the Académie Française. In the same year, she decorated the restaurant Boulestin in London with Jean-Émile Laboureur and Allan Walton.

Laurencin's canvases and watercolours were rendered in monochromatic pastel hues, with detailing simplified to the point of elimination. Her paintings were often included in the ensembles displayed by her brother-in-law André *Groult at the annual Salons and the 1925 *Exposition Internationale. Laurencin was one of several French painters who on occasion also designed carpets or textiles.

Laurent, Robert (1890–1970)

Born in Concarneau, Brittany, as a child Laurent moved to New York in 1901 at the invitation of Hamilton Easter Field (1873–1922), an American painter, writer, critic, gallery owner and publisher. Field subsequently sponsored Laurent's study of avant-garde art in Paris and Rome between 1905 and 1909. On his return to the USA, Laurent founded an art colony with Field in Ogunquit, Maine, where he taught in the summers for the rest of his life.

Laurent was one of the first sculptors in America to apply direct carving – his preference for materials being alabaster, walnut and mahogany. His mature works, such as *The Wave* and *Torso* in the 1920s, frequently depicted the human form or birds and animals, rendered in a reductive style that in its anatomical distortion evoked the works of Constantin Brancusi and American folk art. In 1942 he became a professor at the University of Indiana, and from 1954 to 1955 he served as an artist-in-residence at the American Academy in Rome. One of America's first truly 'modern' sculptors, Laurent's work cannot be grouped entirely within an Art Deco context, but exemplifies the wider tastes of the period nonetheless.

Lavroff, Georges (1895–1991)

Lavroff was born near Enisseyske, Siberia, and studied at the School of Fine Arts in Moscow. He exhibited in Siberia in 1919, and then regularly in Moscow until 1927, at which time he moved to Paris. There Lavroff exhibited at the 1928 Salon des Indépendants and the 1928 *Salon d'Automne. His subject matter included silver-patinated bronzes of animals and women rendered in a spirited Modernist style.

Le Chevallier, Jacques (1896–1987)

Born in Paris, Le Chevallier studied at the city's École des Beaux-Arts from 1911 to 1915, then joined Louis *Barillet (1880–1948) in the stained-glass studio that he founded in 1919 – a collaboration that lasted until 1945.

A member of the *Société des Artistes Décorateurs and the *Salon d'Automne from 1925, Le Chevallier became a founder-member of *Union des Artistes Modernes (UAM) in the late 1920s. During the same period he designed table lamps in a brazenly avant-garde style, some in collaboration with Raymond Koechlin, probably for display at UAM's annual exhibits. In his versatile career, Le Chevallier also painted, created wood engravings and designed carpets for Aubusson. After the Second World War, he opened his own stained-glass studio in Fontenay-aux-Roses.

Utilitarian to a fault but with unquestionable charm, Le Chevallier's lamps were composed of aluminium panels assembled with undisguised screws, their bases and tops in black Bakelite. Although their rudimentary industrial appearance suggests that some models were prototypes, they served as provocative Machine Age design statements.

Le Corbusier (Charles-Édouard Jeanneret) (1887–1965)

Born in La-Chaux-de-Fonds, Switzerland, Charles-Édouard Jeanneret attended the local art school before serving a fifteen-month internship with the renowned

Paris architect Auguste Perret from 1908 to 1909. During a trip to Germany the following year, he met Heinrich Tessenow, the director of the Deutscher Werkbund, who introduced him to the problems involved in standardizing mass-production furniture.

Jeanneret settled in Paris in 1917, and in 1920 took the name Le Corbusier on founding the magazine *L'Esprit Nouveau* with the painter Amédée Ozenfant. The magazine's offices were located at 35 rue de Sèvres. Twenty-eight issues were published at irregular intervals within the next five years, the most celebrated of which was Le Corbusier's 1921 manifesto, *Une Maison est une machine à habiter*, where he replaced the word 'furniture' with the word 'equipment' in offering new solutions to old problems of design.

At the 1925 *Exposition Internationale, the magazine's pavilion in the Cours-la-Reine on the Right Bank was entitled 'L'Esprit Nouveau'. In its design Le Corbusier was joined by his architect cousin Pierre Jeanneret (1896–1969). The pavilion's interior consisted of standardized living units, in particular a series of bookcase components (*caisses métaliques*) manufactured by Thonet. These were

> standardized units designed to be combined in a multitude of ways, they could be sold at the bazaar de l'Hôtel de Ville or on the avenue Champs-Elysées. They can stand to any height against a wall or form the wall itself.

The public's reaction was predictable: Le Corbusier's designs were far too intellectual and surgical, even 'orthopedic' in appearance. Viewers expected to be shown how they should live in the present, rather than in the future. Beyond the exhibition the new style had few adherents. By 1930, however, this initial resistance and incomprehension begun to soften. The cold and impersonal lines of Le Corbusier's furniture suddenly appeared svelte, logical and timeless. Within years the revolution was won and tubular furniture *de rigueur*.

Pierre Le Faguays
Faun and Nymph, patinated
in bronze issued in an edition
by La Style, 1924.

In the late 1920s, Le Corbusier, Jeanneret and CHARLOTTE PERRIAND designed half a dozen furniture models that they included in many of their subsequent interiors. These models are now recognized as classics of 20th-century design. Three chairs, in particular, have received universal recognition: the first, the 'Grand Confort' model, credited generally to Perriand, in which bulky square cushions were contained within a chromed tubular steel chassis, was manufactured by Thonet. Introduced in 1928, the model was reproduced in 1959 by H. Weber and in 1965 by Cassina. The second model, an armchair with adjustable back ('Fauteuil à dossier basculant') resembled Marcel *Breuer's 1925 'Wassily' chair. Comprising a tubular-metal frame with leather or ponyskin upholstery and arm straps, it was introduced in 1929 and reissued in 1959 and 1965. The third was Le Corbusier's celebrated chaise-longue, model 'LC-4', a chair of stepped shape that matched the human body and rested on a detachable metal stand. The prototype, introduced in 1922 by Le Corbusier for his Immeubles-Villas, was refined for both his 1928 Villa à Carthage and 1929 Maison de Mr X in Brussels. Another important model created by the partnership, again credited to Perriand, was the swivel chair (*siège tournant*) which made its début in a dining room at the 1929 *Salon d'Automne.

A founder-member of *Union des Artistes Modernes (UAM), Le Corbusier remained active in the organization throughout his life, continually expanding the group's theories and researching functional solutions to design problems. In the year of Le Corbusier's death, Cassina was granted the reproduction rights to certain of his chair models.

Le Faguays, Pierre (1892–1925)
Le Faguays was born in Nantes and studied under James Vibert. He exhibited from 1922 at the Salons of the *Société des Artistes Français, later becoming a leading member of La Stèle and L'Évolution groups, with whom he exhibited in *Arthur Goldscheider's pavilion at the 1925 *Exposition Internationale.

In constant demand as one of the most diverse and prolific sculptors of the inter-war period, Le Faguays generated a large volume of domestic sculpture in bronze, bronze-and-ivory, marble, terracotta and ceramics for Paris's foremost *éditeurs d'art*, including Arthur Goldscheider, *Etling et Cie, Max *Le Verrier and *Les Neveux de J. Lehmann (LNJL). His style, however, was easily mistaken for that of Alexandre *Kelety or Marcel *Bouraine.

Le Faguays's subject matter included allegorical and mythological figures, Crusaders, odalisques and nude dancers, the last often serving as the bases for lampshades in glass, alabaster or horn. Despite the high volume of his commercial work, Le Faguays also found the time to undertake commissions for public monuments and statuary. He married one of his pupils, Andrée Guerval. Their address in the 1920s was listed as 5 villa des Camélias, Paris.

Legrain, Pierre-Émile (1888–1929). *See under* Paintings, Graphics, Posters and Bookbinding.

Legras et Cie
The experienced glassmaker Auguste-Jean-François Legras took over the Verreries et Cristalleries de Saint-Denis et des Quatre-Chemins in 1864. The glassworks prospered under his direction, producing a wide range of somewhat nondescript commercial domestic glassware. The firm exhibited at some of the international exhibitions in the late 1880s: for example, the 1888 Barcelona Exposition and the 1889 Exposition Universelle in Paris. Its stock-in-trade was coloured glassware decorated with marbled, gold, flecked, mottled or streaked accents, as well as an assortment of curious bottles in clear crystal shaped as buildings or boats. By 1900, Legras et Cie listed about 1,400 employees, including decorators. At the 1900 Exposition Universelle, it was awarded a *grand prix*. In 1909 Auguste Legras retired and was succeeded by his son Charles.

In this era Legras et Cie used more than one trade name to market its glassware. 'Montjoye' was the signature that identified a graceful series of moulded clear or tinted glassware adorned with enamelled and gilded motifs, mostly botanical, in the prevailing Art Nouveau style. After 1900 much of Legras's production was in cameo glass, some with enamelled detailing, much like Émile Gallé's commercial wares. The firm exhibited at the 1910 Exposition de la Verrerie et de la Cristallerie Artistique in Paris, and then at the 1911 Turin International Exposition. Closed at the outbreak of war in 1914, the company re-opened in 1919 as the Verreries et Cristalleries de Saint-Denis et de Pantin Réunies.

Post-war production focused largely on table glass, which included interesting vessels in clear or transparent coloured crystal with acid-etched floral or Cubist-inspired Art Deco imagery. Opaque vessels were similarly decorated with wheel-carved or etched friezes, oblique geometric bands or stylized motifs. The company also offered editions of artistic glassware with bubbled and streaked internal decoration.

Leleu, Jules (1883–1961)
Born in Boulogne-sur-Mer, Leleu succeeded his father in the family painting firm in 1909, where he was joined by his brother Marcel; together they entered the decorating field. In 1914 both were mobilized. After the war, Leleu decided to specialize in furniture-making, while his brother Marcel remained in Boulogne to manage the atelier.

Following his participation in the 1922 *Salon d'Automne, Leleu opened a gallery in 1924 on the avenue Franklin Roosevelt in Paris. At the 1925 *Exposition Internationale he took stand 46 on the Esplanade des Invalides, displaying a dining room

Jules Leleu

(*left*) Cheval mirror
in amboyna, 1920s.

(*right*) Desk and *tabouret* in
burl amboyna, exhibited at the
1927 Salon of the Société des
Artistes Décorateurs, Paris.

(*below left*) Cabinet in
mahogany with ivory trim,
1920s.

(*below right*) Wool carpet,
1920s/1930s.

with a carpet by IVAN DA SILVA BRUHNS. In the Ambassade Française pavilion, Leleu contributed furniture for the reception hall and music room. Warm woods became his hallmark – walnut, macassar ebony, amboyna and palisander – the furniture's richness derived from the material itself.

In due course, lamps, carpets and fabrics were introduced to the family business; by 1929, the firm had moved to 65 avenue Victor Emmanuel, where it remained until the Second World War. Leleu's sons, Jean and André, succeeded him some years later. A wide range of collaborators were listed through the years, including Leleu's wife, sons and daughter Paule; da Silva Bruhns (carpets) and Anatole Kasskoff (murals, tapestries and leather upholstery).

In 1936 Leleu furnished the Grand Salon des Ambassadeurs at the Société des Nations, Geneva. The room, still in existence, is known as the Salon Leleu. Many embassy and ministry commissions followed, the most prestigious a dining room at the Elysée Palace. Ocean liners – including commissions for the *Île-de-France*, *L'*Atlantique*, *Pasteur* and *Normandie* – provided Leleu with further eminence and publicity.

A strict traditionalist, Leleu married unimpeachable sobriety and elegance with the dictates of modern good taste. His designs have been criticized as derivative of JACQUES-ÉMILE RUHLMANN's work. Certainly some models show an unapologetic resemblance, but Leleu's cabinetry was always of an unsurpassed quality and his designs combined harmony, sophistication and prudence.

Lempicka, Tamara (de) (1898–1980). *See under* Paintings, Graphics, Posters and Bookbinding.

Lenci
Established in Turin in 1919 by Enrico Scavini and his wife Elena König Scavini, the Lenci studio's hand-painted and stuffed dolls achieved great popularity

in the mid-1920s. From 1928 until its closure in 1964, the firm concentrated a large part of its ceramic production on figurines, masks and wall plaques decorated with fashionable young women, animals, angels and other religious subject matter, designed initially by Elena König Scavini in the distinctive graphic style of her native Hungary.

Lenci's output included a series of Art Deco style figurines, some signed by decorators Adele Jacopi, Giovanni Grande, Sandro Vacchetti and Mario Sturani. Despite being hit by financial problems in the early 1930s and bombed during the Second World War, the firm re-opened after the hostilities ended.

Lenoble, Émile (1875–1939)
Born in Paris, Lenoble studied with Jean-Baptiste Say before working as a draughtsman for the industrial ceramist Loebnitz. In 1903 he was exposed to *grand feu* ceramics in the Choisy-le-Roi studio of the renowned potter Ernest Chaplet, whose daughter he married two years later. In 1905 responsibility for the pottery was turned over to Lenoble when Chaplet lost his eyesight.

Lenoble's work was inspired by ancient Korean and Chinese Song Dynasty wares; from c. 1910 to 1913, he produced imitative pieces in enamelled *grès* with engraved *champs* (fields) of decoration. The shapes of his vessels were always irreproachably pure and simple, and their scale generous. To these vessels Lenoble applied exquisitely refined glazes in rich turquoise, brown, ochre and ivory hues that he incised with symmetrical geometric patterns.

Leleu was captured during the First World War. After the armistice he displayed again at the Salons of the *Société des Artistes Décorateurs, the *Salon d'Automne and the Salon des Tuileries. Lenoble's inter-war pottery was characterized by compositions of interlacing chevrons, spirals, zig-zags and arabesques overlaid in *slip* clay that was incised or painted with broken-line patterns.

Lenoir, Pierre-Charles (1879–1953)
Paris-born Lenoir was a pupil not only of his father, Charles-Joseph Lenoir, but also of Jules-Clément Chaplain and Antonin Mercié. He exhibited regularly at the Salons of the *Société des Artistes Français, winning second-class medals in 1905 and 1907 and a travelling scholarship in 1911.

Beyond the Paris Salons, Lenoir also exhibited in cities such as Brussels (1910–24), Copenhagen (1909–24), New York (1910), Rome (1911) and Ghent and Tokyo (1913). A member of La Stèle group, he designed small works in bronze, including medallions, for *Arthur Goldscheider, and ceramics for *Sèvres. Several of Lenoir's commissions were for monuments and memorials, including a plaque to celebrate the centenary of the Argentine republic.

Lepape, Georges (1887–1971)
Initially a trainee in Humbert's Paris atelier, Lepape entered the École des Beaux-Arts, studying under Fernand Cormon. His 1909 meeting with Paul *Poiret was propitious: he was hired to provide fashion designs and advertisements for the couturier, a collaboration that produced several illustrated fashion books, including *Les Choses de Paul Poiret vues par Georges Lepape* (1911), which brought Lepape international fame.

In 1912 an expanding clientele brought commissions from Jean-Louis Vaudoyer to design the stage sets for *La Nuit Persane* at the Théâtre des Arts, programme illustrations for the Ballets Russes and graphics for the magazine *La Gazette du Bon Ton*, which continued the arrangement until 1925. Lepape also executed countless covers and fashion illustrations for *Vogue*, *Harper's Bazaar*, *Femina*, *House & Garden*, *L'Illustration*, *Lu* and *Vu*. One of the first illustrators to formulate a fluid Art Deco graphic style, Lepape employed hot colours and cutting-edge fashion in his idealized portrayal of the racy and romantic lifestyles to which his readership aspired.

Georges Lepape

(*opposite left*) *Vogue* magazine cover in gouache on paper, 15 March, 1927.

(*opposite centre*) *Le miroir rouge*, gouache on paper, 1914.

Émile Lenoble

(*opposite right*) Vase in glazed stoneware, c. 1925.

Lenci

(*below*) Accordion player, in glazed earthenware, 1936.

(*right*) *Girl on a Globe*, in glazed earthenware, 1936.

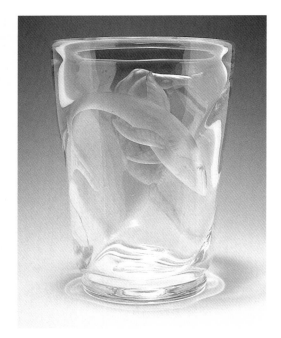

In addition to his graphic work, Lepape applied himself to stage and costume design for productions including the *Le Coup manqué* ballet-pantomime at the Théâtre de l'Athenée (1915), and *L'Oiseau bleu* by Maeterlinck (1923). Notable in this busy schedule were Lepape's costumes for the fashion ball staged at the Théâtre des Champs-Elysées during the 1925 *Exposition Internationale in Paris.

Les Neveux de J. Lehmann

Les Neveux de J. Lehmann (LNJL) was a prominent foundry and *éditeur d'art* in Paris in the inter-war years located at 26 rue de Paradis. The company specialized in editions of bronze and bronze-and-ivory statuary generated by artists such as Pierre *Le Faguays, Amadeo *Gennarelli, Alexandre *Kelety and Alfredo Pina. In addition to producing its own works, LNJL co-manufactured others with *Etling et Cie, for which it occasionally cast bronze components.

Le Sylve (Au Bûcheron)

The design studio Le Sylve, located on the rue de Rivoli, was set up in early 1925 when the director of the Au Bûcheron department store, M. Boutillier, ordered a modern interior for its stand at the 1925 *Exposition Internationale. The 1926 commission to design and furnish the second-class dining room on the *Île-de-France* ocean liner served as a further incentive to the management to create its own furnishings.

Under the direction of Michel *Dufet and the art critic Léandre Vaillat, the studio produced works by Gaston Guérin, Seneschal and Dufet; sculpture by Émile-Antoine Bourdelle, Chana *Orloff and Pierre Traverse; glass by Jean Sala and Capelin; ceramics by Georges *Serré and Marcel *Goupy; silver by *Jensen; *dinanderie* by JEAN DUNAND; and paintings by Maurice Utrillo, Maurice Vlaminck and Kees van Dongen. Dufet remained director until 1939.

Lévard, **Georges** (*fl.* 1903–35). *See* Lahalle & Lévard.

Leveille, **André** (1880–1962)

Born in Lille, Leveille became a specialist in fabric design while working in a textile factory from 1905 to 1925. During this time he taught himself to paint by copying works in museum collections; by 1911, he exhibited his own compositions regularly at the annual Salons. In a jewelry context, Leveille is best known for the series of dynamic Cubist designs he created for Maison FOUQUET in the inter-war years, examples of which won him a *grand prix* at the 1925 *Exposition Internationale.

Le Verrier, **Max** (1891–1973)

The son of a goldsmith, Le Verrier was born in Neuilly-sur-Seine, and studied at the École des Beaux-Arts in Geneva before training as a sculptor. Around 1922 he inherited a small foundry that he built into a successful business, making a variety of decorative objects and lamps designed by sculptors such as Pierre *Le Faguays, André Vincent *Becquerel, Marcel *Bouraine, Jules Masson and himself. These were marketed through the firm's showroom at 100 rue du Théâtre in Paris. Such works, which were executed in bronze, bronze-and-ivory, spelter, ceramics and terracotta at Le Verrier's workshop at 30 rue Deparcieux, were also displayed at the Salon of the *Société des Artistes Décorateurs, of which he was a member. At the 1925 *Exposition Internationale, he took a stand in the Grand Palais, and exhibited again at the 1937 Exposition des Arts et Techniques, where he was awarded a gold medal of honour.

Likarz-Strauss, **Maria** (1893–1956)

Born in Przemysl (now in Poland), Likarz-Strauss was educated at the Kunstschule für Frauen und Mädchen in Vienna from 1908 to 1910, and at the city's Kunstgewerbeschule from 1911 to 1915 where she studied under A. von Kenner and Josef Hoffmann. From 1912 to 1914 she was a member of the Wiener Werkstätte, after which she taught at an art school in the Schloss Giebichstein, Halle, from 1916 to 1920. In 1920 Likarz-Strauss returned to the Wiener Werkstätte, where she designed textiles, leather, lace, pearl jewelry, bookbindings, ex-libris, posters and other graphics until 1931. She was particularly noted for a range of wallpapers using both stencilled and freehand decoration. In 1938 she left Vienna for Italy.

Lindstrand, **Vicke** (1904–1983)

Lindstrand was born in Gothenburg, Sweden, and studied at the city's School of Arts and Crafts before working as a newspaper and book illustrator. The first designer to be added to the Gate-Hald dynasty, in 1928, he brought to *Orrefors a rigorous Modernist style. An early series of enamelled and frosted glassware (1930) captured precisely the 'high-style' Art Deco of the French capital, and specifically that of the graphic artist JEAN DUPAS, in its portrayal of gambolling nymphs, circus elephants, jugglers and the ubiquitous *biche* (doe). In the 1930s Lindstrand turned his attention to the vogue for uneven thick-walled crystal, to which he applied the same Modernist imagery by engraving. By applying an undulating surface to his vessels, he generated a heightened illusion of movement within the crystal, a technique shown at its best in two celebrated works, 'Pearl Fishers' and 'Shark Killer', both designed in the early 1930s.

Lindstrand showed the same easy facility with the *Graal* and *Ariel* techniques developed by Orrefors. In Graal, tribal and mythological subjects were rendered in a loosely flowing yet highly spirited Modernist style. Two typical models executed using the Ariel technique, 'Zebras' and 'Penguins', incorporated brown and opaque-white decoration on an icy, clear, aerated ground, which provided a crisply contrasting and eye-catching effect.

Georges Lévard

(*top left*) Grand Salon, in collaboration with André Fréchet, shown at the Studium—Louvre pavilion at the 1925 Exposition Internationale, Paris.

(*top right*) Dressing table and *tabouret*, 1929.

(*left*) Dressing table in sycamore and coromandel lacquer with silvered-metal mounts, in collaboration with Mlle de las Cazas, exhibited at the 1928 Salon d'Automne, Paris.

(*above*) Table in walnut with burl wood veneer, late 1920s.

Raymond Loewy
(*above*) Prototype pencil
sharpener in chromed metal,
1933.

Claudius Linossier
(*top left*) Vases in patinated
copper with *dinanderie*
decoration, *c*. 1925.

(*top right*) Vase in patinated
copper with *dinanderie*
decoration, *c*. 1925.

Charles Loupot
(*right*) *Fourrures Canton*,
lithographic poster, 1949.

Josef Lorenzl
The Captured Bird, glazed
earthenware figure for
Frederick Goldscheider, 1920s.

In 1940, at the height of his creative powers, Lindstrand left Orrefors for the Uppsala-Ekeby ceramic firm, where he remained for ten years before joining *Kosta Glasbruk as a senior designer.

Linossier, Claudius (1893–1953)

Born in Lyons into a working-class family, Linossier was apprenticed at the age of thirteen as a metalworker in a local workshop that manufactured liturgical articles. On completion of his training, he moved to Paris where he worked in two studios before returning after the First World War to Lyons, where he opened an atelier. In Paris he showed his works through the *Salon d'Automne, the *Société des Artistes Décorateurs and Maison *Geo. Rouard.

Linossier took *dinanderie* – the craft of metal encrustation – to new heights, developing alloys that provided a richer range of tones and colours than those of silver and copper. Eschewing enamel and lacquer in his surface treatments, he employed only the traditional techniques of metal encrustation – hammering and patination. The patination he could vary with a blow torch to extend his range of colour effects to achieve gold, crimson and grey tones. Linossier's mix of crisp geometric motifs and archaic figural compositions rivalled on occasion that of JEAN DUNAND, the period's premier metalworker.

Loewy, Raymond (1893–1986)

Paris-born Loewy underwent three years of specialized training as an engineer before mobilization in the First World War. Following the armistice and an unsuccessful search for employment in Paris, he set sail in 1919 for the USA. A chance meeting on board ship afforded him an introduction to the publisher of *Vogue* and a job as a fashion illustrator for the magazine.

Loewy's career as a commercial artist began to shift toward industrial design in late 1929, when he was hired by Sigmund Gestetner to modernize the appearance of the Gestetner mimeograph machine. In 1930 Loewy opened his own office in Manhattan. Assorted commissions for firms such as Shelton Looms (a textile company) were forthcoming. By the time that he designed the 'Hupmobile' for the Hupp Motor Co. in 1932, Loewy had reached the audience he was seeking, injecting a Gallic flair into the beleaguered American consumer market.

In 1935 Loewy's revamped design of the Sears, Roebuck & Co.'s box refrigerator assured his success. Sparklingly modern, the Coldspot 'Super Six' broke existing sales records, bringing him to the attention of executives in other industries. By 1936 Loewy employed a staff of twelve with branch offices in London and Chicago.

Many of Loewy's 1930s designs were blatantly commercial with aerodynamic forms that gave them a futuristic appearance, especially vehicles that showed a preoccupation with speed in preference to practical design considerations. Charges of showmanship and opportunism masked his more serious accomplishments, such as the series of locomotives he designed for the Pennsylvania Railroad, ferryboats for the Virginia Ferry Corp. and ships for the Panama Line. Later Loewy designs, many now considered American classics, were those for a pencil sharpener (1934), the Greyhound motorcoach (1940) and the Lucky Strike cigarette package (1942).

Longman, Evelyn Beatrice (1874–1954)

Born in England, Longman settled in the USA, where she studied under Lorado Taft at the Art Institute of Chicago, later becoming assistant to the sculptor Daniel Chester French. She modelled memorial sculpture in the fashion of Augustus Saint-Gaudens. Longman's model *Electricity* won the competition for a monumental bronze figure to be installed on the top of the AT&T Building in Manhattan.

Lorenzl, Josef (1892–1950)

Lorenzl was born in Vienna, where he trained as a sculptor and in the inter-war years generated a large volume of bronze, bronze-and-ivory and ceramic models exclusively for *Friedrich Goldscheider. The figures in his groups – often fashionable young women accompanied by greyhounds or borzois; or acrobats, archers or exotic dancers portrayed with the same *joie de vivre* – are characterized by their vibrant costumes.

Lorenzl also created ceramics for the Austrian manufacturer Keramos Wiener Kunst Keramik und Porzellanmanufaktur AG. From the mid-1920s, his early preoccupation with detail yielded increasingly to simplification of form and features.

Loupot, Charles (1892–1962)

Born in Nice, Loupot studied at the École des Beaux-Arts in Lyons. Wounded in the First World War, he joined his parents in Lausanne, and found employment at the Wolfensberger printing plant in Zurich as a lithographer, where he gained considerable experience in the poster medium.

Loupot's first poster dates from 1918. In 1923, at the request of the printer Devambez, he returned to Paris, where his experience as a fashion illustrator led to work with *La Gazette du Bon Ton* and *Femina*. During this time Loupot also created two posters for Voisin automobiles, one of which was rendered in the colourful Art Deco style that became his signature. In 1925 he was appointed art director of the Belles Affiches agency, and five years later joined CASSANDRE and Maurice Moyrand in their Alliance Graphique art and advertising studio. While there, Loupot exhibited his posters with Cassandre at the Salle Pleyel.

During the Second World War, Loupot became art director of *Les Arcs*, for which he designed numerous magazine covers and posters before and after the Second World War. From 1945, Loupot continued to design magazine covers and to work as a poster artist.

Lovet-Lorski, Boris (1894–1973). *See under* Sculpture.

Luce, Jean (1895–1964/65)

Paris-born Luce began his career in his father's ceramic workshop at 29 rue de Châteaudun, exhibiting his works from 1911 at the Musée Galliera and then, from 1913, at the *Salon d'Automne and the *Société des Artistes Décorateurs. In 1923 he left to open his own atelier and shop at 30 rue la Boétie.

In his early glass creations, Luce painted his designs onto the surface of his vessels in clear enamels, but from 1924 he introduced sandblasting into his repertoire. His designs, consisting of abstract or geometric patterns and stylized flora, were mathematically formulated and arresting in their crisp refinement. Many pieces were in black mirrored glass. Because he was not a trained glassworker, his designs were wheel-cut or etched by other craftsmen under his supervision. Luce exhibited *hors concours* at the 1925 *Exposition Internationale and the 1937 Exposition des Arts et Techniques. During his career he produced a considerable volume of ceramic wares.

Retained by the Compagnie Générale Transatlantique to design porcelain and glass tablewares for the ocean liner *Normandie*, Luce's models were so well received that they were employed subsequently by the company on all of its passenger ships. He was elected a *chevalier* of the French Légion d'Honneur in 1937.

Lucet, Maurice (1877–1941). *See* Lahalle & Lévard.

M

McArthur, Warren, Jr (1885–1961)

Raised in Chicago in a Frank Lloyd Wright house commissioned by his father, Warren McArthur, Sr., McArthur studied mechanical engineering at Cornell and graduated in 1908. Between 1911 and 1914 he filed

no less than ten patents for lamp designs, including one still in production today in a slightly revised version by the R. E. Dietz Lantern Co. of Chicago.

In 1913 McArthur moved to Phoenix to work with his brother Charles. Among their first business ventures was a string of Dodge automobile dealerships; another was the 'wonder bus', one of the first recreational vehicles to promote tourism and the newly formed highway system with access to national parks. The brothers also launched the first radio station in Arizona.

In 1929 McArthur moved to Los Angeles, where he started a metal furniture business. Focusing initially on customized pieces, he soon turned his attention to new methods of standardized furniture assembly. A catalogue published at the time reveals technical innovations in his speciality – tubular aluminium furniture, including notched tubes and milled washers. To these McArthur applied an anodizing process that made aluminium hard and relatively impossible to tarnish. This allowed him to offer a lifetime guarantee for his products and to introduce a colouring technique that would not crack or chip. Colours included shades of golf green, Alice blue and grenadine.

McArthur's tubular aluminium furniture, with its distinctive curved frames and leatherette upholstery in dramatically contrasting colours such as red, black and canary yellow was seen on film sets and in film stars' homes and became popular in Hollywood for its chic Machine Age aestheticism. Lounge seating, *tête-à-têtes*, end-tables and smoke-stands proved especially successful in the marketplace. Two of the best-known models were the 'Ambassador' armchair and ottoman (1932), designed for the Ambassador Theatre in Los Angeles, and the 'Biltmore' chair (1933), which took its name from the Arizona Biltmore Hotel in Phoenix. The 'Biltmore' chair was designed by McArthur's older brother, Albert Chase McArthur, with a patent provided by Frank Lloyd Wright for its concrete-block construction – a signature building material used by Wright.

Financially strapped after his father's death, in 1933 McArthur moved his furniture-making enterprise to Rome, New York State, where he continued to design and manufacture aluminium furnishings. In 1937 he moved the factory again to Bantam, Connecticut. During the Second World War, he produced aluminum and magnesium seating for aircraft bombers. After the war he founded Mayfair Industries in Yonkers, near Manhattan, where he continued producing aluminum furnishings into the 1960s. Some of his models are still reproduced by ClassiCon.

McKnight Kauffer, Edward (1890–1954)

Born in Great Falls, Montana, Kauffer was raised in Evansville, Indiana, where he got his start as a scene painter at the town's Grand Opera House. In 1910 he moved to San Francisco, where he attended evening classes at the Mark Hopkins Institute while working in a bookshop. There he met Professor Joseph E. McKnight, a philanthropist who recognized Kauffer's artistic potential and offered to subsidize his studies in Europe. Kauffer subsequently adopted the second surname of McKnight out of gratitude for his patron's support.

He arrived in Paris in 1913, where he studied briefly at the Académie Moderne. The next year, following the outbreak of the First World War, McKnight Kauffer moved with his first wife, the American concert pianist Grace Erhlich, to the UK, where he earned a living as a graphic designer. His work now showed the influence of new movements, including Cubism and Surrealism. In 1915 he received his first commission from the London Underground, for which, and for its successor London Transport, he designed more than a hundred posters over the next twenty-five years to promote the city's underground train system. He signed his posters, which brought him name recognition.

For his graphic and poster work in the turbulent years around the First World War, McKnight Kauffer borrowed elements from most of the major recent

Jean Luce
(*top left*) Vase in etched and gilded glass, *c.* 1925.

Edward McKnight Kauffer
(*above*) Hand-knotted wool carpet, manufactured by the Wilton Royal Carpet Factory, 1930s.

(*left*) Wool carpet, manufactured by the Wilton Royal Carpet Factory, 1930s.

Page 430
Warren McArthur, Jr
(*above left*) Desk in tubular anodized aluminium and Formica, for the library in the State of Virginia's office building, 1930s.

(*above right*) Table in tubular aluminium with Formica top, *c.* 1930.

(*below*) Chairs in tubular anodized aluminium, rubber and oilcloth, designed for the Arizona Biltmore Hotel, *c.* 1929.

Page 431
Furniture in tubular anodized aluminium designed by Harry Lund for Harry's New York Bar, Chicago (Ecklander & Brandt, architects), 1930s.

Louis Majorelle
Cabinet illustrated in an advertisement in *Les Échos des Industries d'Art*, June 1926.

and current movements in painting, including French Cubism, British Vorticism, Italian Futurism, Russian Contructivism, Art Deco and Art Moderne. He never committed to a single style, opting to draw on elements from each in forging his own mode of artistic expression. In this, his simplification of machine forms, in bold and legible compositions suggesting the power and movement of electrical generators and engines, was especially dynamic.

In 1921, on a trip to New York, McKnight Kauffer met Marion *Dorn (1899–1964), with whom, after the dissolution of his marriage, he lived in London, where she was pursuing a career as a rug and furniture textile designer. He likewise ventured into the interior design field, creating rugs for the Wilton Royal Carpet Co. with bold rectilinear designs composed of intersecting planes and stripes. In the late 1920s, he was retained by Shell-Mex BP to design posters for the company's trucks; termed lorry bills, these were large customized posters placed on the sides of their delivery trucks.

In the run-up to and during the Second World War, commissions dried up for both McKnight Kauffer and Dorn, prompting their return to the USA, where McKnight Kauffer failed to re-establish his poster career, even following his 1937 one-man exhibition at the Museum of Modern Art, in New York. He spent the last fifteen years of his life in New York, producing a sizeable body of graphic work for publishers such as Random House, Doubleday, Pantheon and Modern Library. In the late 1940s and early 1950s, McKnight Kauffer produced a series of posters for PanAm.

Magnussen, Erik (1884–1961)

Born in Copenhagen, Denmark, Magnussen apprenticed at his uncle's art gallery, Winkel & Magnussen, from 1898 to 1901, and then studied sculpture with Stephen Indig and **chasing** with the silversmith Viggo Hansen. Between 1907 and 1909 he was employed as a chaser

by Otto Rohloff in Berlin, following which he left to open his own workshop in Denmark. He exhibited his work frequently from 1901.

Magnussen moved to the USA in 1925, where he worked as a designer for the Gorham Manufacturing Co. in Providence, Rhode Island until 1929. Then he worked for the German firm of August Dingeldein & Son, which had a retail outlet in New York City. In 1932 he opened his own workshop in Chicago, and also worked in Los Angeles before returning to Denmark in 1939.

Most of Magnussen's Modernist designs show a restrained and classic formality that reveal his Danish heritage in their scrolled floral accents and reeded ivory stems and finials. Other more spartan designs are comparable to those produced by Marianne *Brandt at the Bauhaus. Magnussen is especially renowned for his atypical 'Lights and Shadows of Manhattan' tea service, which he designed for Gorham in 1927. It had triangular panels in burnished silver with gold and oxidized grey sections that evoked the kaleidoscopic effects of sunlight and shade on the 1920s American urban skyline. The service's popular success generated a host of imitations, such as the Apollo 'Skyscraper' service by Bernard Rice's Sons Inc. and a coffee service with Cubist panelling by the Middletown Silver Co.

Majorelle, Louis (1859–1926)

The undisputed master cabinet-maker of the period after 1900, Majorelle survived the First World War despite the 1916 bombing of his Nancy atelier at 6 rue de Vieil-Aître. He returned from Paris in 1918 to rebuild both the workshop and his confidence, the latter undermined by the ferocious post-war obloquy heaped on the very Art Nouveau movement that had swept him to international celebrity. Whether out of economic necessity or buoyed by the challenge of working within the new Modernism, Majorelle continued to design and manufacture furniture. But the 1920s did belong to the new generation, and the master *ébéniste* slipped

into obscurity. Although he exhibited sporadically at the annual Salons, he preferred to offer his furniture directly through the firm's outlets in Nancy, Paris, Lyons and Lille. Turning sixty years old in 1919, and seeing the need for continuity, he appointed Alfred Lévy, one of his students, a co-director of the firm.

At the 1925 *Exposition Internationale, Majorelle served as a member of the jury, while exhibiting two ensembles *hors concours*: an office-library in the firm's stand on the Esplanade des Invalides; and a dining room marketed by Chambray. The critics were harsh: his post-war designs were bourgeois, soulless and, a recurring condemnation of his *fin-de-siècle* furnishings, a trifle too monumental.

On Majorelle's death, Lévy assumed the directorship of the firm. Retrospective exhibitions at both the 1926 *Salon d'Automne, and the 1927 Salon of the *Société des Artistes Décorateurs paid tribute to Majorelle's work. At these exhibitions the contrast between the total luxuriance of Art Noveau and the total constraint of Art Deco became especially significant when viewed within the life's work of a single cabinet-maker, whose masterpieces of the 1900s were displayed alongside his designs from the 1920s.

Les Ateliers Majorelle continued to exhibit at the Salons, also participating in the third La Décoration Française Contemporaine exhibition in 1929. Lévy was joined at this time by Majorelle's nephew Pierre, a graduate of the École des Beaux-Arts in Paris, who had been working in the family's cabinetry shop in Nancy. The two presented an office at the 1930 Salon d'Automne.

Maldarelli, Oronzio (1892–1963)

The son of a goldsmith, Maldarelli was born in Italy and emigrated with his family around 1900 to New York, where he was eventually awarded a Guggenheim Fellowship to study in Paris from 1931 to 1933. On his return to the USA he worked on the ceiling of the

Erik Magnussen

(*right*) 'Lights and Shadows of Manhattan', coffee service in burnished silver with gold and oxidized grey panels, for the Gorham Manufacturing Co., 1927.

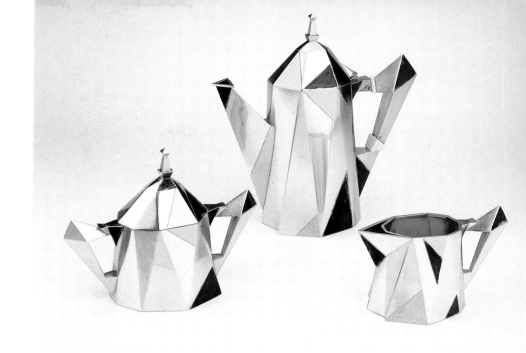

Kazimir Malevich

(*above*) Teapot and matching tray designed for the State Porcelain Factory, 1923, reproduced in silver in an edition of 50 by Rossi & Arcandi for Cleto Munari, 1985.

Louis Majorelle

(*right*) Cabinet in rosewood with ebony and mother-of-pearl veneers, 1920s.

Paul Manship
(*far left and left*) *Indian Hunter*
and *Pronghorn Antelope*,
pair of figures in patinated
bronze, 1914.

Paul Manship
(*left*) *Diana*, patinated bronze
group cast by the founder
Valsuani, 1921.

(*above*) *Acteon* in *verdigris*
bronze cast by the founder
Valsuani, companion group
to *Diana*, 1925.

Center Theater at Rockefeller Center and designed
the figure of an airmail postal carrier for the Federal
Post Office Building in Washington, DC.

Two of Maldarelli's monumental figures were
exhibited at the 1939 New York World's Fair, and
he was awarded many public commissions, including
reliefs for the Hartford Public Library in Hartford,
Connecticut and, in New York, the New York State
Insurance Fund Building and the Martin Birdbath
in Central Park. After the Second World War, his highly
abstracted style of the early 1930s yielded to
representational portrayals of the female nude.

Malevich, Kazimir (1878–1935)

Born to Polish parents near Kiev, Malevich studied at
the city's School of Art and the Moscow Academy of
Fine Arts. In 1913 he developed an abstract geometric
style of painting that he termed 'Suprematism',
through which he sought to resolve the 'dissonances'
between shapes. In 1926 he published his manifesto,
The Nonobjective World, in which he advocated pure
cerebral compositions that would 'free art from the
burden of the object'.

Malevich is known in an Art Deco context for the
teapot and demitasse cups that he designed in 1923
for the State Porcelain Factory in Petrograd.
Resembling a Cubist steam engine, the teapot was
reissued in a silver edition by Cleto Munari in 1985.

Mallet-Stevens, Robert (1886–1945). *See under*
Furniture and Interior Design.

Manship, Paul (1885–1966)

Manship was born on Christmas Day in St Paul,
Minnesota, and studied painting and modelling at the
St Paul Institute before moving in 1905 to New York.
There he enrolled in the Art Students League and
gained practical experience by working as an assistant
to Solon Borglum, the noted sculptor of the American

West. Further tuition at the Pennsylvania Academy
of Fine Arts under Charles Grafly followed, along with
an apprenticeship in the studio of the Viennese-
American sculptor Isidore Konti. Having applied to the
American Academy in Rome for a scholarship, Manship
was awarded the Prix de Rome in 1909. While based
in Rome from 1909 to 1912, he travelled throughout
the Mediterranean to study the iconography and
techniques of archaic and Greco-Roman sculpture,
which considerably influenced his evolving style.

Through the architects Charles Platt and Welles
Bosworth, Manship received several commissions
for garden sculpture on his return to the USA; he also
worked on a series of small-scale bronze models based
on classical themes. In 1915 and 1916, two successful
exhibits gave rise to a further series of commissions.
By 1925 a brilliant and prodigious body of work had
propelled him to pre-eminence within the American
sculpture establishment.

Noteworthy commissions in the 1930s included
'Moods of Time', executed in 1937–38 for the 1939
New York World's Fair, and a celestial sphere for the
Woodrow Wilson Memorial in Geneva, Switzerland
in 1939. In 1934 he created a series of charming animal
and bird studies for a pair of gates commissioned
by Mrs Grace Rainey Rogers for the main entrance to
the New York Zoological Park in the Bronx; these were
a considerable deviation from his usual highly personal
style of design.

Mare, André (1887–1932). *See* Süe et Mare.

Marfurt, Leo (1894–1977)

Born in Switzerland, Marfurt studied at the Aarau
School of Arts and Crafts, before undergoing a printing
apprenticeship between 1910 and 1914. This was
followed by graphics and painting studies at the
École des Beaux-Arts in Geneva. In 1921 Marfurt went
to Belgium where two years later he began a fifty-year

association with the tobacco firm Van der Elst, for
which he produced advertising, packaging and posters,
while accepting commissions for other firms.

In 1927, Marfurt founded his own advertising
agency, Les Créations Publicitaires. A major contributor
to the revival of Belgian poster art, he created some
superb designs for Van der Elst, Remington typewriters,
Chrysler automobiles and British Tourist Board
campaigns. Marfurt's Swiss background may have
accounted for his choice of bold colours, elegant
designs and sparse lines within his compositions.

Marinot, Maurice (1882–1960). *See under* Glass.

Martel, Jan and Joël (both 1896–1966). *See under*
Sculpture.

Martin, Charles (1884–1934)

Martin studied at the École des Beaux-Arts in
Montpellier, the Académie Julian and the École des
Beaux-Arts in Paris before emerging as a premier
graphic and poster artist, fashion designer, and set
and costume designer for ballet and theatre. His work
in all of these areas was rendered in a lively Art Deco
style. He was also a regular contributor to *La Gazette
du Bon Ton*, *Le Journal des Dames et des Modes*, *Vogue*
and *Modes et Manières d'Aujourd'hui*.

Martine. *See under* Furniture and Interior Design.

Marty, André-Édouard (1882–1974)

A student of philosophy and art, Marty was educated
at the École des Beaux-Arts in Paris, after which he
became a graphic artist and contributor to *La Gazette
du Bon Ton*, *Fémina*, *Vogue* and *Le Journal des Dames
et des Modes*. Marty also created stage sets and
costumes, posters, illustrated books and a range of
enamelled vases and jewelry, much of it rendered in
a geometric, Cubist-inspired style.

Matet, Maurice (1903–1989)

Born in Colombes on the Seine, Matet had by 1925 established himself as a decorator at Le *Studium-Louvre, the art studio of Les Galeries du Louvre department store on rue de Rivoli. He participated in the firm's pavilion at the 1925 *Exposition Internationale, showing a dining room in collaboration with Jacques *Gruber (stained glass), EDGAR BRANDT (wrought iron) and Mlle Chameaux (carpets).

In late 1928 Matet and Étienne *Kohlmann, collaborators for the previous five years, were listed at Studium-Louvre, with Matet as consultant designer and Kohlmann as director. It appears Matet may have left the firm within months, since his exhibit at the 1929 Salon of the *Société des Artistes Décorateurs was marketed by *Saddier et ses Fils. He later accepted a professorship at the École des Arts Appliqués in Paris, and continued to design furniture until after the Second World War.

Matet exhibited regularly at the Salons from 1923 to 1929, showing a range of ensembles and individual pieces that were often neat and somewhat bland – the rooms' vibrancy and femininity being provided by Max Vibert's carpets and decorative panels. Matet's most distinctive furniture was included in a 1928 boudoir: open armchairs in tubular steel, upholstered in a ribbed rubber fabric. Many of his interiors were illustrated in the review *Répertoire du Goût Moderne*. Included in a 1929 issue was his sketch for a 'gentleman's gymnasium', complete with punching bag, dartboard, dumbbells and parallel bars.

Mathsson, Bruno (1907–1988)

Swedish-born and a descendant of a long line of Swedish woodworkers and carpenters, Mathsson was trained as an architect and furniture designer. He worked in his father's atelier at Värnamo as an apprentice from 1923, and was influenced by the functionalist doctrines espoused by Marcel *Breuer,

*Le Corbusier and Ludwig *Mies van der Rohe, to which Mathsson applied an organic stylisation. He was also interested in Alvar Aalto's work with curved wood laminates. Mathsson refused to sell his earliest works through large Swedish retailers, and instead used his family enterprise. In 1930 he was commissioned to design a chair for the Värnamo Hospital. Lacking the traditional form of sprung upholstery, the chair, which was called 'The Grasshopper', consisted of a frame covered with plaited webbing and supported by arms and legs in solid birch. He employed the same technique in many of his later models.

In the 1930s he produced a series of ergonomic chairs, notably model 'T 102' (1934), in laminated beechwood secured with webbing, whose sinuous ribbed contours anticipated those by Carlo Mollino some years later. In this, Mathsson went beyond the medium's traditional methods of design and manufacture into new modes derived from physiological research on comfortable sitting. This led him to bent and laminated wood and woven webbing, which he incorporated in the chairs he exhibited at the Röhsska Art Museum, Gothenburg, in 1936. Mathsson's chair designs eventually drew the attention of Edgar Kaufmann, Jr., the director of the Department of Industrial Design at the Museum of Modern Art, New York, who commissioned models for a new museum extension.

Mathsson also designed beds, tables and shelving systems in bentwood. Toward 1940 a chaise-longue on metal feet marked his embrace of metal. Between 1945 and 1957, he concentrated mainly on architecture, designing houses with simple constructions in glass, wood and concrete. Although architecture then became his principal focus, in the 1960s he conceived a series of metal tables made by Fritz Hansen. Mathsson participated in the 1937 Exposition des Arts et Techniques, where he was awarded a *grand prix*,

and in the 1939 New York World's Fair. In 1955 he was awarded the Gregor Paulsson Medal in Stockholm. He continued to exhibit his works nationally and internationally until the early 1980s.

Matter, Herbert (1907–1984)

Born in Switzerland, Matter studied at the École des Beaux-Arts, Geneva, and the Académie Moderne, Paris. Working as a graphic artist, poster designer and photographer in the French capital, he collaborated on occasion with CASSANDRE on posters and *Le Corbusier on architecture and exhibition design while working for the design firm of Deberny & Peignot from 1929 to 1932.

In the 1930s Matter was among the first to employ photography and photomontage in advertising, incorporating the techniques in many of his travel posters for the Swiss national tourist board. To the heightened imagery obtained by photomontage, he added colour and his own spare typography. He later employed the same techniques in the posters and advertisements he designed for Knoll furniture (1946–66).

In the late 1930s Matter settled in New York, where he did freelance photography for *Harper's Bazaar* and *Vogue* as well as exhibition design for the Museum of Modern Art (MoMA) in New York. From the 1940s he was a major contributor to the Container Corp. of America's advertising campaigns, and, from c. 1950, was responsible for the typography and book covers for MoMA and the Guggenheim Museum. Matter later became a professor of photography at Yale, while continuing to work as a designer.

Mauboussin (Noury-Mauboussin)

The history of Maison Mauboussin can be traced to 1827, when a M. Rocher and his cousin Baptiste Noury took over an existing jewelry manufactory at 64 rue Greneta, Paris. By 1850 this manufactory was administered solely by Noury.

.WOLFSBERG ZÜRICH

matter

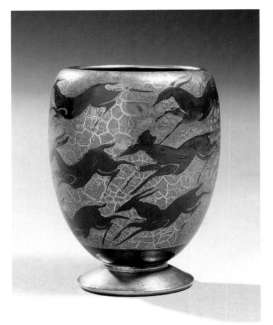

Jean Mayodon

(*top left*) Vase in glazed
earthenware, 1920s.

(*top right*) Plate and vase in
glazed earthenware, 1920s.

Luciano Mauzan

(*above*) *Casa America Pianos*,
lithographic poster, 1930.

Mercier Frères

(*right*) Armoire in burl maple
with ivory inlay, early 1920s.

His nephew Georges Mauboussin joined the firm in 1877, initially as an assistant, then as a partner to his uncle. In 1903 he became sole proprietor.

In 1923 Maison Mauboussin purchased two adjoining premises, an expansion that was followed by showrooms in New York, Boston, Buenos Aires and Rio de Janeiro. The firm also participated in many of the foremost exhibitions of the inter-war years, showing work in Milan (1923, 1924), New York (1924 and 1939) and Paris (the 1925 *Exposition Internationale, the 1931 Exposition Coloniale and the 1937 Exposition des Arts et Techniques).

After 1925 Maison Mauboussin was located in the Place Vendôme, with a workshop in rue de Choiseul. The firm embraced a spirited Modernist style in which stylized images of fountains, vases of fruit, floral bouquets, chinoiserie and the 'Iribe' rose, rendered in carved gemstones, were perennial favourites in a jewelry repertoire that also included pendant watches and seal watches.

Mauzan, Luciano (Achille) (1883–1952)

Born in Milan, Mauzan studied painting and sculpture in France before dividing his time between Milan, Paris and Argentina. Between 1920 and 1940, his graphics, including more than 2,000 postcard and 1,000 poster designs, combined a Cubist influence with a bright palette and witty caricatures. Among Mauzan's most notable poster designs were 'Carpano', 'Cirio', 'Persil', 'Tonson', 'Couple' and 'Fernet-Branca, prolonga la Vida'.

Mayodon, Jean (1893–1967)

Mayodon was born in Sèvres and taught himself to be an artist. In 1912 following a trip to England, he undertook his first ceramic models, using a kiln that he had constructed at his home. Drawn to Hellenistic, Persian and Middle Eastern figurative themes, Mayodon developed an engaging painterly style in which his subjects – mostly archers, nudes and

animals – were portrayed in relief on jade-green and turquoise-blue grounds lavishly highlighted in gold. In addition to tableware items such as vases and plates, he undertook commissions for architectural works: fireplaces, fountains, sculptures and tiled decorative panels that he executed in stanniferous stoneware.

Mayodon exhibited through the *Salon d'Automne (from 1920), the Salon of the *Société des Artistes Décorateurs (from 1922), the Salon des Tuileries (from 1936) and at Maison *Geo. Rouard in Paris. His commissions included tiled ceramic murals for the ocean liners *Normandie*, *Flandre* and *Pasteur*. Retained as artistic consultant by the *Sèvres Manufactory from 1934 to 1939, he also served as its artistic director for a year in 1941. Between 1935 and 1937, Mayodon taught ceramics at the Lycée Elisa Lemonnier.

Mercier Frères

Claude Mercier's furniture-manufacturing firm at 100 rue du Faubourg Saint-Antoine was well established by 1850. It reproduced a wide range of late 18th- to early 19th-century styles – everything from Louis XVI to Empire – the shameless stock-in-trade of most of the quarter's cabinet-makers. Both Art Nouveau and Art Deco furniture were later manufactured. By 1900 the business, now presumably managed by two or more of Claude's sons, was named Mercier Frères.

In the 1920s the firm adapted readily to the prevailing Art Deco style, offering a range of 'modern' interiors in addition to its traditional wares. It participated at the Salons of the *Société des Artistes Décorateurs, showing lamps, furniture, paintings and wall panelling. The September 1926 issue of *Les Échos des Industries d'Art* illustrated a palisander commode veneered with ivory and ebony. Its contours – fundamentally Louis XVI, down to the elongated *toupie* feet – were adapted judiciously to the modern style

by the application of a central ivory panel depicting two maidens kneeling among flowers. Further interiors, including studios designed by H. Aribaud and ERIC BAGGE for Mercier Frères at two of the 1929 Salons, reminded visitors that the firm was a manufacturer of traditional wooden furniture.

At the 1925 *Exposition Internationale, Mercier Frères took stand 48 on the Esplanade des Invalides, close to other commercial manufacturers such as Sormani, P.A. Dumas and Evrard Frères. Its display included a dining room designed by Raymond Quibel. In the late 1920s Mercier Frères opened the gallery Palais de Marbre, at 77 avenue des Champs-Elysées.

Mere, Clément (1861–1940)

Born in Bayonne, Mere was apprenticed in Gérôme's Paris atelier and then returned to family life in the provinces. A selection of his landscapes painted in the Basse-Pyrénées and Franche-Comté were displayed at the Salon of the Société Nationale des Beaux-Arts. His style was restful, if undistinguished. Visits to old colleagues in Paris drew him back there at the turn of the 20th century, at which point he began to produce leatherware and fabric patterns.

Around 1900 Mere joined Julius Meier-Graefe's upmarket gallery, La Maison Moderne, where he worked closely with Franz Waldorff, a designer of bookcovers and embroidered silks. Some time later he introduced small examples of his new *métier*: letter openers, toiletry items, fans and bookcovers in *repoussé* leather, *galuchat* and ivory. A 1912 article by Émile Sedyn in *Art et Décoration* traced this evolution from the fine to the applied arts. The objects, exquisitely rendered, showed refinement and femininity. An Oriental influence was likewise discernible, particularly in Mere's patinated leather floral designs.

Mere introduced furniture into his repertoire *c.* 1910 at the Salons of the *Société des Artistes Décorateurs and the *Société Nationale des

Clément Mere

(*top left*) Jewelry cabinet
in palisander with tooled
and lacquered leather panels,
1920s.

(*left*) Cabinet-on-stand in
macassar ebony and tooled
and lacquered leather,
with ivory trim, *c.* 1925.

(*top right*) Sideboard in
macassar ebony and tooled
and lacquered leather, with
gilt-bronze mounts, *c.* 1925.

(*above*) Commode in macassar
ebony and tooled and
lacquered leather, the interior
in gray ash, 1920s.

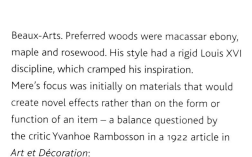

Paul-Louis Mergier
(*right*) Vase in copper with *dinanderie* decoration, marketed by Évolution, 1920s.

(*far right*) Vase in copper with *dinanderie* decoration, 1920s.

Beaux-Arts. Preferred woods were macassar ebony, maple and rosewood. His style had a rigid Louis XVI discipline, which cramped his inspiration. Mere's focus was initially on materials that would create novel effects rather than on the form or function of an item – a balance questioned by the critic Yvanhoe Rambosson in a 1922 article in *Art et Décoration*:

> There are a large number of knick-knacks which are decorated without regard to the intrinsic beauty of the materials that were used. He tries to prettify a commonplace shape with unnecessary additions, and he forgets that the decoration should enhance the lines and surfaces of the objects and not cover them needlessly. I saw a little powder box that was successfully worked, but otherwise there were so many pieces with bits of colour stitched in randomly with no apparent reason. These are good examples of false luxury, to be avoided at all costs.

Around 1924 Mere received two important commissions: a cabinet for Lord Rothermere, and a desk, now in the Musée des Arts Décoratifs, Paris, for Robert de Rothschild, an ardent patron of contemporary furniture. Little is recorded of Mere after 1925: he no longer participated in the Salons and appears to have retired.

Mergier, Paul-Louis (1891–1981x6)
Mergier was born in Orthez (Pyrénées-Atlantiques) and studied engineering at the École Brequet in Paris, after which he undertook graduate studies at the city's École Supérieure d'Aéronautique and the science faculty at the Sorbonne. Conscripted during the First World War and demobilized in 1920, Mergier began to work in cabinet-making and *dinanderie*, where his knowledge of science and metallurgy stood him in good stead.

He exhibited a wide range of objects at the Salons from 1925, including vases, paintings, screens, doors and furniture. Mergier's preferred medium was enamelled copper, which he frequently employed for vases executed to his designs by Goetz or La Monaca Guy. He also designed lacquered screens with *repoussé* decoration, some encrusted with mother-of-pearl, *coquille d'œuf*, pewter, gold or silver.

In his furniture, Mergier revealed his metalware expertise by incorporating copper panels inlaid with semiprecious metals into palisander cupboard doors. One such work at the Salons caught the discerning eye of Jacques *Doucet, who commissioned a similar filing cabinet for his studio in Neuilly. The piece, now in the collection of the Musée des Arts Décoratifs, Paris, incorporates Mergier's entire metalware repertoire, along with leather doors and a parchment-lined interior. For his screens and vessels, Mergier drew on classical mythology for many of his decorative themes, including Nessus, Neptune and the Bacchantes. Some of his work was made by Évolution.

Metthey, André (1871–1920)
Largely self-taught and inspired at the turn of the 20th century by Jean Carries, Metthey established his own stoneware studio in 1903 at Asnières, near Paris. From 1907 he invited a host of noted artists and sculptors – among them Pierre Bonnard, Maurice Denis, André Derain, Aristide Maillol, Henri Matisse and Odilon Redon – whom he had met through the dealer Ambroise Vollard, to decorate much of his work. This freed him to concentrate on the development of new glazes and on modelling and stamping techniques. His *flambé* glazes were especially successful.

Participating at the *Salon d'Automne from 1907, Metthey exhibited also through the Galerie E. Druet in Paris. Many of his pre-war designs anticipated the Art Deco period in their crisp symmetrical patterns.

Louis Midavaine (1888–1978)
Born in Roubaix, where he studied at the École des Beaux-Arts, Midavaine worked in his family's painting and decoration enterprise in the village of Grièvement. Injured and left for dead on the battlefield behind German lines during the First World War, he learned the techniques of lacquer through his German captors, who forced him to work with Asians in a workshop where they lacquered aeroplane propellers. After the hostilities, he moved to Issy-les-Moulineaux, where he decorated objects in lacquer sold to benefit the Red Cross. The Duchesse de la Rochefoucauld, the organization's director, set him up in 1917 in an atelier in the rue des Acacias, in Paris's 17th *arrondissement*, where he created modern works in lacquer, mainly screens and panels. His commissions included murals for first-class cabins on the *Normandie and *Pasteur* ocean liners, and the Côte d'Azur residence of Bao-Dai, the Emperor of Annam in Vietnam. In the 1940s Midavaine's address was listed as 6 rue d'Oran, Cannes.

Mies van der Rohe, Ludwig (1886–1969)
Born in Aachen, Mies van der Rohe worked as a draughtsman of stucco ornaments before moving to Berlin in 1905 to study under Bruno Paul. From 1908 to 1911 he worked in the office of Peter Behrens. In 1926 he became a vice-president of the Deutscher Werkbund, the following year organizing the group's Stuttgart exhibition.

For the 1929 Barcelona Exposition Mies van der Rohe designed the German pavilion, which he furnished with X-framed chairs constructed of chrome-plated steel strips. Soon considered an icon of Modernist design, the 'Barcelona' chair MR90 model, as it became known, has been produced by Knoll since 1947. In 1930 Mies van der Rohe became the last director of the Bauhaus, which he moved from Dessau to Berlin. In 1938 he left for the USA to teach at the Illinois Institute of Technology.

André Metthey
(*below*) Plates in glazed
earthenware, 1920s.

(*bottom*) Bottles in glazed
earthenware, 1920s.

Louis Midavaine

(*below*) Buffet in mahogany with lacquered door panels, probably 1920s.

(*bottom*) Wood panel in lacquer, *c.* 1925.

Pierre-Paul Montagnac
(*above*) Reception hall,
with furniture manufactured
by Robert Sangouard, c. 1927.

(*left*) Cabinet in rosewood
with brass inlay, late 1920s.

Carl Milles
(*right*) *Europa and the Bull*,
verdigris bronze, c. 1926.

Carl Milles
(*left*) *Dancing Maenad*, frieze in sandstone, c. 1914.

Bruce Moore
(*below*) *Black Panther*, bronze, 1929.

Miklos, Gustav (1888–1967). *See under* Sculpture.

Milles, Carl (1875–1955)

Although born in Sweden, where he created a considerable body of work, Milles was claimed by America, as he lived and worked there from *1931* to 1951 as director of the sculpture department at the Cranbrook Academy of Art in Bloomfield Hills, Michigan. He trained under Auguste Rodin in Paris from 1897 to 1904, drawing on Scandinavian folklore and Classical Greek mythology for many of his subjects, which he interpreted in a fluid Modernist style.

Milles's first American exhibit was in 1929 at the 56th Street Galleries in Manhattan. Many of his commissions were for monuments or fountain groups, including his 'Triton' (1916), 'Europa' (1924) and 'Folkunga' (1924) fountains. Among Milles's best-known works was his monumental figure, *The Astronomer*, exhibited at the 1939 New York World's Fair.

Montagnac, Pierre-Paul (1883–1961)

References in the 1920s to Montagnac list both Paris and Saint-Denis as his birthplace. He obtained his painting and decorative skills in Paris at the Académie Carrière and the Académie de la Grande Chaumière, and made his début at the Salons in 1912. His address from 1919 was listed as 58 rue de Rome, Paris.

Montagnac designed a wide range of commercial and domestic interiors, choosing a select group of artist–designers, including IVAN DA SILVA BRUHNS, Raymond *Subes and JEAN PERZEL, to provide ancillary furnishings. Magazines such as *Nouveaux Intérieurs Français* and *Petits Meubles Modernes* show a sober but anonymous modern style inspired by the late 18th century. Among the cabinet-makers who executed his designs, Montagnac chose Robert Sangouard of 116 avenue des Batignolles, Saint-Ouen, to build the majority of his pieces, which were marketed through Le Confortable and Les Galeries Lafayette.

At the 1925 *Exposition Internationale, Montagnac took the stand next to Sangouard's on the Esplanade des Invalides, displaying a hallway and gallery. He also participated in the Grand Salon of the Ambassade Française pavilion and, to show his diversity, designed a selection of chased bronze key escutcheons, window bolts and hinges for *Fontaine et Cie, a Paris locksmith.

The 1930s brought two prestigious ocean liner commissions: in 1931, a deluxe bedroom and drawing room for L'*Atlantique, and the 'Caen' suite on the *Normandie. A 1934 article in *Mobilier et Décoration* traced other recent interiors, in which Montagnac had placed heavy emphasis on architectural lighting. Appointed president of the *Société des Artistes Décorateurs in 1930, he organized its pavilion at the 1937 Exposition des Arts et Techniques.

Moore, Bruce (1905–1980)

Born in rural Kansas, Moore moved to Wichita in 1917, then east to study at the Pennsylvania Academy of the Fine Arts. In 1926 he returned to Wichita, where he produced some of his finest animal sculptures in a pronounced Art Deco style. Between 1929 and 1931 Moore lived in Paris, his work increasingly less dependent on the Art Deco idiom for its decorative vernacular. He then moved to Connecticut, where he worked as an assistant to James Earle Fraser, while pursuing his own projects.

Moreux, Jean-Charles (1889–1956)

Moreux was born in Mont-Saint-Vincent in Burgundy and moved to Paris, where he established himself at 11 *bis* rue de Rome. A renowned architect, he designed a wide variety of private residences, villas and hotels for clients from all income groups, occupying himself with every aspect of interior decoration.

Ultramodern, if not 'minimalist', Moreux's furniture can be defined as fiercely rational and formal: no ornamentation was included beyond the selection of suitable veneers. He exhibited only once at the Salons (1924), receiving frequent magazine coverage, especially in *Les Arts de la Maison* and *Répertoire du Goût Moderne*. In a 1927 article in *Art et Décoration*, Moreux maintained he had solved the problems of modern construction by: 'the maximum use of space, with sliding doors, sash windows, folding tables on the walls and furniture hung from the ceiling by rope'. Superficial decoration was proscribed, Moreaux claiming to have 'banished high fantasy and extreme audacity'.

Gone was every semblance of ornamentation; in its place were razor-sharp angles and functionalism. Despite these spartan tendencies, Moreux was persuaded to design a lavish table for Jacques *Doucet's studio in Neuilly, in which he incorporated a sumptuous mix of macassar ebony, crocodile skin, ivory, *galuchat* and crystal within an illuminated table. At the 1925 *Exposition Internationale, Moreux designed the furniture in a library exhibited by Auguste Perret.

Muller Frères

Members of the Muller family, who came from Kalhausen (Moselle), were traditional glassworkers. The two oldest brothers, Désiré and Eugène, joined Gallé's workshops in Nancy c. 1885 and were followed there by three other brothers, Henri, Pierre and Victor. When Henri established his own glass workshop c. 1895 on rue Sainte-Anne in Lunéville, he was joined shortly thereafter by his siblings, all by this time skilled glass decorators. Muller Frères had its vessels blown to its instructions at the Hinzelin glassworks in nearby Croismare, which it then decorated at the Lunéville works, employing carved, etched and cased glass techniques.

The firm exhibited at the 1908 Franco–British exhibition in London and at the 1910 Exposition de la Verrerie et Cristallerie Artistique in Paris. In the same year Muller Frères moved into larger premises

in Lunéville on rue de la Barre, which the brothers closed during the First World War when they dispersed to other glass shops. After the armistice, they returned to Lunéville and in 1919 purchased the Hinzelin plant. Production now focused on commercial wares, with mass-produced ceiling fixtures, bowls and shades in addition to a line of acid-etched wares with sandwiched colour or crushed foil decoration, some with highly stylized Art Deco imagery. The Wall Street financial crash of 1929, and the Depression that followed, forced Muller Frères to cease production in 1933; it closed its doors finally in 1936.

Müller-Munk, Peter (1907–1967)

Born in Germany, Müller-Munk studied at the University of Berlin and the city's Kunstgewerbeschule under the noted silversmith Waldemar Raemisch. After participating in the 1925 *Exposition Internationale, he emigrated to the USA the following year. There he designed briefly for Tiffany & Co. before setting up his own studio in 1927 for manufacturing handmade silver, which he produced for a private clientele.

Müller-Munk participated in the 1928 Macy's International Exposition of Art in Industry and the 1929 Modern American Design in Metal show at the Newark Museum. In an article in *The Studio* in October 1929, he called for greater harmony of design and technique, criticizing contemporary manufacturers in the silver and associated metal industries for striving to imitate handmade pieces with mass-production methods instead of adapting their product designs to display the strengths of their machines. Müller-Munk despised the application of handmade ornament to a spun or stamped object, and advocated simple lines and a refined Neoclassicism. He claimed, further, that the machine would not put the silversmith out of business, a prophecy that soon proved emphatically wrong as consumer

demand for silver dried up in the Depression. Perhaps for this reason, he entered the industrial design field in the early 1930s.

In his new vocation, Müller-Munk designed industrial metalware for the Revere Copper & Brass Co., and a range of other appliances, such as the well-known 'Waring' blender, in plastics, as well as interiors and transport vehicles. He is known best for his 'Normandie' pitcher, whose streamlined shape was inspired by the ocean liner's stacks (funnels). This, he claimed, provided 'a perfect harmony of efficiency, material and the machine process'.

From 1935 to 1945, Müller-Munk taught at the Carnegie Institute of Technology in Pittsburgh, leaving to establish the industrial design firm Peter Müller-Munk Associates. His exhibit at the 1946 Philadelphia Art Alliance included electrical household goods such as sewing machines and industrial canteens.

Munchley, Robert (*fl.* 1935–43)

Munchley was a member of the Federal Art Project (FAP), a division of the Works Project Administration (WPA) implemented by President Franklin Delano Roosevelt from 1935 to 1943 to subsidize American artists during the Depression. In addition to posters, the FAP commissioned thousands of murals for public buildings, all of which were intended to generate optimism. Munchley, like others, tried to instil in his poster art a positive attitude through dynamic stylized images of labourers, education, travel and, in the early 1940s, the war effort.

Murray, Keith Day Pierce (1892–1981)

Born in Mount Eden, near Auckland, New Zealand, to a stationer and his wife, Murray studied architecture at King's College in Remuera, Auckland, before moving to England with his family in 1906. At the advent of the First World War, he enlisted in the Royal Flying Corps and was awarded the Military Cross in 1917.

Returning to London, Murray completed his architectural studies at the Architectural Association in Bedford Square in 1921 before joining the firm of Simpson & Ayrton.

Toward the end of 1931, when architectural commissions were scarce, Murray developed designs for contemporary glassware, ceramics and silverware. His initial designs for glass were rejected as they were not suitable for the production process at the Whitefriars Glassworks. During his search for other manufacturers, he was put in touch with Felton Wreford, the London showroom manager of Josiah Wedgwood & Sons Ltd, of Burslem, Staffordshire, with whom a formal arrangement was drawn up in 1933 for Murray to submit designs for ceramic vases and tablewares.

Murray's first pieces, thrown and finished on a lathe, were conceived on architectural lines and featured lathe-cut horizontal ridges or incised bands that made them appear machine-made. For these pieces, a range of matt overall glazes was chosen – the glazes having been created earlier at the firm by Norman Wilson and advertised as 'Siennese' – in colours including grey, straw, deep ivory, green, turquoise, black basalt, champagne and silken 'moonstone'.

Murray's models were included in Wedgwood's displays at the 1933 British Industrial Art in Relation to the Home exhibition at Dorland Hall, London, and in the same year at the fifth Venice Triennale. Two years later he exhibited pieces at the Royal Academy of Art and at the Medici Gallery in Grafton Street. In addition to his ceramics for Wedgwood, Murray designed industrial glassware for Stevens & Williams and silverware for Mappin & Webb in the 1930s. Throughout the decade, Murray added new models for vases, bowls and beakers in simple Modernist shapes, but toward the end of the 1930s he began to revert to his architectural practice.

Keith Day Pierce Murray

(*opposite left*) Cocktail shaker set in silver designed for Mappin & Webb and manufactured in Japan, c. 1935.

(*opposite right*) Vases in glazed earthenware, shapes No. 4217, 4200 and 3842, for Josiah Wedgwood & Sons Ltd, mid-1930s.

Muller Frères

(*below*) Vases in etched cameo glass, 1920s.

Peter Müller-Munk

(*right*) 'Silvermode' pitcher in silver-plated metal manufactured by Poole Silver Co., Taunton, Massachusetts, c. 1934.

Peter Müller-Munk

(*right*) Coffee service in silver, gold and ebony, c. 1930.

Robert Munchley
(*above*) *Work with Care*, lithographic
poster for the Works Project
Administration (WPA), 1930s.

Jacques (Lehmann) Nam
(*right*) *Naja dressé*, wood panel
in lacquer and gold- and silver-
leaf with intaglio-carved
decoration, 1920s.

(*below*) *Singes*, wood panel
in lacquer, in ebonized wood
and burr wood frame, 1920s.

Jacques (Lehmann) Nam
(*right*) Four-panel lacquered
wood screen, *c.* 1930.

Mybor

The Mybor carpet retail business was founded by
Marie Cuttoli (née Bordes) (1879–1973) in her home in
Algiers, c. 1910, and then moved to nearby Sétif. After
the First World War Mybor specialized in avant-garde
carpet and tapestry designs commissioned from artists
such as Jean Lurçat, EILEEN GRAY, Francis *Jourdain
and IVAN DA SILVA BRUHNS, which were offered through
the Mybor gallery that opened in Paris in 1926. Later
the firm introduced a series of woven *tapis de maîtres*
designed by the era's foremost painters and sculptors,
including Pablo Picasso, Fernand Léger, Joan Miro,
Raoul Dufy, Jean Arp, Louis Marcoussis and Josef *Csáky.

In the late 1920s the firm commissioned various
tapestry manufacturers in Aubusson to execute its
designs in an attempt to revive the local carpet-making
industry, then in decline. In 1929 Lurçat was retained
to design a new Mybor store at 17 rue Vignon in Paris,
where paintings and decorative objects were shown.

N

Nam, Jacques (Lehmann) (1881–1974)

Painter, book and fashion plate illustrator, sculptor
and poet, Nam is today known especially for his
depictions of cats, rendered in a wide array of materials,
including pencil, charcoal, gouache, pastel and bronze.
A member of the *Société Nationale des Beaux-Arts
from 1906, and later also of the *Salon d'Automne,
he is known in an Art Deco context primarily for his
depictions of wild animals in their natural habitat, such
as monkeys and gorillas, which served as screens and
murals. Among Nam's graphic works were illustrations
for *La Vie Parisienne* (c. 1915) and woodblocks for the
satirical revue *La Baïonette*.

Nathan, Fernand (1875–post 1950)

Born in Marseilles, Nathan studied architecture,
painting and sculpture before settling on a career as

an interior decorator. On moving to Paris, he made
his Salon début in 1913 and established a studio at
112 boulevard de Courcelles.

Nathan designed entire rooms – the furnishings
manufactured by a wide range of artisans. Stylistically,
his furniture drew on English Regency, Restauration
and Louis-Philippe influences. The pieces that he
showed at the Salons in the early 1920s were light
and charming, with unpretentious forms and light floral
marquetry. By 1926 his furniture had lost its earlier
appeal and critics no longer reviewed it in their Salon
coverage. Nathan's wallpapers and carpets, however,
which dominated his interiors, provided the vibrancy
that his furniture lacked; they incorporated repeating
patterns of large flowers that imparted colour
in a manner similar to the styles of L'École MARTINE
and SÜE ET MARE.

As an independent designer, Nathan negotiated
with various retailers to market his furnishings,
including *Primavera, Bianchini–Férier, Cornille Frères
and Les Galeries Lafayette. At the 1925 *Exposition
Internationale, he served as an architect, designing
boutiques for Les Établissements Florina and La
Compagnie des Perles Électriques, also contributing
to their interiors, for which his furniture was executed
by Jeist and L'Art du Bois. In the Ambassade Française
pavilion, Nathan joined a host of co-members in
decorating the Grand Salon.

Nathan-Garamond, Jacques (1910–2001)

Paris-born Nathan-Garamond was a versatile graphic
artist whose body of work included posters, magazine
covers and sales catalogues. His clients included Mazda,
the Ducretet–Thompson Co., Telefunken, Cinzano and
Air France. Posters such as 'L'Habitation' for exhibitions
at the Grand Palais in 1934 and 1936, reveal
CASSANDRE's influence in their angular images and
palette. In 1951 Nathan-Garamond became a founder-
member of the Alliance Graphique International (AGI).

Navarre, Henri (1885–1970/1)

Born in Paris, Navarre studied architecture and
woodcarving under his father. He attended the École
Bernard Palissy in his native city, apprenticed with
a gold- and silversmith, studied at the École des
Beaux-Arts in Paris and took a stained-glass course.
Now a multimedia artist–craftsman, from 1924
Navarre focused on glass, which he exhibited at the
Salons from 1927.

Influenced by MAURICE MARINOT, Navarre worked
with massive thick-walled glass, favouring plain simple
shapes, which he pressed rather than threw. The
essence of his creations lay in their internal decoration,
characterized by swirls and whorls of colour, internal
granulations and *intercalaire* textures. He created
these with powdered metal oxides that were patterned
on the **marver** and then encased within the outer
layer of the *paraison*.

In addition to a large number of vessels, Navarre's
repertoire included large glass sculptures – for example,
a figure of Christ for the chapel on the liner *Île-de-
France* (1927), a large gate for the 1925 Exposition
Internationale, windows, portraits of his wife and
African-inspired masks. His first exhibit of vases was
staged at EDGAR BRANDT's gallery, after which he
switched to Maison *Geo. Rouard. His later glassware
was executed at the Verrerie de la Plaine Saint-Denis,
near Paris.

Nics Frères

Nothing is known of the early years of Michel and
Jules Nics beyond that they were born in Hungary.
On moving to Paris, they became naturalized French
citizens and opened a metal workshop at 98 avenue
Félix-Faure in the early 1920s.

Exhibiting through the Salons of the *Société
des Artistes Français, a high percentage of the work
of Nics Frères was architectural: gates, grilles, elevator
cages, ramps and shop fronts, including a front for

Marcello Nizzoli
Campari, lithographic poster,
1926.

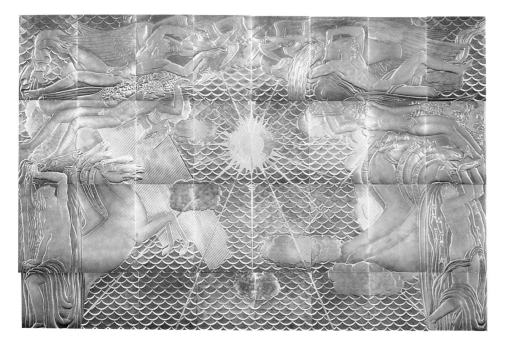

Normandie

(*left*) *The Chariot of Aurora*, 32-panel mural in wood designed by Jean Dupas and executed in gold and silver lacquer by Jean Dunand, for the Grand Salon on the ocean liner *Normandie*, c. 1935.

Nics Frères

(*right*) Gate in wrought iron, 1920s.

the premises of the Société Anonyme des Gants. Smaller items included light fixtures, consoles, *guéridons* and fanlights. Examples of the firm's work, commissioned by such architects as Sébille, Azéma, Petit and Grossard, were illustrated in two editions of *La Ferronnerie Moderne*, published by Charles Moreau c. 1926.

At the 1925 *Exposition Internationale Nics Frères took a stand on the Pont Alexandre III, elsewhere providing wrought-iron furnishings for a hairdressing salon designed by JACQUES-ÉMILE RUHLMANN. Never overly ornate, much of the firm's ironwork was in an angular style embellished with symmetrical volutes and spirals. A deeply *martelé* (hammered) finish served as a further identifying hallmark.

Nielsen, Harald (1892–1977). *See* Jensen.

Nizzoli, Marcello (1887–1969)

An Italian graphic artist, Nizzoli employed a bold palette and catchy typography in his posters for Campari, Moto Sacoche, Citroën and the OM roadster in the inter-war years. By the 1950s he had become a successful industrial designer, producing a wide range of machines for Olivetti and other manufacturers of office and household appliances, including the Diaspron typewriter, Lettera 22 portable typewriter and Lydia MK2 sewing machine.

Normandie

This luxury ocean liner made its maiden voyage from Le Havre on 29 May 1935, gaining New York harbour on 3 June, a trans-Atlantic record at an average speed of more than 30 knots per hour. The *Normandie* arrived for the last time at its New York berth on 28 August 1939, four days after Germany's invasion of Poland precipitated the Second World War, and consequently was unable to make the return trip to Le Havre.

In 1941, after Pearl Harbor had been bombed, the United States government commandeered the *Normandie* for use as a troop carrier. Conversion began on 24 December 1941; the furnishings were to be stripped and stored. On 9 February, however, a welder's acetylene torch ignited a pile of hessian-wrapped life jackets, setting the Grand Salon on fire. Firefighters pumped in so much water than the vessel capsized. Some eighteen months later the hull was towed to Newark and sold as scrap. The rest of the ship, including its surviving furnishings, was sold by the government in a series of public auctions between 1942 and 1943. Lost or dispersed were major works by JEAN DUNAND, JEAN DUPAS, Ernest-Marius *Sabino, Jules *Leleu, Louis *Süe, *Dominique, René *Prou and many others. In recent years several pieces have emerged at auction, generating great nostalgia as poignant reminders of France's golden era of ocean liners.

During the inter-war years, the French government had sponsored and subsidised a string of luxury passenger ships as emblems of national pride, starting with the *Paris* in 1921. Described variously by an ecstatic and jingoistic press as floating palaces, museums of decorative arts, 'dream machines', or, in the theoretical context of *Le Corbusier, as *machines à habiter*, the ocean liners afforded France's foremost interior designers an excellent international showcase. As such, they became extensions of the annual Paris Salons. The interior of the *Paris* was, in fact, organised by the Société de l'Art Français Moderne, the furnishings of the cabins and public areas parcelled out to its members. After the *Paris* came the *Île-de-France*, *Lafayette*, *Le Champlain*, and *Le Colombie*, each in its turn heralded as being more splendid than its predecessor.

As in the case of the *Normandie*, reality often failed to survive the dream. *L'Atlantique*, launched from Bordeaux in September 1931 to service South American ports with its sister ships, the *Massilia* and *Lutétia*, was gutted by fire within fifteen months. A substantial amount of the finest of modern French decorative arts was lost. The next in France's proud line of 'largest, fastest, grandest and most modern' was the *Normandie*, even more unsinkable, its promoters promised, than the ill-fated *L'Atlantique*.

NV Vereenigde Glasfabriek Leerdam

The Royal Dutch Glass Works was established in 1765 in Leerdam, near Utrecht, to produce tablewares, bottles and ornamental crystal. Under the direction of P. M. Cochius from 1912, the firm received no recognition until c. 1915, when it approached designers to create lines of modern glass for mass-production; those commissioned included Cornelius de Lorm, C. J. Lanooy, the architects Hendrik Petrus Berlage and K. P .C. de Bazel and, from 1922 to 1923, Chris Lebeau. Around 1925 NV Vereenigde Glasfabriek Leerdam established the Unica studio, where it developed free-form modern glassware; initially the studio operated under Berlage, who was succeeded by Andries Dirk *Copier. The firm became a part of (Dutch) United Glassworks in 1938.

O

Öhrström, Edwin (1906–1994)

Educated at the Institute of Technology and the Royal Academy of Art in Stockholm, Öhrström arrived at *Orrefors in 1936 as an accomplished sculptor and industrial artist. Within a year of his arrival he had introduced *Ariel*, a variation on the traditional *Graal* technique. Öhrström's initial array of Ariel pieces, in heavily walled crystal decorated with Impressionist images of long-necked tribal women, birds and animals, were included in Orrefors's 1937 catalogue. The images were not new to canvas but were deemed progressive on glass. A similar range of colourless Ariel pieces depicted spidery people and animals in silvery air bubbles that recalled the Surrealist abstractions

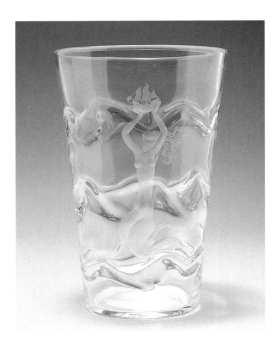

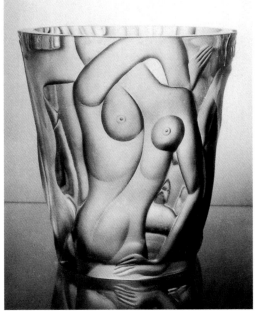

of Salvador Dalí. Öhrström's versatility manifested itself also in a range of crystal vases decorated with engraved themes, such as ballerinas and Viking warriors, on the obverse only.

In the 1940s Öhrström continued to generate a wide range of deeply blasted Ariel models. Several were embellished with repeating geometric patterns, such as cubes or triangles, which accented the refractive powers of the glass. A classic, 'The Gondolier' (also called 'Serenade'), appeared in the mid-1940s, blending light wit with powerful imagery. Later Öhrström introduced heavy globular forms into his designs for functional objects.

The diversity of Öhrström's designs continued in the 1950s: selections of Ariel models were interspersed with lightly engraved crystal wares and undecorated household items such as stoppered bottles and stemware. Öhrström left Orrefors in 1958 and retired to Stockholm, which boasts several of his works, including a 37.5 metre glass pillar on Sergels Torg.

Old, Maxime (1910–1991)

The son and grandson of cabinet-makers, Old was apprenticed in one of JACQUES-ÉMILE RUHLMANN's cabinetry shops after graduating from the *École Boulle. A generation younger than most of the artists who embraced the Art Deco idiom in the inter-war years, his furniture designs in the late 1930s, while indeterminately classical, showed a modern stylistic tendency in their well-balanced and sober lines; for example, in the massive Cubist-inspired chairs that Old later designed for the Marhaba Hall in Casablanca (1954).

Around 1960 Old introduced metal into his many commissions for ministries, for the French ambassador in the Hague and for the French Legation Building in Helsinki. He exhibited regularly at the Paris Salons, including those of the *Salon d'Automne, *Société des Artistes Décorateurs, *Société Nationale des Beaux-Arts and the Salon des Arts Ménagers.

Orloff, Chana (1888–1968)

Born in Tsare-Konstantinovka, Ukraine, Orloff emigrated with her family in 1905 to Palestine, moving again in 1910 to Paris. There she enrolled at the École Nationale Supérieure des Arts Décoratifs and studied sculpture at the Académie Russe in Montparnasse, where she made the acquaintance of the circle of immigrant Modernists who resided there. Orloff met Amedeo Modigliani in 1912 and made her début at the *Salon d'Automne the next year. In 1916 she exhibited alongside Henri Matisse, Georges Rouault and Kees van Dongen at the Galerie Bernheim-Jeune.

From 1919 to 1924 Orloff undertook her first portrait commissions – many of Paris celebrities – in which she displayed a very personal style that mixed Cubism with realism. The busts, although made up of a series of flat planes, were recognizable as portraits. Early works were in carved wood; later ones were in bronze, marble or stone.

Orloff also created stylized animals reminiscent of the work of JAN AND JOËL MARTEL and François *Pompon. In 1925 she became a naturalized French citizen, and again exhibited at the Salon d'Automne, at which she was elected a *chevalier* of the French Légion d'Honneur. From 1942 to 1945, during the Nazi occupation of Paris, she lived in exile in Switzerland, where she created some fifty sculptures, many of which she displayed at the Galerie Georges Moos in Geneva. In 1949 Orloff left for Israel, where from 1950 to 1960 she modelled several memorial commissions, working in a variety of media.

Orrefors

The Orrefors factory began in 1726 as an ironworks on a stream flowing from Lake Orrenas in the glass-making region of Småland in southern Sweden. The name Orrefors was a combination of *orre*, an indigenous blackcock or grouse, and *fors*, the Swedish word for a ford or river crossing. In 1898 the plant

was converted into a glassworks for the manufacture of medicine and ink bottles, window panes and cheap domestic glass; this line of production was subsequently discontinued.

Orrefors was acquired in 1913 by Johan Ekman, an industrialist from Gothenburg, who, with the firm's manager Albert Ahlin, changed Orrefors's direction to decorative glass. The firm also hired the artist–designers Simon *Gate (in 1916) and Edward *Hald (in 1917). Neither of them had any knowledge of glass-making and both therefore had to learn appropriate techniques from Orrefors's master blower Knut Bergqvist.

Initial designs were inspired by the Art Nouveau floral confections of Émile Gallé and his École de Nancy, and by the work of Val Saint-Lambert. Almost immediately the technique of *Graal* was developed, in which superimposed layers of coloured glass were applied to a small layered blank or 'stock' and decorated by engraving. The blank was then reheated, blown up into its final shape and encased in an outer sleeve of clear crystal, following the technique perfected in the 18th century by France's three classical paperweight houses – Baccarat, Saint-Louis and Clichy. To subsidize its 'Graal' line of art glass, day-to-day production at Orrefors in the 1920s, as now, comprised a large volume of utilitarian household crystal with cut or engraved decoration.

Orrefors participated in the 1923 Gothenburg Exhibition and the 1925 *Exposition Internationale in Paris, where it received a *grand prix*. Later in the decade the firm also staged exhibitions of its works in Amsterdam, Barcelona and New York, while establishing agencies in European cities and as far afield as South Africa and Australia.

The functionalist philosophy that evolved at Orrefors following the 1930 Stockholm Exhibition helped it to ride out the Depression. In keeping with the austere times, and corresponding Funkis

Orrefors

(*above*) Panel in etched glass designed by Vicke Lindstrand, probably 1930s.

Maxime Old

(*right and below*) Low table in oak veneered in palisander with leather top and gilt-bronze mounts, 1930s.

Jean Pascaud
(*below*) Armoire in rosewood, lacquer and gold leaf with gilt-bronze mounts, *c.* 1935.

Orsi
(*right*) *Théâtre de l'Étoile, La Revue Nègre*, lithographic poster, 1928.

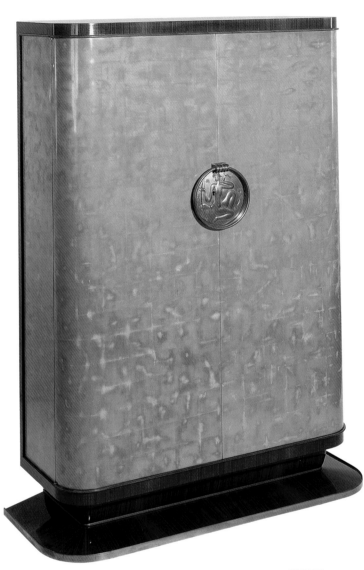

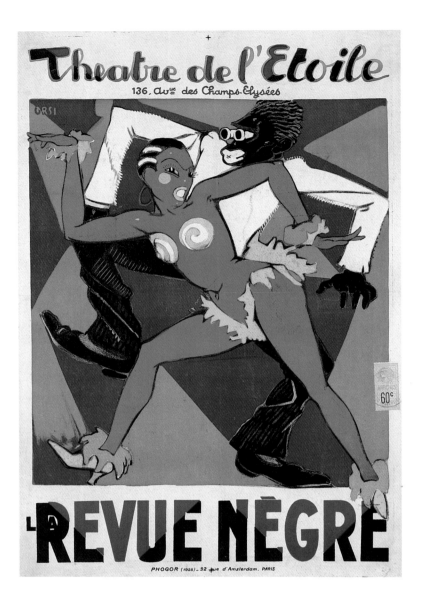

Jean Pascaud
(*right*) Cabinet in palisander with parquetry veneer and bronze mounts, in collaboration with Jean Debarre (sculptor), *c.* 1937.

functionalist design ideology, the public was asked to reconsider the aesthetics of glass. The wafer-thin crystalware of the 1920s, with its complex engraved ornamentation, became outmoded. A thicker variety of glass was introduced, either undecorated or lightly cut, rather than engraved. Less was now more.

'Graal' was followed in 1937 by the *Ariel* technique, derived from the word 'air spirit' and created by Edwin *Öhrström, who was at Orrefors for 22 years. In an extension of the *Graal* process, various parts of the design were sandblasted with deep channels or holes, leaving trapped air bubbles in the recesses, which formed part of the design. Later came 'Kraka' (1944), 'Ravenna' (1948), and 'Centrifuge' or 'Fuga', all techniques developed initially by Sven Palmqvist, who had joined Orrefors in 1936.

Orsi (1889–1947)

Born in Le Raincy (Seine-Saint-Denis), Orsi studied painting and design under Paul Sérusier and Maurice Denis. He later became interested in advertising and posters, which occupied a large part of his work. More than one thousand of his posters were published, executed in a lively, colourful and simplified style. Many were for cabarets and music halls, such as Le Grand Guignol and Théâtre de l'Étoile, or for individual stars, including Josephine Baker, Falconetti, Mistinguett and Dranem.

Oscar Heyman Bros.

Oscar and Nathan Heyman were born in Russia and completed five-year apprenticeships in the jewelry business under their uncle in Kharkov, who was a supplier of objects to Fabergé. In 1906 they emigrated to the USA, where they settled in New York. Fortunate to have learned the skills of making platinum jewelry at a time when the metal was becoming fashionable, they were joined in 1912 by their brother Harry, likewise a skilled jeweller, forming the family partnership of Oscar

Heyman Bros. Eventually the three youngest brothers – George, Louis and William – also joined the firm, which for seventy-five years offered well-designed and crafted jewelry. Its designs emphasized the stones, which were usually set in platinum, but sometimes in gold as a concession to the dictates of fashion.

Ostertag

Maison Ostertag was founded after the First World War by a Swiss jeweller, Arnold Ostertag, in the Place Vendôme, Paris. Maison Ostertag enjoyed rapid success because of the quality of its stones and the popularity of a series of jewelry inspired by Indian prototypes, which especially featured hard stones, such as jade, mounted in gold.

The firm's most distinctive designs incorporated rubies, emeralds and sapphires which, when engraved and juxtaposed in bright floral compositions, gave rise to the phrase 'tutti-frutti' within the marketplace. Maison Ostertag commissioned the famous Paris clockmaker Georges Verger to produce a range of innovative objects of *vertu* – clocks, stands, frames and watches. (Verger worked in partnership with his brother Henri for many of the top jewelry houses in the 1920s.)

A measure of the pre-eminence of Maison Ostertag was afforded by its invitation to participate in the 1929 Exposition des Arts de la Bijouterie, Joaillerie, Orfèvrerie at the Musée Galliera in Paris. Maison Ostertag did not re-open after the Second World War.

P

Paris. See Normandie.

Pascaud, Jean (1903–1996)

Born in Rouen, Pascaud graduated in engineering in 1924 from the École Centrale des Arts et Manufactures. An interest in the decorative arts led him into furniture design and increasingly, from the late 1920s, into the

broader field of interior design. His address at the time was listed as 1 rue de la Villa l'Évêque. A traditionalist, Pascaud eschewed the tubular metal and glass slabs then in vogue: for him simplicity and technical virtuosity represented contemporary taste and the non-imitative continuation of tradition. Today, his furniture, crafted in woods such as violetwood, palisander and American walnut, appears ultramodern, indistinguishable from that of Jean Royère, André-Léon *Arbus and *Dominique.

Pascaud presented his conservative furniture in surroundings that gave it necessary warmth and ambience. The walls of a 1935 bedroom, for example, were lined in mauve fabric, its doors lacquered in gold, its linens and upholstery in grey silk. Reactions were divided: some critics saw this as preciosity; others as warmth and luxuriance. Pascaud's participation at the Salons was limited to the early 1930s; he later concentrated on developing an elite clientele which included government officials and foreign ambassadors. Commissions for the ocean liners *Pasteur* and *Normandie* brought prestige. His collaborators included Mme Bouissou (decorative glass panels), Pierre Lardin (engraved mirrors) and Léon Lang (panelling).

Patou, Jean (1880–1936)

Patou was born in Normandy and joined his uncle's fur company in 1907. In 1912 he opened La Maison Parry, which offered tailoring, dressmaking and furs, but sold it in 1914 to an American. After Patou was demobilized in 1918, he established his own couture business on rue Saint-Florentin, Paris.

Recognized as the designer who did away with the flapper look by lengthening the skirt and returning to a natural waistline, Patou also designed high-end sportswear for the tennis star Suzanne Lenglen and is credited as the inventor of the knitted bathing suit. His designs were geared especially toward wealthy

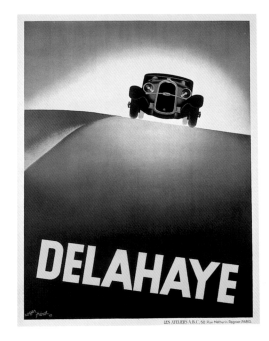

American women. When the stock market crashed, taking with it the luxury goods and fashion industry, Maison Patou survived through its perfumes, including 'Joy' and 'Sublime'. 'Joy' was created at the height of the Depression in 1935 by Henri Alméras for those of Patou's former clients who could no longer afford his *haute couture* clothes. Each ounce purported to contain the essence of ten thousand flowers, including Bulgarian roses, Grasse jasmine and the *Michelia champaca* 'Alba' tree – the last touted as the source of the world's most exquisite fragrance. On Patou's death, his sister and her husband, M. and Mme Barbas, continued the business. Maison Patou's perfume licence is now owned by Proctor & Gamble.

Peche, Dagobert (1887–1923)

Born in Saint Michael, near Salzburg, Peche studied architecture at the Technische Hochschule in Vienna from 1906 to 1908, and then at the Akademie der Bildenden Kunst until 1911. By 1913, as a freelance designer in Vienna, he had produced textile designs for Johann Backhausen & Sohne and Philipp Haas & Sohne, wallpapers for Max Schmidt and ceramics for the porcelain manufactory of Josef *Boch. In 1913 he made his public début with a display of wallpapers and a lady's salon at an exhibition in the Österreichisches Museum für Kunst und Industrie, and displayed his interiors in a Secession exhibition. As a member of the Wiener Werkstätte from 1915 until 1923, Peche continued to participate in exhibitions, including the 1920 Vienna Kunstschau and the 1922 Deutsche Gewerbeschau in Munich. Between 1917 and 1919, he managed the Zurich branch of the Wiener Werkstätte.

One of most versatile and prolific decorative artists of the early 20th century, in spite of a tragically short life, Peche produced almost three thousand designs for the Wiener Werkstätte across the entire gamut of the applied arts, including furniture, silver, ceramics, glass, textiles, jewelry, bookbindings,

costumes and wallpapers. Much of his work was characterized by dense and rich ornamentation that drew on Austrian Baroque and Rococo antecedents for its subject matter. Other designs were playful and modern, rendered in bright colours. In the years immediately after the First World War, Peche and Josef Hoffmann abandoned the Wiener Werkstätte's pre-war geometric style for an exuberant and mannered approach that was more in keeping with the decorative vernacular of the Paris Salons.

Perot, Roger (1908–1976)

Nothing is known of Perot beyond that he was a French architect who designed a handful of automobile posters in an appealing Art Deco style. In particular, he produced a poster of the Delahaye roadster, in which the haloed vehicle is shown at an angle as it crests a distant hill. Perot also designed an automobile poster for Ford.

Perriand, Charlotte (1903–1999). *See under* Furniture and Interior Design.

Perzel, Jean (1892–1986). *See under* Lighting.

Petit, Philippe (d. 1945). *See* DIM.

Poertzel, Otto (1876–1963)

Born in Scheibe (Thüringerwald), Germany, the son of a porcelain designer–decorator, Poertzel studied under Professor R. Möller before setting up his own studio in 1900 in Coburg. There he created works shown at the 1904 St Louis World's Fair and the 1910 Brussels Exposition Universelle et Internationale. Poertzel moved in 1908 to Munich to study at the city's academy with Adolf von Hildebrandt and Professor Erwin Kurz, the latter at the time a renowned teacher and sculptor of public statuary.

Poertzel is best known for his 1920s and 1930s **chryselephantine** statuettes of cabaret, burlesque

and circus performers, film stars and winsome young women promenading with their dogs. Among his commissions were portrait busts for members of the reigning ducal family of Saxe-Coburg-Gotha, garden statuary and monuments. Many of Poertzel's smaller decorative pieces, modelled from photographs, were made by Preiss–Kassler or Rosenthal & Maeder.

Appointed an honorary professor by the state – the reason that some of his pieces are signed 'Professor Poertzel' – Poertzel served on the Coburg Art Association committee for some twenty-seven years, and received other honours such as the Knight's Cross of the Bulgarian National Order for Civil Merit.

Poillerat, Gilbert (1902–1988)

Poillerat was born at Mer (Loir-et-Cher) to parents who owned the town's railway station hotel. In 1921 he received his diploma as an engraver and **chaser** from the *École Boulle in Paris. For the following six years he was a model designer in EDGAR BRANDT's workshops, where he worked closely with the foreman, Roger Caussimon, and married one of the secretaries, Rosette.

In 1927 Poillerat joined Baudet, Donon & Roussel, a firm specializing in lifts and construction frameworks. He was appointed head of its newly formed decorative ironwork division, where he oversaw the manufacture of grilles, tables, screens, andirons and lighting. Commissions included the doors for the Palais Chaillot, grilles for the Bibliothèque Nationale and the Hôtel des Tabacs, grilles and lighting for the restaurant at the Eiffel Tower and ironwork for numerous private residences. In 1934 Poillerat began to design jewelry for the couturier Jacques Heim. The following year he executed patinated bronze doors for the swimming pool on the *Normandie*.

Poillerat's highly distinctive style drew its inspiration from the Louis XIV era in its choice of *flambeaux*, arabesques, scrolled acanthus and a host of other 17th-century motifs. After the Second World War,

Otto Poertzel
(*right*) Figurine in cold-painted bronze and carved ivory, on a marble base, 1920s.

Gilbert Poillerat
(*far right*) Console in patinated and parcel-gilt wrought iron with marble top, *c.* 1940.

(*below left*) Four-panel screen in silvered- and gilt-metal, for an interior by André-Léon Arbus, *c.* 1935.

Otto Poertzel
(*below right*) *Snake Charmer*, figure in cold-painted bronze and carved ivory, 1920s.

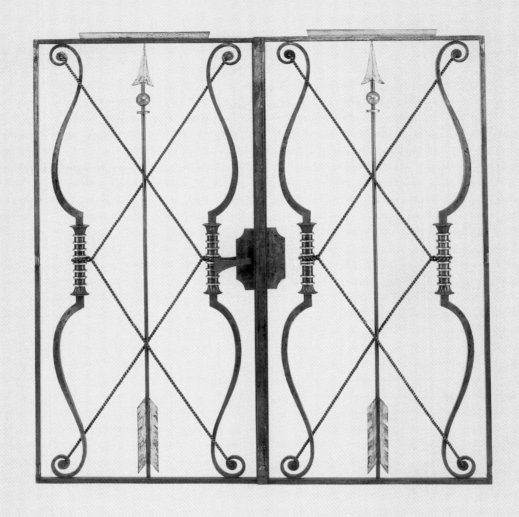

Gilbert Poillerat

(*opposite above*) Pair of gates in patinated and parcel-gilt wrought iron, probably 1940s.

(*opposite below*) *Arc, flèches et passementeries*, occasional table in patinated and parcel-gilt wrought iron, with marble top, *c*. 1943.

(*below*) Pair of andirons in wrought iron, 1930s.

(*right*) Wall ornament in patinated and parcel-gilt wrought iron, late 1930s.

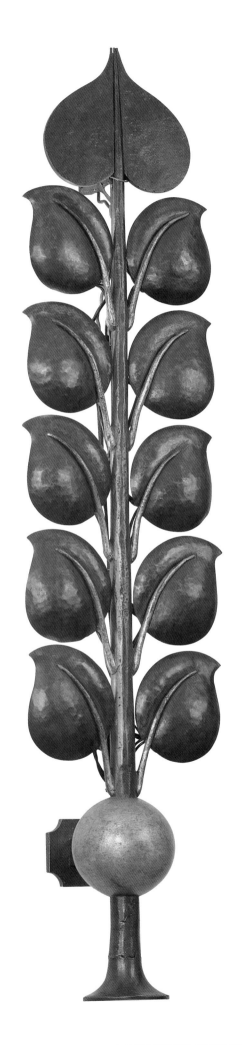

Pomone

(*right*) Mantel clock in gilt-
wood, designed by Albert
Guénot, marketed by the Au
Bon Marché department store,
Paris, 1920s.

(*below*) Mantel clock in gilt-
wood, marketed by the Au Bon
Marché department store,
Paris, 1920s.

LASSITUDE
Robe de diner, de Paul Poiret

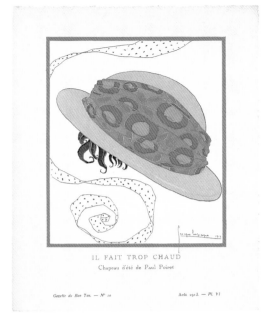

IL FAIT TROP CHAUD
Chapeau d'été de Paul Poiret

he accepted a professorship at the École Nationale Supérieure des Arts Décoratifs in Paris and left Baudet, Donon & Roussel. Between 1945 and 1947 Poillerat presided over the *Société des Artistes Français while collaborating on individual projects or ensembles with his friend Jacques *Adnet and the era's other foremost artist–designers, including Serge Roche, Hubert Yencesse, André-Léon *Arbus, Christian Bérard, Vadim Androusov and Jean Royère.

Poiret, Paul (1879–1944)

Born in Paris, the son of a draper, Poiret revealed from an early age a strong aptitude for drawing and costume design. At the age of nineteen, he was invited by Jacques *Doucet to join his fashion house, where Poiret managed the firm's graphic production and participated in its dress designs. Around 1904, after a brief association with Gaston Worth, Poiret set up his own business, La Maison Poiret, at 5 rue Auber, Paris. There he gained recognition for a new natural look that liberated women from their corsets.

From 1909, in his showroom in a townhouse at the corner of rue du Faubourg Saint-Honoré and avenue Victor-Emmanuel II, Poiret hosted dazzling parties for the city's social elite and avant-garde artists. His signature dress designs at the time included high waistlines, *décolleté* necklines, flowing and shimmering fabrics and turbans and large embroidered coats in contrasting colours. In 1911 he added to his couture business by founding l'École MARTINE, a school of interior decoration for young women, through which he marketed naive and colourful fabric and wallpaper designs created by the pupils.

Although out of style after the First World War, Poiret nevertheless found a way to briefly recapture the public's eye: he introduced three barges – *Amour, Délice* and *Orgue* – on which he staged his display at the 1925 *Exposition Internationale. His address at the time was listed as 1 Rond-Point des Champs-Elysées, Paris.

Pomone (Au Bon Marché)

Pomone was set up in 1922 to serve the Au Bon Marché department store, founded in 1848 by Aristide Boucicaut on rue du Bac, Paris. Paul *Follot was appointed its design director in 1923. He was succeeded in 1928 by René *Prou who, in turn, was replaced in 1932 by Albert Guénot who remained at Pomone until 1955. Among its noted designers in the inter-war years were Mme René Schils, Germaine Labave and Mme Émile Roussel. The studio participated in the 1925 *Exposition Internationale.

Pompon, François (1855–1933)

The son of a French cabinet-maker, Pompon learned the basics of carving at an early age while apprenticed to a marble cutter in Dijon, after which he studied architecture, etching and sculpture. In 1875 he moved to Paris, where he worked as an assistant successively to Antonin Mercié, Jean-Alexandre-Joseph Falguière, René de Saint-Marceaux and, finally, Auguste Rodin. Pompon was encouraged by Rodin to model his own figures – some portraits, but mostly animals – which he rendered in an Impressionistic style similar at the time to that of Rembrandt Bugatti. He later developed a fluid style in which superfluous detailing was systematically pared away.

Pompon is regarded today as the quintessential Art Deco animalier-sculptor, but it was not until 1922, when he was sixty-seven years old, that his work finally gained widespread recognition and acclaim. This recognition was largely due to the exhibition that year of his striding marble figure *Ours Blanc* ('Polar Bear'), which was displayed again at the 1925 *Exposition Internationale and later produced in a porcelain edition by *Sèvres. On his death, Pompon bequeathed more than three hundred examples of his work to the French state, which subsequently established a museum in his name.

Ponti, Giovanni (Gio) (1891–1979)

Having served in the Italian army in the First World War, Ponti received his diploma in architecture from the Politecnico in Milan in 1921, after which he opened an office in the city with fellow architects Mino Fiocchi and Emilio Lancia. Instead of pursuing a career in architecture, however, in 1923 Ponti accepted the position of artistic director at *Richard–Ginori, where his father-in-law was employed. Ponti's job was to modernize the firm's porcelain production. Success was immediately forthcoming: the display of his ceramics won the firm its first award at the decorative arts exhibition in Monza that year. Further prizes followed at subsequent Milan and Monza triennales.

Ponti continued to design ceramics for Richard–Ginori until 1930. He adopted a mannered style in which he sought a synthesis between the traditional values of Italian Classicism and the structural logic of the Machine Age. Archaeological finds and architectural elements drawn from Renaissance majolica, such as columns, pedestals and arches, were repeated themes that Ponti translated in a witty and eye-catching contemporary style on his vases and dishes. He described some of these pieces as 'Palladium'. Also evident in his designs is the stylistic influence of the Vienna Secession and Wiener Werkstätte.

Recognized as Italy's most prominent 20th-century decorative-arts designer, Ponti also promoted Modernism as a writer and as a professor in the architecture faculty at the Milan Politecnico from 1936 to 1961. He founded the widely read architecture and design magazine *Domus* in 1928, and authored nine books on architecture and some three hundred articles on related topics.

Ponti designed a prodigious number of post-war household wares for manufacturers such as Cassina, Knoll, Artflex and Techno, including furniture, metalware, glass, ceramics, textiles and light fixtures.

François Pompon

(*below*) *Pintade* in patinated bronze, *c*. 1910–12.

(*bottom*) *Ours blanc* in white marble, *c*. 1922.

Giovanni (Gio) Ponti

(*right*) Vase in glazed porcelain manufactured by Richard–Ginori, *c*. 1930.

Giovanni (Gio) Ponti

(*opposite above*) Vase, model No. 1175, in glazed porcelain, from 'Le Mie Terre' series, manufactured by Richard–Ginori, *c*. 1929.

(*opposite below*) 'Donatella', *coupe* in glazed porcelain, from 'Le Mie Donne' series, manufactured by Richard–Ginori, *c*. 1925–27.

Henry Varnum Poor
Ceramic plate with underglaze decoration on slip clay, *c.* 1930.

His most celebrated design was an espresso coffee machine for La Pavoni in 1948. In 1952 he joined with Antonio Fornaroli and Alberto Rosselli to form the architectural firm Studio Ponti–Fornaroli–Rosselli, which was operational until 1976. Ponti's last major architectural commission was in 1972 for the Denver Art Museum, in association with James Sudler.

Poor, Henry Varnum (1888–1970)
Born in Chapman, Kansas, Poor studied painting at Stanford University (1903–1906), the Slade School of Art in London (1910) and the Académie Julian in Paris (1911). On returning to the USA, he taught art at Stanford from 1911 to 1918 before enlisting during the First World War. After the war, Poor settled in New York.

Unable to survive on the sales of his paintings – his first one-man show in 1920 at the Kevorkian Galleries in New York was a commercial failure – Poor taught himself the craft of ceramics. His technique was to coat the clay model with a white- or cream-coloured *slip*, which was then fired and painted with decorations in one or more metallic oxides, usually cobalt, manganese, copper or iron. From the mid-1920s the addition of a second brown or black slip allowed Poor to articulate his images with carved *sgraffito* detailing, such as cross-hatching, which provided variation in his designs. A final colourless or lightly tinted lead overglaze accompanied the second and final firing.

Poor brought the fundamentals of his formal painting background to his new medium. His compositions – nudes, still-lifes, landscapes and portraits – remained deeply rooted in French Modernist painting, with many subjects showing a Fauve influence. Elsewhere, Paul Cézanne, Georges Braque and Juan Gris appear to have provided inspiration. Poor's ceramic style did not vary greatly; he remained more a painter-on-pottery than a ceramist *per se*, although he was identified repeatedly by contemporary critics as 'the best potter of the time'.

By the winter of 1920 Poor had installed a homemade kick-wheel in his painting studio at Crow House, his rustic home in New City, New York State (in Rockland County, north of Manhattan). By Christmas the following year, a selection of his wares was on sale in the Bel Maison Gallery at Wanamaker's department store. This was followed in 1922 by a one-man show at the Newman Emerson Montross gallery.

Poor participated in various shows around the end of the decade, including the 1928 International Exhibition of Ceramic Art, organized by the American Federation of the Arts at the Metropolitan Museum of Art in New York; 1928 and 1929 exhibitions at the American Designers' Gallery, where he displayed a tiled ceramic bathroom fired by Thomas Maddoc's Sons, a luncheon set and a selection of plaques; and the 1931 Contemporary American Ceramics exhibition at W. & J. Sloane on Fifth Avenue, New York.

Among his diverse achievements, in 1958 Poor wrote *A Book of Pottery: From Mud into Immortality*. In addition to his ceramic household wares, he accepted architectural commissions such as a mural entitled 'Sports' for the Hotel Shelton in Manhattan. Other projects included an eight-tile mural entitled 'Tennis Players and Bathers' for the financier Edgar A. Levy and a fresco for the Department of Justice Building in Washington, DC.

Porteneuve, Alfred (1896–1949)
Trained as an architect, Porteneuve lived and worked in the awesome shadow of his uncle JACQUES-ÉMILE RUHLMANN. Porteneuve appears to have joined the family firm in the early 1920s, and participated in the Hôtel du Collectionneur pavilion at the 1925 *Exposition Internationale; with two other architects (Bourquin and Haranguer), he was responsible for the building's interior architecture. He gained his uncle's confidence and the two collaborated on various interiors from 1926. Porteneuve's special duties

were to design the settings for Ruhlmann's interiors and to coordinate the firm's participation in local and international expositions.

On Ruhlmann's death in November 1933 Porteneuve was charged with the liquidation of the remaining inventory. His uncle had left explicit instructions that the office at 27 rue de Lisbonne be closed and that the name of Ruhlmann & Laurent be discontinued. Porteneuve installed himself nearby at 47 rue de Lisbonne, where he worked under his own name, designing his own models while reproducing a range of models that Ruhlmann had authorized to be made posthumously with the qualifying identification, 'modèle de Ruhlmann édité par Porteneuve'. Porteneuve's own models bore a branded signature, 'A. Porteneuve'. His designs from 1934 were virtually indistinguishable from earlier Ruhlmann prototypes so it is difficult today to determine whether Porteneuve's own preferred style happened to match that of his uncle or whether he continued these designs for commercial reasons.

Before 1934 Porteneuve had sometimes exhibited independently at the Salons of the *Société des Artistes Décorateurs – in 1930, for example, collaborating with Henri *Rapin on the exhibition hall with RENÉ LALIQUE (illuminated fountains), Thonet (garden furniture) and Brunet, Meunie et Cie (fabrics and carpets). At the 1937 Exposition des Arts et Techniques, Porteneuve showed an office for the president of the Syndicat des Soiereries de Lyons and collaborated with JEAN DUNAND in an ensemble in the Société des Artistes Décorateurs exhibit.

Pougheon, Robert-Eugène (1886–1955)
Born in Paris, Pougheon studied under Charles Lameire and Jean-Paul Laurens at the city's École des Beaux-Arts and then at its Académie Julian, where he made his first contact with the Nabi movement. He made his début at the *Société des Artistes Français in 1911, and in the same year was awarded the Theodore Ralli prize. In 1914 Pougheon received the prestigious Prix de Rome; after

Robert-Eugène Pougheon

(*below*) *Femmes et faunes*, oil on canvas, 1920s/1930s.

(*right*) Maquette in ink, chalk and gouche on paper, for the painting *Amazone*, late 1920s.

Alfred Porteneuve

(*below right*) Storage cabinet in macassar ebony and burled amboyna, with ivory key escutcheon, 1930s.

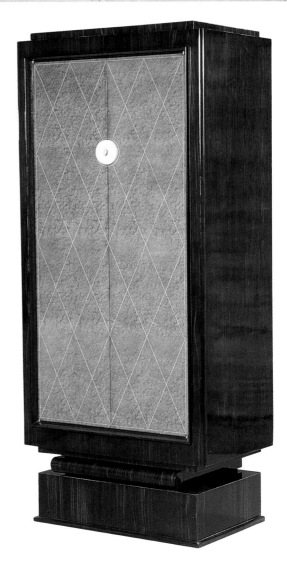

Gaston Priou
(*above*) Wall panel in lacquered
wood, *c.* 1925.

(*above right*) Screen in
lacquered wood inlaid with
coquille d'œuf, c. 1925.

René Prou
(*right*) Console in gilt-wood
with marble top, *c.* 1926.

René Prou
(*opposite left*) Fall-front desk
in burled wood, *c.* 1929.

(*opposite centre*) Lady's desk
and chair in burled wood,
c. 1929.

Primavera
(*opposite right*) Vases in glazed
earthenware, manufactured by
the Faïencerie d'Art de Sainte-
Radegonde for the Au Printemps
department store, Paris, 1920s.

the war he therefore joined the French Academy in Rome, where he studied under Paul-Albert Besnard. On his return to France, he continued to exhibit at the Salons. In 1928 his *Fantaisie italienne* was acquired for the Musée de Saint-Quentin by the French state, which later acquired his *Amazons* for the Musée du Luxembourg in Paris.

Pougheon worked in both Paris and Bordeaux and joined with JEAN DUPAS, Jean *Despujols and RENÉ BUTHAUD as a member of the loosely knit group that came to be known as the Art Deco Bordeaux school. His early Neoclassical style evolved in the 1920s into a Modernist approach in which the human figure – invariably that of a lithesome young woman, clad or nude – was sharply elongated. Although he had absorbed the geometric forms of Cubism, Pougheon ensured that his human forms remained recognizable.

In 1935 Pougheon became a professor at the École des Beaux-Arts in Paris, and in 1942 was elected a member of the Institut Français. At the 1937 Exposition des Arts et Techniques, he painted the complete interior of the Pavillon du Bâtiment, including a fresco for a ceiling measuring 180 square metres. Pougheon is best known for his lithographic work, 'Le Cheval Libre' (1932), which depicted a nubile young woman standing on a beach beside her prancing black steed, its discarded bridle in her left hand.

Powolny, Michael (1871–1954)

After an apprenticeship as a potter in his father's firm, Sommerhuber, in Judenburg (Styria), Austria, Powolny attended the technical school for the pottery industry in Znaim (1891–94) and the Kunstgewerbeschule in Vienna (1894–1901). Employed by F. Metzner from 1903 to 1906, Powolny left to form the Wiener Keramik with Bertold Löffler.

Powolny participated in various exhibitions, including the 1900 Exposition Universelle; the 1925

*Exposition Internationale in Paris; the 1908, 1909 and 1927 Kunstschau in Vienna and the 1914 and 1939 Deutscher Werkbund in Cologne, while undertaking commissions in various media for the Wiener Keramik, Wiener Werkstätte, Sommerhuber, Augarten, Wienerberger and Lobmeyr, among others. Popular among his designs are his series of figurines in glazed stoneware depicting putti with cornucopia. In 1913 the Wiener Keramik merged with the ceramic factory Gmundner Keramik.

A seminal figure in the development of 20th-century ceramics in Austria, Powolny influenced a generation of ceramic artists as a professor at the Kunstgewerbeschule, where he taught from 1909 to 1936.

Preiss, Johann-Philipp (1882–1943). *See under* Sculpture.

Primavera (Au Printemps)

Primavera was established in 1913 by René Guilleré as the design studio for Au Printemps on boulevard Haussmann in Paris. On his death in 1931, he was succeeded by his widow, Charlotte *Chauchet-Guilleré and Colette Guéden. Other designers associated with the studio included Philippe *Petit, Marcel *Guillemard, Louis *Sognot, Georges *Lévard, Claude Lévy, Sigismond Olesiewicz, Madeline Sougez and RENÉ BUTHAUD. Primavera's pottery enterprises at Longwy in Meurthe-et-Moselle and at Sainte-Radegonde were organized by Buthaud. The studio displayed through its own pavilion at the 1925 *Exposition Internationale.

Printz, Eugène (1889–1948). *See under* Furniture and Interior Design.

Priou, Gaston (b. 1899)

Priou remains relatively unknown. Born in Paris, he emerged in 1922 at the Salon of the *Société des Artistes Décorateurs as an accomplished artist in lacquer. Ten years later he was still exhibiting the same

range of screens, trays and small furniture in lacquer and *coquille d'œuf*, for example, for deluxe cabins on the ocean liner *Félix Roussel*. Why Priou remained unnoticed is uncertain. Only one brief reference to his work appeared in the critical press – a black lacquered table reviewed in a 1922 article in *Art et Décoration*.

Although Priou's output was less prolific than contemporaries such as Louis *Midavaine and Paul-Étienne *Sain, his designs incorporate a careful interplay of lavish dark lacquers accented with *coquille d'œuf*. The few surviving examples of his work show excellent craftsmanship, as in the ornamentation of the tropical landscapes, mountain citadels and enchanted isles depicted on his room partitions and panels.

Prou, René (1889–1947/8)

Born in Nantes (Loire-Atlantique), Prou settled in Paris after graduating from the École Bernard Palissy in 1908. After this he joined Maison Gouffé, where he was appointed artistic director. In 1912 Prou was awarded two prestigious decorating commissions: the Salle du Conseil du Comptoir d'Escompte de Paris; and the residence of the Paraguayan ambassador. The First World War interrupted his career, although he managed to continue his research into new materials and techniques. In 1919, listed at 26 rue de Lyons, Prou exhibited a first-class dining cabin for the ocean liner *Paris* at the *Salon d'Automne; the furniture had been executed by Schmit et Cie. A string of ocean liner commissions followed in the next few years: the *Paris*, *Volubilis*, *Roussillon*, *Cuba* and *De Grasse*, for which he showed his interiors at the Salons. Further exposure was afforded at the time by the 1922 Exposition Coloniale in Marseilles.

The 1925 *Exposition Internationale drew widely on Prou's skills as an architect and decorator. He was involved in numerous exhibits: his own stand on the Esplanade des Invalides, and those of *Fontaine et Cie,

L'Art du Bois, Le Pavillon de l'Art Colonial, the Société des Chaussures 'Cecil', the boutique Élégance, the Pavillon des Alpes-Maritime, Le Palais de la Ville de Paris, a governor's apartment for the Pavillon de l'Indo-Chine and a boudoir and bathroom in collaboration with Eric *Bagge for the Ambassade Française pavilion.

In 1928 Prou succeeded Paul *Follot as artistic director at *Pomone, where he remained until 1932. His principal collaborators there were Henri Martin, Albert Guénot, Jean C. Colosiez, Pierre Paschal and Jean Merot de Barre.

Prou made the transition from wood to metal in the late 1920s, when he began to favour wrought iron and sumptuous veneers in tortoise shell, lacquer, **duralumin** or pigskin. A booklet published by Pomone in the 1920s, *Le Secret du succès de l'atelier René Prou*, listed his architectural and decorating commissions in the previous twelve years: three hundred apartments, sixty private residences, thirty banks, four hundred train compartments for La Compagnie Internationale des Wagon-Lits and fifteen ocean liners. His 1930s commissions included the Waldorf-Astoria hotel in New York, and interiors in Geneva, Tokyo and Le Havre. From the late 1930s until his death Prou taught part-time, most notably at the École Nationale Supérieure des Arts Décoratifs.

Puiforcat, Jean (1897–1945). *See under* Silver, Metal, Lacquer and Enamel.

R

Ragan, Leslie Darrell (1897–1972)

Ragan was born in Woodbine, Iowa, and attended the Cumming School of Art in Des Moines and the Art Institute of Chicago, before joining the Office of War Information (OWI). A painter, illustrator and poster artist resident near Monterey, California, he was known primarily for his poster designs in which he employed

aerodynamic images of locomotives speeding through the countryside. These posters included advertisements for the Cleveland Union Terminal and the New York Central Railroad's 20th Century Limited and Empire State Express services.

Rapin, Henri (1873–1939)

Born in Paris, Rapin studied under Jean-Léon Gérôme. Emerging as an accomplished painter, illustrator and decorator, he exhibited at the Salons from c. 1903. His early furniture in oak was overly large and bourgeois; its stiff frames were carved with floral mouldings and panels by Charles Hairon and Gaston-Étienne Le Bourgeois, and inset later with ceramic and marquetry medallions. Rapin's importance as a decorator diminished steadily from 1919. His interiors, awash with colour and detail, appeared almost Victorian to the Salon critics, who found them too fussy at a time when the dictates of the modern style demanded reduced decoration. Rapin's furniture from this period was executed by Evrard Frères.

By 1924 Rapin had been appointed artistic director of both the Manufacture Nationale de *Sèvres and the École Nationale Supérieure des Arts Décoratifs. He continued to apply himself to all aspects of decorative arts and architecture. The reviews *Intérieurs Modernes* and *Décors et Ameublements du Goût du Jour* showed a wide variety of his contemporary interiors, in which his previous tendency towards over-ornamentation had been checked. At the 1924 Salon of the *Société des Artistes Décorateurs, for which he designed the exhibition hall and rotunda, Rapin displayed ensembles for ministerial offices that were expressively modern. Two addresses were listed for him at the time: 274 boulevard Raspail and 99 rue du Bac.

At the 1925 *Exposition Internationale, Rapin participated widely. In the Ambassade Française pavilion he designed the Grand Salon with Pierre Selmersheim, as well as a dining room. Elsewhere,

he decorated the pavilion of the Librairie Industrielle et des Arts Décoratifs, the *Arthur Goldscheider and Paul-René stands, and the displays of the École du Comité des Dames de l'Union Centrale des Arts Décoratifs. For the Sèvres pavilion, Rapin designed carpets, ceramics, lamps and furniture; his furniture designs were executed by the Association des Anciens Élèves de l'École Boulle. He continued to exhibit into the 1930s, collaborating on some projects with Jacques Rapin, presumably a family member. Their exhibit at the 1935 Exposition de Bruxelles was one of his last.

Rateau, Armand-Albert (1882–1938). *See under* Furniture and Interior Design.

Ravinet–d'Enfert

The metalware enterprise founded in 1845 by E. Tonnelier was acquired in 1882 by Louis Ravinet (1854–1925), who in 1891 formed a partnership with Charles d'Enfert (1865–1960). The firm, renamed Ravinet–d'Enfert, was located in the old Hôtel Caumartin at 83 rue du Temple in the Marais quarter of Paris.

Known initially for its silver dinnerware, to which Ravinet–d'Enfert later added silverplate, the firm's wares were manufactured from 1895 through the Mouroux workshops in Seine-et-Marne. The company participated in the 1895 Lyons and 1897 Brussels exhibitions and the 1900 Exposition Universelle, Paris.

In 1923 management of Ravinet–d'Enfert passed to the founders' children, André Ravinet and Jacques d'Enfert. The firm continued to exhibit internationally, participating in the 1925 *Exposition Internationale and the 1937 Exposition des Arts et Techniques, both in Paris. Ravinet–d'Enfert closed in 1984.

Reeves, Ruth (1892–1966)

Reeves's life was peripatetic in the extreme: she ran away from her home in Redlands, California, before the age of ten, and she died in New Delhi, where,

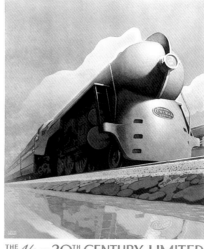

Henri Rapin
(*opposite left*) Bedroom exhibited at the 1926 Salon of La Société des Artistes Décorateurs, Paris.

Ruth Reeves
(*opposite right*) Selection of patterns, including *Nudes in a Pool*, *Dinette*, and *Bestiary*, included in the Exhibition of Contemporary Textiles at W. & J. Sloane & Co., New York, 1930.

(*far left*) *Manhattan* pattern for an office, offered in block-printed cotton, glazed chintz, Osnaburg cloth, or voile, designed for W. & J. Sloane & Co., *c.* 1930.

Leslie Darrell Ragan
(*left*) *The New 20th-Century Limited*, lithographic poster, 1938.

Ruth Reeves
(*right*) *Electric* pattern in hand-printed cotton, felt or billiard cloth for furniture upholstery and in duo-print felt for curtains in a radio room, for W. & J. Sloane & Co., *c.* 1930.

Henri Rapin
(*far right*) Vase in glazed porcelain modelled by Marcel Prunier, for La Manufacture Nationale de Sèvres, 1925.

Frederick Hurten Rhead
(*below*) Fiesta Ware in glazed earthenware for the Homer Laughlin China Co., *c.* 1936.

Albert Reimann
(*right*) Four-light candelabrum in copper, and candlestick in brass, designed for the Chase Brass & Copper Co., *c.* 1930–31.

Richard–Ginori
(*opposite left*) Grottesca covered urn in glazed porcelain designed by Gio Ponti, *c.* 1930.

Lucie Renaudot
(*opposite right*) Games table and chair in burled wood, marketed by P. A. Dumas, *c.* 1923.

as one of the first Fulbright scholars to work on the Indian subcontinent, she had served for ten years as a handicraft adviser.

Reeves attended the Pratt Institute in Brooklyn from 1910 to 1911, the San Francisco Art Institute from 1912 to 1913 and the Art Students League in Manhattan until 1915. She then spent the years between 1920 and 1927 in Paris, where she studied further under Fernand Léger at the Académie Moderne. Returning to the USA, Reeves taught briefly in Redlands before settling in Rockland County, north of Manhattan. There she specialized in printed textile and carpet design, bringing a colourful blend of Modernist impulses to Classical, primitive, figural and abstract subject matter.

She participated in the 1928 inaugural exhibition of the American Designers' Gallery, the 1931 American Union of Decorative Artists and Craftsmen (AUDAC) exhibition at the Brooklyn Museum as well as the 1932 National Alliance of Art and Industry at the Art Center in New York, where she showed paintings, drawings and textile designs. Reeves's first one-woman textile exhibition, staged in 1930 at the W. & J. Sloane furniture store, included block-printed designs such as 'Nudes in a Pool', 'Abstract', 'Dinette' and 'Bestiary' on thirteen types of fabric, including hopsacking and monk's cloth. Her 'Electric' textile design for Sloane's, for utilization in different materials such as curtain fabric, billiard cloth or furniture upholstery, was an instant success with its pattern of triangular lightning bolts that symbolized the power of electricity. Also popular was her 'Manhattan' office fabric, which in its Cubist collage of the city's panoramas effectively evoked its dynamism. In 1932 Reeves provided carpet and wallpaper designs for Radio City Music Hall in New York.

Reimann, Albert (1874– c. 1971)

Reimann was born in Gnesen, Germany (now Poland) and trained as a sculptor and architect. In 1902, with his wife Klara, he founded the Schulerwerkstätten für Kleinplastik (School for Small Sculpture) in Berlin. This was a private institution, as distinct from the state-run Bauhaus. In 1912 the Reimann school was expanded into twenty-three departments, each with its own instructor. The revised curriculum included courses in the decorative arts, design and architecture. When forced by the Nazis in 1935 to sell the school because he was Jewish, Reimann moved with his family to London, where his son opened a new Reimann school at 4–10 Regency Street, SW1. It was bombed in 1942.

In the late 1920s, Reimann visited the USA, where he was commissioned by the *Chase Brass & Copper Co. to design silver and brass household accessories, such as candlesticks, for its new product line. Most of the models he submitted were generated by members of the metalware workshop at his school, including the shop's director, Karl Heubler.

Renaudot, Lucie (d. 1939)

No apparent record of Renaudot's maiden name or her early years has survived, although Salon catalogues list her place of birth as Valenciennes. She appears to have emerged unannounced on the Paris scene at the end of the First World War, making her début as a decorator at the 1919 *Salon d'Automne. Soon thereafter, Renaudot formed a fruitful liaison with the cabinet-maker P. A. Dumas, of 24 rue Notre-Dame-des-Victoires, for whom she designed furnishings until her death.

Renaudot's style was classically inspired, part English Regency and part Louis XVI, and a gentle formality predominated. She preferred a combination of woods, often a light burl veneer juxtaposed with a darker one. Alternative decoration was achieved by patterning within a veneer: the unusual grain in Brazilian jacaranda, for example, providing an arresting effect when running the vertical length of adjoining drawers on a commode. Her ceilings were a distinctive aspect of her interiors; many contained circular or square recessed frosted panelling to provide concealed lighting.

Renaudot received broad coverage at the 1925 *Exposition Internationale – both in a studio shown on Dumas's stand on the Esplanade des Invalides and in a child's room in the Ambassade Française pavilion. On the latter, she had collaborated with Laure Albin-Guillot, Paule Marrot and Évelyne Dufau. In the early 1930s Renaudot was commissioned to design cabins on the ocean liners France and *Normandie. She participated in the seventh exhibition of Artistes de ce Temps in 1935.

Rhead, Frederick Hurten (1880–1942)

Born in Staffordshire, Rhead followed family tradition in becoming the art director of Wardle Art Pottery in Hanley. After studying under Marc Solon and working as a designer for Josiah Wedgwood, he emigrated in 1902 to the USA, where he worked for Weller & Co. in Zanesville, Ohio (1903–1904), Roseville Pottery (1904–1908), Jervis Pottery (1908–1909) and a string of other factories into the mid-1920s.

Rhead's significance in an Art Deco context began in 1927, with his appointment as artistic director of the Homer Laughlin China Co. in Newell, West Virginia, for which he designed the 'Fiesta' line of tableware. Introduced in 1936 in festive colours such as persimmon, scarlet, orange, chartreuse and sunflower, and with sleek Art Deco contours and sculpted concentric rings, 'Fiesta' became the world's highest-selling tableware service. Discontinued in 1973, it was re-introduced in 1986. Rhead's daughter Charlotte also designed ceramics in the Art Deco style.

Richard–Ginori

In 1737 the Tuscan marquis Carlo Ginori established a porcelain factory next to his country residence and named it 'Doccia' after its location in the borough of Sesto Fiorentino, six kilometres north of Florence. For this reason the Società Ceramica Richard–Ginori is still often referred to as Doccia. In 1896, after five generations of family ownership, the factory passed

Robj
'Portugais aux citrons', covered
jar in enamelled earthenware,
1920s.

to the Richard Corp., a Milanese manufacturer of
stanniferous faïence. Around 1900 Richard–Ginori
added a line of Art Nouveau wares to its classical
repertoire and two years later was acclaimed for its
Modernist display at the 1902 Turin Exposition.

Richard–Ginori is known in an Art Deco context
almost exclusively for Giovanni (Gio) *Ponti,
who on his appointment as artistic director in 1923
immediately set about updating the company's
porcelain production. Ponti was not the only one to
transform the firm's designs; Salvatore Saponaro
and A. Sibau also designed hardpaste porcelain wares
for Richard–Ginori in the Modernist idiom during
the inter-war years. In 1950 the site of the original
factory was abandoned and a new plant built
three kilometres away. The firm remains active under
the name Richard–Ginori.

Riemerschmid, Richard (1868–1957)

Born in Munich, Riemerschmid studied painting
at the Munich Academy (1888–90) before turning to
industrial design. In 1897 he became a founding
member of the Munich Vereinigte Werkstätten für
Kunst im Handwerk, established to generate and
market items for mass-production. From 1902 to 1905
he taught at the Nuremberg Kunstgewerbeschule,
two years later becoming a founding member of the
Deutscher Werkbund, and later its chairman from
1921 to 1926.

Among Riemerschmid's early interiors was a music
room noted for its harmony, which he exhibited in
1899 at the Dresden Deutsche-Ausstellung. Later
interiors included a revolutionary programme of
machine-made furniture. Until the First World War,
his practice was highly varied; he designed household
wares in numerous media, including metal light fixtures
for the Dresden Studio, porcelain for the Meissen
factory, glassware for the firm of Benedikt von
Poschinger and ceramics for Reinhold Merkelbach.

As an architect and industrial designer,
Riemerschmid developed a formula for furniture design
in which smooth, simple and undecorated forms
bridged the gap between the exuberant Jugendstil
(in rapid retreat from c. 1905) and industrial products,
setting the standards for progressive German design
in the first decades of the 20th century. After the First
World War, Riemerschmid was active principally as
an architect and teacher, serving as the director of the
Munich Kunstgewerbeschule from 1912 to 1924 and
as head of the Cologne Werkschule from 1926 to 1931.

Rietveld, Gerrit Thomas (1888–1964)

Rietveld was born in Utrecht in the Netherlands and
apprenticed in his father's cabinetry shop between 1899
and 1906. He then worked as a draughtsman in a jewelry
firm before setting up and operating his own cabinet-
making business between 1911 and 1919, while managing
also to study architecture with P. J. C. Klaarhamer.
During this period, Rietveld continually experimented
with designs for buildings, interiors and furniture,
translating into three-dimensional shapes the Neoplastic
principles of rectangularity and reliance on primary
colours formulated by the De Stijl group of Dutch artists.

He introduced his famous 'Red-Blue' chair c. 1918,
and the following year joined De Stijl, of which he
remained a member until 1931. In 1923 Rietveld showed
his 'Berlin' chair – more a piece of sculpture than a
functional seat – at a Bauhaus exhibition in Weimar,
and the following year designed the Schröder house in
Utrecht. These and other 1920s and 1930s designs were
spatially and technically innovative, exerting a profound
influence on both his contemporaries and later designers.

Most of Rietveld's furniture between 1917 and 1971
was made from readily available, inexpensive wood
products by one cabinet-maker, G. A. van de Groenekan.
Thereafter the rights were purchased by Cassina of
Milan, which continues to reproduce his landmark
models.

In 1927 Rietveld began to experiment with
moulded fibre and later with plywood. Among his most
notable later designs was his 'Z' (or 'Zig-Zag') chair
(1934). As his career progressed after the Second World
War, he increasingly turned his attention to
architecture. In the 1950s and 1960s, as his earlier
designs began to receive recognition, Rietveld expanded
his operation. In 1961 he formed a partnership with
J. van Dillen and J. van Tricht.

Robj

The firm's early history is sketchy; surviving records
indicate that an inventor of electrical ignitors,
Jean Born, who changed his name to Robj, decided to
add an art division to his business shortly after the
First World War. On his death in a car accident in 1922,
the firm was taken over by Lucien Willmetz, one of its
shareholders, who commissioned sculptors and
modellers to design a wide selection of table-top items,
including lidded jars, inkstands, tobacco pots, perfume
burners, *veilleuses*, decanters and bonbonnières.
Robj also staged an annual competition between 1927
and 1931 for which it invited new designs, mainly in
ceramics and enamelled glass.

Success was immediate. Robj's speciality was
novelty items, which were described in an
advertisement in *L'Illustration*, December 1924, as: 'Les
bibelots à la mode en vente dans toutes les maisons
d'élégance'. Located at 3 cité d'Hauteville, Paris, the
firm offered a selection of fashionable and witty
decorative items, including decanters modelled as
costumed women with stoppers as their headgear,
sombreroed Mexican mariachi players, Japanese geishas
holding parasols that served as lampshades, and visibly
puffed weightlifters holding aloft dumbbells whose
two spheres were made of frosted glass and internally
lit. These were produced by various manufacturers,
including the *Sèvres manufactory, Villeroy & Boch and
in Robj's own workshop in Boulogne-sur-Seine.

Robj
(*right*) 'Nanouk' sweetmeat jar
and 'Mandarin' inkwell in
enamelled earthenware, 1920s.

Robj
(*below*) Four flacons in
enamelled earthenware:
'Benedictine', 'Général de
Brigade', 'Rhum' and 'Guignolet',
1920s (*right*), shown with two
pairs of dancers in glazed
porcelain by Aime La Maîtrise,
1920s (*left*).

Robj
(*right*) 'Nanouk' sweetmeat
and 'Mandarin' inkwell in
enamelled earthenware, 1920s.

Robj
(*below*) Four flacons in
enamelled earthenware:
'Benedictine', 'Général de
Brigade', 'Rhum' and 'Guignolet',
1920s (*right*), shown with two
pairs of dancers in glazed
porcelain by Aime La Maîtrise,
1920s (*left*).

Rookwood

(*right*) Vase in glazed earthenware decorated by William E. Hentschel, 1918.

(*far right*) Vase in glazed earthenware decorated by Wilhelmine Rehm, 1930.

Rosenthal Porzellan

(*below left*) 'Pierrette' in glazed porcelain designed by Constantin Holzer-Defanti, *c.* 1920; and figural clock in glazed porcelain designed by Gustav Oppel and modelled by Kurt Severin, *c.* 1925.

(*centre right*) Covered urn in glazed porcelain designed by Kurt Wendler, *c.* 1922.

(*below right*) Covered urn in glazed porcelain, the form by Hans Küster, *c.* 1923.

Gilbert Rohde
Clock in aluminium and black
lacquer, for the Herman Miller
Clock Co., early 1930s.

Rohde, Gilbert (1894–1944)

Born in New York to Prussian immigrant parents,
Max and Mathilda Rohde, Rohde grew up in the Bronx,
where he attended high school. He graduated in 1913,
after which he worked as an apprentice photographer,
newspaper cartoonist and advertising illustrator for
W. & J. Sloane and Macy's. In 1923 Rohde was hired by
the Brooklyn department store Abraham & Straus as
a furniture illustrator. There he met Gladys Vorsanger,
another employee, whom he married in July 1927.

In 1927 Rohde visited Paris, where he familiarized
himself with the Modernist movement before returning
to the USA, and setting up a workshop c. 1928 to
produce tables made of chromium-plated metals and
Bakelite. Among his early interior design commissions
was the highly publicized Norman Lee penthouse
on Sheridan Square in Manhattan, which included his
'Rotorette Cellarette', a cabinet designed to conceal
contraband liquor.

In the 1930s Rohde reduced his custom work to
concentrate on designs intended for mass production.
His client list included the Heywood–Wakefield Co.
(of Gardner, Massachusetts), the Koehler Manufacturing
Co. and the Herman Miller Furniture Co. He exhibited
interiors at the Design for Living house at the 1933
World's Fair in Chicago, and played a major role in the
design for the administration centre at the 1936 Texas
Centennial Exposition. Although secondary to his
role as a furniture designer, Rohde designed a series
of streamlined Modernist clocks in the 1930s for the
Herman Miller Clock Co., and these are now eagerly
sought by collectors.

Rohde, Johan (1856–1935). *See* Jensen.

Rollin, Lucien (1906–1993)

Rollin studied at the *École Boulle from 1919 to 1923,
and then worked briefly for JACQUES-ÉMILE RUHLMANN.
After collaborating with Michel Roux-Spitz, with whom

he designed a bathroom in 1928, Rollin opened his own
design office in Paris and made his début at the Salon
of the *Société des Artistes Décorateurs. In 1929, at the
same Salon, he showed an office for a technician and
ensembles for a dining room, bedroom and office, in
which he was assisted by Gilbert *Poillerat, JEAN PERZEL
and Max Ingrand. His style – contemporary with
classical overtones – was more restrained than that
of many of his colleagues.

Beyond the Salons, Rollin also participated in
displays at W. & J. Sloane's in New York in 1934, in the
Pavillon du Bois at the 1937 Exposition des Arts et
Techniques and in the French pavilion at the 1939
New York World's Fair. During the Second World War,
he stayed in Aubusson, and in 1946 designed an elegant
ensemble for the Élysée Palace. Rollin later abandoned
furniture design to dedicate himself to architecture.

Rookwood

Founded in 1880 by Maria Longworth Nichols in an
abandoned schoolhouse on Eastern Avenue in
Cincinnati, Ohio, the Rookwood Pottery Co. is best
known for its ceramics of the Arts and Crafts period.
In the 1920s, however, the firm's decorator–modellers,
including Lorinda Epply, William E. Hentschel, Jens
Jensen, Wilhelmine Rehm, Sara Sax, Edward T. Hurley
and Harriet E. Wilcox, responded with enthusiasm
to the modern style, carefully reviewing the current
decorative arts magazines issuing from Paris. These
provided illustrations of the newest stylistic and
technical developments at the annual Salons, including
RENÉ BUTHAUD's figurative subject matter and ÉMILE
DECOEUR's glazes.

Rookwood Pottery remained prosperous for most
of the 1920s, producing editions of expensive hand-
painted wares in matt glazes that gave the pieces a
fresh look. The firm's repertoire of glazing techniques
included **Tiger Eye**, *flambé*, *sang-de-bœuf*, **jewel
porcelain** and **Wax Mat**. Toward 1930, however, moulds

were introduced and surface decoration eliminated in
an attempt to cut costs. The Depression had a severe
impact on the firm. In 1934 it registered its first loss;
by 1936 it was operating only one week per month.
Filing for bankruptcy in 1939, Rookwood Pottery closed
in April 1941. Later attempts to revive it, initiated by
Walter Schott, were unsuccessful.

Rosenthal Porzellan

Rosenthal Porzellan AG was founded in 1879 in Selb,
Bavaria, by Philipp Rosenthal (d. 1937), who had
recently returned to his native Germany after working
with a porcelain importer in Detroit. Following family
tradition – his father had owned a porcelain factory
in Werl – he created Philipp Rosenthal & Co. in
Erkersreuth for the decoration of porcelain blanks.
As business flourished, he built his own factory in
nearby Selb, which was operational in 1891. A further
plant opened in Kronach six years later.

The firm's early wares were imitative of the
Jugendstil floral style and palette adopted at the
fin de siècle by Scandinavian factories such as
Rörstrand and *Bing & Grøndhal, alongside which
Rosenthal Porzellan exhibited at the 1900 Exposition
Universelle. Although affected by the restrictions
on raw materials and the difficulties of international
commerce during the First World War, Rosenthal
Porzellan rebounded afterward. The firm transferred
its main offices to Berlin in 1920 and established
showrooms in major capitals.

Rosenthal Porzellan's series of Art Deco models,
especially the exaggerated figures sculpted by Gerhard
*Schliepstein and the painted decorations of Tono
Zoelch, represent the best of the firm's Modernist
designs from the 1930s. With the rise of the Nazi party,
Rosenthal Porzellan moved its offices back to Selb.
During the Second World War, production was geared
to simple household wares and items supporting the
nation's war effort.

In the post-war years the firm was revived. In 1950 Rosenthal Porzellan was again headed by a family member, Philipp Rosenthal Jr., who commissioned internationally renowned designers, including Raymond *Loewy and Tapio Wirkkala, to provide contemporary models. The firm remains in operation, despite numerous corporate name changes, re-organizations and the purchase and sale through the years of its factories and outlets.

Roseville

Founded in 1890 by George F. Young, the firm was incorporated in 1892 as the Roseville Pottery Co.; it moved to Zanesville, Ohio in 1898, near rich deposits of natural clay. Its first pieces were produced under the name Rozane. The years before 1920, following the Arts and Crafts period, saw the start of what became known as the firm's 'middle period' when the newly appointed art director, Frank Ferrell, began to phase out the Rozane line and introduce one entitled Rosecraft, which included multicoloured models with embossed or moulded floral designs in matt glazes. Patterns included 'Sunflower', 'Wisteria' and 'Pinecone'.

A distinctive Art Deco pattern that was strikingly out of character with Roseville's standard repertoire of models – most of which incorporated floral patterns – was 'Futura', introduced by Ferrell c. 1928 in a mix of matt earth-toned glazes. Included in the line was a broad selection of vases, jars, bowls, jardinières, window boxes and candlesticks in stark terraced and angular forms that echoed the contours of modern metropolitan skyscrapers. Other designs in stepped spherical configurations anticipated Buck Rogers's 1930s rocket ship. Described in a 1929 advertisement in *House & Garden* as 'adventurous … modern … fashioned with today's appreciation of beauty', 'Futura' remained in continuous production until Roseville was sold in 1954.

Rousseau, Clément (1872–1950)

Born in Saint-Maurice-la-Fougereuse (Deux-Sèvres), Rousseau was trained as a sculptor by Léon Morice and exhibited at the *Société des Artistes Français. Furniture appears to have been a natural extension of his sculptural abilities, given legitimacy in the early 1920s by commissions from Jacques *Doucet and Baron de Rothschild, examples of which are now in the Musée des Arts Décoratifs, Paris, and the Metropolitan Museum of Art, New York. The majority of Rousseau's commissions were apparently for private clients, as he did not participate in the annual Paris Salons, although he did exhibit a selection of his furniture and objects at the Galerie Charpentier, Paris, in 1925. No later reference to him appears in contemporary reviews.

An air of excitement greets the infrequent arrival of a piece of Rousseau furniture on the auction block. No major Art Deco collection is considered quite complete without an example of his work – be it table lamp base, pedestal or small *meuble de barbier*. Aside from the extreme rarity of his pieces, their magic lies both in their form – they show a very personal, somewhat whimsical, interpretation of late 18th-century furniture styles – and in the superb interplay of Rousseau's preferred materials. Richly grained palmwood or rosewood provide the framework for furniture veneered with stained **galuchat** or snakeskin intersected by thin ivory banding – a technique that Rousseau adopted in 1912. His style is easily mistaken for that of the cabinet-maker Adolphe *Chanaux; most of Rousseau's pieces, however, are signed in an incised wavy scrawl, often with the year of manufacture.

Royal Dux

The Royal Dux porcelain factory was founded in 1853 in Duchcov (Dux), Bohemia, north-west of Prague. In 1860 it was renamed the E. Eichler Thonwaren-Fabrik after its new owner, Eduard Eichler, who two years later purchased a small factory in Selty for the manufacture of terracotta, **faïence** and majolica wares. In 1898 the firm was transformed into a public company, the Duxer Porzellan-Manufaktur AG with headquarters in Berlin. A porcelain factory was purchased in Blankenhain, near Weimar, and the Selty plant liquidated.

Specializing in matt ivory and bronze over- and under-glazes, Royal Dux produced a wide selection of figurines c. 1900 depicting maidens, nudes, sportsmen, socialites and wild animals modelled in the prevailing Jugendstil style. For these the company was awarded a *grand prix* at the 1904 St Louis World's Fair.

The First World War generated an enormous financial crisis for Royal Dux, and the factory in Blankenhain was sold in 1918. In the 1920s, although the quality of its wares had diminished, the firm continued to manufacture figurative and decorative porcelain, drawing mostly on existing models. It also introduced a limited number of models in a graceful Modernist style, such as those by Schiff and Elle Strobach. By the time of the Nazi invasion of Czechoslovakia in 1938, the factory could draw on more than twelve thousand existing models for its porcelain and faïence production. In 1992 Royal Dux was renamed the Porcelain Manufactory Royal Dux Bohemia AS. The company is now fully privatized.

Ruhlmann, Jacques-Émile (1879–1933). *See under* Furniture and Interior Design.

Russell, Sir Gordon (1892–1980)

Born in England, Russell began to design furniture in 1910 and after the First World War made contact with the Design & Industries Association. His furniture was shown at the 1924 Wembley British Empire Exhibition and at the 1925 *Exposition Internationale. In 1926 Russell became a member of the Art Workers' Guild and in the same year formed his company, Gordon Russell Ltd.

Clément Rousseau

(*below*) Pair of side chairs in rosewood inlaid in ebony, shagreen and mother-of-pearl, c. 1925.

(*right and below right*) *Guéridon* in burl walnut and palmwood inlaid in shagreen, mother-of-pearl and ebony, c. 1920.

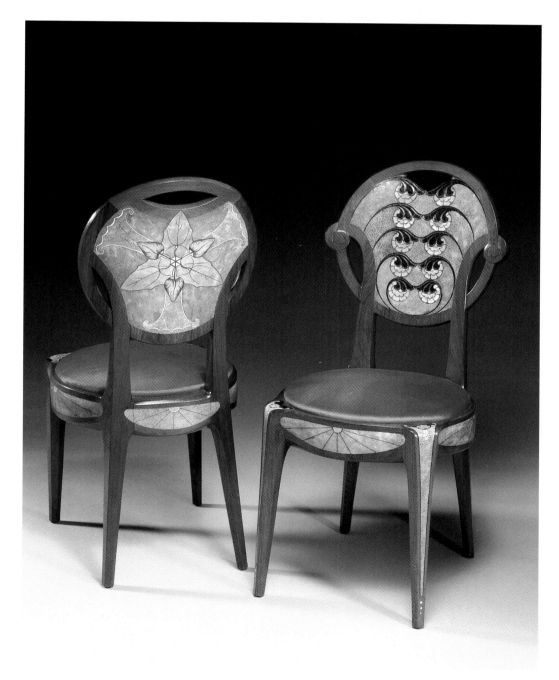

In 1930 Russell began to work in the modern style, and in 1931 was commissioned by Murphy Radios to produce a series of radio cabinets designed by his brother, R. D. Russell. From 1942 he was a member of the Board of Trade committee which initiated the production of 'utility' furniture.

S

Saarinen, Eero (1910–1961)

Saarinen was born in Kirkkonummi, Finland, to Loja and Eliel *Saarinen and in 1923 moved with his family to the USA. He studied sculpture at the Académie de la Grande Chaumière in Paris between 1929 and 1930 and architecture at Yale from 1931 to 1934, after which he worked on furniture designs with Norman *Bel Geddes.

Saarinen joined his father at the Cranbrook Academy of Art in Bloomfield Hills, Michigan, in 1936, where the two often worked in association with J. Robert F. Swanson. Their office was listed between 1944 and 1947 as Saarinen, Swanson & Saarinen, then as Saarinen, Saarinen & Associates. Saarinen taught at Cranbrook between 1939 and 1941, participating in various exhibitions with his mother, Loja *Saarinen. In 1941 he won the two first prizes in the organic design competition sponsored by the Museum of Modern Art in New York. He later worked for the Office of Strategic Services in Washington, DC, from 1942 to 1945, before returning to Cranbrook.

Saarinen, Eliel (1873–1950)

Born in Rautasalmi, Finland, Saarinen studied painting at the University of Helsingfors and architecture at the Polytekniska Institute from 1893 to 1897, after which he went into private practice in Helsinki and Kirkkonummi. In 1904 he married Loja *Saarinen (née Gesellius). He emigrated with his family in 1923 to the USA, where he started a limited practice in Evanston, Illinois, and served as a visiting professor of

architecture at the University of Michigan in Ann Arbor from 1923 to 1924. After this he moved to Bloomfield Hills, Michigan, north of Detroit. Between 1932 and 1942 Saarinen served as president of the Cranbrook Academy of Art in Bloomfield Hills, where he remained as director of the department of architecture and urban design until 1950. Between 1944 and 1947 he was a partner in the firm of Saarinen, Swanson & Saarinen with his son Eero *Saarinen.

During his career in the USA, Saarinen participated in several contemporary design exhibitions, including the 1929 The Architect & The Industrial Arts show at the Metropolitan Museum of Art in New York, in which he presented a modern interior setting comprising standardized metal units. He also exhibited at the 1931 American Union of Decorative Artists and Craftsmen (AUDAC) show at the Brooklyn Museum and the 1934 Contemporary American Industrial Art exhibition, again at the Metropolitan Museum of Art.

Saarinen, Louise (Loja) (1879–1968)

Loja Saarinen (née Gesellius) was born in Helsinki, where she received art training at the Konstföreningen and the Suomen Taideyhdistyksen Piirustuskoulu from 1898 to 1902. Moving to Paris, she studied further at the Académie Colarossi under Jean-Antoine Injalbert. In 1903 she returned to Helsinki, where she joined her brother, Herman Gesellius (an architect and partner of Eliel *Saarinen and Armas Lindgren), for whom she worked on commissions for interiors, photography and sculpture. She married Eliel Saarinen in 1904.

Saarinen emigrated with her family in 1923 to Evanston, Illinois, two years later moving with her husband to Ann Arbor, Michigan, where he had accepted the directorship of the Cranbrook Academy of Art. In 1928 she opened the Studio Loja Saarinen, where for the next three years she worked on textile and carpet designs for the academy's Kingswood School. In this she was assisted by Maja Andersson,

whom she hired in 1929 to supervise a team of largely Scandinavian weavers. Saarinen administered the studio until 1942, participating in numerous exhibitions through the years, often with her daughter Pipsan and son Eero *Saarinen.

Through her studio, Saarinen designed and manufactured textiles, window treatments, upholstery and floor coverings, including those for her family residence at Cranbrook, which was completed in 1930. Important commissions included the Chrysler showroom in Detroit and Frank Lloyd Wright's office for Edgar Kauffmann in Pittsburgh. Her carpet designs, which incorporated rectilinear and asymmetrical geometric patterns or stylized plant and animal motifs, often mixed Modernism with Scandinavian Arts and Crafts traditions.

Sabino, Ernest-Marius (1878–1961)

Born at Acireale, Italy, to a sculptor and his wife, Sabino trained as a woodcarver before moving c. 1900 to Paris, where he studied at the École Nationale Supérieure des Art Décoratifs and, briefly, at the École des Beaux-Arts. He enlisted in 1914 and was wounded. After demobilization at the end of the war he set up a firm to make light fixtures.

Sabino exhibited his work at the 1923 Biennale Internazionale d'Arte Decorativa in Monza, and again in 1925 and 1927. He first displayed a range of his lighting effects in Paris at the 1925 *Salon d'Automne and the 1925 *Exposition Internationale; at the latter he had his own stand in the Grand Palais. By the advent of the Second World War, his range had become more diverse even than the work of RENÉ LALIQUE or JEAN PERZEL, though it remained somewhat inferior in quality. Sabino initially designed everything himself, but by 1930, because of expansion at his studio, he had appointed a production manager. In a 1930 Lux article, the firm's goal was described as being to rescue the illuminated objet d'art from its banality.

Eliel Saarinen

(*opposite left*) Table in mahogany and ebonized wood, manufactured by Tor Berglund in 1931.

(*opposite right*) Pair of side chairs in fir with black ochre paint and red horsehair upholstery, manufactured by the Company of Master Craftsmen, New York, 1929–30.

Ernest-Marius Sabino

(*right*) Vase in moulded glass, 1920s.

(*far right*) Vase in moulded and enamelled gold glass, c. 1930.

(*below*) *La Danse*, bas relief luminaire in moulded satin glass with metal base, 1920s.

Ernest-Marius Sabino

(*right*) Illuminated console in *dalles de verre* with metal mounts, 1920s.

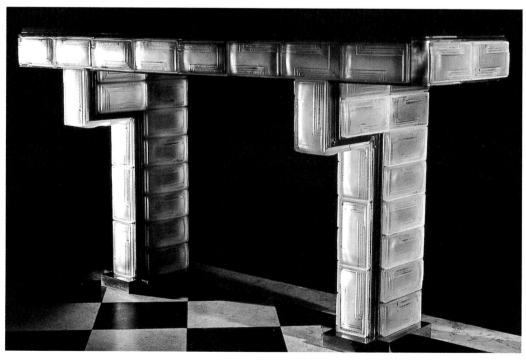

Sabino discovered a new form of glass that 'amplified, embellished and sublimated' the naked light source. Unlike Perzel, who advocated an even diffusion of light by employing a glass of uniform thickness and opacity, Sabino used pressed and moulded patterned glass in bas relief. The resulting variation in the thickness (and hence the translucency) of the glass was intended to generate a multiplicity of moods.

Pressed glass was Sabino's preferred medium, although cut, blown and engraved variations were introduced on occasion for special effects. No form of lighting, from the minute to the gargantuan, was beyond Sabino's capabilities. He applied himself to illuminated *bibelots*, menu-holders, clocks, statuettes, *potiches* (large vases), panels, doors, ceiling tiles, columns, pilasters, stelae and belvedere-shaped fountains. Spheres composed of facets of pressed glass, either as chandeliers or architectural lighting, singly or in series, were perennial favourites. Motifs included various themes from nature: bouquets, cascades, rain, waves and garlands; these were patterned in relief on panels or florets of glass.

It was for his larger fixtures that Sabino became best known. He was responsible for all the general lighting in the passageways and antechambers of the annual *Salon d'Automne exhibitions, and he also undertook commissions for the ocean liner *Normandie and various hotels and restaurants.

Saddier et ses Fils

Little information exists on the decorator and furniture wholesaler Saddier *père* prior to the First World War. In 1919 he appears to have turned over the management of his firm at 29–31 rue des Boulets, Paris, to his two sons Fernand and Gaston.

Saddier et ses Fils began to receive attention from the critics in the early 1920s, particularly for its dining room, 'Les Cerises', in contrasting Ceylonese lemonwood and coralwood, which was displayed in

1923 at the first Exposition de Décoration Française Contemporaine in Paris. At the second exposition, in 1924, the firm again displayed a dining room. At the 1925 *Exposition Internationale, it took stand No. 39 on the Esplanade des Invalides, showing a bedroom in *bois des îles*, which was advertised as 'modern'. Saddier et ses Fils was also represented in the colonial section of the exhibition by the Tunisian retailer Boyond, which exhibited a Saddier dining room designed by the Rouen painter Raymond Quibel. The room's decorative theme was not modern, but rustic, and therefore very suitable for a French colony.

The firm presented a bedroom in mahogany and sapelli at the 1926 *Salon d'Automne, in which pastel wallpapers by Marianne Clouzot added femininity and elegance to the neat composition. In the same year the revue *Les Échos des Industries d'Art* illustrated two ensembles: a dining room and a suite of furniture. Other designers for Saddier et ses Fils in 1926 were listed as J. & J. *Adnet and Quibel. The following year, the firm displayed a bar at the Salon of the *Société des Artistes Décorateurs, and a palisander bedroom and 'studio on the Côte d'Azur', both designed for the firm by Ghislane Rinquet, as well as a studio by J. & J. Adnet.

In 1928 Saddier et ses Fils produced a *chef d'œuvre*: a dressing table in sycamore at the Salon d'Automne, part of a boudoir that was at once avant-garde and feminine, with lighting by Dunaime. An article in 1929 in *Mobilier et Décoration* underlined the celebrity status acquired by the firm at that time. Illustrated were ensembles and individual pieces, often designed in collaboration with EDGAR BRANDT, André Adam (decorative panels) and Lehucher & Chabert Dupont (window shades). Everything was ultramodern and sumptuous.

From 1930 the firm's interiors became more anonymous. Clean, angular furniture in Honduras mahogany or burled cherry, often with pronounced metal mounts, was complemented by the talents of

other decorative artists to achieve the desired effects: Quibel (decorative panels), Renée *Kinsbourg (carpets), Mlle Cettier (wall hangings and curtains), Ernest-Marius *Sabino (lighting) and Marcel *Goupy (tableware marketed by Maison *Geo. Rouard), all in a dining room marketed by Brunet, Meunie & Cie.

Sain, Paul-Étienne (1904–1995). *See* Sain & Tambuté.

Sain & Tambuté

This firm was run by Paul-Étienne Sain (1904–1995) and one of his pupils, Henri Tambuté (1911–1987). Sain was a member of a celebrated Parisian family of artists and sculptors, and he studied at the École Bernard-Palissy and the École des Beaux-Arts in his native city. Utilizing his knowledge of chemistry, Sain experimented with pigments and minerals that would extend the palette of his chosen *métier*, lacquer. The technique, which provided a rich surface luminosity, was termed **laque de Beka**.

In the 1940s, assisted now by Tambuté, Sain opened a workshop at 192 rue de Vaugirard, Paris. At Sain & Tambuté he produced panels, doors and screens that were often decorated in a distinctive mix of brown, gold and blue lacquers depicting Muses, hunters and fauna in pastoral landscapes. These were for a wide range of clients, including offices, hotels and ocean liners such as the *France*.

Sakier, George (1897–1988)

Sakier studied engineering at Columbia University in New York, then worked as a commercial illustrator, as art director for *Harper's Bazaar* and as an interior decorator. In the 1920s he directed the office of design at the American Radiator and Sanitation Co., specializing in luxury bathroom accessories and fittings. He was then hired by Fostoria, in Ohio, in the late 1920s to design inexpensive glassware for mass production.

Édouard-Marcel Sandoz
Condor in black Belgian marble
on granite base, 1920s.

Among Sakier's early designs were stemware and dinnerware services. He described some of his designs in a 1933 article, 'Primer of Modern Design', in *Arts and Decoration*, as 'functional modern', 'geometric, classic and romantic modern'. His glassware for Fostoria was offered in several colours, including amber, rose, green, silver mist and ebony. Some editions remained in production after the Second World War.

Salon d'Automne

The Salon d'Automne, founded in 1903, was held annually from late October until December, initially at the Petit Palais, in Paris, and then at the Grand Palais. Like the *Société des Artistes Français and the *Société Nationale des Beaux-Arts, the Salon's emphasis was on sculpture and works on canvas and paper, although admission was also open to artist–designers within the applied arts.

Sandoz, Édouard-Marcel (1881–1971)

Sandoz was born in Basle, Switzerland, and was the son of the founder of Sandoz Bale SA, a large pharmaceutical company set up in 1886. His initial education in Munsterberg was cut short due to ill-health, but he did manage to attend high school in Lausanne between 1895 and 1900 before going to the École des Arts Industriels in Geneva. There he studied sculpture under B. Caniez and A. -J. Huguet and ceramics under J. Mithey from 1900 to 1903. The following year Sandoz left for Paris, where he was apprenticed under the painter Fernand Cormon and the sculptors Jean Antoine Injalbert and Antonin Mercié, while attending classes at the École des Beaux-Arts. He made his début at the 1906 Salon of the *Société Nationale des Beaux-Arts.

A shortage of stone and bronze during the First World War encouraged Sandoz to switch to porcelain for his sculpture. This change also signalled the start in 1916 of a collaboration with *Haviland et Cie that lasted until 1952. The joint venture resulted in a comic, playful and highly stylized menagerie of animals, fish and birds rendered in bright monochromatic glazes that were fashioned into porcelain table-top wares such as tea and coffee services, ewers and candlesticks. From 1921 Sandoz modelled a similar mix of geometric and organic *animalier* subjects for Porcelaine de Paris and, later, for the Manufacture Nationale de *Sèvres (1927–36), *Richard–Ginori, Langenthal (from 1925) and Nyon.

Following the First World War, during which he served in the artillery, Sandoz returned to Paris, where he resided at 171 boulevard Montparnasse and took a studio at 2 villa d'Alésia. In 1921 he made several trips to North Africa. He remained a member of the Société Nationale des Beaux-Arts during the 1920s and exhibited internationally. Sandoz was awarded a *grand prix* at the 1925 *Exposition Internationale, and he participated in both the French and Swiss pavilions at the 1939 New York World's Fair.

Classically trained, Sandoz executed numerous memorials, public monuments and portrait busts, although he is remembered especially for his *animalier* studies – large figures of birds and animals of prey, groups of dancing frogs, fennecs (desert foxes) and monkeys – rendered in a poignant and often humorous personal style. He also designed a charming series of table-top items including glassware, boxes and tea and coffee sets. The tea and coffee sets were modelled as birds, animals and babies in swaddling clothes and manufactured in polychromed porcelain by Theodore Haviland in Limoges.

An adherent of direct carving, Sandoz interchanged materials frequently in his search for optimum effect, using Belgian black marble, plaster, tree trunks, rock crystal, Siennese yellow marble, stone, limewood, Dolomite marble, silver, gold, tulipwood, Brazilian jacaranda, nephrite, malachite, lapis lazuli, obsidian and olive-tree wood among other materials. Works produced in bronze were cast by Valsuani, the Paris founder, using the *cire perdue* process.

Sandoz, Gérard (b. 1902)

Paris-born Sandoz came from a family of jewellers and watch- and clock-makers from the Jura. His grandfather, Gustave, and father, Gustave-Roger, successively ran a watch and jewelry shop in the Palais Royale from the early 1860s. After attending art schools in Paris, where he exhibited an early aptitude for painting and design, Sandoz joined his father in the family business. There he trained as a jeweller and silversmith, assisted in part by his uncle, the noted designer–decorator Paul *Follot.

At eighteen years of age, Sandoz began to design jewelry, hollowware and small enamelled and lacquered accessories, such as cigarette cases and compacts, in stark geometric configurations in two-colour gold, frosted crystal and onyx. Examples were displayed at the 1925 *Exposition Internationale. In the 1920s he participated also as a painter at the *Salon d'Automne and the Salons of the *Société des Artistes Décorateurs, his canvases revealing a preoccupation with mathematical solutions in their precise compositions. Sandoz became a member of the *Union des Artistes Modernes (UAM) at its inception in 1929. In 1931 he closed Maison Sandoz to devote himself to painting and film-making.

Sarreguemines

Situated in an ancient ceramic centre in Sarreguemines, a small town located at the confluence of the Saar and Blies rivers just inside north-east France, the Sarreguemines workshops were well established by the 19th century, with new plants in nearby Digoin and Salins. In 1871 Paul de Geiger, the son of the founder, took over the firm's management and initiated a major increase in *faïence* production. The factory, which on de Geiger's death in 1919 was

Édouard-Marcel Sandoz
(*left*) 'Fennecs' in patinated bronze, cast by the founder E. Robecchi, 1930.

(*below*) Tea service in enamelled porcelain, manufactured and marketed by Theodore Haviland, Limoges, 1920s.

Gérard Sandoz

(*right*) Cigarette case in enamelled silver inlaid in *coquille d'œuf*, manufactured by the atelier Gustav Sandoz, c. 1925.

Gérard Sandoz

(*left*) Brooch in enamelled gold, onyx and diamonds, 1928.

(*above*) Pendant in gold, aventurine and onyx, c. 1930.

renamed Les Faïenceries de Sarreguemines, Digoin et Vitry-le-François, produced vibrantly coloured Art Deco wares designed either by or for the art studios of Paris department stores. The firm participated in the 1925 *Exposition Internationale.

Schenck, Édouard (1874–1959) and Marcel (1898–1946)

Born in Toulouse, where he trained as an architect, Édouard began his career as a decorative metalworker in Paris at the turn of the 20th century. He operated out of a studio on rue Vergniaud and exhibited at the Salons of the *Société des Artistes Décorateurs and the *Salon d'Automne alongside Brindeau de Jarny and EDGAR BRANDT. Édouard's preferred interpretation of the prevailing Art Nouveau style included entomological and vegetal themes that he applied to jardinières, andirons, screens, lamps and architectural elements.

In the early 1920s Édouard was joined by his son Marcel. Together they produced a full range of consoles, fire-screens, radiator covers and floor and table lamps. They later transferred their workshop to Toulouse, where they remained active until after the Second World War.

Scheurich, Paul (1883–1945)

Born in New York, Scheurich was the second of three children of German immigrant parents, who returned to their homeland shortly after his birth. He studied the plastic arts and in 1909 modelled his first work in porcelain for the Schwarzburg workshops, managed at the time by Max Adolf Pfeiffer.

Scheurich was offered an exclusive contract with the Meissen manufactory by Pfeiffer, when the latter moved there. The relationship between the two worked well for Scheurich, who enjoyed the artistic freedom afforded him in the 1920s and early 1930s. At this time he produced numerous models, either

entirely in white porcelain or accented sparingly in colour, in a distinctly mannered style with meticulous detailing. In 1933 matters changed, however, when Meissen's artistic licence was partly revoked by the Saxon state treasury because Adolf Hitler's new National Socialist party had introduced revised standards of decency for all works produced under its domain. Some of Scheurich's creations were found to be too piquant, if not overtly sexual; his equestrian group 'Stürzende Reiterin' ('Lady Falling off a Horse') of 1932–33 was rejected for this reason, although it was included in the Meissen exhibit at the 1937 Exposition des Arts et Techniques in Paris, where it was awarded a *grand prix*. In 1934, after Pfeiffer was dismissed by Meissen, Scheurich cancelled his contract and became a freelance modeller.

Schliepstein, Gerhard (1886–1963)

Born in Braunschweig (Lower Saxony), Germany, Schliepstein was one of the outstanding German sculptors of the first half of the 20th century. He shared a studio with Fritz Bernuth from 1925 to 1945. Most of his models, comprising figurines or lamp bases in white-glazed earthenware or porcelain, were commissioned between 1925 and 1937 by *Rosenthal Porzellan. From 1929 Schliepstein designed exclusively for the firm in an abstract style in which the human form was reduced to sweeping curvilinear planes from which all superfluous features had been pared away.

Schmidt, Joost (1893–1948)

Born in Wunstorf (Hanover), Germany, Schmidt from 1910 to 1914 attended the Großherzoglich-Sächsische Hochschule für Bildende Kunst in Weimar. Between 1919 and 1925 he was a student in the wood-carving shop at the Bauhaus and from 1923 also studied in the school's typography workshop. From 1925 until shortly before the school's closure in Dessau in 1933, Schmidt served as a teacher and later as a master in both its

sculpture workshop and advertising department. He then rented a studio in Berlin, where he worked as a cartographer for a publishing house. After the Second World War, he was appointed a professor at the city's college of visual arts.

Schmidt is best known as a typographer who integrated different fonts and photographic images into his graphics in ingenious compositions highlighted by stark colour contrasts.

Schmidtcassel, Gustav (1867–1954)

Schmidtcassel was born in Kassel, Germany, and studied at the Berlin Kunstgewerbemuseum and the Berlin Akademie der Künste. He then travelled through Italy and Russia before returning to Berlin, where he became a pupil and assistant of Ernst Herter. In 1907 Schmidtcassel began to exhibit in group shows in the city, and in 1910 received his first commission for a public monument – an equestrian group of Peter the Great for the Baltic city of Riga. Around this time he also modelled a standing figure of Emperor Frederick for the city of Grätz (now Grodzisk Wielkopolski) in Poland.

In the 1920s Schmidtcassel designed a number of sculptures of exotic dancers in the Art Deco style, similar to those by Gerdago (Gerda Iro) – their ornate costumes accented in vivid **cold-painted** enamels. He also executed a series of figurines in bronze and ivory for both Preiss–Kassler and Rosenthal & Maeder.

Schmied, François-Louis (1873–1941). *See under* Paintings, Graphics, Posters and Bookbinding.

Schnackenberg, Walter (1880–1961)

Born in Bad Lauterburg, Schnackenberg determined his vocation as a draughtsman and painter at a young age. At nineteen he attended Heinrich Knirr's painting school in Munich, before enrolling in the Franz von Stuck academy. Fine draughtsmanship and a lively

Joost Schmidt
(*right*) *Staatliches Bauhaus Ausstellung*, Weimar, lithographic poster, 1923.

Gerhard Schliepstein
(*below left*) *Märchen*, group in porcelain for Rosenthal Porzellan, 1928.

Walter Schnackenberg
(*far right*) *Bonbonnière et Eremitage*, lithographic poster, c. 1920.

Gustav Schmidtcassel
(*below right*) Exotic dancer in cold-painted and carved ivory, 1920s.

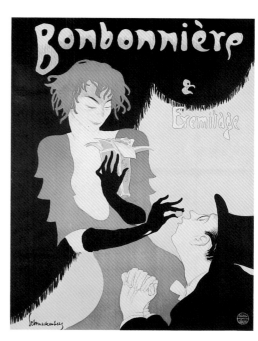

Eugene Schoen

(*far left*) Armchair in maple in black lacquer or cherry stained black, manufactured by Schmieg, Hungate & Kotzian, 1930.

(*left*) Settee manufactured by S. Karpen & Bros., 1929.

Schneider

(*above*) Vase with applied and internal decoration, 1920s.

(*right*) Vase in etched cameo glass, marketed under the trade name Le Verre Français, late 1920s.

Jacques Schnier
The Kiss, later edition in
patinated bronze from the
original in teak, on granite
base, 1933.

imagination allowed Schnackenberg to excel as a
caricaturist in his artwork for magazines such as *Jugend*
and *Simplizissimus*.

Also a print-maker and stage-set and costume
designer, Schnackenberg's best work between 1911 and
1934 was in poster design, where he often portrayed
fashionable society in a gay and frivolous graphic style
similar to that of the medium's *fin-de-siècle* masters,
Henri de Toulouse-Lautrec and Jules Chéret.

Schneider

Ernest and Charles Schneider (1877–1937 and
1881–1953, respectively) purchased the plant of a
closed glassworks at Épinay-sur-Seine in 1913. Both
brothers had at an earlier stage in their careers worked
as glass designers for DAUM FRÈRES in Nancy. They
quickly re-equipped the works, hiring old colleagues
from the Daum and *Muller glassworks as glass
artisans. Their initial production focused on fancy glass,
acid-etched cameo vases and lamps.

Drafted at the start of the First World War, Ernest
and Charles were forced to close the works during
the hostilities. When they were demobilized in 1917,
they were commissioned by the state to manufacture
badly needed hospital and laboratory utility glass.
Ernest took over the firm's administration, Charles its
technical and artistic side. By 1923 the number of staff
had grown to four hundred.

After the armistice, a range of artistic wares was
quickly produced by the firm, which changed its name
to Le Verrerie Schneider and revised its customer list.
New outlets included major Paris galleries, such as
Maison *Geo. Rouard, Delvaux and Damon's Le Vase
Étrusque and an overseas chain of retailers.

Charles was elected a member of the *Société
des Artistes Français, where from 1927 he displayed
a selection of wares in a distinctive palette of red,
saffron, orange, green, yellow and tango, mixing floral
Art Nouveau and geometric Art Deco motifs. Included

was a line of wares marked 'Le Verre Français' produced
from 1918; it comprised a series of cameo glassware
in two or three opaque layers that were acid-etched
or engraved in highly stylized geometric repeating
patterns and then polished. The line was designed
specifically for sale in major department stores
and in the firm's showroom at 14 rue de Paradis, Paris.
Meanwhile glass under the Schneider name was on
view at a nearby showroom at 54 rue de Paradis.
In addition to the trade names Schneider or Le Verre
Français, some of the firm's wares bear the signature
'Charder', a contraction of CHARles and SchneiDER.

At the 1925 *Exposition Internationale, the firm's
exhibit included stained-glass panels 100 square metres
in size for the Vins de France pavilion. In 1926 the
Degué glassworks enticed away Schneider's workers
and copied the firm's designs and techniques,
which generated a copyright lawsuit. In the action,
which lasted from 1926 to 1932, Schneider prevailed,
although both firms were by then facing bankruptcy.

In 1940 invading German forces took over
the Schneider works; destroyed its contents, including
all records and documents; and turned the building
into a brewery.

Schnier, Jacques (1898–1988)

Born in Romania, Schnier was a self-taught sculptor
influenced greatly by the art of Polynesia and the
Hawaiian Islands, where he worked for two years.
Many of his pieces were carved in teak with boldly
silhouetted and deeply carved detailing.

His major commissions included a gilt bas relief
for the Anne Bremer Memorial Library in San Francisco
(1936), eight monumental figures and reliefs for
the Golden Gate International Exposition on Treasure
Island, San Francisco (1939) and decorative bas reliefs
for the Hawaiian Room and the Congressional Club
in Washington, DC (1949). Schnier later modelled large-
scale works in stainless steel.

Schoen, Eugene (1880–1957)

A native New Yorker, Schoen earned a degree in
architecture from Columbia University in 1901. He then
won a scholarship to travel in Europe, during which
he visited Josef Hoffmann and Otto Wagner in Vienna.
On his return, he established his architectural practice,
Eugene Schoen Inc., in New York, in 1905. Sympathetic
to the Modern movement long before it was popular,
Schoen was inspired by the 1925 *Exposition
Internationale to set up an interior decorating business
at 115 East 60th Street, New York, which included a
gallery. He remained there until the Depression in
the early 1930s forced a move to 43 West 39th Street.

By the late 1920s, when Modernism made its
initial forays into the American home, Schoen was
perfectly placed to capitalize on its advances. Despite
his adherence to the Modernist principles of mass-
production, however, he believed in 'no duplication'.
Each piece was individually made, thereby restricting
the scope of his work. Yet he managed a unique blend
of the old and new: modern furniture with Neoclassical
proportions, which incorporated ebonized wood
veneers, precise ornamental detailing, lacquers, metals
and synthetic materials. These showed both French
and German influences. His designs were executed by
S. Karpen & Bros and Schmieg, Hungate & Kotzian, a
New York firm specializing in quality revival furnishings.

Schoen participated in the 1928 Livable House
Transformed exhibition at Abraham & Straus, the 1929
Architect and the Industrial Arts show at the
Metropolitan Museum of Art in New York, the 1931
American Union of Decorative Artists and Craftsmen
(AUDAC) exhibition at the Brooklyn Museum and
the 1931 Decorative Metalwork and Cotton Textiles
exhibition at the Metropolitan Museum of Art.

His son Lee (b. 1907) joined him in 1929. In the
early 1930s, the firm was commissioned to design
the RKO Center Theater in Rockefeller Center, which
opened in 1933.

Schreckengost, Paul (1908–1983)

Like his celebrated older brother Viktor, Schreckengost studied at the Cleveland Institute of Art, following which he joined the Gem Clay Forming Co. of Sebring, Ohio, manufacturers of china tableware, in the early 1930s. He remained with the firm, finally as its chief designer, until his retirement in 1979.

In an Art Deco context, Schreckengost is known primarily for a streamlined tea service in glazed earthenware with silver detailing (c. 1938), which in its aerodynamic form embodies the streamlined aesthetic of the period.

Schreckengost, Viktor (1906–2008). *See under* Ceramics.

Serré, Georges (1889–1956)

Information on Serré is sketchy. He trained as a colourist at the *Sèvres manufactory from 1902, after which he went to Saigon, where he discovered Khmer ceramics. He returned to Sèvres c. 1920, where he operated his own studio and divided his production stylistically between pieces with a high technical refinement, executed in the manner of ÉMILE DECOEUR, and those inspired by the coarse baked clay that he had seen in Southeast Asia.

Serré decorated his vessels with symmetrical geometric compositions in a very personal style. Any firing flaws were allowed to remain if he felt that these vagaries provided felicitous results. He marketed his wares through Maison *Geo. Rouard in Paris.

Sèvres

The Manufacture Nationale de Sèvres was founded in 1738 at the Château de Vincennes by local craftsmen from a nearby porcelain factory at Chantilly. Its production was aimed at the wealthy and privileged. In 1745 Louis XV granted the factory a twenty-year exclusive contract to produce porcelain in France, using

the title of royal manufacturer of porcelain. In 1756 the factory was moved to Sèvres, a commune in the south-west suburbs of Paris, where it produced soft-paste porcelain with underglaze decoration until 1770. Later Louis XV was pressured into loosening his edict on Sevrès's exclusive right to produce porcelain when new natural deposits of kaolin were discovered near Limoges, ensuring independence for French producers within the medium.

With the French Revolution and the nation's subsequent economic collapse, Sèvres was in ruins and declared the property of the state c. 1798. In the early 1800s it flourished again under the administration of Alexandre Brongniart. The company began to shed its dependence on the aristocracy and, during the reign of Napoleon III, adapted to the needs of the nation's growing bourgeoisie with the cyclical offering of historicist patterns. In 1876 the factory moved to its present location near Saint-Cloud.

Overhauled in 1891, Sèvres underwent a remarkable rejuvenation at the turn of the 20th century following years of experimentation with new soft- and hard-paste formulae, mixing traditional and Modernist influences within a large repertory of glazed and painted forms of decoration. At the 1900 Exposition Universelle, its presence was ubiquitous: in addition to its own pavilion, the firm participated in the state's joint display of its three national manufactories (Sèvres, Gobelins and Beauvais), in the display in the general ceramics section, and in architectural projects dispersed throughout the exhibition grounds. Sèvres likewise showcased its newest creations at the annual Salons.

During the inter-war years, the firm was administered by Georges Lechevallier-Chevignard, whose directive was that it participate in the modern art movement, thereby breaking with the firm's tradition of revivalist styles and techniques. From 1918 new vase shapes were presented by Félix Aubert

and Henri *Rapin, decorated in an understated contemporary style in both porcelain and *faïence*. The latter was introduced in 1924 under the direction of Maurice Gensoli (1892–1972) to provide customers with a less expensive choice of material. Gensoli, who had worked as a decorator at Sèvres since 1921, served as its artistic director from 1928 to 1959, in which capacity he oversaw the creation of a wide range of progressive designs, including some Cubist ones.

The economic downturn in the late 1920s affected the firm's sales, initiating a further search for new designs and techniques. In 1931 a new clay, named *grès fine* or *grès tendre*, was produced in parallel with the faïence. Both were decorated with simple patterns commissioned from freelance designers such as Jean *Patou, Almeric *Walter, André Naudy and Jane Lévy. Launched at the same time were new dinner and tea services by David Weill and a series of light fixtures that exploited the translucency of porcelain, designed by Eugène and G. L. Capon, Gensoli, Rapin, JACQUES-ÉMILE RUHLMANN and Jean *Chauvin.

Sèvres's standard repertory of products was likewise expanded: jewelry, *flacons*, chess sets, mahjong and smoking services were designed in the modern idiom by artist–decorators such as MAURICE DUFRÈNE, Gustave-Louis *Jaulmes, Robert *Bonfils, Suzanne Lalique, Eric *Bagge and Raoul *Dufy. After 1925 the firm also undertook monumental commissions, such as a series of faïence panels for the Paris Métro stations (for example, those designed by Rapin in 1933 for the Pont de Sèvres station, and by A. M. Fontaine in 1937 for the Mairie de Montreuil station), and murals by Jean Beaumont and François Quelvée for the ocean liner *Normandie*. Sculptors were likewise retained to produce works in *biscuit*, terracotta and *grès*, including artists such as François *Pompon (*Ours blanc*, 1922), Émile Just *Bachelet (*Condor*, 1939) and JAN AND JOËL MARTEL (*Joue'r da accordéon vendéen*, 1932).

(opposite left) Pitcher with
cups in glazed earthenware
with silver detailing,
manufactured by Gem Clay
Forming Co., Sebring, Ohio,
c. 1938.

Georges Serré
(opposite right) Vase in glazed
earthenware, 1920s.

Although tradition-bound – and therefore perhaps hesitant to implement an Art Deco grammar of decorative ornament into its repertoire – the works that Sèvres did produce in the idiom show the easy facility and refinement with which it could do so.

Shoesmith, Kenneth Denton (1890–1939)

Born in Halifax, Yorkshire, Shoesmith was raised in Blackpool, where in 1906 he enlisted as a naval cadet. This largely self-taught artist, who supplemented his training by correspondence art courses, showed an early talent for drawing. This enabled him to pursue a secondary career as a poster artist and illustrator for the English publisher Thomas Forman, while serving as a merchant marine officer. Among Shoesmith's many ocean-liner posters were those for the Anchor Line, Holland Lines, the Royal Mail Steam Packet Co. and Royal Mail Line. He also designed posters for British and Canadian railways, and postcards for the Cunard Line. All were rendered in vivid primary colours with sharply contrasting images.

Simard, Marie-Louise (*fl.* 1920s–early 30s)

Paris-born Simard was raised in Monaco, where she learned the rudiments of carving from a local stonecutter but was otherwise self-taught. She exhibited from 1927 at the Salon des Tuileries and the Salon des Indépendants, including portrait busts and groups such as *Saint George and the Dragon*, *The Four Horsemen of the Apocalypse* and *Don Quixote on Rosinante*. The Don Quixote sculpture was purchased for the French state by the Musée du Luxembourg. Simard also exhibited through the EDGAR BRANDT and Danthon galleries in Paris and held one-woman shows in Madrid, Prague and Tokyo.

Among Simard's smaller commercial works, rendered in a rigorous Art Deco style, were figures of nudes, dancers and fashionable socialites, some in gilt-bronze or silvered bronze with intricately enamelled or *damascened* detailing.

Simmen, Henri (1880–1963)

Born in northern France, Simmen trained in architecture before turning to ceramics. He first studied stoneware techniques under Edmond Lachenal and then travelled to the Far East. He made his début at the Paris Salons in 1911.

Applying his vessels with fiery *sang-de-bœuf* and *fourrure de lièvre* glazes, Simmen was the consummate potter in an Arts and Crafts context as he handled every stage of the manufacturing process himself. He was responsible for the creation of the glaze, the mixing and throwing of the clay, and its decoration and firing. His pre-war pottery was restrained, incorporating symmetrical black and brown motifs on monochromatic salt-glazed grounds, some enhanced with aventurine.

Simmen's career fell roughly into two periods: from 1910 to 1914, when he worked at Meudon with salt-glazed glazes; and from 1923 to 1935, when, at Marseilles, he developed speckled glazes, including celadon, imperial yellow, *rouge flambé* and aventurine. Between 1919 and 1921 Simmen visited the Far East, including Japan, where he integrated eastern influences into his work and met his future wife, Eugènie O'Kin (1880–1948). She was a Japanese-born sculptress who created a delightful array of stoppers and covers carved from ivory, horn and precious woods to serve as decorative fillips for Simmen's vessels. Illness forced Simmen's retirement in the mid-1930s.

Simonet, Albert (*fl.* early 1920s–35). *See* Simonet Frères.

Simonet Frères. *See under* Lighting.

Singer (Singer-Schinnerl), Susi (1891–1965)

Singer was born in Vienna and attended the Kunstschule für Frauen und Mädchen in the city between 1905 and 1915. In 1917 she joined the Wiener Werkstätte, where she learned the craft of ceramics. From 1921 Singer designed many figurines, busts and table-top items for the workshops in a humorous, bright and idiosyncratic style similar to that employed by Vally *Wieselthier, Gudrun *Baudisch-Wittke and Ena Kopriva.

After her 1924 marriage, she added her husband's surname and called herself Singer-Schinnerl. The following year she left the Wiener Werkstätte and established her own workshop in Grünbach, where she designed postcards and textiles in addition to ceramics. Forced to leave Austria in 1937 as she was Jewish, Singer emigrated to the USA, where she settled in California.

Slater, Eric (1902–1984)

Born and raised in the Stoke-on-Trent area, Slater was the son of a Royal Doulton designer who transferred in 1905 to Wileman & Co. After his formal education, Slater took a position in the drawing office of the North Staffordshire Railway Co., but, lacking the degree in engineering required for advancement, in 1919 he joined Wileman & Co. and enrolled in a design class at the Hanley School of Art. In 1925 Wileman changed its name to Shelley's and opened a showroom in Holborn, London. In 1928, when the showroom became a limited company, Shelley Potteries Ltd, Slater replaced his father as art director. His responsibility was to update bone china production with the introduction of an appealing blend of modern patterns, shapes and glazes. Several Art Deco designs were forthcoming, including 'Sunray' (1930) and 'Blocks' (1931), as well as important new shapes such as 'Vogue' (with its striking triangular handles), 'Mode' and, later, 'Regent'.

In the Second World War Slater enlisted in the Home Guard. After the war he focused on rebuilding the firm's sales, especially in foreign markets, again with new shapes and decoration. He remained with Shelley Potteries until 1972, even as it underwent mergers and name changes. He left a legacy of fine design, especially during the Art Deco era.

Société des Artistes Décorateurs

(*above left*) Maquette in chalk, gouache and ink for the poster by René Buthaud for the 1931 Salon of the Société des Artistes Décorateurs, Paris.

(*above right*) Lithographic poster by Jean Dupas for the 1924 Salon of the Société des Artistes Décorateurs, Paris.

Henri Simmen

(*left*) *Visage au voile*, bust in glazed stoneware on a steel base, 1920s.

Louis Sognot

(*top left*) Chest-of-drawers and filing cabinet, in collaboration with Charlotte Alix, *c.* 1928.

(*top right*) Side table in oak with metal mount, marketed by Primavera, Paris, 1929.

(*above*) Desk and chair, in collaboration with Charlotte Alix, *c.* 1928.

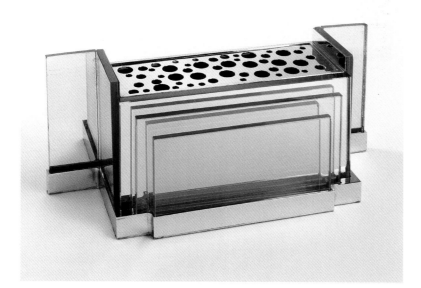

Louis Sognot
Jardinière in chromed metal
and tinted glass, in collaboration
with Charlotte Alix, 1930.

Société des Artistes Décorateurs

The Salon of the Société des Artistes Décorateurs (SAD) provided one of four French forums through which an artist could display his or her newest creations. The other three forums were the *Société des Artistes Français, the *Société Nationale des Beaux-Arts and the *Salon d'Automne.

Inaugurated in January 1904 at the Palais de Beaux-Arts, the SAD moved two years later to the Pavillon de Marsan on rue de Rivoli, and then to the Union Centrale des Arts Décoratifs, on the present site of the Musée des Arts Décoratifs. In the 1920s the SAD emerged as the preferred venue through which many of the *sociétaires* in this book exhibited their works.

Société des Artistes Français

Of the principal annual Salons that of the Société des Artistes Français (SAF), staged at the Grand Palais, was the oldest and most illustrious. Founded in the early 1670s to show the works of living artists – especially paintings and sculptures – from 1881 the SAF began to include a wider range of disciplines, including gravure, lithography, pastels, public monuments, miniatures and a selection of applied arts.

Société Nationale des Beaux-Arts

Established in 1890, the Société Nationale des Beaux-Arts (SNBA) added applied works of art to paintings and sculpture in its second year. Situated from the mid-1890s on the corner of avenue d'Antin and rue Jean Goujon, the Salon of the SNBA provided artists with an alternative venue to that of the *Société des Artistes Français. Many artists, in fact, participated in both exhibitions.

Sognot, Louis (1892–70)

Born in Paris, Sognot was educated at the École Bernard Palissy, after which he trained at Krieger, a furniture manufacturer on the rue du Faubourg Saint-Antoine.

In the early 1920s he joined *Primavera. His designs were exhibited under his own name at the Salons from 1923.

Sognot's style was always impeccably sharp, matching the bold and clean sweep that tubular chrome brought to furniture. His quick grasp of the metal's aesthetic potential propelled Primavera to the forefront of the modern movement. At the firm, Sognot worked closely with Charlotte *Chauchet-Guilleré, Marcel *Guillemard and Charlotte Alix. Sognot and Alix created numerous designs together, especially chairs in tubular or flat metal, with high and angular frames upholstered in leather or rubberized fabric.

Sognot presented two rooms – a boudoir and adjoining bedroom – in the Primavera pavilion at the 1925 *Exposition Internationale. Colourful carpets softened and complemented his angular suites of furniture in warm woods. At the exhibition he also designed a piano for the Gaveau stand. A co-founder of the *Union des Artistes Modernes (UAM) in 1929, Sognot displayed a range of innovative furniture at the group's yearly exhibitions, examples of which were illustrated in *Répertoire du Goût Moderne IV* and *V*. Where possible, his pieces were dual- or multipurpose: desktops opened to show interiors fitted as dressing tables; and pedestals enclosed compartments housing smoking accessories. Even Sognot's walls were movable – his administrator's office at the 1930 UAM exhibition could be converted into a recreation room.

Sognot's notable commissions included an interior for Jean *Carlu (1930); furniture for the Maharajah of Indore (1931); offices for the newspaper *La Semaine de Paris* (1930); and the first-class cabin for the resident doctor on the *Normandie. His celebrated 1931 double bed for the Maharajah of Indore was made in **duralumin** and had twin glass end-tables. Its design evolved from two earlier models: the first a single

bed for a colonial house shown at the 1930 Semaine de Paris Exposition; the second, with a coverlet by Hélène *Henry, for a first-class cabin on the ocean liner L'*Atlantique (1931). In 1932 Sognot experimented with a new material: his set of dining chairs at the Salon of the *Société des Artistes Décorateurs was made of moulded and lacquered Lakarmé, an incombustible plastic. He lectured part-time as a professor of decoration at the *École Boulle from 1926.

Sornay, André (1902–2000)

Born in Lyons into a family of merchants and furniture-makers, Sornay entered the École des Beaux-Arts in his native city, where he studied under Jean Larrive. Taking over the family enterprises after his father's death, he set out to add a line of modern furniture to the firm's repertoire of revivalist editions.

In spite of negative reviews from several critics, Sornay, with the assistance of his future wife Suzanne Lunet, researched modern design and became inspired by PIERRE CHAREAU, Francis *Jourdain and other avant-garde designer-decorators. In 1923 Sornay made his début at the *Salon d'Automne, showing a bedroom in white sycamore designed on a massive scale. In 1925 he opened a workshop in Villeurbanne, and decorated numerous apartments in Paris and Lyons, as well as retirement homes and libraries. At the 1925 *Exposition Internationale, he collaborated with the architect Tony Garnier on the Pavillon de la Ville de Lyons.

Much of Sornay's furniture was solid and rigorously geometric, invariably functional and often multifunctional and convertible, sometimes with a Cubist or African tribal accent. His choice of veneers included macassar ebony, palisander, burled elm, mahogany, *loupe de thuya*, Oregon pine and walnut.

From the late 1920s Sornay used synthetic lacquers, plastic fabrics, *caoutchouc* (India rubber),

André Sornay

(*right*) Pair of armchairs in Oregon pine with copper mounts, 1930s.

(*below left*) Easel in macassar ebony with bands of brass nail-head decoration, 1930s.

(*below right*) Armchair in Oregon pine with bands of brass nail-head decoration, 1930s.

André Sornay

(*right*) Commode in burl wood with brass nail-head decoration, 1930s.

(*centre*) Desk in palisander and rosewood with bands of brass nail-head decoration, 1930s.

André Sornay

(*left*) Desk in mahogany with bands of brass nail-head decoration, 1930s.

Séraphin Soudbinine
(*below left*) *Naïade au Dauphin*,
plaster group, 1924.

Mart Stam
(*below right*) Chair in tubular
chrome-plated steel and
lacquered wood, manufactured
by Thonet, *c.* 1935.

John Henry Bradley Storrs
(*right*) *The Spirit of Walt
Whitman*, study in bronze for
a monument to the poet, cast
by the founder Valsuani, *c.* 1920.

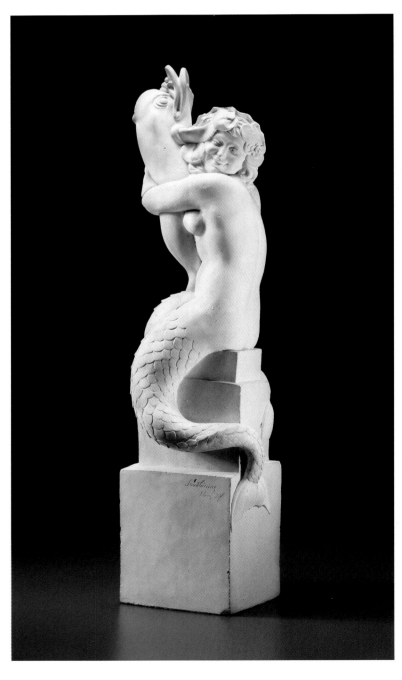

William Spratling
Tea and coffee service
with pitcher and tray, silver
with wood mounts, 1930s.

Formica, Permatex and a diverse selection of industrial manufacturing techniques. Between 1930 and 1933 he introduced a very simple and effective form of ornamentation: bands of brass nail-heads composed in infinite patterns, to which he added inlays of leather, copper and lacquer. To provide his furniture with novel dimensional effects, Sornay commissioned metalware mounts from Claudius *Linossier and Michel *Zadounaisky, among others. In 1932 Sornay patented a method of furniture construction in which a wooden frame was supported by a metallic internal structure. The frame was then covered by twin veneered panels affixed by visible brass nails organised in rows and spaced 5 or 10 millimetres apart. This new technique, known as *cloutage*, became a signature feature of Sornay's furniture.

Never afraid to follow his instincts and to reveal his independent spirit, Sornay nevertheless remained rational in his approach to furniture design. He was at the height of his creativity from 1933 to 1938. His firm is now administered by his children.

Soudbinine, Séraphin (1870–1944)
Born and raised in Russia, Soudbinine later moved to Paris, where he became a protégé of Auguste Rodin, in whose studio he worked for ten years as a stone-carver. He also created bronze portrait busts, including one of Rodin entitled *Bust of the Master*, cast by the founder Alexis Rudier.

Following a visit to New York, in which he saw the Pierpoint Morgan collection of Asian ceramics at the Metropolitan Museum of Art, Soudbinine built a workshop for high-fired sandstone and porcelain in Paris. He set about sculpting works that he applied with thick crackled glazes – his preferred subject matter being animals. Collaborating on occasion with the potter Paul Jeanneney (1861–1920), he designed **biscuit** busts for the *Sèvres

manufactory from 1915 to 1943. Soudbinine also created compositions for JEAN DUNAND's lacquered screens and panels, two of which, entitled 'Battle of the Angels: Fortissimo' and 'Battle of the Angels: Pianissimo', are in the collection of the Metropolitan Museum of Art, New York.

Spratling, William (1900–1967)
Spratling was born in Sonyea, New York State, and studied at the Art Students League in 1915. Two years later he entered the school of architecture at Auburn University in Auburn, Alabama. Graduating in 1921, Spratling afterward served as an adjunct professor of architecture at Tulane University in New Orleans, visiting Mexico *c.* 1926 to study Spanish colonial architecture. In subsequent trips there he befriended the artists Diego Rivera, Miguel Covarrubias and David Alfaro Siqueiros, whose idiosyncratic styles influenced him.

In 1929 Spratling moved to Taxco, Mexico, where two years later he established a workshop, La Aduana, in an old customs house. His silver jewelry, hollowware and flatware, which drew primarily on pre-Columbian and Spanish colonial ornamentation, single-handedly resuscitated the local silver manufacturing industry and its related mining industry. In the early 1930s, as his business expanded, Spratling hired goldsmiths from Iguala and renamed his workshop Taller de las Delicias (Shop of Delights). During the Second World War, when European imports were banned, American department stores commissioned their silverware from Spratling.

In 1945 the firm's name was changed to Spratling y Artesanos, after which it became financially strapped and was dissolved. Two years later Spratling set up another shop, Taxco-el-Viejo, which remained in production until his death, at which time an old friend, Alberto Ulrich, bought the business from its employees, to whom Spratling had bequeathed it.

Stam, Mart (1899–1986)
Born in Amsterdam, Stam studied drawing at the Royal School for Advanced Studies from 1917 to 1919, then worked as an architectural draughtsman in Rotterdam until 1922. He is best known for the cantilevered tubular-metal chair, constructed of gas pipes, which he designed in 1926. The same year he moved to Berlin, where he met several avant-garde architects, including Hans Poelzig (1869–1936) and Bruno Taut (1880–1938). He took part in an exhibition at the Bauhaus in 1923 and between 1925 and 1928 published frequent articles on design and architecture. In 1926 he produced the first prototype of his revolutionary cantilivered tubular chair, made from welded gas pipes. This construction was later refined by Ludwig *Mies van der Rohe and Marcel *Breuer. With Gerrit Thomas *Rietveld and Hendrik Petrus Berlage, Stam became a founding member of the Congrès Internationaux d'Architecture Moderne in 1928. The following year he exhibited chair designs in Stuttgart. Between 1931 and 1932 he worked as a town planner in Russia. Before his retirement in 1966 he taught design and architecture in Berlin and Dresden. He died in Goldbach, Switzerland.

Stölzl (Stadler-Stölzl), Gunta (1897–1983).
See under Textiles.

Storrs, John Henry Bradley (1885–1956)
Storrs, who was born in Chicago, was the last of seven children of an architect–real estate developer. His art training began in earnest in 1905 after he graduated from University High School and embarked on a trip to Europe. This was the first of countless trans-Atlantic crossings in a peripatetic lifestyle that divided his career between Chicago and Europe, where he spent most of his time in Orléans, France, with the family of his fiancée, Marguerite Chabrol.

Raymond Subes
Mantel clock in wrought iron
and marble, c. 1921.

John Henry Bradley Storrs
(*opposite*) *Bathers*, group in
bronze, c. 1916–19.

He studied in Hamburg and in Paris, possibly at the Académie Montparnasse, between 1906 and 1907. In 1908 Storrs returned to Chicago, where he enrolled in night classes at the city's Academy of Fine Arts, and in 1909 at the School of the Art Institute of Chicago, where he studied anatomy and modelling with the sculptor Charles J. Mulligan. His formal education continued unabated: in 1910 he studied under Bela Pratt at Boston's School of the Museum of Fine Arts; and in 1911 under Charles Grafly at the Pennsylvania Academy of Fine Arts in Philadelphia. The following year he returned to Paris, where he registered for courses at the Académie de la Grande Chaumière, the Académie Julian, the École des Beaux-Arts and the Académie Colarossi. In 1914 this protracted series of educational ventures culminated with an invitation from Auguste Rodin to join his atelier. Storrs later travelled to San Francisco to install the master sculptor's exhibit at the 1915 Panama–Pacific International Exposition.

Having launched his career in Paris, Storrs staged his inaugural American one-man show at the Folson Gallery in New York in 1920. His versatility allowed him to move easily between figurative and abstract art, drawing both on a classical iconography and on a blend of themes from avant-garde abstract art, including Cubism, French Modernism and the machine aesthetic.

In the 1920 and 1930s Storrs added paintings and rug designs to his artistic repertoire. His career by this time was studded with gallery exhibitions on both sides of the Atlantic. By 1920 he had already developed a distinctive non-representational style which simplified form into planes and volumes. In the 1920s he also introduced a series of sheer architectural models inspired by the setbacks on skyscrapers, including *Forms in Space* and *Study in Forms*. His thirty-metre aluminium figure of Ceres (1928), designed to surmount the Chicago Board of Trade Building,

displayed a more fluid interpretation of the Modernist idiom. In 1929 he was elected to full membership in New York's American Union of Decorative Artists and Craftsmen (AUDAC) group. His last trip to the USA was in 1939. During the Second World War he was arrested by the German infantry and confined in a military prison.

Studium–Louvre (Le Louvre)
Studio Studium–Louvre was established in 1923 as a decorating workshop by the department store Le Louvre, which had been founded in 1855 on rue de Rivoli. Its director until 1938 was Etienne *Kohlmann, who retained a team of consultant designers, including Georges *Djo-Bourgeois, André *Fréchet, Pierre *Lahalle, Georges *Lévard and Maurice *Matet. The studio's display at the 1925 *Exposition Internationale also included works designed by EDGAR BRANDT, Laurent Malclès and Albert Laprade.

Subes, Raymond (1893–1970)
Paris-born Raymond Subes attended the *École Boulle, where he studied metal engraving, and then moved to the city's École Nationale Supérieure des Arts Décoratifs. His first job set the course of his career – a three-year apprenticeship in Émile Robert's atelier in Enghien-les-Bains. Here, theories of metallurgy were put into practice and the traditions of the medium were absorbed and later adapted by Subes, who learned quickly. In 1919 he was appointed director of the metal studio of Borderel & Robert, a prominent architectural construction company. Business flourished as commissions poured in from architects throughout France.

A cursory glance at Subes's 1920s commissions shows the wide range of work that he undertook, including churches, cemeteries, monuments, exhibition halls and hotels. Many of his *tours de force*, however, remain unidentified on building façades and in the

bold sweep of unsigned hotel balustrades. Many more were stripped and scrapped when the ocean liners *Île-de-France*, *L'*Atlantique*, *France* and *Normandie* met their ignominious ends.

Subes showed a range of furnishings at the annual Paris Salons. His displays included commissions for other exhibitors; for example, a steel frame for a bookcase by JACQUES-ÉMILE RUHLMANN and a wrought-iron doorway for Michel Roux-Spitz. Later, he undertook work for Maurice *Jallot and Alfred *Porteneuve. At the 1925 *Exposition Internationale, Subes provided ironwork for the pavilion of the Ambassade Française, the Hôtel du Collectionneur and the pavilion of the Société de l'Art Appliqué aux Métiers. His preference was for wrought iron, which he interchanged on occasion with bronze, patinated copper and, in the 1930s, aluminium and steel – the last either oxidized or lacquered in Duco.

Süe, Louis (1975–1968). *See* Süe et Mare.

Süe et Mare. *See under* Furniture and Interior Design.

Suisse, Gaston (1896–1988)
Suisse is best known for his lacquered paintings, which he described as '*après Nature*', depicting birds-of-paradise, lush forests inhabited by monkeys, and streams teeming with tropical fish. Although he had entered the École Nationale Supérieure des Arts Décoratifs in Paris in 1913, he soon enlisted in the French infantry. Demobilized in 1918, he returned to complete his diploma under Paul Renouard and Albert d'Ys. Graduating in 1925, Suisse made his début the following year at the *Salon d'Automne, of which he was elected a *sociétaire* the following year. He was also a member of the *Société des Artistes Français, the *Société Nationale des Beaux-Arts and the Société des Artistes Animaliers and exhibited in Paris at the Drouant, EDGAR BRANDT, Georges Petit,

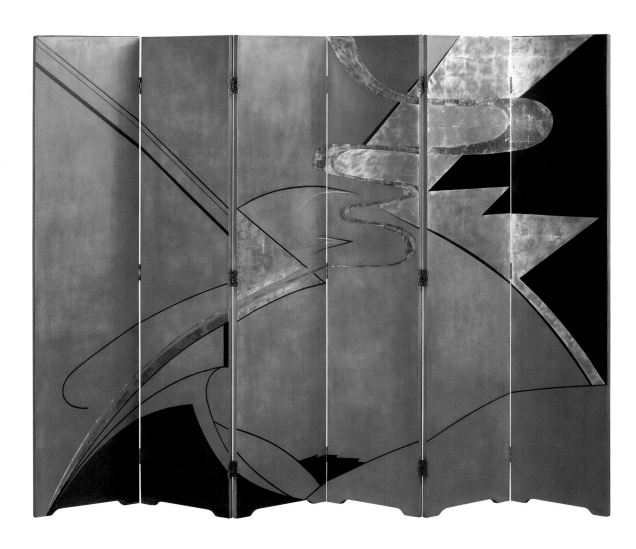

Gaston Suisse

(*right*) Table in lacquered wood
inlaid with *coquille d'œuf*,
c. 1930.

Gaston Suisse

(*below*) Murals for the reception hall of the Conseil Municipal in the Palais de Tokyo at the Exposition des Arts et Techniques, Paris 1937.

(*right*) *Poissons japonais*, lacquered and gold leaf wood panel with engraved detailing, 1939.

Walter Dorwin Teague
(*below left*) Pair of candlesticks in pewter manufactured by Plymouth Pewter, commissioned by the Marshall Field & Co. department store, Chicago, c. 1934.

Elsa Tennhardt
(*below right*) Centrepiece and matching candlesticks in silvered- and gilt-brass manufactured by E. & J. Bass Co., New York, 1928.

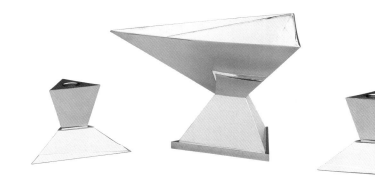

Jean Charpentier and Malesherbes galleries. His atelier in the 1920s was listed as 42 rue de Tolbiac; he later moved to 47 boulevard Saint Marcel, near the Jardin des Plantes.

At the Salons, Suisse showed a wide selection of screens, panels, *étuis* and boxes in lacquer and eggshell. Private commissions included furniture in both modern and Oriental styles. He worked on wood or Masonite, applying a base coat of gold or silver lacquer to which he added polychrome or incised decoration. In the early 1930s he switched from lacquer to nitro-cellulose, a synthetic varnish that dried more quickly than traditional lacquer and was easier to work with.

Suisse exhibited frequently outside the Salons in the 1930s, providing the mural decoration for the Temple d'Angkor at the 1931 Exposition Coloniale and a reception hall in the Palais de Tokyo at the 1937 Exposition des Arts et Techniques, the latter in collaboration with the artist Cottet. A touring museum exhibition of his work visited Brussels, Zurich and Cairo.

Szabo, Adelbert-Georges (*fl.* 1906–38)

Hungarian-born Szabo became a naturalized French citizen and established his metal workshop at 15 rue Émile-Dubois, Paris. As early as 1906–07 he exhibited metalware at the Salon of the *Société des Artistes Décorateurs*; and as late as 1938 he showed a wrought-iron door commissioned by a charity institution in Angoulême. His pre-First World War works were inspired by historicism rather than the prevailing Art Nouveau style, but from 1919 his pieces included Art Deco elements.

Szabo's works tended to be small in scale: grilles, chandeliers, radiator covers, mirror frames – even key escutcheons – in wrought iron or, on rare occasions, bronze-on-copper. Only occasionally did he accept commissions for architectural projects, such as a clock for the façade of *Le Temps* Building in 1921, and

elevator doors and stairway ramps for the Banque de l'Union Parisienne ten years later. A major undertaking both in size and importance was the doors for the first-class dining room on the *Normandie*.

T

Tambuté, Henri (1911–1987). *See* Sain & Tambuté.

Teague, Walter Dorwin (1883–1960)

Born in Decatur, Indiana, Teague grew up in Pendleton, near Indianapolis. Graduating from high school in 1902, he moved the following year to New York, where he attended night classes at the Art Students League. In 1908 he joined the art department of the advertising agency Calkins & Holden, and in 1911 opened his own office, where he popularized the use of decorative borders to frame advertisements. In the mid-1920s Teague established himself as a freelance industrial designer and an acknowledged authority on typography.

Teague's first blue-chip client was the Eastman Kodak Co., which in 1928 retained him to redesign its showroom and cameras, including the plastic 'Baby Brownie' model (1933), a commission that established his reputation as an industrial designer. Among his other well-known designs were the 'Marmon' car (1930), the 'Spartan' radio (model 557) with blue-mirrored case and chromed fins (1936), the 'Scripto' pen (1952), Schaefer Beer cans (1957), New Haven Railroad coaches and Texaco gas stations as well as a host of products such as furniture for S. Karpen & Bros., lamps for the Polaroid Corp., pewterware for Marshall Field's department store in Chicago, refrigerators for Westinghouse, pianos for Steinway & Sons and cash registers for the National Cash Register Co. In 1932 Teague was hired by Amory Houghton, the president of Corning Glass Works, as a design consultant to develop a line of modern

colourless crystal tableware and decorative glass for its Steuben division – a radical change from its previous repertory of frosted and coloured glass. Teague's new patterns, all self-consciously upper-class in theme, included 'St Tropez'.

At the 1939 New York World's Fair, Teague served as an in-house consultant for various firms, including the Libbey Glass Co. (for which he designed the 'Embassy' stemware pattern for the state dining room in the Federal Building, in collaboration with Edwin W. Fuerst) and the Ford car company (chairs in aluminium and Lucite for its stand). The most businesslike of America's industrial designers, Teague remained in the forefront of his profession in the post-war years. In 1940 he authored a book on his theories, *Design This Day – the Technique of Order in the Machine Age*.

Templier, Raymond (1891–1968). *See under* Jewelry.

Tennhardt, Elsa (1899–1980)

Tennhardt was born in Germany, but travelled to the USA in her teenage years as a nanny for an English family. By 1920, having settled in or near Manhattan, she became acquainted with the city's Austro-German *émigré* artists' colony. This included the circle around Winold Reiss, in whose art school on Christopher Street she studied drawing and briefly worked c. 1925.

Around this time, Tennhardt was commissioned by E. & J. Bass, a local silver manufacturer, to design a line of Modernist silverware, which was introduced in 1928. Included were a creamer and sugar set, candlesticks and a vanity set in a triangular Cubist style. A silver cocktail shaker set was illustrated in *Harper's Bazaar*. These were apparently Tennhardt's only industrial designs, after which she concentrated on painting, while teaching adult education art classes at the Cooper Union and New York University. Tennhardt moved to Southampton, Long Island in the mid-1960s.

Adelbert-Georges Szabo
(*above left*) Pair of gates in wrought iron, mid-1920s.

(*above right*) *Torchère* in wrought iron and alabaster, *c.* 1930.

Walter Dorwin Teague
(*left*) St Tropez glassware for the Steuben Glass Co., *c.* 1932.

André Thuret

(*above*) Vase in thick hand-blown glass with applied and internally-textured decoration, c. 1930 (*left*); with similar examples by Maurice Marinot and Henri Navarre, late 1920s/early 1930s.

Tétard Frères

(*top left*) Coffee pot in silver with ebony handle, 1936.

(*top right*) Tea service in silver with ivory handles, late 1920s.

Tétard Frères

Founded in 1851 by Hugo Tétard at 4 rue Béranger, Paris, Maison Tétard was administered from 1880 by Edmond Tétard (d. 1901). After Edmond's death, the firm was continued by his sons, Henri, Jacques and Georges, who changed its name to Tétard Frères.

A trio of highly talented designers was added between the wars: Valéry Bizouard, who served as design director until his retirement in 1936, and Louis Tardy, who stayed until 1959, both joined the company in 1919; followed in 1930 by Jean Tétard, the founder's great-grandson. Jean rejuvenated the Tétard product line with an arresting selection of angular and fluid hollowware designs. The highly polished surfaces on his silver were further accented with handles and knop finials in exotic materials such as ivory, rosewood and lapis lazuli. André Mare (of SÜE ET MARE)was one of the noted outside designers commissioned by Tétard Frères.

Thuret, André (1898–1965)

French-born Thuret was employed as an engineer at the Bagneux glassworks and later at another in Bezons. Although trained as a technician in the large-scale problems of industrial glass manufacture, he became fascinated *c.* 1924 with MAURICE MARINOT's work in glass and joined his friend Henri *Navarre in initial experimentations in the medium. Thereafter he worked alone, except with the occasional help of a gaffer, at the Alfortville glasshouse near Paris.

Thuret's creations were mostly in transparent tinted glass which he either blew into free-form shapes or into a mould. To create the internal swirls and patterns of colour that came to characterize his creations, he rolled the parison on to powdered metallic oxides on the **marver**; when it had annealed, he used tools to pinch the glass into graceful folds that framed the central vessel. Awarded a diploma of honour for his display at the 1925 *Exposition

Internationale, Thuret also exhibited at the 1928 *Salon d'Automne and at exhibitions in London, Madrid, Munich and Florence.

Thuret continued to create glassware after the Second World War, varying decorative effects by the interchange of clear, transparent or tinted glasses with bubbled or textured encased decoration. Scientific considerations in these designs interested him as much as aesthetic concerns. In a 1951 glass exhibition at the Pavillon de Marsan, Paris, Thuret showed examples of his mature work.

Tiffany & Co.

The celebrated silver, jewelry and luxury goods retailer Tiffany & Co. was founded in 1837 by Charles Lewis Tiffany and John Young as a stationery and dry-goods store in New York. In the next ten years the partners, joined in 1841 by John L. Ellis, added gold jewelry and silverware to their stock. In 1853 Tiffany bought out his partners, and the store assumed its existing name. It participated in all the international exhibitions in the 19th and early 20th centuries, receiving top prizes for its presentation of Oriental and Aesthetic Movement styles, to which it added native American themes in the 1890s. At the 1900 Exposition Universelle, the Tiffany & Co. exhibit was placed alongside that of Charles's son, Louis Comfort Tiffany. From 1903 the company retailed decorative items produced by Louis's firm, Tiffany Studios.

That America's premier silversmith and jeweller could afford virtually to ignore the Modernist style in the inter-war years shows that domestic demand remained unaffected by Parisian trends. Tiffany's tradition of quiet and elegant restraint – demonstrated in a range of jewelry and period-revival silver tableware and toiletry accessories that served as the bedrock of its business and reputation – remained the proven choice of its patrician New England clientele. Only in the 1930s did the firm add a selection of 'Modern

Classicism' to its repertory, including the faceted trophy weighing 4.6 kilograms, made of platinum and crystal rather than silver, which it presented at the 1933 A Century of Progress Exposition in Chicago.

Examination of Tiffany's sketch books from the 1930s shows that few other Art Deco designs were put into production until 1937, when more examples of Modernist silver were forthcoming, as in the firm's entries for the Contemporary American Design exhibition at the Metropolitan Museum of Art in New York. These included examples by Tiffany's chief designer, Arthur Leroy Barney, and Peer Smed (1878–1943) – the latter a Danish designer who mixed a lightly decorated Scandinavian-inspired style with sheer, rectangular German functionalism. In 1937 the firm also celebrated its centenary with the introduction of its 'Century Pattern' flatware. By 1939 the earlier hesitancy was gone: Tiffany's Modernist silver display in the House of Jewels at the 1939 New York World's Fair, led by Barney and Olaf Wilford, surpassed the Art Deco designs of its nearest competitors.

U

Union des Artistes Modernes

Within two years of the triumphal 1925 *Exposition Internationale, the high-styled grammar of Art Deco ornament that had dominated the exhibition and the annual Salons had faded. In 1928, after *Le Corbusier and others severed their association with the *Société des Artistes Décorateurs, ROBERT MALLET-STEVENS proposed a Secession-like equivalent of the Deutscher Werkbund. As a result of Mallet-Stevens's suggestion, a group of avant-garde artists, designers, architects and sculptors formed the Union des Artistes Modernes (UAM) in 1929.

In addition to Mallet-Stevens, founding members included PIERRE CHAREAU, EILEEN GRAY, André Lurçat, JAN AND JOËL MARTEL, Charlotte *Perriand and

Tiffany & Co.

(*right*) Chinoiserie desk clock, the case in 18-karat gold, lacquer, jade and lapis lazuli, with multi-coloured enamelled dial set with rose-cut diamond hands and Arabic numerals; the movement by Vacheron Constantin, c. 1929.

(*below*) Centrepiece and pair of candelabra in silver, exhibited in the firm's display in the House of Jewels at the New York World's Fair, 1939.

Tiffany & Co.

(*far left*) Cocktail service in silver with cabochon emeralds exhibited in the firm's display in the House of Jewels at the New York World's Fair, 1939.

(*left*) Coffee service in silver and black fibre exhibited in the firm's display in the House of Jewels at the New York World's Fair, 1939.

(*below*) *Tête-à-tête* tea service with tray in silver with nephrite finials and synthetic fibre handles, designed by Albert L. Barney for the firm's display at the New York World's Fair, 1939.

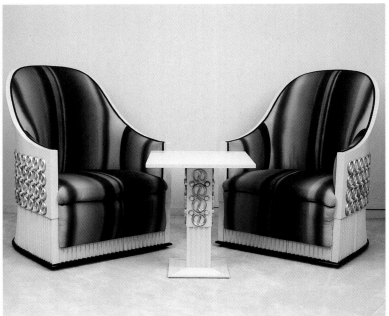

JEAN PUIFORCAT. The UAM's first offices were in the apartment of Hélène *Henry, the textile designer, at 7 rue des Grands Augustins, Paris. Mallet-Stevens was its first president, René *Herbst its second. Through the years a large number of artists joined the organization; by 1932 membership numbered sixty.

Searching for a universal philosophy of design, UAM members advocated a stark functionalism and absence of ornamentation, dubbed 'La Grande Nudité'. In 1930 members showed their works at the UAM's inaugural exhibition staged at the Musée Galliera in Paris. The group's first manifesto – written in 1934 by Louis Cheronnet – served as a partial response to Paul *Iribe's attacks at the time on Modernism. A second UAM manifesto was drafted by Georges-Henri Pingusson in 1949.

Urban, Joseph (1872–1933)

Born in Vienna, Urban studied at the Akademie der Bildenden Künste between 1890 and 1893 with Karl von Hasenauer and at the Polytechnicum in his native city. He first visited the USA in 1901 to design the Austrian pavilion for the 1904 Louisiana Purchase Exposition in St Louis. On returning to Vienna, Urban participated in the Hagenbund exhibitions, but turned his attention increasingly to operatic stage design. In 1911 he accepted the art directorship of the Boston Opera House, and returned to the USA permanently. Around this time, Urban worked also as a designer for the Metropolitan Opera and the Ziegfeld Follies in New York, and designed the New School for Social Research building on West 12th Street. In 1921–22 Urban served as the president of the short-lived Wiener Werkstätte of America gallery at 581 Fifth Avenue in Manhattan.

Urban's furniture, textile and wallpaper designs were theatrical, youthful and exuberant, as in the lady's bedroom in black mirrored glass that he showed at the 1928 American Designers' Gallery. The stylistic

influence of the Vienna Secession is ever-present, with colour predominating. The Urban archives in the Butler Library at Columbia University record a considerable number of furniture commissions that he undertook for hotels and restaurants in the American Midwest and in New York at the time, some of which were manufactured by the Mallin Furniture Co. He participated in the 1929 Architect and the Industrial Arts exhibition at the Metropolitan Museum of Arts in New York and in the 1931 American Union of Decorative Artists and Craftsmen (AUDAC) show at the Brooklyn Museum.

In the 1920s Urban exerted a monumental influence on all aspects of the decorative arts in the USA. A generation older than most of the aspiring Modernists, he emerged as the *paterfamilias* to the movement.

V

Van Cleef & Arpels

This French jewelry house was founded in 1906 by two brothers, Julien (1884–1964) and Charles (1880–1951) Arpels, and their brother-in-law Alfred Van Cleef (1873–1938), who like the Arpels came from a family of diamond merchants. A third Arpels brother, Louis (1886–1976), joined the firm shortly before the First World War. At their showroom at 22 Place Vendôme and their workshop on rue Saint-Martin, Van Cleef took charge of administration and production, while Julien Arpels was responsible for the firm's sales and Charles Arpels for the selection of precious stones.

The partnership quickly earned a reputation for *haute joaillierie*, establishing branches in Dinard, then Cannes, Deauville, Vichy and Monte Carlo. Far less portentous was the opening of a New York showroom on 24 October 1929, the day of the Wall Street crash.

At the 1925 *Exposition Internationale, Van Cleef & Arpels won a *grand prix* for one of its jewelry designs –

a half-open rose in diamond-studded rubies and emeralds. From 1926 to 1942 Renée Puissant, Van Cleef's daughter, served as the firm's artistic director. Gifted with a rich imagination but unable to draw, she worked closely for years with René-Sim Lacaze, a talented draughtsman and designer. The firm's first *minaudière*, an exquisite box of **chased** gold set with precious stones that housed all the accessories a socialite could not do without, was created in 1930 by Louis Arpels for Florence Gould, wife of the American railway magnate.

In 1932 Van Cleef & Arpels expanded its space in the Place Vendôme with the acquisition of RENÉ LALIQUE's adjoining showroom at no. 24, and the following year it signed a contract with Alfred Langlois, a watch- and clock-casemaker of repute, who specialized in making vanity cases. In 1935 the firm revolutionized the art of jewelry by introducing the *serti mystérieux* or serti invisible (invisible setting).

Van Cleef & Arpels participated in the 1937 Exposition des Arts et Techniques, and the following year it received a prestigious commission from the Egyptian court to furnish the jewelry for the marriage of Princess Fawzia (daughter of King Fuad and sister of Farouk) to Reza Pahlavi (the Shah of Iran). Since then a stream of royal and Hollywood clients has secured the firm's position at the pinnacle of the jewelry profession.

In addition to their jewelry, Van Cleef & Arpels produced a vast array of deluxe accessories in the inter-war years, including vanity cases, powder compacts, handbags, pill boxes, *minaudières*, cigarette cases, chatelaine watches, clock lighters, mystery clocks and even bird cages and aquariums. For these it drew on Egyptian, Far Eastern and Persian themes and motifs, in addition to a highly coloured and exuberant array of Modernist designs. Van Cleef & Arpels remains closely associated with its founding families.

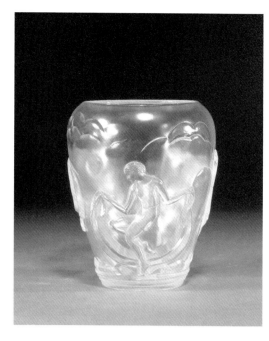

Venini

Paolo Venini (1895–1959) was born at Varenna, near Milan, to a glass-making family from Como, and he studied law at Milan University. He then turned to glass-making, and in 1921 became a partner with the Venetian Giacomo Cappellin (1887–1968) in the Andrea Rioda glassworks in Murano. After Rioda died in the same year, the partners changed the firm's name to Vetri Soffiati Muranesi Cappellin-Venini & Co., and engaged the designer–technician Vittorio Zecchin (1878–1947) to continue the firm's tradition of producing glassware inspired by old paintings.

In 1926, with the partnership dissolved, Cappellin withdrew to form his own glass enterprise, and Maestri Soffiati Muranesi Venini & Co. was formed. Among the changes that were forthcoming, new techniques were developed and the production of **millefiori**, **filigrana** and **latticino** revived. In addition to its own designers – including Paolo Venini himself, who is perhaps best known for his 1950s *vaso fazzoletto* (handkerchief vase) made of Zanfirico glass (*vetro a retorti*) – the firm retained a formidable team of outside designers, including the Finn Tapio Wirkkala, the sculptor Napoleone Martinuzzi, the Swedish potter Tyra Lundgren, Gio *Ponti and Salvador Dalí.

Vera, Paul (1882–1958)

Vera was born in Paris but little is known of his upbringing and education, although it can be assumed that he attended one of the schools of fine arts in the city, because he emerged after 1900 at the Salons as an accomplished artist–decorator. His mural, *Les Trois Grâces*, displayed in 1913, shows both a technical proficiency and a sharp awareness of the prevailing fashion for depictions of young women and flora in a whimsical Art Deco style.

In the 1920s Vera created a wide range of interior decorations, including painted panels and murals, bas reliefs, tapestries, wallpapers, fabrics and wood engravings for book illustrations. Favourite themes included the four seasons, garlanded flowers, fruit-filled cornucopia, and allegorical and mythological figures. Orpheus, in particular, was depicted in various media. The critics approved of these designs, listing among the artist's talents an irrepressible optimism and joyous sense of humour.

Vera is best known for the wallpaper and tapestry designs that he exhibited at the Salons alongside examples by competitors such as Raoul *Dufy, René *Gabriel and J.-E. Labouret. His wallpapers were printed and marketed by the Compagnie des Arts Français; the tapestries were made by Aubusson. A long-standing arrangement was established in the early 1920s with Louis Süe of the Compagnie des Arts Français, for whom Vera provided painted decoration for SÜE ET MARE's furniture: for example, a lacquered dining-room screen entitled 'Le Pain, le Vin, les Fruits, la Viande' shown at the 1922 *Salon d'Automne. Two Paris addresses were listed for Vera in Salon catalogues: 72 rue Blanche and 61 rue de Rome.

Verlys

A division of the American Holophane Co. was established c. 1920 in Les Andelys (Eure), France, for the manufacture of artistic tableware similar to that made as a by-product at the parent company, which specialized in optical lenses and other pressed industrial glassware, such as car headlamps. The trade name Verlys was derived from the first and last syllables of the French company's title, Les Verreries d'Andelys.

Importing skilled artisans from Bohemia, the firm's initial production comprised handblown domestic vases and bowls offered through its showroom at 156 boulevard Haussmann, Paris. The process was industrialized in the mid-1930s with a new line of pressed wares, mostly in a luminescent milky white or layered iridescent glass ornamented with fauna, flora and linear patterns, the last often rendered in a spirited Art Deco style.

Vertes, Marcel (1895–1961)

Born in Budapest, Vertes was a student of K. Ferenczy before moving to Vienna, where he quickly established a fine reputation as a poster artist, painter and illustrator. He moved to Paris in 1925, where he exhibited at the *Salon d'Automne, the Salon de l'Araignée and numerous galleries. While in Paris, he was commissioned by Maurice Exteens (the publisher Gustave Pellet's son-in-law and successor) to illustrate two albums of lithographs: one in black entitled *Maisons*, the other in colour entitled *Dancings*.

Vertes had difficulty establishing himself in France, because of his mordant wit, sharp observation and choice of risqué subject matter, such as brothels, which was not readily received. In the late 1920s he therefore moved to the USA, where he greatly sweetened his range of subject matter and its treatment, portraying circuses, romantic lovers and horseback riders. He painted a number of murals for stores, restaurants and private homes, including one for Gypsy Rose Lee.

Vincent, René (1879–1936)

Vincent was born in Bordeaux and studied architecture at the École des Beaux-Arts, Paris. He then worked as an illustrator for *La Vie Parisienne*, the *Saturday Evening Post* and *L'Illustration*, providing engaging images of the leisured classes, particularly illustrations showing demoiselles playing golf or twirling parasols. He published his first illustrated book in 1905.

Vincent's early work was in the Art Nouveau idiom, but it soon began to feature an angular imagery that evolved into 'high-style' Art Deco. From c. 1920 he concentrated on poster design; the giant Paris department store Au Bon Marché was among his clients. He signed his works 'René Vincent', 'Rageot' or

'Dufour'. In addition, he designed a number of household
accoutrements, including vases, table services
and clocks, some of which were executed in ceramics
by Jean *Besnard at Ivry. In 1924 Vincent opened
a workshop in Sèvres, which he named Vinsard.

Von Eiff, Wilhelm (1890–1943)

German-born von Eiff was the son of an artisan
at the *Württembergische Metallwarenfabrik (WMF)
glassworks in Göppingen. He was trained in glass
and metal engraving early in his career while attending
the local art school. He then travelled around Europe,
stopping en route to work at RENÉ LALIQUE's glass
studio in Paris, among other firms. In 1913 von Eiff met
Stefan Rath, a nephew of the owner of J. & L. Lobmeyr,
which operated glassworks in Vienna and Bohemia.
After the First World War, Bohemia became part
of an independent Czechoslovakia, where Stefan Rath
opened a new glassworks in Steinschönau. Von Eiff
joined the firm briefly as a designer before being
appointed a professor in cutting and engraving on glass
and precious stones at the Stuttgart art school in 1922.

Proficient in engraving and *Hochschnitt* (high-
relief carving), von Eiff designed and executed a large
volume of glass vessels throughout the inter-war years,
generally in simple shapes with superbly cut and
polished abstract or geometric patterns, including
images of waves.

Von Nessen, Walter (1889–1943)

Born in Germany, von Nessen trained with Bruno Paul
in Berlin. Early commissions included the city's subway
stations and, during a sojourn in Stockholm from
1919 to 1923, furniture for Swedish clients. In 1923 he
emigrated to the USA, approximately four years later
establishing Nessen Studios at 151 East 38th Street,
New York, where he designed and produced a wide
range of contemporary metal furnishings and light
fixtures, principally for architects and interior designers.

In 1930, when most businesses were retrenching
in consequence of the Depression, Nessen Studios
expanded to service orders from the retail trade.
Von Nessen's lamps, especially, drew praise for their
brazenly innovative forms and choice of bright metallic
finishes, which together provided a powerful
interpretation of the modern aesthetic. Swing-arm
shades in frosted glass or parchment were mounted
on chromium- or nickel-plated metal, brass or brushed
aluminium bases. Decorative fillips, such as vertical
tiers of discs in Formica, Bakelite or rubber, provided
a futuristic look to lamp columns and ash-stands.

Beyond the designs for his own firm, von Nessen
also served as an industrial designer of household
products for retailers such as the *Chase Brass &
Copper Co., Miller Lamp Co. and Pattyn Products Co.
Chromium-plated copper and plastic wares provided
an affordable alternative to silver in the collapsed
economy of the Depression era.

Von Nessen participated in several of the museum
and department store exhibitions that promoted the
new design aesthetic in the late 1920s and 1930s.
These included the American Designers' Gallery shows
in 1928 and 1929; the 1929 Architect and the Industrial
Arts, an exhibition of Contemporary American Design
at the Metropolitan Museum of Art, New York; and
the 1931 Exhibition of Contemporary Industrial Art
staged by the American Union of Decorative Artists
and Craftsmen (AUDAC) at the Brooklyn Museum.

Vörös, Béla (1899–1983)

Vörös was born in Hungary and was initially
apprenticed to a cabinet-maker. During the First World
War, he obtained a job as a delivery boy for a
pharmacy whose owner was a sculptor. Vörös began
to assist him in his studio and then enrolled in the
Academy of Decorative Arts in Budapest. After the war
he studied with the Hungarian sculptor Stróbl, staging
exhibitions of his works.

In 1925 Vörös arrived in Paris, where he exhibited
at the annual Salons. From 1932 to 1938 he lived
in Nice, working with an ivory-carver and modelling
figurines and decorative objects. After the Second
World War, he retired to the town of Sèvres, where
he devoted himself to his own scuptural work. Vörös
is today best known for his bronze groups of pigeons.

W

Wagenfeld, Wilhelm (1900–1990)

Bremen-born Wagenfeld was apprenticed to the
silverwares firm of Koch & Bergfeld in Bremen while
attending classes at the city's Kunstgewerbeschule
between 1916 and 1917. In 1923 he entered the Bauhaus
at Weimar, where he specialized in metalwork under
the direction of László Moholy-Nagy. From 1923
to 1924 Wagenfeld designed lamps and tea services
in a spartan functionalist style. When the Bauhaus
moved to Dessau the following year, he remained
in Weimar as an assistant in the metal workshop of
the Weimar Staatliche Bauhochschule, and from 1927
designed independently for industry, including for
the firm of Walter & Wagner in Schleiz.

Opening his own studio in 1930, Wagenfeld
produced a number of designs for the Bauhaus.
He had begun to work in glass *c*. 1927 and in 1930
had submitted designs to the Jenaer Glaswerke
Schott & Genossen, and later to the Vereinigte
Lausitzer Glaswerke in Weisswasser. He also designed
porcelain for the Furstenberg and *Rosenthal
Porzellan factories in 1934 and 1938, respectively.
In 1938 his 'Kubus' series of modular glass containers
was introduced.

Because he refused to join the Nazi party, during
the Second World War Wagenfeld was sent to the
Eastern Front, where he became a Russian prisoner
of war. From 1947 to 1949 he served as a professor
of industrial design at the Landesgewerbeamt in

Walter von Nessen

(*below*) Table lamp in chromed metal with glass finial, for the Miller Lamp Co., *c.* 1930.

(*right*) Floor lamp in aluminium, manufactured by Nessen Studios, late 1920s.

(*far right*) Floor lamp in chromed metal, manufactured by Nessen Studios, *c.* 1930.

(*bottom*) Desk in birch with silver leaf, commissioned by Mr & Mrs Glendon Allvine for their home in Long Beach, Long Island, New York, *c.* 1929.

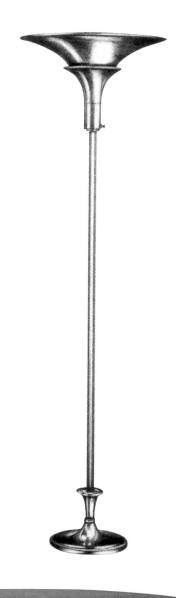

Stuttgart, while taking commissions from various companies, including the *Württembergische Metallwarenfabrik (WMF). He resigned from the Deutscher Werkbund in 1955, believing that it now designed only for the wealthy; he had been a member since 1925. Wagenfeld established his Werkstatt Wagenfeld design studio in 1954, where he later designed passenger food utensils for Lufthansa.

Walter, Almeric (1870–1959)

Born in Sèvres, the son and grandson of porcelain decorators at the Manufacture Nationale de *Sèvres, Walter attended the manufactory's school before entering it as an apprentice. In 1895 he set up a small workshop at 39 rue des Binelles in the town of Sèvres, where he decorated **faïence** with *cloisonné* enamels, a selection of which he showed at one of the 1895 Salons. Around 1900 he moved to 9 rue des Écoles, where he began to experiment with *pâte-de-verre* in association with one of his former teachers, Gabriel Levy. Together they exhibited – without notable success – at the 1903 Salon of the *Société Nationale des Beaux-Arts.

While in search of new techniques, Antonin Daum at some point saw Walter's work in *pâte-de-verre* and offered him employment at DAUM FRÈRES in Nancy, where a special kiln was built for him when he began work in 1905. Walter successfully adopted the technique of applying powdered metallic oxides to the surface of the parison to achieve bright colours, but struggled for some time to overcome certain technical difficulties such as vitrification. Daum's chief decorator at the time, Henri *Bergé, designed a wide range of table-top accessories for Walter, including ashtrays, *vide-poches*, Tanagra figurines, ring stands, bookends, paperweights and inkwells, as well as miscellaneous items such as plaques for insertion into furniture, and window panes. For these, Walter employed the *cire perdue*

(lost wax) process to achieve the highest possible level of detailing.

At the start of the First World War, the Daum Frères works closed and Walter joined the French army. Once demobilized after the armistice in 1918, he decided against returning to Daum and instead set up on his own. Leaving his old workshop on rue du Point-Course, he set up a new one at 20 rue Claudot. By 1922, he employed three assistants; by 1925, ten.

The French post-war grammar of decorative ornament – its simplifications, stylizations and abstractions – held no appeal for Walter or Bergé, who continued to generate a range of objects in the Art Nouveau idiom. In the 1920s Walter also executed designs for Joseph Mougin, Jules Cayette, Jean-Bernard *Descomps, André Houillon, the *Adnet twins and Joe *Descomps, whose works like Walter's, were distributed through *Arthur Goldscheider's Paris showroom. At the 1925 *Exposition Internationale, he showed a small selection of plaques designed by Bergé.

Walter was greatly affected by Bergé's death in 1936. At this time he also faced two further adversities: he was gradually losing his sight and his pieces had become *démodé*. Forgotten, he later moved from Nancy to Lury-sur-Arnon (Cher).

Walters, Carl (1883–1955)

Walters trained and then worked as a painter until he was nearly forty, after which he taught himself the art of ceramics and built his own studio and kiln in Woodstock, Vermont. There he modelled decorative sculptures in terracotta and lead-glazed earthenware, especially a humorous menagerie of speckled animals that were produced in small editions from the same mould, a fact that he cleverly disguised by adding small details to the final wet clay and by glazing them differently. His work is noteworthy for its translucent blue glaze which closely resembled that on ancient Persian ceramics .

Walters participated in several shows, including the 1928 International Ceramic Exhibition (which opened at the Metropolitan Museum of Art, New York, before travelling to seven other cities) and the annual National Ceramic exhibitions in Syracuse. His entries of a bull and a warthog at the 1933 A Century of Progress Exposition in Chicago brought wide acclaim for their 'pleasing unity of basic form, surface modelling and glaze texture'.

Waugh, Sidney Biehler (1904–1963)

One of six children born to a history professor, Waugh grew up in Amherst, Massachusetts, where he attended Amherst College before studying architecture at the Massachusetts Institute of Technology (MIT). In 1925 he travelled to Europe, where he studied in Paris under Émile-Antoine Bourdelle at the École des Beaux-Arts and later was an assistant to Henri Bouchard. In 1928 and 1929 Waugh was awarded bronze and silver medals at the Salon du Printemps, and in 1929, the Prix de Rome, which provided three further years of study at the American Academy in Rome.

Waugh returned to the USA in 1932, where he worked briefly on sculptural commissions for various federal buildings in Washington, DC. The following year he was hired by Arthur A. Houghton (president of the Steuben division of the Corning Glass Co.) and John Gates (the firm's director of design) to create a new series of glassware. This was the start of a fruitful collaboration in which one of Waugh's first designs was the 'Gazelle Bowl' (1935). Bold and weighty, in clear crystal with a pronounced Art Deco sensibility, the piece embodied the beauty and unfailing taste inherent in Waugh's designs. This was followed by other works for Steuben, such as the 'Zodiac Bowl' (1935), which married mythological and other traditional themes to modern forms, some evocative of earlier works by Simon *Gate and Edvard *Hald at *Orrefors.

Valerie Wieselthier
(*right*) Mirror frame in glazed terracotta, manufactured by the Wiener Werkstätte, *c*. 1928.

(*far right*) Figure in glazed earthenware, before 1929.

By 1935 Waugh's early classicism had yielded completely to a robust contemporary style in which the human body was given exaggerated muscular emphasis – its definition accentuated by deeply carved detailing. The secondary areas of a composition, such as trailing drapery and background foliage, were reduced to basic geometric elements.

Noted among Waugh's architectural commissions at this time was his group of friezes designed for the Buhl Planetarium and Institute of Popular Science in Pittsburgh, Pennsylvania. For the 1939 New York World's Fair, he designed a 136-kilogram sculpture, *Atlantica*, cast in clear crystal, which symbolized the coming of glass-making to the New World; he also exhibited a monumental group entitled *Manhattan*. Waugh was later appointed president of the National Sculpture Society and was the director of the Rinehart School of Sculpture in Baltimore from 1942 to 1957.

Weber, **Karl Emanuel Martin (Kem)** (1889–1963)
Born in Berlin, Weber was apprenticed in 1904 to Eduard Schultz, one of Potsdam's royal cabinet-makers. On receiving his journeyman's diploma, he studied under Bruno Paul in Berlin from 1908 to 1910. He left for San Francisco in 1914 to assist in the construction of the German pavilion at the Panama–Pacific International Exposition.

Trapped in California by the outbreak of the First World War, Weber took whatever jobs he could find before opening a design studio in Santa Barbara, before moving to Los Angeles in 1921. There he found employment in the design studio at the Barker Bros. store. In 1927 he resigned from Barker Bros. and opened an office in Hollywood, listing himself as an industrial designer. His style was soon seen as extremely distinctive as he was almost the sole designer on the West Coast to embrace Modernism. Weber lived in California throughout the 1920s, participating during the decade in many national

design exhibitions, including the 1927 Art-in-Trade exhibition at Macy's in New York, in which he showed 'Six Rooms in Three' as his solution to the problems of inner-city living.

As an innovator of multifunctional furniture for modern apartment-dwellers, Weber's early work showed a certain Parisian influence – it was termed 'zigzag moderne' by the critics. However, in the 1930s he settled into a mature streamlined style based on horizontal rather than vertical planes. He preferred wood to metal, often with a lacquered finish. In 1930 Weber introduced his 'Bentlock' line of furniture, based on the elimination of traditional wood joints, which was manufactured by the Higgins Manufacturing Co. in Oakland, California. The line enjoyed a short-lived popularity.

Wegener, **Gerda Gottlieb** (1886–1940)
Danish-born Wegener attended the Royal Art Academy in Copenhagen where in 1904 she married a fellow student. In 1912 the couple moved to Paris, where she found employment as a poster artist and graphic designer for fashion magazines, including *Vogue*, *La Vie Parisienne* and *Fantasia*.

Wegener used a sensuous, sometimes erotic, illustrative style that depicted the city's high society at play. Her husband, who dressed in female attire had served as her model, later declared himself a transsexual and underwent a sex-change operation. Following their divorce, Wegener married an Italian officer. After her second marriage had dissolved, she returned to Denmark in 1938.

Wende, **Theodor** (1883–1968)
Wende served his apprenticeship as a gold- and silversmith in Berlin and then worked as a journeyman in Dresden, before studying at the Königliche Preussische Zeichenakademie in Hanau and, under Bruno Paul, at the Vereinigte Staatsschulen für Freie und Angewandte

Kunst in Berlin-Charlottenburg. In 1913 he joined the artists' colony in Darmstadt of the Grand Duke Louis IV of Hesse-Darmstadt. Of the twenty-three artists who worked at the colony during its fifteen years of existence, only he and his successor, Ernst Riegel, were goldsmiths. In 1921 Wende was appointed a professor at the Badische Kunstgewerbeschule in Pforzheim.

In the inter-war years, at his workshop in Pforzheim, Wende created a range of table-top silverware – tea and mocha services, tureens and gravy boats – decorated with Cubist-inspired abstract motifs, and with a robust hammered finish applied to unornamented surface areas.

Wieselthier, **Valerie (Vally)** (1895–1945)
Born in Vienna, Wieselthier studied from 1914 to 1918 under Michael *Powolny at the Viennese Kunstgewerbeschule before joining the ceramic workshop at the Wiener Werkstätte, which she left in 1922 to set up her own workshop. She exhibited in Germany in the same year and was awarded gold and silver medals at the 1925 *Exposition Internationale. Two years later, after a series of reversals, Wieselthier returned to head the Wiener Werkstätte's two ceramic departments.

In 1928 Wieselthier visited the USA, where her works were being included in the travelling International Ceramic Exhibition staged by the American Federation of the Arts. Following this trip, she decided to emigrate, and in 1929 she settled in New York. There she joined the Contempora and the American Union of Decorative Artists and Craftsmen (AUDAC) groups, and she marketed her wares through Rena Rosenthal's gallery. Wieselthier later served as a designer for the Sebring Pottery Co. in Ohio, and also produced designs in various other media, including glass, textiles, paper mâché and metal. Among her designs in metal were the elevator doors for Ely Jacques Kahn's Squibb Building in New York.

Karl Emanuel Martin Weber (Kem)

(*right*) Digital clocks in chromed metal, brass and copper, manufactured by Lawson Time Inc., Pasadena, c. 1933.

(*below left*) Airline armchair in birch, ash and oilcloth, manufactured by the Airline Chair Co., Los Angeles, 1934–35.

(*below right*) Dressing table in burl walnut, maple, cedar, chromed metal, mirrored glass and silvered- and painted wood. Designed for the home of Mr & Mrs John Bissinger, San Francisco, 1928–29.

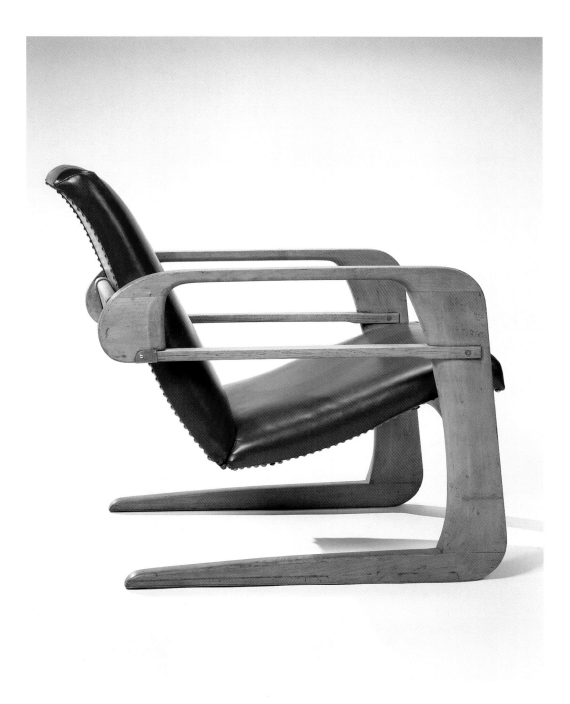

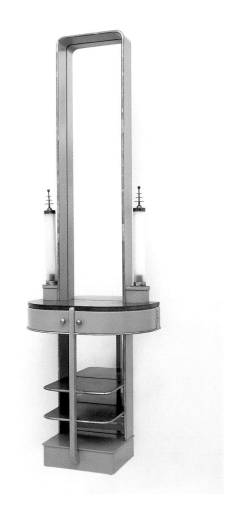

Valerie Wieselthier
Figure in glazed earthenware,
c. 1928.

Gerda Gottlieb Wegener
Untitled, oil on canvas,
dated 1925.

Wolfers Frères

(*right*) Five-piece tea service
with tray in silver with ebony
handles and finials, *c.* 1930.

(*below*) Four-piece tea service
with tray in silver with ivory
finials and handles, *c.* 1930.

Württembergische Metallwarenfabrik
(*below*) 'Ikora' vase in etched chrome-plated metal, *c.* 1928.

(*right*) Vase in nickel-plated brass, the design attributed to Fritz August Breuhaus de Groot. *c.* 1930.

Russel Wright
(*right*) Cocktail set, model No. 326, in spun aluminium, cork and wood, manufactured by Russel Wright, New York, *c.* 1932.

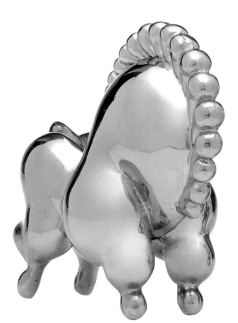

Wieselthier created figurines, masks, tableware items and busts in the highly idiosyncratic style peculiar to post-1900 Vienna. Her work was at once vital, spontaneous, fanciful and carefree and, although modelled coarsely and in discordant colours, was chic and sophisticated.

Wolfers Frères

The Wolfers dynasty of silversmiths was founded by Louis Wolfers in 1812, and in 1890 it passed to his grandson Philippe (1858–1929), the renowned Art Nouveau jeweller–sculptor–silversmith. His son Marcel (1886–1976) was born in Brussels and began his career in his father's studio in La Hulpe, south of the city, before transferring to work with the Belgian sculptor Isidore de Rudder. Choosing sculpture (and later lacquer) as his *métier*, Marcel had by 1909 completed a series of monumental statues in stone. These were followed after the First World War by more than a dozen monuments and portrait busts in various materials, including stone, **faïence** and gilt- and lacquered bronze.

On Philippe's death, the firm, renamed Wolfers Frères for Marcel and his brother Lucien, continued its production of silverware, to which Marcel contributed Modernist designs for lacquered household wares such as coffee services, boxes, *coupes*, vases and bracelets. In the inter-war years, the workshop also produced liturgical objects in silver designed by Dom Martin, a priest from the abbey in Keizersberg.

Wright, Russel (1904–1976)

Born into a Quaker family in Lebanon, Ohio, Wright took summer painting courses with Frank Duveneck at the Art Academy of Cincinnati before moving in 1920 to New York. There he enrolled in painting and architecture classes at the Art Students League before entering Princeton University the following year.

Wright began his career in 1924 as a theatrical designer, assisting the costume and set designer

Norman *Bel Geddes. In 1930 he established his own workshop in New York, where he designed furniture and household accessories in chrome, ceramics, glass and spun- and brushed-aluminium. He participated in the 1930 Third International Exhibition of Contemporary Art at the Metropolitan Museum of Art in New York, and in the 1931 American Union of Decorative Artists and Craftsmen (AUDAC) exhibition. Around this time Wright was commissioned by the *Chase Brass & Copper Co. of Waterbury, Connecticut, to design informal serving accessories, such as cocktail shakers, in chromium-plated metal.

In the 1930s Wright showed his versatility in designs for a wide range of household products, including wallpapers, fabrics, floor coverings and furniture. Furniture designs included his 'Modern Living' line for the Heywood–Wakefield Co. in 1935, which comprised sectional units that could be arranged to meet the space constraints of inner-city living. Employing an understated Modernist style, Wright sought to create designs for a casual lifestyle.

In 1935 Wright, with his wife Mary and the designer and businessman Irving Richards, formed the partnership Russel Wright Associates. One of its first commissions was the dinnerware service 'American Modern', designed in 1937 and put into production two years later at the Steubenville Pottery in East Liverpool, Ohio. Comprising asymmetrical shapes with sweeping curvilinear contours and unconventional colours, from which the consumer was encouraged to 'mix and match', the service was initially unsuccessful, but following a large advertising campaign demand soared. Over the next twenty years more than 80 million pieces were produced, establishing 'American Modern' as the most popular-ever mass-produced pattern for informal dinnerware.

After the Second World War, Wright introduced another successful dinnerware set, 'Casual China', for the Iroquois China Co., in which some sets were

made of melamine plastic, and the 'Easier Living' collection for the Statton Furniture Co., both aimed, as previously, at the casual American lifestyle. In the 1950s his austere and simple designs became unfashionable.

On closing his studio in 1958, Wright became an environmental consultant for developing countries and created an experimental programme for the National Park Service entitled 'Summer in the Parks'.

Württembergische Metallwarenfabrik

The metalware firm founded by Daniel Straub in 1853 evolved in 1880 into the Württembergische Metallwarenfabrik (WMF) following the merger of Straub & Schweizer of Geislingen and A. Ritter & Co. of Esslingen. Production concentrated on metal and electroplated household wares, and electrotyped reproductions of historical metalwares.

From the late 19th century until the First World War, WMF's design studio was administered by the sculptor Albert Mayer. He oversaw a team of designers, modellers and craftsmen in the mass-production of historical and Jugendstil wares in silverplated Britannia metal – a lightweight alloy of tin, antimony and copper that could be oxidized to provide a matt finish. In 1905 WMF took over Orivit, manufacturers of hollowware and cutlery in machine-pressed pewter. A review of the firm's catalogues from the period shows that whereas much of its Jugendstil production was adapted from the creations of outside artists such as Albino Müller of Darmstadt, some pieces were strikingly original. The catalogue was published in German and English – the latter for an export market that included Liberty & Co. in London.

WMF's 1920s production included a range of similarly contemporary models in silver, including, toward 1930, some credited individually to Fritz August Breuhaus de Groot, Paul Haustein and Richard *Riemerschmid.

Evelyn Wyld
'Orages' wool carpet,
exhibited at the 1928 Salon
of the Société des Artistes
Décorateurs, Paris.

Ossip Zadkine
Sainte Famille, study in
patinated bronze cast by the
founder Susse Frères, 1912–13.

Wyld, Evelyn (1882–1973)

Wyld was born in England and learned the rudiments of the weaving craft in North Africa before settling in Paris, where in 1910 she set up a workshop with EILEEN GRAY on the rue Visconti. In 1927, after Gray withdrew from the venture, Wyld formed a new partnership with Elizabeth Eyre de Lanux (1894–1996), in which they designed carpets for decorators such as JEAN DUNAND, Albert Fournier and EUGÈNE PRINTZ.

In 1932, following the closure of their workshop, Wyld and Eyre de Lanux opened Décor, a short-lived decorating shop in Cannes. Later, after Eyre de Lanux moved to Rome, Wyld became a market gardener, while continuing to exhibit her rugs at various exhibitions in the USA and Europe.

Z

Zach, Bruno (1891–1935)

Little biographical information exists on Zach, an Austrian sculptor who is best known for his titillating figures of cabaret dancers and other members of the *demi-monde*. Many of his sculptures are provocative, depicting women wearing leather suits and high heels, smoking cigarettes and wielding leather whips. Some are coquettish, others sexually charged with sado-masochistic overtones. Other themes in Zach's *œuvre* are more conventional: bobsledders, equestrians and circus figures. He worked both in bronze and bronze-and-ivory. His works were manufactured by the Viennese firms of Argentor-Werke, S. Altmann & Co. and Bergmann, among others.

Zadkine, Ossip (1890–1967)

This Russian sculptor and engraver worked in Paris. He created ceramic bas reliefs for the Manufacture Nationale de *Sèvres from 1936 to 1938, notably two **faïence** squares on the theme of 'Le Tourneur et la Décoratrice'.

Zadounaisky, Michel (1903–1983)

No information has emerged to date on Zadounaisky's early history, including his education and training, despite the recent recognition within the marketplace of his accomplishments as a *ferronnier* who applied a robust Art Deco decorative vernacular to many of his works in wrought iron. He is known to have worked in the mid-1930s with the glassmakers Dumaine, two brothers who had founded their factory in the 1920s and specialized in the production of mirrors decorated with gilt foliate scrolls. In 1937 Zadounaisky was awarded a silver medal at the Exposition des Arts et Techniques, Paris.

Zig (Louis Gaudin) (d. 1936)

Little is known of Zig, except that he was known as Louis Gaudin before adopting this pseudonym. He was a *habitué* of Montmartre, where he sang and recited. Zig then became involved in set and costume design and, finally, poster design.

Zig (Louis Gaudin)

(*left*) *Casino de Paris Joséphine Baker*, lithographic poster, undated.

Michel Zadounaisky

(*above*) *Naja dressé*, panel in forged and hammered steel, 1930s.

Michel Zadounaisky

(*right*) Pair of three-light candelabra in wrought iron, 1930s.

(*below*) Fireplace surround in patinated and hammered steel, with marble top, 1932.

SOURCES OF QUOTATIONS

INTRODUCTION
p. 9 Paul Follot, quoted in an unpaginated sales brochure for Waring & Gillow, London, 1928

FURNITURE
p. 14 André Mare, quoted in Léon Deshairs, 'Notre enquête sur le mobilier moderne: La Compagnie des Arts Français', *Art et Décoration*, vol. 34 (January–June, 1920), pp. 65–72, at p. 70

p. 19 Jacques Porel, *Fils de Réjane-Souvenirs: 1895–1920* (Paris: Plon, 1951), p. 223, as quoted in Léopold Diego Sanchez, *Jean-Michel Frank – Adolphe Chanaux*, tr. John D. Edwards (Paris: Éditions du Regard, 1980), p. 40

p. 48 Paul T. Frankl, 'Furniture of the Fourth Dimension Designed for the New Interior', *House and Garden*, vol. 51 no. 2 (February, 1927), pp. 76–79 and 140, at p. 140

p. 49 Paul T. Frankl, 'Furniture of the Fourth Dimension Designed for the New Interior', *House and Garden*, vol. 51 no. 2 (February, 1927), pp. 76–79 and 140, at p. 140

p. 81 Jacques-Émile Ruhlmann, quoted in *An Exposition of Modern French Decorative Art*, Lord & Taylor, (New York, 1928) [unpaginated exhibition catalogue]

pp. 89–90 André Mare, quoted in Leon Deshairs, 'Notre enquête sur le mobilier moderne: La Compagnie des Arts Français', *Art et Décoration*, vol. 34 (January–June, 1920), pp. 65–72, at p. 70

PAINTINGS, GRAPHICS, POSTERS AND BOOKBINDING
p. 148 Cassandre in a letter to M. Stahly, dated 11 March 1935, as translated in Henri Mouron, *A. M. Cassandre* (London: Thames & Hudson, 1985), p. 48

p. 157 Marcel Valotaire, 'Jean Dupas – His Work and Ideas', *Creative Art*, June 1928, pp. 386–389

LIGHTING
p. 237 Jean Perzel in an article in *Lux,* September, 1928, p. 119, quoted in Alastair Duncan, *Art Nouveau and Art Deco Lighting* (London: Thames & Hudson, 1978), p. 180

TEXTILES
p. 255 Marcel Weber, 'Les Tapis de Da Silva Bruhns', *Art et Décoration*, vol. 46 (July–December 1924), pp. 65–72, at pp. 65–66

p. 255 Ivan Da Silva Bruhns's carpets described by Gabriel Henriot, 'Le Salon d'Automne', *Mobilier et Décoration*, December, 1928, p. 303

SILVER
p. 266 Napoleon III, as quoted in Princess Pauline Maria Walpurga von Metternich-Sandor, *The Days That Are No More: Some reminiscences* [English translation of *Éclairs du passé*, Zurich: Amalthea-Verlag, 1922; with a preface by Edward Legge.]. (London: Eveleigh Nash & Grayson, 1921)

JEWELRY
p. 299 Paul Poiret, quoted in Alastair Duncan, *Art Deco* (London: Thames & Hudson, 1988), p. 162

p. 299 Elsie Bee, 'The New Art in Jewelry. Influence of "Cubist" and "Futurist" and Dominance of the Oriental Note. How the radical changes may be shown', *The Jewelers' Circular-Weekly*, March 26, 1913, p. 53

A–Z
p. 318 Louis Cheronnet, *Jacques Adnet* (Paris: L. Danel, 1948) [unpaginated monograph for *Art et Industrie*]

p. 352 Marcel Coard, interviewed in *L'Oeil*, 1975 [issue date unknown]

p. 364 Piet Mondrian, quoted in Andrei B. Nakov, *Felix Del Marle* (Paris: Galerie Jean Chauvelin, 1973), p. 16

p. 400 Léon Deshairs, 'Les Tapisseries de Jaulmes', *Art et Décoration*, vol. 37 (January, 1920), pp. 17–26, at p. 22

p. 419 Le Corbusier, *L'Art Décoratif d'aujourd'hui: Collection de 'L'Esprit nouveau'* (Paris: G. Crès, 1925), p. 21

p. 445 René Chavance, 'Jean-Charles Moreux Architecte et Décorateur', *Art et Décoration*, vol. 51 (January–June, 1927), pp. 48–55, at p. 49

p. 441 Yvanhoë Rambossen on Clément Mere, 'Le XIIIe Salon des Artists Décorateurs', *Art et Décoration*, vol. 41 (January–June, 1922), pp. 13–128, at p. 127

p. 446 Peter Müller-Munk describing his 'Normandie' pitcher, quoted in Dianne H. Pilgrim, 'Engineering a New Art', in *The Machine Age in America 1918-1941*, ed. Richard Guy Wilson, Dianne H. Pilgrim and Dickran Tashjian (New York: The Brooklyn Museum in association with Harry N. Abrams, Inc., 1986), p. 307

p. 474 Advertisement for Robj in *L'Illustration*, vol. 164 (July–December, 1924), p. 31

p. 478 Advertisement for Roseville Pottery in *House & Garden*, vol. 55 (May, 1929), p. 152

p. 483 George Sakier, describing his designs in 'Primer of Modern Design', in *Arts and Decoration*, vol. 40 (November, 1933), pp. 36–37, at p. 36

p. 517 Carl Walters's entries in the 1933 A Century of Progress Exposition in Chicago reviewed in *Design*, June 1934, pp. 16–17

ACKNOWLEDGMENTS

Appreciation is extended to the following in Paris for their considerable assistance: Robert and Cheska Vallois, Martine Baverel, and Laetitia de Galzain at the Galerie Vallois; Dominique Suisse, grand-daughter of Gaston Suisse; Jean-Marc Maury and the photographer Pascal Faligot; Lorraine Aubert at Tajan; Sabrina Dolla at ArtCurial; Alexandra Jaffre and the photographers Philippe Sebert and Stephane Briolant at Camard et Associés; Marceau Delaage at Millon et Associés; and M. & Mme. Jacques de Vos.

In New York, especially, to Jack Rennert and Terry Shargel at Posters Please, Inc.; Simon Wills and Mark Lynch at Christie's Images; Megan Whippen and Sarah Stein-Sapir at Sotheby's; Jason Jacques, Yoni Ben-Yosef and Claire Cass at Jason Jacques Inc.; Gérard Widdershoven at the Maison Gérard; Nathan and Rena Krishtul at Ark Restoration & Design, Ltd.; Tara DeWitt at Phillips de Pury & Company; Phyllis Elliot; and Mark Schachner of AJ Fine Arts. Elsewhere in the U.S., to Frederick Brandt and Howell W. Perkins at The Virginia Museum of Fine Arts; The Norwest Corporation, Minneapolis; Heather Carr and the photographer Gary Kirchenbauer at the Viktor Schreckengost Studios, Cleveland Heights, Ohio; and Herbert and Eunice Shatzman of Durham, North Carolina. In Toronto, Canada, to Nicola Woods and Robert Little at the Royal Ontario Museum; and to Fedora Horner and Janice Passmore at Homeculture, Ltd.

In London, Sue Daly at Sotheby's; Michael Jeffrey at Woolley & Wallis; and Ray Perman of SevenArts, Ltd. Also in England, to the photographer Peter Greenhalf of Rye Harbour and Pam Henderson at the Antique Collectors' Club in Woodbridge, Suffolk. Elsewhere, to José Berardo and Zaid Abdali in Lisbon; Gaby Lourie and the photographer Somin Makwela in Johannesburg; Dr. Rene Wanner in Switzerland; Maria Granström at the Stockholm Auktionsverket; Faridah Younès at the Quittenbaum auction house, Munich; and Alberto Shayo in Rio de Janeiro.

Finally, my gratitude to the staff at Thames & Hudson, without whose enthusiasm, guidance and overall professionalism this project could never have reached fruition. In particular, to Jamie Camplin, Ian Jacobs, Robert Adkinson, Flora Spiegel, Susanna Friedman, Sally Paley and, from his retirement in Florida, Stanley Baron.

In conclusion, especial thanks is extended to the book's designer, Karolina Prymaka, whose masterful layout skills jump out at the reader from every page.

Alastair Duncan

GLOSSARY

Ariel glass. A type of glass decoration in which a design is deeply carved into cased glass by sandblasting, which results in embedded air bubbles (the name takes up this characteristic in referring to Shakespeare's trapped sprite in *The Tempest*). It was developed c. 1936 by Edvin Öhrström at the Swedish glass manufacturer Orrefors Glassbruk. *See also* **Graal glass**.

au point noué (Fr.: 'hand-knotted'). A type of pile rug knotted by hand. Handmade knotted carpets continued to be produced in France during the first half of the 20th century, in contrast to a shift in Germany towards industrial mass production.

aspiré-soufflé (Fr.: 'suck-and-blow'). A partially automated process for making glassware, which involves sucking molten glass into a mould with the aid of a machine in order to create a vacuum. This technique of glassblowing was used by René Lalique to mass produce glass vessels.

au point dit 'de Cornély'. A semi-mechanical embroidery technique in which a tightly twisted yarn is attached to a fabric backing. The stitch was invented in 1865 by Emile Cornély and adapted to carpet making in the 1920s by Ernest Boiceau.

biscuit de Sèvres. Unglazed white porcelain with a texture similar to marble, often used for figures and busts. Produced at the Manufacture Nationale de Sèvres since 1753.

bijoutier (Fr.). Jeweller.

cabochon. A gemstone with a smooth round surface as a result of having been shaped and highly polished. Stones of this type have no facets, and are usually opaque or have a special optical effect enhanced by polishing. This style of cutting gems was popular from antiquity until the 15th century, and was revived in Art Nouveau jewelry.

cartonnage (Fr.). Hardcover bookbinding.

champlevé. A type of decoration in which the surface of a metal object is pitted with grooves which are then filled in with powdered enamel. The object is fired to fuse the enamel to the metal, and polished to achieve an even, level surface. *See also* **cloisonné**.

chasing. A technique of decorating the front surface of a malleable metal, most often silver, by hammering it to indent or raise a design. As the silver is merely pushed aside rather than carved, the surface remains continuous. A range of shaped tools are used to create the decoration, and the marks made by these tools remain visible on the metal surface. This process is the reverse of **repoussé**, and the two methods are often used together.

chryselephantine. A material used in figurative sculpture, which is made of a combination of ivory and bronze. It was very popular to combine the two materials in the early 20th century owing to the then relatively low cost of ivory in relation to bronze. The word derives from the Greek *chrysos* (gold), and *elephantinos* (ivory), and initially described the overlay of gold and ivory employed in classical Hellenistic statuary, but by 1900 was extended to encompass any sculpture combining ivory with another material.

cire perdue (Fr.: 'lost wax'). A method for casting highly detailed glasswares. A model of the object to be cast is carved out of wax, encased in a mould and then heated, allowing the melted wax to run out. The hollow chamber of the mould is then filled with molten glass which takes its shape. The process was originally developed in the 4th millennium BC and used to cast metal objects, and was later adapted to glass.

cloisonné. A type of enamel in which the surface of the metal object to be enamelled is covered in a network of wire bands forming *cloisons* (compartments), which are filled with powdered enamel. The object is fired to fuse the enamel to the metal, and polished to achieve a smooth surface, with the tops of the bands remaining visible, dividing the different areas of colours from each other. *See also* **champlevé**.

cold-painting. A technique of decorating ceramics or glassware through the application of lacquer colour or oil paint to the surface of an object, which is left unfired. Decoration created in this fashion is often worn away over time, as the unfired surface colours are vulnerable when cleaned, though stoneware often holds this decoration longer than glass. Also known as applying 'cold colours'.

coquille d'œuf (Fr.: 'eggshells'). A process used to create a white-coloured surface decoration by crushing eggshells and inlaying the shards into a top layer of lacquer. This labour-intensive process was developed by Jean Dunard c. 1925 as a means to achieve a previously elusive pure white lacquer. By using both the outside and inside of the eggshells, and by varying the arrangement of the pieces, Dunard was able to produce highly detailed surface designs on furniture and portraiture.

craquelure. A type of decoration used on ceramics which is characterized by an all-over patterning of fine, hairline cracks throughout the surface glaze. The effect is achieved when the body object and the glaze expand and contract at different rates during firing and cooling, and the more rapidly shrinking glaze surface cracks at random. The technique was developed in China as early as the Song Dynasty (960–1279). Also known as 'crackle'.

dalle. A slab of glass, either clear or coloured, through which natural light can be filtered as an interior lighting mechanism. *Dalle de verre* faceted-style windows are those that use thick blocks of hollow, cast glass, arranged in decorative patterns borrowed from traditional stained glass techniques, to allow light into a building. The first faceted slab-glass windows were produced in France in the 1920s, and were initially used to light churches.

damascening. A technique to inlay threads of a soft precious metal, such as gold or silver, into a harder metal, usually bronze, to create an intricate and delicate pattern of contrasts. The term derives from the ancient technique practised in Damascus of creating detailed inlay patterns on sword blades, and was popular in Art Deco sculpture and jewelry production

dinanderie. Brassware objects, often vases, which may be decorated through various processes, including **repoussé**, inlay of other metals, or the application of a lacquer or patina finish. The term is named for the Flemish city of Dinant where the practice, which originally used bronze, was developed in the medieval period. There was a large-scale revival of *dinanderie* in France in the early 20th century.

duralumin. An aluminium alloy composed of copper, manganese and magnesium, which becomes resilient and rip-resistant after hardening for a few days. It was developed in 1903 by the German metallurgist Alfred Wilm, and used in aircraft during the 1930s, and occasionally in Art Deco bookbinding.

ébéniste (Fr.: 'cabinetmaker'). The term was originally used in the 17th century to identify one who constructed cabinets and other case furniture in the luxury wood ebony, but it has come to mean, more generally, a furniture maker working in wood.

en tuyau de poêle (Fr.). Stovepipe style.

engobe. A type of **slip** which is used primarily as an underglaze, and applied to a clay body before firing the object. May also refer to slip containing gum or flux, which is used to adhere additional layers to the underlying clay body.

ensemblier (Fr.). Interior designer.

étui. A small ornamental case, or a small handbag for holding personal items or accessories.

faïence. A type of decorated earthenware which is tin-glazed. The technique used to produce these ceramics is the same as that used for Delftware and Italian maiolica. Of French derivation, the term probably comes from the Italian town of Faenza which began exporting ceramics of this style in the 15th century.

ferronnier (Fr.). Craftsman working in iron.

filigrana. A type of glass decoration created through the embedding of fine threads or ribbons of coloured glass into clear glass. The embedded designs often resemble netting. This process was originally developed in Murano, Italy, in the 16th century, and is generally known in English as 'filigree'. *See also* **latticino**.

flambé. A type of ceramic glaze which uses a copper reduction in the firing process, resulting in distinctively rich coloured surfaces. First developed in China in the Song Dynasty (960–1279), this technique was not used in Europe until the late 19th century. *See also* *sang-de-bœuf*.

fourrure de lièvre (Fr.: 'hare's fur'). A type of ceramic glaze which is characterized by a deep black ground streaked with rusty brown. This technique of glazing was developed in China during the Song Dynasty (960–1279), and was adopted in Japan, where it is called *temmoku*. It influenced subsequent Japanese ceramic design, and by extension, European design in the 20th century.

galuchat. The untanned skin of a shark or spotted dogfish, used as a luxurious finish in Art Deco furniture production. The skin could be left in its unbleached state, or varnished or tinted to accentuate its granular surface pattern. Also known as 'shagreen'.

galvanoplastie (Fr.: 'electroplating'). A process that uses electrical current to coat a conducive metal object with a thin layer of another metal. The process was invented by the Italian chemist Luigi Brugnatelli in 1805, and patented by George and Henry Elkington in 1840. Charles Christofle bought the patents in 1842, developed silverplating – metal electroplated in sterling silver – and began mass producing silverplated goods.

Graal glass. A type of glass decoration in which cased glass is carved or etched with sand or acid and then heated in a furnace to produce a smooth and fluid design, entirely integrated into the glass. Developed in 1916 by Albert Ahlin and Knut Bergvist at the Swedish glass manufacturer Orrefors Glassbruk, the name derives from the legend of the Holy Grail.

grand feu (Fr.: 'high fired'). A process to decorate ceramics, usually tin-glazed (**faïence**), in which the object is painted with colour and fired at a high temperature. This process is more economical than the alternative *petit feu* method which requires an extra enamel firing.

grès (Fr.: 'stoneware'). Very hard, non-porous pottery consisting of clay and fusible stone, fired at a high temperature between 1200 °C and 1400 °C. Unlike porcelain, it is not usually more than faintly transparent, and can range in texture from smooth to coarse. This type of ceramic was first produced in China in the 4th century and was being produced in Germany by the 9th century.

grès fine. A clay introduced in 1931 at the Manufacture Nationale de Sèvres. Also known as *grès tendre*.

guilloché. An engraved decorative pattern produced by mechanical etching of a repetitive plait-like ornamentation into an underlying material. The decoration is used as a border design on metalwork and jewelry. The name may derive from a French engineer named Guillot, who is said to have invented the machine that creates the pattern. It is directly related to guilloche, a braided decoration found in Greek and Roman architecture, revived during the Renaissance, and prominently featured in 19th and 20th century Neoclassical buildings.

Hochschnitt (Ger.: 'high engraving'). A process of decorating glass by carving a design into the surface with the use of a rotating wheel, which grinds away the surface glass, resulting in high-relief engraving. This technique has been used in glass decoration since Antiquity.

intercalaire (Fr.: 'inserted'). A type of decorative effect used in glass design, created by using two layers of glass. A first internal layer of molten glass (a *paraison*) is rolled into powdered metal oxides on a **marver** to create the embedded decoration, and a second external layer is applied to encase the decoration.

jaspé (Fr.: 'mottled, marbled'). A type of decorative opaque glass that resembles marbled semi-precious stones such as jasper, onyx, lapis lazuli and agate. The effect is achieved by blending multi-coloured metals or glasses together to create variegated designs. Variations of the technique have existed since Antiquity, but the modern techniques were developed in Venice in the 15th century. Also called 'agate glass' or 'imitation stoneware' in English.

jewel porcelain. A type of decorative ceramic glaze characterized by bubbles trapped within the glazing layers. The technique was introduced by Rookwood Pottery *c*. 1915.

laque arracheé. A type of decorative lacquer characterized by a rough, chipped finish. To create this effect, applied lacquer is lifted from the surface of a piece of furniture with a flat wooden spatula, resulting in an uneven surface and texture. The process can be repeated with several colours to create a tonal range.

laque de Beka. A type of decorative lacquer characterized by a rich surface luminosity. It was developed by Paul-Étienne Sain in the 1930s after extensive experimentation with lacquer pigments.

latticino. A form of *filigrana* glass decoration in which the embedded patterns are formed uniquely with threads of opaque white glass. The white glass is known as 'lattimo', derived from *latte*, the Italian word for 'milk'. The process was originally developed in Murano, Italy, in the 16th century.

marqueterie. A technique for decorating glass, which involves embedding pre-shaped, cut pieces of hot, coloured glass into the body of a differently coloured glass object, resulting in a flat surface. The process was patented by Émile Gallé in 1898, and is derived from similar marquetry decoration used in woodworking.

martelage. A decorative finishing technique for glassware, which produces a surface similar to hammered metal. Glass is textured with indentations in order to achieve patterns that appear to have been beaten with a hammer.

martelé (Fr.). Hammered.

marver. A smooth, flat surface of polished iron or marble on which a *paraison*, attached to the end of a hollow iron blowpipe or rod, is rolled in order to smooth it, create symmetry or apply decoration.

millefiori (It.: 'a thousand flowers'). A style of decorating glass that produces multicoloured patterns usually in floral designs. The effect is achieved by embedding thin rods or canes of coloured glass in clear molten glass to form mosaic-like patterns. It is a labour intensive process which was developed in Murano, Italy, in the 16th century based upon ancient techniques.

orfèvre (Fr.). Silversmith or goldsmith. The products of their work are known as *orfèvrerie*: silver or gold crafts.

ormolu. Gilded metal, in particular bronze, created by fusing the base metal with an amalgam of gold and mercury. The process is used to ornament metal furniture fixtures and decorative objects, and is also known as 'gilt-bronze' and 'bronze doré'.

paraison. A partly inflated gather of molten glass collected on the end of a hollow metal blowpipe.

pâte-de-cristal (Fr.: 'crystal paste'). A material similar to *pâte-de-verre* but composed of a powdered glass of very fine quality. When fused, this results in highly translucent glass.

pâte-d'émail (Fr.: 'enamelled paste'). A material similar to *pâte-de-verre* but made of a combination of soft porcelain paste and glass which results in a fine opaque glass paste. When the paste is fired, the resulting compound resembles porcelain.

pâte-de-verre (Fr.: 'glass paste'). A material produced by grinding glass into a fine powder and adding a catalyst to lower the melting point. The resulting paste is coloured by using tinted glass or by adding metallic oxides. In paste form, *pâte-de-verre* is as malleable as clay, and is modelled by being packed into a mould, where it is fused by firing. It can likewise be moulded in several layers or refined by carving.

parure (Fr.). Finery. Also, parure, which in English is a matched set of jewelry, including pieces such as earrings, bracelet, brooch, necklace and ring.

patination. The chemical process through which a patina – a discoloured coating – forms on a metal surface. This may naturally occur after prolonged exposure to weathering, or may be artificially achieved through the application of a chemical treatment.

pavé (Fr.: 'paving stone'). A style of jewelry setting in which many small gemstones are placed very close together, covering the entire setting. The emphasis in this style is on the cumulative effect of many stones together, rather than on any one individual stone.

peau de serpent (Fr.: 'snakeskin'). A type of decorative ceramic glaze which resembles snakeskin through its patterned, cracked surface. The technique was developed by René Buthaud in the early 1930s, and was influenced by indigenous art. *See also* **craquelure**.

petit point. A type of needlework characterized by fine cross-stitches used to achieve maximum detail and shading. This form of embroidery has been used for tapestries since the Middle Ages.

Plakatstil (Ger.: 'poster style'). A German style of graphic art characterized by an uncomplicated visual language, bold fonts and simplified design. First used by Lucian Bernhard in 1905, it marked a shift away from the complexity of Art Nouveau graphic design.

pochoir (Fr.: 'stencil'). A technique used to create prints or to add hand-colouring to pre-existing prints. Characterized by crisp lines and vibrant colours, and produced primarily in Paris in the 1920s and 1930s, these prints were used in French fashion journals, and collected in illustrated folios about interior design, textiles and architecture.

pressé-soufflé (Fr.: 'press-and-blow'). A partially automated process for making glassware, which combines mould-blown and pressing techniques. Molten glass is blown into a mould by mouth or with bellows, and then a metal plunger is pressed inside the glass to create the interior shape. This technique of glassblowing was used by René Lalique to facilitate mass production of glass vessels.

repoussé (Fr.: 'pushed back'). A method used to produce decorated relief on malleable metallic surfaces by hammering and punching from the back in order to raise a design on the front. Also known as 'embossing', this technique has been used since Antiquity and was among the first developed by metalworkers. It is the reverse of **chasing**, and the two methods are often used together.

rocaille. An ornamental style featuring elaborately stylized shell and rock motifs. It is one of the more prominent aspects of the 18th century Rococo style of architecture and decorative arts.

ronde-bosse (Fr.). Sculpture in the round.

rouge flambé. See **flambé**.

sabot. A decorative metal shoe used to enclose the end of the leg on a piece of wooden furniture. Often made of cast **ormolu**.

sang-de-bœuf (Fr.: 'oxblood'). A rich, glossy, blood-red ceramic glaze created by a copper reduction in the firing process. The best-known **flambé** glaze colour.

serrurerie décorative (Fr.). Decorative household hardware.

serti mystérieux (Fr.: 'mystery setting'). A style of jewelry setting in which the supportive metal prongs are entirely hidden underneath the gemstones. In order to achieve this, each gem is grooved and faceted to fit together precisely. The technique was developed by Van Cleef & Arpels in 1935, and is also known as *serti invisible*, or 'invisible setting'.

sgraffito (It.: 'scratched'). A technique used to decorate ceramics, which consists of scratching a design into an applied top layer of coloured clay (a **slip**) in order to reveal a different colour clay below. The resulting pattern or design is the colour of the lower layer. This practice is widespread throughout the history of ceramics, and has similar applications in painting and glass decoration.

shagreen. *See* **galuchat**.

slip. Pottery clay diluted with water to achieve a semi-liquid, creamy consistency. It is often a different colour from the main clay body, and it can be washed or brushed on to the surface to create ornamental decorative effects or an all-over colour. It can also be applied in several layers of different colours. *See also* **engobe**.

spelter. A type of zinc alloy, in use since the 1850s, which is the most common commercial form of the metal. As it is soft and easily breakable, it is used only to make small sculptural pieces such as figurines and candlesticks, and is often painted or bronzed.

tapis de maître (Fr.: 'artist-designed carpet'). A term applied specifically to a series of carpets commissioned by the Mybor carpet company from the leading visual artists of the 1920s–1940s. Artists whose designs were used for these woven rugs included Picasso, Léger, Miró and Klee.

tapissier (Fr.). Tapestry or carpet maker or upholsterer.

tête de nègre (Fr.: 'negro's head'). A shade of dusty brown popular in textile design in Europe in the late 1920s.

Tiger Eye. A type of decorative ceramic glaze characterized by gold streaking which resembles the markings in a tiger's eye. Developed by Rookwood Pottery in the late 19th century, this unstable glaze was difficult to reproduce on a regular basis, and as a result, ceramics decorated in this glaze are quite rare and highly collectible.

tous les Louis (Fr.: 'every Louis'). A reference to the opulent style of interior design and decorative arts popular during the reign of three successive French Bourbon kings named Louis: Louis XIV (1643–1715), Louis XV (1715–1774) and Louis XVI (1774–1792). The style during this 150 year period is most often characterized by sumptuous materials and craftsmanship, and is marked by the emergence of the Rococo and Neoclassical styles.

verde antico. A vibrantly coloured blue-green patina, formed when bronze, copper or brass is weathered. Also known as *verdigris*.

vermeil. A type of gilded silver, also known as 'silver gilt', which is produced by coating or plating a silver object in a layer of gold. The original process, which involved fire-gilding, was developed in France in the 18th century, but has been supplanted by a safer modern process, which uses electrolysis to bind the gilding. Gilded silver is resistant to tarnish.

verre églomisé. A process of glass decorating in which the backside of a glass surface is covered in gold or silver leaf and engraved with a fine needle, but left unfired. The fragile decorated surface is often covered in varnish or metal foil, or a secondary protective layer of glass. The style was in use by late Antiquity, but derives its name from the artist Jean-Baptiste Glomy who re-popularized it in France in the 18th century.

vieil argent (Fr.: 'antique silver'). A silver-coloured finish, coated with Duco, an artificial lacquer impermeable to heat or cold. Duco was a range of quick-drying automotive lacquers developed by the DuPont company in the 1920s, and this finish was used on lamps designed by Félix Aublet in the 1930s.

Wax Mat. A type of decorative ceramic glaze characterized by a dull, flat (rather than shiny) finish. This particular type of matt glaze was the tradename for a glaze developed by Rookwood Pottery *c*. 1900, and became a predominant form of decoration in the ceramics produced by the company, usually painted on light-coloured clays.

SELECT BIBLIOGRAPHY

Ader Picard Tajan, *Collection Alain Lesieutre . . . Hôtel George V, Paris, 13 Décembre, 1989* [auction catalogue]

Adler, Rose, *Reliures présentées par Rose Adler*, L'Art international d'aujourd'hui, vol. 17 (Paris: Charles Moreau, 1930)

Alexandre Alexeïeff (Edinburgh: National Library of Scotland, 1967) [exhibition catalogue]

Arwas, Victor, *Art Deco* (New York: Abradale Press, 2000)

Arwas, Victor, *Art Deco Sculpture* (London: Academy Editions, 1992)

Arwas, Victor, *The Art of Glass: Art Nouveau to Art Deco* (Windsor: Andreas Papadakis, 1996) [exhibition catalogue]

Badovici, Jean (ed.), *Harmonies: intérieurs de Ruhlmann* (Paris: Éditions Albert Morancé, 1924) [trade portfolio]

Badovici, Jean (ed.), *Intérieurs de Süe et Mare* (Paris: Éditions Albert Morancé, 1924) [trade portfolio]

Badovici, Jean (ed.), *Intérieurs français* (Paris: Éditions Albert Morancé, 1925) [trade portfolio]

Barré-Despond, Arlette, *UAM: Union des artistes modernes* (Paris: Éditions du Regard, 1986)

Battersby, Martin, *Art Deco Fashion: French Designers 1908–1925* (London: Academy Editions, 1974)

Bayer, Patricia, *Art Deco Architecture: Design, Decoration and Detail from the Twenties and Thirties* (London: Thames & Hudson, 1999)

Bayer, Patricia, *Art Deco Interiors: Decoration and Design Classics of the 1920s and 1930s* (New York: Thames & Hudson, 1998)

Bayer, Patricia, *Art Deco Source Book* (Hoo, Kent: Grange Books, 2005)

Bayer, Patricia, and Mark Waller, *The Art of René Lalique* (London: Grange Books, 1996)

Bendazzi, Giannalberto, *Alexeieff: Itinerary of a Master* (Paris: Dreamland, 2001)

Benedictus, Édouard, *Nouvelles variations: soixante-quinze motifs décoratifs en vingt planches* (Paris: A. Lévy, [1929?])

Benedictus, Édouard, *Relais, 1930: quinze planches donnant quarante-deux motifs décoratifs* (Paris, Vincent, 1930)

Benedictus, Édouard, *Variations: quatre-vingt-six motifs décoratifs en vingt planches* (Paris: A. Lévy, [1924?])

Berents, Catharina, *Art Deco in Deutschland: das moderne Ornament* (Frankfurt: Anabas-Verlag, 1998)

Bobritsky, Vladimir, *Taxco Mexico: 12 Pastels for V. Bobri* (Milano: Author, 1949)

Bony, Anne (ed.), *Les années 20 d'Anne Bony*, 2 vols. (Paris: Éditions du Regard, 1989)

Bouillon, Jean-Paul, *Art Deco, 1903–1940* (Genève: Éditions d'Art Albert Skira, 1989)

Bowman, Sara, *A Fashion for Extravagance: Art Deco Fabrics and Fashions* (London: Bell & Hyman, 1985)

Brega, Vanna, *Robj Paris: le ceramiche 1921–1931* (Milan: Leonardo Periodici, 1995)

Bröhan, Torsten, and Thomas Berg, *Avantgarde Design, 1880–1930* (Cologne: Taschen, 1994)

Burkhalter, Jean, *Jean Burkhalter: soixante-dix motifs décoratifs en dix-huit planches* (Paris: A. Lévy, [1930])

Caeymaex, Martine (ed.), *L'Art Déco en Europe: tendances décoratives dans les arts appliqués vers 1925* (Brussels: Société des Expositions du Palais des Beaux-Arts, 1989) [exhibition catalogue]

Caws, Mary Ann (ed.), *Manifesto: A Century of Isms* (Lincoln: University of Nebraska Press, 2001)

Céramiques de Robert Lallemant (Bordeaux: Musée des Beaux-Arts, 1992)

Czech Art Deco, 1918–1938 (Prague: The Municipal House, 1998) [exhibition catalogue]

Clair, Jean (ed.), *Les Années 20: l'âge des métropoles* (Montreal: Musée des Beaux-Arts, 1991); Eng. trans. as *The 1920s: Age of the Metropolis* (Montreal: Museum of Fine Arts, 1991)

Clouzot, Henri (ed.), *Le Style moderne dans la décoration intérieure: 36 planches empruntées aux décorateurs modernes* (Paris: Charles Massin, [1921?]) [trade portfolio]

Clouzot, Henri (ed.), *La Ferronnerie moderne à l'Exposition Internationale des arts décoratifs* (Paris: Charles Moreau, [1926?]); Eng. trans. as *Art Deco Decorative Ironwork* (Mineoa, NY: Dover, and London: Constable, 1997)

Day, Susan, *Art Deco and Modernist Carpets* (London: Thames & Hudson, 2002)

Day, Susan, *Jean-Charles Moreux: architecte-décorateur-paysagiste* (Paris: Norma, 1999)

Delacroix, Henry, *Intérieurs modernes* (Paris: S. de Bonadona, n.d.)

Delaunay, Sonia, *Tapis et tissus* (Paris: Charles Moreau, 1929)

Deshairs, Léon (ed.), *L'Hôtel du collectionneur, groupe Ruhlmann, exposition des arts décoratifs de 1925* (Paris: A. Lévy, 1926) [exhibition catalogue]

Deshairs, Léon (ed.), *Intérieurs en couleurs, exposition des arts décoratifs, Paris 1925* (Paris: A. Lévy, 1925)

Deshairs, Léon, *Modern French Decorative Art: A Collection of Examples of Modern French Decoration, with an Introduction*, 2nd series (London: London Architectural Press, 1931)

Djo-Bourgeois, Francis Jourdain and E. Kohlmann, *Répertoire du goût moderne: ouvrages sur l'architecture et l'art décorative moderne*, (Paris: A. Lévy, 1928–29)

Drouot Montaigne, *Les Ruhlmann de Geneviève et Pierre Hebey: Jeudi 28 Octobre 1999 . . . Paris, Drouot Montaigne* [auction catalogue]

Dufet, Michel, *Meubles, ensembles, décors: recueil de documents et de commentaires sur la décoration d'intérieurs moderne contemporaine*, 2nd edn (Paris: Éditions du Décor d'Aujourd'hui, 1946)

Dufrène, Maurice, *Authentic Art Deco Interiors from the 1925 Paris Exhibition* (Woodbridge, Suffolk: Antique Collectors' Club, 2002)

Dufrène, Maurice, *Ensembles Mobiliers: Exposition Internationale 1925*, 3 vols. (Paris: Charles Moreau, 1925) [trade portfolio]

Dufrène, Maurice, *Ensembles Mobiliers: Exposition Internationale de 1937*, 18 vols. (Paris: Charles Moreau, 1937–60) [trade portfolio]

Dufrène, Maurice (ed.), *Les intérieurs français: ou, salon des artistes décorateurs* (Paris: Charles Moreau, 1926) [trade portfolio]

Dufrène, Maurice and J. J. Adnet, (eds.), *Meubles du temps present; présentés par M. D.* (Paris: Charles Moreau, 1930) [trade portfolio]

Duncan, Alastair, *American Art Deco* (London: Thames & Hudson, 1986)

Duncan, Alastair, *Art Deco* (London: Thames & Hudson, 1988)

Duncan, Alastair, *Art Deco Furniture: French Designers* (London: Thames & Hudson, 1992)

Duncan, Alastair, *Art Nouveau and Art Deco Lighting* (London: Thames & Hudson, 1978)

Duncan, Alastair and Georges de Bartha, *Art Nouveau and Art Deco Bookbinding: The French Masterpieces, 1880–1940* (London: Thames & Hudson, 1989)

Du Pasquier, Jacqueline (ed.), *Céramiques de René Buthaud* (Bordeaux: Musée des Arts Décoratifs de la Ville de Bordeaux, 1976) [exhibition catalogue]

Dybdahl, Lars, *Dansk Design: 1910–1945: Art Déco & Funktionalisme* (Copenhagen: Danske kunstindustrimuseum, 1997)

Eliel, Carol S., *L'Esprit nouveau: Purism in Paris, 1918–1925* (Los Angeles: LACMA/Harry N. Abrams, 2001) [exhibition catalogue]

Ellis, Anita J., *Rookwood Pottery: The Glaze Lines* (Atglen, PA: Schiffer, 1995)

Ellis, Anita J., *Rookwood Pottery: The Glorious Gamble* (Ohio: Cincinnati Art Museum, 1992)

Encyclopédie des Arts Décoratifs et industriels modernes au XXème siècle, 12 vols. (Paris, 1932; repr. London and New York: Garland, 1977) [official edition for the Paris *Exposition Internationale des Arts Décoratifs et Industriels Modernes*, 1925]

Encyclopédie des métiers d'art: décoration et style, 2 vols. (Paris: Éditions Albert Morancé, [1930?])

Ercoli, Giuliano, *Art Deco Prints* (New York: Rizzoli, 1989)

Exposition Internationale des Arts Décoratifs et Industriels Modernes, Paris, 1925: Une ambassade française: organisée par la Société des Artistes Décorateurs, preface by R. Chavance (Paris: Charles Moreau, 1925) [exhibition catalogue]

Exposition Internationale des Arts et des Techniques dans la Vie Moderne. Paris, 1937, 2 vols. (Paris: R. Stenger, 1937) [exhibition catalogue]

Follot, P. (ed.), *Intérieurs présentés au Salon des Artistes Décorateurs, 1930* (Paris: Charles Moreau, 1927) [trade portfolio]

Fontaine et Cie, *Album de Serrurerie Décorative Moderne* (Paris: Fontaine et Cie, 1932)

Fouquet, Jean, *Bijoux et orfèvrerie: Présenté par Jean Fouquet* (Paris: Charles Moreau, 1931)

French Art Deco Fashions in Pochoir Prints from the 1920s (Atglen, PA: Schiffer, 1998)

Gabardi, Melissa, *Art Deco Jewellery 1920–1949* (Woodbridge: Antique Collectors' Club, 1989)

Galerie Printz: meubles, objets d'art, 1 (Paris: Atelier, 1934) [exhibition catalogue]

Geddes, Norman Bel, *Horizons: On Design in Machines and Objects of Common Use* (Boston: Little, Brown, 1932)

Guidot, Raymond, (ed.), *Le luminaire par Guillaume Janneau [et] Luminaire moderne par Gabriel Henriot*, (Paris: Charles Moreau, 1992) [combined reprint of Janneau's 3 vols. (1925–1930/31) and Henriot's 1937 volume.]

Halén, Widar, *Art Deco, funkis, Scandinavian design* (Oslo: Orfeus Forlag, 1996)

Halouze, Édouard, *Costumes of South America* (New York: French & European Publications, 1941)

Heller, Steven and Louise Fili, *Deco Type: Stylish Alphabets of the Twenties and Thirties* (San Francisco: Chronicle Books, 1997)

Heller, Steven and Louise Fili, *Euro Deco: British Modern, French Modern, Spanish Art Deco, Dutch Modern, German Modern, Italian Art Deco* (London: Thames & Hudson, 2004)

Herbst, René, *25 Années U.A.M.: Les formes utiles: l'architecture, les arts plastiques, les arts graphiques, le mobilier, l'équipement ménager. Union des artistes modernes, Paris, 1930–1955.* (Paris: Salon des Arts Ménagers, 1956)

Herbst, René, *Pierre Chareau* (Paris: Éditions du Salon des Arts Ménagers, 1954)

Hillier, Bevis, *Art Deco of the 20s and 30s* (London: Studio Vista, 1973)

Hillier, Bevis and Stephen Escritt, *Art Deco Style* (London: Phaidon, 1997)

Hiriart, J. (ed.), *Interieurs au Salon des artistes décorateurs, 1931* (Paris: Charles Moreau, 1931) [trade portfolio]

Horneková, Jana, *Art Deco: Boemia 1918–1938* (Milan: Electa, 1996)

Intérieurs en couleurs, France: cinquante planches en couleurs, preface by Léon Deshairs (Paris: A. Lévy, 1926)

Janneau, Guillaume, *Technique du décor intérieur moderne* (Paris: Éditions Albert Morancé, 1929)

Janneau, Guillaume, Luc Benoist and Paul Vitry, (eds.), *L'Exposition Internationale des Arts Décoratifs et Industriels Modernes* (Paris: Publications de Beaux-Arts, 1925) [exhibition catalogue]

'Jean Dunand' *L'Illustration* (1940) [special issue]

Jourdain, Francis, *Intérieurs présentés par Francis Jourdain*, L'Art International d'Aujourd'hui, vol. 6 (Paris: Charles Moreau, 1929)

Karshan, Donald, *Csáky* (Paris: Dépôt 15, 1973) [exhibition catalogue]

Kery, Patricia Frantz, *Art Deco Graphics* (London: Thames & Hudson, 1986)

Kery, Patricia Frantz, *Great Magazine Covers of the World* (New York: Abbeville Press, 1982)

Kjellberg, Pierre, *Art Déco: les maîtres du mobilier, le décor des paquebots* (Paris: Amateur, 1998)

Krzysztofowicz-Kozakowska, Stefania, *Art Deco in Poland* (Krakow: Muzeum Narodowe w Krakowie, 1993) [exhibition catalogue]

Labbé, E. (ed.), *Photographies en couleurs. Exposition Internationale des Arts et des Techniques Appliqués à la Vie Moderne, Paris 1937: album officiel* (Paris: La Photolithe, 1937; repr. Colombes: J. Chaplain, 1987)

Lacroix, Boris J., *Magasins & boutiques, documents réunis et présentés par Boris J. Lacroix* (Paris: Charles Massin, [193-?])

Le Corbusier, *L'art décoratif d'aujourd'hui* (Paris: Éditions Crès, [1925?])

Le Corbusier, *Vers une architecture* (Paris: Éditions Crès, 1923)

Lesieutre, Alain, *The Spirit and Splendour of Art Deco* (New York: Paddington Press, 1974)

Lucie-Smith, Edward, *Art Deco Painting* (Oxford: Phaidon, 1990)

Lucius, Wulf D. von, *Bücherlust: Buchkunst und Bücherluxus im 20. Jahrhundert: Beispiele aus einer Stuttgarter Sammlung* (Stuttgart: Württembergische Landesbibliothek, 1998)

Lussier, Suzanne, *Art Deco Fashion* (London: V&A Publications, 2003)

Malevich, Kazimir, *The Non-Objective World* (Chicago: Theobald, 1959)

Mallet-Stevens, Robert, *Dix Années de réalisations en architecture et décoration* (Paris: Charles Massin, 1930)

Mallet-Stevens, Robert, *Vitraux modernes: Exposition Internationale de 1937* (Paris: Charles Moreau, [1937?])

McCready, Karen, *Art Deco and Modernist Ceramics* (London: Thames & Hudson, 1995)

Menton, Theodore, *The Art Deco Style in Household Objects, Architecture, Sculpture, Graphics, Jewellery* (New York: Dover, 1972)

Meubles et objets d'architectures dans les années 1925, Galerie Maria de Beyrie, 19 November–31 December, 1976 [exhibition catalogue]

Morgan, Sarah M., *Art Deco: The European Style* (New York: Dorset Press, 1990)

Moussinac, Léon, (ed.), *Intérieurs*, Collection documentaire d'art moderne, 4 vols. (Paris: A. Lévy, 1924–26)

Moussinac, Léon (ed.), *Croquis de Ruhlmann* (Paris: A. Lévy, [1924?])

Neuwirth, Waltraud, *Glass, 1905–1925: From Art Nouveau to Art Deco* (Vienna: W. Neuwirth, 1985) [exhibition catalogue]

Novi, A. (ed.), *Ensembles choisis: mobilier, décoration, nouvelles creations de goût moderne* (Paris: Charles Moreau, [1920?]) [trade portfolio]

Olmer, Pierre, *Le Mobilier français d'aujourd'hui (1910–1925)*, Architecture et arts décoratifs (Paris and Brussels: G. Van Oest, 1926)

Olmer, Pierre and Henri Bouché-Leclerq, (eds.), *L'Art décoratif français en 1929* (Paris: Société Artistique de Publications Techniques, 1929)

Ozenfant, Amédée, and Charles-Édouard Jeanneret, *Après le cubisme* (Paris: Éditions des Commentaires, 1918)

Pavillon Société des Artistes Décorateurs. Exposition Internationale, Paris. 1937, preface by Anatole de Monzie (Paris, 1937) [exhibition catalogue]

Perlein, Gilbert, *Art Déco belgique, 1920–1940* (Paris: Édition Musée d'Art Moderne Villeneuve d'Ascq, 1989) [exhibition catalogue]

Pérez Rojas, Javier, *Art Déco en España* (Madrid: Cátedra, 1990)

Perrin, G. M. (ed.), *La Ferronnerie française contemporaine* (Paris: 1961)

Pierre Chareau (Paris: L'Arc en Seine, 1991) [exhibition catalogue]

Pinsard, Pierre, (ed.,) *Meubles modernes en métal*, Librarie des arts décoratifs (Paris: A Calavas, [n.d.]) [trade portfolio]

Poor, Henry Varnum, *A Book of Pottery: From Mud into Immortality* (London: Bailey & Swinfen, 1959)

Powers, Alan, *Front Cover: Great Book Jacket and Cover Design* (London: Mitchell Beazley, 2001)

Préaud, Tamara and Serge Gauthier, *La Céramique, art du XXe siècle* (Paris: Fribourg et Éditions Vilo, 1982); Eng. trans. as *Ceramics of the Twentieth Century* (New York: Rizzoli International Publications, 1982)

Price, Matlack, *Design and Craftsmanship in Metals: The Creative Art of Oscar Bach* (New York: Bartlett Orr, 1928)

Quénioux, Gaston, *Les Arts décoratifs modernes (France)* (Paris: Larousse, 1925)

Rapin, Henri (ed.), *Intérieurs présentés au Salon des artistes décorateurs, 1930* (Paris: Charles Moreau, 1930) [trade portfolio]

Rapin, Henri, *La Sculpture décorative moderne*, 2 vols. (Paris: Charles Moreau, 1925)

Raulet, Sylvie, *Art Deco Jewelry* (London: Thames & Hudson, 1985)

Roche, Antoine (ed.), *Paris 1929: Documents sur la décoration plane* (Paris: Librarie des Arts Décoratifs, 1930)

Sekler, Eduard F., *Josef Hoffmann: das architektonische Werk: Monographie und Werkverzeichnis* (Salzburg: Residenz, 1982); Eng. trans. as *Josef Hoffmann: The Architectural Work: Monograph and Catalogue of Works* (Princeton: Princeton University Press, 1985)

Skinner, Tina, *Art Deco Textile Designs* (Atglen, PA: Schiffer, 1998)

Société des artistes décorateurs, *Nouveaux intérieurs français*, 2e série (Paris: Charles Moreau, 1934) [trade portfolio]

Société des artistes décorateurs, *Nouveaux intérieurs français*, 4e série (Paris: Charles Moreau, 1936) [trade portfolio]

Sonia Delaunay: Art into Fashion, introduction by Elizabeth Morano; foreword by Diana Vreeland (New York: Braziller, 1986)

Sternau, Susan A., *Art Deco: Flights of Artistic Fancy* (New York: Todtri, 1997)

Stevenson, Greg, *Art Deco Ceramics* (Princes Risborough: Shire, 1998)

Süe, Louis and André Mare, *Architectures: recueil publié sous la direction de Louis Süe & André Mare* (Paris: Éditions de la Nouvelle Revue Française, 1921)

Tapisseries: Sonia Delaunay (Paris: Musée d'art moderne de la ville de Paris, 1972) [exhibition catalogue]

Teague, Walter Dorwin, *Design this Day: The Technique of Order in the Machine Age* (New York: Harcourt, Brace, 1940)

The Official Pictures of A Century of Progress Exposition, Chicago 1933, (Chicago: The Reuben H. Donnelley Corporation, 1933)

Troy, Nancy J., *Modernism and the Decorative Arts in France: Art Nouveau to Le Corbusier* (New Haven: Yale University Press, 1991)

Uckerman, P. d', *L'Art dans la vie moderne* (Paris: Flammarion, 1937)

Vegesack, Alexander von, Stanislaus von Moos, Arthur Ruegg and Mateo Kries, (eds.), *Le Corbusier: The Art of Architecture* (Weil am Rhein: Vitra Design Stiftung, 2007)

Vos, Jacques de and D. Cohendet, *Robert Lallemant (1902–1954), ou La Céramique mécanisee* (Paris: Galerie Jacques de Vos, 1984) [exhibition catalogue]

Weber, Christianne, *Art Deco Schmuck: die internationale Schmuckszene der 20er und 30er Jahre* (Munich: Wilhelm Heyne, 2000)

PICTURE CREDITS

Images. © 2008 Artists Rights Society (ARS), New York; **290tl, tr, b** Christie's Images. © 2008 Artists Rights Society (ARS), New York; **291t** © 2008 Artists Rights Society (ARS), New York; **291bl** Galerie Vallois, Paris. © 2008 Artists Rights Society (ARS), New York; **291br** S.V.V. Camard et Associés, Paris. © 2008 Artists Rights Society (ARS), New York; **292t, bl, br** © 2008 Artists Rights Society (ARS), New York; **293t, b** © 2008 Artists Rights Society (ARS), New York; **294** Royal Ontario Museum. © 2008 Artists Rights Society (ARS), New York; **295t** Virginia Museum of Fine Arts, Richmond, VA. © 2008 Artists Rights Society (ARS), New York; **295b** © 2008 Artists Rights Society (ARS), New York; **296t** © 2008 Artists Rights Society (ARS), New York; **296b** S.V.V. Camard et Associés and Stephane Briolant, Paris. © 2008 Artists Rights Society (ARS), New York; **297** Sotheby's. © 2008 Artists Rights Society (ARS), New York **299tr** Christie's Images; **301l** Christie's Images; **302l, r** Sotheby's. Courtesy Denise Laurent; **302c** Sotheby's. © 2008 Artists Rights Society (ARS), New York. Courtesy Denise Laurent; **303l** © 2008 Artists Rights Society (ARS), New York; **304l** Sotheby's. Courtesy Denise Laurent; **308t, b** Christie's Images; **309l, b** Tajan, Paris; **310t** ArtCurial, Paris. © 2008 Artists Rights Society (ARS), New York; **310b** © 2008 Artists Rights Society (ARS), New York; **311tl, br** © 2008 Artists Rights Society (ARS), New York; **311tr, bl** Sotheby's. © 2008 Artists Rights Society (ARS), New York; **312t** Virginia Museum of Fine Arts, Richmond, VA. © 2008 Artists Rights Society (ARS), New York; **312b** Musée des Arts Decoratifs, Paris. © 2008 Artists Rights Society (ARS), New York; **313tl** © 2008 Artists Rights Society (ARS), New York; **313tr** Sotheby's. © 2008 Artists Rights Society (ARS), New York; **313cl** Christie's Images. © 2008 Artists Rights Society (ARS), New York; **313b** Primavera Gallery, New York. © 2008 Artists Rights Society (ARS), New York; **314tr, c** Sotheby's. Courtesy Stéphane Guilloteau; **314bl** Christie's Images. Courtesy Stéphane Guilloteau; **315tl, tr** Courtesy Stéphane Guilloteau; **315b** Virginia Museum of Fine Arts, Richmond, VA. Courtesy Stéphane Guilloteau **318** Tajan, Paris. © 2008 Artists Rights Society (ARS), New York; **319t** © 2008 Artists Rights Society (ARS), New York; **319bl** Christie's Images. © 2008 Artists Rights Society (ARS), New York; **319r** © 2008 Artists Rights Society (ARS), New York; **320** Poster Photo Archives, Posters Please Inc., New York; **321b** © 2008 Artists Rights Society (ARS), New York; **321tl, tr** Quittenbaum Art Auctions, Munich; **322tr** Sotheby's; **322bl** Thierry de Maigret and Jean-Marc Maury, Paris © Seventh Square, photo Pascal Faligot; **322bc** Virginia Museum of Fine Arts, Richmond, VA; **322br** Sotheby's; **323** © 2008 Artists Rights Society (ARS), New York; **324tl, tr** Poster Photo Archives, Posters Please Inc., New York; **324b** S.V.V. Camard et Associés, Paris; **325** Christie's Images; **326l** Sotheby's; **326r** Norwest Corporation, Minneapolis. © 2008 Artists Rights Society (ARS), New York; **327** Poster Photo Archives, Posters Please Inc., New York. © 2008 Artists Rights Society (ARS), New York; **328l, r** © David Behl, 2008, courtesy Verdura, New York; **329tl** Phillips de Pury & Company; **329tr** Royal Ontario Museum, Toronto; **331tr** Sotheby's; **331bl, br** Poster Photo Archives, Posters Please Inc., New York; **332l** Galerie Vallois, Paris. © 2008 Artists Rights Society (ARS), New York; **332tr** Boisgirard et Associés and Jean-Marc Maury, Paris. © Seventh Square, photo Pascal Faligot. © 2008 Artists Rights Society (ARS), New York; **332cr** Poster Photo Archives, Posters Please Inc., New York. © 2008 Artists Rights Society (ARS), New York; **332br** Tajan, Paris. © 2008 Artists Rights Society (ARS), New York; **334l** Christie's Images; **335tl** Sotheby's; **335br** Poster Photo Archives, Posters Please Inc., New York; **336t** Christie's Images; **336bl** Galerie Vallois, Paris; **336br** Poster Photo Archives, Posters Please Inc., New York; **337r** Christie's Images; **338r** Phillips de Pury & Company. © 2008 Artists Rights Society (ARS), New York; **339tl** Christie's Images; **339tr** Norwest Corporation, Minneapolis; **339b** Phillips de Pury & Company; **340l** Poster Photo Archives, Posters Please, New York; **341tl** Phillips de Pury & Company; **341tr** Poster Photo Archives, Posters Please, New York. © 2008 Artists Rights Society (ARS), New York; **341b** S.V.V. Camard et Associés, Paris; **343t** Sotheby's; **343b** Poster Photo Archives, Posters Please Inc., New York. © 2008 Artists Rights Society (ARS), New York; **344** © 2008 Artists Rights Society (ARS), New York; **345l** Poster Photo Archives, Posters Please Inc., New York. © 2008 Artists Rights Society (ARS), New York; **345r** Christie's Images; **346l** S.V.V. Camard et Associés, Paris; **347** Tajan, Paris. © 2008 Artists Rights Society (ARS), New York; **349** Sotheby's; **351l** Galerie Vallois, Paris; **351r** Phillips de Pury & Company; **352c, r** Galerie Vallois, Paris; **353** Christie's Images; **354tl** Christie's Images; **354c** Berardo collection, Lisbon; **355l** Christie's Images; **356** Tajan, Paris; **357** Sotheby's. © 2008 Artists Rights Society (ARS), New York; **358** © 2008 Artists Rights Society (ARS), New York; **359l** Sotheby's. © 2008 Artists Rights Society (ARS), New York; **359tr** Christie's Images. © 2008 Artists Rights Society (ARS), New York; **359br** © 2008 Artists Rights Society (ARS), New York; **360l** Claude Aguttes and Jean-Marc Maury, Paris. © Seventh Square, photo Pascal Faligot **360r** Christie's Images; **361r** Olivier Coutau-Begarie and Jean-Marc Maury, Paris. © Seventh Square, photo Pascal Faligot; **362tl** Sotheby's; **362br** ArtCurial, Paris. © L & M SERVICES B.V. The Hague 20080913; **363** Christie's Images; **364** © 2008 Artists Rights Society (ARS), New York; **365** Courtesy Denise Laurent; **366** © 2008 Artists Rights Society (ARS), New York; **367tl** Christie's Images; **367bl** Tajan, Paris. © 2008 Artists Rights Society (ARS), New York; **369tl** Berardo Collection, Lisbon. © 2008 Artists Rights Society (ARS), New York; **369bl** Poster Photo Archives, Posters Please Inc., New York. © 2008 Artists Rights Society (ARS), New York; **369br** S.V.V. Camard et Associés, Paris; **370** Christie's Images; **371tl** © 2008 Artists Rights Society (ARS), New York; **371tr** Christie's Images; **371bl** J.-J. Dutko. © 2008 Artists Rights Society (ARS), New York; **371br** Sotheby's; **372** Claude Aguttes and Jean-Marc Maury, Paris. © Seventh Square, photo Pascal Faligot. © 2008 Artists Rights Society (ARS), New York; **373t** Christie's Images. © 2008 Artists Rights Society (ARS), New York; **373b** Sotheby's. © 2008 Artists Rights Society (ARS), New York; **374bl** Poster Photo Archives, Posters Please Inc., New York; **374br** Phillips de Pury & Company; **375** Christie's Images; **376** Tajan, Paris; **377t, b** Christie's Images; **380l** Claude Aguttes and Jean-Marc Maury, Paris. © Seventh Square, photo Pascal Faligot; **380r** Sotheby's; **381** Claude Aguttes and Jean-Marc Maury, Paris. © Seventh Square, photo Pascal Faligot; **382l** Sotheby's; **383r** Galerie Vallois, Paris. © 2008 Artists Rights Society (ARS), New York; **385l** © 2008 Artists Rights Society (ARS), New York; **385r** Virginia Museum of Fine Arts, Richmond, VA. © 2008 Artists Rights Society (ARS), New York; **386l** Galerie Vallois, Paris. © 2008 Artists Rights Society (ARS), New York; **386tr** © 2008 Artists Rights Society (ARS), New York; **387** Tajan, Paris; **388l, r** Christie's Images; **389tl** Sotheby's. © Franz Hagenauer Estate, Courtesy Ronald Hagenauer; **389tr** Royal Ontario Museum, Toronto; **389bl** Christie's Images; **389bc, br** Sotheby's. © Franz Hagenauer Estate, Courtesy Ronald Hagenauer; **390** Galerie Vallois, Paris; **391tr** Christie's Images; **391b** Sotheby's; **392tl** Christie's Images; **392br** © 2008 Artists Rights Society (ARS), New York; **393l** Claude Aguttes and Jean-Marc Maury, Paris. © Seventh Square, photo Pascal Faligot; **393r** Tajan, Paris; **394t** Poster Photo Archives, Posters Please, New York. © 2008 Artists Rights Society (ARS), New York; **394b** Phillips de Pury & Company; **395r** Mme de Beyrie, Paris; **396l, r** Christie's Images. © 2008 Artists Rights Society (ARS), New York; **397tr** Phillips de Pury & Company; **397b** Sotheby's; **398t** © 2008 Artists Rights Society (ARS), New York; **399l, r** Tajan, Paris; **400l** Christie's Images **400r** Sotheby's. © 2008 Artists Rights Society (ARS), New York; **401** Tajan, Paris. © 2008 Artists Rights Society (ARS), New York; **402l, r** Christie's Images; **403** Phillips de Pury & Company; **404l** Christie's Images. © 2008 Artists Rights Society (ARS), New York; **405tr** S.V.V. Camard et Associés, Paris; **405b** Sotheby's © 2008 Artists Rights Society (ARS), New York; **406tl** Christie's Images; **406tr** Norwest Corporation, Minneapolis; **406b** Sotheby's; **407r** © 2008 Artists Rights Society (ARS), New York; **408tl** Sotheby's; **408br** Maison Gerard Ltd., New York; **409l, r** S.V.V. Camard et Associés, Paris; **410** The Whitney Museum of American Art, gift of Gertrude Vanderbilt Whitney; **411** Sotheby's; **413t** Christie's Images; **413b** Tajan, Paris; **414tl, br** S.V.V. Camard et Associés, Paris; **414tr** Norwest Corporation, Minneapolis; **414bl** Christie's Images; **415** S.V.V. Camard et Associés, Paris. © 2008 Artists Rights Society (ARS), New York; **416** Virginia Museum of Fine Arts, Richmond, VA. © 2008 Artists Rights Society (ARS), New York; **417tl** Tajan, Paris. © 2008 Artists Rights Society (ARS), New York; **417tr** Millon ey Associés, Paris; **417bl** S.V.V. Camard et Associés, Paris. © 2008 Artists Rights Society (ARS), New York; **417br** Sotheby's. © 2008 Artists Rights Society (ARS), New York; **418tl** Norwest Corporation, Minneapolis © 2008 Artists Rights Society (ARS), New York; **418tr** Galerie Vallois, Paris © 2008 Artists Rights Society (ARS), New York; **418b** Phillips de Pury & Company. © 2008 Artists Rights Society (ARS), New York; **419l, r** Christie's Images; **420** Christie's Images; **421tl** Maison Gerard Ltd., New York; **421br** Maison Gerard Ltd., New York. Christie's Images; **422l** Poster Photo Archives, Posters Please Inc., New York. © 2008 Artists Rights Society (ARS), New York; **422c** © 2008 Artists Rights Society (ARS), New York; **422r** Galerie Vallois, Paris. © 2008 Artists Rights Society (ARS), New York; **423l** Sotheby's; **423r** Gabe Lurie collection, Johannesburg; **426tl, tr** Christie's Images. © 2008 Artists Rights Society (ARS), New York; **426bl** Christie's Images; **426br** Poster Photo Archives, Posters Please Inc., New York. © 2008 Artists Rights Society (ARS), New York; **427** Christie's Images; **428** Maison Gerard Ltd., New York; **429tl** Christie's Images; **429tr** © Simon Rendall; **429b** Christie's Images. © Simon Rendall; **430tl, b** Phillips de Pury & Company; **430b** Phillips de Pury & Company; **433l** Christie's Images; **435l** Poster Photo Archives, Posters Please Inc., New York; **436l, r** Christie's Images; **437** Poster Photo Archives, Posters Please Inc., New York. Courtesy Alex Matter; **438tl** Tajan, Paris; **438tr** S.V.V. Camard et Associés, Paris; **438bl** Poster Photo Archives, Posters Please Inc., New York. © 2008 Artists Rights Society (ARS), New York; **438br** Christie's Images; **439l** Virginia Museum of Fine Arts, Richmond, VA; **440br** Tajan, Paris; **441l** Sotheby's; **441r** Christie's Images; **442t** ArtCurial, Paris; **442b** Tajan, Paris; **443b** Galerie Vallois, Paris; **444br** © 2008 Artists Rights Society (ARS), New York; **445l** Detroit Institute of Arts. © 2008 Artists Rights Society (ARS), New York; **446l** Sotheby's; **446r** Christie's Images; **447tl** Sotheby's; **447tr** Phillips de Pury & Company; **448** Poster Photo Archives, Posters Please Inc., New York; **449** Christie's Images; **450t** S.V.V. Camard et Associés, Paris. © 2008 Artists Rights Society (ARS), New York; **450bl** Christie's Images. © 2008 Artists Rights Society (ARS), New York; **450br** Sotheby's. © 2008 Artists Rights Society (ARS), New York; **451** Poster Photo Archives, Posters Please Inc., New York; **452** Poster Photo Archives, Posters Please Inc., New York; **453l** Courtesy of Romain Lefebvre © 2008 Artists Rights Society (ARS), New York; **454l** Sotheby's; **455c, b** Tajan, Paris; **456tl** Phillips de Pury & Company; **456tr** Poster Photo Archives, Posters Please Inc., New York; **456b** Tajan, Paris; **457l** Tajan, Paris. © 2008 Artists Rights Society (ARS), New York; **458** Poster Photo Archives, Posters Please Inc., New York; **459tl** Christie's Images; **459tr** Sotheby's. © 2008 Artists Rights Society (ARS), New York; **459bl** Christie's Images. © 2008 Artists Rights Society (ARS), New York; **459br** Christie's Images; **460t** Sotheby's. © 2008 Artists Rights Society (ARS), New York; **460b** Tajan, Paris. © 2008 Artists Rights Society (ARS), New York; **461tl, bl** © 2008 Artists Rights Society (ARS), New York; **461r** Galerie Vallois, Paris. © 2008 Artists Rights Society (ARS), New York; **462t** Maison Gerard Ltd., New York; **462b** Claude Aguttes and Jean-Marc Maury, Paris. © Seventh Square, photo Pascal Faligot; **463l, r** © 2008 Artists Rights Society (ARS), New York; **464tl** Christie's Images; **465t** Phillips de Pury & Company; **465b** S.V.V. Camard et Associés, Paris; **467br** S.V.V. Camard et Associés, Paris. © 2008 Artists Rights Society (ARS), New York; **468l, br** Phillips de Pury & Company; **469r** S.V.V. Camard et Associés, Paris; **471tr** Poster Photo Archives, Posters Please Inc., New York; **472t** Sotheby's; **474** Olivier Coutau-Begarie and Jean-Marc Maury, Paris. © Seventh Square, photo Pascal Faligot; **475t** Claude Aguttes and Jean-Marc Maury, Paris. © Seventh Square, photo Pascal Faligot; **475b** S.V.V. Camard et Associés, Paris; **476bl** Sotheby's; **476cr, br** Quittenbaum Auctions, Munich; **477** © 2008 Artists Rights Society (ARS), New York; **479tr, br** Christie's Images; **480l** Christie's Images; **480r** Cranbrook Academy of Art/Museum; **481tl, tr** Christie's Images; **482r** Tajan, Paris; **483** © 2008 Artists Rights Society (ARS), New York; **484t** © 2008 Artists Rights Society (ARS), New York; **484b** Thierry de Maigret and Jean-Marc Maury, Paris. © Seventh Square, photo Pascal Faligot. © 2008 Artists Rights Society (ARS), New York; **485t** © 2008 Artists Rights Society (ARS), New York; **485bl** Virginia Museum of Fine Arts, Richmond, VA. © 2008 Artists Rights Society (ARS), New York; **485br** Sotheby's. © 2008 Artists Rights Society (ARS), New York; **486l** Sotheby's; **487tl, tr** Poster Photo Archives, Posters Please Inc., New York. © 2008 Artists Rights Society (ARS), New York; **487bl, br** Christie's Images; **488bl** Sotheby's. © 2008 Artists Rights Society (ARS), New York; **488br** © 2008 Artists Rights Society (ARS), New York; **489** Sotheby's; **490l** Norwest Corporation, Minneapolis; **490r** Tajan, Paris; **491** Christie's Images; **492l** Poster Photo Archives, Posters Please Inc., New York; **492r** Christie's Images; **493tr** Courtesy of Romain Lefebvre; **493b** ArtCurial, Paris; **495** Sotheby's; **496t** Tajan, Paris. © 2008 Artists Rights Society (ARS), New York; **49bl** Galerie Vallois, Paris. © 2008 Artists Rights Society (ARS), New York; **496br** © 2008 Artists Rights Society (ARS), New York; **497t, b** Tajan, Paris. © 2008 Artists Rights Society (ARS), New York; **497c** S.V.V. Camard et Associés, Paris. © 2008 Artists Rights Society (ARS), New York; **498t** Courtesy Estate of John Storrs; **498bl** Christie's Images; **498br** Phillips de Pury & Company; **499** Christie's Images; **500** © 2008 Artists Rights Society (ARS), New York; **501** Courtesy Estate of John Storrs; **502t, b** Dominique Suisse. © 2008 Artists Rights Society (ARS), New York; **503t, b** © 2008 Artists Rights Society (ARS), New York; **504l** Phillips de Pury & Company; **504r** Norwest Corporation, Minneapolis; **505tr** Christie's Images; **506tl** Christie's Images; **506tr** Tajan, Paris; **506b** Sotheby's; **507** Phillips de Pury & Company; **508t, b** Christie's Images; **509b** Christie's Images; **512** Poster Photo Archives, Posters Please Inc., New York; **513c** Christie's Images; **513r** Poster Photo Archives, Posters Please Inc., New York; **514r** © 2008 Artists Rights Society (ARS), New York; **515tc** Sotheby's; **516** © 2008 Artists Rights Society (ARS), New York; **518l** Christie's Images; **519bl** Phillips de Pury & Company; **520t, b** Sotheby's; **521t, b** Christie's Images. © 2008 Artists Rights Society (ARS), New York; **522l** Quittenbaum Art Auctions, Munich; **522tr, br** Phillips de Pury & Company; **523** Sotheby's; **524l** Christie's Images; **524r** Tajan, Paris. © 2008 Artists Rights Society (ARS), New York; **526l** Poster Photo Archives, Posters Please Inc., New York; **526r** S.V.V. Camard et Associés, Paris; **527t** Maison Gerard Ltd., New York; **527b** Tajan, Paris.

INDEX

Page numbers in **bold** refer to artists' biographies; those in *italics* refer to illustrations.